CW00541850

THE STORY OF LOTUS
1961-1971
Growth of a Legend

THE STORY OF LOTUS

1961-1971: Growth of a Legend

by

Doug Nye

MOTOR RACING PUBLICATIONS

MOTOR RACING PUBLICATIONS LTD
28 & 32 Devonshire Road, Chiswick,
London W4 2HD

ISBN 0 900549 15 7
First Published 1972
Reprinted 1978

Printed in Great Britain by
Page Bros (Norwich) Ltd, Norwich

Chapters

The author and publisher wish to thank the following photographers and companies whose pictures have helped to illustrate this book: Artricia Industrial Pictures, Kenneth Bieber, Michael Boys, S.J. Brown, Bernard Cahier, Noel Conlon, A.R.F. Cooke, Michael Cooper, Keith Duerden, Floyd Photographic, Ford Film Library, Albert Foster, Geoffrey Goddard, Guido Haug, Michael Hewett, Peter Hulbert, Ronald Hunt, Indianapolis Motor Speedway, Nicholas Loudon, T.C. March, Victor Meeussen, Lynton Money, Motor News and Features, Malcolm Parnell, Malcolm Pendrill, David Phipps, Victor Robertson, Euan Sarginson, Nigel Snowdon, Sports Graphic, F. David Stone, Gerry Stream, Herbert Suendhofer, Colin Taylor, E. Johnson Taylor, Fred Taylor, Toni Temburg, Peter Tempest, J. Thomas, John F. Whitmore, Stewart White (Monitor), and David Winter.

Preface

Together with its companion, 'The Story of Lotus 1947-1960—Birth of a Legend', by Ian H. Smith, this book sets out to record and pay tribute to the first quarter-century of Lotus history. Apart from the obvious milestone of the 25th year, the end of 1971 was a most appropriate moment in which to sign-off this second volume for it marked the point of time when the major emphasis of Group Lotus activities swung away from racing to the manufacture of passenger cars, and Lotus designed and built racing cars ceased to carry their own name and emerged in new colours as 'John Player Specials'.

Prior to that momentous decision Team Lotus and their sponsors from the tobacco world had enjoyed a fruitful association as partners in Gold Leaf Team Lotus, and in recognition of the importance of this venture to this period of the Lotus story the jacket of this book carries the Gold Leaf colour scheme of red, white and gold, whereas the earlier volume was jacketed in the traditional Team Lotus green and yellow colours. The superb drawings in each case are by David James, and the book design by David Murray.

In view of the wealth of information which the Lotus story has generated between 1961 and 1971 I have, I hope, simplified the reader's task by sub-dividing each chapter (one is devoted to each year) into three sections. The first section covers Lotus road car developments, general business aspects and company politics, as well as overall policy; the second details all Lotus' major single-seater activities and development during the year; and the third discusses the Lotus competition record in the remaining leagues of motor racing and other branches of motor sport. A number of appendices have been added at the back of the book to enhance its reference value.

Although one person has written the final manuscript, many others have eased his task, and I would like first of all to offer my sincere thanks to Colin Chapman for being so informative and helpful when finally I managed to pin him down. Of those who spared time from their Group Lotus responsibilities to be helpful my appreciation in particular goes to Martin Walter, Peter Warr, Trish Strong and Jim Endruweit, and equally to former Lotus men Dick Scammell, Andrew Ferguson, Mike Warner and David Lazenby, and to Duncan Rabagliatti of the Formula One Register, whose assistance was invaluable in preparing the appendices.

The original research into this period of Lotus history was carried out by the late Gregor Grant, former Editor in Chief and founder of 'Autosport' and 'Speedworld International' magazines, during the months prior to his tragic death in 1969; I dedicate this book to Gregor in the hope that it is worthy of his memory.

Finally, my thanks to publisher John Blunsden for convincing me that all the sweat and drudgery was worthwhile, and to my wife Valerie who had to put up with the screwed-up papers and cursing when I thought it wasn't.

DOUG NYE
Lower Bourne
Farnham, England

Introduction

The story of Lotus is essentially the story of one man's achievements, and of the products which his fertile and imaginative mind created. It is a great success story, tinged with moments of extreme sadness, as have been so many pages of motor racing history before it.

Colin Chapman, whose influence on the world of motor sport has been greater than that of any other man during the second half of the twentieth century, is a unique combination of engineer-designer, businessman and motor racing enthusiast. It is doubtful whether anyone else could have steered Lotus from a backyard in North London past so many seemingly insurmountable obstacles to its present stature as one of the world's leading manufacturers of high-performance cars.

There is no doubt whatsoever that without its competition pedigree the Lotus marque would have meant little if anything today, and so inevitably this story, which concludes the first quarter-century of Lotus, is to a great extent one of motor racing achievements. During the 11 years covered by this volume Lotus Grand Prix cars and their drivers became motor racing's World Champions on four occasions. Lotus racing car design achieved major breakthroughs which repeatedly sent their rivals scurrying back to their drawing boards. And inevitably, the Lotus road cars which have emanated from the same talented design team and have benefitted from the cross-fertilisation of ideas tried and proved on the World's race tracks have also become pacesetters in their own right.

Interlinked with the Lotus success story, of course, have been the brilliant careers of racing drivers of the calibre of Jim Clark, Graham Hill and Jochen Rindt, and before them of Stirling Moss; all contributed substantially to the growth of the Lotus legend.

But this is not an undiluted success story, and while I have striven to provide a comprehensive and accurate record of Lotus accomplishments in motor sport I have also attempted to reveal some of the trials and tribulations, the problems and the imperfections of a mushrooming company. The collective intensity of these might well have sunk Lotus without trace had it not been for Colin Chapman's myriad talents and unbelievable energy, and his extraordinary ability to inspire loyalty and accomplishments far beyond reasonable bounds from those around him. Such has been his magnetism that even the most outrageous of anti-Chapman stories by disgruntled ex-employees or associates invariably carry the rider '... but for all that he's a marvellous bloke', or '... but you can't help admiring him'. At least some of the magnetism stems from his sheer guts and determination and his inability to admit defeat, even when all seemingly has been lost.

In the early 'Sixties Team Lotus used to travel Europe with a small Ford Zephyr-powered transporter, which invariably was overloaded and towed a double-decked two-car trailer. One of its trips to France developed into a typically Chapmanesque saga and revealed vividly the never-say-die character of the man who forged Group Lotus . . .

One of the drawbacks of the transporter was

that it could only be driven up the loading ramp into one of the Channel Air Bridge Bristol Freighters by giving it peak revs and popping the clutch. Understandably, it objected to such treatment, and regularly the engine would judder and poke its fan through the radiator. When it performed this trick during a typical Lotus last-minute dash to the French Grand Prix at Reims, Dick Scammell and another mechanic found themselves stranded at Le Touquet airport with the radiator well and truly punctured.

Eventually Colin appeared in his Raymond Mays-modified Ford Zephyr, which had a multiple-Amal carburettor conversion and was a very powerful conveyance. Colin's instant decision was that he should tow the two-car trailer, so it was coupled-up and off they belted. At the first corner the Ford and its wildly overloaded fellow-traveller careered straight on, with Dick cowering under the dash panel while Colin sorted it all out, muttering 'no brakes, no brakes', forgetting the massive weight behind him!

Colin is a fine driver, and Dick recalls the journey as a kind of high-speed obstacle race. As speed built-up to around 85 mph the trailer began to weave, but undeterred Colin charged along the undulating roads of the French coast. The Ford was darting wildly from kerb to kerb and to this day Dick swears that Frenchmen were pulling off the road ahead as they saw the apparently wildly out of control car and trailer approaching.

Over one crest a fork appeared in the road ahead, and Dick scrambled for the map as Colin called for directions. Dick Scammell: 'I was very young and overawed by it all, and couldn't pronounce the road signs. I ummed and aahed, and Colin suddenly snatched the map, controlled a big weave with the other hand and yelled, "I suppose I've got to read the bloody map as well!" I think more by luck than judgment we took the right fork, and so we went on.'

Somehow Colin found his way into a narrow country lane, still boring along at unabated speed, and Dick was searching for something under the dash when he heard Chapman mutter 'She's just got to stop this time!',and tremendous braking forced him down into the parcels shelf!

When he finally fought back upright he saw the trouble—a farm tractor towing a wide trailer blocking the lane ahead. The Lotus vehicles were almost on their side on the bank, but the phlegmatic French farmer studiously took to the verge on his side and carefully picked his way round without batting an eyelid.

Colin was now determined to make-up lost time, and as he powered past a lorry the trailer took a big swing, and this time Dick was convinced that all was lost. 'You could see the side of the trailer out through the side windows of the car, and there was no way anybody could get it back in shape . . . but Colin did.'

But this tremendous side-swipe was too much for one of the four trailer wheels, and soon afterwards a tremendous bang and lurch from behind heralded its departure. Colin cursed and slithered to a stop while Dick piled out and ran to examine the damage. The remaining wheel and tyre on that side looked undamaged, so out came the pump and the tyre was inflated to about 50 psi to compensate for the extra load it would have to carry. While this was being done Colin stamped about impatiently, and a lorry driver stopped to return the missing brake drum!

Colin climbed back behind the wheel and rushed off at unabated speed with Dick by this time resigned to his fate in the passenger's seat. The remaining wheel could stand only a few more kilometres at 85 mph and an even bigger bang than the first one and a tremendous grating and clattering noise announced its departure. 'You bloody fool', ranted Colin, '. . . you over-tightened those wheel nuts, you must have done'. Dick was spared a fate worse than death when the wheel studs and nuts were found to be intact, for the tortured wheel had pulled clean off over them. Now the trailer was stuck with two wheels, but both on the same side, and there were still miles to go to the circuit.

The two Grand Prix cars on the trailer miraculously were still undamaged, so they were unloaded and Colin detailed Dick and Mel, the other mechanic, to drive them to the circuit on the road. The trailer was jacked-up and the wheels fitted one on each side, and he set off to tow it along behind. Some peasants were enlisted from the fields to give the two 2.5 litre Lotus 18s a push-start, and since they probably had never seen such cars before, far less push-started them, the Lotuses' take-off left a cloud of rubber dust hanging over a big heap of French peasants lying in the middle of the road . . .

Eventually, the cars arrived safely in the paddock at Reims, as did the trailer, after an episode very typical of the dramas and disasters which have followed Team Lotus over their colourful years of racing. That they reached their destination on this, as on so many other occasions, was due to the indefatigable character of Colin Chapman who throughout the whole saga summoned his natural abilities to save himself and his fellow-travellers from apparently irretrievable situations while he steadily grew angrier and angrier!

Colin, naturally and understandably, takes life very seriously when it is agin him. Andrew Ferguson (ex-Team Lotus manager): 'Colin has a terribly serious approach to his business and to his racing, which the rest of us often didn't share. While we were seeing the funny side of things he'd be getting more and more serious and uptight. And yet if you recall it afterwards, then Colin will see the funny side and he'll curl up just like the rest of us. He's an incredible man; let's face it, you could have an evening out on Chapman stories alone!'

The Chapman abilities as driver, designer, engineer and businessman are well-known. They are demonstrated by the successes of his cars and of his company, but such genius can be capricious.

With all the Lotus people to whom I have spoken in preparing this book, one sentiment seems common. To a man they all throw up their hands in horror and say 'Ooh, Colin Chapman; the things he's done to me! He doesn't play by your rules. He's got this fantastic knack of manouevring people. Impossible man sometimes . . . BUT I WOULD GIVE MY RIGHT ARM FOR HIM'.

This love-hate relationship has been instilled by innumerable incidents; the love stemming from respect for a man who is a winner every inch of the way, and the hate from a staggering ability to do anything better than the average man, an apparent inability to plan things to avoid last minute rush and panic, and an inability to appreciate that the normal mortals working under him perhaps aren't quite as quick and accomplished in all things as he is.

Perhaps two Andrew Ferguson stories explain the mixed regard but the deep respect which Lotus men hold for 'The Old Man' (who, incidentally, is a mere 43 years of age as I write!) . . .

'I used to prepare Colin's flight plans when he flew himself to some Continental race meetings, and on one occasion he had to fly to a small military field where there were no proper passenger facilities. I fixed up a hire car to be available there for him from the nearest town, but about two hours after he'd left the 'phone rang.

'It was Colin. "Andrew, where's my car, it's not here!" I said the hire company must have got their wires crossed and told him the telephone number was on his flight plan. "I haven't got time for that", he said, "I'm doing a job sheet, you ring them".'

So Andrew had to ring the French hire company from England while Colin did his job sheet on the airfield a few miles from their offices. 'When I got through I found myself exchanging fractured French with some chap who couldn't understand a word I was saying. Suddenly there was silence and then this terribly English voice said "Hello, can I help you, the butcher doesn't speak English!"—I'd been put through to the wrong number! This had taken about five minutes, and I was just about to dial again when the operator came through saying Mr Chapman was on the line for me. I said I'd just taken that call but she said, "No, this is another one!". I picked up the 'phone and there was Colin roaring "Andrew! Where's my bloody car?".

The other occasion was at Indianapolis, in the middle of a hectic day of mechanical disaster and political strife. A weary Chapman paused pensively, then said to Ferguson, 'You know Andrew, we're mad going racing like this. What do we do it for? We've got £150,000 capital investment here for a return of about two per cent . . . it's stupid. Point is, we couldn't have as much fun doing anything else . . .'

This is the story of this remarkable man, and of the other talented men who have helped him forge Group Lotus and build its reputation and its strength. It is also the story of Lotus racing accomplishments over 11 frantically busy and memorable years . . . I hope it does them justice.

1961

Backbone for prosperity

In January 1961 the Lotus Group of Companies were just half-way through their second year at their purpose-built works in Delamare Road, Cheshunt. The old Roman town, 14 miles North of London, had grown into a centre of light industry in modern times, and Lotus had moved there in June, 1959. They were to stay there for seven years, during which time the Group and its products were to grow to full maturity and win Worldwide success and acclaim.

The new year found Lotus Cars fully involved with the assembly of the Elite road and racing GT, while Lotus Components were laying down their production lines for the new Formula Junior Lotus 20 single-seater. They also built the Lotus 19 sports-racers and the Lotus Seven fun cars, while tucked away in their own shop were Team Lotus, maintaining their old Lotus 18s for the start of the new 1.5 litre Formula 1, and preparing to cut the first metal on the new Lotus 21 Grand Prix car.

Already the international racing season was under way, and down in New Zealand Team Lotus mechanics Jim Endruweit and Dick Scammell were looking after the cars driven by Clark, Ireland and Surtees in the Tasman Series. They had an hilarious trip, punctuated by a blast along New Zealand's only strip of motorway just outside Auckland which ended with both of them receiving speeding tickets from a somewhat out-of-breath traffic cop. On the tickets the 'vehicle' was described as 'Formula 1 Lotus' . . . This, of course, was one of the old 2.5 litre cars.

The announcement of the new formula, with its high minimum weight and one-litre-smaller engines, had caused a furore among many of the leading constructors, and this had led to the adoption of an additional 3 litre InterContinental Formula for certain British events, but when the new Grand Prix formula proved so successful the 3 litre class was quietly dropped. Colin Chapman had not been one of its supporters: 'I realised that Formula 1 was going to be 1.5 litres and that there wasn't much we could do about it. There was no satisfactory engine available with which we could compete against Ferrari, and so we just had to treat the year as an interim season during which we ran a four-cylinder Coventry Climax the same as everybody else. Ferrari just ran away with the races, but we were secure in the knowledge that Climax were coming along with their V8 for the following season. This was the year when Jimmy Clark really showed his virtuosity as a Formula 1 driver. I already knew he was good, but it became apparent that he was really something very special . . . he was brilliant.'

While Team Lotus won their first World Championship-qualifying round during the year, and Stirling Moss was the only man to beat the Ferraris in his old 1960 car, Lotus Components' customer cars were selling like hot cakes. Lotus as a whole was still very competition-orientated, and even the Elite road car was really a racer in disguise . . . it was also rapidly becoming a threat to the Group's existence . . .

Chapman: 'The Elite was really a road-going racing car, and used many of the racing components. We didn't have much experience of road-car economics when we designed it, and without long-range tooling, long-range buying and strict cost-saving it was finally just uneconomic to build. I believe we lost over £100 on each car we built. Something had to be done, and so we started work on the Elan.'

The Lotus 26 Elan was to prove probably the most significant car in the Group's history. From early chassis developments with this car there stemmed the Lotus 25 monocoque, and even before that certain other developments on the touring car had found their way into racing.

When the new Lotus 21 made its debut at Monaco it featured a lightweight ZF transmission and rubber-doughnut drive-shaft joints for the first time. During 1961 the Special Equipment Lotus Elite Series 2 had used a ZF transmission as standard, and the whole deal with the German company came from some earlier business. During the previous year Colin's own Lotus gearbox for the Formula 1 car had continued to prove troublesome. It suffered from selection and engagement problems, and consequently the drivers didn't like it very much. In an effort to overcome these problems Colin went to Friedrichshafen to talk ZF into producing parts for his own gearbox. While he was there he happened to see a transaxle lying in their experimental shop which looked suitable for adaptation to a mid-engined Grand Prix car application. The German engineers proved willing and able to produce suitable lightweight four-and five-speed all-synchromesh gearboxes, and so the Lotus 21 appeared with ZF transmission.

The rubber doughnuts were an Elan prototype development, in which Colin decided to do away with troublesome splines and add a cushioning element in the drive-line. 'It then occurred to me that if you ran the same thing on a racing car you could cushion the drive, run a lighter gearbox, suffer less incipient wheelspin from irregularities in the road surface, and save weight and complication. They worked beautifully, and we continued to use them for a number of years until space problems (like when we wanted to fit inboard brakes) prevented us doing so. The original Elan prototype had inboard rear brakes with doughnut drive-shaft joints, but we soon found that they wouldn't work. If you parked on a hill and yanked the handbrake on, the car would roll back a yard before the doughnuts wound-up and stopped it!.

While the all-glass-fibre Elite was rapidly losing the money the racing cars were making—which was considerable—design of the Elan revolved originally around another chassisless construction, but it soon became obvious that this was unsound commercially, and Colin was still working on the basic considerations which had spawned the Elite; light weight, reasonable cost, and good handling. The tooling cost for a pressed-steel body would have been prohibitive, and a tubular spaceframe chassis with separate body panels would have been both heavy and complex. So the two concepts of a unitary glass-fibre body-shell and a separate load-bearing chassis had to be combined, and the result was a fabricated steel backbone. During the year development proceeded with this type of construction, and as Chapman and his design team delved further into the backbone -chassis idea the more promising it looked.

Meanwhile, Steve Sanville, who was in charge of Lotus powertrain developments, was progressing with the engine intended for the new car. The idea of a Lotus engine had been in the air since 1958, and it was intended to build a unit using as many proprietary components as possible. Early development work was carried out on a 1,600 cc Ford Consul, fitted with a Raymond Mays-modified cylinder head, but when Ford announced their 997 cc 105E engine for the new Anglia in 1959 this looked to be a much more promising subject. Harry Mundy—formerly with Coventry-Climax—was called in as a consultant, and he directed the design of a twin-overhead-camshaft cylinder head for the new engine.

Mike Costin was Lotus' Technical Director at the time, working out his three-year contract before leaving to join Cosworth Engineering, the company he had formed with Keith Duckworth to tune and develop racing engines. One of Keith's Cosworth Formula Junior engines was craned into Mike's Anglia at this time to see how the device would perform; apparently it was terrifying, and work proceeded . . .

The original twin-cam-headed engine retained the standard Ford bottom-end, but before any serious testing started the design team already had set their sights on bigger fry.

Ford had just announced their 1,340 cc 109E Classic engine, and the first Lotus-Ford twin-cam was completed on this block, and ran for the first time on October 16, 1961. It produced 87.3 bhp at 5,500 rpm by the time all the tweaks had been completed, but once again Ford developments had outstripped the Lotus team. The new 116E five-main-bearing engine for the Capri and Cortina was on the stocks, and this was then projected as the base for the new twin-cam. The original 109E experimental unit was bored-out to 1,477 cc in just under a month from first firing, and in this form it produced a reliable 97.1 bhp at 5,500 rpm.

There were some problems, particularly with the standard 1,340 cc bottom-end, but the aluminium head itself was not stiff enough and caused recurrent gasket failures. It was stiffened with webs across the central plug well, and struts were later added within the water jacketing, spreading loads from between the combustion chambers to the vertical flanks of the plug well. This new head proved extremely rigid, and offered more gasket loading than even the standard iron head. Other problems mainly involved crankcase breathing, for the first unit acted like a huge oil pump and blasted all its lubricant out of the breather at high rpm. The problem was solved with a breather chamber Araldited to the head, and things then seemed to be set fair for 1962 and the announcement of the Elan . . .

In the meantime, the Elite was continuing to amaze the sceptics with the strength of its glass-fibre body/chassis unit, and as well as proving a popular, if expensive, road car it still excelled in circuit work. The S2 version had been announced in October, 1960, with revised rear suspension. The original suspension layout had been virtually identical to that of the original front-engined Formula 2 cars, with tall 'Chapman struts' combining telescopic dampers and coil springs, located laterally by fixed-length drive-shafts and longitudinally by single radius rods. But this system had its shortcomings, and allowed the rear wheels to toe-in, making the car unstable at speed, so the new system used two-piece radius rods on either side, resembling swept-back reversed wishbones in plan form, which located the wheels much more effectively and gave much improved stability.

The Coventry-Climax light-alloy FWE engine was retained, fitted with a single SU carburettor as standard and producing 75 bhp at 6,100 rpm from its 1,216 cc. A high-performance Special Equipment (SE) Elite was also offered, with the ZF gearbox replacing a BMC 'B' Series unit, and twin 1½-inch SUs boosting power output to 83 bhp at 6,500 rpm. The price of this version was £2,118, compared with £2,006 for the standard model, and the old 1960 price of £1,949 . . . some measure of the way costs had soared.

In October the Elite was offered in component form

Formula 1 Lotuses came in various shapes during 1961. Above: Dan Gurney drove Mrs Louise Bryden-Brown's modified Lotus 18 when his works Porsche contract permitted. On this occasion it was the Silver City Trophy race at Brands Hatch. Below: In the same race Stirling Moss, the winner, chases Jim Clark's Lotus 21 with the re-bodied UDT/Laystall Lotus 18.

in an attempt to reduce assembly costs, and the price of £1,299 offered a tremendous saving. The 'B'-series gearbox from the MGA was retained, and one road-tester returned figures of 17.2 seconds for the standing-start quarter-mile, 10 seconds from 0-60 mph and 30.5 mpg in an early kit-built car. Top speed was a splendid 115 mph, and with speeds of 80 mph in third, 51 mph in second and 32 mph in first the Elite owner/builder was certainly given value for his money . . .

At the same time a new, slightly more sophisticated and more habitable Super Seven was introduced. The stark, lightweight little Seven had been produced in Series 2 form in June, 1960, using a revised tubular chassis-frame and modified suspension, with a choice of BMC 'A'-series or Ford 100E side-valve engines. A new S2 was offered at the Racing Car Show in London in January, using the new 105E Ford ohv engine and gearbox and selling for the first time in component form for £499—a race-bred Lotus for under £500!

Now the Super Seven used the same basic structure, but added power was provided by a Cosworth-tuned 1,340 cc Ford Classic engine. This was fitted with twin Weber carbs, had a compression ratio of 9.5:1 and produced a fierce 85 bhp at 6,000 rpm. With an all-up weight of only 8 cwt this flared-winged little monster had a power-to-weight ratio exceeding 200 bhp per ton, and it could be yours (in component form only) for as little as £599. These Lotus kit cars were to prove very popular, but numerous disgruntled customers found bits missing and had a long wait before Lotus Components could catch-up and offer them the truant bits and pieces as spares.

Amid all this road-car activity Lotus pursued a generally highly successful competitive programme, and Team Lotus' trusty old Zephyr transporter with its invariably overloaded two-car double-deck trailer was a familiar sight all over the Continent. Dick Scammell and Andrew Ferguson both recall the problems, the alarms and the excursions with this old wagon, such as the occasion when a steering arm broke at 80 mph along Belgium's Jabbeke highway. 'We suddenly turned hard-left, missed the end of the barrier and shot straight into a parking area . . . Good job there was nobody parked in it at the time. We ground to a stop against the wall just before it took us back out on to the motorway!'.

The hard-pressed truck regularly blew its brake seals, and on one occasion an on-the-ball German pump attendant saw it approaching along the autobahn at its standard 80 mph cruising speed and had his pump ready as he saw the indicators signalling a stop. Much to his surprise the wagon roared into his filling station, roared straight past his pump and roared back on to the autobahn, its white-faced driver pumping desperately on a limp brake pedal!

Lotus' flying incident of the year was probably Innes Ireland's flight back from the Nurburgring for the Brands Hatch August Bank Holiday meeting. He, Colin and Jimmy were all tired and dispirited after a hectic German Grand Prix and one by one they nodded off. Their light 'plane droned on through the darkness, until Innes woke up and snapped 'Who's flying?'. Colin jerked awake with a muffled 'I thought you were!', and Jimmy realised there was nothing he could do anyway and nodded off again . . .

The Springbok Series at the end of the year was a light-hearted venture for Colin, Jimmy and Trevor Taylor, and for mechanics David Lazenby and Cedric Selzer who looked after their cars. The two drivers, Chapman and Max Caplan (who managed a garage in Johannesburg) hired a Zodiac for a trip round the Kruger National Park, and one of their hosts took them deep into the wild-life preserve in his VW. They sighted some giraffe and Jimmy clambered on to the roof to take some cine shots while the animals fled and his driver gave chase. The VW was doing about 20 mph when the driver swerved to miss a bush, which launched the Scotsman straight ahead—solo! He reckoned he was running like the devil before he touched the ground . . .

During 1961 Team Lotus had achieved the guv'nor's primary ambition of winning a World Championship round in their own right, and with development of a new touring car, and a new engine to power it, well advanced the company was about to enter a new phase in its history. Stirling Moss had proved that a brilliantly driven obsolete Lotus was a match for the strongest opposition, and with V8 engines promised for the new year Chapman's sights were fixed firmly on the World Championship. With a victory in that under his belt, what better way to launch a new road car . . .

Moss launches his attack on Ginther's Ferrari during the closing minutes of the Dutch Grand Prix, and is about to claim fourth place with his venerable Lotus.

1961 RACING RECORD
Grands Prix and other major formulae

Team Lotus began their racing programme just one week into the New Year, when Stan Chapman took Jimmy Clark, Innes Ireland and John Surtees down-under for the Tasman series in New Zealand and Australia.

They were running a pair of 2.5 litre Lotus 18s, and their first race was the New Zealand Grand Prix at Ardmore on January 7th where they were faced with Moss in the 2.5 litre Walker 18 and the works Cooper-Climaxes of Brabham and McLaren. Moss was the pre-race favourite, and he led the Grand Prix from laps 5 to 30 before retiring with Colotti transmission troubles, leaving the race to the works Coopers. Brabham won with Bruce second, and Innes was running third in the works Lotus 18 before quitting with transmission trouble. Clark's car wouldn't run properly, and he spluttered home an unhappy seventh.

The following week the Tasman circus moved to Levin for the Vic Hudson Memorial Trophy race, where Jimmy was second behind Jo Bonnier's Yeoman Credit Cooper and ahead of future World Champion Denny Hulme in Feo Stanton's Formula 2 Cooper.

The unheard-of happened a week later at Christchurch for the Lady Wigram Trophy—it rained! Not since 1952 had there been a wet Wigram, but Brabham was undismayed and demonstrated his mettle by winning at 78 mph, with a battered Walker Lotus splashing home in second place.

Jimmy Clark had snatched pole position in practice, and chopped past Bonnier's spinning Cooper to threaten Brabham's lead before spinning off himself in the treacherous conditions and failing to restart a dead engine. Meanwhile Moss had been shunted by McLaren at the first corner, which had put the Walker Lotus' front wheels out of alignment. This made the car a pig to handle, but Moss the Showman performed superbly for the drenched crowd, pressing on in seventh place and pulling up the leader board as cars ahead dropped out. Then he was shunted again, this time having the left-rear radius rods bent and carburettor intakes mangled, but he struggled on to take second place from local man Angus Hyslop's Cooper just before the finish. Brabham set the fastest lap at 1min 39sec, but Moss' virtuoso performance in the crippled 18 brought him second fastest time, only 0.2 seconds slower. Surtees drove the second works 18, and he retired after 26 laps with engine trouble after running as high as third.

Immediately after the race at Christchurch's airfield circuit, the circus took a ferry across the Tasman Sea for the Warwick Farm International at Sydney, Australia. The new course, laid out around Sydney's famous horse-race course, saw staggering temperatures on race day, 110 degrees in the open and an insufferable 148 degrees on the track surface!

In these conditions the race was as much a test of a driver's stamina as of his skill, and again Moss proved he had a surfeit of both, leading virtually from start to finish in the dark-blue 18 while only three other cars finished, Innes being the best works Lotus finisher with a gritty second place. Austen Miller's local Cooper was fourth, and he was so shattered by the heat that he spun across the finish line and fell out of his car's cockpit . . .

Two Tasman events remained, at Teretonga back in New Zealand and at Ballarat in Australia. Roy Salvadori drove Yeoman Credit's 18 into second place behind team-mate Bonnier's Cooper at the former, while at Ballarat the race was a BRM walkover with the 2.5 litre P48 cars of Gurney and Hill first and second.

Back home a bronzed Stan Chapman announced his retirement as team manager and moved to Devon to enjoy it, and Andrew Ferguson—late of Cooper Cars and the Camoradi team, joined in his place, taking up the position he was to hold with Lotus for the following nine years.

The team's Formula 1 plans had been announced by Colin Chapman, with Innes Ireland and Jimmy Clark as regular drivers in a two-car team, and Trevor Taylor as reserve. The early races were to be contested by the 1960 Formula 1 Mark 18 chassis updated with 1,500 cc Coventry-Climax four-cylinder FPF engines, self-starters and other modifications to comply with the new FIA regulations which had just been introduced, replacing the old 2.5 litre Formula 1 of 1954-1960. Lotus, and several of the other British works and independent teams, retained their old 2.5 litre engines for British InterContinental Formula events.

The British clung steadfastly to the idea of an InterContinental Formula, with a capacity limit of 3 litres, in place of the unpopular new small-engined Formula 1. The new GP class had been much berated, but the 'one-and-a-halves' were to prove so closely competitive during 1961 that it was the 3 litre class which was destined to die on its feet. Colin never felt that Formula InterContinental would provide a successful alternative to Formula 1, and his new 1,500 cc Formula 1 design was to prove the most potent of the year's Ferrari-baiters.

The first major race of the European season was the InterContinental Lombank Trophy held at Snetterton in March. This included a separate Formula 1 class, but Jack Brabham won handsomely in Tommy Atkins' privately owned InterContinental Cooper-Climax, nearly a lap ahead of Cliff Allison, who was making a welcome return to racing in UDT-Laystall's 2.5 litre Mark 18; he had been badly injured while practising at Monaco in a works Ferrari the previous year. Ireland's works 2.5 litre Lotus 18 set the fastest lap at 1min 33.6sec, 104.23 mph, while Henry Taylor's 1.5 litre UDT-Laystall 18 was placed second in the Formula 1 class behind John Surtees' Yeoman Credit Cooper. Clark drove a similar car for Team Lotus, and was just pipped for fifth place overall by Salvadori's Formula 1 Cooper, which had been driven furiously after two stops to cure misfiring.

Just over a week later came the Easter Monday Goodwood meeting, coinciding with the non-Championship Formula 1 Pau Grand Prix in Southern France—the first serious race of the new 1.5 litre formula.

In Sussex, a large crowd saw a 21-lap Inter-Continental race for the Lavant Cup and the inaugural 1,500 cc Formula 1 event over 42 laps for the International '100' Glover Trophy. Moss' Walker Cooper won the InterContinental event, and the best-placed Lotus was Salvadori's Yeoman Credit 18 down in fifth place. A Cooper also won the Formula 1 race, with the forceful Surtees keeping well ahead of Moss in the re-engined Walker 18. The ex-motorcyclist maintained a 2.5 to 3 seconds lead until the Walker car began to misfire on lap 32 and drop behind Graham Hill's BRM-Climax and Salvadori's Cooper finally to finish fourth; Ireland's works Lotus 18 was fifth and Henry Taylor's UDT 18 sixth. Dan Gurney gave Louise Bryden-Brown's 18 an outing in the Lavant Cup race and bent it quite severely, fortunately without suffering any personal harm.

Meanwhile Jimmy Clark was scoring Team Lotus' first victory of the 1,500 cc formula down at Pau, where Trevor Taylor was having his first Formula 1 race as Jimmy's team-mate; while Innes drove chassis 372 at Goodwood, Jimmy used 371 and Trevor 374 at the picturesque French town circuit. Brabham took pole position for Cooper in practice, with Jimmy beside him and Trintignant's older Cooper on the outside, but the French veteran's clutch failed on the warming-up lap and race director 'Toto' Roche relegated the unfortunate 'Petoulet' to the back of the grid, moving everybody else up one place. While all this shuffling was going on the panicky Roche suddenly realised that Jimmy's car was sitting completely alone on the centre of the front row, with nary a soul near it.

Clark was at the pits sorting out his helmet and goggles, and with most of the engines running and Roche's flag-hand itching he sprinted across to his car, leapt into the cockpit and was still pulling his gloves on as the start was given. Roche raised five fingers to indicate there were as many seconds to go, then immediately waggled the flag and scampered for cover as the field screamed away!

Despite his hasty preparations Jimmy led Brabham into the first corner, closely followed by Jo Bonnier in a brand-new Lotus 18 owned by the German driver Wolfgang Seidel. When the fuel pump spindle on Brabham's Cooper failed Jimmy's works Lotus was left with a long lead over the Swede's similar white-painted car, and they finished in that order. Meanwhile, Trevor Taylor had a great scrap with Bianchi and Gendebien in their Emerysons until both Belgians crashed under pressure but Trevor retired later with a broken gearbox output shaft when running fourth. Both the Pau 18s were aged and well-used machines, running Coventry Climax Mark I FPF four-cylinder engines and five-speed Lotus transmissions.

The season was getting into its stride, and the weekend after Pau saw the Brussels Grand Prix on the public-road Heysel circuit near the famous Atomium of the World Fair. Innes ran the car which Trevor had used at Pau while Jimmy retained his winning car, the Yorkshireman being on hand more or less as an extra mechanic.

Rob Walker Racing arrived at Brussels with both of their Lotus 18s, Moss deciding to use the car which retained the standard Lotus transmission in preference to the Walker 'Special' with its Colotti gearbox. Tim Parnell's standard 1960 Formula 2 18 was on loan to the Belgian Andre Pilette, and an interesting home-developed 18 was entered by Tony Marsh, the hill-climb specialist.

This had been fitted with a 1960 Cooper gearbox, splined half-shafts and top links on the rear suspension to relieve the drive-shafts of their normal duties as locating members for the uprights. Stronger steering arms were also fitted, and the front anti-roll bar was attached to the lower wishbone by a long link in place of the normal fitting in which the roll bar just sat in an eye on top of the king-post. These modifications added some weight, but made the car look safer and rather better-engineered . . . they proved to be rather prophetic of later Lotus developments.

Trintignant become a non-starter in Seidel's 18 because the mechanics forgot to put oil in the gearbox and it chewed-up the differential during practice, while Ireland was feeling off-colour and consequently was slow, and Clark's car suffered gasket failures. Moss was despairing of getting his car running properly, and in fact the misfiring problem was not identified and cured until some time later. The trouble was mainly at high speed, and the fault lay with the Weber carburettors' recent transition from an almost hand-made product to a mass-production item. Minor flaws in the mass-produced carburettors caused the floats to stick intermittently and the inlet tract would flood or starve dependent upon where they stuck. Alf Francis, Walker's famous chief mechanic, eventually traced the problem and cured it rapidly by smoothing-off the inside of the float chambers, but in the meantime the problem was to remain a frustrating mystery.

Out of all these problems Marsh's 18 Special came through as the fastest Lotus qualifier, on the inside of row three for the first of the three 22-lap heats, the overal result being decided on aggregate. Marsh, Ireland and Cliff Allison in the UDT 18 finished fifth, sixth and seventh in Heat 1; Marsh and Ireland were third and fourth in Heat 2; and Moss finally got going sufficiently well to take second place behind Brabham's Cooper in Heat 3 with Marsh finishing fourth. Overall results put the English privateer in a fine third place behind the works Coopers of Brabham and McLaren, with Allison fifth, Moss sixth and Ian Burgess in the Camoradi Team's 18 seventh. Clark's car was put out by a broken gearbox input shaft in Heat 1, while Ireland actually led Heat 3 on the opening lap but spun in a big way on the autoroute and bent the rear-end against the bankings.

Later in April the Aintree '200' was run at Liverpool

Left: Extra trunking was used to feed more air to the engine of Moss's rebodied Lotus at Spa, but without success. Below: Clark's first big race win came at Pau in 1961. Bottom: Clark gives the Lotus 21 its debut at Monaco; relaxed concentration.

in dank and miserable conditions which mirrored Lotus fortunes. Brabham's works Cooper scored another win and the best Lotus performance was Tony Marsh's seventh place in his 18 Special. The works Coopers ran with the new Dunlop D12 high-hysteresis wet-weather tyres and the Lotus entries were handicapped by the lack of them. Innes found 371 unmanageable in the wet—conditions he hated anyway—and finished a tardy ninth, while Jimmy's 372 was holding a consistent fifth place before his engine began to misfire. He stopped for attention and dropped well back while the best that Trevor Taylor could manage with 374 was a lowly 20th place.

Three days later came the Italian Liberation holiday and the XI Gran Premio Siracusa in Sicily. This was the day which the British constructors had been awaiting with some trepidation, for it was to mark the debut of the new V6 Ferrari which, apart from the German Porsches, was the only car fully-developed for the start of the new formula. Many of the Aintree cars were air-freighted direct to Sicily, although Moss' Brussels 18 was sent by road from Belgium. Clark was given 374, which had a canted engine and enclosed carburettors, and Ireland had the earlier 371 with the upright power unit, but both Team Lotus 18s were now looking very tatty and hard-raced. There were only two mechanics available to look after the cars and the pit, so Gregor Grant, late editor of Autosport, took over the time-keeping and lap-scoring duties for the race. The only other Lotus entries were Seidel's older 1960 18 and Ernesto Prinoth's Formula 2 model which he practised but didn't start.

The sensation of practice was the performance of the solitary V6 Ferrari driven by 25-years-old Giancarlo Baghetti. During 1960 the Italian racing teams had clubbed together to form a confederation called FISA, and Ferrari had agreed to make available a 1961 Formula 1 car to their chosen driver, to be selected on the basis of 1960 national results. After much argument Baghetti, a successful Formula Junior driver, was their choice, and this was to be his Formula 1 debut.

Even with such a responsibility on his shoulders, the taciturn Baghetti responded well and only Gurney's works Porsche qualified faster in practice. Surtees' Cooper took an early lead in the race, chased hard by Gurney and team-mate Bonnier in their Porsches, and Baghetti. But the Italian quickly proved that he could catch and pass the other Formula 1 cars as he liked, and he was soon dictating the pace of the race. After disposing of the Porsches with ease he drove on to a tumultuously popular victory.

Brabham, Ireland and Graham Hill had a great scrap for fourth place, while Moss' Walker car misfired its way round at the back of the field, where it was accompanied by Jimmy's works car which was also ailing. After Innes had held a strong fourth place for eight laps his fuel pressure began to rise from around 2 or 3 psi to nearer 10 psi. The throttle had also been sticking and he was having to hook it back with his toe, so he stopped before he had a crash or something in the fuel system burst. The pit stop dropped him to 13th place, and then his throttle stuck open again and powered him into some straw bales, bending the front suspension and retiring the car. Just before the finish Moss' magneto drive sheared and he had to push across for a miserable eighth place, while Clark soldiered on into sixth position.

There was no letting-up in the hectic international calendar, and the following Saturday the BRDC ran their International Trophy race for InterContinental Formula cars at a wet and gloomy Silverstone. This was another Cooper-dominated race, with Moss winning in the Walker car, followed by Brabham and Salvadori. Henry Taylor was fourth in one of the Walker 18s, loaned to UDT-Laystall for the occasion, and John Surtees was an heroic fifth after spinning the Vanwall 'Whale'. This car had been built up after experience gained with a Vanwall-engined Lotus 18 chassis the previous year, using a 2.85 litre version of the powerful 2.5 litre Formula 1 engine, mounted behind the driver.

In practice Mike Parkes shunted the Yeoman Credit 18 when the track rod broke, and Dan Gurney smashed Mrs Bryden-Brown's 18 once again. It had been straightened-out after the Goodwood accident but was handling diabolically and thumped the bank at Becketts. In the race Clark's works 18 (372) expired with crownwheel and pinion failure when running an unhappy ninth, and both Allison in the UDT car and Ireland's works 374 spun into the ditch and out of the race at Maggotts.

While the ageing 2.5 litre machinery had been given another outing at Silverstone the new 1.5 litre cars were being carefully prepared for the first Grande Epreuve of the year under the new formula, the Monaco GP, one week later.

Monte Carlo saw the first appearance of the new Porsche chassis with coil-spring front suspension, the 120-degrees V6 Ferraris developed from the original 65-degrees models, and the 1961 Lotus Formula 1 contender, the brand-new type 21.

Colin had been hard at work on a design to reduce the frontal area and aerodynamic drag of the boxy 18, and the first step towards this improvement had been the Formula Junior Lotus 20, released at the Racing Car Show in London back in January. The new 21 was based closely on the Junior, but shared few components. It used an entirely new small-diameter multi-tubular spaceframe chassis, with the main longerons used to carry oil and water from the front-mounted radiators to the rear-mounted engine.

A major departure from conventional practice came in the front suspension for the coil-spring-damper units were tucked away within the body and were operated by bell-crank extensions of the upper suspension arms, the latter being one-piece fabrications in sheet steel which pivotted on the upper chassis rails. A very short anti-roll bar was attached to the inboard arms so that this, too, was tucked away well out of sight and out of the air-stream. This was not a complete innovation in

Stirling Moss' two greatest Formula 1 drives took place during 1961. His victory in the Monaco Grand Prix (above) with Rob Walker's Lotus 18 with side panels removed was an epic of on-the-limit driving. Moss' mastery of the wet helped him to another victory in the German Grand Prix (below), the Lotus now with its smoother body.

Grand Prix car design, for the 4CLT/48 Maserati of 1948 had used a similar system, but with the new low, compact and sleek Lotus body the saving in drag must have been much more worthwhile.

At the rear Chapman had scrapped the use of the drive-shaft as a transverse locating link in the suspension, the shaft being relieved of these duties by a single top link on either side, effectively forming very wide-based wishbones with the upper radius rods. These were higher-mounted on a taller upright than on the Lotus 18, but the lower reversed wishbones and radius rods were much the same as before.

The geometry of the new rear suspension layout normally would have required a sliding-spline drive-shaft, but Colin evolved a lighter alternative, with one-piece drive-shafts coupled to the transmission through large-diameter rubber doughnut couplings. The 'bunge' in these couplings gave the in-and-out movement required of the drive-shafts as the wheels rose and fell.

The latest Coventry-Climax Mark II FPF engines were used in both works cars at Monaco, and were fitted upright in the chassis frame. They could be mated to a new four-or-five-speed transaxle (dependent on the circuit) built to Lotus requirements by the ZF company of Friedrichshaven in Germany. Fuel tanks were provided on either side of the driver, their large capacity giving a bulkier midriff than on the Lotus 20 Formula Junior, and the seat itself was formed in a third central tank. Both cars, number 930 for Clark and 931 for Ireland, were beautifully finished and immaculately turned out for their debut.

Reappearing at Monaco were the Laystall five-speed transaxles fitted to UDT's two Lotus 18s, these being in effect the first Hewland transmissions, Mike Hewland having been approached to produce them by Bob Gibson-Jarvie of UDT; the new five-speed unit had already made its debut on one of the UDT cars at Aintree. Hewland transmissions were later to become almost universal in all classes of sports and single-seater motor racing.

Climax had produced eight of their new Mark II engines for Monaco, using a strengthened bottom end developed from the large 2.5 litre engine which allowed higher revs and a gentler torque curve than the standard Mark I 1.5 litre unit. Lotus and Cooper received two engines each, and Yeoman Credit, UDT-Laystall, R.R.C.Walker and BRM each received one.

The first practice session on Thursday saw both the new 21s going very quickly, and Jimmy Clark covered a lap in 1min 39.6sec before crashing heavily next time round at Ste Devote. The chassis had to be stripped and straightened for the race, but worse was to follow . . .

Innes Ireland snubbed his 21's nose on Gendebien's Emeryson on the Friday, but the damage was repaired and the nose cone repainted yellow in time for the last session on the Saturday. But Innes wasn't very happy with the new ZF transmission, and when he changed down instead of up in the Tir aux Pigeons tunnel the new Lotus went wild, slamming from barrier to barrier before finally rolling out into the sunlight and pitching its unfortunate driver on to the road. Innes was picked up with cuts and bruises and understandably severe shock, and was out of the Grand Prix.

Meanwhile, Jimmy's car had been rebuilt with a five-speed gearbox installed, and his Thursday time was sufficient for the outside of the front row of the grid. Ginther's Ferrari was in the middle with Moss' Walker 18 on pole position.

The Walker mechanics had removed the 18's side panels in anticipation of a hot race, and fixed up a drinking bottle in the cockpit. Ferrari had their problems, but Moss knew he was giving away 20 bhp to them, and if they were going to win he was determined to give them a run for their money and make them work hard all the way. Just before the grid formed up a cracked chassis tube was found on the Walker car, but despite the 30 gallons of fuel in the tanks Alf Francis calmly welded the crack solid in time for the start.

One of Jimmy's plugs oiled-up on the warming-up lap, presumably due to damaged piston rings, so he was wheeled on to the grid with three hard plugs and one soft plug fitted to his engine. He started-up only 10 seconds before flag-fall and accelerated away into second place behind Ginther's fleeing Ferrari. But on the next lap he stopped with a shorting fuel pump, a wire having been crimped under a chassis tube in the hasty rebuild. The soft plug had oiled-up again and was changed, but Jimmy was in after another stuttering lap to have yet another plug fitted and finally he rejoined the race seven laps behind.

Moss had inherited his early second place, and as the 100-lap race progressed he breathed harder and harder down the freckled little American's neck. On lap 14 he nipped by the red car, towing Bonnier's hard-charging Porsche with him, and from then on he pulled away. The Ferraris of Hill and Ginther soon displaced the silver Porsche and began a vengeful chase of the dark blue Lotus. Ginther was forcing Phil Hill along, and the pair of them closed on the 18, getting to within 4½ seconds by lap 55. Three laps later Moss could see the Ferraris' shark noses clearly in his mirrors, and he opened the gap to 5 seconds by driving as hard as he knew. He was bulleting through slower traffic, making good use of his superb reflexes and judgement, and every split-second the Ferraris lost among the back-markers evened-out their power advantage on the short straights and climbs.

Hill was looking hot and bothered in his V6 and as the gap opened to 6 seconds Ginther began to pressure his compatriot for he was being baulked. On lap 75 the gum-chewing American slid ahead at the Gasworks Hairpin and began to reel-in the Walker car. By lap 80 the gap was down to 4½ seconds, another half-second coming off on lap 81. By this time the lap record was already down to 1min 37sec, faster than practice, and on the 85th lap Ginther set the fastest lap of the race at 1min 36.3sec, only a tenth of a second slower than the outright 2.5 litre lap record of the previous year.

With 10 laps to go the valiant Ginther tossed his gum

overboard for one final attack on Moss. By lap 96 the gap was still 4½ seconds, on lap 98 it was down to 4 seconds, then Moss responded and held his lead into the 100th and final circuit. Around the Tabac left-hander for the last time, and Moss flashed across the finish line with the Walker Lotus 18 just 3.6 seconds ahead of the Ferrari, winning against all the odds after a classic among the classic races.

Moss' obsolete Lotus had totally outclassed all the other British Climax-powered cars, but Allison finished way down in eighth place in the UDT 18, and the delayed Jimmy Clark was tenth, the last runner to finish, 11 laps behind. The only other Lotus in the race was Wolfgang Seidel's 18, driven by the Swiss engineer Michel May, who had retired on lap 42 with a broken gearbox oil pipe.

Lotus had won their first Grande Epreuve of the 1961 season and of the new formula, but once again the victory had belonged to Moss and Walker and not to Team Lotus. Stirling had proved that the Ferraris and Porsches could be beaten, but it was Colin's burning ambition that his green cars should do the beating.

After this classic race there was another mad scramble to prepare the cars for the Dutch Grand Prix at Zandvoort on Whit-Monday. Moss had been the moral winner of the previous year's event in trusty old 912—his Monaco-winning 18—and he held the lap record at 1min 33.8sec, although he had lapped in 1min 33.2sec during practice with the 2.5 litre car. With Ireland still in hospital Team Lotus were running Clark in 930 and Taylor was to feel his way round quietly in 371, the old Lotus 18 works car fitted with a Mark II engine. Jimmy used the unraced Mark II engine salvaged from Innes' wrecked car, while Moss had his usual choice of Lotus or Cooper, but remained faithful to the Monaco-winner. He got down to 1min 36.2sec in practice with this car, a time he couldn't approach in the Cooper, but the three works Ferraris were in a class of their own, monopolising the front row with times in the 1min 35sec bracket.

Stirling's time was fourth fastest, and the quickest works Lotus was Clark's at 1min 36.9sec, which put him back on the fourth row behind the BRMs, Gurney's leading Porsche and the Coopers. Taylor was on the back row with his ancient warhorse, and the other Lotus entry of Ian Burgess in the Camoradi 18 failed to make the race after the throttle had jammed open in practice and the car had ploughed through the fencing, without injury to the driver.

Despite his lowly grid position Clark made a searing start, and although at the end of the lap Wolfgang von Trips' Ferrari had built a sizeable lead from Phil Hill's car, Graham Hill's BRM-Climax and the green Lotus 21 were right on the tail of the second Ferrari. Ginther had muffed his start and was back in the following bunch which included Moss, who had been squeezed-out by the Ferraris at the start.

Hill and Clark took on the Phil Hill Ferrari with a vengeance, and on lap 7, with its fuel tanks still nearly full, Clark's Lotus set the fastest lap of the race at 1min 35.5sec, a time which Jimmy had been unable to approach in practice. Moss was challenging Ginther for fifth place, but as the leading BRM dropped back Clark was being held up in the Lotus, which allowed von Trips to consolidate his clear lead.

But on lap 21 Jimmy upset Ferrari plans by splitting their two leading cars, and with only 3½ seconds covering the trio von Trips was forced to set a faster pace than should have been necessary, or prudent. Moss had managed to pass Graham Hill, and then Ginther—handicapped by a collapsing seat—did likewise and then hauled-in the Walker Lotus 18. By lap 55 Phil Hill reckoned he had done his job of covering von Trips' tail and during the next two laps he closed on the leader, leaving Jimmy floundering in his wake but in an unchallenged third place. The Ferraris finished the 75-lap race less than a second apart with Clark 1.2 seconds back in a fine third position for four championship points. Near the end Ginther spun at the Hunzerug, which allowed Moss into fourth place, and Stirling managed to hold his advantage by a tenth of a second as Ginther ducked out of his slipstream and attempted to sprint ahead over the finish line. Trevor Taylor soldiered on reliably in his creaky old 18, finishing 13th, two laps behind the winner.

There followed a four-week break before the next championship round in Belgium, but in the meantime there was the Silver City Trophy Formula 1 race at Brands Hatch. Team Lotus entered Jimmy in the 21 and he shared the front row of the grid with Surtees' Cooper and Graham Hill's BRM. UDT-Laystall had the services of Stirling Moss in their slippery-bodied 18 Special, while Trevor Taylor was in his Zandvoort car and other 18s were handled by May, Marsh, Gurney, Henry Taylor, Seidel, Bonnier and Parnell. May stalled on the line and had to be pushed away, while Surtees and Clark led wheel-to-wheel on the first lap. Moss consolidated his third place, while Bonnier stopped with split fuel tanks, Trevor Taylor with a chronic misfire and Seidel with gearbox problems. Henry Taylor fell away with misfiring and Gurney's engine was also stuttering, while Tony Marsh was delayed by over-heating. Tim Parnell was slow but reliable in his car, which was being well ballasted by the hefty Derbyshire farmer.

Meanwhile the battle up front had raged fast and furious between Clark and the Yeoman Credit Cooper, and Jimmy nipped ahead on lap 26. Two laps later Surtees missed a gear, found neutral, then stuffed the lever into first in error as he was entering Stirling's Bend. The Cooper spun savagely into the bank, losing its nose, and this left Clark leading with Moss chasing him hard. Trying too hard Jimmy took the edge off his engine, and Moss took the lead along the top straight and pulled away to another popular win. Jimmy held on to place second, and a bevy of Lotus 18s filled fifth to ninth places, in the order Gurney, Marsh, Parnell, Henry and Trevor Taylor, with Bonnier eleventh. Moss set a new Brands Hatch long-circuit record of 1min 42 sec in his chase of the works Lotus 21.

The Belgian Grand Prix at Spa-Francorchamps followed two weeks later, and again Ferrari utterly dominated the race, starting four cars from the first four grid positions and finishing them in the order 1-2-3-4.

The organisers invited 16 entries and a further nine to qualify for the three remaining places on the grid. Of the Lotus contingent Clark and the recovered Innes Ireland were invited in the works 21s, along with Moss in the modified Walker car. The Team Lotus cars included the original 21 as raced at Monaco and Zandvoort, with two brand-new and slightly modified cars using very large front suspension ball joints in place of the original smaller components, and sliding-spline drive-shafts replacing the original rubber doughnuts, which for the moment had fallen from favour. All three cars were fitted with five-speed ZF transmissions and Clark's 932 used SU instead of Weber carburettors. The Walker car had been modified with Mark 21 suspension to become an 18/21 Special; it retained its Colotti transmission, but single top links and sliding-spline drive-shafts at the rear were in line with the latest works specification and a more streamlined type 21 nose cone was fitted, similar to those on UDT's Specials.

The nine attempting to qualify included UDT-Laystall's 18 driven by either Allison or Henry Taylor, Tony Marsh in his Special, straight from a Shelsley Walsh hill-climb success, Ian Burgess in the slim-nosed Camoradi 18, and Seidel with a similar 1960 Lotus 18.

Near tragedy struck on the first practice lap, for the unfortunate Cliff Allison lost the UDT 18 on the embankment curving downhill to Burnenville suffering serious injuries, destroying the car and covering the roadway with debris, mud, oil, petrol and water. This was a distressing accident for his old friends at Lotus, and although he was in no danger it marked the end of his racing career.

The Walker and works teams both experimented with ram trunking to the carburettor intakes on their cars, while Equipe Nationale Belge had a lot of trouble with their Emerysons and finally made a deal with Marsh and Seidel, Mairesse driving the Englishman's car and Bianchi the German's, both hurriedly plastered with yellow paint. Moss' 18/21 was the fastest Lotus, sixth quickest overall,while Clark and Ireland in the works cars were back on the seventh row.

Graham Hill's BRM-Climax led away towards Eau Rouge from the third row of the grid, but was soon swamped by the Ferraris. Clark stopped at the end of his first lap with gearchange problems, while Moss and Ireland were well down the field. Jimmy rejoined on the leaders' fourth lap, but had to stop again to have the mechanism re-adjusted, and eventually he finished 12th, six laps down on Phil Hill's winning Ferrari.

Innes' engine broke a rod and blew up in a big way on the tenth lap, while Moss' car was simply not fast enough on a circuit such as Spa-Francorchamps, although it ran reliably into eighth place. Mairesse retired his borrowed Lotus on lap 8 with engine troubles, and Bianchi had an oil pipe fail on lap 10.

Spa had been a non-event so far as Team Lotus were concerned, and a disaster for UDT who had lost both a car and a driver. But two weeks later came the French Grand Prix at Reims, another high-speed circuit where the Ferrari's power advantage would really show itself.

The two Spa cars reappeared at Reims for Innes and Jimmy, with the earlier 21 as a spare. Clark's car retained its SU carburettors while Ireland's was still on Webers.

The UDT-Laystall finance house team arrived there in surprisingly good order, with Lucien Bianchi joining Henry Taylor in place of the injured Allison, and three cars, two of them with the sleeker body-panelling. All three used Lotus sliding-spline transmissions, the Laystall 'box having been shelved for the time being. Camoradi International had their old Lotus 18 for Burgess, Seidel obtained an entry for Michel May in his 18, and Mairesse arrived with an eye on the spare Team Lotus 21.

Moss was not happy with the handling of his revised car, but in a superb piece of gamesmanship he irritated von Trips into going faster and faster and towing him round for a fine practice lap at 2min 27.6sec, which put him fourth fastest behind the Ferrari-filled front row which was led by Phil Hill at 2min 24.9sec.

Juan-Manuel Bordeu—Fangio's protege who never really made it—did some exploratory laps in the spare UDT car. Clark had some trouble with his car which was repaired in time for the Friday evening session, and this allowed Mairesse to get his hands on the spare works Lotus. Late in the session the Lotus works drivers got into a high-speed slipstreaming dice with the Coopers of McLaren and Surtees, Brooks' BRM and Gurney's Porsche, and Jimmy managed to leap-frog his way round them to record the fifth fastest time at 2min 29.0sec, and join Stirling on the second row.

From the start Moss, Surtees and Clark chased hard after the works Ferraris while Baghetti, having his first Championship race in the FISA Ferrari, was up with the bunch from a mid-field starting position. Henry Taylor stopped early on with a fuel leak, and on lap 4 Ginther in the third Ferrari spun at Muizon, allowing Moss by, but putting Surtees off into the rough and bending his suspension.

This incident broke up the field, but Moss was driving really hard in third place, ducked down behind his screen just like Brabham in the Cooper. Clark and Ireland led the rest of the field, but Baghetti was biding his time, gaining experience among the slipstreaming mid-field bunch.

He moved up and pushed Ireland on to the grass at Muizon, but one lap later Innes was back in the bunch again and soon their battle had brought them closer to Moss and the steadily-pacing leaders. By lap 13 Phil Hill had let von Trips into the lead,following team orders, while Ginther was trailing in third place, and Baghetti was heading the pursuers with Ireland and Clark on his tail and Moss dropping back.

The Walker Lotus was losing its brakes, and Moss stopped at his pit where it was found that the bridge pipe connecting the two sides of the right-rear disc caliper had fractured, letting the pressure and fluid escape. While a new pipe was fitted molten tar centrifuged around the inside of the rear wheel rim, dripped to the bottom and solidified, so that when Stirling restarted the wheel was badly out of balance. He did a slow lap with this terrible vibration, then stopped to have the wheel nuts tightened. He stopped a third time since the vibration wasn't any better and it was some time before the blobs of tar were noticed, clinging to the inside of the wheel. He continued way down the field.

Meanwhile, von Trips' engine had broken after a stone had holed the radiator and Phil Hill was left leading until he spun on melting tar at the Thillois hairpin, with Moss on his tail; the two cars collided, buckling the Ferrari's nose and bending the Lotus 18/21's suspension. Hill couldn't restart for some time, while Moss crept along to retire at the pits, waving to Ferrari team chief Tavoni as he trundled down the pit road.

When Ginther's leading Ferrari also suffered engine failure the race was left between the solitary FISA Ferrari of Baghetti and the Porsches of Bonnier and Gurney, with the two Team Lotus 21s spaced out behind. With two laps left Bonnier slowed with his engine cooked, and Baghetti out-fumbled Gurney at the last corner to lead across the line and so win his one-and-only Grande Epreuve. Jimmy and Innes were third and fourth to a great reception from the Lotus crew, while Taylor was tenth (behind Phil Hill, who had managed to restart his Ferrari), May was 11th and Burgess 14th. Bianchi went out on lap 22, while Mairesse came into the pits with fuel vapourisation and caused great confusion. The '4' of his number 48 had been peeled off by the slipstream, and as he entered the pits it looked as though number 8 (Clark) had stopped and press, public and timekeepers all became confused. Jimmy himself had been hit in the face by a flying stone, and he had lost contact with the eventual leaders while struggling to fit his spare goggles; he finished with blood encrusting his cheek and nose. Reims had not been the expected Ferrari walkover, and while the Climax-engined cars were well down on power the Lotus 21's good shape had contributed to a fine performance.

The following Saturday saw another Inter-Continental Formula race run in damp and dreary conditions at Silverstone, victory going to Moss' Cooper-Climax once again. Innes and Jimmy ran works 18s while the UDT-Laystall InterContinental cars were driven by Taylor and Bianchi. Mike Parkes practised the Yeoman Credit Lotus 18 but Tim Parnell handled it in the race. Ireland stopped his 371 early on with clutch-slip, while Taylor ran fifth until the final-drive failed. Parnell spun-off just before Abbey Curve and Bianchi was flagged in to hand over his car to Taylor, but Henry restarted far behind with the car trailing thick smoke . . . Jimmy snatched fifth place near the finish in 372, while Ireland finally was ninth ahead of the Bianchi/Taylor car. Not an auspicious outing, and a dull 23rd British Empire Trophy race.

England was the true home of wet-weather racing during 1961, and a week after Silverstone came the British Grand Prix, run in a steady downpour at Aintree. Team Lotus took their two latest 21s, 933 for Innes and 932 for Jimmy, while Moss again ran 912—the 18/21 Walker Special. Taylor and Bianchi were in UDT's two entries, the friendly Belgian running the old 18 spare car with the Hewland transmission to give modified internals some race testing. Burgess was out again in the Camoradi 18, and Seidel, Ashmore, Parnell and Maggs all had 1960-type 18s, the latter's being Mrs Bryden-Brown's usual car, giving the young South African Formula Junior star his Formula 1 debut. Tony Marsh was also running his much-modified 18 Special.

Ireland had injured his hand on his aeroplane but was otherwise fit and he and Jimmy Clark both recorded laps in 1min 59.2sec to take the inside positions on the third row of the grid. Ahead of them was Moss, fourth fastest once again, the three works Ferraris and Bonnier's Porsche. Innes spun on the first lap, hurting his damaged hand as he piled on corrective lock, so having frightened himself and being no lover of racing in the rain anyway he lost all interest in the proceedings. Moss forced his way into third place among the Ferraris by the end of lap 6, and then poor Henry Taylor came through the murk into Melling Crossing in a big slide, spun, ploughed into the hoardings lining the track and broke several ribs as the UDT Lotus crashed to a halt.

On lap 10 Moss splashed into second place to a tremendous cheer from the sodden crowd, Clark was a lonely ninth, and Ashmore was already out with drowned ignition. Parnell's clutch expired two laps later as Moss was pushing von Trips hard and feinting to pass, but the German was well in control and was not being pressured into any mistakes. On lap 24 Stirling hit a puddle at Melling Crossing and spun twice, halting the gyrations as the nose whipped round straight and charging off after von Trips, after losing about 10 seconds.

As conditions began to improve Ginther took Moss for second place, and on lap 45 Stirling stopped after Phil Hill went by, with a repeat of the Reims brake pipe failure, this time on the left-rear caliper. The car was retired, and so the only man capable of challenging the Ferraris was out of the race. Jimmy had moved up into fifth place through all the watery mayhem around him, but on lap 63 the works 21 developed a massive oil leak and his consistent run ended in retirement. The Ferraris came home in line-astern, while the best-placed Lotus was Ireland's in a miserable tenth place; Maggs was 13th, Burgess 14th and Seidel 17th and last. Marsh had stopped after 26 laps and Bianchi retired 20 laps later with gearbox failure after a big spin across Mrs Topham's lawn at Melling.

There was little time to brood on Team Lotus' failure at Aintree, for the following Saturday came the

Solitude Grand Prix just outside Stuttgart, where Ireland was to score the works team's first victory with the Lotus 21.

Innes and Jimmy ran their regular cars, and Trevor Taylor was given an outing in the earlier spare 21, number 930. UDT-Laystall had Moss driving one of their 18/21s, and Wolfgang Seidel's Scuderia Colonia ran both its 18s for Michel May and Seidel himself.

The main opposition came from four works Porsches, and Bonnier and Gurney annexed the front row of the grid, with Bruce McLaren alongside them in a Cooper. Innes and Moss were on the second row with Clark flanked by Herrmann's Porsche and Brabham's privately owned Cooper behind them.

This was a rough, tough and thrilling race from start to finish, with Innes snatching the lead from the flag. Into the first corner, at Glemseck, McLaren dived inside the Lotus, forcing it wide and in turn shouldering out Herrmann who had been trying to run round outside him, while Brabham got into a big slide right in the middle of the pack . . . the tone of the whole race was set!

May crashed on this opening lap, bending his 18's chassis, and Ireland led McLaren's Cooper and the Porsches across the timing line. Colin was running the Dunlop D12 rain tyres on his cars in the hope that their softer compound would give more grip, and despite Dunlop fears that the covers would overheat and break-up the Lotus' handling proved extremely good.

Innes and Bruce continued to lead the Porsches, but Gurney and Bonnier strode determinedly forward and on lap 7 Ireland, Gurney, Bonnier, Brabham and McLaren were all in the leading bunch, pushing and shoving and shouldering their way though the corners. Moss' car just wasn't fast enough on the straights to maintain contact, and Clark was off-colour although he managed to pass the light green UDT car.

Brabham's engine suddenly starved on lap 20 and as the Cooper faltered the pack exploded round him, Innes rushing away in the lead with Bonnier and Gurney swerving round the Cooper on either side. McLaren had to brake to avoid his works team-mate and lost contact, leaving the green Lotus and two silver Porsches at daggers-drawn. On the penultimate lap Bonnier forced ahead of the Lotus, and the Team Lotus pit crew groaned as the trio howled away into the forest with Innes sandwiched between the two works Porsches. Downhill through the swerves on the back stretch Bonnier used all the road to prevent Innes scratching past, but the Scot was determined, threw all caution to the wind and made his move.

As the trio rushed down to the hairpin at the end of the main straight Innes shot off onto the grass, ploughed past the startled Swede and chopped back onto the road, braking savagely and skittering through the turn barely under control. Weaving all over the road to prevent the Porsche repassing he held his advantage through the twists and turns to the finish, and the Lotus pit just exploded in delight at this marvellous motor race. No quarter had been asked and none given, and with Innes' magnificent victory backed up by Jimmy's seventh and Trevor's ninth places there was good cause for the Team Lotus celebrations which followed. Moss had dropped out almost unnoticed in the excitement with final-drive failure, and Seidel had retired his 18 when the steering wheel broke.

In high spirits the works team headed for the Nurburgring and the German Grand Prix two weeks later, when the prototype 1.5 litre Climax V8 engine appeared in the stern of Brabham's Cooper. Team Lotus, of course, were still using their Mark II four-cylinder engines in their two regular cars, and in the original 21 which Taylor had driven at Solitude, which was now being used as a spare. Moss was in the regular Walker Special, and Mrs Bryden-Brown once again entered her old-style 18 for Tony Maggs. Marsh had his Special and Ashmore, Seidel and May their normal Lotus 18s.

Practice revealed chassis problems for the Ferraris which were handling badly over the humps and bumps of the 'Ring, but on one lap Phil Hill landed his car well every time to break the nine-minute barrier with a shattering 8min 55.2sec lap. Moss had gearbox trouble but managed 9min 1.7sec, and Clark got down to 9min 8.1sec before his car's steering broke and he crashed heavily, damaging the car severely but fortunately not himself. Seidel's 18 broke a rear upright, and he borrowed the spare 21 for a few laps, but was soon called in to hand it over to Clark when Jimmy got back to the pits. The Colonia team were most unlucky, for May somersaulted his car and on the Sunday Seidel had to race a Lotus built from parts salvaged from the two damaged cars.

Race day was wet but changeable, and during the morning Dunlop encouraged all the runners to fit D12 rain tyres, but when the skies brightened everyone was advised to change back to R5 dry tyres for fear of excessive wear and possible tread chunking. But Moss and Walker decided to gamble on the extra grip of the D12s, and as Colin had run the 21s very successfully on D12s at Solitude he wasn't going to change them for anybody!

Ferrari and Porsche refitted the normal R5s, and the grid formed-up with Phil Hill, Brabham, Moss and Bonnier sharing the front row with four different chassis and engines. Clark was back on the third row in 930 with Ireland—who had little experience of the circuit—on the fifth row in 933.

Moss, Gurney and Brabham went away side-by-side from the start, but only 5 kilometres down the road the V8 Cooper hit a wet patch and spun viciously into the hedge. Moss went by with Bonnier and Phil Hill vying for the lead, and by the Karussel the Walker Special was in the lead for good.

Tony Marsh had already stopped with ignition problems and Innes lost his 21's engine cover on this fateful first lap. Next time round his oil pressure line burst and the car caught fire leaving the Schwalben-schwanz. Innes stopped as quickly as he could and hopped out with scorched arms, but the marshals allowed the 21 to burn to a cinder. Seidel's steering became deranged in his 'bitsa' so he gave Innes a lift on the tail of the white car as he retired to the pits.

Stirling Moss was putting on the performance of his life in maintaining his lead over the Ferraris. He set a fastest lap of 9min 13.8sec on the second lap while he still had a clear run although the track was wet in places and he had a full fuel load. By the end of the third lap he had a 10 second lead, but three laps later von Trips took 5.7 seconds off Moss' time to close on Hill, and pruned another 3.8 seconds off the 1.5 litre record next time round as the circuit dried. Clark was a consistent fourth behind this grimly struggling trio, but on the eighth lap Moss went round in 9min 2.8sec to which von Trips replied with 9min 1.6sec in second place. The German took off another half-second next time round to close to within 10 seconds of the flying Walker Lotus, and then both Ferraris lapped in under 9 minutes to close to within 9 seconds of the leader.

Von Trips could see Moss on the hump-backed straight on lap 11, but two laps later it began to rain hard and the D12-shod Lotus suddenly had a marked advantage over the Ferraris. The race was over, but Moss had driven magnificently to stay ahead of the Ferraris in the dry and the rain now made his lead safe. Von Trips and Hill fell back, but continued to dice with each other, von Trips managing to take second place but Phil Hill smashing the record yet again on the very last lap, a great flood of adrenalin forcing the Italian car round in 8min 57.8sec. Moss won by a margin of 20.4 seconds, and Jimmy's fourth place in the spare 21 gave Colin some consolation for the loss of the other car. Maggs and Burgess splashed home through torrential rain for 11th and 12th places, while Marsh managed to revive his car and finally finished 15th and last.

The works drivers flew back to England overnight in a scarifying excursion to compete in the August Bank Holiday meeting at Brands Hatch. The race was the Guards Trophy for InterContinental Formula cars, and Team Lotus entered 2.5 litre Mark 18s for Ireland and Clark, while similar cars for Masten Gregory and Gurney were entered by UDT-Laystall. Moss was in the Walker Cooper, and he trailed Surtees' similar Yeoman Credit car until Brabham made up for his misfortune the previous day and blasted past them both to win. When Surtees spun into the bank at Clearways and Moss retired with gearbox trouble the works Cooper driver was left unchallenged. Ireland's crownwheel and pinion failed, Gurney also suffered a transmission breakage, and Clark soldiered through it all to take second place. Gregory was slow out of Druids on the fourth lap and McLaren booted his Cooper straight into the Lotus' tail, spinning the American off into the bank with a badly bent Lotus. There were only seven finishers in this 76-lap race, which marked the end of the InterContinental Formula's brief and unsuccessful life.

August 20 found Team Lotus in Sweden for the Karlskoga Kannonloppet races, run over the short distance of only 80 kilometres. Ireland ran 930, the works 21, and Clark was in 371, the old Mark 18, while Moss once again was appearing in a UDT-Laystall Lotus. All three had driven in the Tourist Trophy at Goodwood the day before and were rather tired when they arrived in Sweden, but Moss was in good form, as usual, and went on to win from Bonnier's Porsche and Surtees' Cooper after sharing the fastest lap at 1min 30.4sec with the Yeoman Credit car. Ireland's engine mountings broke and Clark's tired old battle-wagon had a front wishbone collapse, both Team Lotus cars dropping out early in the race.

One week later the Scandinavian tour took the teams to the tight and tiny Roskildering in Denmark, where the track writhed for 1.2 kilometres around the bottom of an old gravel pit. Lap times were near the 40 seconds mark and the Formula 1 event was run in three heats, with the overall result on aggregate. Moss won again in the UDT Lotus, taking all three heats—the first from Brabham and the second two from Ireland in 930 after the Cooper's transmission had broken. Masten Gregory also drove for UDT (his Camoradi drive having dissolved when the team collapsed), and Henry Taylor made a welcome return after his Aintree accident, finishing fourth in another of the UDT cars. Tim Parnell was fifth in his private 18 and Jimmy placed fourth in one of the heats in the ancient works 371.

There followed a long haul South for the non-championship Modena Grand Prix in Northern Italy just one week after Roskilde. Team Lotus arrived with two 21s for Ireland and Clark and a new car, number 934, as a spare, which was intended for the Italian Grand Prix at Monza the following weekend. Moss was back in the Walker Special, and Gregory and Taylor appeared again in the UDT 18/21s. Privateers included Parnell and Giorgio Scarlatti, both with old Lotus 18s, the latter in Prince Starraba's Maserati-powered device.

The grid was limited to 14 starters, including three Italians whether they qualified or not, and this system caused Innes to be dropped after a troubled session. Gurney (Porsche), Moss, Surtees (Cooper), Graham Hill (BRM-Climax) and Gregory ran in close company from the start of the 100 laps, but by lap 12 Moss had tired of pleasing the public and just ran away with the race, leaving the Porsches when he wanted. Both UDT cars retired, Moss set a lap record of 57.8 seconds, and another win was chalked up for the Walker equipe. Jimmy was fourth in his works car, while Scarlatti retired the ill-begotten Lotus-Maserati after only a handful of laps.

It was at the 32nd Italian Grand Prix at Monza that Phil Hill and Ferrari finally clinched the 1961 World Championship, but tragically this final success was clouded by the death of 'Taffy' von Trips, whose car collided with Jimmy's new works 21 on the second lap and spun along a fence packed with spectators, killing 14 of them and injuring many more.

Colin had brought the new car from Modena still unraced, for Clark to use at Monza, while the other 21 was prepared for Ireland. Brabham was giving his new Cooper-Climax V8 its second outing, and Rob Walker had obtained a similar engine for Stirling Moss which had been installed in the team's spare chassis, which had been lying in the racing shop at Dorking for some months, awaiting its new engine. Ferguson Research had cut off the whole of the rear part of the chassis and grafted on an entirely new rear end to accept the larger V8 engine. Lotus 21-type rear suspension had been added, and Hardy-Spicer sliding-spline drive-shafts were mated to a Colotti Type 32 gearbox. Detachable tubes over the engine and transmission stiffened the rear end of the frame, and like the works Cooper engine Walker's new V8 used four Weber IDF downdraught carburettors mounted within the vee. The car had been finished off quite hurriedly in order to take it to Monza, and the original engine cover was retained, modified with an unsightly hump over the carburettors and retaining the original open bulge for the four-cylinder engine's sidedraught carburettor system. The other Walker Special which Moss had driven at Modena was present as a spare.

UDT-Laystall took along three 18/21s for Henry Taylor and Gregory, the former's having one of the original Colotti transmissions and the latter's a brand new one. Parnell, Gerry Ashmore, and Seidel all had their old 18s and Gaetano Starraba decided this time to drive his Lotus 18-Maserati himself.

Five Ferraris were running,four of them with 120-degrees V6 engines for Phil Hill, von Trips, Ginther and Baghetti, while the young Mexican sports car driver Ricardo Rodriguez was running an older 65-degrees version. He proved extremely fast, qualifying second quickest behind von Trips to take his place on the front row of the grid. Jimmy put the brand-new 934 on the fourth row and Innes was behind him with the other works Lotus 21. However, there was to be some post-practice shuffling of cars and drivers.

Moss' new V8-engined Lotus had been troubled by overheating and he wasn't happy with it, while the old 18/21 Special was rather tired after its Modena win. Moss was the only Lotus driver remaining with a chance in the World Championship so Colin and Innes got together and offered Walker the works 21. The change was made behind closed garage doors in the paddock, the works car being fitted with the dark blue body sections from 921, and the number 28 pasted on its two-tone flanks. Meanwhile, 921 had been fitted-up with Lotus 21-type body sections borrowed from UDT-Laystall because the works panels wouldn't fit properly, and the number 38 was applied to this car. It was Moss' first drive in the latest Lotus, and after Jimmy's good practice showing in his car the maestro looked all set for another crack at the Ferraris.

The Maranello team cars' high axle ratios gave them slow starts and Hill's BRM and Clark's Lotus were in amongst them as they howled away into the Curva Grande. On the second lap as the bunched leaders swept down into the Parabolica, the 180-degrees final turn of the circuit, Jimmy and poor von Trips collided.

Jimmy was slightly behind as they swept into the braking area at the end of the flat-out 165 mph straight from Vialone, and he dived inside von Trips as the lightweight Lotus could brake later than the Ferrari. Suddenly he realised that the German hadn't seen him and was moving over into the green car. Instantly the two cars locked wheels, broadsided and spun wildly to the outside of the circuit with such tragic results. Clark staggered unhurt from his wrecked car, but was badly shaken and horrified by the awful carnage wreaked behind him.

After the accident only Jack Brabham was able to stay in contact with the remaining Ferraris with Moss next up in sixth place. Ashmore had already gone over the bank and into the trees at the Parabolica and was hospitalised, his car being written-off, and then Ireland had the chassis break on the Walker–works car, the flexing of the frame making gear-changing a hit or miss operation from then on. Gregory was in what he thought to be plug trouble but which, in fact, was something more basic, and when Brabham retired the Cooper after nine laps Moss was left duelling for fifth place with Gurney's Porsche, hard on the Ferraris' heels.

Baghetti and Rodriguez both retired, moving the Moss/Gurney battle into third place, and as these two towed each other round the Ferraris were in a difficult position. With two cars out from mechanical failure Phil Hill and Richie Ginther couldn't afford to press on too hard, and yet they couldn't ease up and allow the Lotus and Porsche to catch them. Vague hopes began to dawn of another Lotus victory, and when Ginther's engine broke after only 24 laps it seemed a distinct possibility.

Phil Hill had about 20 seconds in hand over Moss and Gurney, who were thoroughly enjoying their co-operative efforts at slipstreaming. The Ferrari team leader tentatively pushed his car into a 23 seconds lead, but after 33 laps Moss was trailing Gurney and clearly something was wrong with his car. On lap 37 Stirling headed into the pits, and a disappointed Alf Francis found that the left-front wheel bearing had failed and was allowing the wheel to wobble. The stresses of the right-handed, high-speed banking had proved too much for the lightweight Lotus, but it had been a good try.

Phil Hill went on to win the race by over half a minute and with it the World Championship, but it was a bitter victory with the death of the popular German Count and so many spectators to mar it. Of the remaining Lotus drivers Parnell finished 10th and Taylor 11th, but Gregory finally gave up with a broken lower rear wishbone, and both Seidel and Starraba also retired.

Jimmy Clark and Team Lotus were badly shaken by that second-lap collision, and more unpleasantness was to follow when the police impounded the wrecked 21 for technical inspection by the coroner's court. Later still, actions were begun on behalf of some of the victims' dependants, and Clark and Lotus were both named as culpable. It was to be two years before the future World Champion's name and Lotus' reputation were finally absolved of all blame.

On the way home from Monza, several teams took in the non-championship Austrian Grand Prix on the Zeltweg airfield circuit, Team Lotus taking along the 21 which Mcss had driven at Monza for Ireland while the old spare 21 which had raced at Monaco and Zandvoort was brought out from Cheshunt for Clark. Parnell, Seidel and Ernesto Prinoth also took along their 18s, and they were faced by the Yeoman Credit Coopers, Brabham's works Cooper, Tony Marsh's new BRM and Bonnier and Carel Godin de Beaufort in Porsches.

Innes took pole position in practice, with Jimmy 0.7 second behind but Ireland was insisting that his car felt funny and the mechanics finally discovered that one front wheel had positive camber and the other one negative!

Race day was broiling hot, and after Ireland had muffed his start Clark led Surtees, Brabham and Salvadori in their Coopers, with Innes right behind at the end of the first lap. In two laps the annoyed Lotus number-one was pushing Clark and Surtees, and after disposing of the Yeoman Credit Cooper he signalled to Clark to let him by. Jimmy dutifully moved over but

Innes Ireland drove magnificently to beat a strong Porsche effort in the Solitude Grand Prix (right) and two months later scored another non-championship win at Zeltweg, Austria (below) after displacing Clark and Surtees.

the wily Surtees saw his chance and slipped through behind Ireland, relegating Clark to third. Surtees had to stop when he began spilling fuel, leaving the works 21s running one-two ahead of Marsh, Brabham and Bonnier. But after 50 laps Clark's steering column worked loose and he had to stop to fix it, then the clamping bolt broke off and he stopped again. Brabham was in trouble by this time and Innes waited for him on the straights to tow him away from Bonnier (a friendly race this one!) and so the Lotus team leader came home to his second victory of the season, with Brabham and Bonnier second and third, Clark fourth and Parnell seventh.

Back home the Oulton Park Gold Cup was dominated by Moss in the experimental Ferguson P99 entered by the Walker team. It was wet and damp yet again, conditions which ideally suited the Ferguson's four-wheel-drive transmission and Maxaret anti-lock braking system. Ireland ran the Zeltweg-winning 933 and Clark 930, while Trevor Taylor reappeared in Formula 1 with 371, the old Mark 18. UDT ran their 18/21s for Henry Taylor and Gregory, and Seidel, Parnell and a recovered Ashmore reappeared.

Jimmy led from the start, while David Piper spun his Gilby on the first lap, contacting Jack Lewis' Cooper and Taylor's UDT Lotus. Henry carried on but thought the car was handling oddly—he was right, a radius rod had been broken and he had three wheels helping to steer the car.

Clark's engine went off-song dropping him back, and Trevor Taylor had to stop when his exhaust system came adrift. Parnell and Ashmore had transmission failures, and on lap 26 Ireland retired with a broken tappet when lying eighth. . . it was raining! Jimmy's car suddenly became barely controllable and he retired with a broken radius rod, and after Trevor had spun the surviving works car at Esso the race finished with Masten Gregory in the best-placed Lotus in fifth position with team-mate Taylor cork-screwing along eighth and Seidel tenth.

The following weekend a small national Formula 1 race was held at Brands Hatch over 30 laps of the 2.65 miles long circuit for the Lewis-Evans Trophy, which Tony Marsh won with his new BRM in front of Tim Parnell in his old Lotus 18. Peter Procter drove Anthony Brooke's old front-engined Lotus 16 near the tail of the field, but had a good dice with Graham Eden's Cooper, finally forging ahead only to drop out when the offside rear wheel oil seal burst.

This closed the European Formula 1 season, with Colin's ambition for a works win in a championship race still unfulfilled. The final race of the series was to be the United States Grand Prix, which was being held for the first time at the Watkins Glen circuit, near Lake Seneca in upstate New York. Having clinched the title under the shadow of tragedy Ferrari stayed in Maranello and so the British Climax-powered brigade were given their best chance of victory of the season, having only the Porsches of Gurney and Bonnier to oppose them.

Team Lotus arrived at the circuit with no less than four cars, two of them being 21s for Jimmy and Innes, and the others 18/21s which were to be hired by the promising young Canadian Peter Ryan and Jim Hall, the Texan sports car driver, whose car had a Mark II FPF engine. UDT-Laystall entered their 18/21s for Gregory and Olivier Gendebien, since Henry Taylor had not been considered a sufficient 'name' by the organisers' publicists.

Lloyd Ruby ran an old 18 painted a lurid gold with blue stripes, and Rob Walker Racing brought along both their Lotus Specials, the V8 and four-cylinder cars, for Moss. Coventry-Climax had traced the V8 engine's overheating problems to differential expansion of the liners and block, allowing the cooling system to pressurise and blow all the water out of the overflow. Walter Hassan's team had quickly produced longer liners with better bottom-end location, and were hoping the problem had been cured.

Early in practice Colin and Huschke von Hanstein of Porsche had something of an argument with the organisers over the mass of regulations which had been directed at the pit crews, and to their credit many of the organisers' rules were relaxed instantly and the remainder of the meeting was held in an extremely amicable atmosphere.

Gendebien tipped over his UDT 18/21 early in practice, but Tony Robinson and his men quickly straightened it out, and then practice was stopped when Ireland crashed many yards into the scrub and saplings and had to have the car extracted. He was unhurt and the accident was traced to a broken knuckle joint on the left-hand steering arm. Damage was otherwise slight and the car was soon running again. Jimmy went very quickly the following day until oil fouled the clutch, and then Innes' repaired car suffered a transmission breakage which spread oil everywhere. These continual problems were mirrored in the Walker camp, and Moss was still unconvinced by the performance of his V8 car and decided to run 912 in the race.

Brabham was much happier with his V8 and started from pole position alongside Graham Hill's BRM-Climax. Moss was on the second row, his time having been equalled by McLaren's Cooper, and Clark was on the next row with Ireland on row four.

Moss led for six laps until Brabham's V8 screamed by as Clark stopped at the pits with a slipping clutch. Jimmy rejoined three laps behind the leaders as Moss and Brabham were having a rare battle for the lead, with Ireland established in fourth place, running alongside Graham Hill in pursuit of McLaren. Moss took the lead again on lap 34 as Innes took third place from McLaren, and on lap 39 Brabham began to slow with his V8 engine overheating. He stopped six laps later for water to be added.

This left Moss holding a 40-seconds lead over the works 21 with which Ireland was fighting off Hill's BRM. Then Moss' engine suddenly stopped and he coasted in to retire with run bearings and no oil

The biscuit-box-shaped Lotus 18 Formula Junior car was replaced by the much sleeker Lotus 20 for the 1961 season. Technical changes included the substitution of the scuttle fuel tank by side tanks, and the transfer of the rear drum brakes inboard. The frame diagonal in the engine bay was removable.

Above: Junior grows up. The improved aerodynamics of the Lotus 20 over the 18 is shown clearly as Peter Arundell drives out of the Brands Hatch paddock ahead of 'last year's model'. The race, which Arundell won, was for the John Davy Trophy. Below: Arundell and the Lotus 20 were a formidable combination in Formula Junior during 1961.

pressure. This left Ireland with a narrow lead over Hill's BRM, and when the BRM's magneto cap fell off on lap 74 joy was unconfined in the Lotus pit. Innes eased off considerably, allowing Roy Salvadori to close up in the Yeoman Credit Cooper; the 20-seconds gap was down to only 5 seconds on lap 97 but then Roy's engine broke and Innes was able to tour round to win the works' first-ever championship race victory, from Gurney and Brooks. Jimmy finished down in seventh place, while Gregory had relieved Gendebien (after his own car had broken its gear selectors) and finished 11th and last. Jim Hall had retired with fuel leaking from split tanks, a not-uncommon Lotus 18 failing, and Ruby stopped with a sheared magneto drive. An ecstatic Ireland won a huge cup, and after Colin's brief punch-up with a policeman patrolling Victory Circle the pair of them thoroughly enjoyed their first Grande Epreuve victory. Team Lotus, at long last, had arrived . . .

Shortly after the Watkins Glen race the BARC announced the well-deserved award of their Gold Medal to Stirling Moss, while 7,000 miles away the Mexican Grand Prix, due to be run on a new circuit in Mexico City, was cancelled.

Soon afterwards a change was announced at Team Lotus with the departure of Innes Ireland, despite his three victories during the season, culminating in the American success. In Colin's words: '. . . we used to go motor racing because we enjoyed it, and to travel the World together you had to get on well. There was a certain amount of rivalry between Innes and Jimmy. Both were Scots, and I think Innes was a little jealous of Jimmy's promise. Anyway, they didn't get on well together and this atmosphere got on the team's nerves. Eventually it became a case of deciding which one should go. I felt that Jimmy showed such tremendous promise he should stay, and since I knew the UDT/British Racing Partnership set-up would be running Lotus cars the following season it seemed sensible to have Innes driving for them as number-one and so spread our driving strength over two Lotus teams. I had decided on the change before Innes won at the Glen, but I don't think he took it very well and he wasn't happy for some time. The decision still seemed fair and sensible to me . . .'

So Innes made his departure, and at the end of the season Jimmy became team-leader with Trevor Taylor as his number-two for the Springbok series of Formula 1 races in South Africa. The first of these was the Rand Grand Prix at Kyalami, where Lotus should have been faced by a Porsche works team, but the freighter carrying the German cars was delayed and they failed to arrive at the circuit until a mere hour-and-a-half before the race. After some hasty practice Edgar Barth just made it to the line in time, but Jo Bonnier was unable to start until half a lap of the race had been completed.

Jimmy and Trevor had qualified fastest, with Masten Gregory's UDT 18/21 outside them on the front row. It was blisteringly hot and the Lotus' side panels were removed giving spectators an instructive view of the works drivers' backsides and legs. Clark led Taylor all the way, and after Gregory retired due to overheating the pair nearly dead-heated for first place. Bonnier was third and Barth fourth, and poor Taylor was so badly affected by the heat that he had to be lifted from his cockpit. Syd van der Vyver's Lotus-Alfa Romeo was placed seventh and Bob van Niekerk was ninth in a Formula Junior Lotus-Ford.

The following week saw the first Natal Grand Prix held at Durban's brand-new Westmead circuit, where Bonnier split the works 21s on the front row although Jimmy ran away to an uncontested win, leading Moss' UDT 18/21 across the line by about 34 seconds. Moss had to start from the back of the grid for he had missed practice, and he had seared his way through the field as the works 21s ran away from Bonnier.

Gregory's UDT car had blown a gasket on the first lap, which allowed first Maggs' Cooper and then Moss' Lotus by, and Masten retired on lap 16. Clark and Taylor had pulled out a huge lead on the Porsche when suddenly Trevor's rear suspension collapsed, and he had a huge moment, although he escaped unharmed.

Moss had just gone on record as saying that he thought Clark was the most under-rated driver in the World, and despite some frantic efforts he could not catch the new Lotus number-one. Van der Vyver was another Lotus finisher in fifth place behind the Porsches of Bonnier and Barth.

The major race of the tour followed one week later with the South African Grand Prix at East London. This non-title round was run over 195 miles and Clark, Moss and Taylor occupied the all-Lotus front row. Bonnier and Gregory were behind them, and at the start the works 21s squeezed-out the plae green private car. Jimmy spun in avoiding somebody else's spin, and Moss built a 20-second lead, with Taylor second and Jimmy third. Jimmy's gearbox was damaged, and occasionally he found second and fourth in the same gate, while on lap 13 Taylor lost his nose cowling at Cox's Corner and retired with a gashed radiator core.

Again Moss was doing his best in an obsolete car, but Jimmy was consistently lapping faster and closing the gap, drawing out more than 40 seconds on Bonnier. On lap 25 he set a time of 1min 33.4sec, and later reduced this to new record figures of 1min 33.1sec. A speed trap on Potters Pass caught both Moss and Clark at 124.3 mph, while the Porsches of Bonnier and Barth could only manage 116.7 mph and 155 mph, respectively. Van der Vyver's Lotus Special was clocked at 110 mph,and on the main straight Jimmy was touching 150 mph.

On lap 38 the two Lotuses were neck-and-neck leaving Beacon Bend, but despite Moss leaving dirt and stones all round the circuit he couldn't hold-off Clark and the works Lotus 21 scored its hat-trick of wins by 15.7 seconds. Van der Vyver was sixth and Van Niekerk ninth.

The Cape Grand Prix at Killarney closed the four-race series, on New Year's Day 1962, although effectively it formed the end of the 1961 Lotus season. Jimmy and Trevor were on the front row of the grid with Bonnier's Porsche outside them, and the Swede took an initial lead before Clark swept by, followed by Taylor a little later. This time Jimmy was driving with his car's side panels in place although Trevor—more susceptible to the heat—had his removed, and on lap 19 the stripped car took the lead to keep the crowd awake. On lap 34 the pair swopped again, and again, but on lap 51 Jimmy spun at Hoales Hoek while leading. Trevor was left with an unassailable lead, with Bonnier right on Clark's tail. Jimmy really poured on the coals, setting a new lap record of 1min 29.1sec on lap 53 but seven laps later Trevor scored his first Formula 1 victory by just 0.6 second from his number-one, who won the Chris Bristow Trophy for setting fastest lap. Gregory just pipped Maggs' Cooper for fourth spot, Van der Vyver was seventh, Menzler's old Lotus-Ford 13th and Neville Lederle's Lotus-Ford 14th. Lederle gained much experience with the Jim Russell Racing Drivers' School in England and after ordering his own Lotus 21 after the race he looked to be set for great things in the new season.

During 1961 (and including this Killarney race) Team Lotus contested four Tasman races, the five home InterContinental events, including one with a Formula 1 class, 18 non-championship races and the eight World Championship rounds. The team won one of the Grandes Epreuves and seven of the non-title events, while Lotus cars entered by Rob Walker won two other Grandes Epreuves and one non-title event. Moss also won three non-title events for UDT-Laystall, so that 14 of these 35 major events went to Lotus, seven to the slim-line 21, two to a virtually standard 18 and five to 18/21 Specials.

1961 RACING RECORD
Other formulae and classes

At the start of 1961 Formula Junior was entering its second full season in Great Britain after finding its feet and growing to full maturity in Italy and other parts of the Continent. The previous year Junior cars had been racing essentially as a juvenile league, their 1,100 cc engines giving many an aspiring newcomer an introduction to single-seater open-wheeled racing. Formula 2, with 2 litre engines, formed a bridge between FJ and the full 2.5 litre Formula 1, but with the death of the old Grand Prix formula and the birth of its 1.5 litre replacement for 1961, this 'bridging formula' came to an end, and Formula Junior stood alone.

During 1960 Jimmy Clark and Trevor Taylor had made their names in Formula Junior Lotus 18s, and while the Scotsman earned a regular Grand Prix drive for the new season, Trevor stayed on in Formula Junior, and was joined by Peter Arundell, Alan Rees and Mike McKee in works or works-backed cars.

The new Formula Junior Lotus 20 was shown at the British Racing & Sports Car Club's Racing Car Show in London, in January, and in comparison with the successful old Lotus 18 it was a greyhound beside a St Bernard! Gone was the functional biscuit-box bodywork, and in its place was a slim, graceful and aerodynamic fuselage with a pointed nose and curvaceous engine cover. The scuttle tank of the Lotus 18 was removed, and fabricated side tanks took its place, hung on the flanks of a welded mild-steel tubular spaceframe similar in general arrangement to its predecessor, although the top right and lower left main longerons doubled-up as water pipes, carrying coolant between engine and radiator. Suspension fore and aft

Les Leston in 'Dadio' and Graham Warner in 'Lov 1'; their superbly prepared and driven Elites set GT racing alight in Europe.

was similar to that on the Lotus 18, with upper and lower front wishbones, and twin radius rods, reversed lower wishbones and fixed-length driveshafts locating the rear wheels. Cast magnesium 'wobbly-web' Lotus wheels were fitted, 13 inches in diameter at the front and 15 inches at the rear, and drum brakes were used all round, mounted inboard on the cheeks of the gearbox at the rear. This feature reduced unsprung weight and made for improved road-holding and stability. Power came from a 105E Ford-based Cosworth engine, mounted amidships with a detachable Y-shaped frame-member stiffening the engine bay. Bodywork was by Williams & Pritchard, and was formed in three glass-fibre mouldings (nose cone/cockpit surround, undertray and engine cover). Orders were soon flooding into Lotus Components for the cars at £1,450 each, and they had a supremely successful season, the final production run totalling 118 cars.

Trevor Taylor scored a win first time out in the Team Lotus 20 at Goodwood in March, and he went on to seven more major victories during a full season, including one at Reims and another at Solitude, where the Yorkshireman just pipped team-mate Peter Arundell by 0.1 second. Trevor's car ran a new 1,100 cc engine for the first time at Reims, linered-down from a 1,340 cc 109E Ford Classic unit. This gave just on 100 bhp in Cosworth-tuned form, and as the units became more widely available later in the season Formula Junior speeds rose steadily. At Reims Trevor won on aggregate by just 0.8 second from Tony Maggs' Tyrrell-entered Cooper, and although the fastest lap went to the South African at 112.41 mph the winning Lotus 20 was timed at 142 mph on the main straight.

Peter Arundell and the forceful Swiss ex-motor-cyclist, Jo Siffert, both had Lotus Formula Junior seasons almost as successful as Taylor's, with seven victories apiece. Peter's first victory was scored in a wonderful race at Goodwood on Easter Monday, after a massive pile-up on the start-line put out five cars and left Mike Parkes' Gemini squatting on top of Alan Rees' Lotus 20 on the verge! Arundell was hampered by the mass of wreckage strewn across the track, but he soared through the field and dead-heated with Maggs' Cooper on the line.

That same day there was a somewhat prophetic happening at Brands Hatch, where Lotus Components' own Peter Warr—later to return to Gold Leaf Team Lotus as racing manager—spun his Lotus 20 at Clearways; he was torpedoed by Richard Utley's Caravelle and one Maurice Phillippe, driving a Formula Junior of his own design called the Delta. Four years later Maurice was to join Team Lotus as chief designer . . .

Meanwhile, Peter Arundell's greatest success that season was a win in the Prix Monaco Junior, after Trevor Taylor had retired from the final. Some measure of motor racing's progress was provided by Trevor's fastest lap of 1min 45.3sec, which bettered Fangio's Formula 1 lap record in the 1957 Maserati 250F by 0.3 second . . .

Jo Siffert excelled on the Continent, and after scoring an initial win in a Lotus 18 at Cesenatico he invested in a new Lotus 20 and scored six more wins, including the fastest ever recorded in Formula Junior at the time, at Enna, where his race average was 114.63 mph, and his lap record average as high as 116.43 mph. Jo ended the season as joint European Formula Junior Champion, sharing the title with Tony Maggs.

Australian driver Frank Gardner arrived in Britain early in the year, armed himself with a Lotus 18 and had a thoroughly good season, eventually replacing it with a Lotus 20 and scoring four major wins in the teeth of fierce opposition. Bill Moss also shone with his immaculately prepared light blue Lotus 18 and won the John Davy FJ Championship at Brands Hatch. His performances also gave him a works Gemini Formula Junior drive, and late in the season the Chequered Flag team's cars proved a real threat to Lotus' near-domination of the class.

Three wins each were notched by Alan Rees, New Zealander Angus Hyslop and Midlands club-racer Jack Pearce, all in new Lotus 20s, while in France Henri Grandsire won a couple of races and Bernard Boyer one in Ecurie Edger's Lotus 18s and 20s. Poor Mike McKee had an indifferent season in his works-backed Lotus 20, and after scoring a solitary win he retired at the end of the year. Another Lotus driver to hang up his crash-hat was Jim Russell, who tigered a Lotus 20 round until he lost a wheel at Crystal Palace, and then retired to run the successful Jim Russell Racing Drivers' School at Snetterton.

In between running his Lotus 18 in hill-climbs and Formula 1 events, Tony Marsh had a good Formula Junior season with a similar car, and other successful drivers in Britain included Bill Pinckney, Reg Brown and Brian Whitehouse, all in Lotus 20s, while old Lotus 18s proved fantastically competitive in the determined hands of Peter Procter at home, and Walt Mackay, Gaston Andrey, Ed Leslie, Javier Velasquez and Pete Lovely across the Atlantic.

Canadian Peter Ryan showed enormous promise in a new Lotus 20, winning the Vanderbilt Cup race at Bridgehampton, New York, and he secured a European Formula Junior contract with Ian Walker's team for 1962. Harry Carter won the SCCA Formula Junior Championship in the United States, and William Smith Jr, Floyd Aaskov, Jack McAfee and Pat Pigott were top Lotus Junior peddlers opposing him.

Team Lotus' operation generally was limited to home Nationals and Internationals, and unlike the Tyrrell Coopers amongst others they did not take-in a full Continental season. Arundell had a brief lay-off following an accident at the Nurburgring in an Elite, but later became a centre of drama at Karlskoga, in Sweden, the day after the Tourist Trophy meeting at Goodwood. The Formula Junior drivers flew out overnight, and Peter practised his car in the Formula 1 session on the Sunday morning, bettering all the previous day's Formula Junior times and supposedly winning pole position on the grid. However, when the grid was drawn-up the organisers relegated Peter to the back row, for practising out of session. Colin Chapman understood that an arrangement had been made with them to allow Team Lotus' out-of-session times to count, and a tremendous row brewed-up on the grid. The race was delayed while a sit-down strike went on, but it was all to no avail, and a very peeved Arundell blasted away from the back row as the flag fell. Sadly it was all to no avail, and on the second lap he hit a SAAB as he attempted to pass it and crashed into retirement.

Lotus won more Formula Junior events than any other marque during the season, but late in the year the Team Lotus cars had some pretty poor outings, and Gemini in particular seemed very much in the ascendant. Season-long the Tyrrell Coopers had provided the Lotus 20s' stiffest opposition, and such fierce competition saved Formula Junior racing from becoming a one-marque-dominated bore in 1961.

During 1960 Stirling Moss had begun testing a new sports-racing car, the Lotus 19, and during 1961 Lotus Components produced a small batch of these cars. The Lotus 19 was based closely on the Lotus 18 chassis, with the side rails widened to accommodate a two-seater cockpit and carry a chunky all-enveloping glass-fibre-and-aluminium bodyshell. Mechanically the sports-racer was very similar to a Formula 1 Lotus 18, and the 2.5 litre Coventry-Climax FPF engine and five-speed Lotus transmission were pure 'Grand Prix'.

Bob Gibson-Jarvie's UDT-Laystall Racing Team invested in a trio of Lotus 19s, and during 1961 these were a star attraction in the supporting races at major British meetings. In their first outing at Oulton Park in April they scored a runaway one-two-three victory in the hands of Henry Taylor, Graham Hill and Cliff Allison, and they had a similar unopposed win at the Aintree '200' meeting, with Moss coming home ahead of Taylor and Allison. Stirling set a new class lap record of exactly 90.00 mph for the Liverpool circuit, and he won again in the International Trophy supporting event at Silverstone, setting another lap record at 106.22 mph.

In October Moss won at Laguna Seca, California, in a UDT Lotus 19 with Dan Gurney second in a similar car, and although large-capacity sports car racing was on the wane at the time these Lotus 19s enlivened the season considerably. When the car had first been released, it was regarded as a real Cooper Monaco-baiter; so much so that it was jokingly dubbed the Lotus Monte Carlo, and the name stuck—the only racing Lotus ever to carry a name. But during the year the Coopers failed to offer any real opposition, and when the UDT cars appeared the race result was usually a foregone conclusion.

Stirling Moss also raced against Dan Gurney's Arciero Brothers-entered Lotus 19 with the similar car owned by the American Team Rosebud, but Dan was able to avenge his Laguna Seca defeat when they met again for the Bahamas Speed Week in Nassau, when Moss' car broke a wishbone and Gurney's went on to win.

The UDT team had a vast racing programme, for in addition to their Formula 1 and big-banger sports-racing cars they also ran a Lotus Elite in their pale green colours, which normally was driven by Mike McKee or Henry Taylor. It had limited success, but the small GT classes both at home and abroad were almost completely dominated by the Elite. In particular Graham Warner and Les Leston had a season-long battle in home events, with their respective cars 'LOV 1' and 'DAD10'.

Graham Warner, boss of the Chequered Flag sports car dealership in West London, was the most successful Elite peddler of the year, his black-and-white car scoring a string of class and outright victories in everything from club to International events at home and abroad.

The first of several great tussles with Les Leston, the accessory king, was at Crystal Palace on Whit Monday, when Warner forced LOV 1 ahead of DAD10 for the class lead on lap four, then held a narrow advantage to the last corner when a back marker baulked him and allowed Leston to nip by and win the class by half-a-length.

At Silverstone Graham went to the line with an ailing engine, but he held off Leston for 15 of the 25 laps until he was baulked by a back-marker once again and spun at Copse. Les rushed away into a nine second lead, but with five laps to go LOV 1 was back within four seconds! Three laps from the end DAD10 suddenly faltered with an electrical failure and the black-and-white Chequered Flag car whistled by to lead the class. The car rushed out of Woodcote to start its last lap, but immediately blew-up past the pits in a huge cloud of smoke, so that was that!

At Brands Hatch on August Bank Holiday Graham practised the Elite in the wet with German Dunlop SP tyres and was two seconds per lap faster than anything else, including Mike Parkes' Ferrari. But race day itself was dry and sunny, and the usual Warner/Leston duel began for the class lead until, with seven laps to go, LOV 1 skittered on to the grass at Druids Hairpin. This left Leston with a 150-yards lead, and although Graham made up ground through the traffic DAD10 led across the line by just half-a-second.

The best race of Graham Warner's tremendous season was undoubtedly the 50-lap GT World Cup event at Zandvoort in Holland. The car apparently was 'nobbled' in practice when a mysterious piece of aluminium found its way into the Climax engine, but it was rebuilt overnight and finally made ready just 10 minutes before the start. The regulations stipulated a fuel stop to take on one gallon, and the Chequered Flag team decided to bring LOV 1 in as early as possible so as to run on a light fuel load near the finish. Graham came in after 11 laps when running third behind two Porsche Abarths, and he rejoined one minute in arrears. The Porsches boomed away into the distance, and by lap 24 they had a 64 seconds advantage. But Graham lapped faster and faster as the Porsche's compulsory stops approached, and on lap 28 the German Hahnl rushed into the pits, rejoined in second place and spun at the

Above: Stirling Moss was the brilliant all-rounder, and as such was as devastating when he drove a UDT/Laystall Lotus 19 as when he handled Rob Walker's single-seaters. The Lotus sports car was based on the 1960 Formula 1 Lotus 18 with widened chassis. Below: Lotus adopted a ZF all-synchromesh transmission for the 21 and experimented with rubber couplings on the inner ends of the drive-shafts early in 1961.

Hunzerug, which allowed the Elite to close to within 11 seconds. Two laps later Ben Pon's leading Dutch Porsche stopped and restarted with a 33-seconds lead over the third-placed English car.

On lap 31 Graham forced ahead of Hahnl and set off after the leader. With 13 laps left the gap was 19 seconds but two laps later it was down to only 14. The black-and-white Elite was haring round, and the crowd were on their feet at Warner's tremendous performance. With eight laps left the Porsche's lead was down to only four seconds, and although Pon's brakes were fading Warner was lapping at record speed. With four laps to go the Elite outbraked the Porsche into the hairpin, only to be repassed as the cars howled out of sight between the dunes.

The Chequered Flag pit crew were shattered at the end of this lap as Pon appeared at the end of the straight on his own! But their disgust turned to elation as they spotted LOV 1, tucked in so close behind the German car that it had been invisible. As they shot across the line Graham whipped out of the slipstream and rushed ahead, and managed to maintain a good lead to the finish of a splendid race. His new GT lap record of 1 min 49.9sec bettered the previous outright figures held by a Ferrari!

While Warner and Leston had their battles, young David Hobbs ruled the roost in club GT racing with his red-and-blue car. David was the son of the designer of the Hobbs Mechamatic automatic transmission, and the little Elite proved the system's value in no uncertain terms, putting up some fabulously fast and smooth displays. One of David's best performances was in the International Trophy meeting at Silverstone, where his practice time of 1min 56.8sec was approximately five seconds better than Colin Chapman's own GT class record!

Internationally, Elite successes were many and varied. Peter Lumsden/Peter Riley repeated their 1960 success in the Nurburgring 1,000 Kms by winning the 1,300 cc class from Alfa Romeo, but it was there that Peter Arundell injured his ribs when he wrote-off one of Team Lotus' Elites during practice.

At Le Mans a works 2 litre Lotus 19 entry was scrubbed in favour of a pair of Elites for Trevor Taylor/Bill Allen (standard 1,220 cc) and Cliff Allison/Mike McKee (742 cc Climax FWMA engine sporting four Amal carburettors, motorcycle-style). Ecurie Edger entered a standard car for Kosellek/Massenet and Team Elite ran another pair for Dr John Wyllie/David Buxton, and Robin Carnegie/ Louis Malle. The first works car was placed 12th overall, while the UDT-entered 750 led the Index of Performance until the oil pump failed after ten hours. Edger's car was 13th, equal runner-up with a DB in the Index of Energy, which finally fell to a Sunbeam Alpine. Both the Team Elite cars dropped out.

Finally, the little Lotus sports cars, the Sevens and the older Lotus 11s, 15s and 17s, ran in events of varying status virtually wherever there was motor racing for fun. Roy Pierpoint's 2 litre Lotus 15 was a potent club contender in Britain, where Mike Beckwith also shone with a Lotus 11, while Jon Derisley, Mike Adlington and Peter Mitchell all used Sevens to terrorise their club classes.

Throughout the motor racing spectrum the marque Lotus was well to the fore, and while Lotus Components' racing cars won many sales as well as races the Elite's racing reputation helped considerably to sell road cars across the World.

The master demonstrates. Jim Russell shows what a Formula Junior Lotus 20 should look like when it is cornered on the limit. This very talented driver was soon to retire from competition to concentrate on developing his very successful racing drivers' school, which is still based at Snetterton but has associated schools in other parts of the world.

1962

Dawn of the monocoque

This year was to see the dawn of the monocoque age in motor racing, sired by Colin Chapman's Lotus 25. Tests with the prototype backbone chassis for the Elan had shown it to be tremendously rigid and very light, and the adoption of a single-seater version—the so-called 'monocoque'—was a logical step. Its design and conception are described in the following race section, and while Colin and draughtsman Alan Styman laid-out the car almost everybody had a hand in building it. Dick Scammell recalls: 'None of us really knew quite what we were doing, but it all took shape very nicely and it certainly looked right. Mike Costin was in there wielding a riveter because he had experience in the aircraft industry, so we all thought he must know what he's doing . . . it was that kind of project!'.

It seems he did, because Colin recalls the original Lotus 25 as: ' . . . quite the cleanest and nicest-looking car we'd ever made. There were no holes in the bodywork, the engine and gearbox were beautifully cowled-in and it all worked very well . . . What some of our customers didn't seem to realise at the time was that it was very experimental. Although people keep telling me there had been monocoque racing cars in 1912 as far as I was concerned this was the first monocoque racing car. We didn't know whether it would work or not, and the Lotus 24 customer car was a spaceframe chassis which we knew would work, designed after the 25 to pick up the same suspension'.

In fact the effectiveness of the new form of construction was astonishing. Just as the Elan backbone had proved light and extremely rigid, so the Lotus 25 was a vast improvement over the Lotus 21 spaceframe of 1961. The latter had weighed 82 lbs bare, rising to 130 lbs with the addition of brackets, mounts and the separate aluminium tanks, but its torsional stiffness was only 700 lb ft/degree. The new Lotus 25 hull scaled a mere 70 lbs, yet its bare torsional stiffness was 1,000 lb ft/degree, rising to 2,400 lb ft/degree with the Climax V8 engine installed!

While this car was setting the racing world on its ear and coming so close to winning the Formula 1 World Championships, it was also the catalyst of another racing project which was to have far-reaching consequences in later years.

At the debut of the Lotus 25 in the Dutch Grand Prix, Porsche driver Dan Gurney was full of admiration. Colin Chapman: 'Dan came to me and said "My God, you know if someone took a car like this to Indianapolis they could win with it. Would you like to come to Indy to see what it's like?" '. Dan was driving a Buick-powered mid-engined car for Mickey Thompson in the Memorial Day 500-miles race that year, the car having been inspired by Jack Brabham's good performance in the 1961 race when he finished ninth in a very underpowered Cooper-Climax. Dan saw the promise of the new Lotus design, and paid Colin's air fare to Indy for him to study the whole USAC (United States Automobile Club) track-racing scene. 'I went over just for the race, and just couldn't believe it. I thought I'd gone back 15 years or something . . . I could imagine this must have been what it was like to watch the Mercedes and Alfa Romeos pre-war at Tripoli. Having seen these old-fashioned and antiquated cars trundling round I thought, well, all you've got to do is to get an engine with about half the power these great lumps of junk had, build a decent chassis and you've won the race . . .'.

Coincidentally, Ford of America were just getting interested in competition, and development engineers Don Frey and Dave Evans were at Indy that day, watching the World's richest motor race falling—as it had for so many years—to front-engined, beam-axled, Offenhauser-powered roadsters. While Colin and Dan jetted back to Monaco and began to evolve their plans for a monocoque Indy contender, Frey proposed a Ford engine for the '500' based on existing experimental aluminium V8 blocks for the Ford Falcon. Evans approached the leading roadster constructors in search of a suitable chassis, but back at Cheshunt Colin quickly finalised his own ideas for a mid-engined Indy car.

With Dan Gurney he presented himself and his plans at Ford's Dearborn door on July 23. Don Frey and Bill Innes, head of Ford's foundry and engine division, listened with scarcely concealed scepticism, for the mystique of Indianapolis was such that even experienced engineers felt there was only one way of succeeding there.

The Lotus proposals were simple in the extreme. The idea was that the car should complete the race with only one pit-stop, and would therefore have to be economical, demanding petrol instead of alcohol fuel. It should carry and consume 400 lbs of petrol, carry 24 lbs of oil (while the Offies needed 80 lbs) and have a minimum power output of 325 bhp from 4.2 litres. Carburation was proposed instead of fuel-injection in the interests of simplicity and economy, and an agreement was reached which allowed Colin to begin serious development of a suitable chassis.

Back at Dearborn the Ford engineering hierarchy talked to roadster-builder A.J. Watson, and his proven formula for winning at Indy seemed attractive. But after taking a close look at the USAC scene Ford began to appreciate the effects of design stagnation and leant towards the Gurney-Chapman-Lotus proposals.

Ford arranged a detailed survey of the Speedway, and bought an Offenhauser four-cylinder engine for comparative testing. They found that it produced 407 bhp at 6,000 rpm on alcohol, and when their own V8 produced 351 bhp on petrol and 400 bhp on methanol they felt they had the power for whichever approach they chose – the Watson, or the Chapman . . .

What finally loaded the dice in the Lotus' favour was Jim Clark's superb victory in the 1962 United States Grand Prix, and subsequent tests at Indianapolis with the 1.5 litre Formula 1 car. During these trials the Lotus mechanics had a look round one of the leading roadster emporiums, and watched in polite silence as a massively-proportioned spaceframe was heated and warped for maximum cornering power!

Ford originally wanted to buy the Lotus 25 for evaluation, but since there was no driver available with rear-engined single-seater experience they dropped the idea and instead fitted one of their experimental engines in a Galaxie stock car. Nelson Stacy tested it at Daytona in November, and lapped at 154.8 mph on methanol as against 146.7 mph on straight pump petrol, but fuel consumption was improved from 2.22 mpg to 6.41 mpg with the use of standard-grade, and so the decision to 'go gasoline' was taken.

Bill Gay, one of the chief engineers, flew to England to finalise engine and chassis designs with Colin, and moved on to Bologna where he talked Weber into making special 58mm twin-choke carburettors for the new car, to close the gap between petrol and methanol performances. Thus the stage was set for the Lotus-powered-by-Ford Indy assault of 1963.

Meanwhile, the Lotus-Ford twin-cam engine had been approaching full development back home. Early in the year Jim Clark had been stuck for a car to drive home and asked if a company vehicle was available. He was offered a Ford Anglia saloon, which he reluctantly accepted, but despite his resignation to a slow trip to Scotland he realised that this was something different in Anglias as soon as he turned the key. He had a look under the bonnet, and there were two 'Lotus'-lettered cam covers gleaming up at him. He had a record run home and left a wake of terrorised Jaguars behind him!

At this time Colin's own Jaguar was to be seen rushing about with a curious pop-up headlamp system fitted, being development-tested for the Elan, while one day this same car brought the first five-main-bearing 116E Ford block back from Ford's Aveley plant for twin-cam modification. The cam-drive had to be redesigned to cater for the block's increased height, and in a great hurry the engine was assembled and prepared and fitted in the Lotus 23 for Jimmy to drive at the Nurburgring . . .

This race experience proved the engine to be every bit as good as its designers had hoped, and in mid-Summer the production go-ahead was given and work began to turn out engines for the new Elan line.

Almost simultaneously Ford of Britain approached Colin with the idea of fitting the twin-cam engine into one of their production saloons, and building 1,000 of them to qualify for Group 2 homologation. The choice lay between the Anglia and the Cortina, and the latter was chosen for its up-market appeal. Lotus took on the job of chassis and suspension modification, while race engine development was placed squarely in Cosworth's lap – to whom Mike Costin had finally departed in July.

'I know Jimmy's smaller than me, but I didn't think he was that small!' Colin Chapman has difficulty trying the brand-new Lotus-Climax 25 for size at Zandvoort. Mechanic Derek Wilde tries not to notice.

The Elite had been revised, and the new Super 95 model was introduced in May. This featured a cold-air duct in the bonnet, long-range fuel tank as standard and servo-assisted disc brakes. Power output from the 1,216 cc engine was raised to 80 bhp at 6,100 rpm with twin SUs, and in component form the car was priced at £1,595.

In September a new Super Seven 1500 was released, using the five-main-bearing 116E Ford engine fitted with a single Weber carburettor and producing 65 bhp at 5,200 rpm. This made for a rather smoother and less temperamental performer than the Cosworth projectiles, and with the latest all-synchromesh Ford gearbox the new model sold for £868 complete or £645 in component form. The twin-carburettor engines were still available, and despite the Seven's brick-like aerodynamics these gave it a top speed of just on 104 mph and acceleration from 0-50 mph in the 5-seconds bracket!

The Elan was announced at the London Motor Show in October and revealed Lotus' maturity as a serious motor company in that it was a refined touring car as distinct from a schizophrenic road-racer such as the Elite.

Its backbone chassis was fabricated from 16- and 18-gauge pressed steel, welded into a box-section girder 11½ inches deep. The front forks provided engine and gearbox mounts and carried pillars for the front suspension, while shorter forks and a cross-beam at the rear carried the final-drive and rear-suspension pillars. The new unstressed body allowed convertible styling, something the Elite could never have accepted since its roof panel was so vital to its strength. The new shell sat over the chassis like a saddle, and was bolted to it at 14 points. Two wide-opening doors were fitted, and in order to eliminate scuttle shake as a penalty of providing such large door openings the rigid facia panel joined the scuttle to the backbone. Full-width glass-fibre padded bumpers promised better protection than the skimpy pressed-steel affairs used on most production cars, and reasonable luggage capacity was provided by the compact boot and space behind the two seats.

The nose-line was very short and gave superb visibility, but it was so low that vacuum servo-operated pop-up headlamps had to be developed to combine legality with good aerodynamics; the minimum legal headlamp light was 24 inches, and these just qualified.

Power came from the now fully developed and race-proved Lotus-Ford twin-cam engine in 1,498 cc form with two twin-choke 40 DCOE Weber carburettors. It produced 100 bhp at 5,700 rpm in this trim, and drove through the all-synchromesh Ford gearbox to a BRD propellor-shaft running within the backbone. The hypoid final-drive unit was suspended on two rubber mountings beneath the rear cross-beam, and had a pair of steady bars to add rigidity. Each drive-shaft used a pair of Metalastic rubber-doughnut universal joints, but the Girling disc brakes were now outboard all round! They were 9½ inches in diameter at the front and 10 inches at the rear in an unusual combination.

Front suspension was by double wishbones with interposed co-axial coil-spring/dampers, and an anti-roll bar, while at the rear the chassis pillars provided top mounts for Chapman strut units—rather shorter than those used on the Elite—while very wide-based lower wishbones with robust cross-braces provided positive location. The steering was through a rack-and-pinion and pressed-steel perforated disc wheels were fitted, wearing 5.20-13 tyres as standard. In this trim, the Elan was offered at £1,499 complete.

About 50 of these early 1,498 cc twin-cam engines were completed, and these appeared in the first 22 production Lotus Elan 1500s before Group 2 saloon car racing requirements resulted in a larger 1,558 cc unit being standardised. The Group 2 class division stood at 1,600 cc, and maximum over-boring took the production engines to this 1,558 cc capacity although later race developments increased this to a full 1,593 cc. All 22 of these original Elans subsequently were recalled and fitted with 1,558 cc engines, while J.A. Prestwich— famed for their JAP engines—swung into full production of the Lotus-Ford twin-cams. Special Equipment and Super 95 Elites continued to be built as Elan production was built up.

At the time of the London Motor Show at Earls Court all the British Formula 1 teams received a shock when Leonard Lee of Coventry-Climax announced his company's impending withdrawal from racing. Lee explained that it was completely impossible for Climax to continue what had become a virtual

Enthusiasm for the Lotus Seven received an uplift in 1962 with the announcement of a Super Seven 1500 with Cosworth-modified five-bearing Ford engine. Though still starkly functional, the Super Seven at least offered a reasonable measure of weather protection and luggage space.

subsidy of Formula 1 racing, and to keep some 40 highly-skilled engineers involved in non-profitable work. This announcement came as a body-blow to British Grand Prix hopes, and the constructors—Lotus included—banded together in talks with Lee and his engineers, and finally agreed to pay more for their engines. The good old days when you could buy a Formula 1 engine for £1,250 and have it overhauled regularly for £80 a time were over, and the final agreement provided for rebuilds of 1962 V8 engines to 1963 specification for £3,000, while new heads would be made available at a further cost of £2,000. Brand-new 1963 engines were to cost £5,000 each . . . and Climax stayed in racing for three more years.

In the midst of the new Elan release and the Coventry Climax scare, Len Terry rejoined Lotus as chief design and development assistant to Colin Chapman. He had been with the company in the late 'fifties, but left when his freelancing activities clashed with the Lotus sense of commitment. Now he was back in the fold, and he was to continue development on the Lotus 25 series of cars and culminate his second spell with the company in the winning Indy cars of 1965.

Sadly, 1962 saw the deaths of two prominent and popular members of the Lotus team. Mechanic Dick Violet lost his life in a road accident shortly before he was due to be married, and in November 'Nobby' Clark died at the early age of 42. 'Nobby' had joined Lotus Engineering in 1953 as the first employee, and had become director and general manager of Lotus Components when the move to Cheshunt was made in 1959.

Lotus were growing up as car manufacturers, the new Elan (left) making an impressive contrast with the Super Seven (below), but the management remained young at heart (above). Colin's prowess as a designer was matched by his accuracy as a bread-roll thrower at social functions. Hazel Chapman on this occasion acted as enthusiastic observer of her husband's bomb-aiming activities.

1962 RACING RECORD
Grands Prix and other major formulae

One week after the New Year's day Cape Grand Prix served to close the 1961 Formula 1 season, a new season of international racing began with the New Zealand Grand Prix at Ardmore. Stirling Moss flew there from South Africa, and Rob Walker gave him a choice of his 2.7 litre Cooper-Climax or a brand-new 2.5 litre Lotus 21; he chose the Lotus. On race day there was a cloudburst just before the start and the Ardmore aerodrome was soon awash, but Moss managed to insert the new dark-blue Lotus in the lead and as he was the only driver with a clear view of the road ahead he was able to pull inexorably away from the Coopers of Surtees and McLaren. He was motor-boating along the back straight at 138 mph, and set the fastest lap at 1min 32.8sec, on his way to his first win in a Lotus 21.

The Ardmore race had been shortened to 50 laps because of the conditions, but the Vic Hudson Memorial Trophy race at Levin the following weekend was even worse hit, and was chopped to only eight of its programmed 28 laps for the public's safety. The circuit was very bumpy, and Moss decided to run the Cooper this time; he was placed second behind Brabham's winning car, and the best-placed Lotus was young Ross Greenville's Formula Junior in sixth position.

One week later in vivid contrast the Lady Wigram Trophy took place at Christchurch in scorching weather and once again Moss was the victor, running the Lotus 21 on Dunlop D12 tyres. He led the 150-miles race from start to finish, and shared a new lap record of 1 min 20.1 sec with Surtees' Bowmaker-Yeoman Cooper, but Stirling was lucky, for he finished with bald rear tyres and little tread remaining on the fronts. Ron Flockhart ran the ex-Bryden-Brown 2.5 litre Lotus 18 but retired after lying sixth, while the Ford Classic-engined Formula Juniors of Jim Palmer and Greenville ran well down in mid-field. Bruce McLaren beat Moss in the Cooper at Teretonga one week later, when Hamilton youngster Palmer took fourth place in his Lotus 20 behind Brabham's Cooper.

Moss used his Cooper again when the Tasman series moved to Australia in February, and won the Warwick Farm International '100', where Ron Flockhart was fifth in the old Lotus 18 behind the three leading Cooper-Climaxes and Bandini's Centro-Sud Cooper-Maserati. This was the Scot's last international race success, for shortly afterwards he was killed when his modified Mustang fighter-plane crashed on a test flight in preparation for an attempt on the Australia-to-England air record.

Team Lotus made their only entry of this Tasman series at Melbourne for the Sandown Park International in March. Jim Clark drove 933, the Mark 21, and was fifth after being handicapped by transmission problems. In New Zealand Jim Palmer won the coveted NZCC's Gold Star award driving his Lotus 20. His

ove: Jim Clark gave the Lotus 24 its first win in the mbank Trophy race at Snetterton. Below: Jack Brabham used a Lotus 24 pending the completion of his own GP car l took fifth place in the British Grand Prix.

bored-out 105E Ford engine had been taken out to 1,495 cc by the use of a 109E crankshaft, and he used it most capably.

Back at Cheshunt Team Lotus were hard at work on the new season's Formula 1 designs, and both Clark and Taylor were testing vigorously the new V8-engined car. This was the spaceframe-chassis Lotus 24, and it made its racing debut in April in the Brussels Grand Prix at Heysel. This was the team's first experience of the V8 engine under race conditions.

The Lotus 24 was hailed as the sleekest and lightest Lotus yet produced, although externally it was very similar to the now-obsolete 21s, apart from the humped engine cowling with two megaphone exhausts protruding above the neatly-covered ZF transaxle.

Despite its similarity to the 21, none of the Lotus 24 components was interchangeable. The front uprights were completely different although the upper rocker arms and inboard coil-spring-damper units were similar, while the forward-mounted track-rod was mounted higher on stronger steering arms. The rear-suspension geometry was similar to that of the 21, and rubber doughnuts reappeared on the inboard ends of the one-piece drive-shafts. The wheelbase had been increased by an inch, to 7ft 6in.

The second car was something of a Special, with a late-series 21 production chassis-frame (number 938), a four-cylinder Climax Mark II engine and a Colotti five-speed transmission. Trevor Taylor was to drive it in his first European appearance as works number two, and it was to be delivered to Jo Siffert, the 1961 Formula Junior star, after the race.

Because Team Lotus were using his new Formula 1 car, Colin loaned the Swiss a special 1,500 cc Ford engine for his Lotus 20 Formula Junior chassis, Cosworth-developed but basically similar to Jimmy Palmer's Tasman engine. Other Lotus entries came from UDT-Laystall with their old four-cylinder 18/21s for new team leader Innes Ireland and Masten Gregory, and 912—the famous ex-Moss/Walker car—appeared under a coat of red paint, entered by Count Volpi's Scuderia SSS Republica di Venezia for Sicilian lawyer Nino Vaccarella. Walker Racing appeared with their neat V8-engined Special for Moss, as seen at Monza and Watkins Glen in 1961, but now wearing a neat new low-line engine cover and tail cowling with the exhaust protruding through a rectangular slot.

Once again the Brussels Grand Prix was run in three 22-lap heats, and practice times put Jimmy's brand new 948 on pole position, 0.2 second quicker than Moss' Special, 906, with Graham Hill's new V8 BRM on the outside. Moss led away from the start only to lock-up his front wheels and charge straight up an escape road. He rejoined and rocketed back through the field and was gaining on Hill when his V8 began to lose revs. He finished second in this first heat, and in the interval the Walker boys raised the final-drive ratio to preserve the engine. Clark's Cfimax suffered a valve-gear derangement on the first lap, and Gregory's UDT car went out on lap 19 with suspension problems.

There was a start-line kerfuffle at the beginning of the second heat as the Hill and Tony Marsh BRMs stalled and were illegally push-started. Moss led until his valve gear followed Clark's into limbo on lap 7, although Mairesse in the solitary V6 Ferrari had been challenging him hard until he spun off. Rather than wait for a gap in the traffic the Belgian shot back on to the course just as Trevor Taylor came by, and the two cars collided. Trevor had already made a long stop with gear-change trouble in the first heat, and when Mairesse booted his car wildly into the Lotus' path, smashing one of its wheels and tearing away the tyre and inner tube, an understandably furious Yorkshireman was to be seen shaking his fist at the fast-departing Ferrari. . .

The Belgian went through the field to win this heat, with Ireland a close third behind Bonnier's Porsche. Mairesse was untroubled in winning the third heat and took the race overall. Trevor started from the back of the grid with a new wheel and tyre and finished fourth behind the UDT car. Innes was third on aggregate.

Siffert excelled himself in the new Ecurie Filipinetti's over-engined Junior, and was sixth overall. Moss made fastest lap in the first two heats, his second-heat time of exactly two minutes being the new circuit record. During practice Vaccarella broke Moss' old car by spinning in the wet and hitting a marker post.

A fortnight later came the first British Formula 1 race of the season, the Lombank Trophy at Snetterton. Team Lotus entered 948 for Clark and 949, their second 24 chassis fitted for this occasion with a four-cylinder Climax engine, for Taylor. UDT-Laystall had borrowed the Walker V8 Special and hired Moss to drive it, and regular drivers Ireland and Gregory were in the team's four-cylinder cars. Jack Brabham, having left Coopers to form his own manufacturing business, was waiting for his own Formula 1 car to be completed, and had bought a Lotus 21 to tide him over, but sadly it was seriously damaged in a workshop fire before this race and he became a non-starter. Two other Lotuses which appeared were Parnell's 18 and Tony Shelly's newly-acquired 18/21 which had been built-up from spare parts.

Moss took pole position, his time of 1min 34.2sec comparing with Ireland's 2.5 litre works Lotus lap record of 1min 33.6sec set the previous year. It was Clark's turn to be 0.2 second slower and Hill's BRM was again on the outside of the row. Hill and Moss led away but Moss soon established a lead for UDT as almost simultaneously Ireland shunted Gregory in the tail at the hairpin and both came in to the pits.

Meanwhile Jimmy was in trouble with his 24, the engine going off-song, the brakes locking and fourth gear baulking, but after five laps everything miraculously righted itself and he really began to fly, catching the BRM and taking second place after 16 laps. Two laps later the dark green car was leading with Moss trailing it closely until a sticking throttle caused him to make the first of three pit stops to attempt to cure it. In between stops he motored furiously, but Jimmy came home to a clear win from Hill's BRM and Bonnier's lapped Porsche. Tony Shelly was fifth and Moss seventh, although he had the fastest lap to his credit at 1min 33.6sec, equalling Innes' 2.5 litre time! Parnell had lost his Lotus 18's coolant and Trevor Taylor retired with engine trouble after running sixth, but the Lotus 24 had proved its designers' faith.

The following weekend there were two Formula 1 meetings on Easter Monday, at Goodwood, and the other at Pau in Southern France. There were two Formula 1 races on the Goodwood programme, the 42-lap Glover Trophy for all-comers, and the 21-lap Lavant Cup for four-cylinder cars. The latter was won by McLaren's works Cooper, Shelly was third in his Lotus 18/21, and Gunther Seifert was minding his own business burbling gently through the chicane when Surtees shunted him from behind in the Lola four-cylinder Formula 1 prototype . . . most undignified. Graham Hill's promising BRM V8 scored its first outright win in the Glover Trophy after taking the lead on lap 3 to win comfortably from McLaren's Cooper and Ireland's four-cylinder UDT 18/21. Gregory was fifth for UDT and Shelly was sixth.

Moss drove the Walker V8 Special, again under UDT colours, and once again he started from pole position but the car was not running well. He was fourth when he stopped on lap 9 with gear selection problems, then rejoined three laps down and set about tackling the lap record. Surtees lost time with a spin in the new V8 Lola but he too was lapping extremely quickly. The Lotus got round in 1min 23sec, and Surtees replied with 1min 22.6sec before stopping with a sticking throttle then set a lap time of 1min 22sec after rejoining. By lap 30 Moss was up into seventh place and had equalled Surtees' new Goodwood lap record, but on the 35th lap came disaster . . .

The pale green Lotus was charging hard after Hill's BRM as Stirling prepared to unlap himself at least once, and he went through the 120 mph Fordwater curve on line, closing on the BRM into the right-hander entering St. Mary's corner. He changed down into fourth, drew almost abreast of the BRM, and then went straight off the course, bounding across the rutted grass for almost 60 yards before plunging head-on into the bank at scarcely diminished speed.

It was inexplicable that Moss should apparently have done nothing to avoid or lessen the impact. The car folded itself into a maze of crushed tubing and punctured oil and fuel tanks, and rescuers took half an hour to cut the unfortunate driver free. He was taken to hospital with extensive head injuries and damaged shoulders, knees and ribs. Although his life was in the balance for several days Stirling Moss survived, but he had driven his last race . . .

Moss' accident overshadowed interest in the happenings that day at Pau, but Maurice Trintignant won in one of UDT-Laystall's four-cylinder 18/21s, loaned to Rob Walker for the occasion in return for the V8 Special at Goodwood. Team Lotus had entered Clark and Taylor in the Snetterton 24s, Trevor's still

Jimmy takes a keen interest during a practice session at Spa as his mechanics sort out a spot of valve trouble with the V8 Coventry Climax engine of his Lotus 25. He went on to win his first Grand Prix, and the first of four consecutive Belgian GP victories.

using a four-cylinder engine due to the intended BRM V8's non-delivery. Jack Brabham had repaired his fire-damaged 21 and was making his Lotus debut, and Venezia had straightened-out their ex-Moss 912 for Vaccarella to drive once more. Jo Siffert was having his first outing in Filipinetti's new Lotus 21 but Kurt Kuhnke's Ecurie Suisse 18 was too slow to qualify.

Despite overheating troubles Jimmy took pole position, 1.9 seconds faster than Ricardo Rodriguez's 120-degrees Ferrari V6 and Bonnier's ancient Venezia Porsche, while Brabham and Trintignant were on the second row, Jimmy held back at the start, allowing Rodriguez to lead until lap 9 when, having got the measure of the Ferrari, he rushed ahead. But Trintignant was charging hard in the old 18/21 and pushed into second place behind the fleeing Clark, and when Jimmy suffered gear-change trouble the 44-years-old Mayor of Vergeze took the lead in his first race of the year. Jimmy's trouble was caused by failure of the brazing securing a gear rod bearing bracket to one of the chassis tubes, and with no way of finding a gear the car was retired on lap 24. Brabham's oil pressure disappeared after only five laps, and Taylor's hastily prepared car ran badly, although it finished the race 11th and last after losing 28 laps in stops to cure misfiring.

The Frenchman was an immensely popular winner for Walker on home ground, and the terrible news from Goodwood did not filter through until the celebrations were almost over. Vaccarella was sixth in his historic racing car and Siffert ran into transmission trouble and finished a limping seventh. Jimmy set fastest lap at 1min 33.4sec around the tight and twisty street circuit.

Five days later Team Lotus' Pau cars lined up again for the Aintree '200', held on the circuit lining Liverpool's famous horse-race course. They were being driven again by Clark and Taylor, and UDT-Laystall ran Ireland and Gregory in their two 18/21s. Brabham's ruined Pau engine had been hastily rebuilt and a varied selection of old Lotuses appeared for Shelly, Jay Chamberlain, Parnell, Bernard Collomb and Gunther Seifert, altogether ten Lotuses taking part in the race.

While waiting for his new engine Brabham completed the necessary qualifying laps in the works Lotus 24 V8, but Trevor had a gasket blow in his four-cylinder, ruining a liner. Jimmy took pole position with the 24 at 1min 53.8sec, with Hill's BRM and Surtees' Lola next up. Ireland qualified his two-year-old car fourth fastest to demonstrate his disgust at being dropped from the works team, with Ginther's BRM alongside.

In fact the two BRMs led away, but Jimmy was ahead by the second lap and just pulled away to win as he pleased. McLaren's four-cylinder Cooper was second, over a minute-and-a-half behind, and he was followed by Phil Hill's sick Ferrari and Baghetti's similar car. Taylor was a consistent fifth, and the works opposition evaporated. Shelly was seventh, Parnell ninth, Collomb 11th and Seifert 12th (26 laps behind) while Brabham's gearbox failed—again after only five laps—and Ireland and Gregory both had engine troubles. Chamberlain's 18 was disqualified for a push-start. On his winning way Clark set a new outright record of 1min 54.0sec, which shattered the previous figures.

There was a fortnight's grace before the International Trophy at Silverstone, which once again was for Formula 1 cars. Team Lotus still had just the one V8 engine for Clark, so the two works cars appeared as before, but UDT-Laystall had taken delivery of a shiny new Lotus 24 complete with Climax V8 engine. Ireland was driving a borrowed V6 Ferrari, and Brabham's mechanics were finishing off his new 24 V8 while he practised in the four-cylinder car. Vaccarella was out again in 912 for Venezia, and Trintignant, Piper, Shelly, Parnell and Chamberlain were the remaining Lotus drivers. Practice suggested that this was to be a splendid battle of the V8s, with Hill's BRM on pole, flanked by Clark, Surtees and team-mate Ginther.

Jimmy made a wonderful start, and he led easily from Hill in the opening stages. But the first World Championship race in Holland was only one week away, and mindful of his V8 engine's rarity Jimmy eased back gently with some 12 laps to go. He began to lose some of his 19 seconds lead, and the BRM pit kept Hill well-informed in second place as the gap narrowed. Colin signalled the danger to his number one, but the BRM was really flying and closed inexorably. With two laps to go the Lotus pit timed the gap at 6 seconds and as Jimmy shot by into his last lap they signalled him '6.0'. This seemed safe with one lap to go, but the next car to come shrieking out of Woodcote, skittering close to the grass, was Hill's BRM and the gap was now only 3 seconds! Down towards Club Corner Jimmy realised the danger, but Gregory was in the way and unwittingly baulked the leader. By now the BRM was on the Lotus 24's tail. Jimmy clung to the inside into Woodcote to force Graham wide, but Hill made a do-or-die effort, held the throttle wide open, and flung his car broadside through the curve. The slithering BRM just got its nose ahead across the line to score a sensational victory.

Both cars were given the same time for the race distance, and Surtees' third-place Lola was the only unlapped runner. Brabham was sixth in his new 24 and Gregory finished eighth in his; Taylor finished tenth, Chamberlain 16th and Piper 17th but all the other Lotus drivers disappeared.

So the new BRM had proved itself a match for the Lotus but Colin's ace card was up his sleeve for the first World Championship round at Zandvoort. The age of the monocoque was about to dawn . . .

Some of the Lotus 24 customers felt rather short-served at the Dutch seaside resort when the Team Lotus transporter disgorged its brand-new Lotus 25 for Jimmy Clark. Gone was the accepted multi-tubular spaceframe,and in its place was the first monocoque chassis in Formula 1 racing.

In fact Lotus type numbers should be reversed around the Marks 24, 25 and 26—the new Elan road car. Colin's development programme on the Elan had

Stirling Moss driving in his last motor race. Seconds after this picture was taken at Goodwood on Easter Monday, 1962, Moss' UDT/Laystall entered, Lotus 21-based Formula 1 car left the track at high speed and crashed into the bank between Fordwater and St Mary's. Stirling survived his terrible injuries, but announced his retirement a year later after a private test drive.

Trevor Taylor had an eventful 1962 season. After taking a magnificent second place in the Dutch Grand Prix (above), the first time he had driven a V8-engined Lotus 24, he survived an alarming accident at Spa, then went to the French Grand Prix at Rouen, where he had to coax his Lotus 25 back to the pits with a broken throttle spring (below). At the end of the race he was an innocent party in another high-speed crash.

shown that its backbone chassis offered tremendous rigidity for a very light weight. He says, 'I began to think about applying the backbone idea to a racing car, and strangely enough I really did draw out the original scheme on the back of a table napkin. I thought, 'Why not space the sides of the backbone far enough apart for a driver to sit between them?' So we drew-up the 25, but despite people telling me ever since that there were monocoque racing cars in 1911, it was the first so far as I was concerned. I'd never seen one before, and we didn't know if it would work. So then we drew the 24 spaceframe car to pick-up the 25 suspension. The spaceframe was a known quantity and so we sold it to our customers. We couldn't be expected to sell them a revolutionary car which might not work at all, and might need a long and expensive development programme. At that time the monocoque—if that's what you want to call it—was really an unknown animal.'

The 'chassis' of the new car was formed by two parallel box members fabricated from 16-gauge L72 Alclad aluminium sheet. These ran the length of the car along either side of the cockpit and were joined by a stressed floor panel, a fabricated bulkhead behind the driver's humped seat pan, the dash panel and a square-tube diaphragm arrangement at either end. The side pontoons carried rubber-bag fuel cells fully-enclosed apart from access panels, and the Climax V8 engine sat between two forks behind the rear cockpit bulkhead. A detachable nose cone, engine cowl and gearbox cover formed the bodywork, the outer panels of the pontoons being exposed on either side. The front and rear suspension geometry and the five-speed ZF 5DS10 transmission were identical to those of the Lotus 24 which had been released earlier while the new car was being built and tested. The whole point of the car was increased torsional rigidity for less weight, giving bonuses in braking, cornering and acceleration.

The carburettor mounting on the engine had been revised with each Weber twin-choke unit now bridging the vee and feeding opposing cylinders in either bank, in place of the original two-by-two in-line arrangement with separate units for each cylinder bank. This improved the inlet tract shape and allowed a simplified throttle linkage.

This remarkably innovative design drew much attention from interested press and public and disgruntled 24 customers alike, and all sat back to see how it would perform.

Meanwhile Trevor Taylor was having his first race with V8 power in 948, the Snetterton and Aintree-winning Lotus 24, and Brabham was giving his 24 its first World Championship outing. UDT-Laystall put Ireland in their 24 V8 which had been shaken-down at Silverstone by Gregory, and Masten was back in one of their 18/21 Specials. Rob Walker had taken delivery of a new Lotus 24 V8 for Maurice Trintignant, but the car was not ready to race and the entry had to be scratched.

Cooper introduced their new V8 engined car for McLaren and Porsche had their new flat-eight car for Gurney, but the sleek and beautifully clean Lotus 25 was queen of the piece.

Surtees' Lola took pole position ahead of Hill's BRM and Jimmy's new car, and Jack Brabham was fourth quickest in his promisingly competitive Lotus 24. Trevor only completed one practice lap before the camshaft drive broke, and Gregory's car suffered a piston collapse; Colin flew Trevor's engine back to England and brought out a replacement, while UDT also did some aerial shuttling to collect a spare for the American.

From the start Jimmy's Lotus 25-R1 hacked across to the inside to lead around Tarzan Hairpin and back behind the pits, through the left-handed Hunzerug corner and away through the dunes. He rapidly pulled out a 3.5 seconds lead from Hill, while behind them Ricardo Rodriguez spun his Ferrari in Brabham's path and put the private 24 into retirement with frontal damage. Trevor Taylor became involved in a great scrap for fourth place until he spun and dropped to seventh.

Jimmy's lead was not to last, for on lap 12 the Lotus 25 slowed out of Tarzan and Hill went into the lead. The Lotus' clutch had not been engaging properly so Jimmy limped round to the pits where Jim Endruweit and the mechanics set about the clutch adjustment; Clark rejoined the race just as Hill flashed by on his 20th lap.

By this time Taylor had caught and passed Ireland and was now after Phil Hill, while Masten Gregory latched on to the leading BRM's tail as it lapped him and closed-up on Baghetti's Ferrari. Taylor was going splendidly in third place, and by lap 61 he was right on the Ferrari's tail just as Ireland lost his 24 under braking for Tarzan and somersaulted crazily into the infield, escaping with nothing worse than a cut face but quite bemused by sudden disaster.

But Lotus followers were soon cheering again as Taylor appeared in second place, 27 seconds behind the BRM, but Hill was pacing the race carefully and was fully aware of any threat. He went on to score his first World Championship round victory, while Trevor came home into second place to score his first six Championship points, 27.2 seconds behind; Jimmy was finally 10th, ten laps down.

Two weeks later came another trip to Monaco, and Team Lotus filled their two invitations with R1 for Clark and 948 again for Taylor, while the UDT drivers, Brabham, Trintignant, Vaccarella and Siffert arrived there knowing that they would have to qualify for a place on the grid. Ireland and Gregory both had brand-new Lotus 24s, one with the engine from the crashed car and the other with a new BRM V8 with Weber carburettors and stub exhaust pipes. Both cars had Colotti transaxles, and one of the 18/21s was present as a spare.

Brabham had his bright green Lotus 24 repaired after its Zandvoort collison, and Trintignant's Walker 24 was making its debut with the borrowed UDT 18/21 which had won at Pau as spare. Vaccarella had little chance of qualifying the Venezia 912 which had won in 1960 and 1961, and Siffert was also unsuccessful in his efforts to make his first Championship appearance in his Lotus 21.

Clark was fastest in the first Thursday practice session, and both drivers tried the works' spare car, a brand new Lotus 24 with BRM V8 engine and six-speed Colotti gearbox. Graham Hill was quickest on Friday morning when Vaccarella crashed his famous car once again in the rain, and on the Saturday Team Lotus were embroiled in film-making which rather annoyed Jimmy. Towards the end of the session BRM and Graham Hill started to get involved in the film, and Jimmy nipped out in anger and stole pole position from the Bourne team by 0.4 second!

The BRM-engined 24 had not run well during practice and so both Team Lotus starters were Climax-powered. As usual, the start was on the quayside, with the road curving gently left before the first corner, the tight 180-degrees Gasworks Hairpin. Mairesse catapulted his Ferrari into the lead, bouncing through from the second row between Clark and Hill, and entering the hairpin far too fast and broadsiding. Jimmy virtually stopped in avoiding him as McLaren and Graham Hill dived by. Mairesse gathered his car up and snapped on to their tails as the Lotus 25 also cleared the corner, but behind there was chaos.

The leaders' unexpectedly heavy braking caught the pack unawares,and as Ginther's throttle stuck wide open in the BRM all hell broke loose. Gurney, Ireland and Taylor were all involved in a wild collision as Ginther pushed Trintignant into the sea wall. Innes bounced backwards into the straw bales while poor Trintignant careered along the wall, ending up with the brand-new Walker car totally wrecked, its radiator torn right off. One of Ginther's wheels was torn off and very sadly it struck and fatally injured a marshal. Taylor's nose cowling was bent upwards but he pressed-on and stopped to have it removed at the pits. Ireland also continued and meanwhile Mairesse spun again at the Station Hairpin and there was more pushing and shoving.

Jimmy was sixth at the end of the traumatic first lap with Brabham eighth, but Jack soon powered by and towed the Lotus 25 and its shaken driver through into fourth and fifth places, respectively, at the ten-lap mark. On lap 12 Phil Hill spun the third-placed Ferrari, at which point both Lotuses slipped by, and when Jimmy passed Jack on lap 22 he stormed away in third place, and closed on McLaren and Hill's leading BRM.

Taylor's oil tank had been damaged during the first-lap accident and he retired at 25 laps with his pedals covered in oil, which had caused his feet repeatedly to slither off them. At that point Jimmy had just taken second place. He had suffered early gear-change problems, but the trouble seemed to have disappeared and he closed right up on the BRM, only to lose out through the traffic and then have the change stiffen-up once again. The Lotus 25 dropped to 15 seconds behind the BRM and on lap 56, when his clutch

Above: 1962 World Championship rivals Jim Clark and Graham Hill looked relaxed enough before their vital final race, as do BRM boss Alfred Owen and his chief designer—later to join Lotus—Tony Rudd.

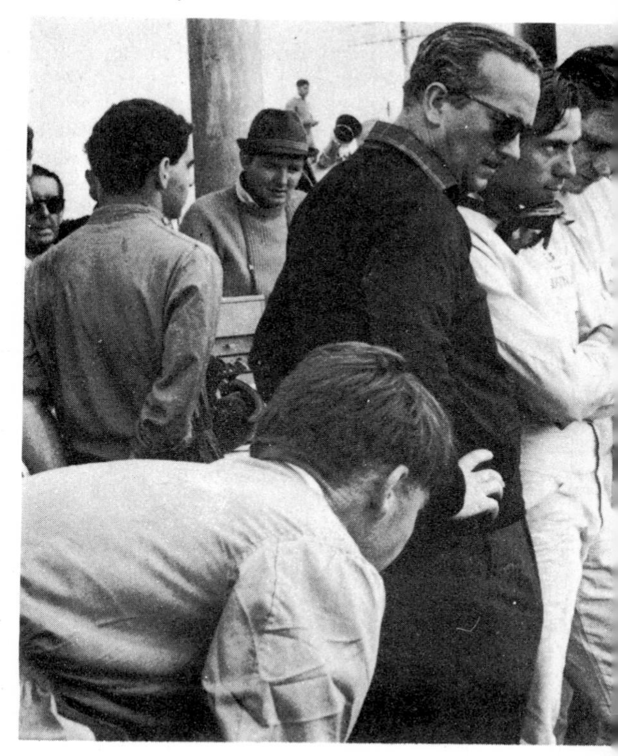

Below: Not so many smiles from Colin Chapman, Jim Clark and Trevor Taylor in the East London pits after Jimmy had reported a misfiring problem during practice for the South African Grand Prix.

broke, Clark's race ended abruptly after he had set a new lap record of 1min 35.5sec.

Brabham was now third behind McLaren, and staving off Phil Hill's Ferrari, but he was getting hot and uncomfortable in the process, and on lap 77 he spun in the Casino Square and bounced up a grassy bank, bending the front suspension and retiring. Ireland's miserable ride had ended after 64 laps with fuel pump trouble; the rear-end damage had caused a fuel leak, and fumes entering the cockpit had made Innes sick several times before he finally gave up. Finally, Hill's BRM failed after 93 of the 100 laps and so McLaren won for Cooper. Of the other Lotus hopefuls Gregory had failed to qualify, and Siffert was also unlucky even though his 1min 38.9sec practice lap was faster than those of the guaranteed starters Ginther, Taylor, Bonnier and Maggs.

Just over a week later came the Whit-Monday meetings in England, where two Formula 1 events were organised, the lucrative Mallory Park 2,000 Guineas and the London Trophy at Crystal Palace.

In Leicestershire Jimmy took pole position in R1, 0.6 second faster than Brabham in his Lotus 24, while Hill forsook his BRM for Walker's borrowed 18/21 and was 0.4 second slower, Surtees' Monaco-nosed Lola completing the front rank another 0.6 second down. Fearless John was in dazzling form for the race, and after making a lightning start he led all the way. Gregory's UDT 18/21 dashed into an early third place behind Brabham, but was then displaced in turn by Graham Hill and Jimmy. But on lap 19 the Lotus 25's oil pressure dropped in the turns and Clark made a pit stop, continued for four tentative laps, then stopped again for good. Brabham finished second, and Hill's Lotus 18/21 was third for Walker. Gregory was fifth, and also-rans included Colin Davis in Venezia's 18/21, Tony Shelly in his 18/21 and John Dalton with Parnell's old 18.

Down at Crystal Palace Taylor put the works Lotus 24, 949, on the outside of the front row, 0.2 second slower than McLaren's four-cylinder Cooper and 0.4 second down on Salvadori's Bowmaker Lola in pole position. Innes Ireland had to start from the back of the grid in UDT's BRM-engined Lotus 24, having just returned from racing a Ferrari in Canada. Gerry Ashmore entered the now tatty Marsh Special 18 for Graham Eden, similar to those of Gunther Seifert, David Piper and Jay Chamberlain, and Brian Hart ran his Formula Junior 20 fitted with a 1,475 cc Ford engine.

Ireland shot through the whole field at the start to take third place behind the leading Lola and Cooper from the front row, with Taylor fourth. Eden in the old Marsh Special was left on the line and then pushed to the pits, while Ireland took the lead on lap 3 and just ran away to an easy win, breaking the lap record several times. Trevor's car went sick towards the finish when challenging McLaren for third place, and stopped on the circuit during the last lap, while Piper was sixth. Ireland's race average for the 36 laps was nearly 4 mph faster than the previous best figures, and his lap record of 57.2 seconds was faster than the best practice time.

It had been another disappointing weekend for Team Lotus, but three days later they arrived at the Spa circuit for the Belgian Grand Prix in a mood of optimism. Clark was again in the 25 while Trevor ran 948, his usual 24. Jimmy's Climax engine used the transverse-carburettor layout while Trevor's had the original in-line arrangement. UDT-Laystall had their Lotus 24s with Climax engine for Ireland and BRM for Gregory, and Rob Walker had rebuilt his wrecked Monaco car with a new frame for Trintignant, while his old 18/21 was loaned to Equipe Nationale Belge for Lucien Bianchi. Brabham and Siffert were in their personal cars and at the last moment Wolfgang Seidel's new Autosport team entered the spare BRM-engined Team Lotus 24 for Dan Gurney since the Porsche works were giving the race a miss. Finally, John Campbell-Jones did a deal with Gunther Seifert and drove his usual Lotus 18.

Jimmy had trouble in the first practice session when a cam-drive dowel sheared and damaged the engine, but Trevor settled in and impressed everyone by lapping really quickly on his first visit to this daunting circuit. None of the private Lotus 24 owners were happy with the cars' high-speed handling, and when Gurney's 24 finally arrived, painted white for the occasion, he quickly decided it wasn't raceworthy. Jimmy tried Trevor's 24 since his own car was not ready in time for the final session and he drove very gently in order not to break anything. Then, on the way back to the Lotus garage, the transmission locked in two gears at once and the mechanics were faced with more work.

Trevor's lap in 3min 59.3sec was the third quickest behind Graham Hill's and McLaren's so the 24 was on the front row of the grid while Jimmy's 25 was buried back on the middle of the fifth row.

Hill led from the flag with Taylor second and McLaren third, but Clark scratched away like mad in the 25 to take fourth place up the hill, with Mairesse on his tail in the Ferrari. Mairesse quickly moved up and came to grips with Taylor, and on the second lap Trevor led past the pits with the red Ferrari on his tail. After four laps the Ferrari was leading from the Lotus, while Jimmy sat back in the 25 gaining experience of the monocoque car's high-speed handing characteristics. But suddenly Clark rushed through into second place and by the ninth lap he was leading with Taylor and Mairesse locked in combat some distance behind. So Team Lotus were leading a Grande Epreuve fair and square against the might of all the major teams apart from Porsche. Trevor, however, was being harried mercilessly by Mairesse, the two cars passing and repassing repeatedly.

On lap 21 the red Ferrari screamed past the pits in second place, downhill into Eau Rouge, and still led Taylor away over the pine-clad ridge at Les Combes. But on lap 22 Taylor was back in front, and he was still leading narrowly four laps later when the Lotus 24 jumped out of gear in the left-hander at Blanchimont, just before the Club House above the pits. In an instant the Lotus was sideways, skewered by the Ferrari, and spinning wildly into the banks and ditches. The car thudded to a halt with a telegraph pole felled across the engine bay, while the Ferrari rolled over, threw out its fearless driver, and came to rest upside down and burning furiously. Mairesse suffered slight burns and concussion,while Taylor miraculously walked down to the pits, his yellow overalls torn and stained, and a cigarette held in unsteady hands.

Surtees reassured the Lotus crew by slowing and giving them a thumbs-up before Taylor appeared, and as a pall of smoke drifted over the valley Jimmy rocketed round, consolidating his lead and coming home to win his first Grande Epreuve, the first victory for the Lotus 25, and the first for a Grand Prix car of monocoque construction.

Brabham was sixth, but was two laps behind, as was Trintignant in eighth place, and Bianchi, Siffert and Campbell-Jones filled the next three places. Ireland stopped with his 24 handling strangely and when Tony Robinson found a wishbone anchorage pulling out of the chassis the team wisely withdrew Gregory's sister car.

Jimmy beat Hill's BRM by a convincing 44 seconds, and set a new 1.5 litre lap record in 3min 55.6sec. Both works Lotuses had run without their tail cowlings as gearbox oil temperatures had proved frighteningly high during practice.

The weekend after the Spa success was enlivened by the Le Mans 24-Hours and the unfortunate 'Affaire Lotus' fully described elsewhere but the outrage on the Sarthe was forgotten temporarily the following Sunday for the non-Championship Reims Grand Prix, run over 50 laps of the fast Reims-Gueux road circuit in the heart of the Champagne country.

Trevor Taylor had recovered from his Spa shaking, which was more than his car ever would, and he was in a brand-new Climax-engined Lotus 24 with five-speed Colotti transmission—number 950. Jimmy retained the 25, R1, and the spare BRM-engined 24 had been painted green again after its brief appearance in white at Spa, and was to give Peter Arundell, the Formula Junior star, his first experience of Formula 1.

Brabham and Trintignant were in their usual 24s and UDT also had their regular cars—the Climax for Ireland and the BRM for Gregory—and both had reinforced rear suspension mounts. Venezia entrusted Carlo Mario Abate with 912 for this race, and Siffert and Shelly were entered with their usual four-cylinder cars.

As the works Lotuses were late arriving Jimmy tried the Walker 24 after Trintignant had complained of its high-speed behaviour; he found it terrifying! Eventually the Team Lotus transporter arrived and Jimmy took his car for just five laps. Hill's BRM was down to 2min 24.8sec at this stage, and Jimmy's five flying laps began at 2min 24.9sec, then came down to 2min 24.3 sec fourth time round and ended-up at 2 min 24.2sec on the fifth. Then he pulled in, having left the opposition looking thoroughly demoralised.

The following day he did another five-lap cycle right near the end of the session and got down to 2min 22.9sec to take pole position ahead of Hill and Surtees. Taylor's hastily-completed 24 arrived from Cheshunt that morning with the Spa Climax engine installed, and Peter Arundell prepared for his Formula 1 debut in the BRM car.

Masten Gregory was to have an unfortunate race in his UDT 24. He was late on the grid, and by the time he settled himself engines were bellowing all round him and he couldn't hear if his starter was turning. Consequently he flooded his engine, and despairingly raised his arms to show he couldn't move. As the flag fell de Beaufort in his old Porsche tried to dodge the Lotus, but Maggs didn't leave enough room for him in the works Cooper and the Dutchman thumped the 24's rear wheel as he bounced by. Masten retired on the line with a dead engine, a cracked upright and two 'S'-shaped radius rods.

Meanwhile, Surtees had fled into the lead from Hill with Jimmy third, Brabham fourth, Ireland fifth and Trintignant sixth, but as Taylor came down into Thillois he found fuel slopping over the pedals from a leaking scuttle tank; his feet slipped and the car went sideways and hit the fence, crumpling the nose. Clark was now in second place, keeping the leading Lola in sight, but on lap 5 he dropped out when the swirl-pot in the cooling system spilt. This left Arundell on his own in a works car, but he stopped almost immediately with the fuel pressure gauge feeder pipe adrift. He had to drive in the Formula Junior final after this main race, so Clark took over the car, but in the heat of the moment nobody thought to top-up the fuel tanks, and Jimmy ran out of fuel after 37 laps.

This long fast race made the cars very thirsty, and Brabham lost his third place to Ireland when he forgot to flip his reserve tank switch and his engine died momentarily. Surtees broke a valve spring, leaving McLaren to win for Cooper, with Hill's BRM second, Ireland third for UDT, Brabham fourth and Trintignant fifth. Siffert was ninth, lacking the power of the V8 cars on this muscle circuit. Shelly's engine had been bodged after practice and failed on the second lap, and Abate spun the poor abused 912 yet again, parking it among the corn fields on lap 23. This was a most unsatisfactory race for Team Lotus, but one week later came the serious business of the French Grand Prix at Rouen-les-Essarts.

A new Lotus 25—R2—arrived there for Clark, and Taylor took over R1 for his first race in the latest monocoque car. The works 24-Climax was present as a spare but the 24-BRM had been sold to Filipinetti for Jo Siffert. UDT-Laystall's second transporter came out with a brand-new 24-Climax with five-speed Colotti gearbox for Ireland, and Gregory's mangled Reims suspension had been replaced. Trintignant and Brabham were in their normal Lotus 24s.

Ireland ran his older car while the new one was finished-off in the paddock, and he had a fright when the steering rack broke and prevented any right lock. Jimmy had a similar fright with the new 25, and Siffert's clutch hydraulics failed him on his first lap in his new acquisition and stranded him out on the circuit. The next day Brabham left the road and filled his 24's nose cone with mud and foliage, but Jimmy rocketed round in 2min 14.8sec to take yet another pole position ahead of Hill's BRM and McLaren's Cooper.

On race day he completed his warming-up lap with the car running perfectly and then found the engine refusing to fire on all eight when he restarted. The plug leads had been crossed, and they were hastily corrected, Jimmy showing a Fangio-like serenity although the same couldn't be said of Colin and the mechanics!

Down through the fast curves to Nouveau Monde Hill led from Surtees and Clark while Ireland slid sideways in the pack, held it, and then spun at the hairpin with a puncture. Jimmy's car was not handling well and he pointed despairingly at the front end as he passed the pits on lap 12, but when Surtees stopped he inherited second place and he set a new lap record on lap 22 at 2min 18.4sec, which was to be bettered later by Hill. Meanwhile, Taylor had stopped at the hairpin with throttle linkage trouble and drove back to the pits leaving the engine cowl down on the infield, and on lap 30 the BRM was involved in a minor collision and Jimmy appeared in the lead. But in only three laps Hill had caught and passed the Lotus and Jimmy stopped with a faulty ball-joint on the left-upper front wishbone. Sadly, the car was retired, and Trevor was signalled-in to have Clark's engine cowl fitted to his car, as the regulations forbad running without a cover—how times have changed!

Gurney's Porsche inherited the lead when the BRM faltered and went on to win both his own and his team's first Grande Epreuve. But immediately after the finish came mayhem. Surtees had finished fifth, travelling very slowly with the car stuck in third gear, and he tried to pull into his pit immediately after crossing the line. But he was prevented from doing so by a wall of Gendarmes, and as he couldn't see where his pit was anyway he shuddered to a halt. Trintignant came over the brow to finish (also on the right-hand side of the road even though he was still racing) and seeing the Lola in his path he suddenly swerved to the left, and straight into the path of Trevor Taylor, who came boring over the hill at 120 mph. The Walker Lotus was doing about 40 mph and Trevor chose to hit it rather than swerve and chance the bales or the police.

He braked desperately hard and slammed into the Walker car's tail, and the two shattered machines careered into the straw bales beyond the pits. Both drivers were shaken but otherwise unhurt, but the front of the original 25 was badly distorted and the right-front wheel torn off, while the 24's rear-end was crushed and the left-rear wheel torn off. Poor Taylor had now completed a hat-trick of accidents, two of them writing-off his cars, but he couldn't conceivably be blamed for any of them.

Trintignant was seventh and Taylor eighth, while

Ireland's race had ended on lap two, Siffert had retired on lap six with another clutch failure, Brabham on lap 11 when the right rear spring unit broke away at its top mounting, and Gregory on lap 15 when his BRM engine just died under him.

Again there was just a week between races, the Formula 1 circus moving this time to Solitude for the race which had been won by Ireland the previous year. Team Lotus had to scrub their third entry as they now had only two surviving cars—R2 for Clark and Taylor with the 24 in which he had covered only one lap at Reims. Siffert was in his new BRM-engined 24 and lent the four-cylinder 21 to Gerhard Mitter, while Kuhnke and Seifert reappeared in their aged Lotus 18s.

Colin and his drivers missed first practice due to aeroplane problems, and in his first session on Saturday Jimmy had a strange puncture. A front brake pad became dislodged and the metal back-plate scored through the wheel rim until it found its way into the inner tube! Nevertheless he took pole position from the works eight-cylinder Porsches of Gurney and Bonnier.

The race began with Jimmy running between the two Porsches, but his fuel mixture was wrong and two plugs were burning. In a brief rain shower Gurney spun while in the lead and Trevor also spun off on to the grass. He came into the pits to have the tyre pressures lowered, and was about to leave when he was seen to be trailing a length of wire, which was removed before he pressed on. Then Jimmy spun at Schatten, touched the fence and retired with the exhaust pipes and right-rear radius rods crumpled. This left the Porsches with a one-two victory before their home crowd, with Taylor a lucky third. Mitter finished sixth but Siffert spun early on, then retired when petrol sprayed over the electrics and caught fire, fortunately with little damage. Kuhnke retired with engine trouble after five laps, and Seifert was ninth and last, seven laps behind the winner.

The following Saturday, Team Lotus ran the two Solitude cars, suitably repaired, in the British Grand Prix at Aintree. Brabham's new car was complete but hadn't been tested so he stuck to the 24, and UDT had a pair of 24-Climaxes for Ireland and Gregory. Wolfgang Seidel had a brand-new BRM-engined 24 while Ecurie Excelsior entered Jay Chamberlain in a Lotus 18 and Tony Shelly in Dalton's ex-Parnell 18/21.

During practice Jimmy and R2 had soon equalled his Aintree '200' lap record, and he ended up with a tremendous lap in 1min 53.6sec for pole position, with Surtees' Lola in the middle and Ireland on the inside of the front row, pole position at Aintree being on the outside of the circuit.

Late in practice Innes' gearbox had shown slight wear on the dogs and so the transmission was rebuilt overnight, but on the warming-up lap his new selector forks broke and all that could be done was to remove the broken pieces, leaving Innes without second and third gears. But on the starting grid he found that he had no gears at all, so he put his hands in the air and prayed . . .

As the flag fell everyone avoided the stranded pale green Lotus and Jimmy shot into the lead, driving with a speed and precision which left the opposition floundering. Surtees settled into a consistent second place, and Brabham was fourth, but Trevor was way back and he stopped on lap 7 brandishing a carburettor choke tube which had popped out of one of his front Webers and fallen into his lap! He carried on a lap behind.

As Jimmy lapped Trevor for the second time he began to tow him through the field, and when the Lotus 25 came up behind Graham Hill in fourth place he decided not to lap him, but instead allowed Taylor, who was now really in the groove, to pass both of them to unlap himself once. Jimmy remained unchallenged to the end, so the British Grand Prix fell to Team Lotus, less than a year after they had won their first Grande

épreuve at Watkins Glen. Jimmy averaged 92.52 mph for the 225 miles, and set fastest lap on lap 36 at 1min 55.0sec, 93.91 mph.

Brabham was fifth and Gregory seventh, just ahead of Taylor in the works 24. Chamberlain was 15th and the unfortunate Innes Ireland finally finished 16th and last. Shelly went out on lap 6 with head gasket failure, and Seidel retired on lap 11 without brakes and with overheating.

On the first weekend in August the fabulous 14.2-miles Nurburgring circuit through the Eifel Mountains was host once again to the German Grand Prix. Team Lotus ran the Aintree cars for Clark and Taylor, but UDT-Laystall and the organisers couldn't agree on starting money so the pale green Lotuses didn't run. Jack Brabham forsook the Lotus fold to make his debut in his new Brabham-Climax, and Rob Walker's team had again rebuilt their 24 around a new chassis frame. Filipinetti put Siffert in the old 21 and allowed Heinz Schiller to take over the BRM-engined 24 (a sad waste of talent), Seidel had his new 24-BRM and Chamberlain and Shelly were running their older cars once again.

Clark was unable to put a really fast lap together in R2, but he managed a rather unsatisfactory second-quickest time to Gurney's Porsche on Friday afternoon. On the Saturday Trevor's car suffered a valve breakage, wrecking a brand new engine, so the old Aintree unit was fitted overnight.

Race day was horribly wet and the start was delayed while landslips and wrecked GT cars were cleared from the circuit and some of the puddles pumped dry.

1962 South African Grand Prix. Jimmy and Graham share the front row for their all-important race.

Chamberlain, Shelly and Seidel non-started through insufficient practice, and the timekeepers ruled-out Taylor for having completed only four laps, but later Colin managed to persuade them he had covered the minimum of five and so Trevor was allowed to start after all, although his old engine wouldn't run properly.

It was at the start of this race that Jimmy probably lost the 1962 World Championship. He tried to stop his goggles from steaming up as he sat in third place on the four-strong front row, flanked by Hill and Gurney to his right and Surtees to his left. He started his engine, but forgot to switch on his fuel pumps, and as the flag fell the Climax V8 died. The field surged away as Jimmy sat and waited furiously for the float chambers to refil. He was last away, and meantime Taylor was also having a bad time. He was struggling round with his engine spluttering and banging, when suddenly it chimed-in on all eight, took him by surprise, and poked the Lotus 24 straight through the hedge and down a bank into a tree and out of the race.

Jimmy passed 17 cars on that first streaming lap, the Lotus 25 screaming through the woods, slithering and skating from lock to lock. His progress was fantastic, and after three laps he was eighth, worrying the works Ferraris. By lap 8 he was fourth, and still gaining five seconds a lap on the leaders. He closed to within 14 seconds of the leading trio, driving the 25 right on the limit, but then he had a couple of really big slides at high speed in top gear and decided to settle for a safe fourth place rather than risk the car any more. Graham Hill won from Gurney and Surtees to score nine points while Jimmy took three for fourth place. Siffert was 12th in the four-cylinder 21 while Schiller retired the team's Lotus 24 after four laps with no oil pressure. Trintignant's car stopped with a broken gear selector—a repeat of Ireland's Aintree trouble.

One week later there was a small Formula 1 meeting at Karlskoga, in Sweden, where Masten Gregory scored a rare win for UDT-Laystall's Lotus 24-Climax. Graham Hill drove the Walker 24 but retired, while Ireland was fourth with the other UDT car. The following Sunday the Mediterranean Grand Prix was run at Enna, far South in Sicily, where the works Ferraris of Bandini and Baghetti led the way home, with Siffert's Lotus fourth after a dice with Vaccarella in Venezia's 18/21 which later retired.

Back in Scandinavia the Copenhagen Grand Prix at Roskilde was won by Jack Brabham, giving his bright green Lotus 24 a final outing; Jack won all three heats and set a new lap record of 42.7 seconds, while Gregory was second on aggregate, narrowly ahead of Ireland's sister car. Gary Hocking, the young Rhodesian motor-cyclist, was fourth in a Lotus 18 which he had just acquired from Tim Parnell, while Trevor Taylor drove R2, had a miserable time, and couldn't do better than sixth place.

In September Team Lotus were back in England with three cars for the Oulton Park Gold Cup—Clark's R2, Taylor's 24 and a brand-new 25—R3—for practice. Once again poor Trevor had an engine failure in the 24 and he had to race the untried, untested new monocoque car. Jimmy shared fastest practice time with Ginther's BRM but took the lead straight away from second place on the grid and won comfortably, averaging 97.64 mph for the 73 laps and setting a new record lap at 1min 40.0sec, 99.34 mph. Both UDT cars had clutch trouble on the line, Gregory's new 24-BRM stalling completely, but he slashed back through the field into fourth place, despite suffering a badly burned right foot, an inoperative clutch and dicey brakes. Bonnier drove the Walker 24 and retired with gearbox trouble, Ireland's clutch failed completely, and Taylor retired when a radius rod pulled loose after many earlier stops with gear-selector trouble. Gary Hocking led the four-cylinder race from the rear of the eight-cylinder group, waving the inside front wheel high through the corners, but he stopped for water and finally went out when an oil pipe parted. . . his talent clearly was tremendous. Shelly went on to win the four-cylinder race, finishing fifth overall, with Gregory sixth, Ashmore eighth and Seifert tenth.

Team Lotus were in a terrible state two weeks later as they prepared for the Italian Grand Prix at Monza. Jimmy had R2, Trevor R3 and the 24 was present as a spare, but on Friday Jimmy's 25 was way over-geared. The ZF transmissions did not have quick-change drop-gears, a selection of assembled units with varying final-drive ratios having to be taken to each race instead. So the mechanics set about swopping the transmission, and then the replacement broke so they had to change the lot again. In between his troubles Jimmy set the second fastest time, and then Trevor had a rear suspension ball-race seize and break-up. Meanwhile, Colin had arranged for another gearbox to be flown out overnight, and on Saturday this broke before the car even left the paddock! As soon as Jimmy got going his Climax broke a tappet, and in desperation his number 20 was pasted on Taylor's car and in seven desperate laps he bettered Hill's fastest BRM time and equalled the outright record of 1min 40.4sec. Then, right at the end of the session, Trevor tried Jimmy's repaired R2 and the gearbox seized yet again, so the weary mechanics dragged it away once more.

Team Lotus were running a lubricant additive in the ZF transmissions, which had the only synchromesh in Grand Prix racing at the time, and the failures were traced to overheated cones. Inaccurate assembly was blamed at the time, but the use of the additive certainly contributed. The team found not only the weather to be dismal on race day, for after running second to Hill for three laps Jimmy's transmission tightened up once again. He stopped, rejoined the race, then finally retired on lap 13 with the gearbox ruined!

Meanwhile, UDT were doing considerably better. Their 24s occupied the third row of the grid, and Ireland led the slipstreaming group pursuing the leaders until he stopped with carburettor trouble. Then he rejoined and led the lot on the road, although one lap behind, and towed his team-mate with him, his Climax engine being slightly quicker on the straights than

Gregory's BRM. Masten tucked in right behind to get the best possible tow, but unfortunately this caused his 24 to overheat and he stopped to blow-off steam. Later he had gearbox trouble and continued with the car jammed in one gear to finish 12th and last, while Innes went out when a front suspension upright cracked.

Vaccarella was the highest-placed Lotus finisher in a 24-Climax with six-speed Colotti gearbox, newly built by the Walker team and loaned to Venezia for this race. Trintignant drove his usual Climax-engined 24 and pushed it into the pits with electrical failure shortly before Trevor Taylor stopped his 25 with yet another transmission breakage. Siffert, back in the Filipinetti BRM-engined 24, Shelly in Seidel's similar car and Jay Chamberlain, Gerry Ashmore and Ernesto Prinoth in their Lotus 18s all failed to qualify.

There followed a dignified pause while cars were repaired, rebuilt and freighted to America for the United States Grand Prix at Watkins Glen in October, during which time the troublesome transmissions were carefully stripped at Friedrichshaven and rebuilt for the two Lotus 25s. UDT took across three 24s, two Climax-engined cars for Ireland and Roger Penske's Team Zerex, and the BRM-engined version for Gregory. Penske's car was repainted in Zerex mustard yellow for this race. Walker Racing took their two 24s, with Trintignant in the car Vaccarella drove at Monza and the older car on loan to John Mecom Jnr for Rob Schroeder, the car being resprayed light blue. Jim Hall entered his own ex-Brabham four-cylinder 21 to complete the Lotus entry.

Jimmy took pole position in R3 by a clear 0.8 second from Hill's BRM, then led the BRM until lap 12 when Graham gained an advantage when they were lapping the tail-unders. But on lap 19 Jimmy retook him to establish the lead he was to hold to the finish, scoring Team Lotus' second consecutive victory in this most lucrative Grande Epreuve. Gregory was sixth, with Ireland, Penske and Schroeder filling eighth to tenth places and Taylor 12th. Innes had a stop with crossed gear selection and Trevor had another unhappy race watching a faltering oil pressure gauge. Trintignant's was the only Lotus retirement when he lost his brake fluid and gave up after some nasty loops across the grass.

With this victory Jimmy still had a chance of beating Graham Hill in the World Championship, everything depending now on the result of the South African Grand Prix at the end of December. In order to win Jimmy had to score another victory at East London, when he would equal Hill's present points total. The fact that he would then have won one more race would give him the title. But of course Graham would have to fail to score in order to give Jimmy the drivers' title in this way, and Team Lotus the constructors' World Championship.

Immediately after the Watkins Glen race Colin and Jimmy took one of the Lotus 25s to Indianapolis, where Jimmy drove the car in some exploratory testing and took his 'Rookie's track test' for the authorities, lapping consistently at 142-143 mph. Colin took copious notes, and in his mind the first Lotus-Ford Indy car began to take shape.

Then, at the beginning of November the first Mexican Grand Prix was held on the new Magdalena Mixhuca circuit in Mexico City as a non-championship event. Team Lotus ran Jimmy in R3 and Trevor in R2, and Clark took his customary pole position. But his engine refused to fire on the grid, and as the rest of the field waited with engines running his battery was changed. The V8 still refused to fire, so he was push-started and quite correctly was disqualified by the organisers. So Colin called in Trevor and Jimmy took over his car, rejoining one minute behind Jack Brabham, who was leading in his new Brabham-Climax. After a sensational comeback drive, Clark's Lotus 25 caught and passed the Australian and went on to win by just over two seconds. Ireland was third after spinning at the hairpin and clouting Salvadori's Lola, Jim Hall was a splendid fourth in his Lotus 21 ahead of Gregory and Schroeder in their Watkins Glen cars, and Jay Chamberlain was ninth in his 18, Jimmy averaged 90.31 mph, leaving the inaugural Formula 1 lap record at 1min 59.7sec, 93.44 mph.

Sadly the Mexico meeting was marred by tragedy, for Rob Walker loaned his latest Climax-engined 24 to Ricardo Rodriguez to drive in his local Grand Prix, and he lost control on the banking in practice, plunged into the guard-rails and died from his injuries.

At the beginning of December Gary Hocking won his home-town Rhodesian Grand Prix at Kumalo, driving his ex-Parnell car, while Neville Lederle was second in his Scuderia Scribante 21. Hocking broke the lap record 36 times during his victorious drive!

A fortnight later most of the major teams were at Johannesburg for the Rand Grand Prix which was opening the International Springbok series. Team Lotus had Clark and Taylor in R3 and R2 respectively, and despite an oil leak Jimmy took pole position by 0.2 second from Trevor, with Hill's BRM 0.2 second slower on the outside. The Lotus twins dominated the race from start to finish and they staged a near dead-heat, mirroring their 1961 Kyalami performance. Jimmy averaged 95.7 mph and set fastest lap at 1min 35.3sec, 96.9 mph. Ireland was lying fourth in the UDT 24 before retiring with front suspension failure, and Gary Hocking took over his place in Walker's surviving 24. Syd van der Vyver appeared in the ex-Brabham 24 and was the fastest local driver in practice, but he went out after 32 of the 50 laps with clutch failure. Lederle was fifth after Ernie Pieterse's similar 21 had failed, and Brausch Niemann raised a few eyebrows by finishing tenth in, of all cars, a 1,500 cc Lotus 7, ahead of Bernie Podmore's Lotus 20 and Bob van Niekerk's 22.

The following weekend came the Natal Grand Prix at Durban's Westmead circuit, and tragedy struck hard at Rob Walker's team for a second time when Gary Hocking crashed fatally in practice, the car breaking in two after hitting a drainage ditch and smashing into a tree. This sad event cast a gloom over the meeting.

Once again Jimmy took pole position, this time in R4—a new Lotus 25 just freighted out from Cheshunt. There were two qualifying heats and after leading the first Jimmy ran into fuel vapourisation problems in the intense heat and retired. Trevor was on the middle of the front row for the second heat in R2, and he just beat Graham Hill to the finishing line by some very forceful motor racing. Trevor began the final flanked by the works BRMs of Hill and Ginther while Jimmy was right at the back. The Lotus number two performed brilliantly, setting a new lap record of 1min 24.20sec, 96.79 mph, on his second lap as he consolidated a good lead. Clark took just 12 laps to carve his way through the field, to take second place behind his flying team-mate. His engine went flat as Team Lotus tried to stage another dead-heat, and he trailed home 6.5 seconds down in a well-won second place. Trevor completed the race with only one gear left! Lederle and Pieterse were fourth and fifth, van Niekerk 11th, Jack Holme 14th in a Lotus 18, while poor Van der Vyver crashed his 24 on lap five, but was lucky to escape unhurt from a badly-mangled car.

So the circus arrived at East London for the all-important last round of the World Championship. Another new Lotus 25 was sent out for Jimmy to drive, numbered R5, while his training car became R4, which had a new Lucas fuel-injection unit on its Climax engine. Taylor was in R2 once again, UDT ran one Climax-engined 24 for Ireland, Lederle and Pieterse had their 21s, and Sam Tingle ran the late Gary Hocking's 18/21 in one of the Grand Prix's supporting events.

Jimmy had misfiring problems with his fuel-injected engine during practice, and something began to seize on his other car. Nevertheless he was the first driver to get under 1min 30sec while Taylor survived two big spins and Ireland discovered that his car was jumping out of third gear. On Friday Jimmy secured pole position at 1min 29.3sec, compared with Hill's 1min 29.6sec, and Trevor practised R4 after pushing R2 home with a partial seizure. He set the third-quickest time with the fuel-injected car, but it wasn't running reliably and Colin decided to run the carburettor engines in the race. Jimmy retained his pole position in R5, but this decision put Trevor back on row five with the repaired R2.

Jimmy led from the start with Hill chasing hard, but the Lotus just streamed away from the BRM. By lap 61 he had a 30-seconds lead, when suddenly the car began to trail smoke past the pits. There were 21 laps to go, but only two laps later the oil pressure began to surge in the turns and on lap 64 Clark rushed the Lotus into its pit. Everybody hurried to examine the engine, and after some time they found a small hole hidden under the exhaust heat shield at the back of the block. A quick check of the spare engine showed that it should have held a two-inch long bolt which retained the jack-shaft bearing. The oil had sprayed out from the hole onto the exhaust. When the bolt was taken from the spare engine it left behind a firm impression of its lock-washer, but there was no such impression o Jimmy's leaking engine; it seemed likely that n lock-washer had been fitted at the works. Clark an Lotus had lost the World Championship.

Graham Hill carried on to win the race and with the title, and BRM took the coveted constructor World Championship. Innes Ireland's was the fir Lotus home, in fifth place, ahead of Lederle wh gained a championship point for finishing sixt Pieterse was tenth after failing to start on the grid an losing time while the battery was changed, and poo Taylor lost seventh place when he abandoned his car o the circuit with crownwheel and pinion failure. Th 1962 racing season was at an end . . .

Team Lotus had contested all nine of the Worl Championship-qualifying races during the year and ha won three of them, adding to their original Grand Epreuve success at Watkins Glen the previous year. N less than 18 non-championship races of reasonab importance were held, and of these Team Lotu contested 14 and won six, four more falling t privately-entered Lotuses. Thus of 27 Formula 1 even during 1962 Lotus cars won 13, and to this total mus be added Moss' two Tasman victories with the Walke 21. The biggest prize had proved elusive, but the yea had proved far from unsuccessful.

1962 RACING RECORD
Other formulae and classes

After the Chequered Flag Geminis had proved such serious threat to Lotus domination of Formula Junio late in 1961, the new season offered the bright prospec of some hard and close racing. Jack Brabham and Ro Tauranac had been encouraged by the good showing o their original MRD Formula Junior prototype, and ha laid down a batch of a dozen improved cars for 1962 which they had decided to call Brabhams after Jack ha been warned of the implications of the original name i the French language!

Lotus had taken a hard look at their successfu Junior, and developed it into the new Lotus 22, whic was shown to the public in London at the BRSCC' annual Racing Car Show in January. The new mode was based closely on the Lotus 20, but differed in usin an inclined 1,100 cc Cosworth-Ford engine as standard along with Lotus 21 rear suspension, a wider track, thicker radiator and outboard disc brakes all round The canted installation of the engine, leaning over at 3 degrees to the right, allowed a smoother induction trac shape to be achieved, thereby giving further scope fo development, and at the same time gave a lower, mor compact line to the rear bodywork. The 1,098 c Cosworth-tuned unit gave a guaranteed 100 bhp a 7,500 rpm, and drove through a choice of eithe Renault or Volkswagen-based four-speed trans missions.

Above: Innes Ireland, having left Team Lotus, drove for the UDT/Laystall (later BRP) team during 1962-63, mainly using Lotus-BRM 24s as seen here at Aintree. Below: Taking time off from Championship-chasing, Jim Clark scored an easy win in the Oulton Park Gold Cup race with the brand new Lotus 25.

Chassis changes were minimal, although both oil and water were now fed through the frame tubes to do away with separate piping. The front suspension was as on the Lotus 20, but at the rear single upper links on either side replaced the drive-shafts as wheel location. The old 15-inch rear wheels were replaced by 13-inch 'wobbly webs', and a half-inch rear anti-roll bar supplemented the standard 9/16-inch front bar. The wheelbase was unchanged at 90 inches, but the track was now 51½ inches at the front and 50 inches at the rear—increases of 2½ and 2 inches, respectively.

During the 1961 season front disc brakes slowly found their way on to the Lotus 20s as they became homologated on the Triumph Herald production car, and on the Lotus 22 similar discs were fitted outboard all round. This was due mainly to the lack of space for inboard calipers at the rear, but the old drum brakes on the cheeks of the gearbox were never very accessible, and were prone to become affected by oil leaks. The price of the new car was £100 more than for the Lotus 20, at £1,550.

Just as Jim Clark had dominated Formula Junior racing in 1960, and Trevor Taylor had done so in 1961, Peter Arundell took over the mantle more effectively than ever before in 1962. Out of 25 starts his Team Lotus 22 scored 18 wins and three second places (by margins of 1 second, 0.03 second and 1.6 seconds) and retired on only four occasions, as a result of a start-line collision, a race collision, a crankshaft failure and a straightforward solo crash. The red-helmeted man from Essex had a really superb season.

Peter was joined by Alan Rees and ex-motorcyclist Bob Anderson in the works team, but neither of them had much of a season, although Rees won at Crystal Palace. He was injured in an early accident at the Nurburgring (which later caused great dramas) but later added a couple of second places to his solitary important win.

Ian Walker's private Lotus 22 team ran cars for Mike Spence and Canadian Peter Ryan, who scored a good win at Mallory Park. He was extremely promising, but at Reims his car collided with Bill Moss' Gemini, and poor Ryan was killed. Mike Spence drove a dogged race to win the final at this tragic meeting, and his smooth performance marked him down as a man to watch . . . Colin Chapman duly took note.

Across the Atlantic Pete Lovely gave the Lotus 22 its racing debut at Daytona in February, and his Team Rosebud car easily beat Floyd Aaskov's Lotus 20. Pat Pigott, Lovely's team-mate, won with a similar car at Sebring, and the Rosebud cars went on to have a fine season, challenged mainly by Rob Nethercutt's private Lotus 22.

In Europe Peter Warr won the Eifelrennen in his ageing but seldom-raced Lotus 20, and John Fenning was another winner in a year-old Lotus 20 owned by film distributor Ron Harris. French privateer Jean Lucienbonnet won at Caserta in his Lotus 22, but later he lost his life at Enna when he crashed in an attempt to avoid a wheel from Norberto Bagnalasta's Lotus. 'Geki' Russo won the Enna race in another private Lotus 2: and like Mike Spence was later to drive a Lotu Formula 1 car. Another future Lotus Grand Prix pil was the Mexican, Moises Solana, who scored numero successes in his own country with a Lotus 22.

What of the competition? The few Brabhams were often sensationally fast, and Frank Gardner's works car beat Arundell in one of the heats at Reims, while once again Ken Tyrrell's Coopers notched a string of victories, and in America Timmy Mayer won the SCCA

A smiling Mike Spence lines up for another Formula Junior race in one of Ian Walker's Lotus 22s. It was Spence's consistent performances in this team which marked him down as a future Lotus Formula 1 driver.

Formula Junior Championship in another Cooper. The season in Europe ended with Lotus winning 23 of the 36 major events, Cooper 11, and Brabham and Lola one each. But such crushing Lotus success earned a kick-back, and in October the German magazine Das Auto Motor und Sport ran a feature by its editor, Richard von Frankenberg. It was headed Die Grosste Blamage im Internationalen Motor Sport ('The Biggest Disgrace in International Motor Sport') and accredited the works Lotus 22s' fantastic turn of speed to the use of 1,450 cc engines! Team Lotus and the private drivers, Kurt Ahrens Jr and Kurt Bardi-Barry, were quoted as known delinquents, though the latter's case was mitigated because his engine was 'only 1,300 cc'. The whole story was based on a shaky interview with a heavily drugged Alan Rees, lying in hospital after his Nurburgring accident, who had refused to sell his engine, saying it belonged to the works. The full text of Lotus' response to the feature is reproduced in an Appendix at the end of this book, and Colin responded in a splendidly British manner, challenging the German to name any circuit on which Team Lotus' Juniors had won and put up £1,000 against their reproducing their speeds before being immediately stripped down and verified as legal.

The ex-Porsche driver accepted the challenge, and understandably chose a sheer power circuit, Monza, where Peter Arundell had won the Lottery Grand Prix at 113.47 mph over 30 laps, and set a lap record of 1min 50.8sec, 115.99 mph. The reproduction run was fixed for December 2, which turned out to be a bitterly cold day, with patches of ice lying under the trees on the empty, echoing Autodrome. Peter's own car had been sold to Harry Martin in the United States so he drove Bob Anderson's usual car, averaging 115.16 mph for the 30 laps and setting a best time of 1min 50.4sec, 0.4 second quicker than before. But then Peter did three more no-holds-barred laps, and shattered his old record at 1min 49.8sec, 117.14 mph!

Under the supervision of the Italian magazine Auto Italiana the Lotus 22's Cosworth Ford engine was stripped in the Monza paddock. The bore and stroke measurements of 85 mm x 48.15 mm gave a true and legal capacity of 1,092.348 cc, and the car was 3 kilograms over the minimum weight limit of 400 Kg. Everything was absolutely legal and Team Lotus were cleared completely of any smear from the whole unfortunate incident. This was splendid publicity for Lotus, in fact the whole exercise was so much more effective than legal action might have been that it turned out to be one of the best publicity stunts ever achieved by a member of the motor industry.

There was not such a heavy demand for the Lotus 22 as there had been for the Lotus 20, but even so 77 of them were produced during the year.

The second new car for the year, the Lotus 23, was very similar to the Lotus 22 in many respects, despite its two-seater bodywork. The engine, transmission, suspension and brakes were all identical in type and layout, although both 1,470 cc and 997 cc engines were available at extra cost. The chassis frame was similar in basic conception to the 20/22 designs, but widened to accommodate the two-seat cockpit and carrying all-enveloping glass-fibre body panels. This complied with Appendix J Group 4 regulations in respect of windscreen height, luggage space (provided alongside the engine), ground clearance and turning circle, and full electrical equipment included head, side, tail and brake lights, windscreen wiper and a horn. Even so the little car scaled just 880 lbs and in initial tests at Silverstone Peter Arundell went round in 1min 7.6sec, well within the 1,100 cc sports car record, without any body panels fitted!

Without a doubt the best Lotus 23 performance of the year was Jim Clark's epic drive in the Nurburgring 1,000 Kms race. This marked the debut of the Lotus twin-cam-headed Ford engine, developed by Harry Mundy and originally tested on a 997 cc 105E Ford Anglia unit. For the Nurburgring the 'works' Lotus 23 was entered by the Essex Racing Team, but Mike Costin was directing operations and the little car packed a full 1,498 cc twin-cam engine. This was based on the new 116E Ford block, yet to be released in ordinary production trim in the 'big' Classic, due in July. This had a five-main-bearing crankshaft—a bottom-end fully capable of carrying the power which a twin-cam top-end could provide—and in practice Jimmy blasted round in 9min 48.9sec, 86.51 mph, easily quickest of the 2 litre cars and seventh-fastest overall.

The weather broke for the race and the 14-mile circuit was soon damp and treacherous. Jimmy won the Le Mans-start sprint to the cars, but was beaten into the first corner by the Essex Racing Team's giant Aston Martin DBR1/300 driven by Bruce McLaren. Out of the South Curve the tiny Lotus 23 scuttled past, and it led the remainder of the lap ahead of Ferraris, Maseratis and Porsches, all of which dwarfed it completely.

Jimmy burst out of the Tiergarten with a staggering 27 seconds lead from the Porsches, Ferraris and the Aston Martin, and during the second lap the Lotus 23 pulled out another 20 seconds. After five laps it held a secure 88 seconds lead over Bonnier's Porsche, and during the next three laps Jimmy's lead had grown to more than two minutes and he was just walking away with the race.

But then the sun came out and the circuit began to dry, allowing Mairesse's 4 litre Ferrari to close the gap on Clark. At the end of 10 laps he was 54 seconds behind, and next time round the gap was down to 42 seconds. While Mairesse was happier with the Ferrari on the drying surface, Jimmy was suffering in the Lotus 23 and slowing up; the exhaust pipe had broken, and fumes were blowing into the cockpit and beginning to poison him. He was feeling really groggy when his slowed reflexes allowed a slide to develop just a shade too far in the Kesselchen, and the gallant little car skated off the road into a ditch and out of the race before co-driver Trevor Taylor could take over.

Clark's fastest lap of 9min 46.3sec, 86.94 mph, was

The two extremes of Lotus racing endeavour. Above: Jim Clark giving the monocoque Lotus 25 its race debut at Zandvoort in the Dutch Grand Prix. Below: Clive Lacey proving that the Lotus Seven (with much-modified suspension) could still beat most opposition on the Club scene.

unbeaten in the 2 litre sports car class, while the 1 litre class was won by Ian Walker's standard Lotus 23 driven by Peter Ashdown/Bruce Johnstone. Fastest lap in this class went to the sister Walker car shared by Paul Hawkins/Peter Ryan, at 10min 26.6sec, which gives some measure of the difference between a 997 cc push-rod engine and the 1,498 cc twin-cam.

This tremendous performance encouraged Colin to run a 997 cc twin-cam-engined Lotus 23 at Le Mans for Clark and Taylor, while UDT-Laystall added another string to their comprehensive bow with a similar 750 cc model for Les Leston and Tony Shelly.

The cars were presented for scrutineering, but the organising club's officials rejected both of them because the front wheels had four-stud fixings and the rears had six studs so that the spare wheel could only replace wheels on one axle. So Colin had the wheel fixings standardised front and rear with four studs each, but then the scrutineers said that since the rears had originally been designed to use six studs they were now dangerous, and they refused to re-examine the cars and rejected them out of hand.

Colin was aghast and brought over Dean Delamont of the RAC to protest his case, despite the presence of French-speaking Harold Parker, who seemed unable to get through to Secretary Acat and his men. French journalist and long-time Lotus supporter Jabby Crombac also pleaded Team Lotus' case, but it was clear that the Automobile Club de l'Ouest had made up their minds. With Bonnet and Panhard, both French makes, prime contenders for the Index awards it did not take much imagination to realise that the Lotus 23s were just too hot to handle.

L'Affaire Lotus was made even more murky by the fact that the list of verified runners was at the printers before the Lotus 23s had been re-scrutineered, and it included a Bonnet which was written-off in subsequent practice, but omitted both Lotuses . . .

Colin understandably was furious, and initially he intended to take legal action against the club before cooling-off, telling them to 'stuff their race' and swearing that Team Lotus would never again return to the Sarthe. They never have . . .

Strangely enough, the race brought poetic justice, for the Team Elite cars of David Hobbs/Frank Gardner and Dr John Wyllie/Clive Hunt finished eighth and 11th overall, finished one-two in the Index of Thermal Efficiency, and took third place in the Index of Performance behind a Panhard and a Bonnet!

Internationally the Lotus 23s went on to make a considerable name for themselves. Paul Hawkins practised the Walker car faster than a Ferrari and Arundell in the works twin-cam at Clermont-Ferrand in July, but unfortunately suffered gearbox trouble in the race and finished 22nd. Arundell crashed in the Formula Junior race there so Alan Rees took over the Lotus 23 and finished second despite never having sat in the car before. Also in France the ex-UDT Le Mans car, fitted with a 997 engine, won its class in the Montlhery 1,000 Kms driven by Jose Rosinski and Bernard Consten. Jack Brabham handled a 1.5 litre Holbay-engined Lotus 23 to win the 2 litre class in the sports-car Canadian Grand Prix at Mosport at the end of the year, and in the hilarious Bahamas Speed Week at Nassau Dan Gurney drove a similar car while his usual Arciero Brothers' Lotus 19 was run by Phil Hill.

A major tragedy for American motor racing occurred in the November Riverside meeting when Pat Pigott was killed when his Team Rosebud Lotus 23 dived under a crash barrier.

The old Lotus 19s were a very big deal in the United States at this time, particularly after Dan had won at Daytona in his usual car at the start of the year, although he had been lucky, for his crankshaft broke just before the start of his last lap, and he trickled across on the starter motor to win! Jim Clark drove Hobbs' Mechamatic Elite in this race, but lost the class lead after a long stop when the car refused to restart. The two big Mosport sports car races both fell to Masten Gregory in UDT's Lotus 19, while Gurney and Canadian Francis Bradley ran similar cars, and in relatively minor British events Innes Ireland cleaned-up regularly with one of the UDT cars.

Gurney won the North West Grand Prix at Pacific Raceways in the Arciero Lotus 19, and won one heat at Laguna Seca, on the Monterey Peninsula. Lloyd Ruby won the other in another Lotus 19, but the aggregate overall victory went to Roger Penske's Cooper Zerex Special, which was second in both. Innes appeared in the Bahamas to drive Team Rosebud's 2.5 litre Lotus 19, and won the main 252-miles Nassau Trophy quite easily. In all, ten other major wins were scored by the cars.

Graham Hill also drove a UDT-Laystall Lotus 19 during the 1962 season, and won the Archie Scott-Brown Trophy race at Snetterton, during the course of which he set the circuit's first 100 mph sports car lap record.

Jimmy Clark probably received the fright of the year on the line for the 'Autosport' three-hours race at Snetterton. His Lotus 23 twin-cam stalled on the front row, and with a ridiculous RAC ruling placing the ranks of cars so far apart that the back of the grid was out of sight at Coram Curve, he just sat there while the back numbers whistled by through the rubber smoke at near their maximum speed. Miraculously everyone avoided him and he sped through the field to score a typically smooth and unflurried victory.

On the home club front Mike Beckwith proved to be the outstanding driver of the year in his Normand-sponsored Lotus 23. Roy Pierpoint was one of his leading opponents in a well-prepared 2 litre Lotus 15, but Mike's direct competition in the 1,100 cc class came from Tony Hegbourne's incredible front-engined Lola. They were to join forces in Normand Lotus 23s for the following season.

Test pilot Dizzy Addicott proved a great crowd-pleaser in his 3.5 litre Buick-engined Lotus 15—precursor of 'big-banger' sports car racing in England in the mid-'sixties—and flocks of Elites shone

The Lotus 23, based on a widened version of the Formula Junior chassis, became as popular and successful a small-capacity sports-racing car as had the Lotus 11 during the 'Fifties. The new car received a tremendous boost when Jim Clark led the 1962 Nurburgring 1000 Kilometres race with the aid of the new Lotus Twin-cam engine.

in club events.

Bill Shaw, Mike Johnson, David Buxton, Sid Taylor and Dick Fores all impressed in their cars, and young Roger Nathan won a string of races before crashing heavily at Brands Hatch when a half-shaft broke and he lost a rear wheel. Autosport staffer Patrick McNally lent his Elite to Roger for the rest of the seaon, and at Snetterton he upset the Team Elite cars by finishing between them, which was very creditable for a newcomer with such limited experience. Team Elite had Clive Hunt's Tourist Trophy class win under their belts, and in the Spa Grand Prix for GT cars Sir John Whitmore won the 1,300 cc class in an Elite owned by band-leader Chris Barber.

At club level John Fenning was the most successful Formula Junior driver of the year, winning the John Davy Championship in Ron Harris' Lotus 20, while Jack Pearce ran his Lotus 22 later in the year with a 1,500 cc twin-cam Ford engine for Formule Libre races. He notched a string of successes, and retained the car for several years. Two Lotus Seven drivers made their names during the 1962 season, and both were to become famous in later years. They were Piers Courage and Peter Gethin . . .

Below: Business end of the Formula Junior Lotus 22 with outboard disc brakes and canted Cosworth-Ford engine. Bottom: Dawn of a new age. The Elan backbone chassis proved so strong during 1961 development testing that Colin Chapman began to study ways of adapting it for Formula 1 use. The result was the Lotus 25 monocoque.

1963

Champions of the World

In two short years the Lotus Group had progressed from a very competition-orientated company into a much better-balanced concern, still doing tremendous customer business with racing designs while a considerable road-car range was growing around the name.

In January Lotus' type 28—the 'Cortina-developed-by-Lotus'—was released. Based on the light and rigid two-door Cortina bodyshell, the twin-cam-engined Lotus-Cortina used the full 1,558 cc unit as standard, providing 105 bhp at 5,500 rpm. Macpherson-strut independent front suspension was retained, with zero wheel camber and a stiffer anti-roll bar as Lotus modifications, while at the rear the live axle was mounted on coil springs and located by radius rods and a hefty A-bracket. Larger disc/drum brakes were fitted, using servo-assistance, while 5½J wheels, a wood-rim steering wheel, special front bucket seats and full instrumentation completed an almost uncompromisingly 'sporty' saloon. Top speed was 108 mph, 0-50 mph acceleration occupied only 7.5 seconds and fuel consumption was still reasonable at 21 mpg. The Lotus-Cortina rapidly became the ideal road car for an enthusiastic family man and production finally brought Group 2 homologation late in the year.

Meanwhile, Lotus' prime target for 1963 was the Indianapolis '500'. While the prototype Lotus 29 hull was being completed at Cheshunt, Ford craned one of their two development V8s into Dan Gurney's Cobra for the Daytona Continental, but they encountered nothing but trouble, and there was little impetus to the programme until the first symmetrically-suspended Lotus 29 was shipped to the Kingman test track for evaluation. It lapped at 165 mph, but the engine was still unreliable and Colin began to have some misgivings about the Ford side of the deal.

It was agreed that there should be one final shake-down test at Indy in March, and Bill Gay specially prepared one of his engines only to have it snap a camshaft on the test bed. He was shattered, but hastily dreamed-up some modifications and built-up a replacement just in time for it to be air-freighted to Indiana where Chapman, Gurney and Clark were waiting for it with their car.

The engine was a last-gap effort, and was turned into a runner at the Speedway with wiring looms and bits and pieces cannibalised from a pair of hired Fairlanes. Few people realised how makeshift this Lotus-Ford debut at the Speedway really was, particularly when the car and engine began to fly!

Jimmy drove the car in initial tests on March 24, and next day worked it up to laps at 146 mph. Two days later Dan took it round at 149 mph, and overnight the final-drive ratio was lowered and with Dunlop tyres fitted Gurney howled round to set the second fastest lap ever of the Hoosier Bowl, at 150.501 mph, just as the computer had predicted. The car covered 457 trouble-free miles, and two weeks later the engine design was finalised as Ford Project AX230-2. The Indy project meant a reorganisation of Team Lotus, and David Lazenby became Indy Chief Mechanic while Jim Endruweit continued to run the Formula 1 team.

While the full story of the race itself is told in the following section, the qualifying period was a troubled time. Since the March tests offset suspension had been adopted, with longer front suspension links on the right-hand side and equal-length links with the hull mounts offset at the rear. This feature countered the centrifugal effects of Indy's four left-hand turns. New 15-inch Firestone tyres were fitted on Dunlop perforated disc wheels, and when the two new Lotus 29s specially built for the race proved so fast the roadster establishment screamed!

They petitioned Firestone, demanding that the 15-inch tyres be withdrawn or made available to all, and claimed they were being handicapped by being 'forced' to use obsolete 16-inch wheels and tyres. It was significant that no complaints were made about the 12-inch tyres specially made for Mickey Thompson's cars, which were no threat to the big front-engined roadsters; the petition was a compliment to the Lotus-Fords' competitiveness.

After a lot of flak had flown around Gasoline Alley Firestone agreed to produce sufficient 15-inch tyres for all, and then a scramble began to find suitable wheels in sufficient quantities. Ted Halibrand was the Speedway wheel specialist, and he forced through a batch of 15-inch castings as quickly as he could, but this was not quick enough for many people, Lotus included. Problems had been encountered with the Dunlop wheels cracking across the cooling holes, and only one set of suitable Halibrands was available for the two cars, these having been borrowed from Smokey Yunick, whose own car had been wrecked by Curtis Turner in practice.

It was agreed to share the wheels between the cars in qualifying, but on May 18 Dan Gurney ruined them when he crashed on his qualifying attempt, smeared the Lotus along the Turn One wall and wrote-off its right side. Jimmy then had to qualify on the narrower Dunlop wheels while Lotus mechanics and Ford engineers set about building the 'Mule' prototype car into a racer. He set fifth fastest time for a four-lap average of 149.750 mph, and after running out of time that day Gurney scraped in on the fourth row on Sunday with an average of 149.019 mph before joining Colin and Jimmy in a mad dash to Monaco!

The final panic prior to the '500' concerned the assembly of a practised pit-crew to handle the scheduled stop. Team Lotus' own mechanics had no experience of this kind of work, and Bill Stroppe's Mercury stock car racing crew were finally enlisted from Atlanta, while Pete Wiseman—later to become famous as a transmission designer—was detailed to handle the fuelling hose. It was remarkable how such a scrambled operation looked so smooth and professional on the surface, and but for yellow lights, oil on the circuit and indecisive officialdom it could so easily have resulted in a first-time win.

As it was Jimmy finished second, and earned 55,000 dollars for his day's work. Colin's silver tongue had forged a handsome deal with Ford, and the Lotus coffers collected another 20,000 dollars for the qualification of both cars, plus a 25,000 dollars bonus for second place and all expenses . . .

Meanwhile, back home the Elan had made a tremendous impression, and with original 1500 kits available at £1,095 demand among the cognoscenti was high. Maximum speed was just under 110 mph, and 0-60 mph acceleration in 8.6 seconds felt remarkable, though it was quite understandable with 100 horsepower in an 11½ cwt motor car; fuel consumption was around the 20 mpg mark when hard-driven. In May the first 1,558 cc cars became available and production finally got into top gear, and with 105 bhp at 5,500 rpm and 108 lb ft torque at 4,000 rpm, the new Elan 1600s were good for 112 mph, and could dash from 0-60 mph in a regular 8 seconds dead, all for £1,312.

Meanwhile the Elite models were still in small-quantity production, and the Sevens were going as strong as ever. One road test of the Super Seven 1500 in March showed a maximum speed of 102.2 mph, 0-60 mph acceleration in 6.8 seconds and 20 mpg fuel consumption. Its Cosworth twin-carb engine screamed up to 41 mph in first gear, 60 mph in second and 82 mph in third. The main source of criticism was the

bracket-mounted headlights, which wobbled alarmingly at speed and turned fast night driving on twisty roads into a mind-bending stroboscope of light and shade.

In April a long-standing disagreement with the Sports Car Club of America finally brewed-up. During 1962 their class system had placed the Lotus Sevens in among such production sports cars as AC and Arnolt-Bristols, Zagato Alfa Romeos, Daimler SP250s, Stage 3 Elites and Porsche Super 90s. This was hardly fair, but Dave Clark and Horace Pettit drove their 1,340 cc Sevens to such effect that they were placed first and second in their Championship class.

For 1963 the SCCA refused point-blank to accept the Seven for American production sports car racing, and Colin issued a statement pointing out the deception of the Club's claim that it hadn't received the necessary application forms in time. In fact the forms, including those for the new Elan, had been submitted the preceding November, and the Elan had been accepted so the forms must have arrived. The statement also drew attention to the classification of the Elan among the 4.5 litre cars of Class B and the Elite among the 3 litres of Class C. Minor mods such as oil coolers, front wheel disc brakes and magnesium wheels were also refused, and the SCCA hung its whole case on what was 'within the spirit of club racing regulations'. The Lotus statement pointed out that 'the impecunious SCCA amateur can with approval purchase, for instance, six Weber carburettors for his 14,000 dollars 250GT Ferrari—and still stay within the spirit of club racing!'. But the SCCA still refused to accept the cars;

Top left: Lotus' version of the Cortina was a popular 'Q' car on the road and a sensation on the track. Left: Jimmy was bowled over by the Elan! Above: The Elan in hardtop form paved the way for the Coupe.

the penalty of being too fast.

Further American opposition to Lotus aspirations came in the portly shape of Anthony (Andy) Granatelli, head of the Studebaker Corporation and a long-standing Indy entrant of the wailing supercharged Novi-engined roadsters. He led the Establishment owners in proposing a new minimum-weight regulation to USAC which effectively would have ruled-out Lotus-type cars and protected many entrants' vast investments in what had become obsolete machinery virtually overnight. His proposal was not accepted, and later he was to give up his efforts to beat Lotus . . and joined them.

During the year the first Elans began to appear in circuit races, but the apple-cart was upset when it was found that they didn't handle, and heaved and wallowed as only hard-driven road cars can. Colin Chapman: 'When we announced the Elan we said "this is a touring car, it is not intended for racing and we have done no competition development on it." The fact that customers bought them and tried to race them was originally no concern of ours, but in the second year we thought, well, if these people insist on racing them then we'd better get down to some proper development. They were too softly sprung, too softly damped, tore their doughnuts apart and had all sorts of drama, but it was the name, and people just thought they must be racing cars!'.

The Chequered Flag's Graham Warner gave the Elan its racing debut, and his at least was a well-developed car although, of course, a private venture. Carrying the famous old 'LOV 1' number, the white-and-black car used a Cosworth-developed 144 bhp twin-cam engine. A NACA duct on the bonnet fed a cold-air box for the twin Weber carburettors, and other modifications included moving the radiator further forward, replacing the pop-up headlamps with small-diameter units behind transparent farings, cutaway wheel arches for wider tyres, thick anti-roll bars at front and rear and adjustable-toe-in rear wishbones. This car was the first of many.

The Lotus quote of the year came from a Le Mans newspaper at the time of the French Grand Prix: 'L'Anglais Jimmy Clark est Ecossais Volant. Le jeune chef d'agricole sera au Grand Prix de l'ACF sur Lotus—Team Lotus est la meme chose "Ecurie Ecosse", les anciens vainqueur du vingt-quatre heures du Mans . . .'. This gem was accompanied by a photo of Innes Ireland!

During the year Team Lotus' Zephyr transporter continued its epic life, and the most dramatic of its many journeys took place during the week between the Roskilde Formula 1 race in Denmark and the Mediterranean Grand Prix in Sicily. On the way South the brake seals failed and once again the little wagon was hauled to a stop on the handbrake and gears. Then its habit of boiling developed from the merely chronic into the seriously acute, and high in the mountains its crew were reduced to groping their way through the darkness towards the sound of running water. Finally the back-axle dropped off, and the crippled truck was ferried across to Sicily as a very definite non-runner. Andrew Ferguson borrowed De Beaufort's Chevvy Impala and trailer and hired a truck to carry the other car, then set off from Palermo to Enna with Trevor Taylor driving one and Peter Arundell the other in a desperate dash to arrive at 6 am on the last day of practice! On the return run in the repaired transporter the weary mechanics parked it where they shouldn't in France and finally spent the night in jail!

But despite all the alarms and excursions, 1963 was a brilliantly successful year for Lotus Cars and for Team Lotus. Jimmy ended the year as World Champion and the first driver ever to be awarded the Ferodo Trophy for an outstanding contribution to British motor sport. He was voted Driver of the Year by the Guild of Motoring Writers and won the British Racing Drivers' Club's Gold Star. Martini-Rossi also gave him their own Driver of the Year award, and the grateful Esso oil company—Team Lotus' major sponsor—presented him with a Michael Turner painting of himself in action, and awarded Colin, the new World Champion Constructor, a beautiful Bassett-Lowke model of the Lotus 25. Jimmy's three USAC appearances also gave him sixth place overall in the American Championship Trail track series at the end of the marque's greatest year.

Elans and Cortinas awaiting delivery from Cheshunt, and the last of the Elite bodies awaiting assembly.

1963 RACING RECORD
Grands Prix and other major formulae

One week after the South African Grand Prix had decided the 1962 World Championship, the 1963 season began in New Zealand, where the Grand Prix was being held for the first time at the new Pukekohe circuit outside Auckland. Tony Shelly had dropped a 2.5 litre engine in his Lotus 18/21 and he had a brief moment of glory when he jumped the start, led to the hairpin and then spun off! Later he retired with bearing trouble.

Team Lotus gave the Tasman Championship a miss this year, but Shelly contested most of the rounds with limited success, while Jim Palmer shone again with his 1,500 cc-engined Formula Junior Lotus 22. In Australia and Tasmania Frank Matich's Lotus 19 was a dominating star performer in the supporting sports car races.

As the Tasman series came to a close the prototype Lotus 29 Indianapolis car was nearing completion at Cheshunt, and early in March Jimmy Clark tested it at Snetterton. The 4.2 litre stock-block Ford V8 engine proved immensely powerful and Jimmy found that on a conventional track the 29 handled remarkably well. Serious track testing began at Phoenix, Arizona, towards the end of the month.

The Lombank Trophy race at Snetterton opened the Formula 1 season at the end of March. After their successes of 1962, which had begun with victory in this very race, Team Lotus were understandably keen to do the double. Clark drove R3 fitted with a carburettor Climax V8, and the pale green UDT cars appeared under the old management but a new name. The finance house had withdrawn its sponsorship and Alfred Moss and Ken Gregory were now entering the cars under their own British Racing Partnership banner. Both Lotus 24s had BRM engines, and were to be driven by Innes Ireland and his new team-mate from Texas, Jim Hall. Innes's engine was fuel-injected with a low-level exhaust system, and Hall's was an older unit with upswept stub pipes. Tim Parnell, now recovered from a long illness, was fielding a Lotus-BRM 24 for the first time, and Adam Wyllie, a good Scots club driver, was running an old four-cylinder 18/21 for the Jim Russell Racing Drivers' School, Phil Robinson being out again in a similar machine.

At the start of a very wet race Jimmy was beaten off the line by Ginther's BRM while Hill, who had missed practice, and consequently had to start from the back of the grid, began to forge through the pack. Jimmy took over the lead from Ginther, but the Lotus 25 was not running well in the flooded conditions, and Hill managed to splash by with his BRM and hold his lead to the end. Innes fought-off McLaren's Cooper and Ginther's BRM to finish third while Jim Hall drove headily into sixth place, having made his Formula 1 V8 debut in diabolical conditions. Parnell and Robinson retired and Wyllie was seventh, 6 laps down.

Two weeks later came the annual double-billing on Easter Monday, with the Goodwood meeting in England and the Pau Grand Prix in France. Team Lotus took two cars to Pau, R5 with a new short-stroke fuel-injected Climax engine for Clark, and R3 for Taylor. Rob Walker had a new Cooper on hand for Jo Bonnier, and a Climax-engined 24 for Trintignant which had been built-up from the salvaged remains of the two written-off 1962 cars. Jo Siffert was in Filipinetti's BRM-engined 24 and Herbert Muller ran the team's Lotus 22 Junior fitted with a 1,500 cc Ford engine. Parnell had the ex-UDT 18/21s for himself and Andre Pilette, and Bernard Collomb was in the Climax-powered 24 (949) which Taylor had used occasionally for the works in 1962.

Clark was much faster than the rest of the field during practice, but Siffert's mechanics had their 24 well sorted-out at last and he was third quickest for some time, while little Muller surprised everyone with sixth fastest time in the Formula Junior car. Jimmy lined-up alongside Bonnier while Taylor had bettered Siffert's time after some suspension tweaking. The Team Lotus drivers arrowed into the lead under a blistering sun, and after dominating the race they covered the last lap almost side-by-side and crossed the finish line with 0.1 second between them, Jimmy slightly ahead after recording the fastest lap at 1min 35.5sec, 64.61 mph. Muller drove brilliantly, the baby-faced 22-year-old skating round in grand style to

Victory grin. Jimmy takes Colin Chapman and Mike Spence for a lap of honour at Monza after clinching the 1963 World Championship in the Italian Grand Prix.

finish fifth, despite having to stop for fuel. Pilette was sixth, while Collomb's fuel tanks ruptured, and Trintignant lost third place when his gear linkage came adrift. He was using a Colotti six-speed gearbox (this transmission usually being mated to BRM engines) which meant using a rather devious linkage. Siffert also held third place for a time until a leak in the rear brake system put him into the bales at the station, while Parnell retired with a blown gasket.

Innes Ireland ran BRP's Lotus 24-BRM at Goodwood, and won the main race at 102.44 mph after both works BRMs had failed while leading. There were only 10 starters after Seifert's Lotus had failed to appear, and Tony Maggs drove Parnell's 24 into third place, while Jim Hall was placed fifth in the second BRP car, and Robinson was further behind in his 18/21.

One week later the non-championship Imola Grand Prix in Italy lost its sting when the works Ferrari and ATS entries failed to materialise. The Pau Lotus 25s were run by Team Lotus, Siffert's BRM-engined 24 was present with repaired brakes, and Seifert was trying his hand in Seidel's similar car which had gone so poorly during 1962. Baghetti tried the Filipinetti 22 but it was tired after Muller's Pau performance and he refused to race it, so Collomb, Prinoth and Starrabba completed the Lotus runners with their 24 and 18s, respectively, the latter's retaining its Maserati engine.

Jimmy and Trevor were one-two on the grid but Taylor ran into transmission trouble on the second lap of the race as Clark just ran away into the middle distance. Trevor rejoined after ten laps, but his car was consistently jumping out of gear at one point on the circuit, and he made further stops until the fault was corrected, and finally began lapping very quickly indeed. He caught his team-leader on the road and sailed by, setting the fastest lap at 1min 48.3sec, 102.56 mph. Siffert was second after Bonnier's Walker Cooper blew-up, and he finished on the same lap as Clark. Prinoth was eighth, Taylor ninth, Starrabba had his throttle cable break after only six laps, and Collomb motored round in his Lotus 24 until the ignition failed.

Four days later came the Italian Liberation Festival and the Syracuse Grand Prix in Sicily, and with Team Lotus missing this event in favour of Aintree it became a privateers' delight. Siffert took pole position with the Lotus-BRM, 1.1 seconds faster than fellow ex-motorcyclist Bob Anderson in a Lola-Climax, Bonnier was in the Walker 24, Collomb had his similar Climax-engined car and Seifert the BRM-engined 24, Starrabba's Lotus-Maserati making the score five Lotuses among the ten starters.

Siffert took the lead from Anderson on the second lap and held it all the way in the rain to win the race and set the fastest lap at 2min 00.4sec, 102.13 mph. Bonnier had a terrible race for Rob Walker, being thoroughly put to shame by the Swiss in his comparable car, and eventually finished fifth, seven laps down after stopping to complain of an untraceable vibration, while Starrabba was sixth and last. Collomb's left-front wishbone broke and Seifert's gearbox casing split.

The Aintree '200' found Jimmy and Trevor running the fuel-injected R5 and the carburettor-equipped R3 once again, and Clark shattered his own record with a lap in 1min 52.4sec for pole position. The race was a near-repeat of the first Mexican Grand Prix as Clark's battery refused to turn over his engine on the grid, and he was pushed into the pits for a new battery to be fitted as the rest of the field rushed away. Jimmy joined the race over a lap behind Graham Hill's leading BRM and was soon carving his way through the back markers, but his was a hopeless task and so Colin signalled in Trevor Taylor. Trevor was on his 18th lap as Jimmy went by on his 16th, and he came in and was out of his car and ready for the changeover as Clark hurtled into the pits. The drivers' seats were swopped, and Jimmy leapt into R3 and rushed off in fifth place after only 17 seconds in the pits.

This really enlivened the race, and Jimmy got down to some scorching motoring which underlined his supreme class. On lap 39 he passed McLaren's Cooper for fourth place, and with 11 laps to go was 12 seconds behind Ginther's third-placed BRM. With five laps to go he was on the American's tail, and three laps later he snicked ahead to take third place, receiving an immense ovation from the enthralled crowd. He finally left the lap record at 1min 51sec, 96.60 mph, three seconds under his nine-month-old figures.

Innes had taken second place early on and held it to the finish, while Trevor finished seventh in R5. Jimmy Blumer was eighth, making his Formula 1 debut in Parnell's Lotus-Climax, Hall retired after one lap with the BRP 24's throttle jammed, and Robinson went out after only two more laps. Campbell-Jones' 24 lost its oil on lap 13 and Scotsman Jock Russell had suspension problems on his 18. Parnell was disqualified for a push-start and Andre Pilette's 18/21 failed to make it to the start-line.

On the first Saturday in May a prophetic event took place in America, for Lloyd Ruby shook the USAC track-racing establishment with an ex-Formula 1 Lotus-Climax at Trenton, New Jersey, in which he led all the regular Offenhauser-powered cars for the first 40 laps round the one-mile oval before retiring with transmission trouble. He turned a record 106 mph practice lap and really made the track-racing establishment look up and ponder on what the monocoque Lotus 29 might do at Indianapolis at the end of the month.

The whole month of May is taken up by practice and qualifying runs at Indy, with qualifying periods being held on successive weekends, times on the first weekend counting towards pole position and the leading positions on the 33-strong grid. Later qualifiers can record higher speeds but still be relegated to starting positions down the grid if they miss this first weekend. So May saw Jimmy and his Indy team-mate Dan Gurney commuting between Europe and

Above: Clark and Taylor perform a quick-change act during the Aintree '200' race as mechanic Ted Woodley changes seats after Jimmy's car had been delayed by a flat battery. Clark finished third and Taylor seventh after the switch. Below: Jimmy lapped the field in the course of winning the Dutch Grand Prix, his Lotus 25 racing with an air-deflector screen for the first time.

Above: Another runaway Clark victory, this time at Spa, where a violent thunderstorm later flooded the circuit; this time Jimmy won by almost five minutes! Below: Mike Beckwith drove one of the BRP Lotuses in the Oulton Park Gold Cup, but crashed into a bank after locking his transmission.

Indianapolis, testing and qualifying their new cars.

Dan lapped at 150 mph while testing the prototype 29/1, and while the USAC establishment entertained dark thoughts about the Lotus threat two new cars were built-up at Cheshunt while Ford race-prepared their engines at Dearborn. All three cars ran in early practice and qualifying, Jimmy and Colin flying out between the Aintree and Silverstone races for the first weekend's trials, then returning for the qualifying weekend of May 18-19.

Meanwhile, at Silverstone Clark and Taylor appeared once again in their ageing Lotus 25s, but Innes Ireland was on sparkling form with his BRM-powered 24 and took pole position a whole second faster than Hill's works car, which must have made the Bourne team regret selling BRP their engines! Jimmy crashed and damaged Trevor's R3 at Copse Corner after his own engine had failed, and Team Lotus had a sleepless night rebuilding both engine and chassis. The two cars formed up on the second row of the grid, with Surtees' new Ferrari outside them.

After his good work in practice Ireland fumbled his start, and Clark shot through to trail McLaren's leading Cooper with Innes fourth ahead of Surtees, and Taylor leading the rest of the field. Jimmy soon took the lead, and then Ireland appeared out of Woodcote, having the most enormous spin, obscuring the track in tyre smoke and seeming about to plunge into the pits. But fortunately he caught the spin and continued, now down in eighth place. Jimmy went on to win the race easily, averaging 108.12 mph, with Taylor third and Ireland an unabashed fourth. In a meteoric drive back through the field Innes had set a new 1,500 cc Formula 1 lap record of 1min 35.4sec, 110.45 mph on the very last lap in a desperate attempt to catch Taylor. Campbell-Jones' Lotus-BRM 24 packed-up with plug trouble, Robinson's 18 with rear axle failure, Parnell's with engine trouble, and Jim Hall's BRM-powered 24 with a dead engine out on the circuit.

A few days after Silverstone Jimmy and Colin jetted-out to Indiana to prepare for Indianapolis qualifying. The Lotus 25-based monocoque cars were supremely impressive, and Jimmy set the fastest speed so far of 149.75 mph on his four-lap run, turning 150.025 mph on one lap to hold pole position temporarily. Dunlop had flown over light-alloy 15-inch rear wheels with knock-off attachments for the two Lotus-Fords, but owing to Ford obligations and Indy experience Firestone tyres were fitted. Colin decided to retain four speeds in the Colotti transmission, hoping to save valuable seconds leaving the pits. At the end of qualifying Jimmy's speed was good enough for fifth place on the grid, while Dan crashed his car comprehensively. It was later rebuilt, and he made the race at a four-lap average of 149.019 mph.

On the same day the Rome Grand Prix was held at Vallelunga, in Italy,where Prince Gaetano Starrabba finished fifth in his Maserati-engined 18, Clement Barrau was sixth in his newly-acquired ex-Filipinetti 21, Parnell was ninth in his 18/21 and Seifert tenth in Seidel's 24-BRM. Collomb also ran but retired, as did Campbell-Jones, whose gearbox broke.

During the next few days Lotus teams and drivers journeyed from Italy, Indiana and Cheshunt to Monaco for the opening race in the 1963 World Championship series. Chassis R4 had been completely rebuilt and refurbished for Clark while Taylor took over R5, the carburettor-engined R3 being relegated to spare-car duties. BRP fitted a five-speed Colotti gearbox to Ireland's BRM-engined 24 while Hall's retained a six-speed transmission, both cars being fitted with abbreviated nose cones in anticipation of some pushing-and-shoving around the tight street circuit. Finally, Siffert and Collomb had their BRM and Climax-powered 24s, respectively.

During first practice Jimmy bettered his 1962 time by 0.1 second at 1min 35.4sec then took out Taylor's car and set the second fastest time at 1min 36.7sec. The next day he lapped in 1min 35.2sec in the carburettor-equipped spare car but ended up on pole position with 1min 34.3sec recorded in his own R4, 0.7 second faster than Graham Hill's BRM. Taylor was on row five, and Colin loaned R3 to Brabham for the race after poor Jack had blown two engines in his own team cars; this was the first time that a non-works driver had had his hands on a Lotus 25.

The works BRMs out-accelerated Jimmy's Lotus from the line, but after five laps he repassed Ginther and chased after Hill. They began to pass and repass each other in a tremendous battle for the lead, while Siffert's BRM engine threw a rod, Brabham was in gearchange trouble, and Hall's final drive sheared. On lap 17 Jimmy passed the BRM at the Gasworks and finally drew away from Hill.

Ireland was running sixth ahead of Taylor, but when he was hard on the brakes under the Portiere, where the road goes hard right on to the sea-front, his Lotus 24 jumped out of gear and smashed straight into the sea-wall. Innes was unhurt, but the car was wrecked.

By half-distance (50 laps) Jimmy was 8.5 seconds ahead of Hill, Trevor was fifth, and Brabham was at the pits having his gear selectors checked. On lap 69 Clark lowered the lap record to 1min 34.9sec, and at 75 laps, with the 25 holding a 17-seconds lead, hopes were high for another Lotus Monaco win, but as Jimmy came down the quayside into the Tabac the Lotus jammed in gear. He was struggling with the lever as the car coasted behind the pits and as he neared the Gasworks the selectors suddenly clicked into second and fourth at the same time and the Lotus skated to a halt with the rear wheels locked. He had been easing off, and changing gear gently, but because the ZF plunger movements were very small and light they needed quite a bit of inertia to engage properly, and this was usually imparted by flicking the lever quickly. Clark's gentle movements hadn't imparted the necessary inertia, and in that last fateful gearchange the selectors had sprung back the wrong way.

So the race went to Hill's BRM, with Trevor sixth, unhappy about the feel of his gearchange, and Jimmy was classified eighth on distance covered. Jack Brabham was ninth, although 23 laps behind the winner, and near the end of the race John Surtees had bettered Jimmy's fastest lap in the new V6 Ferrari.

The Memorial Day (May 30th) Indianapolis '500' followed four days later, and the impact of the 'Lotus-powered-by-Ford' onslaught on this inner sanctum of American motor sport was enormous. For the first 20 laps Jimmy and Dan took things easily, lapping just fast enough to stay with the second bunch of cars, which were trailing the leaders headed by Rufus Parnelli Jones in his Agajanian-Willard Battery Special.

Jones knew that Lotus planned to make just one pit-stop, and he pulled out as long a lead as possible before making his own first stop. He was lapping at 151 mph and when the yellow caution light came on after an accident on lap 47 the field had to maintain station for 9min 32sec. This allowed Jones' pursuers to close up, although they were not allowed to pass him; Clark was ninth and Gurney 11th under the yellow. Immediately the green light was shown Jones stepped-up the pace, averaging 150 mph before making his scheduled stop after 62 laps. As the other roadsters made their stops the green and white Lotuses moved forward, and on lap 67 Jimmy took the lead with Dan close behind. Jones was third, just 17 seconds behind the white-and-blue American Lotus. At 70 laps Jimmy's average was a record-breaking 141.793 mph, and at the 200-mile mark (80 laps) he had lifted it to 142.566 mph.

On lap 92 Dan came in for the first Lotus stop, stopping squarely over the platform jack which lifted the 29 bodily into the air. It was a slow 42.2 seconds stop for three wheels to be changed and the tanks filled, and Jones shot by into second place.

On lap 95 Jimmy came in, and the crew gave his 29 the same service in 32 seconds, as Jones took the lead. Jimmy rejoined third, but was soon back into second place and at the half-way mark was 40 seconds behind Jones. He was having trouble threading his way through the back-markers and soon found that the USAC drivers rarely used their mirrors. Jones managed to pull away, and when the yellow light came on again at 116 laps he took his second stop and rejoined without losing his lead. After 130 laps Jones was averaging a record 142.495 mph, Dan was in sixth place and everyone was wondering if Jimmy would need another tyre change to last 500 miles; Parnelli was drawing even closer to his inevitable third stop, and while the 29 couldn't catch him he couldn't pull away from it. Dan inherited fourth place, and then under another yellow light Jones made his stop.

He rejoined in 21 seconds, with an 11 seconds lead over Clark and Dan third. The Lotus 29s looked poised for the kill with Jones fighting a desperate rearguard action to protect the roadster establishment. On lap 172 Jimmy was 10 seconds behind the heavier fuel-laden Special; on the next lap it was 7 seconds, and he reeled-him in by half-a-second per lap until on the 177th circuit there were only 5 seconds between the Lotus and the lead.

As Jones lifted for the turns the Offy was beginning to blow smoke, and oil was reported on the left side of the car. Simultaneously Jimmy began to fall back by 2 to 3 seconds per lap until there was a clear 10 seconds between them.

Dan lost third place in a stop for tyres and fuel, did two more laps, then returned for the rear wheels to be tightened. On lap 186, with 14 seconds between the leaders, Jones' car was apparently throwing oil. Jimmy found the turns slick and treacherous and sat back confident that Parnelli would be flagged in. Johnny Poulsen, Jones' mechanic, had a frantic discussion with Chief Steward Harlan Fengler, and when the yellow came out on lap 187 Jimmy found himself baulked by Don Branson and Bob Christie.

Colin pointed out to Fengler that in the pre-race briefing it had been emphasised that anyone dropping oil would be black-flagged. "There's a car streaming oil from everywhere; what are you going to do about it?". Fengler fixed his binoculars on the roadster and said he thought it looked like water dropping on the track, and so the discussion went on. Colin eventually said, ". . . well, it's your decision and we're only the new boys here . . ." and returned to his pit. Jimmy was fed-up with the tactics of the drivers baulking him and passed them—still under the yellow—but the stewards turned a blind-eye to his action. With just seven laps to go the green came on with Jimmy racing to close a 22-seconds gap on Jones. But he couldn't do much with the light car on such a slick surface, and Parnelli thundered across the line to win by just over 19 seconds from the Lotus-Ford debutante. Dan was seventh after his delay, and in Victory Circle Jimmy paid tribute to the winner by saying ". . . he did a damn fine job" while Benson Ford told Fengler ". . . We are delighted with the race outcome and I believe that was the finest decision you could have made". Lotus-Ford had lost their first battle, but they weren't going to lose the Indianapolis war . . .

Back in Europe the Formula 1 circus returned to Spa, the scene of Jimmy's first Grande Epreuve success the previous year, for the Belgian Grand Prix. Team Lotus ran the Monaco cars, but Colin tried something new on Jimmy's car in the shape of an air-deflector windscreen. This took the form of a very low screen with a slot under its leading edge, which funnelled air over an upswept glass fibre section above the dash panel. The effect was to give the driver unobstructed forward vision, with an 'air-curtain' ahead of him to prevent buffeting at speed. Jimmy found it a strange experience, sitting above the screen without any blast of air in his face, but heavy objects such as bugs, small stones and rain-drops tended to break through the curtain.

Practice found Jimmy suffering more ZF transmission problems but Trevor was going very well, and on the Saturday he circulated very quickly despite his memories of the previous year's accident. Then an inboard rear wishbone mounting became detached as he rocketed round the slightly banked bend at Stavelot and Trevor had another high-speed accident, slamming into the stone retaining wall, then ploughing a gaping hole in the wooden observers' hut on the outside of the circuit. He escaped with a shaking and some bruises, but R5 was a write-off, and the observers' hut didn't fare much better!

Meanwhile, BRP had overcome problems with their 24s by building their own 'Lotus 25' based on a new monocoque designed by Tony Robinson and fitted with 24-type suspension. Ireland drove this new car, while Hall retained his normal 24-BRM. Jo Siffert ran his similar car in the smallest Lotus Formula 1 entry for years.

Team Lotus' problems left Clark starting from the inside of row three while a sore Trevor Taylor was on the outside of the fifth row in the spare carburettor car. Jimmy decided to use an old-type windscreen and he made a flying start, shrieking down the pit road straight past the two rows ahead to take the lead from Graham Hill up over the ridge.

Jimmy drew away from his old adversary as thunder clouds encircled the hills around him and on lap 16 he hurtled round in 3min 58.1sec, 132.47 mph. But on the next lap the violent storm erupted over the circuit just as Hill retired with transmission trouble, and Jimmy was left with an unassailable lead in almost impossible driving conditions. The sky was now viciously black, and as lightning flashed every few seconds the circuit began to flood.

Jim Hall ran into the storm downhill towards Malmedy and in an instant spun off the road and into the fields. Siffert wrecked his car on a bank, and amid this carnage Colin and Tony Rudd of BRM tried to get the race stopped before somebody got hurt. There were only six survivors still splashing round, but Jimmy never put a foot wrong and allowed himself to be unlapped by McLaren in the second-place Cooper, which felt OK in the flood. So Clark came home to win, tired and wet, but very happy and nearly five minutes ahead of Bruce!

Taylor retired after only five laps, suffering from the after-effects of his accident, but Jimmy had scored his first nine World Championship points of the year.

Two weeks elapsed before the Dutch Grand Prix at Zandvoort, where Team Lotus appeared with Jimmy in his trusty Spa-winning R4 and Trevor in the ancient R2, now fitted with a fuel-injected Climax V8 and six-speed Colotti transmission. An air-deflector screen appeared on R4, slightly modified to give a stronger up-draught.

While BRP had introduced Formula 1's second monocoque at Spa, BRM introduced the third at Zandvoort, exactly a year after Colin's 25 had introduced the idea.

Reg Parnell's private team brought along a Lotus-Climax 24 with carburettor engine as a spare to their Lola for Chris Amon, and BRP's 24-BRM was present as a training car for Ireland, although an entry was arranged for Jim Hall, and he took over this car for the race. Jo Siffert and his two Swiss mechanics had rebuilt their Spa wreck, adding fuel injection and strapping aluminium fuel tanks on either side as in Brabham and Cooper designs, their outer skins forming the body sides.

Jimmy started from pole position, his 1min 31.6sec lap pruning 0.8 second off Hill's best time. The Lotus led away into Tarzan, pushed the opposition wide through the corner, and from there on Jimmy just marched away as he pleased, winning by a clear lap from Gurney's Brabham, and notching a new record race average of 96.5 mph for the 80 laps and setting the first 100 mph Zandvoort lap record at 1min 33.7sec 100.1 mph. He was untouchable—a man in a class of his own, driving the best available car.

Trevor stopped with misfiring, caused by a faulty high-pressure fuel pump, and finally finished tenth, while Siffert and Hall had a long dice for seventh and eighth places, the Swiss leading after the Texan's pedals began to burn his feet.

Jimmy was now leading the Championship clearly, with 18 points to Ginther's 11, McLaren and Gurney being tied for third place with ten points each; Lotus-Climax led BRM in the constructors' competition by 19 points to 14.

It was a scramble to get to Reims for the French Grand Prix just one week later, where Jimmy was to appear again in R4, and Trevor in R2, while the spare carburettor R3 was present for Peter Arundell to drive. Reg Parnell provided his 24-Climax for Trintignant, and son Tim entered his 24-BRM with fuel-injection for Masten Gregory. Hall and Siffert were in their similar cars, and Ecurie Filipinetti entered a brand-new 24-BRM with fuel injection for Phil Hill who had been without a drive since the Italian ATS team were giving the race a miss.

Team Lotus were riding the crest of a wave, and Jimmy began his fourth Grand Prix meeting on the same set of Dunlop tyres by taking pole position at 2min 20.2sec, 0.7 second quicker than the inevitable Graham Hill in his BRM. Taylor was on the middle of the third row, but the organisers would not allow Arundell to start as he was entered in the Formula Junior race at the same meeting. Due to the prevalence of flying stones at Reims R4 was fitted with a full screen for the Grand Prix.

Jimmy made a scorching start and scratched like mad round those early laps to establish a lead. In two laps he had pulled out 4 seconds, which was a long enough gap to prevent his pursuers getting into his slipstream. After ten laps his lead had grown to 15 seconds, but two laps later his engine went off-song. Taylor had been well up, but had since developed an oil leak and was trailing smoke, so Team Lotus' hopes looked a little shaky.

The works Brabhams led the pursuit of Clark, but Taylor caught them in fourth place. Jimmy found he could lap more quickly by changing-up at 8,000 rpm instead of 9,200-9,500 rpm as his engine still had plenty of punch lower down but tailed-off at the top end.

At half-distance he still had a 15 second lead while Trevor was harrying Brabham for second place, but then it began to drizzle, which was Clark's salvation. The pursuit backed-off while he was able to continue at his already reduced pace. Taylor's alternator failed and his ignition played-up as the battery went flat, so he had to stop for the battery to be changed, but Jimmy went on to win his third consecutive Championship round after his most intelligent and cool race to date. He now led Dan Gurney by 14 points while Lotus-Climax had scored 12 more points than Cooper-Climax in the constructors' table.

Siffert went splendidly for sixth place and a Championship point, while Trintignant was eighth with a badly burned foot. Hall was 11th and officially last, while Phil Hill was still motoring, but too far behind to be classified after making many stops. Taylor's fine drive was wasted when the drop-gears stripped at Thillois after 41 of the 53 laps, and the parked 25 was damaged during the Formula Junior race which followed when one of the Juniors crashed into it. Gregory had been left on the line at the start of the Grand Prix and retired with a split gearbox casing on lap 31.

The British Grand Prix returned to Silverstone later that month after a rather controversial two-year absence, and Clark and Taylor appeared in their usual fuel-injected 25s, both with ZF transmissions following Trevor's Colotti gearbox failure at Reims. Hall was in BRP's normal Lotus-BRM 24 and the Parnells entered a Climax-engined car for Mike Hailwood, making his Formula 1 debut after many motorcycle World Championship wins. Gregory reappeared in their 24-BRM as at Reims, and Siffert made a welcome first British appearance in his modified Lotus 24.

The works Lotuses were resplendent in a new colour scheme with broad yellow stripes along their nose-cones and engine cowls, and Jimmy's deflector-screen car was soon lapping very quickly. On the Friday morning Team Lotus produced a new 25 with six-speed Colotti gearbox and deflector screen, but the transmission had been wrongly assembled and Jimmy spent a frustrating time while it was stripped. Nonetheless he took pole position in R4 by 0.2 second from Gurney, but then threw it all away with an uncharacteristically bad start.

The works Brabhams led initially with Hill and McLaren on their heels and Jimmy fifth, but the Scot gritted his teeth and soon squared the account, taking the lead on lap four and rushing round unmolested to the finish, easing off towards the end as his fuel capacity was somewhat marginal. One of the 25's fuel bags had kinked as it was filled and it had been difficult to get the necessary amount aboard, so Jimmy circulated in top gear as much as possible. The race became an economy run at the finish as Hill lost second place when his BRM's tanks ran dry, and Jimmy won by 15 seconds from Surtees' Ferrari, to score his fourth consecutive Grande Epreuve and his second consecutive British Grand Prix victory. His average speed was 107.75 mph for the 82 laps, but Surtees claimed the fastest lap in 1min 36.0sec.

Hall was sixth, Hailwood a promising eighth and Gregory 11th, while Taylor led the second bunch in seventh place until his electric fuel pump failed again and he stopped for a replacement. He returned later with gear-selection problems and was disqualified for a push-start. Siffert shook off Hailwood and was chasing Hall hard when a ball-race broke up in the gearbox and ruined its internals, so he was forced out after 67 hard laps.

The Solitude Grand Prix followed the next weekend at Stuttgart, where Team Lotus' flow of wins was interrupted when Jack Brabham drove to victory in his old prototype car. Clark and Taylor had their usual cars and Pete Arundell was entered with the spare carburettor car. Hall was out again for BRP, and Tim Parnell entered himself in his Lotus 24-BRM and Robinson and Carter in his old four-cylinder 18/21s. Collomb, Siffert and Seifert were in their 24s, Pilette had a four-cylinder 18, and Filipinetti again ran their troublesome BRM-powered 24 for Phil Hill. Ernst Maring and Kurt Kuhnke ran their 'BKL-Borgward' Specials, which consisted of Lotus 18 chassis fitted with the old Borgward Formula 2 engines from 1959.

In 1962 Jimmy had lapped at 3min 53.9sec, but in nine practice laps he was down to 3min 50.2sec at this meeting. Meanwhile, Taylor was in transmission trouble and took over Arundell's carburettor car for the race, the Formula Junior star being given the experimental fuel-injection 25 with Colotti gearbox.

Team Lotus were testing new drive-shafts on Jimmy's car and as the flag fell he leapt forward from pole position, then flung his hand up as the Lotus died and rolled to a stop. The right-hand drive shaft had stripped its spider and the left-hand shaft was bent and buckled, so the car was pushed to the pits, and the mechanics set about fitting new drive-shafts.

Jimmy helped with the signalling, and Brabham burst into sight leading narrowly from Trevor. But after only seven laps Taylor was in deep trouble, for his ZF gearbox had lost all its oil and the final-drive gears were ruined. This left Arundell running third behind Bonnier's Cooper, with a gear-gate chart taped to his dash-panel to show him the Colotti change path! When the Walker car broke its engine Peter inherited second place and finished close behind Brabham.

As Jack had started his 16th lap Jimmy appeared from behind the pits to start his motor race, and the crowd thrilled as he put on a tremendous show, just to put the Brabham victory in perspective! Half his fuel load was drained off so the car was in ideal trim for some fast motoring and he shattered the lap record repeatedly, leaving it at 3min 49.1sec, 111.41 mph, despite finishing too far behind to be classified, along with the delayed Robinson and Seifert. Kuhnke and Phil Hill were early retirements, followed by Parnell and Ron Carter. Siffert lost fifth place when his gearbox jumped out of engagement, causing the engine

Above: Using the same set of tyres for his fourth consecutive Grand Prix, Jim Clark put on another masterful display on the slippery Reims circuit to claim nine more World Championship points. Below: Congratulations by Colin Chapman, Cedric Selzer and Jim Endruweit for Jimmy on winning the British Grand Prix two weeks later.

to over-rev and bend a valve, and Maring followed him into retirement. Hall was sixth after a poor drive, Collomb 11th and Pilette 12th.

The following weekend Jo Siffert gained just recognition by receiving an invited entry for the German Grand Prix at the Nurburgring. Jimmy was retaining his record-breaking R4 while Trevor took over R2, which Arundell had driven so well at Solitude, still with the Colotti transmission. Hall was out again in BRP's Lotus-BRM 24, Collomb in his Climax-engined 24, Pilette and Parnell in the old 18/21s, and Kuhnke in his doubtful 'BKL'. BRP also had a BRM-engined 24 as spare, and Ireland used it thankfully after creasing his monocoque car early in practice.

Clark's car showed the strain of Solitude early in the practice sessions, and a brand-new fuel-injection engine and ZF transmission were fitted overnight. The new gearbox had reverse gear omitted since the reverse selector was normally on the same shaft as the forward gear selectors and could cause trouble. While Jimmy went from strength to strength, taking pole position at 8min 45.8sec, 0.9 second quicker than Surtees' Ferrari, Trevor got into more and more trouble with his Colotti gearbox, ending-up on row five. Another night session saw a ZF gearbox fitted to his car, and BRP craning a new engine into the spare 24 for Ireland to race.

Jimmy took an immediate lead on a warm and sunny Sunday, but on the return road behind the pits Maggs' Cooper and Ginther's BRM were catching him. Ireland and Bandini (in the red Centro-Sud BRM) collided and were out near the Karussel, and the first lap ended with Ginther leading from Surtees with Clark third.

The works number-ones soon passed the BRM number-two, and pulled away from the rest of the field, but Jimmy's engine had a faulty plug which was causing misfiring, and there was nothing he could do about Surtees. As the race progressed his transmission began to rumble and groan, and he was very relieved to finish the long race in second place.

Poor Trevor's car just would not go and he trailed round at the back of the field to finish a misfiring eighth, while Jim Hall soldiered on into fifth place. Siffert was a rousing fourth when his differential failed, but Collomb trundled round and round to finish ninth, five laps behind.

The Team Lotus run had been broken, but Jimmy still led the Championship table by a clear 20 points from Surtees, and Lotus had a 21-point lead over BRM in the constructors' standings, so everyone looked to Monza for a decision. But in the meantime there were the non-title Formula 1 races at Karlskoga, Enna and Zeltweg, while in America the Milwaukee USAC race was to mark the reappearance of the Lotus-Ford 29s.

At Karlskoga two 20-lap heats were used to give an overall result on aggregate. Jimmy took along R3, the spare carburettor car, for this race leaving Trevor with R2, which had been fitted with a fuel-injected engine. The race was held in the wet, and Brabham's latest car seemed better able to put its power on the road than the 25s, and he was able to lead the first heat until his

engine suddenly faltered, letting Clark and Taylor rush by Jack restarted to finish third, and in the second heat the 25s just shadowed him, Jimmy and Trevor knowing that they needed to do no more to finish one-two on aggregate. Jack won this heat from Trevor and Jimmy, but Clark won on aggregate with Taylor second. Other Lotus runners were Gregory in Parnell's 24-BRM, which he placed sixth, Pilette's 18/21 which was tenth, and Barrau's 21 which was 12th. Kuhnke and Maring broke their BKLs while Carter's Parnell-entered 18/21 was a non-starter.

Colin and Jimmy flew straight out to the United States for the Milwaukee race, where Clark qualified on pole position at 109.307 mph and led from start to finish, lapping all but A.J. Foyt in second place with an Offy-powered roadster. Gurney was third in the second works 29, and Jimmy shattered the USAC opposition by setting a new course record and averaging a record 104.48 mph for the 200-miles.

That same Sunday Team Lotus were running their Formula 1 cars in the Mediterranean Grand Prix on the super-fast egg-shaped Enna circuit laid out around Lake Pergusa. Trevor Taylor was in R4 with fuel injection and Arundell had R2 with carburettors, both cars arriving on the Saturday morning after an epic journey down from Karlskoga. Siffert and Andre Wicky were in Lotus-BRM 24s, the latter's being the unfortunate Filipinetti car, and Collomb was running his 24-Climax once again. FJ exponents Giacomo

Top left: Colin Chapman and his design and build team pose with Jimmy at the unveiling of Lotus' first Indy challenger. Left: Four views of the Lotus 29. Below: Trevor Taylor, out of the Belgian Grand Prix, signals some comforting news to Clark.

Above: Lotus Indianapolis team-mate Dan Gurney and Ford's Don Frey listen to a spot of suspension theory by Jim Clark during one of the pre-race test sessions at the Speedway. Below: Wheel-to-wheel with a traditional Indy roadster, Jimmy and his Lotus-Ford 29 head for a close second place behind winner Rufus Parnelli Jones.

'Geki' Russo and Carmelo Genovese had 1,500 cc Cosworth-Ford engines in Lotus 27 and 22 Juniors, respectively, but Starrabba failed to qualify his Maserati-powered 18. Surtees' Ferrari and Bandini's BRM were quickest in practice with Trevor on the outside of the row.

The race was run in the early evening and Taylor took an immediate lead before Surtees forced by and pulled away. Arundell was third and Siffert was right with the leaders as Bandini forged through the field after a poor start.

By lap 25 the Italian's red BRM was slipstreaming Arundell round the lake, the pair of them gaining on Taylor in second place. On lap 36 Trevor was baulked and Bandini slipped past Arundell and dived inside Taylor on the bend before the pits. The BRM drifted wide and put two wheels off the road, with Trevor right behind showered in a flurry of dust and stones. He lost control and the Lotus 25 slammed into the outside bank at about 140 mph, hurtling across the road in front of a horrified Arundell, with Trevor hanging half out of the cockpit before bouncing off the guard-rail protecting the pits. Trevor was thrown out as the car somersaulted down the road, burst into flames and was destroyed. Once again his amazing constitution spared him serious injury, and he came round in a few minutes suffering nothing worse than some painful bruises and gravel rash. The pits rail saved a massacre, although one mechanic stood speechless clutching a signal board punctured by bits of gearbox and debris from the crashing Lotus!

Recovering from the accident, Arundell kept the pressure on Bandini and passed him to take second place, while Siffert was fifth, Wicky ninth and Collomb tenth. 'Geki' had led the latter pair of 24s before retiring his Lotus-Ford 27, but Genovese was an early retirement with his 22.

The non-championship Austrian Grand Prix at Zeltweg at the beginning of September marked Jimmy's first appearance in the brand-new R6, which was fitted with a flat-crank Climax engine mated to a VW-based Hewland gearbox as used by the latest Brabhams. The new monocoque had modified radius rod mounts, and an aircraft-type throttle control was used giving better response than was available from the rather crude Bowden cable. An ammeter and an extra fuel pressure gauge were added to the instrument panel.

BRP produced Lotus-BRM 24s for Ireland and Hall, saving their monocoque car for Monza, and Siffert, Collomb, Seifert and Parnell were running their usual 24s. Prinoth had his 18 and Pilette the Parnell 18/21. Siffert's never-say-die mechanic had driven from Bourne with a brand-new BRM V8 engine on the back seat of his VW hire car!

Jimmy took pole position, 1.22 seconds quicker than Brabham's Solitude-winning car, after acclimatising himself to the Hewland change, but an oil pipe failed in practice, and then failed again during the race when Jimmy was leading on lap 13. Innes Ireland then took the lead but had an enormous spin, and began a great battle with Brabham. On lap 57 Jack eased-off with fuel vapourisation and a cockpit so hot he could hardly keep his feet on the pedals, but seven laps later the BRP 24's engine broke and Brabham was able to trundle home to an easy win.

Jimmy had rejoined the race after his oil line had been replaced, but the rules forbade adding oil and when he noticed the pressure surging through the corners he wisely retired after three more laps. Collomb was fifth ahead of Parnell, Seifert and Pilette, while Hall's engine had also failed, making this an expensive meeting for BRP, and Prinoth's suspension had collapsed. Siffert was lying fourth when a broken fuel pump mounting forced him out. After the race the Austrian motoring journalists present voted Innes a well-deserved hard-luck trophy for his very fine drive.

At Monza Team Lotus had a driver problem, for Arundell was committed to the Ron Harris Formula Junior team and Taylor was still unfit. So Mike Spence was promoted from the Harris number-two seat to make his works Formula 1 debut. The full circuit including the notorious Monza bankings was used in practice, but after several cars had broken the police thought up a reason for the organisers to revert to the pure road circuit; Formula 1 cars had been seen for the last time on the Monza speed-bowl.

Spence was to drive R6, Jimmy's Zeltweg car, but while Clark was borrowing it to set second fastest time to Surtees' new Ferrari monocoque the Hewland gearbox was damaged, so Mike took over the old hack carburettor-engine R3 to qualify for the race. Jimmy found that his V8 would not pull peak revs along the straights, and despite Walter Hassan's attentions he had to give best to Ferrari and BRM in the power battle, and allow Surtees to start from pole with Hill alongside.

A new engine was fitted in Jimmy's car overnight, and he streaked away from the start, striving desperately not to be dropped by the front row. He split the Ferrari and BRM at the end of the first lap, and by lap 5 Surtees was weaving from side to side in an attempt to throw the Lotus out of his slipstream. But on lap 17 Surtees retired, leaving Jimmy leading, although the Lotus was slower without the tow and was quickly caught by Hill and Gurney. The trio battled for the lead for lap after lap, until Hill fell back on lap 44, his BRM's clutch slipping. By lap 60 Jimmy and Dan had lapped the entire field, and the Lotus was beginning to hold the lead more consistently. Then, two laps later, Gurney's Brabham appeared way behind, stopping with fuel feed trouble, leaving Jimmy with a whole lap's lead. He eased right back allowing Ginther to unlap himself in second place, and took the chequered flag to win his fifth Grande Epreuve of the year and his first World Championship drivers' title, and to give Lotus-Climax the constructors' World Championship.

Jim Hall was next Lotus finisher in eighth place, and Mike Spence was classified 13th, although his oil consumption had been very high and he had had to switch off just before the engine seized on lap 73.

Gregory stoked-up the Parnell 24-BRM as never before, and led the mid-field group before retiring on lap 27, and Siffert's car failed at 41 laps after another good performance.

Unfortunately, Jimmy's victory was soured by the Monza police, who insisted on taking him away after the race to interview him concerning the 1961 von Trips accident, the law-suits concerning which were still pending. But the following Saturday there was a much happier event at Brands Hatch in the BRSCC's Formula Junior finale meeting, when Colin and Jimmy did a lap of honour sitting on—and in—the victorious Lotus 25. They were given a tremendous reception, and Jimmy made a few high-speed demonstration laps in the car, during which he unofficially broke the outright 2.5 litre lap record by 0.6 second.

Team Lotus' next appearance was in the Oulton Park Gold Cup where once again Jimmy drove his regular R4 and Trevor Taylor made a welcome return in R6 with its Hewland transmission. Jimmy started on pole, his time equalled by Hill's BRM, and Ginther and Taylor completed the rank after equalling each other's times. Jimmy led the race throughout the 73 laps winning from Ginther and Hill at the record average of 98.34 mph. His new lap record of 1min 39.1sec, 100.2 mph, was nearly a second under his 1962 time, and put Oulton Park in the 100 mph club.

Once again poor Trevor retired, his Hewland crownwheel and pinion breaking up after he had made a good early showing. BRP ran their 24-BRMs for Ireland and Mike Beckwith, the Normand Lotus 23 sports car driver, but it proved an expensive afternoon for them; Innes missed a gear and wildly over-revved his engine, while Mike found two gears at once and the car thudded into the bank, suffering serious damage. Siffert retired with four laps left and was classified 11th, while Peter Revson, at that time an American Formula Junior Cooper driver, made his Formula 1 debut in Parnell's 24-BRM and finished ninth. Pilette's 18/21 was 12th, and Collomb's 24-Climax 14th. Gregory retired with run bearings in the other Parnell Lotus 24.

Immediately after the race Jimmy and Dan Gurney flew to America for the Lotus 29s' third race of the season, the Trenton '200' where 36 Offy-powered cars were vying with them for the 27 starting places, the best of them lapping the one-mile oval at 35 seconds. Then Gurney fled round in 33 seconds, and Jimmy went out to the skirl of a pipe band to set a new track record of 32 seconds, about 112 mph. The Lotus 29s ran away from the opposition in the race, but at half-distance Jimmy's oil pressure suddenly zeroed and he retired trailing a cloud of blue smoke. Soon afterwards Dan's leading car failed for the same reason and so Foyt's traditional roadster inherited the 11,000 dollars first place. Clark's 29 broke an oil line, while Gurney's engine swallowed a piece of piston, which dropped down and blocked the oil-scavenge pump. His engine drowned in its own oil!

The Team Lotus personnel stayed on for the United States Grand Prix at Watkins Glen the following weekend, where three cars were entered for Clark, Taylor and Pedro Rodriguez, elder brother of the late Ricardo Rodriguez and a fine sports car driver. Reg Parnell ran a 24-BRM for Rodger Ward, the USAC driver, and a similar car for Hap Sharp, Jim Hall's partner in the Chaparral sports car concern. BRP were missing the unfortunate Innes Ireland, who was in hospital following a bad accident in a Lotus-Ferrari 19 at Seattle on the day of the Trenton race, and Jo Siffert completed the Lotus entry in his 24-BRM Special.

Jimmy was second fastest behind Hill during the Friday practice, while overnight Trevor Taylor's engine was rebuilt with parts borrowed from Parnell after it had broken a camshaft. Jimmy's gearbox had played up during practice, and this was also changed, and on the Saturday a tab washer broke-up inside Trevor's gearbox and so that also had to be fixed by the hard-working Team Lotus mechanics. Later, Taylor's engine had a blow-back, and a fierce carburettor fire started in the vee, which fortunately was smothered quickly before doing any damage.

Anticipating what was to become standard Grand Prix practice, the cars were assembled on a dummy grid before rolling forward to the actual starting grid. Jimmy's engine wouldn't fire, and he flattened the battery and was left behind as the other cars screamed away. The battery was changed, and he flew off in pursuit but his fuel pump was working erratically and his lap times varied widely.

Rodriguez was running ahead of Taylor, and was dubious about the rev limit he had been quoted, 1,000 rpm below that of his team-mates, but he didn't realise that he had the long-stroke engine, and he consistently over-revved it until a camshaft dowel broke after 37 laps. Clark was 11th and gaining ground all the time after losing a lap-and-a-half at the start, and he had inherited seventh place by the 43rd lap. More retirements helped him to move into third place by the finish of the 110-lap race, one lap down on Hill's winning BRM. He had a new lap record of 1min 14.5sec, 111.14 mph, to his credit and he was the only Lotus finisher.

Jim Hall was classified tenth, but had abandoned with a broken transmission, and Siffert's drop-gears had stripped. Ward's gear-change seized, and when he forced it into a gear he bent something vital and retired, while Trevor lasted only 25 laps before the transistor box failed, and Hap Sharp was out after just six laps with a broken tappet.

In the three weeks before the Mexican Grand Prix many of the drivers contested the West Coast sports car races, while in South Africa the Rand Spring Trophy at Kyalami and the Van Riebeek Trophy at Killarney both fell to Neville Lederle's Lotus 21.

At Mexico City Team Lotus ran the same car/driver combinations as at Watkins Glen, and the Parnell team ran their Lotus 24s for Hap Sharp and Chris Amon. BRP's solitary 24 was giving Jim Hall his last Formula 1 ride, and Siffert's Special appeared with the

Something to confuse the historians! Above: Dan Gurney's original race Lotus 29 poses before qualification runs with its Halibrand rear wheels. Below: After wrecking his car and those valuable wheels Dan prepares for another attempt with 'The Mule' . . . the Lotus-Ford 29 prototype.

transmission repaired.

Rodriguez's timing chain broke in practice, wrecking the engine, and Team Lotus had to strip and rebuild the unit with parts borrowed from other teams and a length of Renold chain bought from a local dealer. The timing was 180-degrees out as originally reassembled, and then the oil pump drive was found to be broken and the engine had to come out again.

Jimmy's car was jumping out of gear, so the transmission was rebuilt before the race, and Trevor started without first gear as a tooth was chipped and there was no spare available.

Jimmy took an immediate lead from pole position, led all the way, set a record lap of 1min 58.1sec, 95.30 mph, and won at a record average of 93.28 mph for the 65 laps.

Siffert spun avoiding a sliding Rodriguez on the opening lap and had to stop to have deranged fuel pump wiring replaced, and Amon's engine lost so much power it would hardly pull fourth gear on the straights so he retired. Taylor had a cam follower disintegrate and ran his bearings after struggling round in 12th place, and Pedro steamed round in eighth place, delighting the locals, and then the left-front wheel began to lift high in the air through left-hand bends. The right-rear upper link and spring mount were pulling away from the chassis, and he retired at the pits after the suspension had finally collapsed. Sharp was seventh, with Hall eighth and Siffert ninth.

A brand-new Lotus 25—R7—was exhibited at the London Motor Show in honour of Jimmy's World Championship and the company's constructors' title, and on December 14th the car joined Team Lotus in South Africa for the Rand Grand Prix at Kyalami.

Trevor Taylor spent the first practice session there sorting out both R4 and R7, and Jimmy arrived the next day when the weather broke. The fuel injected engines' fuel pumps continually overheated, and Team Lotus used three on Jimmy's R4 and two on Trevor's R7 without solving the problem. Eventually Trevor's car split the works Ferraris on the front row, but Jimmy could not better fourth fastest time, which put him on the inside of row two.

In the first 25-lap heat the Ferraris pulled away from Jimmy and Trevor until the champion's fuel pump problem struck again after 17 laps. Trevor ran third for four more laps until his pump quit, and both cars restarted once the pumps had cooled, but finished way behind Surtees' victorious Ferrari.

Naturally the Lotuses started the second heat way down the grid, but after three laps Jimmy was fifth, despite pointing to his pump as he passed the pits. Taylor was a distant sixth, and the heat ran out with Ernie Pieterse's 21 the first Lotus on aggregate in fifth place overall. Brausch Niemann's meteoric Lotus 22 lost a wheel in the first heat and retired with ignition problems in the second, and also out of the hunt were motorcyclist Paddy Driver, running the borrowed Gunther Seifert 24-BRM, Jack Holme's 18, Dave Charlton's 22 and Clive Puzey's 18. Taylor finished 12th.

The South African Grand Prix at East London, held three days after Christmas, enabled Jimmy to set a new record by winning seven Championship rounds in one season. Trevor ran his new R7 for the last time and Jimmy was in the ancient R4, both cars with the pumps repositioned in the nose cone. Local entries included Pieterse, Driver and Niemann (with 140 pounds of lead ballast to bring the Lotus 22 up to the weight limit).

Jimmy took pole position by a narrow 0.1 second margin from Brabham, while Paddy Driver had a steering arm break and almost tore the Lotus 24 in two as it somersaulted along the verge; he was unhurt.

Clark led throughout, pulling away from Gurney hand over fist, driving calmly and smoothly as ever, as unruffled and consistent as a machine, to win by over a minute. Trevor was running fifth when he missed a gear entering the Esses and spun. He rejoined tenth and quickly swept back through the field, but he had to stop when a pinch bolt in the gear selectors worked loose; the bolt was tightened and he went on again to finish eighth, four laps down. Niemann finished 14th after some long pit-stops, while Pieterse had a neat hole punched through his Climax engine's cam cover by an errant bolt and retired after only four laps in a haze of oil smoke. And so a record-breaking Lotus season came to an end.

During the year Team Lotus had entered their Formula 1 cars in 11 of the season's 15 non-championship races, and had won five of them, two others falling to Lotuses in private hands—Ireland's UDT-Laystall 24 at Goodwood and Siffert's own 24 at Syracuse. All ten Championship rounds had been contested and seven of them fell to Clark's Lotus 25. In addition the Lotus-powered-by-Ford operation had taken in three USAC track races, winning one of them with Clark's 29. So of 27 major races entered during the season, Team Lotus cars had won 16 and privateers two to give the marque a marvellous two-thirds victory record.

1963 RACING RECORD
Other formulae and classes

Formula Junior ran its last season in 1963, and with the prospect of a new Formula 2 replacing it in 1964 Colin produced a new chassis capable of running in production for both seasons . . . the Lotus 27.

This was the first minor-formula monocoque from Lotus, and although the bathtub-type hull was similar in appearance to the Lotus 25, it differed in construction. Rolling the aluminium side panels for the Lotus 25 was an expensive and time-consuming business, and it was obvious that a similar Formula Junior monocoque would be too expensive to produce in any quantity.

Consequently the new car's outer panels were moulded in ¼-inch thick glass-fibre, then pop-riveted to the flat interior panels of 18-gauge aluminium sheet. Fabricated steel brackets within this composite structure accepted suspension stresses, and three main bulkheads gave the structure its torsional rigidity.

At the front end, the bulkhead was a massive fabricated steel structure, enclosing the inboard front suspension. A humped seat pan gave some 'midships' rigidity while a centre bulkhead of aluminium sheet formed a reclining seat-back. The monocoque side pontoons maintained their height along either side of the engine bay, and terminated in another steel fabricated bulkhead, which was completed by a tubular tie-bar, bolted across the chassis above the gearbox, which itself was hung on this member.

The front suspension showed clear Lotus 25 influence, with the coil-spring/damper units tucked away inside the hull and operated by fabricated upper rocker arms. Very wide-based lower wishbones located the foot of modified Triumph Herald uprights, and at the rear the system included twin radius rods, single top links and reversed lower wishbones on either side. The suspension was not easily adjustable . . . Disc brakes were mounted outboard all round, the disadvantage of added unsprung weight being offset by better cooling and easier maintenance. Wheels were in cast magnesium to the faithful old Lotus 'wobbly web' design, 13 inches in diameter all round, and the drive-shafts used Metalastic rubber doughnuts as inboard joints to accommodate plunge.

This sleek little car looked almost impossibly narrow, fully 5 inches slimmer than the preceding Lotus 22. It was obviously a sophisticated and advanced concept, yet the chassis cost only £65 more than the old tubular type. But much more expensive were the engine and gearbox, for the 1,100 cc Formula Junior Cosworth unit now used a fully counter-balanced forged-steel crankshaft, and a Mark 4 Hewland transaxle was adopted, based on the trusty old VW production gearbox. The asking price was £1,890, but as a contemporary magazine said when the car was unveiled '. . . for what is virtually a slightly reduced Grand Prix car this is by no means expensive. If ever a car looked a winner, this is it . . .'.

But in its final comment the magazine was wrong, for in its early races the Lotus 27 was not a winner, and the new Ron Harris-managed Team Lotus Formula Junior operation had a miserable time. There had been a very hard winter, and the usual early testing season was completely snowed-out. This meant that the Lotus 27s were under-developed when they went to the line, and although the same could be said in respect of the Brabham, Lola and Cooper opposition the problem was less serious for these companies as they were at least working on known principles.

Harris ran cars for Peter Arundell, Mike Spence (enlisted from the Ian Walker team) and his own find, John Fenning. But after a lucky start at Oulton Park, where Peter won, things deteriorated, and at Goodwood he could not better seventh place, while in the Aintree '200' meeting he finished a distant third after a series of wild spins.

The problem was inadequate rigidity in the chassis, for the composite construction—which worked on paper—did not work on the race track. With the season well under way there was only one alternative if the cars were to start winning, and that was to replace the glass-fibre outer skins with rolled aluminium panelling.

Peter Arundell drove the first all-aluminium Lotus 27 at the Silverstone International Trophy meeting in May, but his clutch exploded when he was running fourth. In the all-important Prix Monaco Junior Peter and his Lotus 27 worked together to such effect that they won their heat, but to Cosworth's total amazement Arundell's steel crank broke in the final and put him out. But at Rouen in June the Lotus 27 really started to challenge the successful Brabhams, and Arundell pushed Denny Hulme hard in his heat only to spin off into a bank; he was third in the final with a slightly bent car. Then, at the British Grand Prix meeting Peter used his spare car, and although its engine was around 4 bhp down on his usual power its suspension set-up was perfect . . . at last. He had a race-long battle with Denny which finished on the last lap when the Brabham driver overcooked it and crashed at Club Corner, leaving the red-helmeted Arundell to score a fine victory.

He went on to score five more consecutive victories and snatched the British Express & Star Formula Junior Championship from Denny Hulme by just one point.

Of the 37 major European Formula Junior races held during the 1963 season, Brabham won 14, Lotus 12, Cooper eight, De Sanctis two and Lola one. French private entrant Jacques Maglia scored two of the marque's successes, at Chimay and Monza, in his Lotus 22, and Gerhard Mitter, the two-stroke expert, won the Eifelrennen at Nurburgring in his DKW-powered 22, while at Phoenix Park in Eire Scotsman Adam Wyllie notched the first big win for a private Lotus 27. Jose Rosinski's similar production car won at Montlhery in September, but the privately owned Lotus 27s had got off to the worst possible start earlier in the year . . .

Customer cars were held back until development was finally completed on Ron Harris' prototypes, and the first production 27 went to Ecurie Ford-France in time for the Grand Prix des Frontieres at Chimay. Jo Schlesser practised the car extremely quickly, but finally lost it in the biggest possible way and ended-up sitting in a kind of battered wheel-less hip-bath! He drove a Brabham in the race, while Maglia scored the first of his big wins. The Frenchman also scored a couple of second places, and other successful Lotus 22 pilots during the year included John Mastin (in a Jim Russell school car), Pino Babbini, Teddy Dawson, Bruno Deserti (later given a one-off Harris Lotus 27 drive at Brands Hatch), Alain le Guellec and Brian Hart.

One notable if unsuccessful Lotus 27 was the pure white Miss Veedol, won by Bob Burnard in the 1962 Veedol Championship at Goodwood with an AC-Bristol. As with most Lotus kits the car arrived in a bewildering assortment of pieces, and after ages had been spent assembling it and trying to sort it out its unhappy season ended in a multiple shunt at the final Brands Hatch meeting.

In sports car racing Lotus uprated their standard 23 chassis, fitted 1,594 cc Lotus-Ford twin-cam engines as standard, and called the result the Lotus 23B. From early 1963 until production ceased in 1966, all Lotus 23 chassis frames were built to this more robust specification, and the little sports-racer's total production numbered no less than 131 complete cars.

The marque's major sports-racing operation of 1963 was the three-car Normand Racing Team, who ran Lotus 23Bs for Mike Beckwith, Tony Hegbourne and—when available—Jim Clark. Under Mike's capable management the immaculate white cars with their red and blue stripes scored no less than 38 places out of 49 starts, including 15 firsts and eight lap records. Colin Knight and Gerald Southby cared for the cars and they were always spotless.

Jimmy won the Autosport 3-Hours at Snetterton, a 102-miler at Oulton Park and a 50-miler at Crystal Palace, and other successful Lotus 23Bs were driven by Keith Greene, Rodney Bloor and Jack Pearce, while Alan Rees had some good outings in a car owned by Roy Winkelmann. Ian Walker Racing ran a 1,150 cc Lotus 23 for Paul Hawkins early in the season and scored some class wins, and at the end of the year Graham Hill drove the same team's Lotus 23B in Canada and the USA.

Peter Arundell had the odd outing in his former mechanic Ray Parsons' 1,150 cc 23, and the Japanese Grand Prix at Suzuka fell to Peter Warr's 1,650 cc push-rod-engined 23, from customers Arthur Owen and Mike Knight, whose 23s were powered by a full 1,600 cc twin-cam and a small 1,100 cc engine, respectively. In Europe Cesare Topetti had a great Italian season with a Giannini-engined 23, and Toni Fischaber charged round Austrian circuits to great effect with a 1.8 litre BMW engine in his car. One of the Lotus 23's more exotic successes was in the Singapore Grand Prix, in the hands of police inspector Albert Poon, while in Scandinavia Anders Josefsson's 23B just ran away with the Karlskoga and Roskilde sports car races. Scotsman Jimmy Mackay shipped his much-modified Shannon-Lotus-Climax 11 to Denmark during the season, and won the Copenhagen Cup race at Roskilde. Alban Scheiber's Lotus 23 won cleanly at Zeltweg and Fritz Baumann's 23 was second, in among the Fiat-Abarths, in the Nurburgring 500 Kms.

Across the Atlantic Graham Hill drove the Walker car in the Canadian Grand Prix at Mosport, and finished second behind Pedro Rodriguez's 250P Ferrari with Dennis Coad's Lotus 19 in fourth place. This fine performance more than made up for a dismal Lotus showing in the Player's '200' there earlier in the year, when Jimmy Clark flew-in to drive a 23, Graham ran a 19 and Sir John Whitmore fielded an Elan, and all three retired.

Immediately after the Mosport race Graham flew

Below: Peter Arundell and Mike Spence get their Lotus 27 tyres smoking on the line for the Formula Junior finale race Brands Hatch. Arundell won the race and pipped Denny Hulm (on his right) for the Championship. Bottom: Chapman payir homage to Arundell? Right: Arundell getting the maximu out of the Lotus 27 at Goodwood. Below right: Bob Burnard AC successes earned him a Lotus 27 kit . . . and a load trouble!

TEAM LOTUS

3,000 miles across the Continent to run Winkelmann's 2 litre Climax-engined 23 in the North West Grand Prix at Kent, Washington, and in practice there, Innes Ireland crashed Team Rosebud's V12 Ferrari-engined Lotus 19 into a parked marshal's car, and suffered severe leg and hip injuries which put him out of racing for the rest of the year. During the British season Innes had had a series of battles with Roy Salvadori's 2.7 litre Cooper Monaco, driving the ex-UDT—now BRP—Lotus 19, and although he usually had to give best to the Cooper, the pale green car was never far behind. Other Lotus 19s were run in Britain and Europe by Bill de Selincourt and Charles Vogele, but most of the 13 cars built went to the United States, including Dan Gurney's one-off Ford V8-powered Lotus 19B.

Most of the American-owned cars appeared in the West Coast 'professional series', but the races at Riverside and Laguna Seca brought them little joy. Clark was to drive the Arciero Brothers' car at Riverside, but it just wasn't raceworthy, so he ran a Lotus 23B instead, and retired. Parnelli Jones was down to race the same team's unlikely-sounding 2.7 litre Climax-engined Lotus 23, but couldn't qualify it.

The big Arciero Lotus 19 was ready for Laguna Seca, but it broke under Jimmy during the race, while Graham Hill ran the Walker 23B in both these events but was also out of luck. However, young Timmy Mayer's luck was in, for his ex-Normand car won the 2 litre class both at Laguna Seca and at Nassau late in the year.

Frank Matich excelled in Australian races with his privately owned Lotus 19, while Stirling Moss climbed aboard one of the British Racing Partnership's cars at Goodwood for a private test session—his first time in a racing car cockpit since his terrible accident of the previous year. He convinced himself that his customary brilliant mental co-ordination and sense of balance were no longer there, and made the bold and brave decision to retire from racing, a sport which he had served with such distinction, and which had given him everything in return except the elusive world championship.

In South Africa Syd van der Vyver saw his Formula 1 hopes go up in smoke when his rebuilt ex-Brabham Lotus 24—the only V8-engined Formula 1 car on the Continent at that time—caught fire outside his garage and was destroyed.

Lotus Elites were still popular small GT cars, and while Trevor Taylor won his class in an Elite at the Silverstone May meeting, the race was also notable for the new Elan's racing debut, in the hands of Graham Warner. The Elan was the first Lotus to be designed and built specifically as a touring car, and its suspension characteristics were considered to make the car too soft for racing use, but Warner persevered with his car, while the Stirling Moss Automobile Racing Team (SMART) ran a modified hardtop Elan for Sir John Whitmore. His lurid driving of the pale green car was a delight to watch, but his only real success was a win in the August Bank Holiday meeting at Brands Hatch, in a 2.5 litre GT event.

Team Elite ran cars in most of the Europea long-distance races, and Pat Fergusson was sixth overa and winner of the 2 litre class in the Spa Grand Pri: John Wagstaff, Gil Baird, Trevor Taylor and Davi Hobbs shared another of the team's cars to win the class in the Nurburgring 1,000 Kms, and Mik Beckwith walked away with the 2 litre division in th Goodwood TT. Pat Fergusson stuffed the Team Elit car into the sandbanks at Mulsanne Corner in the L Mans 24-Hours and after manfully digging it out he an John Wagstaff finally brought it home in tenth plac overall, and were third in the Index of Therm Efficiency.

During the year the type 28 Lotus-Cortina saloor made their racing debut. Doc Merfield's club car mad the first serious foray at Snetterton, where in practic he clipped a full 10 seconds off the 2 litre lap record The cars were fully homologated in time for the Oulto Park Gold Cup meeting, and Jack Sears and Trevo Taylor finished third and fourth behind the 7 litre For Galaxies of Dan Gurney and Graham Hill. It wa obvious that should the Galaxies defect for any reaso the new Cortinas would be capable of winning outrigh and in the Snetterton 3-Hours meeting Trevor and Jir Clark dead-heated for second place, with Sears fourt in the Willment-entered car. Jack won the covete British Saloon Car Championship for his performance during the season, scoring points in the Twickenhan team's Cortina GT, Galaxie and Lotus-Cortina cars Henry Taylor took an Alan Andrews Lotus-Cortina t Long Island for the Bridgehampton Double-500 race and he must have boosted American sales hugely b battling wheel-to-wheel with 2 litre Porsche Carreras

At club level Jack Pearce was the most successfu Lotus driver of the year, scoring 12 major wins with hi 23B sports-racer and 1.6 litre Lotus 22 Formule Libr car. Maidstone dentist John Mew, who habituall played the part of Father Christmas at Brands Boxin Day meetings, shone in his 1,500 cc Climax-engine Lotus 20, and consistent Formula Junior front-runner included Dennis O'Sullivan (22), Mike de Udy (22) an Melvyn Long (27). The latter pair were Jim Russel pupils, and Long seemed particularly promising unti he had an unfortunate shunt and broke an arm rathe badly. Derrick Colvin won the Anthony Curtis Trophy for 'best loser' in a well-prepared old Lotus 18, and Ray Parsons took the Peter Collins Memorial Trophy a Goodwood with his small-engined Lotus 23. Big Doc Merfield's Lotus-Cortina clinched the Spring Grov Saloon Car Championship, and Roger Nathan becam Autosport GT Champion in an Elite.

Nathan met strong opposition during the year fron John Surtees' brother Norman, and Derek Bennett also Elite-mounted. Bennett was to build his firs Chevron Clubman's car two years later, and th Bolton-based business had virtually taken over th Lotus sports-racing and small GT market before th end of the decade . . .

Young Peter Gethin had progressed from a Lotus 7

to a 23, and he had some success along with Scotsman Bill Stein and Robin McArthur, who had bought Mike Beckwith's old car. One Mike Warner did well in a Lotus 23B, and was later to become boss of Lotus Components.

While Charles Hodgson wrestled manfully to make his Elan competitive, Lotus Sevens still had the small production sports car classes sewn-up. David Porter's independent-rear-suspension Lotus 7/20 was extremely fast, but in the small GT classes uproar was caused by Sevens running with sketchy Fibrepair hardtops fitted. These unsightly creatures were immensely fast, with a tremendous power-to-weight ratio, but were hardly in the spirit of the regulations.

Sadly, the club season in Britain was not without its tragedies, and young Mark Fielden lost his life at Silverstone, while sitting in his newly-acquired Lotus 17 at the pits. Another car spun out of Woodcote and careered into the pit-lane, and this disaster, added to a similar fatal accident at the British Grand Prix meeting, caused the whole Silverstone pit area to be rebuilt, with the pit-lane elevated above road level. In Scotland, promising Bill Carmichael lost his life when he rolled his Lotus 7 at Charterhall . . .

Hill-climbing and sprinting are the only classes we have overlooked so far, and here flocks of generally obsolete Formula Juniors and sports cars abounded. Undoubtedly the most successful was Welshman Peter Boshier-Jones' 1,500 cc supercharged Lotus-Climax 22, and he narrowly missed winning the RAC Hill Climb Championship despite setting several fastest times of the day.

On the English autocross scene Howard Parkin added four-wheel drive to a Lotus Seven, called the result a Parkin-Cannonball, and understandably became a very difficult man to beat.

The Normand Lotus 23 team dominated their small sports car class during 1963. Jim Clark, who joined Mike Beckwith and Tony Hegbourne when available, goes on his winning way at Oulton Park.

1964

Cortina by Lotus

The new year dawned with Team Lotus preparing to defend two World Championships and the Indy team planning a return to the '500' with new cars and modified twin-overhead-camshaft engines, while for the first time ever Lotus were about to enter the saloon-car field with a serious two-car team. A Lotus-Cortina promotional race programme was put in hand with Ford of Dearborn, and the new Formula 2 cars were farmed-out to Ron Harris, while Ian Walker was to look after the fortunes of the new Lotus 30 large-capacity sports-racer and the Chequered Flag ran the quasi-works Elans.

On the touring-car scene the last Elites were sold in January, when the SE and Super 95 models were discontinued, final production totalling only 988 cars (at a loss of £100 a time that was quite enough!).

While the Elan entered its second full year of production a fully race-prepared Lotus-Cortina was one of the centrepieces of the London Racing Car Show display. The Cosworth-developed engine produced 140 bhp at 6,500 rpm from its full 1,593 cc capacity, and suspension modifications included special springs and shock absorbers, a heavy-duty front anti-roll bar and a high ratio steering box. A limited-slip differential was standard with a choice of three axle ratios, and complete with perspex windows, moulded racing seats and a full Irvin race harness the Lotus-Cortina was offered at £1,725. Top speed, on a 3.9:1 final-drive, was quoted as 128.1 mph.

A still unconfirmed rumour had it that Jimmy Clark had rolled a Lotus-Cortina four times at Goodwood, trying to avoid Colin, who had spun his similar car!

Once again the early part of the year was occupied mainly by preparations for Indianapolis, and after the near-miss of 1963 Ford were preparing their new full-race engines and Lotus were building revised and updated chassis to accept them. After the speed shown by the original Lotus-Ford 29s on Dunlop road-racing tyres, the British company moulded special covers for this year's race. These proved considerably quicker than the hard Firestone compounds originally designed to carry the bulk of a front-engined roadster, but in early practice both Clark and Gurney were outshone by Bobby Marshman. Entrant Lindsey Hopkins ha assisted Ford with information on track racing right the beginning of the Indy project, and he had been so the number-two Lotus 29 which Gurney had crashed i qualifying the previous year. Throughout the Wint Hopkins, mechanic Jack Beckley and Marshman ha tested the car and the new twin-cam engines, and the came to Indy at a fine pitch. The year-old car w quickly lapping at a record 157.178 mph, an Marshman was soon through the 158 mph barrier wit Clark's new Lotus 34 right behind.

Meanwhile, the Ford V8 engines also appeared in variety of home-brewed mid-engined cars, but th Speedway's two top-ranking drivers, Parnelli Jones an A.J. Foyt, were still running their Offenhause powered roadsters. Ford wanted Foyt to run the spar works Lotus-Ford, but Colin wanted it available in cas either of his drivers crashed (as had happene th previous year) and therefore was not keen to let hi have it. The Dunlop tyres were another bone c contention, for Jacque Passino, Ford's top compet tions executive, thought they were too soft to last th race and wanted to run on Firestones.

This put Chapman in a difficult position, for both h drivers were happy to run the softer, faster tyres an would have objected to adopting a handicap in th form of Firestone's hard and obsolete rubber. Coli managed to talk Passino round, then persuaded Le Iacocca—General Manager, Ford Division—that hi choice was the right one, and added Fran Zimmerman—Special Vehicles Manager—to his list o converts. He also won his point on the spare car, an Foyt stuck to his roadster . . .

Chief mechanic David Lazenby recalls the confi dence of these few days, when Jimmy alone was second a lap faster than Jones' fastest roadster. But o Monday, May 18, after Clark, Marshman and Gurne had all qualified, Dan went out to try some full-loa running with full tanks. The overloaded Dunlops bega to blister and scatter shreds of tread; they wer 'chunking'. It was thought that this was a pressur problem, but before the race Dunlops were hastil contacted and set about revising their tyre moulds t give a shallower and more stable tread pattern. They modified the moulds and flew the new batch of tyres to Indiana in a tremendous scramble, having made them in a deserted factory over the Whitsun holiday, but perhaps not surprisingly the tyres were faulty, and the subsequent failures put the works Lotus-Fords out of the '500'. Colin withdrew Dan's car after Jimmy's had thrown a tread and the resultant imbalance had collapsed the left-rear suspension, and as he recalled later '. . . I got into terrible trouble with Ford over that . . .'

The day after the race, which an overjoyed A.J. Foyt won in his roadster, Iacocca ordered a complete post-mortem into the failures which had humbled Ford so publicly. He bawled-out his subordinates to such effect that they prepared to meet Chapman and Andrew Ferguson with swords drawn. He in turn had received a considerable broadside from Charles Patterson, Ford's Vice President, who had not only listened to a snide Foyt victory speech taking the rise out of his company, but had been at the receiving end of a very rude gesture as the roadster grumbled past him into Victory Circle!

Andrew Ferguson: 'When we went down to Dearborn to see Ford's next day Colin said to me

Cortina in Cortina! Ford took their Cortina champions to Italy to celebrate their great 1964 season. After driving down the bob-run (right) and posing for a picture (below) they started a mammoth snow-ball fight in which Jim Clark slipped a disc!

"You've never been to one of these meetings before have you? Ooh, they really know how to look after you." I knew there was something wrong as soon as we were shown into the conference room, because there were two chairs on their own, with a ring of chairs facing them . . .'

Leo Beebe and Zimmerman of Special Vehicles, Frey and PR man Bob Hefty confronted the Lotus men, and Colin immediately apologised for his decision to run Dunlop tyres and for their failure. He confirmed that he would like to continue the original USAC programme with the cars, but Frey then confronted him with Ford's new proposal: 'We would like to have you sell us all three cars immediately'.

To Ferguson's amazement Colin agreed. 'I think it was because he was dog-tired after the drama of the previous few days, and he just couldn't fight them.' Ford were not convinced that the only way to redeem themselves was to take over the running of the cars from Lotus, but they were determined to regain lost face. Frey wound-up the meeting, and it was understood that Ford would buy the cars immediately while Colin should present his plans on paper for the Trenton and Milwaukee 200-mile events. Ford would then consider whether it required his services or not.

The Ford executives, a rather tired Chapman and a shaken Ferguson walked from Frey's to Beebe's office to finalise the sale, but with time to think Colin performed one of his agile volte faces and claimed he had not understood that Team Lotus were to sell their cars to Ford immediately!

Beebe and the others were struck dumb. 'But you just agreed to sell them to us' spluttered Beebe, hurriedly checking back the notes of the meeting which had just finished. Colin was in his eloquent stride now and refused point-blank to sell them, stating that he would rather they went under dust covers than lose the opportunity to redeem himself. He was his old self once again, and sure enough he talked the Ford men round and a new set of terms were drawn up for the 200-milers at Trenton and Milwaukee.

Things looked rather shaky as Milwaukee approached, on August 23, for the date clashed with the Austrian Grand Prix and both Clark and Gurney were anxious to score World Championship points. So two drivers had to be found, and a deal was forged with Parnelli Jones' entrant J.C. Agajanian for one car while Colin enlisted sports car veteran Walt Hansgen for the other. Hansgen had crashed one of the Lotus 34s in private practice at Trenton in July, and now he crashed another in qualifying for the Milwaukee race. So A.J. Foyt was brought in to take his place, healing a rift with Ford since the Indy debacle and giving him his debut in the type of car he was later to drive so well.

While these torrid intrigues typified the Indy programme, Lotus were in further problems with a Ford V8-engined car in the shape of the Lotus 30 sports-racer. This was the first really big-engined sports car the company had built, and the attempt to scale-up an Elan-type backbone chassis was virtually an unqualified failure. Chapman: 'We decided to go in for big sports cars partly because we could buy 289 cubic inch (4.7 litre) Ford engines inexpensively, and we set out to make an inexpensive big sports car. It was built around the engine and as you know, it just didn't go. To make it go we had to put a bigger engine in, a 325 cubic inch (5.3 litre) which gave us much more power but also a lot of problems. It was heavier, and so all the springs had to go up, and the wishbones then had to be made stronger. Stronger wishbones then began to tear the mounting points out of the chassis and so we had to strengthen them as well, and then we needed more fuel and then a bigger gearbox. When we got it all more or less sorted the 351 cubic inch (5.8 litre) engine came along from Ford's experimental department and so we decided to build the completely new Lotus 40 and try to sort out all the problems. We had a lot of other projects on at the time and the car never really got the attention it should have had. Fundamentally the car was built for about half the power we finally put into it, and it just tore it all apart . . .'

Ferguson was instructed to sign on a certain driver for the Cortina team at the beginning of the year, and when he met him he couldn't believe this was the chap Colin had meant. Colin's serious, single-minded approach to racing was well-known, and the breezy, boisterous fellow Andrew signed-on just couldn't possibly fit. Sure enough, after charging round in the lead in his first Team Lotus drive this chap crashed his Cortina heavily, and Andrew winced as he sauntered back into the pits, slapped Colin heartily on the back and boomed 'Well, old boy, better wheel out another one, what!' He was out of the team within a week.

Major road-car development of the year was the announcement in November of the Series 2 'Elan S2' model. This featured several refinements such as the addition of a full-width polished veneer facia, a lockable glove box, chrome instrument bezels, handbrake warning light, smaller pedals to give more space in the rather confined foot-well, and a quick-release filler cap. The rear lights were merged into a single oval unit in place of the previous separate circular types, and larger front brake calipers were adopted. Centre-lock wheels were offered as an optional extra, and the very attractive little S2 was priced at £1,436.

During the year a total of 1,195 Lotus cars were produced, which with the 567 Lotus-Cortinas assembled made a grand total of 1,762. Group Lotus turnover for the year was at an all-time high of £1,573,000, and with a pre-tax profit of £113,000 Lotus' modest band of 396 employees were certainly earning their keep! The year was an unusual one for the Group, for while the road cars really consolidated their position, Lotus racing activities were narrowly eclipsed in the World Championships, were overshadowed in American track-race events and took a most decided dive in the customer competition car sector. The day was obviously approaching when Lotus emphasis would be squarely on production touring cars, but as yet nobody could quite predict when the shift would take place . . .

1964 RACING RECORD
Grands Prix and other major formulae

Once again Team Lotus gave the Tasman races a miss, but Tony Shelly reappeared in his aged 2.5 litre Lotus 18/21, and was fifth in the New Zealand Grand Prix at Pukekohe, despite shutting the door on Brabham as he was being lapped and precipitating quite a bad accident from which Jack was lucky to escape unharmed. He was fifth again at Levin, sixth at Christchurch, fourth at Teretonga, eighth in the Australian Grand Prix, seventh at Warwick Farm, fifth at Lakeside and seventh at Longford. In the New Zealand rounds Rex Flowers and Roly Levis went well to corner the 1,600 cc class with their Formula Junior cars, and in Australia Glyn Scott, Leo Geoghegan and Arnold Glass fought hard for the class with their Lotus 27s.

In South Africa Clive Puzey won the Rand Autumn Trophy race at Kyalami with the ex-Hocking Lotus 18 after his main opposition crashed or spun in torrential rain, and then in March came the first Formula 1 race of the year, the Daily Mirror Trophy at Snetterton.

Peter Arundell made his debut as number-two to Jim Clark, for Trevor Taylor had been dropped following his unsuccessful and unfortunate 1963 season. Jimmy's car was much modified, using brand-new suspension uprights and hub carriers, with smaller brake discs fitting inside new 13-inch diameter wheels shod with wide-tread Dunlop tyres. Changing the wheel size had meant altering the suspension and steering geometry to suit, while at the rear the radius rods were now mounted beneath the monocoque instead of on its sides. Both cars used fuel-injected Climax engines and ZF transmissions.

Trevor Taylor was still driving a Lotus, but now it was one of BRP's pale green BRM-engined 24s with a Colotti transmissiòn. Innes Ireland had recovered from his Seattle sports car accident and was in the BRP team's monocoque. For the first time Lotus 25s appeared in private colours, R3 and R7 having been sold to Reg Parnell (Racing) Ltd, now run by Tim Parnell following his famous father's untimely death during the winter. These cars were fitted with BRM V8 engines and the latest Hewland transmissions, and were to be driven by Chris Amon and Mike Hailwood, who part-sponsored the team. American Peter Revson's 24-BRM was cared for by the same team, and Collomb's 24-Climax and Jock Russell's old four-cylinder Lotus 18/21 completed the field.

Race day was diabolical, with incessant rain and glowering black skies, and the Formula 1 race was cut from 50 to 35 laps in order to finish in daylight, while a dummy-grid start was used in accordance with a new FIA ruling. Clark and Arundell flanked Hill's brand-new monocoque BRM on the front row, but Jimmy was left in pole position as his wide tyres spun on the streaming surface. During the race Hill spun and crashed spectacularly with the BRM, leaving Arundell in the lead with Jimmy third but aquaplaning in all directions on his wide tyres. Both Clark and Brabham were using so little throttle on their big-tyred cars that their engines began to drown and both later retired. Peter impressed with a fast drive in the lead until his engine threw a rod, leaving Innes to score a unique win in the BRP-BRM. Amon was fifth while Hailwood, Taylor, Revson and Collomb all gave up. Peter Arundell's fastest lap was a very respectable 1min 51.2sec, 87.73 mph.

Easter Monday brought the traditional Goodwood meeting, and with no Pau race clashing this year Team Lotus ran the Snetterton cars, in which Jimmy was sandwiched by Brabham and Hill on the front row, with Arundell behind. The World Champion trailed the BRM in the race, while Arundell decided he was being delayed by a dice between McLaren and Ireland, rushed past at Madgwick and upset them both, Innes spinning and taking Bruce off into the bank. Jimmy tried really hard to catch the leading BRM, but the Lotus 25B's clutch failed and he fell back. Brabham passed him, only to have a puncture and slither gently out of contention, and with just two laps left Hill's BRM rotor arm broke and he coasted to a stop, leaving Jimmy to take a very lucky first place. Arundell was on his tail to make it a works one-two, and Trevor Taylor's BRP 24-BRM in third place made it a grand-slam for the marque. Hailwood was fifth in the Parnell 25-BRM, Revson retired his own car, and Collomb got it all wrong at the chicane and took Bonnier's Walker Cooper off through the trolley sections.

The following weekend's Pau Grand Prix was the first race of the new 1 litre Formula 2, and from there Arundell went to Syracuse on April 12 to lead the Team Lotus Formula 1 assault while Jimmy returned to England for a sports car race at Oulton Park. Peter took over Jimmy's Lotus 25B, now reconverted to 15-inch wheels and tyres and using a new simplified ZF gearbox, and Mike Spence joined him as number-two in his usual 25. Hailwood and Amon represented Parnell, and Siffert, Wicky and Revson were in their 24s, the good Swiss driver running his for the last time pending delivery of a new Brabham.

Team Lotus were late for scrutineering, and had problems with the organisers, who were justifiably upset at Clark's non-appearance. Siffert tipped his 24 Special over on top of himself and broke his collar bone, while Arundell was very fast on his first acquaintance with this difficult circuit, but as a penalty for late arrival the organisers wouldn't accept the day's times. Second practice day was wet, so Peter and Mike started from the back of the grid, while the injured Siffert and Wicky, who failed to qualify, missed the race.

The race distance was cut from 56 to 40 laps because the circuit was still dotted with puddles on race day, and Arundell shot through the field from the flag to run third behind the works Ferraris of Bandini and Surtees. Revson stuffed his car into some straw bales, and after seven laps Arundell limped into the pits without fourth and fifth gears. Andrew Ferguson immediately called-in Mike Spence and Peter rejoined in his car in sixth place.

He shrieked back through the field to gain inexorably on Bandini's Ferrari in second place, and the very partisan crowd almost had a mass seizure as Bandini shot into his pit with a shattered vizor. Arundell went by into second place, and Bandini returned to the fray with a will, set a new lap record and just pipped Peter for second place by a tenth of a second at the finish of a memorable motor race. Spence continued in the 25B with an adjusted gearchange, only to retire when the trouble recurred, while Hailwood lost his clutch but finished seventh, and Amon had gearbox problems but finished fifth.

From a rainy Syracuse Team Lotus returned home to a sunny Aintree '200'. Jimmy had a brand new Lotus 33 monocoque for this race, numbered R8 in the 25 series. The new design was based very closely on the Lotus 25 and was almost indistinguishable to the casual observer, but many minor suspension geometry changes had been made to accomodate 13-inch wheels and larger heavy-duty drive-shafts, while solid steering arms and extra rivets in joints found suspect on the standard Lotus 25 monocoques were other 33 features.

The Coventry-Climax engine ZF transmission package was unchanged, but Jimmy had practice problems and started from the second row. Peter was on the outside of the front row with his ex-Clark 25B, R6, still on 15-inch wheels, and he was flanked by Brabham and Hill. BRP now had a second monocoque car ready for Trevor Taylor, and Amon and Hailwood had their ususal 25-BRMs. The field comprised 17 Formula 1 cars and nine Formula 2s contesting their own class.

Arundell was fourth at the end of the opening lap but Jimmy was way down in ninth place. Next time round he was seventh, then fifth, and on lap five he nipped by Arundell to take fourth place. On lap eight Jimmy passed Hill, and he soon caught Brabham in the lead but couldn't get by him. For lap after lap the two circulated nose-to-tail, then Jimmy forged through to lead on lap 26. By lap 42 Jack was back ahead again, and five laps later he led the Lotus down towards Melling Crossing, closing on two back-markers. They kept well over to let Jack by, and the second signalled Jimmy through, but Andre Pilette in the leading Scirocco suddenly braked hard and the car behind him had to swerve, putting Jimmy on the grass.

The Lotus 33 was travelling very fast, and it ploughed into the straw bales in front of an old boiler house, and careered to a stop in a mangled heap. Jimmy was OK but furious, especially as it had cost him his new car. Peter Arundell drove on into third place, while Amon retired after only three laps with metering unit troubles and Hailwood's engine stopped after 22 laps.

After the Aintree disaster Team Lotus provided a pair of 25Bs for Jimmy and Peter for the International Trophy race at the May Silverstone meeting. The works Brabhams annexed the inside of the front row, with Hill's BRM alongside and Jimmy on the outside in R6. Peter drove R4 and started on the middle of row two, Jimmy was third into Copse Corner, caught and passed Jack Brabham at Chapel Curve and after two bites got by Hill to lead at Club Corner. He set a new lap record of 1min 35sec, 110.92 mph, on his second lap as he fought to draw away, but by lap six Gurney was going quicker still and took the lead. The 25B began to sound sick and dropped back into fourth place, finally retiring at Becketts after ten laps with a broken engine, a stream of oil dribbling from the left-hand exhaust pipe. Once again Peter was left to soldier on steadily into third place behind Hill and Brabham, while the blue and maroon Lotus 25s of Amon and Hailwood were fifth and sixth, Revson's 24 ninth and a recovered Siffert 11th in his repaired but aged 24-BRM Special (he was still awaiting delivery of the new Brabham).

Team Lotus reliability record was taking something of a battering, and it was with the basically two-year-old 25Bs that they went to Monaco for the opening World Championship round on the following Sunday. The cars had been further modified, and the press gave them 25C and 25D classifications depending on the extent of the modifications. Both had the latest ZF gearboxes with simplified gear-change linkages, and Clark's had 13-inch wheels with the attendant suspension changes, including complete Lotus 33 rear suspension, solid steering arms and heavier drive-shafts. Arundell's R4 arrived with the 1963 suspension set-up on his car, but during practice this was whipped off and modified to accept 13-inch wheels and tyres, although the standard old-style drive-shafts were retained.

BRP were in a similarly sorry state, for Ireland had crashed his monocoque heavily at Silverstone and so he reverted to one of the team's old 24-BRMs to back-up Taylor in the original 1963 monocoque car. Amon and Hailwood were in their regular R3 and R7, respectively, and 24s appeared for Siffert, Revson and Collomb.

Ireland was further bruised in a road accident on his way to Monte Carlo and was in low spirits, and during first practice he had brake trouble with the 24, locked a wheel entering the chicane and had a lurid accident, escaping with a winding and more bruises from his third badly-damaged Lotus at Monaco in four years!

Jimmy and Dan Gurney were commuting between Europe and Indianapolis for '500' practice and qualifying, and the World Champion returned to Monte Carlo on the Friday morning, not very happy since his new Lotus-Ford 34 had not been ready for him in the United States. He took pole position at Monaco by 0.1 second from Brabham with a 1min 34.0sec lap. In this session Hailwood crashed his Lotus 25 slightly, damaging the front end but not hurting himself.

Race morning saw Peter's car being finished off in the garage, and Parnell's mechanics riveting a strengthening plate on to the left front corner of Hailwood's R7 and making-up brand-new wishbone

Not a good day. The Aintree '200' meeting saw Jim Clark giving two new Lotuses their debut. The Lotus 30 (above) proved a much-troubled handful but struggled home in second place in the supporting race, while in the '200' Jimmy was put off the road by a backmarker (below) and demolished his latest Formula 1 contender, the Lotus-Climax 33.

pivot points. Four of the Lotus entries failed to qualify for the select grid of 16; Ireland, Amon, Revson and Collomb.

Jimmy took the lead from the flag and completed a simply shattering opening lap to pull away from the pack. He was on a real knife-edge through the chicane, and the hurtling Lotus bounced off the bales on the exit in a flurry of dust, but he gathered it up and continued at unabated pace. By lap 20 Jimmy held a consistent 6 seconds lead over Gurney, but as the 25B came away from the Gasworks Hairpin on its 23rd lap the rear anti-roll bar was trailing.

Clark instinctively altered his driving style to suit the changed handling characteristics of his car, but every time he rounded the hairpin the scrutineers were staring at the rear of his car and so he gave them reassuring thumbs-up signs as he slid round under their noses at about 30 mph. In the pits Colin gazed anxiously at his leading car, and decided to call it in before it was black-flagged. Jimmy had prepared for a stop by turning on the taps and pulling out a 10.5 seconds lead on Gurney, and just as he was signalled-in on his 37th lap the dangling pieces fell away harmlessly into the gutter. The 25B shot into its pit for the vertical link to be whipped-off, and this let Gurney and Hill go by before Jimmy rejoined.

By the half-way mark there were only 2 seconds covering this trio, and on lap 53 Hill set a new lap record in passing Gurney. Nine laps later the Brabham's gearbox broke, Jimmy's engine was losing power as the fuel pressure dropped, and Hill drew out a 10 seconds lead. By lap 80 Jimmy's V8 was smoking, and with just eight laps left its oil pressure zeroed and he coasted into the pits. He was still lying third, so Colin told him to continue and try to nurse the car to the finish. So he crawled away, coasting down the hills and being passed by Arundell, whose oil pressure was also dangerously low. Peter was worn-out, for his hurriedly finished car felt strange on 13-inch wheels, the brakes were unpredictable, the gearchange suspect and his seat uncomfortable. He stopped at the pits to report no oil pressure, but Colin sent him on as well. He stopped short of the finish line in the hope that Jimmy could last long enough to pass him for an extra championship point, whereupon Peter could trickle over fourth, but R6 was beyond passing anyone, for the engine gave a death rattle and seized on the hill towards the Casino and so Peter trundled over the line to take third place and his first four title points. Jimmy was classified fourth, and Mike Hailwood drove a consistent race in his very efficiently rebuilt car to take sixth place and a single point. Siffert gave of his considerable best with the old Lotus 24 for eighth position.

This result gave Graham Hill nine points to team-mate Ginther's six, Arundell's four and Clark's three, while BRM led Lotus-Climax in the Constructors' Championship by nine points to four.

Immediately after the race Jimmy was winging his way back across the Atlantic towards Indianapolis, where his Lotus-Ford 34 covered the four-lap

qualifying run at 158.82 mph, with a best lap at 159.38 mph, which shattered Parnelli Jones' 1963 qualifying figures of 151.15 mph and 151.847 mph, respectively. In test runs Jimmy broke the 160 mph barrier, and Bobby Marshman, driving one of the ex-works Lotus 29s, now renamed as the 'Pure Oil Firebird Special', lapped at 160.085 mph.

The rear-engined theme had quickly attracted American support, and Rodger Ward's Kaiser Aluminum-Ford was third quickest with 156.867 mph ahead of Dan Gurney's Lotus 34 with 154.487 mph.

Two weeks after Monaco came the Dutch Grand Prix, and Team Lotus arrived with their 25s further modified. Both had strengthened anti-roll brackets, and Arundell's R4 now had Lotus 33 drive-shafts and steering, although its rear suspension was still basically a Lotus 25 set-up. Jimmy's R6 retained the Lotus 33 rear suspension, but perversely featured original Lotus 25 steering geometry!

Parnell's able mechanics had found that Hailwood's repaired R7 was still raceworthy, and so had spent their time converting Amon's R3 to accept 13-inch wheels and the new wider-section Dunlop tyres. Siffert had finally received his long-awaited Brabham-BRM so there were just the four Lotus runners at Zandvoort.

Jimmy lost pole position to Gurney's Brabham by a tenth of a second, but he won the battle to take the

Top left: Mike Spence became Team Lotus' number-two driver while Peter Arundell recovered from his Reims Formula 2 accident. Left: Leading round the Station Hairpin at Monaco Clark was destined for another unhappy race . . . Below: They reverted to narrow tyres for the high speeds at Spa; Jimmy's Lotus 25B and Graham Hill's BRM battle for second place in pursuit of Dan Gurney.

Here we are again! The 1964 Indianapolis Lotus 34s used double-overhead-camshaft Ford V8 engines, new wheel castings and Dunlop tyres. Clark (above) lost the lead when the left rear tyre failed and caused a suspension to collapse; Gurney (below) was withdrawn on safety grounds. Jimmy liked the air deflector screen, while Dan was more traditional in his taste, beginning practice with a wrap-round screen.

inside line round Tarzan Hairpin and gained a lead he was never to lose in a carbon copy of the previous year's Dutch Grand Prix. At half-distance he held a 29 seconds lead over Surtees' Ferrari, and lapped Arundell in a creditable third place on lap 51. So the Lotus pair came home, with Jimmy winning the 208-miles race at a new record average of 98.02 mph and setting a record lap at 1min 32.8sec, 101.07 mph. Chris Amon went well to finish fifth, but team-mate Hailwood drove gently for his crown-wheel and pinion had failed in practice and a used gear set had been substituted without any guarantee that it would last; it didn't, and Mike retired after 58 laps when running tenth.

Jimmy's win and Hill's troubled fourth place in the BRM meant that they shared the top of the championship table with 12 points each, while Peter was third with eight points, and in the constructors' competition Lotus-Climax had gone into a one-point lead over BRM.

Six days later came the Indianapolis '500', and the Lotus 34s looked all set to score the victory which had so narrowly eluded their predecessors in 1963. The Lotus 34 used an improved bathtub-like monocoque similar to that of the 25/29/33 series cars, and was powered by a 'proper' racing version of the 4.2 litre Ford V8 engine used the previous year. Ford felt that their original virtually stock engine had performed so well that a racing version should be a sure-fire Indianapolis winner, and immediately after early tests with the Lotus 29s the Dearborn engineers had begun developing new twin-overhead-camshaft cylinder heads for 1964. In this project they copied the Offenhauser four-cylinder head design quite closely, and so ended up with valves and combustion chambers suited to a 4.2 litre 'four' on each 2.1 litre bank of their V8. Nevertheless, an output of 425 bhp was claimed for the new engine, an increase of over 50 bhp from the pushrod unit, and it ran on straight petrol fed through Ford-modified Hilborn fuel-injection. The Lotus 34 was quite similar in appearance to the 29, with off-set suspension, but had sleeker bodywork and ran on specially-made Dunlop tyres.

Jimmy started from pole position, and after the usual pre-race jamboree he led the 33 starters across the line, his green and yellow Lotus 34 covered in colourful decals and stickers. He led out of Turn Four to finish the lap, but behind him chaos broke out as Dave MacDonald spun into the inside wall and bounced back into a group of following cars as a ball of flame erupted from ruptured tanks. Eight cars collided as a massive column of smoke and flame blocked the Speedway. The red flag came out to stop the race, but the accident had already cost the lives of MacDonald and Eddie Sachs.

It was an hour-and-three-quarters before the restart could be given, with the cars lined-up in single file in the order in which they had completed the first lap. So Jimmy was at the front and stayed ahead for five laps before the meteoric Bobby Marshman rushed by in his modified Lotus 29, the car Dan Gurney had crashed in practice the previous year. The white Lotus set a terrific pace, lapping at 155 mph until an oil leak developed after 33 laps and put it out. Jimmy inherited the lead again, but only seven laps later he felt a peculiar tremor coming from the rear-end, and as he slowed it snowballed into a shattering vibration which ended in a terrific clang as the left-rear suspension collapsed and the wheel fell inwards at the top; the Lotus weaved crazily before Jimmy got it under control and slithered safely on to the infield.

He walked, grim-faced, back to the pits where Colin eventually decided to call-in Dan's car after 114 laps. Examination of the tyres showed that the treads had overheated, chunked and broken-up, and the resultant imbalance had torn the suspension apart. The Dunlop tyres had performed well during practice, but the race tyres belonged to a new batch specially flown-in from Fort Dunlop, and these had revealed a weakness. Jimmy earned 2,100 dollars in lap-leader prizes, but it was a poor reward compared to winner A.J. Foyt's record-breaking purse of 153,650 dollars!

Two weeks later Team Lotus arrived at Spa for the Belgian Grand Prix. Jimmy disliked the dangerous, high-speed circuit through the Ardennes, but he was poised for a hat-trick of wins in the Belgian event; whatever his misgivings, he kept them under control.

He had the choice of two cars, but didn't like either of them very much. One was R6, back on 15-inch wheels to give a higher top-speed, and with the early Lotus 25-type suspension in place of the Lotus 33 arrangement. The other car was the rebuilt Lotus 33 wrecked at Aintree, which naturally featured all the latest tweaks and the ¾-inch longer wheelbase. Peter Arundell's R4 was also on 15-inch wheels, but was otherwise little changed from its Zandvoort trim.

Mike Hailwood was laid low by a throat infection, and so Parnell ran Amon in his usual R3 and turned over Mike's R7 to Peter Revson.

Jimmy spent practice changing from car to car, while Peter Arundell got going well and put his Lotus 25B on the second row of the starting grid, ahead of his number-one, who ended up on the outside of row three. Revson was very fast and was on row four, ahead of Amon on the fifth row.

Jimmy used R6 for the race, and when it began to rain just before the start his front wheels were changed. Then the flag fell and Arundell blasted away to lead briefly before Gurney, Hill and Clark swept ahead. The race developed with the Brabham out-handling the Lotus and having a definite edge on maximum speed, so Dan drew away while Hill's BRM caught Clark, and Arundell couldn't catch either of them. Graham and Jimmy had a great struggle for second place and were soon joined by McLaren's quick Cooper which split them. Peter was a comfortable fifth until lap 19 when he had to stop for water, and lost four laps.

The BRM was quicker on the straights than the Lotus and while Hill was driving comfortably, Clark was having to drive beyond his car's reasonable limit just to stay in contention.

As he finished his 28th lap, with four to go, Jimmy rushed into his pit shouting for water as his temperature gauge was reading dangerously high. The header tank was filled in seconds and he rejoined, still in third place as Brabham had not yet appeared at La Source hairpin above the pits.

Then Gurney, the leader, was overdue, and he spluttered into his pit calling for fuel. McLaren went by in second place making thumbs-down signs as his battery was running flat and affecting his ignition and fuel pumps so that his engine was misfiring. The Brabham team had no petrol in their pit and had to send Gurney back out hoping he could make it, but before he could catch McLaren his V8 coughed and finally died at Stavelot. At the same time Hill's BRM died beyond Stavelot as his pumps wouldn't pick-up the few gallons remaining in his fuel tanks, and McLaren spluttered past the parked Brabham and BRM only for his own engine to expire before he made it to La Source. He just managed to coast to the corner, rounded it and rolled downhill towards the line in the lead.

Pandemonium reigned at the line as first Hill was overdue, then Gurney failed to appear and finally McLaren was seen coasting silently downhill towards the flag. Then with a shriek Clark's Lotus burst out of the woods, slid round La Source and bulleted past the Cooper just before the line, to score both the car's and its driver's third consecutive victory in the Belgian Grand Prix!

Colin and the Lotus crew were jubilant, but Jimmy didn't realise he had won for he hadn't seen the BRM parked beyond Stavelot. He continued on a cooling-down lap, only to run out of fuel by Gurney's parked Brabham at Stavelot. He sat there commiserating with the Californian, then suddenly heard on the public address that he had won; Peter Arundell picked him up and brought him back to the pits! Peter finished ninth while Amon had gone out after only four laps with engine failure, and Revson completed 28 laps but was disqualified for receiving outside assistance after some marshals had pushed him from the Clubhouse, where he had stopped, to La Source so that he could coast down towards his pit for attention.

The French Grand Prix followed this amazing event two weeks later, and Team Lotus took the Spa cars to Rouen-les-Essarts, all three being back on 13-inch wheels and tyres. Both Jimmy's R6 and R8 had the latest rear suspension geometry with the upper links picking-up on the upright at the same level as the upper radius rods, while on Arundell's R4 the older system was retained with the radius rods anchoring halfway up the upright. The Lotus 33's abbreviated engine cover was another point of recognition, with the Lucas fuel injection trumpets laid bare. The Parnell cars were both on 13-inch wheels and Hailwood was now recovered. Dan Gurney and Jimmy Clark dominated practice completely, the Lotus 25B finally taking pole position by 0.5 second, while Peter's similar car was on the second row once again.

Just before the start on a cloudy Sunday the mechanics suddenly spotted oil leaking from a cam-cover joint on Jimmy's engine and hurriedly larded it with 'goo'. By the end of the first lap he and Gurney were clear of the field and the Lotus gradually asserted itself, and drew away from the Brabham. Then, on lap 29 Jimmy felt his engine go onto seven cylinders as he came up the hill from La Scierie, and as he drew into the pits the green-and-gold Brabham whizzed by to take the lead. Jimmy retired after one more lap, for a piston had been holed, probably by an ingested stone.

Gurney won the race for Brabham-Climax while Peter had a torrid battle with Hill and Jack Brabham for second place, getting liberally peppered by dust and stones for his pains. He dropped back and took fourth place after another excellent performance for a number-two driver. Mike Hailwood was eighth after an overnight drive from Holland, where he had won another motorcycle Grand Prix and then been stranded by an airline strike, and Amon was tenth. Jimmy now had 21 World Championship points to Hill's 20, while Ginther and Arundell had 11 each and Gurney 10.

The following weekend poor Peter Arundell was critically injured in a Formula 2 accident at Reims, and seven days later Mike Spence took his place in the British Grand Prix, which was being run at Brands Hatch for the first time. Mike took over R4 while Jimmy had his usual choice of the 25B R6 or 33 R8. Gauze stone guards were fitted over the intake trumpets following the unfortunate Rouen failure.

The Parnell team ran their 25-BRMs for Amon and Hailwood, using R3 and R7, respectively, while Revson's 24-BRM was also entered under their wing. During practice the American Revlon cosmetics heir broke an upright over the bumps before Paddock Hill Bend and gently nosed into the bank, while Trevor Taylor had another high-speed accident in his BRP-BRM when his foot slipped off the brake pedal entering Hawthorns Bend, and he reappeared in the team's spare Lotus-BRM 24 next day.

The battle for pole position left dust and stones all over the circuit, but Jimmy's virtuosity scored again and he took pole by 0.2 second from Hill and 0.3 second from Gurney with a lap at 1min 38.1sec. Spence qualified on the outside of the fifth row, while Jimmy decided to race 'Old Faithful' R6 for the race.

Amon's clutch failed as the field left the dummy grid and a shunting match ensued behind him as up front Jimmy and Dan fled into Paddock Bend side by side. At Druid's Hairpin Clark's inside position gave him the advantage and he went ahead, but a short-circuit took the Brabham into the pits after only three laps, after which a grim race-long battle developed between Clark and the inevitable Graham Hill. Amon retired after ten laps, and on the fourth lap Hailwood bounded off over the grass at Bottom Bend, running over a photographer's camera case and tearing an oil line under the chassis. He pressed on for a few laps, but had to retire, as did Taylor, who was overcome by cockpit heat.

The leading Lotus and BRM rushed round with the gap opening and closing like a concertina, the long battle of concentration and endurance falling to Jimmy as he crossed the line to score a hat-trick of British Grand Prix victories just 2.8 seconds ahead of Hill. Spence felt his way round suffering fuel starvation and finishing ninth, while Revson pressed on steadily at the back of the field until his engine cried enough after 44 laps. Jimmy went into a four-point Championship lead over Graham, while Lotus-Climax now had a seven-point advantage over BRM with five more rounds to run.

There was only a week left to prepare the cars for the non-championship Solitude Grand Prix at the superb public-road circuit outside Stuttgart, where again Jimmy had the choice of the 33 or the 25B with 1964 suspension and 1963 steering, while Mike Spence had his 25B with 1963 suspension and 1964 steering. Trevor Taylor was out again in BRP's old Lotus 24-BRM, Hailwood and Amon had their Parnell 25-BRMs, Revson his Lola-bodied 24-BRM Special and Gerhard Mitter was signed-on to drive Team Lotus' spare car once Jimmy had made his choice. The Lotus entry was completed by the two Borgward-powered, Lotus 18-based BKLs of Ernst Maring and 'Joakim Parker', an American serviceman.

Although not entirely happy with its handling in practice, Jimmy elected to drive the Lotus 33 in its first race since the rebuild, and started from pole position 0.2 second quicker than Surtees' Ferrari, with Hill on the outside of the row, Hailwood on row two and Spence on row three. With Jimmy starting in R8, Spence took R6 and Mitter had old R4.

As the sun came out on a cold and wet race day the field did a reconnaissance lap and Hailwood spun into a ditch, bending a radius rod which was hastily replaced before the race. Jimmy plumed into an immediate lead, trailing a curtain of spray to hinder the pack behind him.

The wide Dunlop tyres aquaplaned on the flooded road, and halfway through that first lap Bandini's Ferrari broadsided and Brabham hit it, splashing into a ditch. Amon collided with 'Parker', and a stray wheel thumped Mitter's 25B, bending the track rod. Further on, Hill careered into a telegraph pole, Ireland crashed the BRP avoiding someone else's spinning car, and Anderson dropped his private Brabham into a ditch.

Fortunately, nobody was hurt, and Surtees closed his eyes and zipped through Jimmy's spray to take an increasing lead. But as the surface began to dry Jimmy fought back and repassed to win by 10.4 seconds at the end of the 20 laps.

Mike Spence survived that horrendous opening lap only to have the left-hand steering arm break, which put him off the road into a ditch with the left-front wheel torn off. Revson tip-toed round for fourth place, while Taylor finished a relieved sixth, Hailwood was ninth after another spin and a stop to replace loose ignition leads, and Maring was tenth; everyone was considerably relieved to leave Solitude after its last Formula 1 race.

Luckily there was a two-week break before the German Grand Prix at Nurburgring, which gave the teams a chance to repair the Solitude damage. A second Lotus 33, R9, was completed for Jimmy's use, and R8 was now intended for Mike Spence, while the 25B R6 was entered for Gerhard Mitter. Amon's Solitude car had been extensively damaged, and Parnell's demon mechanics had straightened the monocoque and strengthened it with riveted gusset plates. Meanwhile, Hailwood had had a two-wheeler accident and was nursing cuts and bruises, so was not looking forward to the arduous race round the Nurburgring. Revson was running his 24 Special once again, but was in early trouble when he spun and hit a tree.

Surtees took pole position by 0.4 sec from Clark in R9, but Jimmy led away through the woods on the opening lap. Back in the pack Hailwood stopped in a spreading pool of oil when his engine burst, and Mitter wetted some plugs and limped round to the pits for a change in R4. Revson's repaired 24 was also misfiring and he had a change of plugs while Surtees pushed ahead of the Lotus 33.

On lap three Gurney also forged ahead, and as Jimmy dropped into fourth place behind Hill's BRM he signalled despairingly to his pit. At the end of lap 8 the Lotus came into sight very slowly out of the Tiergarten and stopped at the pits where something was found to be wrong with the left-hand cylinder bank. When the number three plug was removed it was found to have been hammered by something inside; an exhaust valve had stuck open and been bent by the piston and inlet valve, and the camshaft drive pin had been sheared in the confusion. Earlier Jimmy had been finding fifth gear instead of third when changing up, and it seemed as though chassis flexing had been the cause.

At the half-distance mark Amon's was the best-placed Lotus down in seventh place, and as cars ahead retired he moved into fifth place before R3 began to handle peculiarly. The New Zealander stopped at his pit where the upper right-rear radius rod was found to be pulling away from the monocoque, and he retired on lap 13. Spence came home eighth, lapped, and Mitter was just behind in ninth place after his early delay. Revson was classified 14th, although he had disappeared out on the circuit just after two-thirds distance.

This result put Hill two points ahead of Clark in the World Championship with Surtees third, 11 points behind. Lotus-Climax still led the Constructors' Championship by one point from BRM, with Ferrari 14 points behind in third place.

One week later came the Karlskoga races in Sweden, this year demoted to Formula 2, and the Mediterranean Grand Prix took place in Sicily the following Sunday. Team Lotus produced R6 at Enna for Clark and R4 for Spence, while Parnell entered their usual cars for Amon and Hailwood and prepared Revson's 24-BRM Special. English clubman Brian Gubby journeyed down with his recently-acquired ex-UDT Lotus-Climax 24 (number 943) and Luigi Malanca entered a Cosworth-Ford-engined Lotus 27.

In practice Jo Siffert's Brabham-BRM took pole position ahead of Trevor Taylor's BRP and Jimmy's 25B, while Mike Spence earned a place on the second row and Brian Gubby went well in the old carburettor car to qualify only 0.3 second slower than Hailwood's R7, and 0.7 second slower than Amon's R3 on the third row. Later in practice Gubby ran wide round Revson on one of the slower curves, got on to some loose stones and ended up in the fencing, only slightly cut, but with his car rather bent and a non-starter.

Both the works cars carried gauze screens above the normal windscreens to trap flying stones, and at the start Jimmy and Mike out-accelerated the rest until Siffert swept through and latched on to the Champion's tail. Innes Ireland also pushed his BRP ahead of Spence, and on lap three Siffert dived into the lead.

On lap five Hailwood dropped his Lotus, spun wildly down the road and broadsided through the reeds on the inside of the corner to plunge into the lake. He waded out and stamped back to the pits while the leading quartet rushed round and round, Siffert and Ireland leading most of the time from the Lotus twins. In the second half of the race Jimmy set about Innes with a will and during the battle the BRP driver received a face-full of stones which smashed his goggles and cut his face.

This torrid struggle allowed Siffert to pull away, but before the finish the leading trio closed-up again and whipped across the line as one, Siffert winning by a tenth of a second from Clark, who was 2 seconds clear of Ireland. Spence had to stop for fuel two laps from the end and Amon slipped into fourth place just ahead of him, despite Mike's fastest-lap effort at 1 min 16.0sec, 141.49 mph. Revson was sixth and delighted to finish a race.

During August Parnelli Jones scored his first USAC win since the Indy '500' the previous year when he drove a Lotus-Ford 34 to victory at Milwaukee. He won 13,840 dollars for the 200-miler, but Foyt's second Lotus retired after only two laps with gearbox failure.

As in 1963 the Formula 1 teams drove North from Enna for the Austrian Grand Prix at Zeltweg, but this year the race was a Championship qualifier for the first time. However, when the frost-shattered concrete of the operational airfield circuit was studied most runners were horrified, for it was clear the wash-board circuit would prove a car breaker.

Team Lotus had R9, the Nurburgring car, on hand for Clark while R8 was turned over to Mike Spence and Jimmy's R6, which he had raced at Enna, was a spare. The old R4 was passed over to Parnell as a replacement for Hailwood's drowned Enna car, 'Mike the Bike' taking over Amon's normal R3 while Chris took the new car.

During practice Jimmy's left-front steering arm broke under the battering it received but the damage was repaired in time for Saturday's session. New drive-shafts, modified from Mercedes-Benz 220S units, were fitted on R9 for the first time, and these also appeared on Mike's car. Then Jimmy had another steering arm failure and Chris Amon yet another.

Team Lotus were fresh out of steering arms by this time, so parts were cannibalised from various sources, including BRP's spare Lotus 24. Both works cars started the race with mixed Lotus 24/25/33 steering gear, and Amon's car used the uprights and steering arms from Revson's Lotus, which was in the Parnell transporter on its way back from Enna.

All these problems meant that Clark started from third place on the front row, and as the flag was raised he found he couldn't find first gear. He was about to raise his hand when he found second instead and took off with tremendous wheel-spin. Hill had similar trouble in the BRM and both cars were engulfed as the pack swept away, ending the first lap with Graham 11th and Jimmy 12th. This set-back really fired Clark, who took Graham Hill, Phil Hill and Siffert on successive laps, then shot through a bunch including Ginther, McLaren, Bonnier and Ireland in two more laps to take fourth place. Amon's car started to handle oddly and blew-up shortly afterwards, while up front Surtees' suspension collapsed, leaving Jimmy third behind the works Brabhams. Clark then scorched past Jack, and began to close-in on Gurney, who was now 13 seconds in the lead.

By lap 27 Jimmy was within 8.5 seconds of the Brabham, but three laps later he felt a vibration from the rear of his car. On lap 40 a drive-shaft broke as he accelerated away from the hairpin and his race was run, while two laps later Mike's Lotus 33 suffered an identical failure to lose fifth place.

Hailwood had lost time in an early spin, but later inherited fourth place until a radius rod began to pull out and he had to make a stop for a repair. He finally finished eighth, the only Lotus survivor, while Bandini scored his first and only Championship round win for Ferrari.

None of the main Championship contenders scored points, but the constructors' standings were changed as BRM took a two-point lead from Lotus-Climax, with Ferrari closing-up, six points behind.

There were two weeks before the Italian Grand Prix at Monza, in September, when the Team Lotus 33s arrived in the Royal Park with strengthened Mercedes-type drive-shafts. Old R6 was on hand as a spare, and larger ball-joints were used in all the suspensions following problems at the Nurburgring and Zeltweg. The Parnell team were in a sorry state, for their Lotus 25s were now very tired after a hard season's racing, R3 in particular being in a dreadful state after Zeltweg, with the rivets fidgeting, ball-joints rattling and the car generally needing a complete rebuild. So they ran only one car, the ex-Team Lotus 25B, R4, at Monza, this car having been modified with one of Tim's own BRM V8 engines and a Hewland transmission. Hailwood was to drive it, while Amon

Above: Dan Gurney was not happy with his 1964 Indianapolis drive, and had many problems. Here he has an air deflector screen fitted, giving unobstructed forward vision. The ill-fated Dunlop tyres and offset suspension are clearly seen. Below: Star of the Show. Bobby Marshman's 'Pure Firebird Special' Lotus 29 set fastest race lap before retiring. This brilliant driver lost his life while testing later in the year.

stood down; Revson took over Chris' entry with his 24, but Gubby, who had entered his Lotus 24, stayed in England.

The works Lotus 33s were not quick enough in a straight line to hold the Ferrari and BRM opposition, and Jimmy set his best time in R6 to take his place beside McLaren's Cooper on row two, Spence being next fastest on row three with R8.

The start was scrambled when Hill's BRM clutch jammed on the line to put him out, and Surtees just went away as he liked from Gurney with Jimmy and Bruce scrapping for third place. By lap 25 the Cooper had fallen back and Jimmy was alone, but next time round his engine was stuttering and he retired with a broken piston. Mike Spence was running among the slipstreaming groups in mid-field, and he benefitted from retirements to move up the leader board. Towards the finish he had a close battle with Siffert's Brabham for sixth place, and led across the line to snatch his first Championship point by just a tenth of a second one lap behind the victorious Surtees. Revson was 13th and last, six laps down in his ancient car, while Hailwood's engine failed again after only five laps.

Surtees' win had rocketed him up the Championship table to within two points of Jimmy, while Hill's failure meant that his lead was still only two points ahead of Clark. Ferrari took over the constructors' table lead with 37 points to BRM's 36 (taken from their best six performances as the rules demanded) while Lotus were now one point further behind.

Three Formula 2 races followed before the serious business of the United States Grand Prix at Watkins Glen in October. Jimmy was down to drive R6 once again while the Lotus 33s were to be handled by Spence and the American veteran Walt Hansgen. The Parnell team were up to strength again with the ex-Arundell car for Amon and Hailwood back in his regular R7, dried-out and rebuilt following its Enna immersion.

After Jimmy had recorded equal times with R9 and R6 he chose his favourite car for the race and started on pole position, 0.13 second faster than Surtees' Ferrari, which looked unfamiliar in the blue-and-white colours of the North American Racing Team. Spence was on row three in R9, but he made a scintillating start and was second at the end of the lap, sandwiched between Surtees and Clark. But soon Jimmy was second and closing on the leading Ferrari as Hill and Gurney battled for third place after surging ahead of Spence. Jimmy took the lead on lap 13 and began to draw away in his characteristically smooth but shatteringly fast style. But on lap 40 Surtees began to close the gap and four laps later the Lotus charged into the pits where the fuel injection was adjusted. Jimmy rejoined, did six slow laps next to last, then stopped again with an injection filter blocked. Colin decided to call-in Mike and concentrate on constructors' points, and so Spence came in, losing fourth place, and took over the sick 25B, only to retire with injection trouble after 54 laps. Meanwhile, Jimmy forced R9 into third place but then a non-return valve stuck in the fuel system and

Top left: Peter Arundell, who made a brilliant start to his Formula 1 career before crashing at Reims, heads for fourth place at Rouen. Left: Dan Gurney and Jim Clark look remarkably happy after running out of fuel at Spa. Seconds later Jimmy heard he had won! Top: Clark's anti-roll bar comes adrift at Monaco. Above: Peter Revson's Lotus-BRM 24 always looked smart with its Lola bodyshell.

prevented fuel running into the collector tank, from which the fuel pumps picked-up. He stopped, but nothing could be done without stripping the system, and so he was out, although he was classified seventh after covering 102 laps. During all this drama Walt Hansgen marched on consistently and smoothly to score two points for fifth place, while Hailwood's oil pressure gauge line burst, and he stopped after 101 laps to be classified eighth and last. Amon went out on lap 47 when his car's starter motor bracket broke and damaged the engine after he had been running seventh and challenging Bandini hard for sixth place.

Graham Hill's win put him in the Championship lead with 39 points to Surtees' 34 and Jimmy's 30, while Ferrari's 43 points headed BRM's 42 and Lotus-Climax's 36 in the constructors' table. All now depended on the Mexican Grand Prix three weeks later, for the South African Grand Prix had been moved to

DUNLOP

Far left: Jimmy is elated with his third consecutive British Grand Prix victory. Left: First lap at Brands Hatch, with Clark already well ahead. Middle: Mike Hailwood's Parnell Lotus-BRM 25 suffers hay fever at Zeltweg. Bottom: One lap too many. Jim Clark lost his World Championship on the last lap in Mexico.

New Year's Day, and therefore would be starting the 1965 World Championship series.

In Mexico City Jimmy had his usual choice of R6 or R9, with the spare being earmarked for local man Moises Solana. The Lotus 33 was fitted with a new flat-crank Climax engine, which had a low-level exhaust system in place of the original high-level cross-over system exiting above the gearbox. Mike Spence had his usual R8, while Parnell's cars were as at Watkins Glen.

Jimmy proved fastest in practice in the low-level-exhaust car and he started on pole position, 0.9 second faster than Gurney's Brabham, but before the race the Mercedes-type drive-shafts were replaced by original rubber-coupled components.

Jimmy took the lead at the drop of the flag and drew away from Gurney, while Mike was driving hard for fourth place in his chosen R6, scrapping with Brabham and Graham Hill, whose goggles-strap had broken just as the flag fell. Hill's Championship hopes were dashed when Bandini spun him into a barrier and crumpled his exhaust pipes, while Mike dropped back after a brief spin. Jimmy looked all set to win the race and so retain his World title, but seven or eight laps from the end he saw a streak of oil round the hairpin and changed his line to avoid it. Next time round he saw another streak on the line he had just adopted, and he realised that the oil was his. He eased off, hoping to nurse the car to the finish, but a rubber oil line had split and the Lotus' life-blood was pulsing out on to the road.

In the pit Colin, Jim Endruweit and the Lotus crew were cock-a-hoop, ready to receive another winner and their second World title, but Jimmy came into sight to start his last lap with his hands despairingly in the air. Gurney shot by to win the race, and as Bandini was signalled to fall back, Surtees shot through to take second place, which was sufficient for him to clinch the World Championship. Jimmy's car seized out on the circuit, and was classified fifth, behind Mike Spence in fourth place. Solana was two laps behind, tenth, after a good drive in R8, while Hailwood went out early on with overheating, only lasting 12 laps by switching off and coasting along the straights! Amon lost first and second gears at the start, and lost 11th place when the remaining ratios disappeared after 46 of the 65 laps, while Jimmy set fastest lap at 1min 37sec, 95.14 mph.

So Jim Clark and Lotus-Climax were deprived of their World titles by another oil leak, as in 1962. Surtees took the drivers' title by one point from Hill and eight points from Clark, and Ferrari beat BRM and Lotus-Climax by three and five points, respectively, in the constructors' table.

Meanwhile, back in the 'States Bobby Marshman lapped Indianapolis at a record 161.4 mph while testing Goodyear tyres on his new Pure Oil Firebird Special Lotus 34, this being the car which Jones had driven to win at Trenton. Marshman had recently set a World closed-circuit record in the car on the Ford test track, and later he was to lap Indy at 162.3 mph, reaching 191 mph on the straights. But soon afterwards the brilliant young driver crashed heavily while practising at Phoenix in the Lotus-Ford, and died later from his burns, a tragic end to a potentially outstanding career.

Jimmy slipped a disc in a snow-ball fight at a Ford jolly in Cortina d'Ampezzo to celebrate the Cortina saloon successes during the 1964 season, and consequently was laid low for the Rand Grand Prix at Kyalami in December. Colin offered the number-one car to Jackie Stewart to enable him to make his Formula 1 debut, even though the promising young Scot had signed-up with BRM for the 1965 season in preference to accepting a Lotus contract.

Stewart accepted the drive before he took-up his BRM commitments at East London, and he drove Jimmy's 33 complete with flat-plane Climax engine to take pole position by 0.6 second from team-mate Mike Spence. Tony Maggs drove a Parnell 25-BRM and started on row two with a time 0.5 second slower than Mike, while local men Niemann, Pieterse, Lederle, Puzey and Hay ran their own Lotuses. Graham Hill drove the Willment team's Brabham, but missed practice so started from the back of the grid.

The race was in two 25-lap heats, and when Maggs' engine broke a camshaft on the warming-up lap it looked like a Lotus walkover, but Stewart's left-hand drive-shaft sheared as he left the line. Niemann spun in the confusion, ramming Pieterse's Lotus 21 and putting it out, but Mike Spence led until Hill screamed past on lap 23; Graham pulled out 3.3 seconds by the finish to win from the number-two Lotus-Climax.

Jackie's 33 was repaired for the second heat with five minutes to spare, and with grid positions decided by the first-heat results he had to 'do a Graham Hill' and drive through the field. Spence led from the start, but on lap 2 a ball joint failed and he slewed drunkenly out of the race. On lap 7 Stewart rocketed past Hill's leading Brabham-BRM, but Graham merely had to shadow him to win on aggregate, which he did. Technically speaking, Stewart's first two Formula 1 races resulted in a retirement and a win, but on aggregate he was nowhere. Brausch Niemann was the best-placed Lotus driver with fifth place, while Jackie set the fastest lap at 1min 36.0sec, 95.4 mph, to end a rather frustrating season for the team.

The works Lotuses contested all eight non-championship Formula 1 races, ten World Championship rounds and two USAC track races during the season, winning two relatively unimportant Formula 1 events, three of the title rounds and one of the USAC races. These six victories from 20 races constituted a not very good record compared with Team Lotus' all-conquering 1963 season, but certain other manufacturers must have looked with considerable envy on the achievement!

1964 RACING RECORD
Other formulae and classes

Team Lotus Ltd formed its own group in 1964, splitting itself into four separate operations while two outside organisations took on racing activities which the still compact racing section just couldn't handle. Team Lotus itself prepared and entered the Formula 1 cars, while Team Lotus Racing with Ford of Britain ran the new Lotus-Cortina saloons in selected British and European events. Team Lotus Racing with Ford of America looked after the Indianapolis cars and the Lotus 30 sports car programme in the United States and Canada, and probably the greatest administrative problem of them all was Team Lotus Racing with English Ford Line (Dearborn). This built and entered Lotus-Cortinas in selected American events for a wide variety of 'guest drivers', and while Ray Parsons looked after the cars and commuted regularly between Cheshunt and the United States, Andrew Ferguson drove himself mad trying to keep tabs on all his contracted drivers. Outside organisations were Ron Harris' Formula 2 team, and Ian Walker's sports car operation for Britain and the Continent.

The beginning of the 1964 season saw the wind of change blowing through motor racing, as Formula Junior died and was replaced by two separate divisions, Formula 2 and Formula 3. Formula 2 allowed 1 litre engines of virtually free design, while Formula 3 demanded production-based 1 litre units, retaining such features as standard valve-gear operation and breathing through single-choke carburettors. This was a reasonable arrangement, for it gave two divisions which offered a logical progression towards Formula 1 in terms of power, speed and cost.

Lotus showed little real interest in Formula 3, as it represented a considerable step-down in power from Formula Junior. The old Lotus 22 design was polished up, fitted with engines to customer choice and called the Lotus 31, but during this initial season, when everybody was feeling their way into the new formula, only a dozen cars were built.

But Formula 2 was a different matter, for an important new Grands Prix de France Championship series of races was planned, in addition to Britain's Autocar Championship. Colin supervised the development of a new monocoque car, based closely on the all-aluminium Lotus 27. Changes included the use of 16-gauge steel sheet panelling, and a redesign to incorporate two nine-gallon rubberised fuel tanks within the hull sides. The front suspension was slightly modified, with wider-based lower wishbones, and front uprights came from the Lotus 24/25 Formula 1 cars. The rear suspension had been subjected to a long, hard look, and the new geometry owed more to Brabham than to previous Lotus practice. The upper radius rods were mounted on top of tall uprights, and were no longer parallel to the lower rods as on the Lotus 27. Full suspension adjustment was provided, as its lack on the earlier Formula Junior car had proved a serious drawback. Power came from a brand-new Cosworth SCA—the first Cosworth-designed as opposed to Cosworth-modified engine. This was a four-cylinder 998 cc over-square unit, very distantly based on a Ford block, with twin valves per cylinder operated by a single gear-driven overhead camshaft. Power output was around 115 bhp, and the engine was canted at about 25 degrees in the chassis, giving a near-vertical induction tract from the two Weber 40DCM2 downdraught carburettors.

Lotus Components built a total of 12 Lotus 32s, and the car made a successful debut in the Pau Grand Prix, the first event of the new Formula, when Jim Clark scored his third victory in the French round-the-houses race. The works cars were run by Ron Harris, and as the season progressed the team worked up to a full four-car strength. Jimmy, Peter Arundell, Mike Spence and Peter Procter were the original drivers, but Jackie Stewart, Brian Hart and John Fenning also had outings during the year. In all the team scored seven wins with the Lotus 32s, Clark taking the honours at Pau, the Eifelrennen, Mallory Park and Brands Hatch, while Mike Spence won the Formula 2 division of the Aintree '200', Brian Hart won at Enna and Jackie Stewart at Snetterton.

The tragedy of the year undoubtedly was at Reims, where a huge slip-streaming battle developed for the lead. Jimmy felt that it couldn't be long before somebody went off as there was a lot of pushing-and-shoving within the pack, so he held back and was soon proved very wise. Peter Arundell suddenly put a wheel on the grass on a fast sweep, spun back across the road and was rammed by Richie Ginther's Lola. His Lotus somersaulted over a bank and Peter suffered severe injuries which effectively put an end to his successful racing career.

Jackie Stewart had proved the undisputed king of Formula 3 in a Tyrrell Cooper-BMC, and Ron asked him to try a Formula 2 drive at Clermont-Ferrand, the next French Championship race after Reims. Later Colin asked Jackie to join the Formula 1 team for the Solitude Grand Prix on the same day, but the shrewd Scot stuck by his agreement with Harris and took the Formula 2 drive. He went very well, and finished second to Denny Hulme's Brabham, and later in the season he won the Vanwall Trophy race at Snetterton, then ended the year with a fantastic battle with Jack Brabham at Montlhery. As the cars rushed for the line to start their last lap 'Toto' Roche waved encouragement with his chequered flag. Jackie thought the race had finished and as he hesitated for one fatal moment Jack was away, and Stewart could only tail him to the line to score another second place!

Jack Brabham ended the season as the French Formula 2 Champion, and of the 18 major races that year his cars won nine, Lotus seven, and Lola and Cooper one each. Mike Spence clinched the relatively unimportant Autocar Formula 2 Championship in his Ron Harris Lotus, but this was based purely on home events. Early in the season, before the new Lotus 32s became generally available, Peter Arundell ran a twin-cam Ford-engined Lotus 27, and other older cars which appeared during the year included John Fenning's Lotus 27—fifth at Aspern—Frank Gardner's Willment 22—third at Aspern—and Roy Pike's 22—sixth at Crystal Palace. David Prophet drove a private Lotus 32, which later he swopped for Jacques Maglia's Brabham, but neither driver had much success with the car.

In Australia Leo Geoghegan scored a series of successes in his new Lotus 32, while Les Howard took over his old Lotus 27 and progressed from strength to strength. Frank Matich was overlord of down-under sports car racing with his very quick Lotus 19, and although Brabham influence was growing the Cheshunt cars were still widely popular. Leo's brother, Ian Geoghegan, won the New South Wales Sports Car Championship in a Lotus 23.

Progress during the first season of the new Formula 3 depended almost entirely on the engines being used. Cosworth had concentrated on development of their SCA Formula 2 unit, and had left the Formula 3 field clear for other developers and tuners to do their best with Ford engines. BMC A-series power units proved to be the engines to run that year, and the works-prepared BMCs fitted to Ken Tyrrell's Coopers were virtually unbeatable. Jackie Stewart and Warwick Banks spreadeagled the opposition in a fantastic season, and Lotus won just one of the 36 major European events. This was at Silverstone, where John Fenning used a Janspeed-prepared engine to beat a rather low-class field.

Most of the Ford Formula 3 engines were sleeved-down ex-Formula Junior units, while Holbay were rapidly developing a new downdraught conversion which was to oust the ancient BMC products the following year. Leading Formula 3 Lotus drivers of the year included Piers Courage and Jonathan Williams, who shared a pair of Lotus 22s under the banner of Anglo-Swiss Racing, and prepared and maintained them in Chuck Graemiger's garage at Lausanne. Harry Stiller ran a Lotus 27 until he blew-off the opposition at Monza to such effect that his engine was stripped and found to be oversize, while Frenchmen Jean-Paul Behra and Phillippe Vidal, Italians Luigi Malanca and Franco Ghezzi, and American-in-Europe Bruce Eglinton all ran Formula 3 Lotuses and were consistently well-placed.

In the Argentine Temporada Uruguayan Alberico Passadore drove his newly-acquired Lotus 27 too quickly in an early event at Buenos Aires and was killed, while Italian hope Bruno Deserti was much more circumspect with his similar car and achieved some excellent placings, although sadly he, too, was later to lose his life at the wheel of a racing car.

The year saw a tremendous resurgence of sports car racing in Britain, mirroring the American adoption of 'big-banger' V8-engined cars. Lola were working on a new car and Colin laid down some original plans for his new challenger—the Lotus 30. It was to be a disaster!

Len Terry, often brutally frank, was against the car from its inception, but Colin's drive forced the programme through. The new car was based on a back-bone chassis similar in shape to that used on the Elan. The centre back-bone was a deep box-section girder, considerably flanged and baffled for stiffness and panelled in 20-gauge mild-steel sheet. It was only 6 inches wide at the top, 9½ inches at the bottom and 12 inches deep. A rubberised 13-gallon fuel tank resided within this back-bone, and two further nine-gallon tanks could be added within the door sills of the one-piece glass-fibre bodyshell. Like the Elan, this sat astride the back-bone as a saddle, and with a total tankage of 31 gallons the car had a range of about 180 miles.

At its front end the back-bone carried a transverse box section which picked-up the front suspension, while two prongs diverged at the rear to provide mounts for a 4.7 litre (289 cubic inch) Ford V8 engine. Lotus arranged to buy these from Ford in 271 bhp Hi-Performance trim, and adopted a four downdraught Weber carburettor system with other modifications to produce around 350 bhp. This was transmitted through a five-speed all-synchromesh ZF transaxle, and the highest available final-drive ratio of 3.00 to 1 gave a theoretical maximum speed of 200 mph!

Front suspension was by unequal-length double wishbones with interposed coil-spring/damper units, and at the rear a change from normal practice was the use of upper wishbones, with reversed lower wishbones and lower radius rods on either side which passed through slots cut in the chassis 'prongs'. Four-spoke 13 inch wheels, developed from the Indianapolis designs, were fitted all round, enclosing Girling 11 inch solid disc brakes. The wheelbase was 94½ inches, track front and rear 53 inches, overall length 165 inches and overall width 68 inches. In final Series 2 form the Lotus 30 weighed 1530 lbs. Twin radiators were fitted behind nostrils in the nose, set at an angle so that exhausted hot air escaped into the low-pressure area in the wheel arches.

Problems encountered with the new design were numerous, but after a long prototype build-and-development period the first car was delivered to Ian Walker-Team Lotus, who were to run it alongside their beautiful 'Gold Bug' Elans. Jim Clark raced it for the first time in the Aintree '200' meeting, where the car was finished-off in the paddock with a sign stuck on the tail reading 'Together we Chose a Lotus 30' in a parody of a contemporary Morris Minor advertisement!

Bruce McLaren won the race in his newly-acquired Cooper-Climax with Jimmy second in the new Lotus. George Pitt's old Lotus 19 was fourth, and at Silverstone two weeks later John Coundley's 19 placed third in another McLaren benefit. Jimmy scored the Lotus 30's only major win at Mallory Park against meagre opposition, and later in the year Tony Hegbourne totally destroyed the prototype car in practice at Brands Hatch. The car somersaulted at

Dingle Dell and completely disintegrated although its likable driver walked away with minor injuries.

This was a terrific blow to Ian Walker, for earlier in the year Mike Spence had written-off the team's special-bodied Le Mans Elan at the Nurburgring, and chief mechanic John Pledger had fallen seriously ill. With only a few home Internationals left to run there was little time to sort-out new cars, and so the team withdrew and sold-off their remaining Elans. These had been driven with tremendous verve by Peter Arundell and by Mike Spence, who occasionally drove for the opposition in the Chequered Flag team cars, with which Jackie Stewart also made a great name for himself during the year.

The first Transatlantic outing of the Lotus 30 was in the Canadian Grand Prix at Mosport Park, where Clark stalled on the grid, then retired after four laps with overheating. Team Lotus then took a new Lotus 30 to California for the professional races in October, and Jimmy was third at Riverside (where Bobby Unser's Chevrolet-powered Lotus 19 was sixth), and Dan Gurney's special Ford-powered Lotus 19B was second at Laguna Seca. The Riverside race was hilarious, for the starter held the cars on the grid with their engines running while Jimmy tried to find a gear in the Lotus 30 on row two. While the engines overheated and tense drivers became irate, the Lotus gearbox eventually surrendered and engaged a gear, so the starter waved his flag and away they went. One car blew-up immediately going into the first corner, and when the pack thundered into the turn next time round they raised a huge cloud of cement dust which had been laid down to soak-up spilled oil. Two cars collided and one smashed into the guard rail, so the organisers hurriedly hung out the red flag and prepared to restart the race.

They then figured that the front-row cars would raise an impenetrable cloud of cement dust into Turn One, so eschewing the use of their modern sweeping equipment the official helicopter was brought in to blow the excess dust away. This was too much for the Arciero Brothers' pilot, and he took-off in their private chopper and got in on the act—blowing away the dust. He then contrived to collide with some overhead cables, and his fragile craft plummeted to earth slap in the middle of the track!

He was uninjured, and a flock of marshals rallied round to manhandle the crippled helicopter off the circuit. They took hold of its damaged runners and heaved it off the deck, whereupon one of the runner brackets broke and the chopper collapsed back to earth, laying out one of the marshals with the tip of a rotor blade. He was carried off to recover his senses and eventually, after a carnival act which would have done credit to a Palermo bus queue in the rush-hour, the race got under way!

One of Jimmy's best performances in the works car, before it expired with brake trouble and suspension failure, was at the last Goodwood TT when he led McLaren narrowly for many laps. But generally the car was plagued by overheating—cured by re-piping the radiator system—and poor brakes. The rear suspension was carried on a bridge-piece bolted between the chassis prongs and carrying the gearbox as well. This meant that any transmission work necessitated removing the suspension, and in the revised Series 2 design which was finalised at the end of the season this bridge-piece was dispensed with. As production progressed it was found that the first three chassis were not stiff enough, and 18-gauge panelling replaced the original 20-gauge sheets in all subsequent cars.

At Laguna Seca Gurney's Lotus 19B was placed second, and Billy Krause was fourth in a Lotus 30 entered by Bob Challman, Lotus' US West Coast Distributor; the day before Krause had scored the Lotus 30's first American win in an amateur event. Bobby Unser drove the Arciero Brothers' Chevrolet-engined Lotus 19 and won the consolation non-qualifiers' race. Dan Gurney's associate, Jerry Grant, was racing a Bardahl-backed Lotus 19-Chevrolet for Alan Green at this time, and Bob Bondurant also appeared in a V8-engined Lotus 19.

Above right: Acrobatic Arundell and the works Lotus-Cortina. Far right: Lotus-Cortinas lead the field at Brands Hatch. Right: Sir John Whitmore was to become European Touring Car Champion once he and the Lotus-Cortina were in tune. Below: Formula 2 Lotus-Cosworth 32, Mike Spence at the wheel. Bottom: Hollow victory. Clark and the Lotus 30 won at Mallory but against minimal opposition.

58
BJH 419B

LUCAS
146

BTW 297 B
19

The first Lotus 30 to be sold in Britain went to David Prophet, who took it on a strenuous South African tour and had to have a new chassis on his return. Simon de Lautour and Vic Wilson also had Series 1 cars, and both had their problems. A total of 33 cars were built before production stopped, and they sold at £3,495 in component form. This was quite inexpensive, for Roy Badcock, then Production Manager of Lotus Components, found that each car took some 600 man-hours to construct. The chassis had to be assembled extremely precisely, and a Promecam guillotine and spot-welder both had to be purchased to process the numerous small panels which formed the back-bone.

In touring car racing Team Lotus excelled with their latest Lotus-Cortinas driven by Jim Clark and Peter Arundell. Jimmy scored maximum points in all eight qualifying rounds of the BRSCC's British Saloon Car Championship, and while he and Peter rushed round—inside front wheels waving high in the air—the similar Willment team cars of Frank Gardner and Bob Olthoff were never far behind. These Lotus-Cortinas were always impeccably prepared and were very, very fast.

Initially the cars suffered from severe understeering characteristics, but much development work was carried out on the steering and front suspension. With thick anti-roll bars fitted they became very predictable and 'chuckable' through the corners, although their tendency towards lifting front wheels could cause sudden instability. Only the huge Ford Galaxies proved capable of beating the Lotus-Cortinas, and the Jaguars, which so recently had dominated British and European saloon car racing, were totally eclipsed.

While Team Lotus' touring cars contested the British Championship, Alan Mann Racing mounted a Ford-sponsored assault on the European Touring Car Challenge. Sir John Whitmore, Peter Procter, Henry Taylor and Peter Harper all drove the cars regularly, while Tony Hegbourne stood-in on occasions. Whitmore drove the winning car at Zolder, Karlskoga, St Ursanne and Timmelsjoch, while Henry Taylor won the Mont Ventoux mountain climb. Whitmore and Peter Procter co-drove the winning car in the Brands Hatch 6-Hours, but the European title finally went to Warwick Banks' works Mini-Cooper. Chris Craft drove a bright orange Lotus-Cortina early in the season, but creased it at Goodwood, and Mike Spence took over the second Team Lotus drive after Arundell's Reims accident; he ended his touring car season on lap 13 of the final Oulton Park race, when he rolled his Cortina into a ball at Esso Bend!

Ford's EFLO programme saw Dave Clark driving one of the team's Lotus-Cortinas into second place in the Road America '500', with another team car, shared by David Hobbs and Chris Craft, finishing third. In the USRRC feature event at Indianola Ken Miles' Cobra won only narrowly from Sir John Whitmore's Lotus-Cortina, and Henry Taylor's similar 'sedan' was second in the class!

Although the Americans normally ran the EFLO Lotus-Cortinas out of category as straightforward Ford publicity exercises, the big Marlboro' 12-hours race saw a serious three-car attack directed in person by Colin Chapman. Drivers were Tony Hegbourne/ Sir John Whitmore, David Hobbs/Dave Clark and Jackie Stewart/Mike Beckwith who actually won after three hours' torrential rain at an average of 53.5 mph!

Down-under, Jim Palmer and Paul Fahey won the Wills Six-Hours at Pukekohe, driving a Lotus-Cortina, and a similar car was second crewed by Ronnie Moore and Ray Thackwell. In the Sandown Six-Hours Palmer shared a car with Jackie Stewart, but the Lotus-Cortina was put out after a good showing when the big-end bolts sheared. Jackie also drove a Lotus-Cortina in South Africa in a supporting race before the Rand Grand Prix (the occasion of his Formula 1 debut) and was placed second behind a Ford Galaxie.

Lotus-Cortinas won National Championships both in racing and rallying virtually wherever Ford cars were sold, and at the end of the year Ford ran a 'jolly' to Cortina d'Ampezzo for their successful drivers; it was during this frolic that Jimmy slipped the disc whilst snow-balling which put him out of the Rand Grand Prix, and Sir John Whitmore belted a Cortina down the vertically-banked bob-run!

In slightly more mundane surroundings the club racing scene was, as ever, rich in Lotus successes. Peter Gethin won the Guards Sports Car Championship conclusively in his Lotus 23, and Rodney Banting's Formula 3 Janspeed-powered Lotus 31 won the BRSCC's '500' Trophy. Sverrir Thoroddsson, an Icelandic pupil at the Russell school, won the MRC Club Championship in another Lotus 31, while Jack Pearce and Alan Rollinson both shone in Formule Libre racing with their twin-cam-powered Lotus 22s. Chris Summers shoe-horned a 5 litre Chevrolet V8 engine into an ex-Formula 1 Lotus 24, but found he had problems in putting all that power through to the road, while Melvyn Long did well in his Formula 3 Lotus 27, and Tony Dean, Barrie Hart and Mo Nunn dominated the larger sports-racing classes with their Lotus 23Bs.

Racing Elans flooded the circuits, the outstanding performers being Jackie Oliver, John Lepp, Malcolm Wayne, Sid Taylor and Dick Crosfield. Mike Beckwith drove Chris Barber's pale green car, complete with golden trombone motif on its side, to several successes but concentrated mainly on the major meetings, in between his Normand Team Cooper Formula 2 outings. In club events Lotus-Cortinas could not challenge free-formula Anglias on a power-to-weight basis, but Peter Boshier-Jones shone once more in hill-climbing with his supercharged Lotus 22. He was second in the RAC Championship to Peter Westbury's four-wheel-drive Ferguson.

As the 1964 racing season drew to a close news of more Lotus successes flooded in from all over the World, as work went ahead at Cheshunt on new and updated designs for the coming season . . .

1965

Rocking the establishment

1965 was to be the final year of the 1.5 litre Grand Prix formula, and consequently Colin set about the spade work for providing Team Lotus with a new 3 litre engine for 1966. Coventry-Climax announced their withdrawal from racing in February, when they also released details of their latest 1.5 litre flat-16 engine; this was the unit for which the Lotus 39 was built, but it was still-born and never raced.

Climax had been taken over by the Jaguar Group, and their new design and development commitments were such that the marginal racing activities had to be shelved. At the time their engines had powered 86 winners in International Formula 1 races since 1958, and had appeared in every successful Lotus Grand Prix car during that period.

Colin's close and long-lasting ties with Cosworth Engineering made Keith Duckworth an obvious choice for the design and construction of a suitable new engine. 'I asked Keith if he could produce a Grand Prix engine and he thought he could so I offered to find the money to finance it. He said he'd need £100,000 and I shopped around in several places. On first contact with Ford they didn't want to know, so we then had meetings with David Brown of Aston Martin in London. He was very interested, but he wanted far more control of the project that Keith was prepared to give him; he virtually wanted to buy Cosworth. Then we tried Macdonald of the British Sound Recording company, and there were several other interested parties, but we didn't really seem to be making much progress. We'd virtually made our minds up to go back to Brown and Aston Martin when I was invited to dinner one night with Harley Copp (Ford of Britain's Vice President in charge of Engineering). I said 'Look, you're missing-out on the best investment you have ever made . . . for £100,000 you can't go wrong'. He thought that was nothing like enough to get initial work done, but I managed to convince him it was and that Keith was really someone special. Harley went back to Walter Hayes (Director of Public Affairs) and within a few days it was all under way . . .'

An agreement was drawn up between the Ford Motor Company, Cosworth Engineering and Keith Duckworth allotting £100,000 for the design and development of Ford Formula 1 and Formula 2 engines for international racing. The 1,600 cc Formula 2 unit, intended for the new class coming into effect in 1967, was to be designated the Cosworth FVA and be based on the Ford 120E cylinder block, while a 90-degrees V8 3 litre unit was to be evolved from it for Formula 1 use. Cosworth and Duckworth were to develop the FVA during 1966 and produce at least five engines for racing during 1967, while at least five Formula 1 units were to be built by January 1, 1968. These were to be supplied to Ford, who would equip one Formula 1 team of their own choice.

Colin had wanted a long-term commitment clause written into the contract regarding Lotus' sole use of the engine, but Ford at that time felt they could not undertake such an obligation. Consequently, Walter Hayes wrote him a formal letter of intent, and Lotus were to become the original team of Ford's choosing.

Meanwhile, another agreement had been reached with BRM, concerning the production of racing twin-cam engines. The Bourne concern were to build a series of these power units for use in the Lotus-Cortina, the Elan and suitable single-seaters. Production was to be at the rate of about five units per week, and BRM were also to overhaul customers' engines. Delivery was to start at the end of February, and the BRM-built Lotus-Ford twin-cams were to be identified by dark racing green cam covers. At the same time the seeds were sewn for a Grand Prix engine agreement, and this was finalised when Team Lotus ordered new 3 litre H16 engines to tide them over pending the delivery of the first Cosworth-Ford units. BRM engines had appeared in Team Lotus' second-string cars on and off for several years, and they were intended to introduce the marque to the 3 litre Formula in 1966, but things didn't quite work out that way . . .

In more mundane forms of racing the Lotus stand at the Racing Car Show was packed with interesting exhibits. These included the latest version of the Lotus-Cortina, with more attention to weight-saving, an optional rear anti-roll bar as standard, and stronger con-rods in the 145 bhp 1,600 cc twin-cam engine. A Special Equipment road-going variant was also announced, with a 117 bhp engine, while the 1965 competition Elan (the Lotus 26R) was shown with the latest twin-cam engine as in the Cortina and many detail improvements to body and chassis. Rear suspension revisions accepted wider wheels and larger tyres, while more Rose joints in the suspension aided maintenance and gave greater adjustability. The old vacuum-pump-operated pop-up headlamps had been removed, and were replaced by perspex-shrouded small-diameter Lucas units. Dual-circuit brake hydraulics were adopted, with an adjustable balance bar, and the chassis was stiffened.

After the fiasco at Indianapolis in 1964, Ford of America were very circumspect about their Lotus contract for the 1965 race. Leo Beebe negotiated the deal with Chapman and Clark, and all the old bonuses were gone in a single lump sum out of which Lotus had to pay their drivers and their expenses.

A brief experimental exercise was undertaken involving an Indy car with De Dion rear suspension, the idea being to keep the tyres vertical on the bankings, but it was complex and slow, and was quickly shelved.

David Lazenby flew out with his new Lotus-Ford 38s in April, when they were scheduled to make their debut at Trenton driven by Jim Clark and Roger McCluskey. In practice McCluskey's throttle jammed open and he just went straight on into the wall at one of the turns and damaged the car severely. Rather than risk the other car Team Lotus scratched their entries for the race and headed straight to Indianapolis. The number-two car had to be rebuilt and was held back as the spare, while the original third car was properly prepared and took over second-car duties.

There were 68 cars entered for this year's '500', 45 of them rear-engined and 25 using Ford V8 engines. Gus Scussel, now in charge of Ford racing engine development, was confident of his progeny's power and reliability, but he objected violently to the way in which he saw his engines being misused by many teams' mechanics. The official Ford racing history states that '... The Lotus mechanics were among the major offenders, and since this was the factory team they naturally caused the most grief ... '! It goes on to criticise Lazenby's men for taking a hammer and chisel to the engines to provide clearance for a snug fit in the chassis, and blames them for a 'dangerous modification' of the throttle linkage which they felt caused McCluskey's Trenton accident.

Lazenby admits that some metal was cut back on the engines, but not in quite the crude haphazard way inferred by Ford's historian, while the throttle problem was quite another matter. The linkage used was a modified version of the original 1963 system, and a 60-thou end-float was provided on one of the spindles to allow for engine expansion when running hot. On McCluskey's engine this end-float had not been provided by Ford's assembly, and as the engine heated-up and expanded during Roger's first few laps, so the spindle tightened and eventually jammed—unfortunately it jammed open, but it was hardly a Lotus problem ...

After a rather unhappy qualification period in 1964, and his final withdrawal from the race, Dan Gurney decided to go it alone in 1965, and had a new Lotus 38 backed by Yamaha and entered by All-American Racers—the concern recently founded by Gurney and Carroll Shelby of Cobra sports car fame. The choice of a second driver to back-up Clark was a problem, although Jones, who had driven the Lotus 34s so well in post-Indy events the previous year, was an obvious contender. Unfortunately J.C. Agajanian wanted a big stake in his driver's ride, and with the prospect of three major sponsors for the one car the deal was dropped. Colin finally enlisted Bobby Johns, a veteran stock car pilot, and he drove a consistent and safe race in the second car ... for the first time there were two green-and-yellow Lotus-Fords in the '500' and both finished. When the cars had appeared at the Speedway for the first time the superstitious traditionalists had thrown up their hands in horror at the green cars and their green-overalled mechanics ... green was an unlucky colour at the Speedway. But now Jimmy's superb victory did much to remove the superstition.

Times had changed, too, for one man in particular—Len Terry, who was flown out of Indianapolis and out of Lotus almost immediately the race was over. He joined Gurney and Shelby at AAR, and designed their original Eagles which were to become the Ford Indy works cars in 1966 in an attempt to score an All-American victory for the Dearborn engines.

Team Lotus had a change-round when Jim Endruweit became Racing Manager in charge of their technical side, while Dick Scammell became Chief Mechanic. Andrew Ferguson continued to deal with Team Lotus logistics, bookings and dealings, in addition to running the Formula 1 Constructors' Association in his 'spare' time.

The Lotus incident of the year in the fullest sense of the word was the 'Zandvoort International'—Chapman versus Police. Colin's scuffle on the grid after one of the patrolling policemen had failed to notice the pass tied to his belt was followed by a large contingent asking him to accompany them to the station after the race, which Clark had won. Dick Scammell: 'He was sitting on the pit counter, and the Police were in the back of the pit ordering him to go along. When he refused, they grabbed him and there was the old man roaring 'come on lads'. We had his feet while the coppers had his head and arms and we were all tugging away. Hazel Chapman had one of the Police by the hair and I thought I was doing all right with another one pinned to the wall until somebody else grabbed me under the chin from behind and pulled me backwards over the pit counter. After that I didn't think it was such a good idea.

"Anyway, we all calmed down a bit, and the Police took Colin up to the race control tower where some of the Club officials agreed to go with him to plead his case. Colin wanted us to stay near him, otherwise he thought he'd disappear without trace, and I was standing right beside him in the tower when this big

The Lotus Elan Coupe was a logical development of the basic theme, with very pretty fixed-head styling and many former 'extras' as standard. Above: Centre-lock knock-on disc wheels and chromium-plated bumpers improved external appearance, while the interior (below) was much improved with deep-pile nylon carpeting, more comfortable seats and electrically-wound windows.

bloated chap tried to push in between us. I elbowed him back to stop him separating us, but he pushed in again and so I trod on his toe. He got very angry at this and stamped on mine, which was a mistake because he was wearing sandals and I had my big working boots on, so I retaliated and nearly crippled him, whereupon it started all over again!' Peace eventually was restored, but the incident ended with Chapman spending the night in jail and being fined £25 for assault. Police should not be allowed to run sporting events . . .

Further troubles at Indy were caused when Jones' Lotus broke a rear upright and crashed, causing the USAC Safety Committee to stop the Lotuses running until new uprights could be made. Colin complained angrily that the breakages were on old cars out of works hands, with many new parts fitted, but it was no use and all his cars had to be fitted with revised, heavier components.

In September the Lotus 36 was released. This was the new Elan Coupe, with a pretty fixed-head body and interior modifications including deep-pile nylon carpets, electrically-wound windows and more comfortable seats. Chromium-plated front and rear bumpers became optional extras, while centre-lock knock-on wheels and Dunlop SP tyres were standard. Another option on the Coupe only was a 3.55:1 axle ratio for long-legged cruising. This was mated to a Lotus-Ford close-ratio gearbox with lower first and second gear ratios to maintain acceleration times associated with the standard 3.9:1 final-drive. An air of luxury had been added to the original Lotus tenets of speed, performance and pure race-bred handling, but the Elan was still the only car to put a G-meter off the clock when it was mounted crossways in the car and recorded cornering force!

That same month saw modifications to the Lotus-Cortina, which reverted to leaf springs at the rear in place of coils and dispensed with the A-bracket location. This had caused diff-case distortion and these modifications softened the ride and made the car rather more civilised.

In December the company decided to run a final small batch of Elites in component form less engine and gearbox to clear their stock of body shells, and simultaneously work began on the new Lotus factory. Further expansion was virtually impossible at the current site at Cheshunt, just as it had been at Hornsey back in 1959, and the ideal site was found at Hethel Aerodrome, near Wymondham in Norfolk. There a factory and office block could be combined with a private test track and landing field for the Chapman aircraft, and a £300,000 contract was awarded to build the facility. The factory was to be a 151,000 square foot single-storey building of tubular steel construction with brick walls and aluminium cladding. A fully air-conditioned 26,000 square feet open-plan office was included in the specification, and the target date for completion was October, 1966.

Chris Rawlinson took his glass-fibre body-building section out of Factory 6 at Cheshunt and set-up shop in existing Hethel buildings at about this time, and acted as site co-ordinator on the project while building the prototype Europa and Plus 2 shells.

Lotus were poised on a springboard, ready to venture into a new factory, with new production car plans, and ready for another interim season at the start of a new Grand Prix formula. Once again they had the World Championship titles to their credit, and their racing successes were mirrored by new record production and turnover figures. The total of 2,352 cars produced included 1,234 pure Lotuses, plus 1,118 Lotus-Cortinas. Turnover was up from £1,573,000 to £2,030,000 and profit from £113,000 to £154,000 . . . the company was going places fast.

Third time lucky. Right: The Wood Brothers' pit crew help Jimmy on his winning way at Indy. Below right, top to bottom: The works Lotus-Ford 38s of Jim Clark and Bobby Johns, and Dan Gurney's 'Yamaha Special'. Far right: Johns finished seventh. Bottom right: The Lotus 38 was well offset. Below: Colin Chapman sees a dream come true.

LOTUS POWERED
ENCO
ENCO
T A TIGER
YOUR TANK!
LOTUS
82

82

ENCO
PREMIER

LOTUS
FORD
83
YAMAHA SPL.
17
GOODYEAR

82

Above: An unusually subdued Colin Chapman tries the prototype Lotus-Ford 38 for size at the Cheshunt press showing. Len Terry's full monocoque design included stressed panelling enclosing the driver's legs and a well enclosed cockpit. The outer part of the air deflector screen has yet to be fitted. Below: Same day, same place. The second and third Lotus 38s near completion.

1965 RACING RECORD
Grands Prix and other major formulae

The new World Championship series opened well for Jim Clark and Team Lotus when the South African Grand Prix took place at East London on New Year's Day. A third Lotus 33–R10–had been completed ready for this race for Clark while Mike Spence took over R9. Parnell entered a lone BRM-engined 25–R4–for Tony Maggs, private 21s were entered for Lederle and Pieterse while Clive Puzey had his old Lotus 18. Brausch Niemann and Dave Charlton were in their over-engined Juniors and Jackie Pretorius hoped for a race in his 18.

Jimmy set the fastest time in all three practice sessions, while Charlton, Pretorius and Puzey all failed to better the required 1min 37sec qualification time. Mike Spence found the hairpin very troublesome and spun three times in succession during practice, while Lederle, Pieterse and Niemann also failed to qualify for the race, which meant that all the local Lotus drivers were out of their own Grand Prix.

Jimmy took an immediate lead from pole position, and Mike nipped through from the second row to trail him away from the pack. On lap 43 Mike spun again at the hairpin, which allowed Surtees to catch up and eventually to pass him when he spun again on lap 60. Graham Hill also scratched past as Jimmy went on to win by 29 seconds from Surtees with the BRM third and Mike a further 22.6 seconds down in fourth place. Maggs stopped to have his brakes bled, but finished eight laps down in 11th place, so that all the Lotus starters completed the race. Jimmy won at a record average of 97.97 mph and set a new record lap of 1min 27.4sec, 100.33 mph.

The Tasman series began the following weekend with the New Zealand Grand Prix at Pukekohe, and after a three-year absence Colin decided to return to the series. A single car was entered for Clark, who was provided with a Lotus 32 Formula 2 chassis, modified about the engine bay to accept a 2.5 litre Coventry-Climax four-cylinder FPF engine, which was enclosed in a tall humped cowling.

Jimmy won a preliminary 12-lap race as he pleased from Lex Davison's Cooper after McLaren and Frank Gardner had both spun off on oil, Bruce's Cooper disappearing into a water-filled ditch.

The main race was over 50 laps, and Jimmy blasted away from pole position with McLaren alongside in his second team Cooper, but at the hairpin Bruce clipped the Lotus 32's tail and spun it round and out of the race with buckled rear suspension. John Riley drove the best-placed Lotus, the ex-Shelly 2.5 litre 18/21, into fifth place.

The Gold Leaf International Trophy followed at Levin on January 16th and Jimmy led the eight-lap preliminary from start to finish to take pole position in the 28-lap main race. He scored a decisive win, setting a new lap record of 49.9 seconds on the way.

Next weekend Jimmy scored his second successive victory of the series after leading all the way in the Lady Wigram Trophy at Christchurch. He also won the 25-mile preliminary race, setting a new record of 1min 25.9sec, but this was equalled by McLaren's Cooper later in the day.

This success gave him the lead in the Tasman Championship by three points from Frank Gardner's private Brabham, and one week later he increased his advantage at Invercargill by winning the Teretonga Trophy race. He set a new record of 1 min 1.7 sec in the preliminary heat and in the afternoon's 75-miler he lapped all but Bruce McLaren in second place. But Bruce earned his revenge in a crowd-pleasing flying-start six-lapper at the end of the day, which he won from Clark's Lotus and the Brabhams of Graham Hill and Kerry Grant.

When the Tasman contenders arrived in Australia for the Warwick Farm '100' outside Sydney in February the local Brabham peddler Frank Matich surprised the visitors by taking pole position and leading away from the start. But Hill and Clark soon forged ahead, and although Jimmy lost third gear in the Lotus 32B, the car responded well as its fuel load tightened and he took the lead from Hill's red Scuderia Veloce Brabham on lap 36. After breaking the lap record repeatedly Jimmy left it at 1min 33.7sec, 86.35 mph, and took a long lead in the Tasman Championship.

Sandown Park at Melbourne was the next stop, and the opening race of the day saw Leo Geoghegan's Team Total Lotus 32 beating Roly Levis' Brabham in a 1.5 litre event. Jimmy led the main race from the middle of the front row until Brabham forged ahead in his own car, but Jimmy led again from laps 16 to 19 before Jack re-established the lead and held it to the finish to score his first win on Goodyear tyres. Jimmy had to ease off as his oil pressure sagged, but retained second place to clinch the Tasman title, his lead of 33 points to the 15 shared by Gardner, McLaren, Brabham and Jim Palmer being unassailable.

At Longford, Tasmania, the new Tasman Champion was seventh in the preliminary race and a tardy fifth in the Australian Grand Prix, his hard-used engine being well down on power. The Lakeside '99' near Brisbane ended the tour early in March, but Jimmy and the Team Lotus 32B were the only 'names' to make the 1,000-mile trek North from Longford. Matich led for the first 19 laps until he made a pit stop and handed Clark the race, the Lotus 32B winning from Gardner's sick Brabham and setting fastest lap at 54.9seconds, 98.36 mph.

In between races Jimmy had earned his pilot's licence down under and it was a bronzed and happy Scot who appeared at Brands Hatch one week after Lakeside for the first non-championship Formula 1 Race of Champions.

The race consisted of two 40-lap heats with an overall result on aggregate, and Team Lotus took their three cars down to Kent for Clark and Spence, the spare car having an old high-level exhaust engine and running experimentally on Goodyear tyres while the other two had low-level systems and were on the usual Dunlop rubber. The Parnell team were back up to strength with their 25-BRMs for Richard Attwood and Mike Hailwood, and Dickie Stoop had bought the ex-works Lotus 33, R8, for Paul Hawkins, the rugged Australian driver, the car being entered in DW Racing Enterprises' bright green colours.

Lap times at Brands Hatch mirrored the accelerated development of tyres which had resulted from the intrusion of the American Goodyear and Firestone companies into what had been a Dunlop preserve for many years. Jimmy's 1min 34.9sec lap was the first ever at over 100 mph at Brands Hatch, and was 3.6 seconds under his 1964 lap record.

Graham Hill and Mike Spence were also on the front row for the start of heat one, and the Lotus pair went straight into the lead. Gurney started from the fifth row after practice problems and was boxed in at the start, but he fought his way through the pack and by lap 13 he was third and starting an assault on Spence's second place. Mike held him off for ten laps, but then the Californian charged past and finished 20 seconds behind Jimmy after sharing fastest lap with him at a record 1min 35.6sec. Attwood just pipped Siffert on the line for tenth place, but Hailwood shunted his Parnell-entered Lotus 25 at South Bank. Hawkins was a reserve driver for this heat, but ran in the second heat to make his Formula 1 debut.

All Jimmy had to do in the second race in order to win on aggregate was simply follow Gurney but instead the Lotus and Brabham drivers went for the lead tooth-and-nail, with Mike trailing again in third place. Jimmy led by the narrowest of margins until lap 11 when Dan nosed inside him at South Bank, but couldn't quite get through. He tried again round the outside at Paddock Hill Bend on the next lap, but Jimmy held on round the inside at Druids, and then was outside again round the left-handed Bottom Bend where, under Dan's pressure, he ran wide and understeered on to the grass. He fought to pull the car back on to the road as it bounded across the infield, but the wheels suddenly hit some ruts and the Lotus hurtled head-on into a bank protecting the back of the pits. Poor R10 bounded into the air and crashed to earth completely wrecked, while Clark hopped out unhurt though winded and shaken.

Gurney took the lead, only to drop out with engine trouble, and although Jack Brabham came off the better in a dice with Spence he, too, retired when an oil pipe split, and so handed the heat, and with it the aggregate victory, to Mike Spence and Team Lotus. Mike won the heat by 6.8 seconds from Bonnier's Walker Brabham, and on aggregate from Stewart's BRM and Bonnier after a cool and intelligently paced drive. Attwood's first drive for Parnell ended when a water hose burst, and Hawkins also dropped out in Stoop's Lotus 33.

At the beginning of April Team Lotus again contested the Syracuse Grand Prix, where Jimmy arrived with the latest Lotus 33, R11. Spence was in his Brands Hatch-winning R9, and Innes Ireland re-appeared in a Lotus as team-mate to Mike Hailwood in the Parnell Lotus-BRM 25s. These had been modified during the Winter with revised rear suspension, the geometry of which was closer to Brabham than Lotus practice, with the radius rods mounted closer together on the monocoque. Collomb and Wicky ran their venerable Lotus 24s once again. Clark took pole position by 0.3 second from Surtees' Ferrari, while Siffert and Bonnier shared the Walker team Brabhams and pushed each other to faster performances with the Swede also ending up on the front row.

But it was Siffert who took the lead at the end of the first lap, with Surtees, Clark and Spence charging after him. Jimmy lay third watching Surtees and Siffert swopping the lead until lap 46, when Siffert changed into fifth as the rear wheels momentarily bumped clear of the road, and instantly over-revved and burst his engine. Surtees' engine lost its edge and so Clark took over the lead and by the finish had pulled out 42 seconds over the Ferrari.

Mike ran fourth until he lost first gear, which slowed him out of the hairpin and consequently reduced his maximum speed down the straight which followed. Bandini caught and passed him in the second Ferrari and in trying to regain his place Mike spun into one of the stone walls which lined the circuit, demolishing the Lotus 33's right-front corner. Hailwood's ignition cut-out momentarily at the hairpin and caused him to ram the wall, and Ireland's transmission broke. Jimmy set the fastest lap at a record 1min 46.0sec, 116.07 mph.

Two weeks later the beautiful Goodwood circuit was the scene of its last Formula 1 race after running major-formula events since 1948. Jimmy's Lotus 33 appeared with the brand-new four-valves-per-cylinder Climax V8 engine, but Stewart's BRM took pole position from Graham Hill, with Jimmy's Lotus on the outside of the front row. Graham led for six laps until the Lotus streamed ahead, and although it was hard-pressed by the BRMs and Gurney's Brabham it was never headed, winning at a record average of 105.07 mph and sharing the lap record of 1min 20.4sec, 107.46 mph, with Stewart. This was to become the perpetual Goodwood lap record, for the Formula 2 cars which raced there in 1966 were considerably slower, and the circuit was then closed to racing.

Mike Spence had been fourth quickest in practice only 0.2 second slower than Clark, but his metering unit failed on the warming-up lap and he failed to make the grid. Richard Attwood was sixth in a Parnell Lotus-BRM 25 while Paul Hawkins, who was having his second race for Dickie Stoop in the bright green Lotus 33, retired early with a massive oil leak.

The next Formula 1 race was the International Trophy at Silverstone in May but as this was also one of the Indy qualifying weekends Jimmy and Dan Gurney

Tasman Championship. Above: Seconds before the start of the Warwick Farm '100' outside Sydney, Australia. Jimmy's Lotus-Climax 32B is on the outside of the front row, with local man Frank Matich on pole position and Graham Hill alongside in a similar Brabham. Jack Brabham himself and Bruce McLaren (Cooper) are next up. Below: Clark and Hill had a great race at 'The Farm', the Scot winning and setting a new lap record despite losing third gear.

were both in the United States running the new Lotus-Ford 38 USAC cars. Len Terry had designed the new cars to Chapman's parameters, and around the many changes in specification dictated by the revised regulations for the '500'. The monocoque hull now wrapped round the driver's legs and up behind his shoulders, and the use of gravity refueling systems in place of the outlawed high-pressure methods meant that the multiple fuel cells of the past had disappeared. Three tanks took their place, two in either side of the hull and one under the seat pan. The wheelbase remained unchanged from the Lotus 34 at 96 inches, but the track was increased to 60 inches and the suspension's assymmetry was increased to 3 inches with the hull offset to the left. The Lotus 38 was 156 inches long overall and 31 inches high, and weighed just over 1,250 lbs—the minimum limit. Girling 12½-inch diameter disc brakes were used, and changes to the Ford V8 double-overhead-camshaft engine allowed the use of alcohol fuels and a boosted output of 500 bhp, delivered through two-speed ZF transaxles. The cars had run poorly in the Trenton '100' in April when Roger McCluskey badly damaged one in a practice shunt, and the whole Ford-powered contingent were humbled in the race by Offenhauser-powered cars.

But in Indy qualifying the picture was brighter, for five Lotus-Fords took the first five places on the grid. A.J. Foyt's modified 1964 Lotus 34, dubbed the Sheraton Thompson Special, was on pole with a four-lap average of 161.233 mph, with Jimmy Clark alongside in the Lotus 38 at 160.729 mph; Dan Gurney's blue and white Yamaha Special Lotus 38 was on the outside of the front rank at 158.898 mph. Row two consisted of Parnelli Jones' Agajanian-Hurst Special Lotus 34 at 158.625 mph and Al Miller in Jerry Alderman's old ex-Marshman Lotus 29. Miller was later relegated by rookies Mario Andretti and Billy Foster in a Brabham-based special and a Vollstedt, respectively, but the scene was set for a Lotus '500' success.

Meanwhile, at Silverstone the valuable 32-valve Climax engine was held over in Jimmy's absence, and Mike Spence ran his usual R9 while the Mexican sports car driver, Pedro Rodriguez, took over R6. Mike qualified fifth fastest overall, which at Silverstone put him on the inside of row two, while Pedro was back on the middle of row four 0.1 second slower than Attwood's Parnell 25. Hailwood and Hawkins, in Parnell's Lotus-BRM 25 and DW Racing's Lotus-Climax 33, respectively, were on row five.

The race resulted in Stewart's first Formula 1 win for BRM, beating Surtees' Ferrari and Spence's Lotus 33, while Pedro led the second group throughout and came home a pleased and popular fourth in his first European Formula 1 race. His consistent and smooth drive much belied a rather wild and unruly reputation, and presaged great things to come.

The Memorial Day '500' was to be run the day after Monaco, and this clash of dates led Team Lotus to miss the second round of the World Championship in favour of the lucrative American event. Only 17 runners

arrived in Monaco to contest the 16 places on the grid, amongst which were Tim Parnell's usual pair of Lotus-BRM 25s, R3 and R7, for Attwood and Hailwood. The team also had R4—now completely rebuilt—as a spare.

Jochen Rindt's Cooper was the unfortunate non-qualifier at Monaco, while Attwood was his usual smooth and unspectacular self in taking the inside of the third row of the grid, while Hailwood was back on row six and Paul Hawkins had put Stoop's Lotus 33 behind the Parnell car on row seven.

Hailwood's gearbox broke after 11 laps, and when running sixth after 44 laps Attwood's left rear suspension collapsed, the wheel and brake fell off, and the car crashed into the bales at the Gasworks. Attwood was unharmed, but this left Hawkins in the sole surviving Lotus, and he, too, left the race on lap 80 when he misjudged the chicane, hurtled into and through the bales on the quayside, and plunged into the harbour! Paul switched-off the engine as the bright-green Lotus ditched, and he was hauled into the rescue boats in moments. The car was salvaged that night, and the Australian's presence of mind in switching-off was found to have saved the engine from serious damage; it was exactly ten years since Alberto Ascari's Lancia had gone into the drink at the same point.

At Indianapolis the Lotus trend had been followed enthusiastically by many of the USAC establishment, and 17 of the 33 starters were using Ford V8 engines.

Top left: Lotus-Brabham duels characterised the Tasman Championship. Here Clark, Matich and Hill join battle. Left: Mike Spence scored his first Formula 1 victory in the non-title Race of Champions at Brands Hatch, after Jimmy 'retired' (above).

Jimmy led on the opening lap, but Foyt soon stormed ahead, only to be repassed by Clark in the green-and-yellow car on lap 3. He led all the way apart from nine laps after scheduled fuel and tyre-change stops, and set such a fierce pace that Foyt was almost a lap behind in second place when his transmission failed after 116 laps.

Gurney's Yamaha Special Lotus 38 duelled for third place with Jones' year-old car until he ran into clutch trouble on lap 42. Jones took second place after A.J.'s retirement and eased right off towards the finish as his fuel ran low. Andretti closed-up so much that Parnelli dared not stop for replenishment, and to his relief he just lasted the distance before running out on the

Four in a row! Jim Clark drove the 32-valve Lotus-Climax 33 at Silverstone to win his fourth consecutive British Grand Prix in 1965. Above: The Lotus' front-end layout seen here at Becketts Corner makes an interesting comparison with the original 1962 Lotus 25. Below: Back end, same car, same race. The 32-valve engine's flat-crank configuration gave this neat low-level exhaust layout, and a characteristic whistling exhaust note.

cooling-off lap, making it a Lotus one-two. Bobby Johns drove the second works Lotus 38 into seventh place.

Jimmy came home to a fantastic ovation from the 350,000-strong crowd to win the prestigious Indianapolis '500' at his third attempt, and Al Miller was a fine fourth in the Jerry Alderman Special Lotus 29. Colin's wisdom in hiring the Wood brothers stock-car racing pit crew to handle Jimmy's car was shown in his magnificently brief pit-stop times—19.8 and 24.7 seconds. His 40-lap average speed exactly equalled the 1964 race record of 149.334 mph, and thereafter he went quicker. The 50-lap quarter-distance mark was passed at a record 152.153 mph (the old figures were 146.981 mph), and the 100-lap average was still 5 mph up on the old record, at 152.185 mph. Jimmy won the race at an average of 150.686 mph, and the team collected over 150,000 dollars for his day's work. A special prize for the 'Best-Dressed Pit-Crew' also came Lotus' way, with Dan's Yamaha team taking the award in their natty turquoise-and-black shorty kimonos. Carroll Shelby topped-off this fine example of functional elegance with a tall-crowned hill-billy stetson!

The following month the jubilant Team Lotus arrived at Spa-Francorchamps determined to make good after their enforced omission of Monaco, and three cars were unloaded from the transporter. The latest Lotus 33, R11, carried the 32-valve Climax engine for Clark, and R9 was fitted with a flat-crank, low-level-exhaust V8 for Spence. The spare car used an earlier Climax with the original high-level exhaust and 90-degree crankshaft, and all three cars were hastily converted to knock-off wheel fixings in the paddock. The Parnell team were running Attwood and Ireland in their cars, Dickie being in the rebuilt R4 while his Monaco wreck was still having the creases ironed-out. Hailwood was away at the Manx TT motorcycle races, so Innes was standing-in for him.

Jimmy qualified his car on the middle of the front row, sandwiched between his age-old rival Graham Hill and new boy Stewart in their BRMs, but Spence had a troubled time and couldn't better the centre of row five, 0.6 second quicker than Attwood on the outside. Ireland was two rows back, 4.2 seconds slower again.

The BRM pair had hoped to 'shut the door' on Jimmy into the first corner at Eau Rouge, but he forced Stewart to back-off and was on Hill's tail going up the hill.

It was miserably wet and Stewart fell back in the spray along the Masta Straight as Clark's personal radar took him plunging through the murk past Hill and into the lead. The BRM was handling impossibly on the slippery surface, and as Jimmy pulled away Hill dropped back through the field. The Lotus 33's 32-valve engine sang its raucous song for the complete 32-laps distance, enabling Clark to win by 44.8 seconds from Stewart. Mike Spence was hampered by running Dunlop R7 tyres, which would have been an advantage if the road had flooded but which tended to skate badly in the damp, and he finished seventh.

Once again Dickie Attwood was performing well, but the race was to turn sour on him. He had been scrapping with Spence until the 28th lap, when he went into a big slide leaving the 'S'-bend at Masta hamlet in the middle of the straight, half-caught it, then broadsided into a telegraph pole. The car was almost cut in two and caught fire, and Attwood was very lucky to escape with bruises and mild burns. Ireland finally finished 13th and last in the other Lotus-BRM 25 after an unhappy race.

Two weeks later the Formula 1 circus moved into the Auvergne where the French Grand Prix was to be held for the first time on the fabulously acrobatic Charade circuit in the mountains outside Clermont-Ferrand. Team Lotus' three cars were as they appeared at Spa, while Chris Amon rejoined the Parnell team as replacement for the injured Attwood. Ireland was still standing-in for Hailwood, who was still concentrating on his two-wheelers.

Jimmy had not been out for long, finding his way round this testing mountain circuit, when his rear suspension collapsed and Surtees gave him a lift back on the Ferrari; nevertheless he finished the day fifth fastest on his first visit to the Charade.

Great mirth was caused when Ireland's Lotus 25 broke its transmission. He hitched a lift on Bonnier's Brabham, which immediately ran out of fuel, the pair of them finally returning on Ginther's Honda which toured in on the bump-stops!

During final practice Jimmy lapped in 3min 20.1sec before his 32-valver broke, and the niggled Scot then settled down to real business in old R6 and took pole position with a storming 3 min 18.3 sec, quicker than Stewart. Mike took his place on the outside of row four after he had tried too hard on new tyres and spun into a bank, bending his Lotus 33's suspension. It was straightened-out overnight, while R6 was race-prepared for Clark.

Jimmy made his usual brilliant start and rushed away from the field, despite nursing the old engine as much as possible. By half-distance he was holding a steady 15-seconds lead over Stewart's BRM, which was suffering from excessive understeer, and he had almost doubled his lead over the BRM by the end of the race. On the way he set a new lap record in 3min 18.9sec, 90.69 mph, and left the race record at 89.2 mph.

Mike Spence ran seventh before moving up into fifth place, then he lost control when his injection pump suddenly missed a beat in the middle of a fast sequence of bends and spun to a halt, luckily without hitting anything. He restarted in eighth place and was seventh at the finish, depsite being plagued by misfiring for the latter part of the race. Chris Amon's Lotus 25 was shunted in the tail by Rindt's Cooper, but he continued after a quick check only to retire after 21 laps with fuel-feed problems. Innes' sister car had dropped out two laps earlier with the transmission stuck in gear, but at least Parnell had two intact cars to take back home.

This result gave Jimmy a 10-point lead in the World

Championship over Hill and Stewart, and Lotus-Climax now headed BRM by two points in the constructors' competition.

The British Grand Prix followed at Silverstone, where Team Lotus were aiming for their fourth consecutive victory in their home event. Jimmy had managed it in Belgium; now for the British.

Jimmy and Mike began practising in 'Old Faithful' R6 and R9 while R11 was at Cheshunt having a new 32-valve engine intalled, replacing the damaged French Grand Prix unit. Amon and Ireland were in the Parnell cars once again, and Brian Gubby appeared briefly in his old Lotus-Climax 24. Paul Hawkins was to have run the dried-out Dickie Stoop Lotus 33, but he crashed it in unofficial practice earlier in the week.

Jimmy was quickest in R6 on the first day until Hill took just 0.1 second off his time, and then in the final Friday session Clark wound-up R11 with its new engine and immediately annexed pole position with 1min 30.8sec, 0.2 second quicker than Hill.

Little Richie Ginther booted his Honda into the lead at the start, but Jimmy surged ahead on Hangar Straight and began a classic drive in which he was trailed by Graham Hill in a grim repeat of the previous year's race-long battle at Brands Hatch.

Surtees held third place in his Ferrari for many laps, with Spence and Stewart pressing him hard, and then on lap 41 Mike went ahead while the BRM dropped back. Surtees retook third place shortly afterwards but Mike hung on determinedly in the second Lotus.

Jimmy looked all set for another demonstration drive, but after 60 laps the Lotus' engine began to develop a misfire as it howled past the pits. Hill began to pile on the pressure in response to pit signals, and as the misfire became more pronounced Graham gained about 3 seconds per lap.

Then, to add to his problems, Jimmy noticed that his oil pressure was falling through the corners. The new engine's oil consumption was higher than anticipated, and as the tank level dropped surge was taking the oil away from the pump pick-up. Jimmy had to ease-up to save his engine, and with five laps to go the gap was down to 15.5 seconds. On lap 76 it had fallen to 13 seconds; on lap 77 it was 11.5 seconds and Hill had been baulked. But the next lap the gap was only 9 seconds, and as Jimmy came past to start his 80th and last lap his engine sounded dreadful. Hill's BRM rocketed sideways out of Woodcote on full power only 5 seconds behind, and Jimmy was coasting through the corners, tyres whistling eerily, to save his engine. The tension was almost unbearable during that final lap, until Jimmy coasted round Abbey Curve, gave a final burst of power up towards Woodcote and coasted across the line to score his fourth consecutive win in the British Grand Prix. Hill's brakeless BRM crossed the line 3.2 seconds behind after setting a new record time on that last desperate lap in a real do-or-die effort.

The smooth-driving Mike Spence finished a good fourth, while Attwood was 13th and last in his Lotus-BRM 25 while Innes Ireland had retired the team's other car after 42 laps with engine trouble.

Jimmy now had 36 points to Hill's 23, and in the constructors' contest Lotus-Climax had pulled away from BRM with 36 points to 31.

There was only a week between the British and Dutch Grands Prix, and Team Lotus arrived in Zandvoort with their usual three cars, R11's 32-valve engine having been hurriedly rebuilt at Coventry to correct its oil consumption problems. It consumed a lot of oil in practice, however, and Jimmy took over Mike's R9 with 16-valve flat-crank engine for the race, and Mike fell back on R6, now also using a flat-crank engine. These troubles allowed Hill to take pole position by 0.3 second from Clark, while Ginther equalled Jimmy's time in the Honda and formed-up on the outside of the front row. Mike started from the outside of row three, 1.2 seconds slower than his number-one, and Ireland's Lotus-BRM 25 was two rows behind, while Dickie Attwood, back in the second Parnell car, was right at the back of the grid.

A dummy grid was used, as was now standard practice, and as Colin walked across for a final word with his drivers the local police failed to notice his pass tied to his belt and tried to manhandle him off the grid. He retaliated, there was a brief skirmish, and Colin then broke away to his pit behind a line of green-overalled mechanics . . . and the race began.

Ginther made a scorching start and led out of Tarzan for the first two laps, but then first Hill and thenClark rushed by. Jimmy took the BRM on lap 6, whipping ahead under braking for the hairpin, and immediately began to pull away. For the fifth time this season he was to win a Grande Epreuve, this time by a clear 8 seconds from Stewart's BRM and Gurney's Brabham. Spence and Ireland both had lurid spins behind the pits, continuing in ninth and tenth places until the last lap, when Bandini's Ferrari jammed in second gear and Mike nipped by to steal eighth place on the line. Attwood, still subdued by his Spa accident, was a steady 13th. Jimmy's race average of 100.87 mph was another record, as was his fastest lap of 1min 30.6sec, 103.83 mph.

After this handsome win the German Grand Prix at the beginning of August looked all set to decide the World Championships. The three regular Team Lotus cars were prepared for the race, R11 with the 32-valve engine for Clark, R9 with a long-stroke engine for Gerhard Mitter. Innes Ireland stepped down from the Parnell team due to a family bereavement, and Chris Amon joined Attwood in the team, Mike Hailwood having returned to motorcycles after a none-too-happy dabble with Grand Prix racing. The only other Lotus entry was the DW Racing Enterprises 33 for Paul Hawkins.

The 1964 lap record stood at 8 min 39.0 sec, and in the Friday morning practice Stewart bellowed round at 8min 30.6sec in his BRM, but this electrifying performance was well and truly put in perspective once Jimmy had sorted-out R11, for in the afternoon session he put together an incredible 8 min 22.7 sec lap—16.3 seconds under the old lap record!

All oiling problems with the 32-valve engine seemed to be cured, and Jimmy took the lead from the start, set a new lap record of 8min 36.1sec on his standing lap, lowered it to 8min 27.7sec on his first flying lap, and just ran away from the field. Graham Hill did his usual magnificent job in pursuit with the BRM, and on lap three he and Jimmy set a joint record of 8min 27.4sec, but on lap 10 the Champion-apparent lowered these figures by a further 3.3 seconds to average 101.22 mph, the best of the race, on his way to his sixth Championship victory of the year, his second World drivers' title and Lotus-Climax's second Constructors Championship success. Team Lotus had won each of the six title rounds entered during the season, and when Jimmy, GrahamHill and Dan Gurney did a victory lap of the circuit in an open Mercedes tourer they received a tremendous reception from the 300,000 spectators among the hills of the Eifel.

Mike Spence had been running fourth and leading a huge midfield bunch when his car's left-hand drive-shaft spider sheared after eight laps, and the Lotus 33 clattered to a halt. Mitter rushed into the pits with steam pouring from the underside of his car where a water hose had been ground off by continual bottoming, and Dick Attwood stopped early with misplaced wiring in his ignition system, continued briefly and then had a similar failure. Chris Amon also stopped early on with electrical problems, then had Hawkins retire alongside him with a massive oil leak. Chris borrowed the DW car's transistor box and pressed-on until this box burned-out, just as he came round to where Spence's car lay abandoned. He borrowed a second transistor box from this car, but something in the system was causing the failures and when this one burned out as well he gave up.

Two weeks later the new World Champion appeared in the Mediterranean Grand Prix at Enna, where Team Lotus produced R6 for him and R9 for Mike Spence. Chris Amon was in Parnell's venerable R3 and Innes Ireland was back in harness driving a special Lotus-BRM '25' which had been built up from spares, and the car was given number R13. Lotus allocated R12 to their own new Lotus 39 chassis which lay around in the works awaiting the Coventry-Climax flat-16 engine which had been promised for the 1965 season, but which was suffering insurmountable development problems.

Before practice began on the Saturday the works mechanics had a bad fright when R6 burst into flames while being fuelled, and although the flames were quickly smothered the old car was well roasted. All the damaged components were speedily replaced, but one of the skins was distorted by the heat and when Colin arrived he thought the car should not be run. However, Jimmy tried it gently and said that it felt OK, so it was raced after all.

Jimmy started on pole position, having lapped 0.4 second faster than Mike, with 1964 winner Jo Siffert on the outside of the row. Siffert and Spence led from a scrambled start, in which Clark found third gear and staggered off the line, but within five laps he was back into third place, although he couldn't catch the leading pair who were slipstreaming each other round at a terrific speed. Mike was signalled to 'HOLD P2', and as he eased the pressure Jo slowed and Jimmy caught them, taking second place ahead of Mike on lap 26. Almost immediately Mike was hit between the eyes by a flying stone, and momentarily blinded he ran wide on one of the curves, clipped the bales and spun crazily across the road, toppling over the inside bank and subsiding gently upside-down in the reeds. The marshals made little real attempt to lift the car, and Mike was taking a lot of weight on his head until two mechanics rushed to the scene and heaved the car upright; he was rescued bruised and rather peeved, but otherwise OK.

Meanwhile Clark got ahead of Siffert, but Jo timed his final spurt brilliantly and led across the line to win by a mere 0.3 second in the Walker Brabham—and in 1965 beating Jim Clark alone deserved a medal!

Ireland and Amon had been running sixth and seventh, but swopped places until Chris stopped with a misfire. He rejoined on Innes' tail, only to have his engine cut dead on the fast corner before the pits where Trevor Taylor had crashed two years previously, and the Parnell Lotus 25 took a header into the bales. Amon was unhurt and watched as Ireland lost fourth place to Denny Hulme's Brabham on the last corner of the race, finishing inches behind.

On the way home Jimmy stopped off at the Swiss International hill-climb at St Ursanne-les Rangiers, where he ran the Indy-winning Lotus 38 fitted for the occasion with symmetrical suspension and a five-speed ZF gearbox. The World Champion made six climbs in the wet, fighting all the way to record a best time of 2min 13.1sec. Jo Siffert followed his Enna success by clipping 3.6 seconds off this time, to set FTD at an average speed of 81.4 mph and collect another trophy in the dark blue Walker car.

The last European race for the 1.5 litre Formula 1 cars was the Italian Grand Prix at Monza in September. Jimmy was in R11 with 32-valve Climax power once more, Mike's R9 had a flat-crank engine, and Italian FJ/F3 exponent Giacomo 'Geki' Russo took over old R6, which had a high-level cross-over exhaust engine refitted. Ireland and Attwood reappeared in Parnell Lotus-BRM 25s, R13 and R3, respectively.

Jimmy took his customary pole position by 0.2 second from Surtees' Ferrari, while Mike was on row three and 'Geki' on row eight with his car liberally plastered with 'Salumi Rondanini' salami adverts.

The race developed with Jimmy and Jackie Stewart sharing the lead, and Hill's BRM, Gurney's Brabham and Surtees' Ferrari challenging hard all round the circuit. Mike Spence dropped away from the leading bunch in seventh place, and behind him Attwood and Ireland were towing the mid-field bunch along with both Parnell cars going well.

BRM began to monopolise the lead with their two

cars until Jimmy's traffic ability took him ahead when they caught some tail-enders. Surtees stopped with clutch failure to give Mike a firm sixth place, but 'Geki' dropped out after a sensible Formula 1 debut when his final-drive lost its oil and the crown-wheel and pinion broke up.

Jimmy let the BRMs go ahead again and sat behind them working out his tactics for the final dash to the line, but on lap 63 the BRMs howled past the pits with daylight between them and the Lotus, and next time round they were alone. Jimmy's electrics had failed, killing the high-pressure fuel pump and stopping the engine, and he coasted to a stop on the back of the circuit to post only his second Formula 1 retirement of the season. Almost simultaneously Mike's rectifier burned out and his electrical system also failed. After a while both were able to persuade their cars back into life and limped into the pits to retire, but the race was a gift to the BRMs, Stewart scoring his first Grande Epreuve victory from Hill.

Ireland and McLaren pulled away from their group, and Innes had a magnificent race until his fuel pumps refused to pick up the last remaining gallons in his tanks and he was reduced to limping round with the engine spluttering, hoping he could make it to the finish; he finally finished ninth while Dickie Attwood took a fine sixth place. Jimmy was classified 10th and Mike 11th on distance covered before their retirements.

After a string of Formula 2 races ended the European season Team Lotus were back at Watkins Glen in October for the United States Grand Prix, and after the Monza reversal Jimmy was hoping to equal his record of seven Championship round wins in a season. He was again to race R11 with the 32-valve engine, Mike Spence was in his regular flat-crank R9, and the spare R6 with its older engine was turned over to the Mexican Moises Solana, making his first Formula 1 apearance outside his home territory. Ireland and Attwood were in their usual Parnell Lotuses so it was again a five-strong Lotus entry.

Both Jimmy and Dan Gurney suffered recurrent oiling problems with their multi-valve V8 engines, and while R11 was being attended-to Jimmy took out Mike's car in Friday practice, found fourth gear instead of second entering the tight right-hander by the pits and thumped over the kerb to spin-off on the grass. This caused great amusement in the pits, and glee in the BRM camp for Graham Hill had just set fastest lap!

Jimmy lapped faster on Saturday, but Graham replied still faster and took pole position by 0.1 second. Gurney's troubles were insurmountable, so he had the 32-valve engine taken out of his car, and when Jimmy's stripped a timing gear parts were cannibalised from the Brabham unit.

From the start Jimmy and Graham shot out of sight in line-abreast, and the Lotus finished the lap sandwiched by the two works BRMs; Mike was running fifth behind Bandini's Ferrari. On the second lap Graham ran wide at Pits Bend and the green-and-yellow Lotus flashed through into the lead, but Graham later repassed, and then the new Champion surged ahead until lap 12 when the BRM passed in the lead as Jimmy peeled off into his pit. His hastily rebuilt engine had broken a piston and burst in a cloud of blue smoke. Mike had lost his sixth place when his timing chain broke and he clattered into the pits, and poor Ireland, who was suffering from 'flu and feeling decidedly ropey, retired after leaving the road twice.

This left only two Lotuses, and while Attwood stopped to complain of bad handling, finally finishing a tardy 10th, Solana trundled round slowly and consistently for 12th place.

Time was running out for the 1.5 litre Grand Prix cars, and in Mexico City later in October they had their last race. Team Lotus had the same three cars as at Watkins Glen, but Jimmy's engine had been hurriedly rebuilt in Coventry and was flown out just in time for practice. Solana was entrusted with the flat-crank low-level exhaust engine in 'Old Faithful' R6, while Mike Spence was relegated to running the old 90-degrees high-exhaust engine in his R9. The Parnell runners were the same as at Watkins Glen, so five cars were present to sing Lotus' 1.5 litre swan-song.

Solana went very well before his home crowd to set the fourth fastest time, and the quickest in a Lotus, early in practice, while after running-in his rebuilt engine Jimmy heard it disintegrate at peak revs down the straight. He then took over Spence's car and lapped it at 1min 56.26sec, 0.02 second slower than Gurney in the fastest Brabham. The old 90-degrees crank engine proved as competitive as it had been way back in 1962 when it had made its first serious appearances, and right at the end of practice Jimmy finally took pole position with a lap in 1min 56.17sec.

There had been ructions in the pits earlier in the day. The Parnell and Cooper drivers had lost their way to the circuit and had arrived an hour-and-a-half late. Tim Parnell was not a man to mince words, and his drivers received a rollicking, but Innes Ireland was not a man to accept a rollicking when something was not really his fault, and the incident flared into a remendous row which ended with Innes being fired on the spot, and Bob Bondurant, the American sports car driver, taking his place.

Mike Spence started on the outside of row three in R9 while Solana was on row five, Attwood on row eight and Bondurant right at the back on row nine. Clark's re-engined R11 was beaten off the line by Ginther's Honda from the second row, and the white car streaked away in an impressive display of power. Stewart and Spence were on his tail at the end of the lap, but Jimmy muffed his start and came by in ninth place. Spence was going splendidly, and after taking Stewart for second place he set off after the Honda. After only eight laps Clark felt his engine tighten and all hope of equalling his 'seven in a season' record was gone; he pulled off at the hairpin and retired before the engine seized, Gurney passed Spence to take second place, and Mike finished the 65-lap race in third place while Ginther scored the only win for the 1.5 litre Honda in the last

Above: 'The Lotus 30 with ten more mistakes'. Richie Ginther's description of the Lotus 40 would certainly have been approved by Jim Clark, here fighting the 5.3-litre beast around Brands Hatch during the Guards Trophy meeting. Below: Old R6 at Clermont-Ferrand. Jimmy reverted to the obsolete car for the French Grand Prix after his latest 32-valve engine broke in the Lotus 33; he took pole position, led all the way and set new race and lap records!

race of the dying formula.

Solana looked set for fifth place until lap 55, when his transistor box burned out and his ignition failed, and Bondurant's first Parnell drive ended after 29 laps when a rear suspension bolt from the lower-right upright joint failed and the Lotus 25 slewed to a crooked halt. Attwood produced a typically smooth and consistent performance, and ended the race in sixth place to collect another Championship point.

The final World Championship scorings gave Jimmy a 14-point lead with 54 points to Hill's 40, followed by Stewart's 33 and Gurney's 17, while Mike Spence was equal seventh with Bruce McLaren with 10 points. In the Constructors' Championship, Lotus-Climax finished the season with 54 points to BRM's 45, Brabham-Climax's 27 and Ferrari's 26, while Lotus-BRM took eighth place with the two Parnell points scored by Dickie Attwood. And so the 1.5 litre Formula 1 finished its five-season career, during which Jimmy and Team Lotus became a devastatingly successful partnership.

Back in England plans were announced for a new Ford Grand Prix engine to power the forthcoming 3 litre Lotuses, and since Peter Arundell was back on his feet Mike Spence's temporary stint as number-two Lotus driver came to an end. Mike had been consistently successful in this role, but his performances had not quite compared with Peter Arundell's brilliant but all-too-brief early successes of 1964. Colin stayed true to the promise which had helped Arundell back to health after several painful months in hospital, and kept his seat vacant.

The non-championship Rand Grand Prix at Kyalami in December was the last major formula race of the year. It was run to the new 3 litre regulations although they were not to operate officially until January 1st, 1966. The organisers tried to find Mike Spence a suitable drive, but they could only offer Lederle's aged 21, so Mike demurred and stayed on as a spectator, Jackie Pretorius taking over the car.

Rob Walker originally had entered a 1.5 litre Lotus-Climax and a Brabham-BRM for Bonnier and Siffert, but these became private entries by the individual drivers, Bonnier's Lotus being none other than old 'R4' with the Team Lotus name obscured by black tape. Parnell had patched-up his dispute with Ireland and had entered him in R4, the BRM-engined Lotus 25, and ran R3, fitted with a 2.7 litre Climax 'four', for Paul Hawkins. Clive Puzey had modified his ex-Parnell/Hocking Lotus 18/21 by fitting 13-inch wheels, bigger brakes and a 2.5 litre Climax FPF engine, and 1,600 cc Lotus-Fords were run by the indefatigable small car pair, Dave Charlton and Brausch Niemann.

The race was a battle between Brabham's own car and Johnny Love's Tasman Cooper, both fitted with 2.7 litre Climax engines. Ireland and Bonnier had started alongside each other on row three, with Hawkins right behind his team-mate on row four, and Paul's big engine helped him into third place at the finish behind the winning Brabham and Pieter de Klerk's similar car. Innes finished in sixth place, Puzey was ninth and Bonnier and Pretorius both retired with overheating.

So the 1965 season came to an end. Team Lotus had entered cars in nine of the ten Championship rounds, winning six of them; they had taken part in all eight Tasman rounds, winning five; and five of the six major non-championship events, winning three. They had won both the Drivers' and the Constructors' World Championships and the Indianapolis '500' in a superbly dominant season.

During the five years of 1.5 litre Formula 1 racing, Team Lotus cars had contested 46 Championship races and won 20 of them, two more falling to privately-entered Lotuses. There had also been 65 non-championship Formula 1 races of which 33 had been won by Lotus cars, 23 by Team Lotus entries and ten by private entries. Thus, of the 112 races held under the 1.5 litre formula, Lotus had won no fewer than 55, or fractionally less than 50 per cent success . . . a marvellous achievement.

Right: R6 again, this time in the Italian Grand Prix at Monza which Clark led before retiring. Far right: Farmer Clark after his fourth win of the year at Silverstone. Below right: A relieved wave as he coasts across the line, his engine dead. Below: This winning the World Championship gets you down, y'know.

28

K·TW 413C

Firestone
5

Mike Spence, Team Lotus number-two driver 1964-1965, won the Race of Champions and his last race for the Formula 1 team, the South African Grand Prix of 1966. Above: Singing to pass the time? Jim Clark on his winning way at Spa. Below: Twice World Champion. Jimmy clinched the 1965 title with a faultless winning drive in the German Grand Prix.

1965 RACING RECORD
Other formulae and classes

The record books show that Jim Clark won both the major Formula 2 Championships of 1965. He clinched the Autocar Championship in Britain, and his successes gave the Ron Harris-Team Lotus equipe victory in the Grands Prix de France series on the Continent. Jimmy's new Lotus-Cosworth 35 scored five wins, paralleling the Brabham marque's five victories at the head of the Formula 2 table. There were 14 events in all, Lola accounting for three of the remainder and Alexis one. But Jimmy's successes were more a measure of his own skill than of the quality of the cars he drove, for no other Lotus driver was really competitive with the Brabham opposition.

The new Lotus 35 was very much a rationalised variant of the Lotus 27/32 series monocoque designs, with a minor re-jig to allow a wide range of engines and transmissions to be fitted. In addition to the standard Cosworth SCA Formula 2 engine, the new BRM Formula 2 unit could be fitted, or alternatively Formula 3 engines, a 1,600 cc twin-cam for American Formula B racing, or even a Coventry-Climax 2.5 litre FPF four-cylinder for Tasman racing. Hewland transaxles with four, five or six speeds could also be mounted in the same chassis, and Lotus Components rang the changes to produce a total of 22 cars.

Ron Harris' team began the season with a mixture of old Lotus 32s and the new 35s, but rapidly phased-out the 1964 cars in favour of the later models. But they proved to be slow cars, and only Clark's phenomenal expertise kept them in the hunt to such good effect that he clinched his Championships with wins at Pau (yet again!), Crystal Palace, Rouen, Brands Hatch and Albi, plus two thirds and a sixth place. He was just beaten to the line in one of the Snetterton heats by Graham Hill's John Coombs-entered Brabham, and another thrilling finish at Albi saw him edging-out Jack Brabham's Honda-powered car by just 0.6 second.

The Lotus 35 really lost out along the straights at faster circuits such as Reims or Enna, and a classic example of this was at the Champagne circuit where Cosworth provided Harris with one of their latest engines for Jimmy's use. At the start of the season the SCA, with a redesigned cylinder head, was producing a reliable 125 bhp, but the new BRM Formula 2 unit—virtually one-half of a bored-out V8—offered an honest 127 horsepower. Keith Duckworth managed to squeeze an extra five horsepower out of his SCA in time for the Reims race, and with this behind his shoulders Jimmy should have been able to dominate the race. However, although he found that he could catch the Winkelmann Brabhams and the leading Lola under acceleration and braking, on the straights they just hauled away from him at their top speed of around 145 mph. The Lotus' clean shape, with inboard front suspension and low frontal area did not seem to work as well as the Brabham's and Lola's more chunky profiles at speed, and Clark had a rough time in taking one of his third places.

Other Ron Harris drivers included Peter Revson, Mike Spence and Brian Hart, the American Revlon Cosmetics heir being the most successful of this trio with fourth places at Solitude and Pergusa. Spence snatched a fourth at Karlskoga and a sixth at Enna, while poor 'Nosher' Hart had an unhappy season with no placings in the first six.

A private Lotus 35 appeared in the colours of Tim Parnell, who fitted a BRM engine and gave David Hobbs the drive, but the combination was notably unlucky, and in August Tim sold the car to John Coombs for Graham Hill to drive. Graham was fourth in the now grey-painted car at Brands Hatch and third at Oulton Park, then provided the 'funny' of the season at Albi in the last meeting of the year.

The last practice session there was held in dull and dreary conditions, and nobody (apart from 'Noddy' Coombs) could quite understand why Hill was out on the circuit droning round and round when he couldn't hope to better the previous day's practice times. In fact he was one of the few people to discover that 100 bottles of Champagne were being offered for fastest time in this final practice session, and sure enough they were handed over to G. Hill at the end of the day. The unfortunate aftermath of this dogged performance came on race day, when the Lotus-BRM's oil pressure disappeared on the warming-up lap and the car had to be withdrawn!

Some Lotus 35s appeared in Formula 3 guise, notably in the hands of the Ron Harris and Willment teams. John E. Miles (no relation to John J. Miles who drove for the same team at this time and was later to join Team Lotus) destroyed the Willment Lotus 35 in practice for the Monaco Formula 3 race and had a promising career ruined by a long sojourn in hospital. But this same meeting saw Lotus' only major success in a year utterly dominated by Jack Brabham's products, when Peter Revson won in a Harris Lotus 35. Ron also fielded a Lotus 32 in Formula 3 trim, and both cars were driven by John Cardwell later in the season while Ray Parsons had some outings in a replacement Willment car. The monocoque Lotus designs probably had a slight edge over the Brabhams in outright cornering power, but in the tight-packed and hectic World of Formula 3 drivers needed a forgiving, predictable and swervable chassis which was something the Lotus 32/35 never was.

Actor Peter Sellers ran a Formula 3 Lotus 35 for Brian Hart and a sports-racing Lotus 23 for the unrelated Barrie Hart, but the team met with little success and folded after the two-seater was written-off at Solitude and Barrie ended-up in hospital.

Group 7 sports car racing met its Waterloo in Britain during the 1965 season. Trade support was torn between Formula 2 and the 'big-banger' sports cars, and when the American-engined monsters proved relatively unexciting and unreliable it was purely a question of the survival of the fittest, and Group 7 died . . .

As described in the preceding chapter Lotus Components had developed the basic Lotus 30 design and were now offering a new Series 2 model for 1965. Series 1 production had totalled 21 cars, and a dozen Lotus 30 S2s were produced during the second year. These featured the revised chassis with simplified rear suspension mounts, and a new body with upswept tail spoiler and a vertical oil cooler duct in the nose. Roll-over bars were fitted in compliance with Sports Car Club of America standards, and following the braking problems encountered during the Lotus 30's initial season brand-new 10¼-inch diameter ventilated Girling disc brakes were fitted all round. The Series 2 works car used 15-inch wheels in place of the production 13-inch wheels to provide better brake cooling, but with Dunlop's latest R7 low-profile tyres overall diameters were virtually unchanged.

Further engine modifications resulted in the adoption of Tecalemit-Jackson fuel-injection as standard after an eight-month development programme. Development Engineer John Joyce worked closely with T-J on the project, which replaced the quadruple-Weber carburettor system. Fuel-injection was only slightly more expensive for a rather larger increase in power, and the 4,727 cc Ford V8 in this trim gave a reliable 360 bhp.

However, this was rather less than the competitive Chevrolet V8s used by Lola and McLaren's lightweight Oldsmobile engines. The Ford's iron block also made it a heavy package, and although the Lotus 30 itself was a very light car this engine weight disadvantage brought near parity with the lighter-engined heavier chassised competition.

As the Lotus 30 was underpowered, a 5.3 litre Ford V8 was developed in an attempt to redress the balance, but this blew-up in grand style during practice for the Tourist Trophy at Oulton Park, and a standard '289' was installed for the two-heat race. Jimmy took the lead in the first heat after John Surtees' Lola and Bruce McLaren's own car had both hit trouble, but then he too had to stop when a rear wishbone came loose (the locking nut had not been tightened) and the rear wheels began to steer. He rejoined to finish 16th in the heat, and in the second heat hacked through the field in terrific style to take the lead and work his way into sixth place on aggregate. But shortly after half-distance the Lotus 30's transmission wilted and the green-and-yellow car was out. Clark's drive in the TT was probably his best performance of the Lotus 30's season, although he had won the rained-out Senior Service '200' at Silverstone early in the year and added a second success at the Easter Monday Goodwood meeting.

Private Lotus 30 S2s went to the JCB Excavator Company's team for Trevor Taylor, to Willment and to John Dean. Peter Sadler destroyed the first JCB car in testing but it was quickly replaced and Taylor took part in several races but with limited success, including a lucky escape from the car when it caught fire in practice for the Martini race at Silverstone. Frank Gardner drove the Willment car and won at Mallory Park, but Dean was an also-ran in his and Vic Wilson had all kinds of problems with his Series 1 model.

Something just had to be done so far as the works car was concerned, and Chapman and Joyce evolved the replacement Lotus 40 in time for the Austrian Grand Prix at Zeltweg in August.

The new car had a stronger chassis and suspension revisions in search of improved reliability and a new 5.3 litre Ford V8 engine was adopted as standard and mated to a hefty Hewland LG500 transmission in place of the rather over-stressed ZF unit. Body modifications included cut-outs in the rear deck for two huge exhaust megaphones, which pointed skywards and looked very 'Indianapolis'.

Mike Spence took pole position at Zeltweg with a lap in 1min 8.46sec, which cut 2.1 seconds off Gurney's existing Formula 1 lap record and he led the race for 13 laps until the engine overheated. The car was then brought back home and hurriedly prepared for the Guards Trophy at Brands Hatch on August Monday where Jimmy spun it twice in the first heat before stopping with the gear-linkage adrift. In the second heat he finally gave up the unequal struggle when the brakes played -up and he ended-up against the bank at Clearways.

Team Lotus' final Group 7 fling was in the American 'professional' race series on the West Coast. Jimmy and Richie Ginther shared a pair of works Lotus 40s at Riverside, where Clark managed to snatch second place, after the stocky little American had laconically described the car as '. . . a Lotus 30 with 10 more mistakes'. A.J.Foyt's brand-new Lotus 40 was completely wrecked in practice for this race when being driven by Bob Tattersall.

At Daytona, Ford dropped one of their very experimental 5,261cc engines very secretly into the Pacesetter Homes Lotus 19-based Special, and Dan Gurney and Jerry Grant led the endurance race for 809 miles until the engine finally expired. This sprint car had little left to betray its parentage, and its advanced specification included multiple faired-in headlamps and built-in pneumatic jacks.

In Canada, Bob McLean drove splendidly in a Lotus 23B, while Lotus 30s appeared regularly in American club events, driven notably by Jerry Crawford, who scored several wins, and by Anson Johnson, while a young crew-cut engineering graduate seen at this time in a Lotus 20B was Mark Donohue . . .

A.J. Foyt's Lotus 40 was rebuilt in time for Nassau, and there the pale blue Holman-Moody-entered car heaved and wallowed its way round with its springs set far too soft and finally just fell to pieces!

The Lotus sports-racing success story of the year concerned the American driver George Follmer and his Porsche-engined Lotus 23. He scored a string of victories which finally gave him the United States Road Racing Championship, which he snatched from under the noses of Chaparral team-mates Jim Hall and Hap

Sharp.

In touring car racing, Team Lotus Racing with Ford of Britain ran Lotus-Cortinas for Jimmy and reigning British Saloon Car Champion Jack Sears. These cars reverted to leaf-spring rear suspension, and used 150 bhp BRM-built Phase 2 twin-cam engines; the cars were very controllable in this form although a little hard on tyres. Early in the season the Willment team's vehicles proved more competitive than the works cars, and Gardner caused a sensation when he beat Jim Clark at Snetterton driving one of the old Willment coil-spring, A-bracket cars from the previous year, powered by a Cosworth-developed engine.

Clark and Sears managed to break every class record in the events they contested, and in the wet at Goodwood they won outright from the Mustangs. Another overall victory was notched at Oulton Park, where Jack Brabham's seemingly victorious Mustang was subsequently disqualified, but the British Championship finally passed from Team Lotus to Roy Pierpoint and his privately-entered Ford Mustang. Jack Sears took his class in the Championship, and ended the season fourth overall.

The Alan Mann Cortinas shone once again in the European Touring Car Challenge. Sir John Whitmore led the team, and he shared the winning car in the Nurburgring 6-Hours with Sears, and won solo at Mont Ventoux, Zolder and Setterton to clinch the European title. Peter Procter, Jacky Ickx and Henry Taylor co-drove the cars, but only Whitmore's lurid expertise could hold off the newly-homologated Alfa Romeo GTAs towards the end of the year. These cars were built and homogolated with the European title very much in mind, and were nearer in spirit to GT cars than to touring cars.

This was the second season of the American 'EFLO-Programme' with Team Lotus Racing with English Ford Line (Dearborn), who contested several Stateside events with a great variety of cars. Andrew Ferguson recalls the programme as something of a nightmare, for with the EFLO crews included Lotus had no less than 27 drivers signed-up during the season, including such notables as Parnelli Jones and A.J. Foyt. This caused untold embarrassment on occasions, as even Chapman didn't know about all of them and he had a confusing conversation with Chris Craft before realising he was on the strength! Part of the administrative nightmare was satisfying each driver's personal sponsors, and the chief mechanic in the United States eventually carried 27 personalised overalls with him, to ensure that each man had the right badges and labels affixed 'in case of photographs'!

At club-racing level Derek Bell, Len Gibbs and Teddy Dawson ran regularly in Formula 3 with their Lotus 22 variants, while Chris Summers finally had his fearsome Chevrolet-engined Lotus 24 tamed and won the Leinster Trophy at Dunboyne as well as setting a new 110 mph lap record at Dublin's Phoenix Park. Tony Lanfranchi scored numerous victories with Racing Preparations' 2.5 litre Climax-powered Lotus 24, and Peter Hawtin ran a rather crude Ford V8-engined version. In general, 1,600 cc twin-cam-engined cars proved competitive, and Peter Sadler did very well with a Lotus 32 although the twin-cam-engined Brabhams once again proved far more forgiving.

Twin-cam engines also powered numerous stripped Ford Anglia saloons which dominated their club classes, completely overshadowing the Lotus-Cortinas which could not compete on a power-to-weight basis. But one Lotus-Cortina which really excelled was that driven by novice Tony Gorst in a few Oulton Park meetings. He shook the establishment rigid by scoring some good wins, but his exuberance finally took charge and turned the Cortina on its roof to end a promising season!

In sports-racing circles Tony Dean ran an immaculate Lotus 23B to a string of wins, and Alan Minshaw's similar car picked up eight trophies during the season. Robin McArthur and John Hine excelled in their 1,150 cc Lotus 23s (the former winning the Guards Championship), and Robin Widdows drove some tremendous races at both club and International level in the Hon Eddie Portman's 998 cc Formula 2 BRM-engined Lotus 23.

Perhaps the strangest Lotus 23 of them all was the 12-cylinder two-stroke Rotorvic which appeared spasmodically at the beginning of the season. This project was developed by R.V. Marchant, and consisted of six Ariel Arrow motorcycle engines, disposed at an included angle of 90 degrees. Each air-cooled engine had a straight-cut pinion on its mainshaft which engaged with similar pinion on a shaft which ran down the centre of the Vee. These gears and the shaft itself were all encased, and a clutch/flywheel assembly hung from the end of the shaft, with auxiliary drive belts running the ignition distributors. Transmission was via a Hewland five-speed gearbox, and the petroil-lubricated 'V12' was cooled through huge scoops on the body panelling. This 1,482 cc engine made a ferocious noise, and it was almost impossible to tell if it was misfiring on one or two cylinders, so Marchant rigged up some thermocouple sensors which lit warning lights on the dash panel when any of the exhaust branches fell below working temperature! Bill Hill drove the car in initial tests, but very little has been heard of the project since . . .

In the bigger sports car classes Ben Moore finally bought the Vic Wilson Lotus 30 after racing two Lotus 11 GTs and a Lotus 31. He had several successes in the North-East, while Aintree and Oulton Park were regular hunting grounds for John Scott-Davies and Harry O'Brien in Lotus 19s.

The advent of the lightweight mid-engined Ginettas caused great problems for the Elans in 1,600 cc GT racing, but Jeff Edmonds' car managed to notch 13 wins during the year. Other prominent Elan peddlers included John Harris, who shared Dick Crosfield's Elan to win the 1965 Autosport Championship. Geoff Breakell, Pat Fergusson, Malcolm Wayne, John Lepp,

Digby Martland, Carlos Gaspar and Willie Green (who bought the Team Elite car late in the season) all scored wins in their Elans, while John Hine won the big Dunlop International race at Zandvoort, from Jochen Neerpasch, both in Lotus Elans.

Lotus employee John Berry was top-dog in the Clubman's Formula class, driving the one-off Lotus 37 prototype which had made its debut at the Racing Car Show. This was an independently-suspended Seven, using a Cosworth-Ford dry-sumped engine and numerous light-alloy Elan parts, plus lightweight magnesium wheels and a stiffened chassis frame. The idea had been to put the car into series production for competition use, but demand for the Elan was so high that works capacity could not stand another model, and the price of construction would have been virtually prohibitive. So the Lotus 37 remained a one-off, and it was to have an extremely successful Clubman's career in succeeding years.

Finally, in the RAC Hill Climb Championship, the inevitable Peter Boshier-Jones took second place to Tony Marsh's title-winning Marsh-Buick, at the wheel of his veteran supercharged 1,220 cc Lotus-Climax 22. Peter Meldrum was third in a blown 1,500 cc Ford-engined example, and Bryan Brown also went well in a similar Lotus 22. But while the old Formula Junior Lotuses went so well in this rather parochial contest, the important European Mountain Championship was a complete preserve of Ferrari Dino and Porsche sports cars, apart from Jim Clark's epic St Ursannes appearance in the Indy-winning Lotus Ford . . .

Below left: The Lotus 30 story nearly ended in practice for the British Grand Prix meeting at Brands Hatch in 1964, when Tony Hegbourne crashed the Ian Walker works car. Below and centre: Jimmy Clark during his great 1965 TT drive at Oulton Park and winning in the rain at Silverstone. Bottom: Trevor Taylor goes for a spin in the JCB team's much-modified Lotus 30 S2 at Silverstone.

1966

A Lotus for Europe

This was to be Lotus' last year at Cheshunt before moving into the new factory at Hethel, and while it was another interim year for Team Lotus in Formula 1, it saw Lotus Cars poised on a springboard with new models ready for full production in Norfolk. Lotus Components were making something of a spaceframe comeback with the new Lotus 41 single-seaters, and commercially it was to be another record-breaking year.

In January a new Special Equipment soft-top Elan was released, with a 115 bhp version of the twin-cam engine, a close-ratio gearbox, servo-assisted brakes, centre-lock wheels and indicator repeater lights as standard, but this variant was very short-lived, for in June the new Lotus 45 Elan Series 3 drop-head Coupe was announced, replacing all previous soft-top models. This featured fixed side window frames with electric winders, but was otherwise generally similar to the earlier Elans. Both drop-head and fixed-head Special Equipment models were also announced, featuring fitted carpeting in the cockpit and boot, inertia-reel seat belts and a padded leather-rimmed steering wheel. The final-drive ratio was changed from 3.77:1 to 3.55:1 and the whole SE package added £163 to the basic price, which stood at £1,553 complete or £1,262 in component form.

The new Coupe's shape contributed to improved performance, and with the extra 10 bhp maximum speed was boosted to around 123 mph, and the acceleration time from 0-50 mph reduced to around 6 seconds, matching that of the 4.2 litre E-Type Jaguar!

Concurrent with these changes the Cheshunt development shop was a hive of activity as their new mid-engined coupe neared completion, ready to be phased into production in the new factory. This was the new Lotus 46, known for the two years of its gestation as the P5. Derek Sleath was in charge of its design and development, and with a simple brief to produce a mid-engined 'Lotus for Europe' his small team spent just 18 months to bring the project from initial design studies to prototype production.

Apart from Matra and Lamborghini, Lotus were the first motor company to produce a road-going mid-engined GT car, and with the basic concept outlined the hunt had started for a suitable engine. It had to be a unit suited to mid-engine mounting, preferably with a transaxle incorporated, and the Renault 16 was an obvious choice. In the French production car the engine was mounted about-face in the nose, driving forward via a transaxle to the front wheels. The job of reversing it and driving the rear wheels in a new frame seemed simple enough, and as Renault were agreeable work proceeded.

Regie Renault agreed to supply complete engine/transmission packages, modified to Lotus requirements, and this left Sleath's team free to develop the installation, chassis, suspension and bodywork.

A backbone chassis was adopted, basically similar to that used in the Elan, and welded-up from 16-gauge sheet steel. It differed from the Elan unit in detail in having Y-shaped forks at the tail end to mount the engine, while the front end was just a straight-forward cross-beam without the bracing-fork arrangement of the older model.

The front suspension consisted of proprietary parts as much as possible in order to keep costs down, the double-wishbone arrangement being by Alford & Alder, as used by the Triumph Herald and Spitfire, and the rack-and-pinion steering coming from the same supplier. Front hubs and disc brake assemblies were also as used by Triumph, this time in the GT6 and 2 litre Vitesse.

At the rear a typically Chapman layout was adopted, with long fabricated box-section radius arms pivoting on the sides of the backbone just where the Y-fork divided. Very deep uprights were used with their lower extremities dropping below the wheel rim to carry the lower spring/damper mounts and the outboard end of a very long lower link. This pivoted just over an inch from the chassis centre-line to form a very wide-based wishbone arrangement in conjunction with the radius arm. Wheel location was completed by fixed-length drive-shafts with Hooke universal joints at each end, and the upper ends of the coil-spring/damper units picked-up on a cross-beam mounted over the gearbox. The wheels were 4½J-13s, as on the Elans, carrying 155 Dunlop SP41 radial-ply tyres as standard.

The body was another unitary glass-fibre moulding

similar in construction to the Elan's, and styled by John Frayling, who had been responsible for the Coupe and the latest S3s. It sat astride the chassis in similar style to the earlier cars, and its rather boxy 'breadvan' styling was in fact remarkably efficient aerodynamically, its drag coefficient being the very low figure of 0.29. Air was fed into the engine bay through the rear wheel arches, and into an offset radiator through the nose intake. Coolant pipes ran through the backbone of the chassis, and two electric fans were fitted, one to force air through the radiator core and the other to pressurise the front luggage well which then acted as a plenum chamber to feed the heating and ventilation system.

Double-curvature side windows were used which naturally had to be fixed, so Renault butterfly nozzles were used in a fresh-air ventilation system for the tailored two-seat cockpit. The semi-reclining seats were fixed but pedal adjustment gave a variable driving position, allied to a Triumph adjustable steering column.

The Renault engine was a light-alloy unit weighing only 200 lbs, which made it all the more suitable for the type of car Chapman and Sleath envisaged. It had a five-main-bearing crankshaft, and a bore and stroke of 76mm x 81mm to give a capacity of 1,470 cc. The Lotus version had its compression ratio raised from 8.5 to 10.25:1 and a new high-lift camshaft. Bigger inlet valves with larger ports were adopted, and a twin-choke Solex carburettor with 26mm progressive throats replaced the standard single-choke type. These modifications raised output from 58.5 bhp net at 5,000 rpm to 78 bhp at 6,000 rpm. Gearbox ratios were unchanged apart from a higher final-drive ratio of 3.56 instead of 3.77:1, giving a top-gear speed of 17.7 mph per 1,000 rpm. Top speed was quoted as 115 mph.

Sales Director Graham Arnold explained that it was intended to supply the first 500 cars to French Lotus distributors (not Renault agents), which would account for the first year's production, but it was hoped to raise output to 50 a week in time. Price was set at around NF20,000, with the intention that if the car should become available in Britain at a later date it would have a price tag of about £1,000. The tie-up with Renault was announced in September, and the new Lotus 46 Europa was shown to the press in mid-December just before production was to begin at Hethel in the new year.

Meanwhile, on the competition front the promised 4.2 litre versions of BRM's H16 engine for Indianapolis had failed to materialise. Racing designer Maurice Phillipe recalls that one was actually run at Snetterton in its intended Lotus 42 chassis, but it didn't last more than a handful of laps and was obviously totally unraceworthy.

With the expiration of the original three-year Indy agreement with Ford of America, and the decision of the Dearborn hierarchy to back Dan Gurney's All-American Racers team in their attempt to score a partisan victory in this richest and most prestigious race of all, Colin came to an arrangement with Andy Granatelli of Studebaker and STP fame to run his Indianapolis cars, but with the defection of the BRM engine the new chassis had to be held back and the old Lotus 38s run once again with Ford double-overhead-camshaft engines.

Lotus Components built a pair of type 38 chassis (at 22,500 dollars each) for A.J. Foyt and Mario Andretti's Dean Van Lines sponsor, and in a confused mass of dealings just before the race Foyt and his Sheraton-Thompson team-mate George Snider wound up with two Lotus 38s, while Jimmy Clark had one of the previous year's cars (known as 'The Old Nail') rebuilt and STP team-mate Al Unser had one of the Lotus Components-built cars, dubbed 'The Soft Alloy Special'. This name stemmed from Lotus Components' use of a softer skinning alloy than was used in the Team-Lotus-built cars, although the cars were just as strong.

David Lazenby recalls the string of engine failures suffered in practice and qualifying: 'We had a couple of engines blow for no apparent reason, and it was only after a lot of detective work that finally we found that ZF had made the gearbox quill-shafts too long. As we bolted the gearboxes up to the engine they put an end-loading on the crankshaft bearings and caused the breakages. We cured the problem by fitting spacers to take up the extra length.'

The cars did not handle too well during qualifying, and the rear roll centres were lowered to improve things. This worked OK in the dry, but after that infamous start-line accident, with oil spread all round the Speedway, the cars became real pigs to handle, explaining Clark's two spins which probably cost him the race. David Lazenby: 'We thought from our lap charts that Jimmy was leading, with Graham Hill second and Al Unser catching him in third place. We thought we might have been heading for first and second places, but then Al wrecked his car and we then thought this left Jimmy in the lead with Graham second . . . we were wrong.'

After the race Jimmy's car was sold to Foyt, whose own Lotus 38 had been shattered in the start-line fracas, but the unfortunate Texan slammed it into the wall at Milwaukee and was quite badly burned on the face and hands. The STP-Lotus Indianapolis arrangement was to evolve into Lotus building and running the cars at Indy and then selling them plus the necessary spares to Granatelli, who would race them on his own in the rest of the USAC series. It worked well for a while.

One other interesting competition development during the season was announced during the Italian Grand Prix meeting in September. Colin and expatriate Argentinian engineer Alessandro de Tomaso had joined forces to produce a racing V8 engine, designed from the ground-up to power 'big-banger' sports cars. The philosophy behind the development was that while American production V8s were very reliable in standard trim, they tended to burst expensively

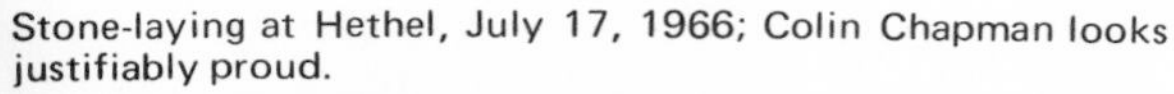
Stone-laying at Hethel, July 17, 1966; Colin Chapman looks justifiably proud.

asunder once race-tuned. The new Lotus-De Tomaso V8 was developed around a 90-degree light-alloy block, extreme rigidity being achieved by carrying the bottom halves of the main bearings in a single casting which bolted up to the block in a style reminiscent of racers of the heroic age before 1914! The bore and stroke were 107.44mm x 76mm, giving a capacity of 5,512 cc, and the pushrod unit developed 'over 500 bhp' at 6,800 rpm. Tecalemit-Jackson fuel-injection was fitted, and the unit's all-up weight, less starter motor, was 347 lbs. As with so many De Tomaso projects (but so few by Lotus) it never got off the ground and the engine was never raced, although one still lies in storage . . . unused.

This participation in an engine-design project was typical of Chapman's versatility as a design engineer. One of his staff: 'One of Colin's greatest attributes is that way in which he can study a problem you've been stuck on for hours; in a few minutes he can grasp all the essentials and come up with a workable solution . . . it's bloody annoying!'.

One example of this grasp of technical matters came at the Dutch Grand Prix, where Jimmy narrowly lost the race when his crankshaft damper came adrift. This was Team Lotus' first season on Firestone tyres and after the race Colin and Jim Endruweit were sitting in the Firestone caravan discussing racing covers with Bob Martin, the company's competitions manager. The outcome of this impromptu conference was that Colin went away and drew-up a new tread pattern, and this was to become the basis of the R125 all-weather tyre which really brought Firestone into the road-racing scene. Initial hand-cut prototypes, to the basic Chapman design, were used at Watkins Glen and Mexico City on the winning Lotus-BRM and Cooper-Maserati!

The move to Hethel took place at the end of the year, and most of the Cheshunt staff went with the company. The new factory was spacious, light and airy and set in a pleasant 40-acre site complete with the 1½-miles test track and ¾-mile runway. The engine assembly lines were laid down with the intention eventually to take over the work which JAP (lately Villiers-owned) had been doing on the twin-cam units, and modern flow-line techniques began to be applied to Elan and Europa models.

Group Purchasing Manager Mike Warner directed the move operations, and with the Elan and Europa releases approaching he recalls it as 'one hell of a programme'.

During their last year at Cheshunt the Group had set new records for the third consecutive time. Lotus production totalled 1,519 cars, which with the output of 986 Lotus-Cortinas made a total of 2,505, 153 up on the 1965 figures. Turnover rose £126,000 to £2,156,000 and gross profit was also up by £97,000 to £251,000. It was a very good year.

Lotus for Europe: The Renault 16-engined Lotus Europa was the first reasonably-priced mid-engined coupe road car to go into production anywhere in the World, and although early numbers were for export only this company road test car impressed all who drove it.

1966 RACING RECORD
Grands Prix and other major formulae

The new 3 litre Formula 1 was only a day old when the cars formed up on the grid for the non-championship South African Grand Prix at East London, a race which brought together new 3 litre cars and old updated 1.5 litre models and gave Team Lotus another success.

Mike Spence made his last appearance for the works team in R11, specially fitted with a stretched 2 litre Coventry-Climax V8 engine. This was the first such engine to come from the Coventry concern, which had officially pulled out of racing; it was designed to tide over Team Lotus until first the 3 litre BRM H16 engine and later the Cosworth-built Ford V8s became raceworthy.

The engine was one of the 1.5 litre short-stroke units of the previous year, fitted with a longer-stroke crankshaft to extract an extra 500 cc. Thick sandwich plates were located between the head and block by taller liners to accommodate this increased stroke, and the unit revved to a modest 8,500 rpm and produced 245-250 bhp.

Peter Arundell, still pale-faced and walking with a limp, took over the second car, R9, which was fitted with a pure 1.5 litre 16-valve flat-crank engine. Bonnier was out again in the ex-Team Lotus R6, and Tim Parnell had his two Rand Grand Prix cars for Ireland and Hawkins, the former's with a 2 litre BRM V8 and the latter's with a 2.7 litre Climax four-cylinder. David Prophet's old Lotus 24 was fitted with a 2.8 litre four-cylinder twin-plug Maserati engine, Clive Puzey's 18/21 had a 2.7 Climax installed and Scuderia Scribante ran a four-cylinder 2 litre Climax in their Lotus 21. Brian Raubenheimer ran a ballasted Lotus 20 Junior fitted with a 1,600 cc Lotus-Ford twin-cam unit.

But Jack Brabham was giving his new 3 litre Repco-Brabham its debut, and he took pole position fully 2.2 seconds faster than Spence. Both Brabham and team-mate Denny Hulme (in the 2.7 Climax car used by Jack in the Rand race three weeks previously) were left by Mike at the start, while Prophet's ancient car broke a half-shaft on the line. On lap 7 Richie Ginther's BRP-BRM spun in the Esses and hit Bonnier's Lotus 25/33 which ground off the road with a wheel ripped off, and two laps later Hawkins retired without gears.

Brabham had passed Spence to take the lead and he pulled away as he liked while Mike staved-off Hulme's less-manageable four-cylinder car. Ireland's extra half-litre proved too much for his transmission after 33 laps, and behind him Peter Arundell and Jo Siffert profited further when Hulme's transmission failed. As Brabham looked all set for a first-time win in his new

David and Goliath. For the greater part of the 1966 season Team Lotus were handicapped by running bored-out 1½ litre machinery against the new 3 litre cars. Jim Clark's prowess made up the deficit in certain races, as at Zandvoort (below) where he proved a match for Jack Brabham!

Above: Jim Clark, the 'Old Nail' Lotus 38 and the Lotus-STP crew at Indianapolis, 1966. Jimmy finished secon after spinning twice; his pit crew thought he had won. The group includes Andy Granatelli (second from left), Coli Chapman, David Lazenby (on Colin's left) and Maurice Phillippe (second from right). Below: Through the Monac chicane go Mike Spence's Parnell Lotus-BRM and Jo Siffert's Walker Brabham.

r the fuel-injection pump spindle seized and broke its ive belt, putting him out.

So Mike Spence was left with a two-lap lead over ffert, and he cruised home to a fine win for Team otus, with Jo's Brabham second and Arundell third; ter was tired and stiff, but he felt good to be back . . .

Meanwhile, Team Lotus' new Tasman contender was st arriving in Auckland for the New Zealand Grand ix at Pukekohe the following weekend. This was the ne-off Lotus 39 chassis, R12, which had been tended for the still-born flat-16 Climax engine. It ffered from the 25/33 series in having no rear chassis gs and in fact terminated abruptly behind the ockpit. Maurice Phillippe had just joined Lotus from e Havilland Aircraft and the Ford Motor Company at is time, and his first job was pencilling a tubular ub-frame to match a 2.5 litre Climax FPF engine to is chassis.

Team Lotus had just come to an agreement with irestone Tyres to run their equipment in place of the unlop rubber which had held a virtual road-racing onopoly since the late-'fifties. The Tasman series was prove a useful test-ground for Firestone's new wares, d Bob Martin was along to tend Jimmy's tyres.

When it rained during practice at Pukekohe Jimmy ied the American 'wet' tyres before pulling into the its rather peeved; he had just been overtaken on the ack straight by a train with a flashing light, running on e main line outside the perimeter fence! But he ualified on the middle of the front row, flanked by pencer Martin's Brabham-Climax and Graham Hill's 2 tre BRM V8. As the flag fell the Lotus 39's ansmission stripped first gear, and by the time Jimmy aggered away he was well behind; after six laps he was the pits, and pulling off helmet and gloves to retire. he 2 litre BRMs of Hill and Stewart finished first and cond, and Jim Palmer was a good third in Jimmy's old otus 32B—the first four-cylinder car home. Jimmy as second at Levin, beaten by Dickie Attwood driving e number-two BRM after Stewart had gone out with earbox trouble. The Lotus 39 was handicapped by its yres, but Jim Palmer was happy with his Lotus 32B in fth place.

The Lady Wigram Trophy followed at Christchurch here Team Lotus' usual engine ran its bearings and ad to be changed. Starting from the second row in the reliminary race Jimmy finished second to Attwood, hile Palmer was third in his heat. The Lotus 39 was on e outside of the four-strong front row for the main ace, and Jimmy took second place from the start right n Stewart's tail. On the fourth lap Clark was hallenging strongly approaching the hairpin, but as he ocked over for the corner Frank Gardner's brakeless rabham careered straight into him, spinning both cars nto retirement. Jimmy began to think that maybe he ould have been better off with the 2 litre Dunlop-shod car Spence had used in South Africa, but here was no changing horses at this stage of the game.

Lotus fortunes improved at Teretonga as Jimmy von his preliminary heat by a short nose from Stewart, the timekeepers being unable to get a watch between them. This put the Lotus 39 on pole position for the main event, and Jimmy led away from Stewart only to hit an unsignalled oil patch on lap 4 and spin off, holing the radiator on a course marker which put him out. Tragically the event had to be stopped after 46 laps following a fatal accident, but Stewart was a deserving winner with Palmer third once more.

Next day the circus flew to Australia, with Palmer lying third in the Tasman Championship and Jimmy equal seventh with Frank Gardner. Palmer's New Zealand performances had already won him the National Championship and the NZRDC title for the third consecutive year.

At Warwick Farm Jimmy took an early lead from Graham Hill, who was back in the 2 litre BRM. The course suited the big four-cylinder car and Jimmy held his advantage all the way to win his first major event of the series; Palmer was sixth, Stewart's 27 points still gave him a comfortable lead, but Hill, Attwood and Clark were now tieing for second place with 15 points each.

At Lakeside, near Brisbane, Jimmy's engine went off-song towards the end of the Australian Grand Prix, and he was beaten by Hill and Gardner. Stewart beat him in one heat, while Palmer was fourth in both his heat and the Grand Prix. Stewart and Hill both forged ahead of Clark in the Championship, but Lotus had some little consolation in seeing Leo Geoghegan's new Team Total 1.5 litre Lotus 32 winning the 1.5 litre supporting event handsomely.

The Exide International Cup at Sandown Park, near Melbourne, one week later decided the Tasman Championship in favour of Jackie Stewart, whose BRM won from Jimmy's Lotus after Jack Brabham's 2.5 litre Repco V8 engine had lost its oil pressure and Jack had switched off before it broke. After his Lakeside misfiring problems Jimmy reverted to his short-stroke Climax engine with which he also finished second in his heat behind Stewart. Palmer was fourth yet again, and local man Les Howard drove very well in a 1,500 cc Climax-engined Lotus 27 to take sixth place and win his class.

The final Tasman round was at Longford, in Tasmania, where the BRMs were quite unbeatable. Stewart won from Hill and Brabham, with Palmer the eternal fourth. Jimmy led initially before the BRMs howled by, and then his engine began misfiring when a plug electrode came loose and he stopped for a plug change, losing two laps and finishing seventh. He ended the series in third place behind the two BRM drivers.

Immediately after the race Leo Geoghegan bought the Lotus 39 for his Total team, and 1,500 cc Brabham driver Greg Cusack took up an option on Palmer's Lotus 32B. Then Jimmy flew off to the United States, where Colin was in deep conversation with Andy Granatelli's STP Division of Studebaker concerning Indianapolis sponsorship. Ford had withdrawn their direct support after the previous year's success, and were now backing Dan Gurney's Eagle project in the hope of an all-American win. Agreement was reached with Granatelli, and a statement was issued saying that STP would be sponsoring no less than six cars, three of them Lotuses powered by 4.2 litre versions of the new BRM H16-cylinder engine!

Although the new Formula 1 had been introduced four months earlier, it was not until the beginning of May that the first 3 litre race was held in Europe. This was the Syracuse Grand Prix for which the works Brabham and Ferrari teams entered new cars, and two customer Cooper-Maseratis also made their debut, although there were no works Lotuses. Tim Parnell, back with his own team after managing the BRM Tasman tour, ran a 2 litre BRM V8 and a 2.7 litre Climax FPF engine in a pair of Lotus 25s, and Jo Bonnier's Anglo-Swiss Racing Team entered old R6 for Giancarlo Baghetti. Mike Spence should have made his debut in the Parnell cars, but he had crashed a Tyrrell Formula 2 Matra at Barcelona and had damaged his foot. A spectator had fallen off a straw bale in front of him, and in avoiding him Mike had driven into a wall. Consequently David Hobbs took his place in the V8-engined car, while Paul Hawkins took the four-cylinder special.

In practice all three Lotuses qualified for a place on the third row, but Baghetti spun backwards into a stone wall, crumpling the monocoque and damaging the gearbox. The car was cobbled-up for the race and collected its starting money, but it was a sad fate for 'Old Faithful' R6, which had been the winner of so many races in Jim Clark's hands.

Baghetti's race lasted just one lap, while the Parnell cars settled into fourth and fifth places with Hawkins leading Hobbs until the big Climax went off-song and the transmission became stuck in fourth gear. Hawkins' oil scavenge pump then broke and oil was pumped all over the road, but Hobbs eventually finished third behind the works Ferraris of Surtees and Bandini, only six of the 12 starters finishing their first serious 3 litre race.

A fortnight later the scene shifted to Silverstone, where the BRDC's International Trophy race gave the 3 litre cars their first English outing. Team Lotus still lacked suitable cars and engines, and only the Parnell cars appeared, Mike Spence making his debut in the BRM-engined car, which ran fourth until lap four when the engine broke, and Mike coasted to a halt at Copse. Paul Hawkins was seen again in the four-cylinder car, rumbling round and round to finish eighth and last.

During the following week the teams began arriving at Monte Carlo for the first World Championship race under the 3 litre formula, Team Lotus providing just one car for Jimmy—R11 fitted with the unique 2 litre Climax engine. Peter Arundell was down to drive the BRM H16-engined Lotus 43, but the power unit was still far from ready, although the works BRM team ran one H16 car in practice. Mike Spence was out again in Parnell's 2 litre BRM V8-engined car, R13, and Phil Hill made a welcome reappearance, this time piloting Bonnier's Lotus R6, fitted with a film camera for John Frankenheimer's epic film 'Grand Prix'.

The 2 litre Lotus 33 was ideally suited to the tigh circuit, and Jimmy took pole position by 0.2 secon from Surtees' 3 litre Ferrari. The reigning Wor Champion made a superb start, but as he tried to snat second the gearchange froze and the other 15 starte all flooded by into Ste Devote.

Surtees and Stewart fled round battling for the lea but Jimmy was soon lapping as quickly and stormi back through the field. He was seventh after 10 lap and then profited from retirements to take fifth plac Next he moved up into fourth place on Graham Hill tail, some way behind Bandini, who was in hot pursu of Stewart's leading BRM, Surtees having retire Jimmy forced Hill round faster and faster in th Tasman car, and the gap behind Stewart closed to 2 seconds. After 60 laps Clark forced the Lotus ahead Hill's BRM at Ste Devote and set off to chase Stewar Jimmy was really flying, and he picked up mo split-seconds on the leader through the Casino Squar down round the old Station Hairpin, hard-right on the sea-front and through the tunnel to the chicane. H rushed along the quayside, slid left through the Taba and rocketed round the long left-hander behind th pits. Hard on the brakes for the right-handed Gaswork Hairpin, and suddenly a dreadful crunch from the re suspension and a lurch signalled the end of his race. rear upright had split in two, and the wheel ha folded-in as the Lotus limped round the Hairpin t retire. Spence's rear suspension had also failed after 3 laps, and Stewart went on to his second Grand Epreuve victory in the BRM.

The Indianapolis '500' took place on its tradition date of May 30th, after the STP-Lotus onslaught ha suffered a troubled month's practice and qualifyin Problems began when it became obvious that th complex BRM H16 engine was going to need man months' development before it would be competitiv in 3 litre Formula 1 form, leave alone in 4.2 litre Ind trim. One engine was delivered to Lotus and teste briefly in its intended Lotus 42 chassis, but it was a fea to complete one lap of Snetterton trouble-free. S Colin fell back on the victorious Lotus-Ford 38s of th previous year, and with the latest 4.2 litre Ford V engines and a coat of lurid dayglo STP paintwork the began practice. Jimmy was unhappy with the handlin of his 'STP Gas Treatment Special' but managed t qualify it on the middle of the front row, with a average of 164.14 mph to Mario Andretti's pol position speed of 165.89 mph in his Brabham-base Brawner-Ford. George Snider was on the outside of th row in his Lotus 38-based 'Sheraton-Thompso Special' at 162.52 mph, and A.J. Foyt's sister car wa back on the sixth row, having been fastest qualifier o the second weekend with a four-lap average of 161.3 mph. Jimmy's STP team-mate in a sister Lotus-Ford 3 was Al Unser, who qualified directly behind Foyt a 162.27 mph, and Al Miller was the final Lotus runner i his splendid old 'Jerry Alderman Special' Lotus 29, th car which had started it all back in 1963. He average

158.68 mph and started on the outside of the penultimate row.

As the 33 starters bellowed round behind the pace car and received the green flag to start the race, Billy Foster's Vollstedt ploughed straight into the outside wall on the pit straight, came back into the pack and caused all hell to break loose with spinning and crashing cars all over the road and wheels, wishbones and half-shafts showering out of the sky. In all, 16 cars were involved in the enormous pile-up and as Jimmy came round in the lead on his first lap the red flags and lights went on, as in 1964, and the race was stopped. Al Miller and A.J. Foyt were put out amid the carnage, the Jerry Alderman car catching fire and Foyt miraculously sustaining the only driver injury when he shinned to safety over the retaining fence and lacerated a finger!

The restart was given after a delay of 1 hour 23 minutes, and five laps were run under yellow caution lights to dissipate much of the cement dust laid down along the straight. The moment the green lights came on Andretti leapt into the lead with Clark and Snider hard on his heels, then the yellow came on again as Johnny Boyd's BRP-Ford slammed into the wall. There were only 21 cars left running after two racing laps!

Andretti dropped a valve on lap 27 and Jimmy inherited the lead, but he wasn't happy with his car's handling, and while slowing for his first scheduled stop on lap 62 he spun out of Turn Four, regained control and pulled into his pit, allowing Lloyd Ruby's Eagle to inherit the lead until lap 76 when it made its first stop. The fluorescent red Lotus was back in the lead, but after only nine laps the unmanageable car broke loose and spun on the back straight, kissing the wall. Jimmy made a rapid stop to check for damage, and pressed on in third place behind Ruby and Jackie Stewart's 'Red Ball Special' Lola-Ford.

On lap 132 both leaders stopped for fuel and Jimmy took the lead once more, but Ruby's Eagle was the fastest on the Speedway in the closing stages of the race, and on the 140th lap Lloyd dived inside Jimmy to take the lead at Turn One. But his car was throwing oil, and 12 laps later the luckless Texan became the first leader of the '500' ever to be black-flagged. Harlan Fengler waved him in with a resolution all too lacking back in 1963 . . .

Stewart had forced his way past Clark so he had inherited the lead on his first appearance at Indy, while behind the STP Special Graham Hill's Lola had moved into a challenging position by a consistent and regular run. George Snider collided with Chuck Hulse's Watson and crashed out of the race, and Al Unser lost his 'Thanks Vermilion' Lotus and stuffed it mightily into the wall, also escaping unhurt.

Stewart looked all set for a first-time victory in the '500' but at the 475-mile mark his oil pressure zeroed and he was out. There was great confusion at this time, for Colin, timekeeper Cyril Audrey and the STP pit all thought Jimmy was in the lead. In fact Graham had got ahead of Jimmy during one of the Lotus 38's spins and was now leading, and he went on to take the flag 44 seconds ahead of the World Champion.

Hill was elated as he pulled the Lola into Victory Lane, but Jimmy crossed the line thinking he had won, pulled into the same lane and found 'his' place occupied! There was great confusion and Granatelli considered protesting, but Colin Chapman has never protested a race result and maintains he never will. The timekeepers checked and rechecked their tapes and discovered where the Lotus crew had gone adrift, so Jimmy was placed second, having completed the full distance. After the race he 'translated' the STP initials, '. . . it stands for Spinning Takes Practice!' and with a payoff of 76,992 dollars he could afford lessons . . .

Two weeks later Team Lotus were back in Europe for the Belgian Grand Prix at Spa, where Jimmy was running his 2 litre R11 once again while Peter Arundell arrived for his first serious run in the new Lotus-BRM 43. Colin was viewing this season very much as an interim year, in just the same way as 1961 had been at the start of the 1.5 litre formula. Nonetheless, the BRM H16 engine demanded a completely new monocoque, and Maurice Phillippe had drawn the Lotus 43 to accept it.

The engine had a completely stressed crankcase capable of carrying rear suspension loads without any rear chassis structure, and the new chassis consisted mainly of a monocoque forward nacelle which terminated at the rear cockpit bulkhead as on the Lotus 39. The H16, comprising in effect two BRM V8 engines, each opened out to 180-degrees and mounted one on top of the other with their crankshafts geared together, was mounted rigidly on the rear face of this bulkhead, and accepted major suspension loadings fed into the heads and gearbox bell-housing. The monocoque wrapped over the driver's legs and formed an enclosed tank section behind his shoulders, and in comparison to BRM's P83 H16 chassis it had a lower frontal area about the cockpit and was much smoother and sleeker. It had a similar weight problem, however, as Maurice recalls, '. . . We knew we were in trouble when the first engine arrived and it took about six mechanics to lift it off the lorry. I believe eventually we put the engine, gearbox and rear-suspension assembly on some scales and found that they virtually made up the minimum weight limit on their own!'

Arundell made a brief appearance in the first practice session with chassis 43/1 and did three laps with a best time of 5min 1.2sec, compared with the lap record of 3min 46.4sec, and then something let go within the complex engine and that was that. Jimmy's engine also broke, and since his best time at that point was 3min 45.8sec he had to start on the outside of the fourth row. Early on race morning he took the repaired car for a trial run, but hadn't gone very far before the suspension collapsed, the tail of the car bottomed and he slid to a halt in a shower of sparks. Team Lotus rushed the car back to their garage and hurriedly rebuilt the suspension, then hustled it back to the circuit just in time for the race.

Rain was threatening at the start, and now Jimmy had another problem on the downhil starting grid. It was normal practice to chock the front wheels to stop the cars rolling forward, saving the driver the irksome task of holding on the brakes before the flag fell. Team Lotus' mechanics suddenly realised they hadn't chocked Jimmy's wheels and rushed on to the grid to do so, harried by start-line marshals who had just cleared the grid. Jimmy was distracted, the flag was dropped prematurely anyway, and the rest of the field rushed off led by Surtees. Jimmy thumped his Lotus 33 into gear and screamed off in pursuit, but he was thoroughly unsettled and before he reached the top of the hill at Les Combes his engine broke and he coasted to a stop; the four-times winner of the race was out after barely a mile.

Mike Spence, meanwhile, having qualified on the middle of the third row in Parnell's R13, was well within the pack as they hurtled downhill towards the right-hander past the Burnenville pub. On the entry to the curve the field suddenly found the road awash with sudden rain, and instantly Bonnier broadsided his new Cooper, Siffert spun his Walker Cooper and Mike crashed into the blue car, spinning down the roadside embankment and out of the race. More accidents decimated the field, Stewart having a particularly nasty one and being trapped in his BRM for several minutes, and only seven of the 15 starters completed that lap, victory finally going to Surtees' Ferrari.

The next World Championship round was the French Grand Prix on the Reims-Gueux circuit in July. Jimmy and Peter had their Spa cars and Mike Spence was in the Parnell 25-BRM, which had been straightened out after its shunt. This time Peter didn't get as far as the paddock gate to start practice when his H16 engine's distributor drive sheared, and in the evening he found the wrong gear leaving the pits and the clutch burned out as he staggered out of sight towards Gueux. Jimmy went out in R11 and returned shortly afterwards with blood and feathers on his face where he had been hit by a bird on the Soissons straight. His left eye was injured and Colin had him flown back to London immediately for treatment by an eye specialist.

Pedro Rodriguez was enlisted again to take his place in the Grand Prix, and David Hobbs took over his car for the Formula 2 event at the same meeting. Peter Arundell tried R11 while Colin, Pedro and the organisers negotiated, and the Mexican finally qualified the car on the centre of the fifth row while Arundell put 43/1 on the last row after it had swallowed another distributor drive.

At the start poor Peter was in immediate gear selection problems, stopped at the completion of the first lap, did two more slow tours searching for gears, and finally retired when the distributor drive failed again. The Lotus 43's racing debut had been inauspicious, to say the least.

Meanwhile, Pedro worked away in mid-field and consolidated sixth place, staying on the same lap as the leading 3 litre cars on this power circuit, and with retirements up ahead he soon inherited fourth place. He was still going very well on lap 41 when an oil pipe burst and he drove round to the pits, unfortunately damaging the engine rather badly on the way. Mike Spence stopped after only nine laps with a slipping clutch, so altogether it was a poor French Grand Prix for Lotus.

Jimmy's eye injury kept him out of the Formula 2 Rouen Grand Prix one week later, but he was fit for the British Grand Prix at Brands Hatch in mid-July. Colin still had problems, for the H16-engined car was obviously of little use until some serious development could be carried out on the transmission, and so he approached Leonard Lee of Coventry-Climax and asked for further assistance on the Company's 2 litre engine. Harry Spiers and Wally Hassan responded by producing sufficient bits to build-up another 2 litre unit, and Colin initiated work on a new Lotus 33 chassis—R14—for Jimmy to drive. It was intended to turn over R11 and the original engine to Arundell, but at the last moment the new unit did itself an injury so the original Climax was dropped into R14 and R11 was left powerless.

BRM then offered a 2 litre V8, which was readily accepted, although the installation job was far from simple, for the gear-change had to be moved from right to left to suit the Bourne-built transmission. Meanwhile Mike Spence began practice at Brands Hatch with Parnell's Lotus-BRM, this team having encountered and solved all these problems way back in 1964.

Jimmy qualified the new Climax car on the outside of the second row, while poor Arundell had to do his best with the hastily-completed BRM-engined car and wound up on the back row, still running it in. With the absence of Ferrari from this meeting the Frankenheimer film people were in trouble, and so on receipt of a large bundle of dollars the Parnell team sprayed their car bright red, Mike Spence wore a helmet similar to Mike Parkes' and the stage was set!

While Brabham ran away to win handsomely Jimmy became involved in a torrid battle for fifth place with Graham Hill's BRM. Graham had been shunted by John Surtees, now in the Cooper team, on the first lap and had a bent front rocker arm. But this affected him little, and the pair of 2 litre cars urged each other round into second and third places with Denny Hulme's number-two Brabham on their tails. Denny had come through the field like a rocket after a bad start, but he took many laps to find a way past the battling Lotus and BRM. Eventually he split them by nosing ahead of Jimmy on lap 37, and then found a way past Graham to make it a Brabham one-two.

Eight laps later Jimmy was in deep trouble. His brakes had been deteriorating for some time, and on the 45th lap the pedal went straight to the floor. He scrabbled into the pits and after an empty master cylinder had been topped-up he rejoined a lap down on the leaders, and finally finished a happy fourth to score his first World Championship points of the season.

The Indianapolis scene. Left: Louis Meyer, three-times '500' winner, stands among some of the dohc Ford V8 engines which his Meyer-Drake company supplied to teams for USAC racing. A total of 32 cars with his engines were entered for the Indy classic—24 qualified. Above: Andy Granatelli, Jim Clark and Colin Chapman agree the STP-Lotus deal. Below: The Lotus 38 looked superb in its vermilion STP livery.

Peter Arundell gave up the unequal struggle with the hastily rearranged gear-change of his car and retired on lap 32 after several stops, while Spence had to give up after 15 laps with a serious oil leak.

Once again there was just a week between the British and Dutch Grands Prix, and in practice at Zandvoort Jimmy rushed round in R14 to set a best time of 1min 28.7sec and take his place on the outside of the front row beside the Repco Brabhams of Jack himself and Denny Hulme. Jimmy also tried the BRM-engined car, and was 1.4 seconds quicker in it than Arundell.

From the start Jimmy split the two Brabhams on the way into Tarzan, and as Jack led away Denny tried for three laps before finding a way past the Lotus. Clark was on dazzling form and the Brabham drivers had to work hard together to stave him off on a circuit which suited his car. On lap 17 Hulme's engine died, and then Jack took off with Jimmy clinging to his tail.

Clark's car was shimmering through the back section curves with the engine shrieking away at peak rpm as he used all the road, right on the limit to offset Brabham's extra litre. On lap 24 the pair came up behind Bandini, Siffert and Spence and Jimmy saw a gap and dived through to take the lead.

By the 40th lap only Graham Hill in third place had not been lapped by the leading duo, and by absolutely first-time overtaking among the back-markers Jimmy had pulled out half the length of the straight on the veteran Australian. The circuit was slick and oily, which suited the Lotus rather than the heavier Brabham, which needed more room through the swerving back section.

Spence was having a great battle for fifth place with Bandini's Ferrari, the Parnell car now painted white with a green stripe and Mike wearing a helmet like Chris Amon's in deference to the film unit fakers. Bandini got away temporarily when Mike was baulked by Surtees, but shortly afterwards the Italian spun and Mike went past him again.

Around the 60-lap mark Jimmy suddenly felt a thump behind him as he braked into the Hunzerug turn behind the pits. It felt as though a half-shaft had gone, but the car accelerated perfectly apart from a vibration so he continued. The vibration damper on the nose of the crankshaft had broken, and flying bits had punched through the water pump casing and allowed the coolant to dribble out.

Jimmy became accustomed to the extra vibration and maintained his lead, but as his temperature gauge began to climb he eased back and Jack closed the gap. He caught the Lotus at the end of lap 75 as Jimmy headed into the pit lane, peeling off the straight near maximum speed and giving a superb display of controlled braking, screaming in with the wheels right on the point of locking-up to stop squarely before his pit. Colin shielded Jimmy's back from escaping steam and water with his lap board as Leo Wybrott and Dick Scammell opened the filler cap and added water, then R14 was away into the race, two laps down on Brabham, one lap behind Hill, but still ahead of

Below: Driver at the peak of his powers—one of the happi
shots of Jim Clark. Bottom: 'We knew we had a weight probl
when it took six mechanics to lift the H16 off the lorry'. Rig
Jimmy, Colin and Peter Arundell discuss the Lotus-BRM 4
promise at Monza. Bottom right: The V8 cars and Lotus peo
at Monza.

20

24

Fighting drives: At Brands Hatch (below), Monza (right) and Zandvoort (bottom) Clark forced his basically obsolete or under-developed cars into challenging positions. He was fourth in Britain, retired in Italy and third in Holland.

Stewart. Jimmy finished third after a superb race, and Mike Spence was fifth after another fine performance in his older car.

Amid all this drama Peter Arundell had been trundling round near the back of the field, and he stopped on the back stretch close to where I had been watching the race when his ignition died after 28 laps. I tried to help him trace the fault, but neither of us realised that the ignition pick-ups beneath the car were covered in oil and so he retired.

The Nurburgring and the German Grand Prix were the next challenge, and after the Dutch failure Climax had modified their 2 litre engine and dispensed with the vibration damper. The revised engine was still mounted in R14 for Jim Clark, and Peter Arundell was running his usual R11 with the side-exhaust 2 litre BRM V8 installed. Spence's Parnell R13 was back in its original colours, and for the Formula 2 race to be run concurrently with the Grand Prix, the Ron Harris-entered Lotus 44s were listed for Gerhard Mitter, Pedro Rodriguez and Formula 3 star Piers Courage.

Jimmy took pole position for the first time during the season with a best lap in 8min 16.5sec, a clear 1.5 seconds quicker than Surtees' Cooper-Maserati. Arundell was slower than Spence and desperately unhappy with his car, and Mitter became a non-starter after a foot injury became inflamed during practice.

Race morning was dull and wet, and Team Lotus fitted Dunlop tyres briefly before returning loyally to the Firestone fold just before the start. Conditions were extremely treacherous as the 3 litre cars powered away from the 2 litres, but Jimmy was fourth at the end of the first lap behind Brabham and the Coopers of Surtees and Rindt. The Firestone-shod Lotus 33 was skating all over the tortuous Nurburgring and first Gurney then Hill went by. Jimmy latched on to his old adversary's tail but when Denny Hulme forged ahead he decided to settle down for a race of attrition. He regained sixth place when the Brabham dropped out, but on lap 12 he lost control of his unmanageable car, and slid off the road down a grassy bank.

Mike Spence went out on lap 13 when his battery died after the alternator drive belt had broken, but Arundell marched round through it all, grimly determined to finish, and was placed eighth and last. In the Formula 2 section Courage dropped off the road into the bushes on lap 4, and Rodriguez lasted only four more laps before his engine failed.

There was a gap in the Formula 1 calendar until September when the Italian Grand Prix took place as usual at Monza. When practice began Team Lotus rolled out their BRM-engined Lotus 43 for Jimmy Clark to make his 3 litre Formula 1 debut. The engine was still an early type which fired as two eight-cylinder units, the two firing cycles coinciding instead of having separate pulses. This had caused all kinds of vibration problems, and although development work with crankshaft balance weights and damper discs had minimised the effect it had not proved a very satisfactory answer.

Consequently BRM had introduced a new engine firing as a pure 16-cylinder, and their gearbox problems had also been carefully researched. Basically the early gearshift problems were caused by mounting the clutch and flywheel assembly on the tail of the gearbox shaft rather than on the engine shaft. When the clutch was disengaged flywheel effect would speed the gearbox internals rather than allow them to slow down, so the driver had to wait for the internals to slow before he could engage another gear, or grit his teeth and force the next cog home. Naturally one could not expect any self-respecting racing driver to count three between changes, and so the engagement dogs were hammered and abused until they broke and refused to hold any gear. Development shifted the clutch body on to the engine shaft, reverting to normal practice, and the problems were largely resolved.

Originally the cable gearchange linkage had been thought to be the culprit, but changes to a rod linkage showed no improvement, and it was then that the Bourne engineers began to look for something more fundamental. Colin retained a cable change on Lotus 43/1, which was equipped with the redesigned transmission.

Peter Arundell was again in the BRM-engined Lotus 33 and Clark's R14 with 2 litre Climax V8 was entrusted to 'Geki' Russo, which seemed rather unfair on the regular number-two. The Parnell team ran two cars for a change, Mike Spence in R13 and Giancarlo Baghetti in R3, with similar 2 litre BRM V8 engines and Hewland transmissions.

Jimmy was encouraged in practice by finding his Lotus 43 to be much more reliable than the works BRMs, and although Colin held R14 in reserve the H16 car did virtually a race distance in practice with nothing worse than a minor oil leak from the gearbox. But at the end of practice the gear-change deranged itself so Jimmy qualified R14, and 'Geki' stood down, biting his nails while the Lotus 43 was examined. However, Jimmy chose to race the 3 litre car and so the Italian was assured of his drive.

Clark started from the outside of the front row, third fastest behind Scarfiotti and Parkes in the works Ferraris, who were 0.2 second and 0.5 second quicker, respectively. Arundell went well and was the quickest 2 litre qualifier on the outside of row five, with Spence 0.9 second slower on the row behind. 'Geki's' limited practice resulted in last place on the grid, and Baghetti broke the Parnell 25's gearbox, so ran the spare works Ferrari V6 under the team's entry.

As the cars rolled forward from the dummy grid Jimmy's fuel pressure was fluctuating wildly and he was frantically checking the inside of the cockpit for signs of a leak. He was caught on the hop as the flag fell and chuntered off the line with his engine almost stalling, his arm held high in warning. He struggled way next-to-last, but as his 16 cylinders came on song he began to shoot through the field. He took two cars on lap 2, another on lap 3, and by lap 5 he was ahead of all the privateers and on the tail of the works cars. He moved into seventh place when Brabham retired after eight laps, then disposed of Ginther's new Honda V12 and Rindt's Cooper-Maserati, to run fifth, but on lap 13 he felt a bad suspension vibration and shot into the pits. Inspection showed that a tyre valve had torn off a rear wheel, deflating the inner safety tube which had bunched on one side and put the wheel wildly out of balance. It was changed and Jimmy screamed back into the race, one lap behind.

Later his gearbox dogs were damaged, and then the battery refused to restart the engine after a further stop which lost him even more time after another quick burst through the field; eventually he retired with the transmission jammed in gear after 59 laps. Both BRM H16 team cars had retired during the first two laps of the race . . .

Arundell had a good race-long battle with Anderson's 2.7 litre four-cylinder Brabham, but with only four laps remaining his BRM engine dropped a valve and broke up past the pits. Anderson went on to take sixth place while Peter was classified eighth. Spence was consistently fast once again to take fifth place, and 'Geki' was ninth after a slow but neat drive at the tail of the field.

The Oulton Park Gold Cup reverted to being a Formula 1 race after a year in the Formula 2 doldrums, and Team Lotus entered the H16-engined 43 for Clark and R14 with the Climax engine for Arundell. Jimmy had the Lotus 43 working well in practice until the gear-change hung up in the gate; before he could catch it the revs went sky-high and the engine turned itself inside out, so Jimmy was forced to take over the 33 and poor Peter stood down.

Jimmy ran fifth behind the works Repco Brabhams and BRMs from the line, and on lap 12 he inherited fourth place when Stewart retired, but he spun at Knickerbrook in his efforts to maintain contact with the 3 litre cars, and finally finished third behind the victorious works Brabhams. Mike Spence went out when his clutch began to slip, caused by a broken piston, which allowed the crankcase to pressurise and blow oil over the clutch plates . . .

The next stop was Watkins Glen for the United States Grand Prix at the beginning of October. Team Lotus arrived with what had now become their three regular cars, 43/1 for Jimmy, and two Lotus 33s, R14 for Peter Arundell to have his first 2 litre Climax drive and R11 with a BRM engine for Pedro Rodriguez. After practising two of the cars Jimmy took second place on the grid, 0.11 second slower than Brabham, in the Lotus 43, but just as he brought the car into the pits after this lap a clonk from the engine heralded trouble and a pool of oil formed under the exhaust megaphones. BRM offered Colin their spare engine to allow Jimmy to take advantage of his good starting position, and this was craned in overnight, the installation being completed in a mad scramble just before the start. Pedro started from the fifth row but poor Arundell was on the back again, with no time in the Climax car after it had been held back for Clark use.

A leaking union was tightened on the Lotus 43 o the grid, and then Lorenzo Bandini led away from th start with the H16 Lotus-BRM second. Jimmy slow dropped back, while Bruce McLaren began to mak ground at the back of the field after a bad start. A Bruce dived inside Pedro's car on a corner he caught th Mexican by surprise and the Lotus turned into his ca losing both body panels in a shower of glass-fibr Pedro stopped, then continued, but without a nos cone his engine ran cold and he stopped again to hav the radiator partially blanked-off with tape. But th was not sufficient, so he stopped again, and when th engine would not restart he retired in the pits after 1 laps.

The leaders were lapping the tail of the field, when Arundell was getting used to R14, and he moved ov to let Brabham and Bandini through but didn't se Surtees and shut the door on him. At the next corne Peter signalled Surtees through, but simultaneously h an oil patch and slid wide. The two cars touched whee and spun crazily into the rough, then continued afte 'Big John' had told Arundell what he thought of drive who didn't use their mirrors.

Meanwhile, Brabham and Bandini had droppe Clark, but the Ferrari retired after 34 laps and this pu Jimmy into a distant second place, and when Brabha retired on lap 55 the Team Lotus 43 was well and trul in the lead. Since both works H16s had already faile the Lotus crew waited with bated breath, but their ca circulated long enough to complete the 108th and fin lap to score their first Grande Epreuve victory of th season, and the only Formula 1 win ever to be recorde by the H16 engine. Arundell finally took a solitar World Championship point with sixth place, but Mik Spence had retired after 74 laps with electric problems, when lying fourth.

A USAC-style race followed the next weekend a Mount Fuji in Japan, where Jackie Stewart's 'Red Ba Special' Lola-Ford won from Bobby Unser's 'STP G Treatment Special' Lotus-Ford. Jimmy's STP Lotus 3 suffered an engine failure in practice and didn't sta the race since for some obscure reason engine chang were forbidden by the regulations . . .

On October 23rd the World Championship seaso was wound-up by the Mexican Grand Prix at Mexic City, although the title had long-since gone to Jac Brabham. Team Lotus ran their three Watkins Gle cars, Arundell and Rodriguez swopping machines an Jimmy having another try in the Lotus 43.

His H16 engine had not been rebuilt between race so it can have come as little surprise when it brok during practice. Jimmy had just lapped in 1mi 54.06sec, 1.78 seconds under Gurney's 1.5 litre recor when the engine burst as he backed-off and boilin water cascaded over his shoulders. There was a gapin hole in the top of the engine where the retaining bol on a balance weight had broken, and the weight ha flown out of the crankcase, accompanied by a show

ew people can have been as surprised as Clark and Chapman when the H16 BRM-engined Lotus 43 survived the race istance at Watkins Glen to win the United States Grand Prix! This was the only victory ever scored by the engine; in his case the BRM team's spare unit had been hurriedly loaned to Team Lotus and fitted the night before the race.

of red hot pieces of metal and scalding water. The engine had covered about 300 miles, the same distance as Stewart's engine when it had suffered a similar failure in the United States, so this appeared to be the fatigue life of the balance weight bolts.

The following day Colin kept practice to a minimum in the re-engined Lotus 43 and Jimmy finished just 0.32 second slower than Surtees on the front row of the grid. Rodriguez got on to the outside of the fourth row while Peter Arundell began his last Formula 1 race, second slowest, on the back row.

Mike Spence was an unfortunate non-starter, for a hub bolt had dropped from the front suspension during practice as he braked for one of the bends, and the wheel and brake caliper had fallen off and sent the car into the guard-rail, where it ended up in a heap although Mike was unharmed.

Jimmy was sixth at the end of the first lap of the Grand Prix, but next time past the pits he was in obvious gear-change trouble; he lasted nine laps before pulling into the pits with the gear-change broken, to retire. Pedro spun early-on at the hairpin, but carved back through the field to the delight of the partisan crowds, and by the half-way stage was lying third. But on lap 49 R14 clattered into the pits with the crown-wheel and pinion broken, and shortly afterwards Arundell pulled in with the temperature gauge of R11 off the clock. But the gauge was faulty, so he rejoined the race and went on to finish seventh.

During the 1966 season Team Lotus had contested all nine World Championship rounds and had won on three of the four non-title Formula 1 events and wc one; all eight Tasman rounds and won one; and the ST Lotus-Ford 38s had run in two USAC-style races with Team Lotus driver and won neither. Therefore, of 2 major events entered, only three had fallen to work Lotuses, the marque's worst record since 1959, whe the old Lotus 16s had had such a disastrous time.

But 1966 had been very much a transitional season pending the arrival of the new Ford-powered ca which were due the following year. Ford were anxiou to back their sponsorship with a strong driver pairin and in November Henry Taylor, Ford's Competitio Manager, was instructed to approach Graham Hill. Th Ford offer was a handsome one, and when BRM fe unable to meet Hill on certain assurances about th structure of their own racing programme he accepte the Lotus-Ford offer, returning to the fold after seve seasons at Bourne.

After his sad season Peter Arundell, once th undisputed king of Formula Junior and the hottest ne driver in Formula 1, left the team to run his ow accessory business. Later he spent some tim instructing trainee drivers at Brands Hatch, then joine the MacNamara racing car company in Germany befor disappearing into obscurity .

Clark's Lotus-BRM 43 howls round Watkins Glen with th Cooper-Maseratis of Jo Siffert and John Surtees and Bruc McLaren's own American Ford-powered car in hot pursuit. Th following year Lotus were to use English Ford power.

1966 RACING RECORD
Other formulae and classes

Cheshunt's new Formula 3 car, the Lotus 41, was the big story before the turn of the new year. Development of the old Lotus 35 had been shelved and a completely new spaceframe was designed. This was regarded as a fundamental reversal in company policy, for the Lotus 27/32/35 series monocoques had completely ousted the old multi-tubular spaceframe since early 1963. The Lotus 31 had appeared briefly as an inexpensive Formula 3 car when the new class was introduced in 1964, but it soon became apparent that a more sophisticated chassis would have to be produced in order to stay competitive. This is what the later monocoques attempted to do—unsuccessfully—and they were not very attractive buys since maintenance could be difficult and chassis repairs were expensive and time-consuming.

So Lotus Components performed a smart about-face and released the new Lotus 41 late in 1965. The basic spaceframe chassis was similar in arrangement to the earlier-type Lotus 22/31 frames, but gained a considerable amount of extra rigidity from sheet-steel panelling around the pedal box and in the undertray. Stressed steel diaphragms formed the front and rear bulkheads and provided cockpit reinforcement, while the rear bulkhead was hollow and doubled-up as an oil catch tank. Further rigidity was gained from solid engine and gearbox mountings, and a low body-line was achieved by canting the Cosworth MAE66 engine at 30 degrees to the right.

Wind-tunnel testing resulted in a sleek and smooth glass-fibre bodyshell, with a steeply inclined one-piece screen (unlike the air-deflector arrangements of other models) and a drooping nose line. It was said to add 3 mph to the top speed compared with the earlier cars, and despite all that had been said about the advantages of monocoque design, the new spaceframe was both lower and narrower than the Lotus 35 hull . . .

The suspension had a very wide track (56½ inches at the front and 56 inches at the rear), and outboard coil-spring/damper units reappeared at the front in a conventional double-wishbone system. The wishbones were slightly angled to give an anti-dive characteristic which would prevent the nose dipping under braking. At the rear the suspension was also conventional, with reversed lower wishbones, single top links, twin un-parallel radius rods on each side and outboard coil-spring/dampers. Six-spoke cast-magnesium 13-inch wheels were used, identical to those on current Formula 1 models, and 10½-inch Girling disc brakes were mounted outboard all round.

Cosworth's latest engine provided 100 bhp at 9,500 rpm, and drove through a Hewland Mark 4 four-speed gearbox. Frame tubes once again were employed to carry oil and water between the engine and radiators, and fuel tankage was provided in a single left-side tank, although twin side tanks and an under-seat reserve tank could be fitted for longer events. The wheelbase was 90 inches, overall length 144 inches and overall width 66 inches, and the new car was far from cheap at £2,475 ex-works, fully-assembled.

During the previous year the Brabhams run by C. Lucas (Engineering) Ltd had been notably successful, and Charles Lucas himself, the youthful team patron, was signed-on by Chapman to run the works-backed Formula 3 team for the new season. So Charles Lucas-Team Lotus came into being, and Piers Courage and Roy Pike were invited to carry the works Lotus 41 banner internationally.

Piers was outstanding among the Lotus 41 drivers, scoring five major wins and clinching the Craven 'A' Championship which was run at the Grands Prix de France Formula 2 events as a supporting feature. Roy Pike, his rapid American team-mate, notched a couple of major wins, and Peter Revson won in a bright green Ron Harris Lotus 41 at Montlhery. Freddy Kottulinsky notched four more tempestuous successes with his Swedish-based Lotus 35, so the marque won a round dozen of the major Internationals of the year. But there were 86 events in all, and the well-established Brabhams claimed 42 of them! De Sanctis, the rather obscure Roman manufacturer, won ten of these events to put the rather meagre Lotus total in clear perspective . . .

In home events the Lotus 41s went very well, and after a handful of races in his own Brabham, Jackie Oliver was selected to run a Lotus Components-backed car. He scored a series of wins at club level, and put up some good International performances against the 'official' works cars. Ron Harris ran Lotus 41s for John Cardwell and Rob Slotemaker as well as Revson, and the former was third at Monaco while private cars were handled by Derek Bell, Morris Nunn and John Hine among others. Bell showed tremendous speed in his bright red car, but crashed it rather often and had a chequered season before maturing into a fine all-rounder in later years.

While Lotus' serious return to Formula 3 racing met with mixed success, the Ron Harris-Team Lotus Formula 2 programme sank without trace so far as major success was concerned. This was the year of the Brabham-Hondas, for Jack Brabham's close second place behind Jimmy at Albi the previous year had been a clear augury of things to come. The sophisticated roller-bearing Honda engine was just untouchable in normal circumstances, and although Cosworth's fuel-injected SCA finally produced 140 bhp and revved to a shattering 11,000 rpm it just could not compete. The Harris team began the season with their old Lotus 35s, but at Barcelona Jimmy made his debut in the new Lotus 44.

In my book this was the most beautiful Lotus single-seater ever produced; unfortunately it was also one of the least successful. It was based on the Lotus 35 monocoque hull, modified to accept wide-track suspension similar at the rear to the new Lotus 41. At the front inboard coil-spring/damper units operated by upper rocking arms were retained, but the upper arms and the lower wishbones were increased in length to give a Lotus 41-like broad track. The nose and tail body sections were also from the 41 and the combined effect was a graceful and slender study in aesthetics.

Clark's engine failed at Barcelona, but after a mid-season absence from Formula 2 racing he returned at Karlskoga and Keimola to place third behind the all-conquering Brabham-Hondas. At Montlhery he actually split them to finish second in the Lotus 44's best performance of the season, and he challenged hard for the lead on the Bugatti Circuit at Le Mans, then placed second at Albi and third in the final meeting at Brands Hatch. Peter Arundell had a regular drive in the number-two Harris car, finishing second to Rindt's Brabham-Cosworth in the Eifelrennen, while the other car was driven by Peter Revson, Pedro Rodriguez, Mike Spence, Piers Courage, David Hobbs, Trevor Blokdyk, Picko Troberg and Eric Offenstadt at various meetings. Pedro was third at Rouen, Mike fourth at Crystal Palace and Blokdyk sixth at Reims while Offenstadt, an ex-motorcyclist, made a tremendous impression.

During the season the Lotus-Cortina also came into its own as a rally car, and although it was never exceptional in this field (it was not really sufficiently robust or reliable) Rod McLennan and Roger Wilson won the gruelling Shell '4000' rally in Canada, and Roger Clark/Robin Edwardes were placed third in this event in a similar car. Bengt Soderstrom and Gunnar Palm won the Acropolis Rally in a Ford works car, and they repeated the success in the RAC Rally of Great Britain. Jim Clark shared a similar car with Brian Melia in this event, and got the hang of rally driving very quickly before the car went out of shape on a series of yumps, landed askew and rolled across a ditch. It came to rest the right way up but there was no way its intrepid crew could get it back across the ditch on to the track so they had to retire. Brian, later to be familiar as the Autolite spark plug representative at all major European race meetings, vividly recalls Jimmy describing how he fought to keep his feet away from the throttle while the car rolled . . . 'to prevent it over-revving, d'you see . . .'! The Geneva Rally also fell to a Lotus-Cortina, crewed by the Belgians Gilbert Staepelaere and Andre Aerts, and the car acquitted itself quite well in this most gruelling form of motor sport.

In club racing John Miles shone in Britain with his John Willment-entered Lotus Elan. He won the Autosport Championship with this car, and a highlight of his season was a superb race at Brands Hatch where he stopped to have a flapping engine cover removed then hared back through the field to win on the line from a 4.7 litre Sunbeam Tiger. Other prominent Elan drivers included Bob Ellice, Keith Burnand, Bill Dryden and Eric Oliver, the former Sidecar World Champion, in the days when he was passengered by Denis Jenkinson of Motor Sport magazine.

The sports-racing car classes were enlivened during 1966 by the presence of 'big-banger' Group 7 cars left high and dry by the abandonment of major races for them. Brian Muir scored several club wins in the much-modified Willment car, while John Berry (of Lotus 37 fame) had graduated to one of the fearsome Lotus 40s. Ken Crook won the Guards Championship in a Lotus 23, and he was also one of the leading Lotus 31 Formula 3 exponents in home events. Jim Morley, Richard Knight and Ben Moore all ran similar Lotus 23s, while Jon Derisley won the British Monoposto Formula Championship in his Lotus 31. Scotsman Willie Forbes shoe-horned a BMW engine into a Lotus 35 and drove it with great verve to win the Bob Gerard Formule Libre Championship, while Peter Deal was the new Lotus 'Three-Seven' owner and he notched a superb string of 15 class victories, 13 of them also being outright wins. Tommy Weber went very well in a BRM-engined Lotus 23, while Tony Dean ran a Lotus 41 and a Lotus-Cortina for the Willment team. He crashed the Formula 3 car repeatedly, but when he kept it on the road he was very competitive.

In hill-climbing circles Peter Meldrum's Shorrock-Ford-powered Lotus 22 took second place to Tony Marsh in the RAC Championship, relegating Boshier-Jones' famous old 'Yellow Peril' down the table.

Right at the end of the season, in the traditional Boxing Day Brands Hatch race meeting, a new Lotus competition model appeared, and in the time-honoured fashion it won first time out. This was the prototype Lotus 47 mid-engined coupe, driven by John Miles. The car was developed directly from the road-going Renault-engined Lotus Europa, which had recently been announced, and was seen as an answer to the mid-engined Ginettas in club racing, as well as a replacement for the Elans in more major events.

It shared the back-bone chassis, glass-fibre bodywork and mid-engined configuration of the Europa, but the rear chassis prongs were remodelled to accept a 165 bhp Cosworth-Ford Mark 13 twin-cam engine. This used Tecalemit-Jackson fuel-injection, and was mated to a five-speed Hewland FT200 transaxle, modified around the rear end to drive an alternator for the electrical system. The double-wishbone front suspension was similar to that of the Europa apart from using fabricated upper wishbones which were fully adjustable. At the rear completely new cast alloy uprights were used, with single top links, reversed lower wishbones and twin radius rods for location. The Europa's fixed-length drive-shafts were replaced by shafts using rubber-doughnut inboard joints and outboard BRD universal couplings. Two fuel tanks were mounted on each side behind the doors, and the oil tank and spare wheel were placed in the nose ahead of the passenger while the combined radiator and oil cooler was offset to the right in the same compartment. Knock-on cast-magnesium spoked wheels were fitted, 8½ inches wide at the front and 10½ inches at the rear, and Girling disc brakes were mounted on the hubs all round.

A total of 55 of these cars were to be built by Lotus Components, and with this early success things looked extremely promising for the forthcoming season... third at Le Mans, fifth at Montlhery and eighth at Brands Hatch. Harris had signed him after he had led the opening laps at Karlskoga in his own Lola, but regrettably all his promise faded in later years.

With the end of the season the 1 litre Formula 2 died, a new 1,600 cc class having been scheduled to replace it when the 3 litre Formula 1 was expected to reach a measure of maturity in 1967, its second season. During the three years of 1 litre Formula 2 racing 48 events had been held, Brabham winning 29 of them, Lotus 12, Lola 4, and 1 each by Cooper, Alexis and Matra. Jim Clark was the second most successful driver of the formula, but his tally of nine wins palled when compared to Jack Brabham's 15 . . .

In touring car racing the BRSCC's British Saloon Car Championship catered for Group 5—virtually 'free-for-all'—cars, while the European Touring Car Challenge retained Group 2 regulations. In Britain the new regulations specified that the body shape and trim above hub height must be virtually identical to production-line standards, but what went on beneath that level and under the bonnet was the entrant's own business!

Consequently, Team Lotus developed their cars with wishbone front suspension, fully ball-jointed throughout, plus a highly-developed and well-located leaf-spring rear end. BRM-prepared dry-sump fuel-injected twin-cam engines were used, developing fully 180 bhp, and with spoked cast magnesium wheels the latest Lotus-Cortina works cars were real racers. Team Lotus won the British Saloon Car Championship entrant's title, but Jim Clark's other commitments caused him to miss the driver's title. Peter Arundell, Jacky Ickx and Sir John Whitmore were among the works drivers during the year, although the English Baronet was also Alan Mann's first-string in the European Touring Car Challenge, defending his title.

The Alfa Romeo GTAs were now fully developed and they stole the European title although Whitmore won at Aspern and Zolder, as well as the mountain climbs at Mont Ventoux and Eigenthal. His Zolder victory, with Ickx in second place in another Alan Mann car, so astonished Alfa Romeo that they protested against the Lotus-Cortinas' eligibility. The scrutineers consequently stripped the red and gold cars, but found them to be entirely legal. They then had a good hard look at Jochen Rindt's third-place works Alfa and disqualified it!

Jackie Stewart and Peter Procter were included in the Alan Mann team during the year, but Peter's racing career came to a horrifying end at the Goodwood Easter meeting when he suffered severe burns in a Broadspeed Anglia.

Left, top to bottom: The Charles Lucas-Team Lotus Formula 3 equipe scored many successes with Piers Courage (top) and Roy Pike driving their Lotus 41s. John Miles' Willment Elan pipped a Sunbeam Tiger on the line at Brands Hatch after a pit-stop to remove a loose bonnet. This staggering drive helped him on the way to a Lotus Formula 1 seat in 1969.

1967

Grand Prix comeback

The Group's first year in its new home saw the labour force growing to a total of 521, and production was stepped up as it had been when the old company had first moved into Cheshunt from Hornsey. While the Elan and Europa formed the Group's mainstay another brand-new model was added in mid-Summer, and as the Ford-engined Grand Prix cars set the pace in Formula 1 racing so the touring cars underlined their splendid reputation. Formula Ford came into being during the year, and Lotus Components adopted it virtually as their own and were to produce more cars for this class in the next three years than virtually all the other interested constructors put together.

The new car was the Elan Plus-2, the original conception of which dated back some three years. The plot was to produce a car combining the best features of the Elan Coupe with the capacity to carry two adults and two children, on a long holiday, in comfort and with reliability. The result was the Lotus 50, with its exceptionally attractive body styling based on the normal two-seater model, but 2 feet longer overall and 10 inches wider. The new body sat astride a redesigned backbone chassis which in general arrangement and suspension geometry was virtually identical to its forerunner. A twin-Weber 40DCOE-carburated 1,558 cc twin-cam engine was fitted, producing 118 bhp at 6,250 rpm, and this was mated to a Lotus-Ford 'semi-close ratio' gearbox connected to a 3.7:1 back axle. The top speed was quoted as 120 mph and 0-60 mph acceleration occupied 7.9 seconds. The new body shape competed with the Europa with a low drag factor of 0.3, and this contributed to some very good touring fuel consumption figures of as much as 28-30 mpg. Servo-assisted Girling 10 inch diameter disc brakes were fitted all round, and 5½J-13 pressed-steel wheels with centre-lock fixings were standard.

The interior of the Plus-2 was fully carpeted, with a fully instrumented polished mahogany facia and a two-wave-band push-button radio adding extra touches of elegance. Well-shaped, fully-adjustable front bucket seats were augmented by two occasional rear seats which were suitable for children, and airflow ventilation systems were built-in. Air horns, windscreen washers and safety-glass windows were other standard features, and with this car Lotus went decidedly up-market and even further away from their original competition-based touring designs.

This was achieved without any loss of performance, handling and the 'swervability' for which the original Elans were so renowned. The prototype chassis was tested at the Motor Industry Research Association's test track near Nuneaton, and was disguised for the occasion with a boxy van-like body. From this ugly duckling emerged an extremely beautiful car whose behaviour and handling certainly matched its looks. The price on its introduction was fixed at £2,113, which matched up pretty well with the old Elites back in 1961 . . . such is progress!

At about the same time as the new car was being shown to the press at Hethel, the 5,000th Elan was rolling out of the production shops. The decision was also taken to discontinue sales of kit cars, as they tended to interrupt the new flow-line production and assembly techniques and generally got in the way. This was another step towards Lotus' full maturity as a major motor manufacturer and one of Britain's most successful exporters.

But the Lotus image took something of a knock at Indianapolis, where the two STP-backed cars for Clark and Hill finished 31st and 33rd out of 33 starters. Once again there had been a great panic to prepare the cars following the non-arrival of special 4.2 litre BRM engines, and new Chief Mechanic Mike Underwood had a devil of a job to produce competitive machinery. Clark's car in fact was one of the two-year-old Lotus 38 monocoques with the normal Ford V8 installation while Graham's car was the Lotus 42F bitsa, consisting of the monocoque nacelle intended for the H16 engine, with a hastily-built spaceframe engine bay to carry the Ford power unit. The whole project was hasty and uncompetitive, and it was Lotus' worst showing at Indy since they had first appeared there.

BRM continued to produce racing versions of the twin-cam Lotus-Ford engine, and their dry-sumped units finally produced as much as 155-160 bhp on carburettors and 185 bhp on fuel injection. Production of the cylinder heads was taken over by the new Hethel engine shop in mid-Summer, while Villiers continued

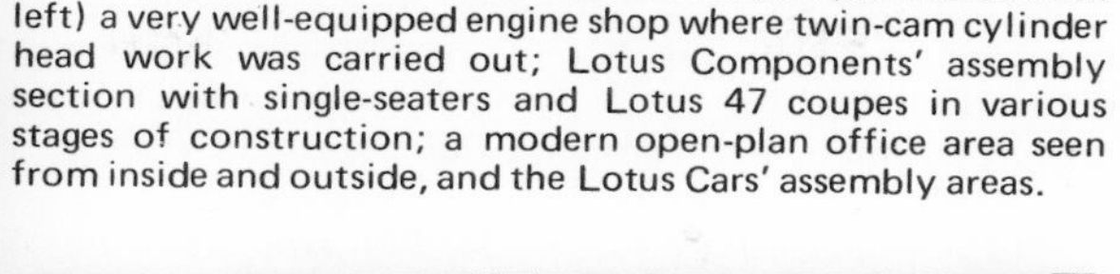

Lotus' new home. The Hethel works included (clockwise from left) a very well-equipped engine shop where twin-cam cylinder head work was carried out; Lotus Components' assembly section with single-seaters and Lotus 47 coupes in various stages of construction; a modern open-plan office area seen from inside and outside, and the Lotus Cars' assembly areas.

to assemble the engines for another year in Wolverhampton. Hethel took over complete twin-cam production in the middle of 1968.

Ford had replaced their original Cortinas with the new Mark 2 body-style in October the previous year, and in February the new model Lotus-Cortina appeared as a very much more civilised vehicle than the original road-racer. Lotus no longer built the chassis and the model became virtually a pure Ford. When 'Twin-Cam' designations replaced the 'Lotus' part of the name in the Escorts and Cortinas of later years, the Lotus part in their development finally became submerged.

Colin was beginning to shape his ideas for the Lotus engine of the future. As far back as 1964 the Lotus powertrain engineering staff had initiated a range of design studies into what eventually could become a 100 per cent Lotus engine, and in late 1966 this had evolved into a clear scheme for a 2 litre double-overhead-camshaft 16-valve unit of slant-four configuration.

While Steve Sanville's staff began to work along these lines, Colin received a shock at the London Motor Show in October 1967. There on the Vauxhall stand was the Lotus engine of the future!

The block was almost exactly what the Lotus design studies had described, and Colin immediately began negotiations to use the Vauxhall crankcase and bottom-end as the basis for the prototype Lotus units. Sanville and Ron Burr—who had joined the company from Coventry-Climax—began work on a new 16-valve twin-cam head for the engine, and for the time being at least plans for a Lotus block were set aside.

A second blow to the strong Chapman constitution was administered at the Motor Show when Esso abruptly announced their withdrawal from motor racing sponsorship owing to high current economic pressures. Esso had heavily subsidised Team Lotus' activities for many years, and new sponsorship was vital for the coming year, so Andrew Ferguson compiled a list of the top 200 British companies and each was contacted with regard to possible backing. Replies were few and far between, but coincidentally David Lazenby, who was now running Lotus Components, heard from somebody else in the office that John Player, the tobacco people, were interested in backing some form of racing promotion.

Lazenby's informant knew someone who worked for Sales Link, Player's PR agency, and David contacted them hoping to find backing for his projected two-car Lotus 47 team for the coming year. He found they were very enthusiastic and reported to Ferguson that something deeper might come from these first contacts. Andrew contacted Player's promotional people, who confirmed that they were very interested, and he drew-up a proposal for Formula 1 sponsorship listing probable cost and intended return. A visit to the John Player headquarters at Nottingham followed, and within two hours the whole deal was agreed and Gold Leaf Team Lotus came into being.

The extent of the backing was very considerable, anc when the details were finalised early in the new year i was announced that Gold Leaf colours were to appea on the Lotus 49Ts in the remaining Tasman Formul events, on the Formula 1 cars in the 11 Grands Prix stil to be run, and on the Formula 2 Lotus 48s in 23 Britisl and European races. Lazenby gained his Lotus 4 backing for a projected 35 events, and Player' marketing director Geoffrey Kent was looking forwar with Chapman, Ferguson and the rest of the team to successful first season . . .

During this first year at Hethel Lotus produce 1,985 cars (none of them Lotus-Cortinas) and th Group's turnover increased by a staggering £647,000 t £2,803,000, while gross profits were up by £73,000 a £324,000. This was achieved although overall ca production was down by 520 units. It had been a unsettled year, but as production began to get into it stride everything was set for the best year ever i 1968 . . .

Left, top to bottom: People in the back! The Elan Plus-2 was designed as a car for a young family. The new backbone chassis was a redesign of the original Elan unit. There was a more spacious boot. Above and below: The 1967 Elan Plus-2 and Lotus-Cortina both represented a move away from Lotus' former 'open-road racers'.

Warwick Farm's Tasman Championship round in 1967 saw Jim Clark and Graham Hill racing as team-mates for only the second time. Jackie Stewart (above) holds pole position in the BRM with Jimmy's 2 litre Lotus-Climax 33 beside him and Graham's brand-new Formula 2 Lotus 48 on the outside. Below: The Cosworth-powered Lotus 48 leads Jack's 1-litre larger Repco-Brabham.

1967 RACING RECORD
Grands Prix and other major formulae

Graham Hill made his debut as Team Lotus' joint number-one driver at Kyalami for the South African Grand Prix in January, the Grand Prix having been moved to the Johannesburg circuit after East London had become unavailable. Graham and Jim Clark had a pair of BRM H16-powered Lotus 43s on hand for what was to be their last appearance, both cars using the older 'double-eight' engines.

Jimmy was in the latest 43/2 while Graham took over the United States Grand Prix-winning 43/1, which suffered a leaking fuel bag and continual overheating problems during practice. Clark spent some time sorting-out his new car, and overnight the water pipes were rerouted outside the monocoque to remove one source of cockpit heat. Despite various problems, Jimmy ended up third fastest on the inside of the second row, but Hill was right back on the eighth row with only 13 practice laps to his credit.

Tim Parnell was to run a 'second-string' BRM team during the 1967 season, but his Lotus-BRM 25, R13, was entered for Piers Courage, who had been promoted from Formula 3 and was to start on the back row.

At the end of the first lap, Jimmy was fifth, Piers 12th and Graham 17th after a poor start, but Hill forged through the field and was dicing with Spence's BRM for 12th place when he thumped over a kerb and bent the front suspension. This allowed the nose of the car to sag and bottom, which wore a hole in an oil pipe, and then he spun on his own oil at Crowthorne and limped home to retire after just six laps.

Clark's Lotus 43 was beginning to overheat, and he stopped to have the nose cone removed and so expose the whole radiator area. He completed three more laps with the temperature gauge showing little improvement, and the final straw came when the metering unit diaphragm broke after 22 laps. Courage 'did a Hill', tore off an external fuel line and gave up after 51 laps. It was not a happy outing for the team, but before the dust had time to settle over Kyalami Jimmy was flying South for the start of a new Tasman series at Pukekohe.

After the crushing success of the 2 litre BRM V8s the previous year Team Lotus finally threw away their four-cylinder Climax engines and shipped the latest 2 litre Climax V8-powered Lotus 33, R14, to Auckland for Clark to drive. BRM had further developed their V8 engine and enlarged it to 2,070 cc, and the series promised a battle royal between Clark and reigning Tasman Champion, Jackie Stewart.

Stewart won the 21-lap preliminary race at Pukekohe from Clark, but in the New Zealand Grand Prix Jimmy led narrowly from the line before the BRM nacked ahead into the first corner. The two Scots drove a tremendous race, running side-by-side along the straight, but with Stewart leading consistently through the corners. But with three laps to go Jimmy clipped a tail-ender, who moved over to let Stewart through then swung back into the Lotus' path. The impact tore the bodyshell, and as the car accelerated out of the hairpin the airstream lifted the glass-fibre and whirled it away over Jimmy's head. He pressed-on, holding his helmet brim with one hand to save his neck and with his overalls billowing in the wind, and despite this handicap he set a new lap record of 1min 0.5sec, 104.1 mph, in an effort to close on Stewart, but finished an honourable second, 5.4 seconds behind. Dene Hollier's Lotus 27 won the 1,500 cc class behind all this drama in the first New Zealand Grand Prix to be run at a 100 mph average.

Jimmy had his revenge the following week at Levin. The Lotus 33 won the 14-lap preliminary race from Stewart to take pole position for the 50.5-miles main event, which Jimmy led all the way, winning by 3 seconds from the BRM number-one at 86.6 mph, and setting his second consecutive fastest lap of the series at 47.5 seconds, 89.05 mph. Hollier's Lotus 27 was second in the 1,500 cc class, and sixth overall.

Christchurch was the next stop for the Lady Wigram Trophy and Jimmy led the preliminary race before first Stewart and then Jack Brabham, in a 2.5 litre Repco V8-engined car, went by. The Lotus driver was thumped on the forehead by a flying pebble and finished with an angry lump above one eye. In the 44-lap main race he took an early lead, but on lap 5 he got too close to the marker tyres inside one corner and hit them. One tyre flew into the air and the hapless Stewart collected it full in the windscreen. It shattered the perspex and ruptured an oil line before bouncing clear, so Jackie was out and Jimmy went on to win at record speed, 16.9 seconds ahead of Attwood's second-string BRM. Hollier was second in the 1,500 cc divison once again and seventh overall, and Jim Clark now led the Tasman Championship by 15 points to Attwood's 10 and Stewart's nine.

Teretonga, the World's Southern-most motor racing circuit, was the scene of the final New Zealand round, and this time Jimmy was blown-off in the preliminary race by Denny Hulme's Repco-powered 2.5 litre Brabham.

He was slightly shaken by the way the bigger-engined car had left him on the straights, and all but jumped the start of the 96-miles main race. This put him in an undisputed lead, and he scored his hat-trick, beating the BRMs of Attwood and Courage and setting another fastest lap, at 1min 3.3sec, 91.1 mph. Hollier drove another good race in his Lotus 27, finishing sixth overall and third in his class behind a brace of Brabham-Fords. Clark's victory did not affect his Tasman points score as only the New Zealand Grand Prix and the Christchurch race counted in this season's revised series.

In the first Australian round at Lakeside in February R14 appeared once again with the original South African Grand Prix-winning Climax engine installed, although the second engine was craned-in for all but one of the remaining races. More Lotuses joined the competition, Leo Geoghegan entering his Team Total ex-Clark Lotus 39 and Greg Cusack making his International debut in the ex-Clark/Palmer Lotus 32B.

At Lakeside Stewart lost the lead to Clark on lap 39 when he missed a gear, and the Lotus 33 won from Brabham at 97.47 mph, with a new lap record of 54.6 seconds along the way. Cusack dropped out when his gear-linkage fell apart, and Geoghegan ran fourth until a wheel bearing broke-up.

The Australian Grand Prix was back at Warwick Farm the following weekend, and Team Lotus fielded two cars for the first time since 1960. Graham Hill had talked Colin into freighting the new 1,600 cc Formula 2 prototype car out to Australia, and was on hand to give it its racing debut.

This Lotus 48 used a sleek and compact full monocoque hull similar in concept to the preceding Lotus 42 and 43 designs. The monocoque nacelle terminated in the rear cockpit bulkhead and Cosworth's brand-new 1,600 cc FVA engine was carried in a multi-tubular steel subframe bolted on to it. Lotus 33-type suspension geometry was adopted, with inboard coil-spring-damper units operated by rocker arms at the front, and twin radius rods, reversed lower wishbones and single top links with outboard coil-spring-dampers at the rear. The new engine represented phase-one of Ford's alliance with Cosworth Engineering, and the twin-cam cylinder head with its four valves per cylinder topped a Ford Cortina block to produce around 200 bhp. 'FORD' lettering featured prominently on the cam covers, and there was no mistaking the unit's parentage.

Team mechanics Leo Wybrott and Alan McCall found an oil pressure problem on the new 2 litre Climax engine fitted in Jimmy's 33, and Graham had problems when his 48 broke its crownwheel-and-pinion. However, both cars were healthy for the race, and while Jimmy was beaten into second place by Stewart the little Formula 2 prototype was queen of the piece in Hill's hands. He raced round in a rousing third place until the crownwheel-and-pinion failed a second time just before half-distance and put him out. Geoghegan was placed fifth despite a time-consuming spin after early delays.

Jimmy clinched the Tasman title at Sandown Park, Melbourne, the following weekend. Although Brabham and Stewart led away from the line both retired within the first dozen laps and Clark was left to streak home to a 101 mph victory. Geoghegan made it a Lotus one-two success, and the Firestone boys popped some Champagne to celebrate their first title victory.

One race remained, at Longford in Tasmania, where Jack Brabham won the 126-mile South Pacific Trophy ahead of Jimmy, who had been third in the first 36-mile preliminary race and second to Stewart in the other, while Geoghegan retired with engine failure and was a regretted non-starter in the main event. Jimmy ran his original engine in this meeting, and rounded-off a fine tour with the Tasman title, five firsts and three second places to his credit.

Back in Europe Team Lotus were still lacking suitable cars while work went ahead on the new Lotus 49 to accept Cosworth's Ford DFV V8 engine, so they missed the Brands Hatch Race of Champions which was held just one week after Longford.

Parnell ran the Lotus-BRM 25B once again, this time for Chris Irwin, who had give Courage a hard time in Formula 3 the previous year. He qualified the old car on the sixth row and drove smooth and steady races in the two 10-lap heats, finishing 13th in one and 11th in the other, then extended the car rather more in the 40-lap final, and finished sixth.

More than a month elapsed before the next Formula 1 race, the International Spring Cup at Oulton Park, the proceeds of which were to be donated to the ambulance services and the newly-formed International Grand Prix Medical Service, whose mobile hospital was making its debut in the paddock.

Team Lotus took a pair of Formula 2 cars to contest their class in this charity race, and entered Graham in his usual 48/2 and Jackie Oliver in the Lotus Components spaceframe 41B, which consisted of a modified Formula 3 frame fitted with the 1,600 cc FVA engine. Piers Courage reappeared in Parnell's R13.

In Heat One Graham charged round to take fourth place behind Hulme's Brabham, Surtees' Honda and Spence's Parnell BRM H16, but in Heat Two the Lotus 48's oil filter bowl worked loose and Graham smoked into the pits. Oliver finished sixth and seventh in the two heats.

In the 30-lap final Hill drove a rousing race which had the crowd on their toes. He disposed of Stewart's H16 so effectively that the Scot crashed in an attempt to stay in contact, and with a best lap of 1 min 33.4sec, 106.42 mph, he shot into second place between Brabham and Surtees. Unfortunately the throttle stop broke and his fuel metering unit linkage slipped over-centre, forcing him into the pits for attention. He rejoined a lap adrift and rocketed round to finish eighth and last, but a great crowd-pleaser. Jackie Oliver finished fourth, beating McLaren's 2 litre BRM V8-powered car and Spence's BRM H16. Graham's best lap equalled the new Formula 1 record set by Brabham and Hulme, which was an indication of how potent the new Formula 2 cars could be!

Two weeks later Team Lotus appeared at Silverstone for the International Trophy race, with Graham driving R11, fitted with one of the latest 2.1 litre BRM V8 engines. Jimmy had drastically reduced his English racing programme on his accountant's advice, and was living in Paris to qualify for exemption from British surtax, but Parnell's old Lotus was entered again for Chris Irwin.

Graham detected a slight misfire on the warming-up lap, before lining-up on the third row of the pitifully small 12-car grid. He was slow away and soon stopped for a plug change, rejoining one lap down but among the leaders on the road. He buzzed Stewart's H16 mercilessly, and went by before the BRM broke. The Lotus-BRM was the fastest car on the circuit and Hil finished fourth after setting fastest lap of the day at 1min 30.0sec, 117.08 mph, just to show who was master. Irwin was seventh, handicapped by indifferent handling.

The following Thursday practice began at Monte Carlo for the Monaco Grand Prix, and Team Lotus were still without their new cars. Jimmy's victorious 2 litre Climax-powered Tasman car had been rescued from the ship's hold which it shared with several hundred tons of fruit, and was hastily prepared for the race, while Graham had his Silverstone car with BRM engine and Hewland transmission.

Both drivers were soon lapping quickly and looked most determined about the whole business, substituting skill and daring for their lacking litre. Jimmy placed R14 on the inside of the third row, while Graham was on the outside of row four with his Friday practice time. His second gear had broken on the Saturday and the mechanics could only remove the pieces, leaving him without second for the rest of the session, before installing a new gear cluster overnight.

Bandini's Ferrari charged into an early lead, but Brabham's Repco engine threw a rod and gushed oil at the Station Hairpin. He spun and then motored round to the pits since miraculously his engine was still running, but this left a trail of oil round the second half of the circuit, and as the leaders rushed into the chicane on lap two they threw up a huge pall of cement dust. Jimmy was down in the field, having been delayed by Jack's original spin, and he thought an almighty shunt had caused the cloud, so he rushed up the escape road. By the time he had reversed out to rejoin the race he was a resounding last.

The circuit was very treacherous, but Jimmy fought his way back through the field, and passed Graham on lap 11 to take seventh place. Four laps later Stewart and Rindt both retired ahead of him, and the Lotus pair inherited fifth and sixth positions.

Surtees' Honda was sick and dropped back, putting Jimmy fourth and chasing hard after McLaren's brick-red 2 litre car, and on lap 38 the Lotus closed right up on the McLaren's tail with a new record lap in 1min 29.5sec, but as Jimmy chased Bruce down into the left-handed Tabac corner on the sea-front his right-hand rear upright failed and in an instant R14 spun like a top and smashed tail-first into the retaining wall. The rear suspension was wiped out, and Jimmy was a spectator from there on.

Graham was in clutch trouble by this time and Chris Amon forced his Ferrari past to take fourth place. As the long race swept on McLaren's battery began to flatten, and as the lack of amps affected his ignition he slowed and let both Amon and Hill go by. Then on lap 82 a tragic accident occurred at the chicane which was to take the life of Ferrari's team-leader, Lorenzo Bandini. Amon ran over some debris and stopped to have a punctured tyre replaced, and this allowed Graham to go through into second place behind Denny Hulme's Brabham. He held the place to the finish to score six World Championship points.

Two weeks later the Syracuse Grand Prix clashed with a Formula 2 round at Zolder and attracted a very indifferent entry, although two of the seven starters were works Ferraris which dead-heated, driven by Mike Parkes and Ludovico Scarfiotti. Chris Irwin ran the Parnell Lotus-BRM 25 once again, and finished fourth, three laps behind.

As always the month of May brought practice and qualifying for the annual Indianapolis '500' and in 1967 86 cars were entered to battle for the 33 places on the grid. After the previous year's debacle it was disturbing to see two cars crashing into each other as they raced to be first out of the paddock gates on the first practice day!

Lotus had been hoping to turn the 4.2 litre BRM H16 engine into a raceworthy proposition in time for this year's race, but it was a lost cause. Consequently the two Granatelli-sponsored Lotuses reverted to running 4.2 litre Ford double-overhead-camshaft V8 engines.

The Ford-engined Lotuses for Clark and Hill were both christened 'STP Oil Treatment Specials', unlike the previous year when Jimmy's car had publicised Granatelli's 'Gas Treatment' additive. Jimmy made the grid on the first day of qualifying with a four-lap average of 163.213 mph, but Graham couldn't work up a competitive speed and decided to come back and try for a quicker average on the second qualifying weekend. He made the field at the last moment as 31st qualifier, with an average of 163.317 mph, quicker than Clark but way down on the grid due to the distinctly peculiar Indy qualification system.

Among the Grand Prix drivers entered, Stewart, Hulme and Rindt all made the race, but Amon, Rodriguez, Bianchi and Bucknum all failed to make the grade. The basically year-old Lotuses were giving their drivers a hard time, but A.J. Foyt's Coyote-Fords on row two had started life as Lotus 38s. 'Ayjay' and his father had modified the cars almost beyond recognition by replacing much of the Cheshunt magnesium with Texan chrome-molybdenum, beefing-up the monocoque, and adding new body panelling, a spoiler under the nose and a duck-tail engine cowling. Foyt drove his Coyote at 166.289 mph to take the inside of the second row, with team-mate Joe Leonard to his right at 166.098 mph.

Beside Leonard sat Granatelli's bet-hedger, the STP-Paxton Turbocar, driven by Parnelli Jones and powered by a Pratt & Whitney ST6B gas turbine. 'Silent Sam, The Whooshmobile' whistled round at 166.075 mph to qualify and was a portent of Lotus things to come. Jimmy wound-up on the inside of row six, while Larry Dickson's old Lotus 38, dubbed the 'Vita Fresh Orange Juice Special' was on the outside of row seven, and Graham was on the inside of the last row.

It was cold and windy on race day, and as the cars went out on their parade lap there in the pit lane sat car number 81, Graham Hill's, with a dead engine. The starter shaft had broken, and as the field rumbled by behind the pace car the STP crew rushed out another starter trolley and fired-up the Lotus. Graham slid into position at the tail of the field as the grid began their rolling lap, thanking his lucky stars he hadn't been somewhere in the middle of the grid!

As the pace car pulled off the grid broke and bellowed into Turn One, but Jones was in the lead and he whistled round at record speed, leaving all the piston-engined cars floundering in his hazy wake. But on lap 16 yellow lights began to flash warning of rain on the back stretch, and as showers engulfed the Speedway the reds came out to call a halt at the end of lap 18 . . . At 4.30 pm, with rain still falling, it was announced there would be no more racing that day, and the '500' would resume at 10.00am the following morning; it was the first time the race had ever been stopped and not restarted on the same day.

Jimmy had been 18th when the race was stopped, and on a sunny Wednesday morning the runners restarted in line astern for the third time in four years, and again Jones' Turbocar left the piston-engined runners for dead. Only 13 minutes after the restart Graham pulled into the pit-lane, out for the day with a burned piston, and on lap 36 smoke streamed from Jimmy's vermilion car and he, too, pulled in to retire with seriously oiled plugs. Larry Dickson finally dropped out on lap 180 and the Turbocar looked all set for an historic win when its gearbox bearings suddenly failed with only three laps to go. Foyt was presented with the lead and he picked his way through a four-car shunt on the last turn to win before the red flag went out again. Leonard was third in the second 'Sheraton Thompson Special', while Dickson's was the best-placed true Lotus, back in 15th place, Jimmy was classified 31st and Graham 32nd among the 33 starters . . .1967 saw a crushing Lotus defeat at Indy.

But faith was soon to be restored for the Dutch Grand Prix followed at the end of the week and the new Lotus-Ford 49s were ready at last. Graham had been testing the first chassis in England while Jimmy was either racing on the Continent or sitting in his Paris flat pondering his problems. Team Lotus took two of the new cars to Zandvoort, and Jimmy saw his 49/2 for the first time when he arrived there for practice.

In basic conception the Lotus 49 was similar to the 42 and 43 models designed for the H16 engine. Once again the engine was a major load-bearing chassis member bolted on to the back of a truncated monocoque nacelle, with the rear suspension and transmission bolted on the back of the engine.

The monocoque was skinned in 18-gauge L72 aluminium alloy sheet shaped over mild-steel bulkheads, and the fuselage side bays carried two 15-gallon fuel bags with a 10-gallon collector tank beneath the driver's seat. An access plate on top of the forward monocoque section opened on to the oil tank and pedals, which were mounted with their master cylinders on a fabricated forward bulkhead. Ahead of this bulkhead a spidery tubular sub-frame carried a combined oil-and-water radiator, while the front suspension picked-up on the forward bulkhead and on a pick-up point sunk in the hull. The suspension layout was similar to that of the preceding cars, but new cast uprights carried thick ventilated brake discs well inboard of the wheels and directly in the air-stream for efficient cooling.

The new engine was attached to the hull at four points, by two strap plates bolted to the cam covers and by studs projecting from a bracing below the auxiliary drive belt. The rear suspension picked-up on triangulated sub-frames bolted to the rear of the engine block and the cam boxes, and the German ZF company provided five-speed-and-reverse ZF 5DS12 transaxles. Two-piece air deflector screens were fitted, and with an impeccable green-and-yellow finish the two brand-new cars looked superb.

Friday practice soon showed that the cars' performance mirrored their good looks, for Graham took 49/1 round in 1min 25.6sec, Gurney's Eagle being the only other car under the 1min 26sec barrier. Jimmy sorted-out his new 49/2, but was worried by a vague feeling of instability late in the afternoon. His 1min 26.8sec best lap was fourth fastest of the session, equalling Hulme's Brabham.

Overnight the suspension of 49/2 was checked and only a slight play in the taper-bearings on the wheels was found. They were adjusted and everything else seemed fine, but on Saturday Jimmy's sensitivity was demonstrated and a more fundamental fault was revealed when a ball-race broke-up within a rear hub and split the upright.

Colin and Maurice Phillippe were most despondent at this failure, for at first it looked as though a design fault had caused the upright to split, but closer examination revealed the true cause and a new hub-carrier assembly was made up and fitted.

Meanwhile Jimmy watched while Graham fended-off all attacks on his pole position, lowered his time to 1min 24.6sec and beat Gurney by 0.5 second and Brabham by a clear second.

It was remarkable how Lotus fortunes were mirrored by adverse reaction in the other pits. When Graham proved so fast all were glum and despondent, and when the new engine began to pop and bang with ignition troubles all were smiles. When the fault was cleared and Keith Duckworth's engine began to sing raucous and clear once more, general gloom descended again! Jimmy's car was completed shortly before the end of practice, and he did a few bedding-in laps, his previous day's best time putting him on the outside of row three

Race morning found the Lotus and Ford hierarchy tense and barely approachable, but from the start Graham howled away from the field. The green-and yellow Lotus bulleted down the long straight past the pits and was in complete command while Jimmy was still playing himself in and acclimatising himself to the engine's sudden surge of power which came in with a bang at around 6,500 rpm.

After five laps Hill led Brabham by 2 seconds, and four cars were on the reigning Champion's tail, Jimmy and his Lotus 49 amongst them. After 10 laps Graham

Left: Jimmy tells all after winning the New Zealand Tasman round at Teretonga. Above: Graham Hill uses that familiar BRM power to take second place at Monaco. Below: Jimmy won the Tasman round at Christchurch's Wigram airfield circuit after 'throwing' a marker tyre at Stewart!

was leading with Jimmy fourth behind Brabham and Rindt, but next time round hearts fell in the Team Lotus pit when Brabham's gold nose appeared first out of the Huzarenvlag.

Rindt, Clark and the rest screamed by, and then the Lotus appeared coasting silently along the straight and into the pits. Keith Duckworth and the mechanics had a close look at the engine, attempted to restart it, and finally decided that the camshaft drive gears had failed, so the car was pushed away.

After 15 laps Jimmy had settled in and began to go motor racing. Brabham was still leading, but Jimmy flashed by Rindt and then stole the lead from Jack next time round. Then he just motored away into the middle-distance, making the job look so easy and effortless.

A win first time out seemed too much to hope for, but Jimmy pulled out 11 seconds on Brabham and then eased off, lapping comfortably in 1min 28sec yet still slowly drawing away. Pulses quickened in the Lotus pit as he went round and round and the race drew on. In the closing laps he eased off and his engine lost its characteristically sharp note, but as his times lengthened to 1min 31sec he still maintained a long lead and won the Dutch Grand Prix by 23.6 seconds from Brabham. He averaged 104.49 mph and set a new record lap of 1min 28.08sec to end a period of Lotus uncompetitiveness in Grand Prix racing and put a whole new perspective on the Formula 1 scene. Within a year the Cosworth-built Ford V8 engine had become the mainstay of the formula and it went on to score four consecutive World Championship victories for its drivers and chassis constructors. Inevitably, the Lotus-Ford performance at Zandvoort completely overshadowed Chris Irwin in the Parnell Lotus-BRM, who finished seventh after another characteristically intelligent and consistent race. At this point Denny Hulme headed the Championship table with 16 points to Pedro Rodriguez's 11 and Jimmy's nine, while in the Constructors' standings Repco Brabham led Cooper-Maserati by 18 points to 11, with Lotus-Ford third with nine points.

A fortnight later the Belgian Grand Prix took place at Spa, and after the previous year's pitiful performance Team Lotus were out for gold with their new cars, and with about 408 bhp from their engines, everybody waited to see how the new Lotus 49s would perform on this high-speed circuit. The lap record stood to Phil Hill's 7 litre Chaparral sports-prototype at 3min 35.6sec but Jimmy soon lapped in 3min 31.5sec and Graham in 3min 32.9sec to put things in perspective!

Both Lotus 49s were using tab spoilers on the nose cone to combat lift at their expected maximum speed of around 190 mph, but Colin was dissatisfied with his chassis' stability and the spoilers were removed for the race. Jimmy took pole position with a shattering 3min 28.1sec, over 151 mph, with Gurney and Hill respectively 2.3 and 4.8 seconds slower; Graham had oiling troubles with his engine. Chris Irwin practised

Birth of a World-beater. Above: Graham Hill discusses prospects for the new Cosworth-Ford engine with Ford director Harley Copp, one of the 'fathers' of the project. Right: A very dapper Graham examines the first Lotus-Ford 49 at Hethel in company with Maurice Phillippe. Bottom right: Graham, Colin Chapman and '49/1', ready for action. Below: Jim Clark gets the feel of the new car at Zandvoort, assisted by Colin and Dick Scammell. Keith Duckworth just stands and thinks.

TEAM LOTUS
LOTUS
Ford

Above: Piers Courage ran this Lotus 35-based Lucas-Martin V8 in practice for the Brands Hatch Race of Champions, lapped 4 seconds slower than Gurney on pole position then scratched from the race with engine maladies. The car was later destroyed in a testing accident. Below: Winner first time out. Jim Clark makes no mistake with the Lotus-Ford 49 at Zandvoort.

Parnell's Lotus 25/33, but raced a Tasman BRM instead.

Graham's car wouldn't start on the dummy grid and he flattened the battery trying to fire it, so was left stranded as the pack rolled forward. But Jimmy made a fine start and rushed ahead over the hill as Graham trundled sadly into the pits for a new battery.

Jimmy's 49/2 shrieked past the pits at the end of the lap, with Stewart and Gurney in distant pursuit, but at the end of the third lap Graham was back in the pits to retire 49/1 with clutch failure. After only ten laps Jimmy had built a 21-seconds lead over Stewart, but at the end of the 12th lap he pulled into the pits with the engine firing on seven cylinders. One of the Autolite plugs had been over-tightened, and another was fitted. The stop had dropped Jimmy to seventh place by the end of the next lap, and then another plug failed, and he stopped again before rejoining in eighth place. Now his clutch was not freeing properly, and with the ZF transmission's baulk-ring synchromesh he was having trouble changing gear, the linkage was damaged in his struggles, and the car limped to the finish stuck with only third and fifth gears. Jimmy profited from problems afflicting Scarfiotti and Rodriguez, and was sixth at the finish, while Gurney eventually won in his Eagle from Stewart's H16 BRM.

After these Spa problems a new clutch assembly was adopted for the French Grand Prix, and a new progressive throttle linkage was adopted to smooth the sudden power surge of Duckworth's engine. The windscreen shape was altered to prevent buffeting at high speed, and the dash panel was mounted on rubber because the new engines had a fierce vibration period. A new control was fitted to this panel, to adjust the front/rear braking ratio, and an interesting addition appeared on the back of the gearbox. An obscure FIA ruling insisted that the exhaust pipes should not protrude more than 10 inches beyond the tail of the car, and in the Lotus' original trim the Cosworth's tail pipes went well beyond this figure. So a double-loop 'crash bar' was added on the back of the gearbox, to bring the 'tail' within the 10-inch limit.

The French Grand Prix was held for the first and only time on Le Mans' new Bugatti circuit, a 2.8-mile loop around the mighty 24-Hour race pit complex, and during practice both the Lotus 49s were dogged by an untraceable misfire. Graham's car cleared long enough for him to take pole position by 0.1 second from Brabham and 0.8 second from Gurney, but Jimmy drove very hard with a sick engine to take his place on the second row, his time of 1min 37.5sec comparing with Graham's 1min 36.2sec.

Jack Brabham took the lead from Hill and Jimmy was third by lap three, second on lap four and first on lap five, towing Graham clear of the pack. On lap 11 Graham went ahead, but three laps later he coasted to a stop with his crownwheel-and-pinion sheared, and on lap 23 Jimmy dropped out with an identical failure when leading handsomely. Graham had set the fastest lap at 1min 36.7sec, 102.3 mph, but that was little recompense.

The failures were thought to have been caused by flexion in the transmission casing, and Colin flew direct to Friedrichshafen with the two broken units, where the German engineers confirmed the diagnosis. This had allowed the mesh to shift with disastrous results, the adoption of internal sliding splines in the differential, to allow for drive-shaft plunge, being a contributory cause. Orthodox splined half-shafts required only a small hole in the transmission casing, but the new Lotus 49 system called for bigger holes to accept even larger ball races. These larger holes naturally reduced the casing's rigidity, and before Colin left Friedrichshafen that Wednesday new casings had been drawn and patterns made for casting. As a stop-gap measure thicker cast-iron side-plates were produced to replace the original magnesium components, cross-bolted together to stiffen-up the whole assembly. Such was the speed at which ZF worked that six modified transaxles were in the Team Lotus transporter at Silverstone for the British Grand Prix less than two weeks after the French race.

The two regular cars had been further modified with revised clutch linkages and throttle operation, but again they suffered terrible misfiring problems in practice. Cosworth's fuel system had a by-pass valve which bled off fuel not required by the injection system and returned it to the tanks. Keith Duckworth puzzled out the problem overnight at Silverstone and decided the by-pass was bleeding off too much fuel, so he reduced the size of the bleed hole by honing down an ordinary household pin and stuffing it in the orifice. All trace of misfiring, for the moment, disappeared . . . but the true cause was deeper rooted.

Jimmy secured pole position with a time of 1min 25.3sec, getting in some much-needed chassis development on 49/2, while Graham took second place on the rank with 1min 26.0sec. He then found 49/1 feeling twitchy and eased off to return to the pits. He cruised into the pit lane at around 70 mph, whereupon there was a fierce jolt from the rear, the car turned sharp right into the wall then bounced back on to the road with the right-front wheel and radiator torn off and a bad crease in the hull. The left-lower radius rod had pulled away from the chassis when a bad weld had failed, and the wheel had turned outwards, putting the car nose-first into the wall.

Back at Hethel two more chassis, 49/3 and 49/4,were on the jigs and Colin made an instant decision to build up one of them overnight for Graham to race the following day. The wrecked 49/1 was rushed back to Norfolk by road and Colin flew the mechanics back to start work on the new monocoque. Hurried 'phone calls brought in help from weekenders, and about 16 men set about building a new car in one night. The engine and rear suspension of 49/1 was grafted on to the 49/3 hull, and final wiring, plumbing and suspension setting was completed in the paddock back at Silverstone next morning. The car looked strange with an old Lotus 33 nose panel fitted, but a cheer went up when the bleary-eyed mechanics unloaded it. It was over-filled with fuel and a flooded cockpit had to be mopped dry before Graham took his place on the grid.

The new car turned a wheel for the first time on the warming-up lap, but Graham was soon following Jimmy round in the race, and from the 10-lap mark they asserted themselves in a firm one-two lead. Graham went ahead after 26 laps, and after 34 laps only six cars remained on the same lap. But on lap 55 Graham was in trouble again, for an Allen screw locating the inboard end of the top link on the left-rear suspension had fallen out and allowed the wheel to lean inwards drunkenly. He staggered round to the pits where the screw was replaced, then charged back into the fray, after losing two laps and dropping to seventh place. But after only ten more laps his engine broke just past the pits and he was out. Meanwhile Jimmy cruised round serenely and won his fifth British Grand Prix by 13 seconds from Hulme's Brabham. There was great rejoicing in the Lotus camp, and even Hill was philosophical. Hailed with a "Hard luck Graham" in the paddock by a sympathetic pressman, he grinned broadly without altering his stride, and growled "Yeah, bugger innit!".

The next Championship round was the German Grand Prix at the Nurburgring in August, and for the first time Team Lotus had three 49s on hand. Jimmy was in his usual 49/2 while Graham's 49/1 had been completely rebuilt and 49/3 was available to either as a spare. The Allen screws in the suspension had been replaced by fixed studs with locking nuts, and all the ignition ancillaries were removed from above the gearbox to within the vee of the engine. In the Formula 2 section of the race Jackie Oliver appeared for Lotus Components in one of the green-and-yellow Lotus 48 monocoques.

Since the previous German Grand Prix a new S-bend had been added at the Tiergarten to slow cars past the pits, and so it was confidently expected that Jimmy's 8min 16.5sec practice record would be unapproachable, but in fact he took pole position yet again with a staggering 8min 4.1sec lap to prove that the sub-8 minute lap of the 'Ring was within sight.

Ever since its introduction the Lotus 49 had been troubled by its brakes, which cooled so well they glazed their brake pads, thereby reducing their effectiveness. The drivers would brake harder and harder to achieve less and less effect, and during the Friday lunch break Jimmy's car was fitted with thin un-ventilated front discs and harder pads, while comparative tests were intended with Graham in his usual car. But on his first lap Hill's gearbox seized through lack of oil. On Saturday 49/3 was prepared for Graham with modified brakes and he set off with a warning that they were different, but he misjudged a corner on the descent to Adenau and thundered from bank to bank, escaping unhurt from a nasty accident which wrecked the Lotus 49. A very ruffled Colin Chapman lent him 49/2 to complete sufficient laps to qualify, and he started from the middle of row four. His 49/1 featured ZF's new magnesium gearbox cheek plates, while Jimmy's 49/2 started with solid front discs.

Clark led away, but Hill's weekend of woe continued as he was nudged under braking for the first corner and spun wildly in the pack, luckily being avoided by everyone. So the first lap developed with the Lotus 49s running first and last, but Jimmy's right-rear Firestone tyre was punctured. He had had no chance to try the car on full tanks in practice, and attributed its strange handling to a full load of fuel, so pressed on. He finished lap 3 craning round to examine his rear suspension, and by lap four the car was weaving and wobbling so badly he was finally convinced that something was amiss and he slowed, letting Hulme and Gurney rush by. Jimmy limped up towards the Karussel, and suddenly saw his right-front wheel lean inwards!

He retired to the paddock with the front suspension rocker arm bent upwards and inwards, and it was only afterwards that the puncture was detected. Meanwhile, Graham very nearly had another accident on the sweeping left-hander after the Flugplatz. As he regained control he saw the right-front wheel jiggling about, and wobbled his way to the pits where the hub nut was found to be loose. It was tightened and he sped away, but on lap 8 an Allen screw dropped out, releasing the top-left suspension frame from the engine's cylinder head and allowing the whole system to collapse. A grim-faced Hill cork-screwed round to the pits to retire. The race went to the Brabhams of Denny Hulme and Jack himself, while Oliver saved the day for Lotus by winning the Formula 2 section after Ickx's incredible Tyrrell Matra had retired.

An addition to the World Championship series, the Canadian Grand Prix at Mosport, followed at the end of August; originally organised as part of the 'Expo '67' celebrations, it was destined to become a regular event.

Team Lotus rebuilt Graham's wrecked 49/3, and while Jimmy ran his usual 49/1 local driver Eppie Weitzes was down to run the spare car. New heavier-gauge rocker arms were fitted after the Nurburgring failure, and misfiring finally traced to blocked fuel filters had been cured. Chapman and Duckworth had found that the tiny fuel filter used in the standard system could compress and block under very high fuel pressure, so this had been replaced with larger filters left in the stores from the old Climax days.

During unofficial practice Jimmy spun 49/1 gently into the bank after the pits and buckled both right-rear radius rods and crumpled the monocoque skin slightly, but the damage was quickly repaired, and after trying both Goodyear and Firestone tyres in practice Jimmy took pole position with 1min 22.4sec to Graham's 1min 22.7sec, 0.5 second faster than Hulme. Weitzes took over R1 and put it on the middle of the last row, while local driver Mike Fisher ran Earl Chiles' newly-acquired Lotus 33, R11, fitted with a 1.9 litre BRM V8 engine, and was slowest of all.

On race day the road was as slippery as ice under an unrelenting drizzle, and Jimmy left the rest in his spray with Graham shadowing Hulme in third place. Denny charged through on lap 4 and Brabham passed Hill and closed on Clark. Then Bruce McLaren's new BRM V12-engined car carved past them all to relegate Jimmy to third place, but as the road dried Jimmy retaliated and rocketed away after the Brabhams. On lap 58 he took the lead from Hulme, but almost simultaneously the heavens opened and ten laps later Jimmy disappeared with drowned electrics. After a while he reappeared, but then his ignition failed again and he retired. Weitzes stopped by the pit barrier almost simultaneously with identical trouble, and Hill spun and stalled while suffering a dodgy clutch. He managed to push-start the car on his own and finally finished a distant fourth, while the Brabhams were again first and second, with Jack ahead. Fisher was slow and reliable in taking 11th place, but the fastest lap went to Clark's 49/2 at 1min 23.1sec, 106.53 mph, equalling the lap record. He was timed at 182 mph on the fastest part of the course, Graham at 178 mph and Weitzes at 162 mph, while Fisher had his old car well wound-up at 161 mph at the same point.

Denny Hulme led the Championship at this point with 43 points to Brabham's 34, Amon's 20 and Jimmy's 19, while Graham was eighth overall with nine points. Repco Brabham headed the Constructors' table with 51 points to Lotus-Ford's 22, but Cooper-Maserati had 21 and Ferrari 20, so it was still close.

Two weeks later the cars were back in Europe for the Italian Grand Prix at Monza, where all three Lotus 49s were fitted with solid discs. Giancarlo Baghetti took over the hire car 49/1, while Jimmy retained 49/2 and Hill 49/3. Rain disrupted practice, but Jimmy took pole position yet again with a best lap in 1min 28.5sec, 0.3 second quicker than Brabham and 0.5 second quicker than McLaren. Graham was on row three due to the rain and Baghetti was on the middle of the back row.

Sunday was the usual Monza mixture of sun and industrial haze, and in a badly scrambled start Jack Brabham broke away with Gurney, Hill and Clark tailing him. Jimmy hadn't extended his car in practice, and on lap three he bulleted past them all to take the lead, swerving from side to side to keep them out of his slipstream as he howled past the pits. When Gurney retired Graham took second place and Team Lotus began to dictate the race from a position of total strength.

But Jimmy's car began to handle oddly in the curves, and Denny Hulme pushed into the lead on lap 10. Next time round Jimmy was in front again but Denny could see the Lotus 49's right-rear tyre changing shape as it deflated, and at considerable risk to himself he dived inside Jimmy braking down from 180 mph into the Curva Parabolica and signalled to the Scot. Jimmy dived into the pits on lap 13 where the wheel was changed and he rejoined 100 yards behind the leaders, one lap down and 15th overall in the race. Jim Clark now began probably the greatest drive of his career . . .

By lap 21 he had caught the leading trio and had passed Bonnier, Ligier and Ickx to run 11th overall. Next time round he had slipstreamed past Brabham, and on lap 24 was ahead of Hulme and Hill. The intelligent New Zealander followed him through to retake the lead from Graham, but Jimmy now had a clear road ahead and on lap 26 he set a new record of 1min 28.5sec.

Spence and Siffert were blasted aside as the Lotus shot into ninth place, while the edge had gone off Brabham's engine and he fell back. On lap 30 Hulme's radiator cap failed and he lost coolant, stopping with overheating, and this left Hill with a 10-seconds lead over Brabham and the distant speck that was Clark's car rushing on to make up its lost lap.

On lap 33 Jimmy thrashed by Baghetti to take seventh place, and with Graham established in his slipstream the pair towed their team-mate round for several laps. Graham was hauled along into a 55-seconds lead over Brabham at the 50-lap mark, but then Baghetti's engine broke a camshaft and he was out.

On lap 59 Jimmy was set to pass the Honda, but then Graham's engine exploded in the biggest possible way just before the Parabolica and he coasted into the pits to retire. This left Brabham with the lead, but he had to complete the lap before actually passing the silent Lotus-Ford, gushing oil in the pit-lane. Jimmy took second place by blasting past Surtees' Honda, then when Jack appeared out of the Parabolica the Lotus was on his tail and Jimmy whipped out of his draught to take the lead on the way towards the Curva Grande! The tension and excitement was almost unbearable, for Jimmy had made up a whole lap on the leaders and had stolen back the lead at Monza, of all places.

Brabham was being towed along a close second while Surtees scratched hard to catch the Australian, and then on lap65 Jimmy slammed right as Jack weaved left and managed to break the tow to draw away from his adversary. The cars were covered by 3.2 seconds at the endof that lap, and on lap 66 Jimmy had pulled out another 0.1 second. But starting the 68th and last lap the gap was only 1.8 seconds and the Lotus 49 was in trouble. Its engine coughed and faltered as the bunch arrowed into the Curva Grande, and Surtees and Brabham dodged it as it slowed. The Honda led into the Parabolica where Jack slid through only to be beaten to the line by 0.2 second in a sensational finale. Jimmy's pumps had refused to pick up the last remaining gallons of fuel in his tanks and with a dead engine he coasted across the line to finish third, 22.9 seconds behind Brabham as the crowds flooded the track, bursting with enthusiasm for a fantastic motor race.

Back across the Atlantic, Team Lotus arrived in Watkins Glen for the United States Grand Prix where Clark and Hill were joined by the Mexican, Moises Solana, in the third car. There was a tacit battle for pole position in practice, and after Jimmy lapped at 1min 6.07 sec, Graham flashed round just as the final session was closing and stole pole position and its 1,000 dollars prize with a lap in 1min 5.48sec.

This pleased the Ford hierarchy not at all, and Public Affairs Director Walter Hayes was alarmed to see his vision of a Ford one-two before the parent company's own crowd apparently threatened. To this point Ford politics had played little part in team direction, but Colin suggested that Walter should tell the drivers of his worries himself. Consequently that Saturday evening they found themselves summoned to Colin's room at the Glen Motor Court, where Hayes suggested tossing a coin to decide which driver should win the race, if both cars should be running well towards the finish. Jimmy and Graham looked at each other and agreed, so Colin tossed, and Graham called and won. Amid some misgivings the result of the 10th United States Grand Prix had been decided . . .

Race day was sunny and the two Lotuses rushed away at the start with Graham ahead. Gurney deposed Clark the second time round, and poor Solana went out on lap 4 when his engine cut, wasting an excellent practice lap which had made him seventh quickest.

On lap eight Jimmy regained second place and the Lotus-Fords were soon leading as they pleased, the Scot going ahead on lap 40. But shortly after this planned change took place Graham found himself in clutch trouble and he had a battle with Chris Amon's Ferrari until lap 96 when the New Zealander retired, leaving Clark leading by 45 seconds from Hill.

While Amon had been forcing the pace Colin had signalled Jimmy not to wait for his team-mate, but with Chris out he slowed-up. But the gap was a big one and he couldn't slow that much. Then, on the 106th lap, with two to go, Jimmy's right-rear suspension failed, the top link broke and the wheel collapsed inwards. His lap times dropped by around 20 seconds as he nursed his car round to the finish, taking the chequered flag just 6.3 seconds ahead of Graham Hill! Walter Hayes and the Dearborn top-brass scored their prestigious one-two victory, although in the wrong order, and the team drivers added Jimmy's 20,000 dollars for first and Graham's 10,000 dollars for second and split their share between them. Graham's record lap at 1min 6.0 sec, 125.45 mph, was good for another 2,000 dollars, while Solana who got going again after a 40-lap pause and finished 18th and last, earned 3,400 dollars. It was a very lucrative trip for Team Lotus, and an American newspaper put it in perspective when a headline proclaimed 'The Ultimate Race Car—It Breaks at the Finish Line!'

But despite his win Jimmy was out of the World Championship race. Hulme now led with 47 points to Brabham's 42 and Clark's 32, and with only the Mexican round left the title had to go to one of the Brabham drivers. Repco Brabham had already sewn-up the Constructors' title, with 67 points to Lotus-Ford's rather meagre 35.

The last round took place in late October, Jimmy having 49/1 for this race with Graham in 49/3 and Solana in the Watkins Glen-winning 49/2, new strengthened suspension brackets being fitted to all the cars. Mike Fisher's Lotus-BRM 33 was trailed all the way down from Canada to make a fourth Lotus entry at Mexico City.

Despite minor problems Jimmy took pole position with a lap in 1min 47.56sec in answer to Amon's 1min 48.04sec, and Hill was on row two and Solana on row five. Old 49/1 crinkled its monocoque skin around the lower right-hand radius rod mounting, which had been damaged in Canada, but it was repaired in time for the race, and Solana's car appeared with a tubular truss strengthening the suspension and running across the gearbox.

Jimmy hesitated at the start, confused by a half-hearted waggle of the flag, and one of his car's long exhaust pipes disappeared up the nose of Gurney's Eagle and did grievous harm to its radiator. Jimmy was third at the end of the lap, while Graham led from Amon, and Solana was a rousing fifth on his home circuit. On lap two Jimmy was second, and next time round was leading from Hill.

Solana dropped out after 13 splendid laps when the connecting pin between the left-front upright and the lower link sheared under braking for a left-hander and the upright broke, and three laps later Graham lurched to a stop from second place when the left-hand drive-shaft yoke broke and the flailing shaft wiped out the coil-spring. Meanwhile, Jimmy just went on and on and he won as he pleased, over a minute ahead of Brabham, with Denny third to clinch his first World Championship title. Jimmy's new lap record of 1min 48.13sec, 103.44 mph, proved the supremacy of the Clark/Lotus combination, and he finished third in the World Championship, five points behind Brabham. Graham was sixth, while Repco Brabham finally took the Constructors' title by a margin of 23 points from Lotus-Ford.

One final Formula 1 race remained, the non--championship Spanish Grand Prix at the new Jarama circuit near Madrid in November. Team Lotus entered 49/1 for Jimmy and 49/2 for Graham, along with a Formula 2 Lotus 48 for local driver Alex Soler-Roig. He was to have bought the car, but negotiations broke down in the paddock and he became a non-starter.

Jimmy started from pole position, 1.5 seconds quicker than Hill, and the Lotus 49s led all the way to finish 15.2 seconds apart, Jimmy winning and setting a record lap at 1min 28.8sec, 85.71 mph.

The 1967 season saw Team Lotus running Formula 1 cars in two of the five non-championship events and winning one, while they contested all eleven World Championship rounds and won four, while Jimmy's superb Tasman record of five wins and three seconds in eight outings made up in some measure for the Indianapolis rout. Counting Indy, the works cars contested 22 major single-seater races during the year, and won ten of them, five with the Lotus-Ford 49 and five with the Lotus-Climax 33—Jim Clark driving every time. A measure of the Lotus 49's Formula 1 superiority was that it took pole position in each of its nine World Championship races, Jimmy six times and Graham three, while the Scot also took pole position and set fastest lap in the final non-title event at Jarama. It had been a very successful year, and few could see the World Championship eluding Jim Clark in 1968 . . .

Below: Jimmy's Lotus-Ford 49 failed at the Nurburgring, but proved nearly invincible at Monza (right) where he retook the lead by unlapping himself after a pit stop! Below: Graham Hill's 49/3 at Silverstone was built overnight after 49/1 had crashed in practice. Here he leads with Jimmy second in a Lotus-Ford demonstration!

1967 RACING RECORD
Other formulae and classes

In Formula 2 the new monocoque Lotus 48 looked a sure winner on its first appearance down-under in the Australian Grand Prix, but when Graham Hill drove the car there the power of Cosworth's brand-new 1,600 cc FVA engine prove too much for the old Hewland Mark 5 gearbox then fitted. In fact the new Hewland FT200 transaxle was to become the usual wear with the Cosworth engine, but Lotus were exceptions to this general rule and subsequently adopted ZF 5DS12 transaxles as standard equipment.

The Lotus 48, with its monocoque forward nacelle and spaceframe engine bay, was very similar in suspension layout to the 1 litre Lotus 44 of the previous season, but it was much more successful. Of the 25 Formula 2 races held during the season—including the classes at the German Grand Prix and the Oulton Park Spring Cup— Lotus won five, four of them with the Lotus 48 and the other with Jackie Oliver's Lotus Components-entered type 41B. This was a beefed-up Formula 3 spaceframe car (as offered for American Formula B racing) fitted with an FVA engine, and it was driven by Oliver whenever Clark and Hill were on hand to run the works 48s. Jimmy won three times, at Barcelona, Jarama and Keimola, and Oliver added another good win with the Lotus 48 in the German Grand Prix class at the Nurburgring. Clark added a second at Zolder (where he lost first place due to the odd system used by the organisers to decide the aggregate result from the two heats) and three thirds at Karlskoga, Hameenlinna and Albi. Graham Hill had a rather unlucky Formula 2 season, mirroring his lack of Grand Prix success, and the best he had to show for some hard racing were second places at Snetterton, in the class at the Oulton Spring race, at Reims and in the Oulton Park Gold Cup. He was also third at Keimola, but his best drive of the season was probably in the second race of the new formula at Silverstone. His car suffered a suspension breakage in the first heat and he started from the back of the grid in the second heat and charged through the field in terrific style to finish second behind the invincible Jochen Rindt. The Brabhams, and Jochen's car in particular, dominated the formula with their tremendous controllability, and won 11 times, compared with Matra's seven and Lola's two.

The upset of the year was undoubtedly at Rouen, where Jimmy had a tyre deflate while battling for the lead with Jack Brabham and Jochen Rindt. He lost control of the Lotus 48 and spun, collecting Brabham in the process and putting both cars out of the race, although with no injury to their drivers.

An interesting 'new' Formula 2 car which appeared early in the season was the Parnell-Cosworth, driven by Mike Spence at Silverstone. Closer inspection revealed this to be none other than R7—the old Lotus 25—hacked about at the rear to accept a Cosworth

FVA engine, but in comparison with the purpose-built Formula 2 cars it was far too heavy and was quickly retired. This car now resides in the Wheatcroft Grand Prix Collection at Donington Park, where it has been restored to its original Formula 1 trim...

In Formula 3 the Lotus 41s continued for another season, with minor rear suspension modifications producing the 41C variant. Including these updated vehicles, Lotus Components produced a grand total of 61 Lotus 41s, but few of them were sold during 1967, when the Formula 3 season was dominated by Brabham and Matra cars.

Charles Lucas severed his arrangement with Team Lotus at the close of the 1966 season, but retained one car which was run in the familiar old 'C. Lucas Engineering' colours of blue with red and white stripes. 'Luke' drove this car himself for much of the season, until his own new Titan production model appeared, and he won the British Grand Prix supporting event with a superb drive after recovering from an early spin.

Ron Harris occasionally produced either a Lotus 41 or one of the evergreen Lotus 35s for John Cardwell or Eric Offenstadt, and on one occasion gave Chris Williams, probably the smoothest of all Formula 3 drivers, an outing. But the team's Formula 3 season was fruitless, in direct contrast to that of privateer Mo Nunn and Lotus Component's own John Miles, who was having his first season of open-wheeled racing.

Nunn's immaculate self-prepared Lotus 41 won an incredible slip-streaming epic of a race at the Silverstone International Trophy meeting, and he added five club successes to this major victory. Miles' season was confined to home events apart from one Continental foray, and he scored 15 wins with the white-and-green Lotus 41 and the works Lotus 47 coupe. But it was left to Fearless Freddy Kottulinsky, the daring Swedish driver, to score more than one international victory in a Formula 3 Lotus—he scored at both Keimola and Hameenlinna in Finland with his new Lotus 41. So the marque's grand total for the year was just four major victories in the 66 Formula 3 Internationals held . . .

With the advent of the 'Mark 2' Cortina body-shell, Team Lotus' touring car operation had to build up completely new vehicles to replace their now obsolete 'Mark 1s'. The first of the new cars made its debut at the Silverstone International Trophy meeting, and Group 5 rules were exploited to the full by the use of a Formula 2 Cosworth FVA engine, producing just over 200 bhp! It was driven by Graham Hill, and in practice he lapped at 1min 45.0sec, 1.2 seconds quicker than Vic Elford's 2 litre Porsche 911!

But the car's race debut was an unhappy one, for Hill's Cortina had a faulty LT lead and refused to start

Top left: Jackie Oliver scoring his only important win for Team Lotus, in the Formula 2 section of the 1967 German Grand Prix. He went very well in this Lotus-Cosworth 48 and retained it during 1968, racing for the Herts & Essex Aero Club. Left: Graham Hill during his great Lotus 48 drive at Silverstone.

Above: Paul Hawkins demonstrating the spectacular road-holding of the Mark 2 Lotus Cortina, which continued the saloon car racing success story of its predecessor. Below: 'Flower Power' was in during 1967. This 'road-going' Lotus 51R Formula Ford car was a promotional gimmick which actually realised some orders!

on the grid until finally being coaxed into life to cheers from the packed grandstands. He was fourth away from the start behind a Ford Mustang and two Falcons, but almost immediately the fault recurred and put him out. Team-mate John Miles was pushed off the grid in the old 'Mark 1' car which was leaking oil, so it was a pretty desperate meeting for the reigning Champion team.

The early BRM Phase 4 twin-cam-engined cars were eventually retired and replaced by a full team of FVA-powered 'Mark 2s', and Hill was joined by John Miles and Jacky Ickx as the season progressed, the pair of them sharing the second car. At Oulton Park in September Roger Clark appeared in a Ford of Britain-entered model, and he was regarded with great suspicion by the works entries. During the season he had put up some lurid performances in a Calypso Cigarettes-backed club-racing Lotus Cortina, and his latest Group 5 car featured many standard high-performance parts such as a bottom-wishbone system in place of the Elan struts used by Team Lotus. The whole effort fizzled out at the end of the second lap when Clark came in to retire with differential failure, but it had caused some interest.

Throughout the season the works Lotus-Cortinas had been battling with Elford's Porsche, and this meeting was notable for both Team Lotus cars leading the red German 'GT' easily until first Ickx and then Hill spun and crashed over the bank at Esso Hairpin! The young Belgian disappeared from sight first, followed by Hill on the very last lap when his brakes failed and he clambered out to find the rears on fire!

The last big saloon car race of the year was the Motor Show '200' at Brands Hatch in late October, where the former Team Lotus cars arrived under new management for Lotus had withdrawn and sold them to Brian Robinson, the youthful North Countryman who took over the entries for Tony Dean and himself. He had been running the old ex-works cars for some time, and went equally well in his newer FVA-engined acquisitions to finish fourth overall in this event, winning his class, and setting himself up for a good saloon car season in 1968. The 1967 season's Championship titles for drivers and entrants went to Frank Gardner and the Cooper Car Company, respectively.

Even at this late date Lotus 19 Specials were still to be seen in America, and Al Unser was running a so-called Lotus 19G—with Ford V8 power—in the second Can-Am series, although without conspicuous success.

In December, Jim Clark tried the STP Turbocar at Indianapolis, but although he professed to be trying as hard as he could he was unable to better a 160 mph average, which would have been too slow to qualify for that year's race!

On a slightly more ponderous note Jim Clark had a drive in one of the big American NASCAR stockers in the Rockingham '500' during the season, sharing a Ford Fairlane with Jochen Rindt, and he found the experience most instructive, although the engine blew before Jochen had a chance to take over...

In GT racing the new Lotus 47 was another flattering but deceptive beast, and it made little impact internationally although in John Miles' hands the works car scored a string of home successes. This was a replacement for a car which burned out completely during early-season tests at Brands Hatch, and its best performance was undoubtedly at the same circuit when John shared the car with Jackie Oliver in the BOAC '500' 6-Hours race, and they finished ninth overall and won the 2 litre class.

Johnny Blades and Malcolm Wayne had successful club seasons in their Lotus 47s, while the Portuguese drivers Carlos Santos and Nogueira Pinto were dominant in their home country with similar cars. Julian Sutton had a none-too-reliable year with a 2 litre Climax-powered car, but finished a good sixth at Karlskoga ahead of two 4.7 litre Ford GT40s.

John Wagstaff resurrected Team Elite during the season, and their Lotus 47, finished in the familiar old white colour with bright green stripes was driven by Trevor Taylor. He looked all set to win the Nurburgring 500 Kms race in the teeth of fierce Alpine-Renault opposition when an obscure electrical fault caused yet another unlucky retirement.

Strangely enough the Lotus name scored many of its major successes of the year in rallying, for Bengt Soderstrom and Gunnar Palm won the Swedish Rally in a Lotus-Cortina, and further victories were notched by Roger Clark in the Canadian Shell '4000' (with Jim Peters), and in the Scottish Rally (with Jim Porter). Ove Andersson and John Davenport crewed another Lotus-Cortina to first place in the gruelling Gulf-London Rally, and one of the finest performances of the year was David Friswell's second place in the Dutch Tulip Rally, when he shared an Elan with Chris Nash; it took a Porsche to beat them. In a vaguely associated sport another Lotus Elan positively excelled, for in Britain Peter Watkin won the National Autocross Championship!

In club racing Peter Jackson, Bob Ellice, Keith Burnand and Mike Crabtree were all leading Elan exponents, while George Silverwood scored eight victories in an immaculate but ancient Lotus 11 GT. Brian Robinson notched seven saloon car wins with his ex-works Lotus-Cortina, and Mike Barnby's Clubman's Formula Lotus Seven had a similar tally. Tim Goss ran the ex-Peter Deal 'Three-Seven' with similar prolific success, and Peter Harrington and Natalie Goodwin, the fine lady driver, also shone with their fully independently suspended Sevens.

In single-seaters Brian Jordan's old Lotus 32/35 topped the Monoposto racing class, while Rod Pickering notched five wins in his 1,600 cc twin-cam-engined Lotus 22, and Willie Forbes defended his Formule Libre Championship with the same total in his BMW-powered Lotus 35.

The new Formula Ford class, for single-seater cars running standard Cortina GT push-rod engines, narrow wheels and road tyres, began during the season, and Lotus Components came to an arrangement with one of the begetters of the class, the Brands Hatch-based Motor Racing Stables driving school, to produce cars for the formula. Once again the old Lotus 22/31 spaceframe design was dusted down, and suitably modified to accept the Cortina engine and narrow wheels. In Formula Ford trim the new Lotus 51 classification was adopted, and the car was offered through MRS at £955 complete. Dan Hawkes drove the school's first car to five wins before the end of the season.

Overseas a surprising win was Tony Maw's success in the Macau Grand Prix at the wheel of an old 1,500 cc Ford-engined Lotus 20B. Steve Holland led the race round the Portuguese colony on the coast of mainland China until his ex-Courage Lotus 41 failed, but the generally light-hearted meeting was ruined when the popular Phillipine driver Arsenio 'Dodjie' Laurel crashed his Lotus 41 twin-cam on the second lap and was killed. It was a bad year for accidents, particularly in the hard-fought field of Formula 3, and at Caserta, Italy lost her leading driver, 'Geki' Russo, when his Matra was involved in a multiple pile-up which cost three lives. 'Geki' had driven Formula Junior Lotuses in the past and also appeared at Monza in the works Formula 1 cars before his tragic death.

1968

Triumph after tragedy

Jim Clark's death at Hockenheim in April 1968 shattered the Lotus world terribly, but Team Lotus' recovery was a tribute to the ability and fortitude of its personnel after receiving such a body blow. Graham Hill clinched his second World Championship and Lotus' third title in the Gold Leaf Team Lotus 49B and salvaged a hard-fought success from a season which had suffered so tragically.

Jimmy's South African Grand Prix win right at the start of the season had given him a total of 25 Grand Prix victories, one more than Fangio's record, and in tribute to this feat the British Racing Drivers' Club awarded him another Gold Star, and the British Automobile Racing Club honoured him with a Gold Medal. This was to have been presented to him at the BARC-organised Thruxton Formula 2 race, but his death the previous week forestalled the ceremony, and the medal finally went to his parents and joined the Jim Clark Memorial Room collection in his home town of Duns, in Berwickshire.

The year also saw Lotus 'go public' with a share issue in September. Group Lotus Car Companies Ltd was to become a holding company from January 6, 1969, and the Group subsidiaries included Lotus Cars, Lotus Cars (Service), Lotus Cars (Sales) and of course Lotus Components. Colin Chapman was Group Chairman, and he was joined on the Board by Fred Bushell, Financial Director since the bad old days of the Elite, and Peter Kirwan-Taylor, who had helped Colin lay-out the Elite way back in 1956 and had been involved in the company ever since. Dennis Austin became Managing Director of Lotus Cars, while John Standen and Graham Arnold ran Service and Sales, respectively, and David Lazenby left Lotus Components to set up his own company to build Hawke racing cars.

Mike Warner, who had left to set-up his own Auto Design Components Company in September the previous year, was bought back by the Lotus Group, and one of his designs became the Brand Lotus alloy road wheels. He took over Lotus Components, which was in a sad state with a £38,000 loss, and by the end of the year it was showing a £10,000 profit.

Dick Scammell was promoted to Racing Manager during 1968 after Jim Endruweit had moved to Service, and Bob 'Lotti' Dance became Formula 1 Chief Mechanic. Arthur 'Jam Butty' Birchall took over as Indy Chief Mechanic, while Mike Underwood eventually took a USAC post under George Bignotti. There was quite a family tree of Formula 1 mechanics, and Leo Wybrott followed Dance, and after he moved to McLaren, Gordon Huckle and Eddie Dennis followed him.

One of the year's first new 'road cars' to see the light of day was the Formula Ford-based Lotus 51R. This was a standard spaceframe single-seater fitted with bicycle mudguards and the necessary Road Traffic Act lights, and with an appropriate 'flower power' paint scheme appeared at the Racing Car Show in London early in the year. Strangely enough Lotus Components offered replicas at £1,085, and actually received an order from an American. However, they were not very keen about fulfilling it because building the 51R had been such a fiddly and time-consuming job, but finally a cable arrived from none other than Henry Ford demanding that the car be delivered quickly, for the prospective customer was a personal friend!

While the Formula Ford production lines were doing very good business, Lotus Components was also building bare cars for motor racing simulators. These were engineless, stationary vehicles perched in front of a screen upon which a 'driver's-eye-view' image of various circuits could be projected. Without moving an inch the simulator pilot could 'drive' round the circuit, setting lap times fast or slow and having harmless solo accidents in the privacy of his own cockpit! The simulators were popular at driving schools, research centres and as plain uncomplicated side-shows, and Lotus Components built 40 'cars' for their promoters.

The new Elan Series 4 was introduced at the end of July incorporating over 50 detail modifications from S3 trim, many of them to bring the model into line with the more luxurious Plus-2. The more noticeable modifications included new rear-light clusters with integral reversing lamps, and opened-out wheel-arches to accomodate low-profile 155-13 tyres. Twin-pipe exhausts were adopted which allowed extra power with

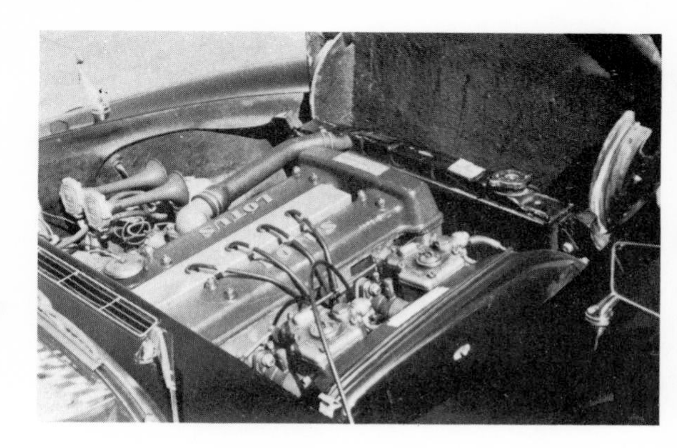

The Elan Series 3 ended its run in July, when replaced by the S4 model. More than 50 detail changes were made but none altered the Elan's legendary road-holding ability, some road testers mounting a G-meter across the car and sending it off the scale while cornering! Engine accessibility has never been a great feature of the Elans. Below: Colin and Hazel Chapman enjoy their flying, but the Lotus founder now finds it a necessity more than a luxury.

less noise, while the dash-panel was redesigned and a bulge appeared in the bonnet. This housed Zenith-Stromberg 'anti-smog' carburettors for the American export version, which had to conform to the new US anti-pollution regulations.

These Federal regulations were the bane of many exporters' lives, and to a comparatively small company such as Lotus the necessity to provide national authorities with cars to test could have been crippling. To protect their own market companies had to submit cars for testing so that these authorities could satisfy themselves that they conformed to whatever new regulations the bureaucrats had dreamed-up. The big problem was that no two countries' safety and pollution regulations were the same, and since the cars involved were almost invariably hand-built prototypes, satisfying every market's test standards was a very expensive procedure. Lotus' sights were set firmly on maintaining their American sales despite the imposition of new standards, particularly in California where the bulk of Lotus sales took place, and in January the Elan passed both the US Federal crash test and the 50,000-miles pollution check.

The 500th Elan Plus-2 was built in February, only eight months after production had started, this being the quickest that any Lotus had passed the 500 mark, and in the same month the 500th Europa rolled out of the Hethel shops.

March saw the Elan passing the full US safety and exhaust-emission tests, clearing the way for continued exports, and in April the Europa followed it through with flying colours. The same month saw the release of a new Series 2 Europa, which was given the Lotus 54 type number. The Lotus 52 had been a one-off Europa prototype powered by a twin-cam touring engine, while the Lotus 53 was a Lotus Components sports-racing project based on the old Lotus 23 which never came to fruition.

An interesting project towards the end of the season concerned the Lotus 57 and 58 De Dion-axled Formula 1 and Formula 2 cars. The Lotus 57 was never completed, but the Lotus 58 with a Cosworth FVA engine, wedge body and tail-mounted radiator covered a considerable test mileage. The De Dion system used a spidery tubular frame in place of the traditional hefty beam, and all its drivers thought it handled marvellously, it was so predictable. But unfortunately it was also very slow, and the car remained under wraps at Hethel . . . unraced.

The new Europa S2 featured many detail refinements, but its greatest advance over the original car was the use of a detachable chassis in place of the original bonded-in backbone. This made major overhauls simpler and cheaper, and the added attractions of electrically-wound opening side windows and extra luggage space behind the engine made the new S2 a much more refined motor car than its predecessor.

Concurrent with the release of the Elan S4, Colin announced the new LV/220 production racing engine.

The Lotus Europa S2 featured many refinements, the greatest of which was a detachable instead of a bonded-in backbone chassis.

The origins of this unit have already been described, but Sanville and Burr had finalised their Vauxhall conversion with a bore and stroke of 3.75 inches x 2.75 inches, giving a capacity of 1,995 cc. A five-main-bearing steel crankshaft was adopted, machined from the solid, and it carried I-section EN24 steel con-rods with 2 inch Vandervell big-end bearings. German Mahle three-ring forged slipper-type pistons were used, with crown cut-outs to clear the four inclined valves per cylinder. Few changes were made to the basic Vauxhall block which appeared in these prototype units, but the LV/220 was dry-sumped and ran an oil pressure of 70 psi. The twin overhead camshafts were run by a lengthy internally toothed rubber belt, and ignition was by Lucas racing distributor and coil on a 12-volt system. Tecalemit-Jackson fuel injection was fitted, and the overall weight of the unit was quoted as 325 lbs. Plans were laid to build an initial batch of 50 units for sale once testing and development had been completed, but after racing had served to prove the cylinder head design but exposed some basic weaknesses in the Vauxhall block the development of Lotus' own die-cast alloy block was hastened while the production ideas were temporarily shelved. At no time did Vauxhall show more than a passing commercial interest in the engine.

Power output was around 220 bhp at 8,000 rpm with peak torque 160 lb ft at 5,700 rpm. The LV/220 classification was derived from the engine's parentage and output, and the forthcoming aluminium-block unit was to be known as the LV/240. New twin-cam classifications included the LF/105 105 bhp unit intended for the Elan and Lotus-Cortina, and the LF/115 Special Equipment unit using modified cams, chokes, jets and exhaust manifolding. The LFR/165 twin-cam was the racing version as fitted in the Lotus 47 (by now also known as a Europa) and the Lotus 41F Formule Libre single-seater.

The Hethel plant took over complete assembly and testing of these LF engines in August when the new dynamometer test house was commissioned, and another happy event during the month was Colin's election as a Fellow of the Royal Society of Arts. This accolade was followed at the London Motor Show by a tribute to the Lotus stylists when the Elan S4 drophead coupe was awarded the Gold Medal in the Coachwork Competition and the Plus-2 carried-off the Bronze Medal, while the marque began the Show with over one million pounds-worth of export orders.

September had seen the introduction of a new Series 3 Seven using the Ford Cortina 1600GT cross-flow engine as standard and with an Escort back axle replacing the earlier Cortina component. This gave a wider rear track and broader glass-fibre wings were adopted to cover the tyres.

While such exciting progress was being made on the production car front, Colin introduced the marque to gas turbine power with the Lotus 56 Indianapolis cars. Granatelli had forged the original ties with Pratt & Whitney with his STP-Turbocar of 1967, and but for pump-drive failures partially attributable to a tie-up with an oil company to run straight pump fuel the new Lotuses might well have won the race. In fact the development was so exciting that initial plans were laid to run a three-car turbine team in 1969 Formula 1 events, but Pratt & Whitney did not have sufficient time available to carry out the necessary turbine modifications to produce 3 litre equivalency, and so the Lotus-Ford 49s went into their third season.

At Indy one of the diabolical 1967 'bitsa' cars stood in front of the Lotus garage with a wry 'For Sale' notice attached, and looking all rusty and horrible, and Ferguson was elated when he took 2,000 dollars for it!

During the year production had been disrupted by extensive flooding and damage to the Lotus factory and office areas after freak mid-Summer storms, while suppliers' labour disputes and strikes caused severe shortages. Nevertheless, Lotus exceeded their sales and production targets, and another record year saw turnover increased by no less than £1,640,000 to £4,443,000. Gross profit rose by £407,000 to £731,000 and a total of 3,048 cars were produced, 1,063 more than during 1967. Profitability soared from 11.5 per cent to 16.5 per cent, and although Lotus as a racing marque had suffered losses which were so hard to bear, the Group as a whole was still going from strength to strength.

Above: The Europa S2's revised interior featured a full-width facia, electrically-wound windows and adjustable seats. Below: The Plus-2 is surely one of the prettiest cars ever built.

1968 RACING RECORD
Grands Prix and other major formulae

Once again the South African Grand Prix at Kyalami opened the new Formula 1 season, on New Year's Day, and Team Lotus freighted two cars South of the equator for their regular drivers, 49/3 for Graham and the brand-new 49/4 for Jimmy.

A year's racing development was amply demonstrated by the Scot's first four practice laps. The lap record stood at 1min 29.9sec (1min 29.3sec in practice) and Clark zipped round in 1min 37.1sec, 1min 31.6sec, 1min 30.0sec and then 1min 27.6sec! By the end of the day he was down to 1min 23.9sec, next day he lapped in 1min 22.4sec and he ended up with a time of 1min 21.6sec to secure pole position. He alternated between Dunlop and Firestone tyres in these sessions and finally set his quickest time on Firestones with the suspension set-up for Dunlops; there should have been more to come . . .

Graham had a troubled practice with fuel pump failure, anti-roll bar linkages coming adrift and clutch failure, but took second place on the grid at 1min 22.6sec. A new threat was Jackie Stewart's Formula 2-based, Ford V8-powered Matra, which took the outside of the rank. The car was run by Ken Tyrrell's Equipe Matra-Elf, Ken having placed an order for Ford engines immediately after Jimmy's first win in the 1967 Dutch Grand Prix!

Jimmy's engine was changed after a cracked liner had been found, and despite an oil leak in the new engine the car seemed healthy as it was wheeled to the line. Stewart out-dragged the Lotuses from the start, and Clark was second and Hill a distant seventh at the end of the lap. But Jimmy was ahead next time round and on lap 13 Graham took third place behind the Matra. On lap 27 he moved up to second, and when Stewart's car threw a rod in a smother of smoke and flying metal after 43 laps the Lotus domination was complete. Clark came home to score his record-breaking 25th victory in a World Championship round (one more than five-times Champion Juan Manuel Fangio's old record). Graham was second, 25.3 seconds behind, and Jimmy's new lap record of 1min 23.7sec, 109.68 mph, trimmed a clear 3.9 seconds off the old figure!

After this crushing demonstration of superiority there came the light relief of another Tasman series, and Cosworth had produced special 2.5 litre short-stroke versions of their V8 engines to power the Lotus 49Ts. These DFW engines were converted from the third and fourth of the seven DFV Formula 1 engines built during 1967.

The New Zealand Grand Prix at Pukekohe traditionally began the Tasman series, and there Jimmy's Lotus 49T (chassis 49/2) was faced by Chris Amon's 2.4 litre V6 Ferrari, works 2.5 litre BRM V12s, Hulme's private Formula 2 Brabham and the Mildren team's Brabham-Alfa Romeo.

Clark was fastest in practice at 59.1 seconds, 106.1 mph, to win 50 bottles of bubbly, but Amon snatched the lead at the start of the main race. However, Clark's Lotus was soon in front and it led for 43 laps until its engine suddenly coughed and died, leaving the New Zealander to win his home Grand Prix. Peter Yock ran the ex-Parnell Lotus-BRM 25/33, R13, but retired after 11 laps with a holed radiator after leaving the road, while Hulme escaped with a shaking from a spectacular end-over-end accident when lapping a backmarker.

Levin saw 49/2 fitted with a new engine to replace the one which had dropped a valve at Pukekohe, and Jimmy won the 14-lap preliminary by 2.6 seconds from Amon. This gave him pole position for the Rothmans International 63-lap race, and he stole the lead from Gardner's Brabham-Alfa after seven laps, only to slither off at the hairpin seven laps later. He streaked back through the field to close on Amon's Ferrari, but it wasn't his day and he retired on lap 32 after hitting a marker tyre and bending a radius rod.

At Christchurch for the Lady Wigram Trophy race, the Lotus 49T appeared for the first time in its brand-new Gold Leaf Team Lotus colours, looking very much like an Indianapolis car with its white undersides, red top and gold striping. Jimmy gave the new GLTL colours a first-time win by one second from Amon in the 11-lap preliminary race, and in the 44-lap main event he won 1,000 dollars for the first 100 mph lap, covering his second lap in 1min 21.8sec, 101.22 mph. He led all the way, beating the Ferrari by 7.7 seconds and sharing the final lap record of 104.02 mph to score Gold Leaf's first International race success.

A harbinger of things to come was seen in practice at Teretonga the following weekend, when a small aerofoil was fitted over the Lotus 49T's gearbox in practice, although it soon disappeared and was regarded by most observers as a leg-pull. It rained on race day, and after Amon was pushed off the grid of the preliminary 10-lap race with his car's electrics swamped Jimmy won from Courage's Formula 2 McLaren. However, because conditions improved for the second heat for 1,500 cc cars the organisers decided to arrange the main race grid on practice times, which relegated Jimmy from pole position to second place between Amon on one side and McLaren's BRM (hurriedly repaired after a crash in the preliminary race) and Gardner's Brabham-Alfa on the other.

Rain began to bucket down in the early stages of the 60-lap race, but by lap 38 Jimmy had pulled out a clear 28.6 seconds on Amon. Then Amon and Gardner both spun and lost a lap, which made McLaren's BRM second. But starting his 53rd lap Jimmy lost control of 49/2 completely, and the car left the straight at about 140 mph, bounced over a ditch and tore down a fence, coming to rest with a smashed nose cone. Jimmy ran round for a quick check, then drove to the pits for the nose cone to be torn off, and rejoined to finish second, Bruce McLaren scoring a surprise win with the V12 BRM. Fastest lap went to Clark at 1min 1.0sec, 94.5

mph. At the end of the New Zealand tour, Amon led the Tasman Championship with 24 points to Jimmy's 15 and Courage's 13.

The first Australian round was at Surfers' Paradise where GLTL had the support of Ford Australia and for the first time fielded two Lotus 49Ts with Graham Hill joining his Formula 1 team-mate. Unfortunately this first Tasman Formula race at the new Surfers' circuit was marred by the Confederation of Australian Motor Sports' attitude to advertising on the cars, and they took particular exception to the Player's sailor insignia on the Lotus-Fords. John Gowland, competitions manager of Ford Australia, finally produced an entrants' licence signed in the name of 'Gold Leaf Team Lotus with Ford Australia' which saved much of the Lotus lettering, but all the decals had to be peeled off, the Player's sailor was blacked out and 'I'm backing Britain' lettering on Graham's Union Jack was also taped over . . . The situation was at its worst when Jimmy had the paddock gate slammed in front of his car as he went out for the ten-lap preliminary, and neither the Lotuses nor the BRMs were allowed to run. It seemed that CAMS would rather call off the meeting than lose face, and only Gowland's intervention brought them to repent. One could imagine the mechanics filing the 'Ford' lettering off the engine cam-boxes . . .

After the trouble had blown over Jimmy and Graham formed up outside Amon on the front row of the grid for the Rothmans 100, and the Scot took an early lead from the Ferrari with Hill third. Chris got ahead momentarily before his head gasket blew, and then Courage led Graham before spinning and letting the bristling moustache go by. Leo Geoghegan forced his old Lotus 39, now sporting a 2.5 litre Repco V8 engine, into third place at one point to make it a Lotus one-two-three, but Courage repassed him before the finish, and Clark won by 6.4 seconds from Hill with Geoghegan fourth. Back in seventh place overall, Glyn Scott's Lotus-Ford 27 won the 1,500 cc class.

The International 100 at Warwick Farm followed and in practice Graham smashed a wheel when he clipped a fence, while Jimmy took pole with a lap in 1min 27.4sec, 92.67 mph. Graham was alongside him, 0.6 second slower, and the race result was a carbon of Surfers', Jimmy taking the Tasman Championship lead with 33 points to Amon's 30 and Courage's 23.

The Australian Grand Prix was held at Sandown Park, 600 miles from Sydney, at the end of February, and Jimmy's rather tired engine (it had completed five races, won two and led them all) could not do better than third fastest time in practice. Melbourne sweltered in a 110-degrees heatwave on race day, but afternoon haze made things more bearable as the grid formed up. Jimmy led away with Amon and Hill on his heels, but Jack Brabham forged through to battle for the lead while Gardner and Graham fought over fourth place. The Londoner was beset by braking and gearchange problems, but up front Clark and Amon had a fantastic race-long battle with the Lotus just winning by 0.1 second. The fastest lap went to the Ferrari, and Graham snatched third place by just 0.2 second from Gardner. Jimmy extended his Championship lead to 42 points from Amon's 36 and Courage's 25, but this tremendous race was the last Grand Prix ever won by Jim Clark . . .

An overnight trip on the 'Princess of Tasmania' took the cars and drivers to Longford for the last race of the series on March 1st. Leo Geoghegan had a bad fright in practice when a wheel detached itself as he braked from 130 mph, but he stopped safely, and Jimmy won 100 bottles of Champagne for the fastest practice time of 2min 12.8sec and Graham was second-quickest with 2min 13.6sec. Mel McEwin was out in Jimmy's old Lotus 32B with 2.5 litre Climax four-cylinder engine, and lapped it in 2min 39.0sec.

Graham won the 12-lap preliminary race from Jimmy to score his first win both for Gold Leaf Team Lotus and in a Lotus 49, after both cars had been timed at 176 mph on the straight.

The Sixth South Pacific Trophy race was run in appalling conditions the following Monday, shortened to 15 laps—67.5 miles—because of the rain and because one of the bridges on the circuit was on fire!

Courage rushed away with the race on new Dunlop 970 compound tyres while the more powerful opposition slipped and slithered in his wake. Jimmy was fifth and Graham sixth, while the Ferrari was seventh and failed to score, so Jimmy took his last Tasman Championship title with 44 points to Chris Amon's 36 and Piers Courage's splendid 34.

Two weeks later the European Formula 1 season opened with the Race of Champions at Brands Hatch and since Jimmy was back in Europe living out his self-imposed exile GLTL made their home debut with just one brand-new Lotus 49—49/5—for Graham Hill. The South African Grand Prix-winning 49/4 had been sold to Rob Walker for his talented Swiss driver, Jo Siffert. The car was repainted in the team's famous dark blue and white colours, but Jo lost control in unofficial practice on Friday and damaged it badly against South Bank. The car was taken back to Walker's Dorking racing shop to be stripped, but a serious fire started there and destroyed the workshop, the Lotus, Rob's just-retired Cooper-Maserati, his racing records and his recently restored ex-Seaman Delage . . . a terrible blow to the greatest sportsman in motor racing.

Graham's car was an experimental model, running with very wide rims and new Firestone tyres and with revised weight distribution. The oil tank and battery had been shifted from the nose of the car to the rear, but early in practice the car was handling very badly. The battery was repositioned forward but with little improvement, and it became obvious to Colin and Maurice that the new wide wheels and the old suspension just didn't mix, and that camber change was tilting the covers and causing sudden loss of adhesion.

Graham put the car on the inside of row three, 1.6 seconds slower than Bruce McLaren's brand-new McLaren-Ford on pole position, and as Bruce drove to a

Below: Graham Hill in the Lotus-Ford 49T at Longford, Tasmania, where he scored his first win in a 49 and his first for Gold Leaf Team Lotus in a preliminary event. Right: Jim Clark leading the field on the way to winning his record-breaking 25th, and last, Grande Epreuve. Bottom: Jimmy winning his last race, and his last Championship, with the Lotus 49T at Sandown Park, Melbourne, Australia. Graham follows.

convincing win in the race Graham, after a good start, held a rather shaky fourth place for 10 laps when the left-hand inboard drive-shaft universal joint broke at Dingle Dell; the flailing shaft punctured the new oil tank over the gearbox and Graham had a nasty moment bringing the car to rest. Once again the Player's sailor was blacked-out, this time by request of BBC TV, and Team Lotus painted a white question mark in his place . . .

Two Formula 2 races followed for the GLTL drivers, and at Barcelona Jimmy made his debut in a one-inch-longer Lotus 48 'special', originally built to accomodate Graham's taller frame but since adopted by the Scot. He was put out of the race at Barcelona when Ickx's Dino shunted him at the hairpin and bent the Lotus 48's rear suspension. Graham ran eighth in this race before retiring, and the team then moved on to the next European Formula 2 round at Hockenheim on Sunday, April 7.

Detail improvements were made to the Lotus 48s' suspension pick-ups after Barcelona, and Jimmy's car had a complete rear suspension assembly replaced. Practice for the German race was confined to three short sessions on the Saturday, and both Gold Leaf cars had metering unit problems which caused misfiring. Jimmy's best time was seventh quickest at 2min 1.1sec, compared with Beltoise's pole position Matra time of 1min 59.3sec. Graham's car had the wrong gear ratios and was 15th, 5.1 seconds slower still.

Race day dawned grey and wet, but the Team Lotus drivers were philosophical and happy as they drove out to the Motodrome. Hockenheim was originally an elliptical high-speed circuit, but had been bisected by a new autobahn. The revised circuit now featured a high-speed slipstreaming back section and a twisty mickey-mouse loop through a stadium complex where the pits and start-line were situated. Consequently the first car out of the woods into the stadium had a slight advantage, but it was a circuit which very much favoured the brave rather than the skilful.

The first heat of the Deutschland Trophy began at 12.30pm, by which time the drizzle had stopped, leaving the circuit glistening and slick. Beltoise slithered into the stadium first with Ahrens' Brabham close behind, then after a gap came Bell and Courage, whose Brabhams led a huge bunch headed by Pescarolo's Matra, Irwin's Lola and Jimmy's Lotus. Graham was 15th at the end of this first lap, unhappy with his car, and it soon became apparent that Clark was in trouble, too, and dropping back. On lap five he was a lonely eighth as he disappeared beyond the pits and accelerated away into the woods, building up to near maximum speed on a virtual straight which led into a tightening right-hand curve.

A lone flag marshal on this so-called Shrimp Curve heard the car approaching after the leaders had screamed by, and then the red, white and gold machine burst into sight twitching from side to side with the driver fighting the wheel. It slewed broadside at around 140 mph and careered off the road, slithered over the

Above: Jim Clark at Hockenheim, just before his tragic last race. Below: Graham Hill led the Gold Leaf Team Lotus Formula 1 attack brilliantly following Jimmy's death, winning the first Championship race after the disaster, at Jarama (right) and following up with another fine win at Monaco (below right). He became a deserving World Champion.

Jeep VIASA
10
STP

P
9
9

Above: Graham Hill, Maurice Phillipe, Dick Scammell and Colin Chapman pause during the first tests at Hethel of the two Lotus 56 Indy turbine cars. Below: Hill, always one to experiment with chassis changes during practice, in deep thought with his Formula 1 car during a pre-race ratio change.

verge and took down some saplings before smashing into a larger tree which it caught full in the cockpit. The car was torn apart, the monocoque crashing to a stop among the bushes while the tubular engine bay and rear suspension were flung round the other side of the tree and bounced to a stop. Jimmy was dead before anyone reached him. . .

The wreckage was hidden from the circuit, and Graham finished 12th having seen some nasty tyre marks but nothing more. But in the pits the shocked mechanics soon knew what had happened, and as the enormity of the disaster dawned, a stunning dullness settled over the paddock and the crowd.

Graham's car was wheeled on to the transporter and scratched from the second heat, and the rest of the meeting was grey and cheerless in the face of motor racing's incalculable loss. Colin flew in soon afterwards, and the wreckage of the car was eventually brought home where a painstaking investigation was begun by a Royal Aircraft Establishment accident inspector. It was so terribly mangled it was difficult to separate cause from effect, but Colin gradually evolved a theory which is the best explanation which can be offered.

Team Lotus had just begun to run tubeless tyres, and as at Nurburgring and Monza the previous year Jimmy's lengthening lap times are now attributed to a slowly deflating tyre. His natural adaptability allowed him to continue driving quickly although there was obviously something wrong with the car. As the pressure within the tyre dropped its bead would be held less firmly on the wheel rim, and at high speed centrifugal force would tend to throw the tyre crown outwards and draw the sides together. With a tubeless tyre this was a very dangerous condition, for if either bead popped inwards off the rim an explosive decompression would occur, the tyre would deflate immediately and collapse. In an instant the tyre would be flailing, a useless rubber bag wobbling round the wheel, and the instant loss of adhesion would throw the car off course. Colin believes that Jimmy was probably the first driver to suffer an explosive decompression of a tubeless tyre, a failure which by definition occurs near maximum speed. Safety bolts which retain tyre beads on the rim, and crash barriers which prevent cars ploughing into trees, have since been adopted on the cars and the circuits, and this tragic wasteful accident which claimed the life of such a great racing driver should never be repeated.

Jim Clark was buried on Wednesday, April 10th, at Chirnside Old Church, near his farm at Duns, Berwickshire. In the town a special commemorative trophy room is his memorial. . . his record in this book is another. . .

Motor racing would never be quite the same, but of course it continued, and the next major event was the International Trophy race at Silverstone on April 27th. Team Lotus ran Graham Hill in 49/1 while Rob Walker had taken delivery of 49/2, the other Tasman car, to replace Siffert's burned-out Brands Hatch wreck. Hill's old car took the middle of the second row on the grid, 1.3 seconds slower than Hulme's McLaren on pole position, while Siffert was on the inside of the third row, 2.0 seconds slower.

One minute's silence was observed in Jimmy's memory before the start as a lone piper played a lament, then the usual babble of voices began, engines coughed and rasped into life, and a new chapter in motor racing and Lotus history began.

Graham was sixth and Siffert tenth away from the line, but the GLTL driver soon rushed into fourth place. When Rodriguez's BRM stopped he took third place and with McLaren put the pressure on Spence's leading works BRM. On lap 11 the Lotus howled past in second place behind Bruce's new car but almost immediately it stopped at Abbey Curve. The metering unit feed had split, filling the engine vee with premium grade fuel, and Graham walked back to the pits. Jo's gearbox broke an oil seal, and as the lubricant leaked away the transmission overheated and broke after 26 laps.

The month of May meant a return to Indianapolis, and after the impressive performance of 'Silent Sam' the previous year Lotus produced gas turbine-powered cars for Granatelli. USAC had been badly shaken by the STP-Paxton Turbocar's performance in 1967 and had hastily altered their rules to protect vested piston-engine interests. Eligible turbines were limited to an effective intake area of 15.999 square inches in place of the original 23.999 inches ruling, and inevitably this limited their power output for with less going in at one end, less came out of the other. Granatelli promptly took legal action against USAC, but lost.

STP sponsored four new Lotus 56 turbine cars, and entered Parnelli Jones in the updated original chassis. The new cars were very striking, with entirely new slab-sided monocoque hulls carrying perfectly wedge-shaped glass-fibre body panelling. The big problem at Indy was to get the cars into the turns at 160 to 170 mph in a stable condition. The earlier cars had all pitched badly as the power was shut-off, and all had aerodynamic lift problems at the very high speeds achieved on the straights. Colin Chapman and Maurice Phillippe gave serious thought to the lift and stability problem, and wind-tunnel tests showed that the simple wedge shape combined the maximum amount of negative lift with a low pitching moment. In other words the car did not drop its nose or tail sharply under acceleration or cornering, and was stable.

Power was provided by suitably modified Pratt & Whitney PT6 gas turbine engines, exhausting through a streamlined chimney behind the driver's head and coupled via a Morse chain drive to a Lotus-prompted four-wheel drive system built by Ferguson Research. Suspension was by upper and lower wishbones and inboard ventilated disc brakes were used all round.

Jim Clark had tested one of the cars at Indy just before the Barcelona Formula 2 race, and had lapped at 161 mph with very little effort. Graham Hill, Jackie Stewart and Greg Weld were listed to drive the other three cars, and after Jimmy's tragic death the new BRM lead driver, Mike Spence, was invited to join the team.

On May 3rd Jones rejected his Paxton Turbocar drive, saying he didn't think the car could be competitive with only two-thirds of its designed power, but next day Spence proved the Lotus' potential by lapping at 164.239 mph. On May 7th he lapped consistently at 169 mph, and his best of 169.555 mph was the second fastest ever at the Speedway.

Later that afternoon Mike was asked to do some shake-down laps on Weld's car. He began at 163.1 mph, and took progressively higher lines into the turns. On his final lap he was so high into Turn One he ran on to some dust and eye witnesses reported he tried to tighten his line and drop down the banking. He then realised he was going too fast and would spin wildly, so tried to lessen the inevitable impact by striking the wall at the smallest angle possible. The car kissed the wall almost broadside at about 125 mph, and the right-front wheel was torn back, bounced on the nose and hit Mike on the head. The Lotus 56 slithered to a stop barely damaged apart from losing both right-hand wheels, but poor Mike Spence was gravely injured and died 4½ hours later without regaining consciousness. . .

A USAC committee, headed by S.A. Silbermann, an eminent metallurgist, immediately inspected the wreck and found no trace of structural failure, but an unfortunate incident concerned Carroll Shelby, whose two Goodyear-sponsored turbine cars had never proved competitive. He took the opportunity to withdraw them, and his statement included the lines '. . . it is impossible to make a turbine-powered car competitive with a reasonable degree of safety and reliability'. This unfortunately sounded like an indictment of the STP-Lotus cars as well as his own.

Meanwhile a distraught Colin Chapman had made up his mind; he announced he was returning to England and handing over his cars and his team to Granatelli. 'I am filled with grief at the loss of my long-time friend and associate Jimmy Clark, and the additional loss, just a month later to the day, of Mike Spence. As an understandable result I want nothing more to do with the 1968 Indianapolis race. I just do not have the heart for it'.

Further troubles struck the team when Silbermann discovered that certain Lotus suspension parts did not meet USAC requirements. Steering and suspension parts should have been in SAE 4130 steel or an equivalent alloy, and the mild steel components used did not meet the regulations, '. . . although they might well be equal or even superior in strength to the specified materials . . .'

The indefatigable Granatelli ordered new parts, while back in Europe the World Championship continued with the Spanish Grand Prix, which had been revived after a 14-years absence, at Jarama.

In the midst of building and testing the Lotus 56s Team Lotus had carried through a six-week development programme on the Lotus 49. The poor Race of Champions performance with 49/5 had prompted the programme and an entire redesign at both front and rear had produced the first Lotus 49B.

This was intended to cure rear-end bump steer with the latest wide wheels and tyres, and to improve stability under braking, which had never been a good point of the basic design. The front suspension rocker arms and links were swept forward to increase the wheelbase by two inches, and the hull modified to remove a built-in anti-dive characteristic. The standard plain-bush rack-and-pinion steering system was replaced by a ball-bearing Indy unit because of the greater loads associated with the wider rims and tyres.

Extensive changes were made at the rear-end. The lack of easy adjustment and ratio changing on the ZF transmissions meant that a whole selection of assembled units had to be taken to each race. Since Graham Hill was particularly prone to experimentation the number of transmissions required had become enormous, and so Hewland transaxles were adopted which were easily adjustable throughout.

A five-speed Hewland DG300 gearbox was fitted, and all suspension loads were fed through its casing, none being fed into the engine cylinder heads as before. Longer lower radius rods were sunk well forward into the hull, and new rear wheels were formed of two conical sections, bolted together by a ring of Allen screws. New-pattern Girling disc brakes were adopted, and aerodynamic aids appeared in the form of small spoiler wings on either side of the nose, mounted on a cross-tube and with adjustable incidence. The combined oil and catch tanks were mounted above the gearbox and an oil cooler fitted above them, fed with air through a NACA duct sunk into an upswept tail cowling. In profile the car had a semi-wedge shape, and it was hoped that it would prove as stable as the true-wedge Indy cars.

But with Colin's absence at Indy and attending Mike Spence's funeral the car stayed in its lock-up at Jarama. He 'phoned instructions that the car was not to be raced, and when Graham arrived from the United States he began practice in 49/1. The only other Lotus runner was Jo Siffert in Walker's 49/2.

Graham qualified on the inside of the third row, 0.5 second slower than Amon's Ferrari on pole position, while Siffert was another 1.3 seconds down on the outside of the fourth row. Jackie Stewart had damaged a wrist in a Formula 2 shunt at the circuit and his place in Tyrrell's Matra was taken by Jean-Pierre Beltoise, who from the start began an intense struggle with Amon and Rodriguez in a BRM. The Matra was called in when it began trailing smoke on lap 13, and after 20 laps Amon was just 0.5 second ahead of Rodriguez, with Graham 3 seconds behind in third place. But on lap 28 Pedro lost control of the BRM on oil and skated into a barrier at Portago, leaving second place to the Gold Leaf car.

Amon drew away while Graham began to be challenged hard by Denny Hulme's McLaren. Denny tried repeatedly to force his orange-coloured car out of Hill's slipstream and past that sunny Sunday, but the Lotus 49 was very wide, and finally Denny began to suffer from the Lotus' exhaust fumes and had to fall back. When Amon's fuel pumps shorted-out Graham rushed into the lead on lap 58, with 2.8 seconds in hand over Hulme.

Denny closed the gap, then Graham began to draw away in the final 12 laps as the McLaren's gearbox played-up, so Graham came home to score his first Grande Epreuve victory in a Lotus and the first for the Gold Leaf team. This triumph against a background of tragedy was a tonic for the team, and Graham took the World Championship lead with 15 points to Hulme's eight, although Jimmy's total of nine still separated them.

The day after the Jarama race the results of an X-ray on Stewart's wrist confirmed that he had a hairline fracture of the scaphoid, and would be out of Indy; another hard blow to Granatelli.

But before the '500' came the next World Championship round at Monaco, where Colin was on hand to supervise the new Lotus 49B's first race. Jack Oliver was promoted from the ranks of Formula 2 to drive the second GLTL 49/1, Graham was in the new 49B/5 and Siffert was out again in Walker's 49/2.

Siffert's crownwheel-and-pinion stripped twice during practice and Oliver walked in with a broken drive-shaft universal joint in his hand. It seemed as though their ZF transmissions were flexing once again, and the heavy-gauge cast-iron cheek plates were fitted for the final session. Meanwhile, Graham had no trouble with his Hewland transmission, and despite clumping a kerb and smashing one of his brand-new wheels he took pole position at 1min 28.2sec. Johnny Servoz-Gavin took over Stewart's Matra for this race and took his place on the front row beside the Lotus 49B, and Siffert blazed round to equal the Frenchman's time of 1min 28.8sec to take the inside of the second row. Oliver was back on row seven, 3.5 seconds slower than his number-one but with minimal practice to his credit.

Beneath a blazing sun Hill was beaten off the line by the dashing Servoz, and the blonde young Frenchman dashed round in the lead for three gloriously partisan laps. First time through the tunnel Bruce McLaren got into a slide, possibly on spilled petrol, and snagged the left-rear wheel on a barrier. He slowed right down towards the chicane, but almost immediately the next group of cars came screaming out of the tunnel with Oliver on the outside and McLaren in his path. The unfortunate Lotus driver had no chance, and slammed straight into the orange car's tail, ending his Grand Prix debut on the first lap.

The Matra was out with a broken drive-shaft on lap four, and Hill and Siffert rushed away into the lead. There were only ten survivors at the ten-lap mark, and two laps later 'Seppi's third crownwheel-and-pinion of the meeting broke up and he was out, leaving Hill alone in the lead.

All this mayhem left Richard Attwood, standing-in at Monaco for the BRM team, in second place and he piled on the pressure as the race progressed. He was on scintillating form, and as his fuel load lightened he pushed Hill harder and harder until both were circulating at near record speed. In a great last lap effort Attwood shattered Clark's existing lap record time by 1.4 seconds, but Graham was well in command and won by 2.2 seconds to give the Lotus 49B a victorious debut, and to score his second consecutive Grande Epreuve victory. This gave Lotus a hat-trick in the first three rounds of the year, and Graham rushed into a clear World Championship lead by 24 points to Hulme's 10 and Scarfiotti's six.

Indianapolis followed four days later, where Joe Leonard had taken over one of the Lotus 56s with a vengeance, taking pole position at a staggering 171.559 mph. Graham was alongside at 171.208 mph and Bobby Unser's 'Rislone Special' Eagle fitted with a 2.8 litre turbocharged Offenhauser four-cylinder engine was on the outside at a 'mere' 169.507 mph. Art Pollard's third 'STP Gas Treatment Special' was on the middle of row four at 166.297 mph, and as the pace car pulled off under an overcast sky Leonard swooshed into an immediate lead. Hill was fourth on that opening lap as Pollard ran in mid-field, happily playing himself in with the strange car.

On lap eight Unser's bellowing Eagle-Offy stole the lead from Leonard and held it until his first stop on lap 56. Graham was running a consistent sixth then moved into fifth place while Pollard tooled round in tenth. It was obvious that the Lotus 56s had been de-tuned from their qualification trim, for they were nowhere as fast as the turbo-charged Offies on the straights and were making up time through the turns. After giving 510 bhp in practice the P&W turbine engineers had detuned their charges to a steady 480 bhp for the race and this couldn't compare with the wailing four-cylinders' 500-plus bhp.

Hill's race ended abruptly after 111 laps when his car threw a wheel after the front suspension broke and ploughed along the wall at Turn Two. At three-quarters distance Unser led Leonard by 10 seconds, and when they stopped Lloyd Ruby took the lead. Unser's gear-lever broke as he left the pits, so he was slow away, and when Ruby's car began to misfire after 175 laps Leonard took the lead. There were only 25 laps left, and then Carl Williams put one of Foyt's Coyotes into the wall at Turn Two, and while the blazing wreck was extinguished the yellow caution light slowed the pace and allowed the pack to close on Leonard.

But as Leonard crossed the timing line after 188 laps team-mate Pollard's seventh-place Lotus 56 died on the back stretch. No sooner had the crowd assimilated this news than the final blow was struck at Granatelli's team, Leonard's Lotus 56 dying on the pit straight and coasting to a silent stop before Turn One. Unser completed the nine remaining laps to win at a record 152.882 mph, while Leonard was classified 12th, Pollard 13th and Hill 19th overall. Leonard had led only 31 of the 200 laps, but had been cheated of almost certain victory.

The failures had been caused indirectly by the slow running under that final yellow light. P&W's fuel pump drive-shafts were designed to shear as fail-safes when used in aircraft should the turbine overheat before take-off. These fail-safe shafts were made of phosphor-bronze tube, and in preparing the race cars Lotus replaced these shafts with steel components. The P&W engineers were horrified at this and demanded that the original fail-safes be replaced. Hill's car started the race with a steel shaft and the other two with the phosphor-bronze types. During the slow-speed running under the yellow the turbines heated-up, and when accelerated to full power after the yellow light had been removed the fail-safe shafts just failed! Another contributory factor was that straight petrol was used in the race rather than kerosene owing to various publicity ties, and so some of the lubricating properties of the practice fuel were lacking in the race. . .

After the bitter disappointments of Indianapolis, GLTL returned to the Formula 1 fray at Spa in June for the Belgian Grand Prix. Oliver's Monaco car had been severely damaged, and while Graham practised his 49B/5 Oliver kicked his heels, waiting for the new 49B/6, which was on its way from Hethel for him. Rob Walker was looking forward to delivery of his new Lotus 49B, but in the interim 49/2 reappeared for Siffert.

Hill's car broke a gearbox bearing early in practice, and since the final Saturday sessions were wet neither Team Lotus driver set very fast times, Oliver having the daunting experience of trying a new car at Spa in the rain! They started on the sixth row of the grid, while Siffert was quicker on the inside of row four.

Graham's car was shorn of its fins and engine cowl for the race, while Oliver had both devices fitted, with the addition of an aluminium spoiler strip on his engine cowl. Hill's mirrors were remounted on struts, but neither Lotus used the latest conical wheels.

Rain held off at the start and Jack Oliver gained his first experience of a Lotus 49B in the dry on that opening lap. Hill lasted only five laps before the left-hand outboard drive-shaft universal joint sheared, but Jackie kept going, moving into tenth place on lap seven, then ninth on lap nine and eighth on lap 11 as leading cars dropped out. When Hulme retired on lap 19 he became seventh, and when Courage's BRM failed he inherited sixth place on lap 23. Siffert was fifth, profiting similarly from retirements, when his oil pressure zeroed with two laps left, so Oliver took his place. But his engine was starving and he stopped for fuel at the end of his 26th lap. As the car accelerated away from the pits his crew noticed the right-hand outer universal joint smoking, and sure enough he failed to complete the lap, retiring when the joint sheared out on the circuit. Nevertheless, he was classified fifth and scored his first two World Championship points, while McLaren was the surprise race-winner after Stewart had run out of fuel.

The next qualifying round was the Dutch Grand Prix at Zandvoort where GLTL and Walker Racing appeared with the cars they had used at Spa. Despite ignition troubles in practice Graham started from the outside of the front row, 0.3 second slower than Amon on pole position, and Oliver was on the outside of the fourth row with Siffert behind him. A rear radius rod had pulled out of the hull of the Walker car during practice, and the suspension and transmission had been rebuilt overnight.

The race started in pouring rain, but Graham stole the lead from Amon on the first lap in celebration of the Lotus 49's first anniversary. However, he was quickly caught by Stewart in the Matra, whose Dunlop tyres proved infinitely superior to Graham's Firestones in the flooded conditions. Graham was also troubled by sand being washed into the throttle slides by the spray and rain and causing the throttle to stick. He spun at the end of the straight, dropping from second to fourth, soldiered on through the rain until the throttle stuck again, and finally spun at Tarzan, knocking a wheel off on the fence posts. Colin didn't even say goodbye after the race. . .

Meanwhile Jack Oliver spent ages in the pits having drowned ignition revived, and stopped on the circuit clearing sand from the throttle slides. He finished too far back to be classified, while Siffert gave up with transmission troubles. Stewart won the race from Beltoise, making it a convincing Matra one-two.

The French Grand Prix followed at Rouen early in July, by which time Team Lotus had rebuilt Graham's shunted 49B/5 with new suspension and steering which gave a higher ratio and smoother action. Jackie's car was basically unchanged, but both carried new aerofoil wings, mounted high above the tail on slender struts. Aerofoils had been introduced at Spa by Ferrari and Brabham, their purpose being to force the road wheels more firmly on to the road, adding traction without any commensurate increase in mass to be accelerated and braked. Oliver's aerofoil was larger than Graham's and both were mounted directly on the suspension uprights to gain maximum effect.

At one point in practice these new wings gave so much downthrust that the cars' noses were almost lifted clear off the ground, and much time was spent adjusting the nose foils to compensate. This cost valuable time, and with Siffert's Walker car handling very badly the fastest Lotus was Hill's, ninth quickest at 1min 59.1sec. Jackie was one row behind on 2min 00.2sec, and because of the limited practice available the organisers were pressured into arranging an extra untimed session early on race morning. Jackie was following Siffert and Attwood in this session when his car suddenly went light and tore out of control across the road, hit a stone gate post at around 120 mph, broke in two and finished up on the verge; Oliver miraculously escaped unhurt. It was thought that his low wing had lost its effectiveness by running into the turbulence of the cars ahead, and his rear tyres had lost virtually all adhesion.

So only two Lotus-Fords started the race, which began in a heavy drizzle, and Graham worked his way into fourth place before retiring on lap 14 when his left-hand drive-shaft sheared. The extra traction

Above: Graham Hill gave this view of the original Lotus 49B to most of his competitors, but the advent of wings rendered this neatly upswept tail cowling obsolescent. Colin gets the latest driver report during practice at Zandvoort. Below: Wings and things at Brands Hatch, Jack Oliver leads a Grand Prix for the first time, trailed by Jo Siffert's brand-new Rob Walker car.

available with a wing had removed much of the 'safety valve' of wheelspin, and without this cushioning effect the transmission was overstressed to the point of failure. Siffert lapped dejectedly without a clutch and stopped by the roadside to borrow Graham's visor, then soldiered on through the rain and finally placed a sorry 11th. The race, won for Ferrari by Jacky Ickx, was saddened by a fatal accident to Jo Schlesser driving an experimental air-cooled Honda.

Two weeks later came the British Grand Prix at Brands Hatch, where Walker returned his 49/2 to Team Lotus for Oliver to race and took delivery of his long-promised 49B/7. Graham was in his usual car, which after Rouen had been given stronger drive-shafts and an even taller rear wing with the wide-span front foils from Oliver's wreck to trim it up. Jackie had similar wings on his car, but Siffert's brand-new Lotus used a lower rear wing and shorter nose foils.

Graham hurled his car round in practice with complete abandon, finding the new Firestone YB11 tyres most forgiving, and took pole position at 1min 28.9sec. Oliver put his specialist knowledge of Brands to great effect to be second-best at 1min 29.4sec and Amon took the outside of the rank 0.1 second slower. Siffert's new car was finished off in the paddock and he was fourth fastest at 1min 29.7sec on row two–Lotus were back on top form. . .

The three Lotus-Fords led away from the line with Oliver darting into the lead from Siffert and Hill. But Graham was second next time round and took the lead at the start of lap four. The works cars pulled away from Siffert, who was locked in battle with Chris Amon's Ferrari, until Hill suddenly slowed on lap 26 and pulled off behind the pits. The Lotus 43-type drive-shafts had not proved man enough for the job, and his left-hand outboard universal joint had failed yet again.

This left Oliver in the lead, driving smoothly and comfortably, and the smoke he had been trailing from a breather had diminished. Jo Siffert had oil over his goggles from Oliver's spillage, but he continued his torrid battle with Amon. On lap 37 Chris dived ahead under braking for Westfield, but there was nothing he could do about Oliver, who had lowered his own lap record to 1min 30.3sec on lap 34. Siffert pushed Amon hard and they both lapped at 1min 29.9sec before Chris made a slight mistake on lap 42, which made 'Seppi' second again. Almost immediately Jackie's crown-wheel-and-pinion stripped as he changed down for South Bank on his 43rd lap and he walked disconsolately back to report to Colin Chapman.

So the Walker-Durlacher Lotus was leading and beginning to pull away from the Ferrari after a lap at 1min 29.7sec, 106.35 mph, which lowered McLaren's old record by a full 1.9 seconds. Jo came home to score Walker's first Grande Epreuve win since Moss' classic German Grand Prix success in 1961, beating Amon by 4.4 seconds. Ickx's French Grand Prix-winning Ferrari was fourth, and the World Championship standings left Graham still ahead with 24 points to Ickx's 20,

First time winner. Jo Siffert's Rob Walker-entered Lotus 49B was having its first race in the British Grand Prix and won. It was Jo's first Grand Prix success. Below: Graham during his gritty drive into second place at the German Grand Prix. The nose fins balanced the downthrust of the rear wing.

Stewart's 17 and Hulme's 15.

The Nurburgring was in one of its foulest moods in this year of wet motor racing, and the track was flooded and fog-bound for the German Grand Prix. Much work had gone on at Hethel to prepare another 49B for Jackie Oliver, based on old 49/2 which he had raced at Brands Hatch. Graham's drive-shaft breakage had wiped-out much of the suspension and this was completely rebuilt with heavier drive-shafts made up from Mercedes and BRD components. Siffert's car was similarly modified, and all three Lotus 49Bs had bracing struts fitted beneath the bell-housing to distribute suspension loads more evenly and relieve the transmission casing of some strain.

Conditions were atrocious for practice, and Jackie dropped his new car on 'Hill's Bend' on the descent to Adenau. The Lotus 49B skimmed along the hedgerow and wiped off two wheels, but it was quickly retrieved and hurriedly rebuilt in time for the race. Graham was on the second row, 42 seconds (it was that kind of weather) slower than Ickx on pole. Siffert was on the inside of row four and Oliver—with wheels pointing in all directions—on the outside of row five.

Graham took the lead from the line, but Stewart's Matra was ahead at the Schwalbenschwanz. The conditions helped the Scot, for narrower wet-weather tyres made his steering lighter and eased the load on his plastered and still painful wrist.

The race splashed on with Stewart leading from Hill, who had Amon constantly in his mirrors. As this battling duo chased Stewart into the 12th lap Chris lined-up to pass the Lotus, but something in his differential failed and the Ferrari spun out at the North Curve. In the general spray and murk Graham failed to notice his absence and pressed on as hard as he could. He slithered over a brow to find a river of water flowing across the road and spun like a top. The Lotus stalled, but the never-say-die Londoner leapt out, turned it in the right direction, pushed and leapt back in. The engine fired and he continued, but it had been a nasty moment, as he thought Amon was about to come out of the murk at any moment!

Just before the finish Stewart had a bad fright when he suddenly came upon Oliver's slow and unmanageable Lotus before Adenauer Forst; he suddenly saw the wing emerging from the mist and just managed to avoid it by braking violently. He went on to win the race with Graham a gallant second, 4min 3.2sec behind! Oliver was one lap down in 11th place and poor Jo Siffert retired with drowned ignition on lap seven after running an unhappy ninth at best. Graham now had 30 World Championship points to Stewart's 26 and Ickx's 23, while reigning Champion Denny Hulme was falling from the fray with his 15.

The Oulton Park Gold Cup race followed two weeks

Below: The Pratt & Whitney gas turbine engine in the Lotus 56 Indy cars came complete with smoke stack! Lotus reverted to open bath-tub type chassis design with this car. Inboard front brakes and rocking-arm front suspension can also be seen. Bottom: Mario Andretti started his first Grand Prix from pole position at Watkins Glen.

later, the Lotus line-up being as in Germany except that Oliver's 49B/2 had been properly rebuilt. Graham took pole position with 1min 29.2sec, 0.6 second quicker than Amon, and Oliver took the centre of row three. Stewart stole the lead at the start and held it to the finish in his pale blue Matra. Hill and Amon began a tremendous tussle behind him, but after only seven laps Hill's crownwheel-and-pinion stripped to put him out. Meanwhile, Oliver improved from an early sixth place to fight hard for and hold third place in another intelligent drive.

On August Bank Holiday Monday a Ford Sport Day at Mallory Park included Formula 1 demonstrations from Hill and Stewart, and Graham's Lotus 49B appeared with a new nose cone with top vents to exhaust radiator air, following the lead set by McLaren and Ferrari, thereby adding downthrust and saving the springs and dampers from being roasted in a hot-air stream.

Early in September GLTL arrived at Monza for the Italian Grand Prix with three cars. Mario Andretti was flown in to drive 49B/5, while Hill took over a brand-new 49B/6 which replaced Oliver's Rouen write-off. Jackie continued with 49B/2, and all three cars had the new nose cones and revised 'four-into-one' Cosworth exhaust systems which gave a slight top-end power improvement for this fast circuit; Jo Siffert had run his car at the St Ursanne-Les Rangiers hill-climb to set FTD at 1min 2.2sec, and Cosworth had not had time to fit his engine with the new system. Extra fuel was required for the long Italian race, and while GLTL provided extra tankage beneath the radiator ducting, Siffert's was within the hull above his legs.

Andretti was a full second quicker than Hill in first practice before rushing back to the United States for a USAC race, then jetting back to Italy for the Grand Prix. But the organisers took a dim view of this rapid commuting and pointed out that drivers were not allowed to contest two International events within 24 hours, so after Andretti and Bobby Unser (who should have run a BRM) had returned to Monza they were told they could not start.

Hill got on to the outside of row two with a lap in 1min 26.57sec and Oliver was back on the inside of row five in Andretti's car with 1min 27.40sec, Siffert being ahead of him at 1min 26.96sec.

At the end of the first lap Graham was second, wheel-to-wheel with McLaren, while Siffert was sixth in the first group and Oliver was third among the mid-field bunch. But after 11 laps Graham dropped out when a badly-made wheel fatigued and the centre tore out, the wheel bouncing away down the road as Graham clattered to a stop with the suspension mangled. Siffert battled with Stewart and the works McLarens for many laps, led for two of them and was a consistent second as the race progressed, but suddenly he pulled into the pits after 59 laps and retired with a broken shock absorber mounting and collapsing suspension. Oliver ran as high as eighth until third gear stripped at Lesmo and put him out after 39 laps.

The 1967 Centennial Canadian Grand Prix was not a one-off as had been thought at the time, and the Formula 1 circus returned to Canada in 1968 to race at the beautiful Mont Tremblant circuit at St Jovite. Graham's Monza car had been renumbered 49B/8 for this trip and his rear wing extended right to the outer edges of the tyres. Jack's 49B/2 had a medium-width wing and the third car, 49B/5, was hired to Canadian Lotus distributor Bill Brack, and was fitted with a similar-size wing. Siffert was in his usual car and for this tight circuit, where torque was at a premium, only Oliver and Brack had the Monza exhaust systems.

In practice Jacky Ickx crashed his Ferrari and broke a leg when his throttle jammed open, and later in the session Graham hit the same bank, crumpling the nose and left-front suspension. Oliver's suspension cross-member was found to be cracked after practice, and all three GLTL cars had gusset plates welded on where the failure had occurred.

A 10-minute test session preceded the race, and when Graham came in after some fast laps his horrified mechanics noticed that his car's drive-shafts were twisted. Oliver came in, and his were twisted, and when Brack returned with the third car his were twisted as well. Some fierce work ensued to swop the shafts around, Hill taking the best of them and Brack the worst.

Jo Siffert was on the outside of the front row, 0.7 second slower than Amon and Rindt's Brabham, while Hill was 0.3 second slower still on row two and Oliver was on the inside of row four.

Siffert and Amon rushed away at the start, battling for the lead while Hill settled himself in to nurse his car round in fifth place. Jo retired after 30 laps when oil loss caused a piston ring to fail, but the Walker crew found his left-front tyre was virtually bald and his drive-shafts badly twisted. Graham was now in third place, and Oliver inherited sixth place on lap 31 when Brabham retired, but his hopes of another World Championship point disappeared abruptly two laps later when a drive-shaft finally sheared. Brack's drive-shafts had broken after 19 laps.

Rindt went out on lap 39 to leave Graham in second place behind Amon, but six laps later he felt a tremendous jolting and banging behind his shoulders and dropped back before calling at the pits. The Lotus mechanics had a good look at the car and found that the top engine mounts had broken; over the bumps the car had been opening and closing in the middle as though it were hinged! They did their best to tighten things up and Graham went back into the race determined to nurse the car to the end; he finished fourth after Amon's jinx had struck yet again and left the race to the McLarens. Jo Siffert earned the consolation of a new lap record in 1min 35.1sec, 100.32 mph.

Hulme's win in Canada combined with his Italian Grand Prix success gave him 33 points, equal to Hill at the head of the table, with Stewart and the injured Ickx within striking distance with 27 points apiece; it was one of the closest Championship battles ever.

The lucrative United States Grand Prix followed at Watkins Glen in October, by which time stronger steel engine mountings had replaced the alloy components on the Lotus 49Bs and new constant-velocity jointed drive-shafts had been fitted. Three works cars were fielded, the usual pair for Graham and Jackie and 49/2 for Mario Andretti.

Jackie's engine had a persistent misfire in the first session, so his Monza-exhaust engine was dropped into Andretti's car and he took the later unit from that chassis. Then Colin arrived from England and ordered the later engine to be refitted in Mario's car, so the weary mechanics had to change it again. More work followed when Graham's clutch broke, and then on the day before the race Oliver crashed heavily when the left-rear wheel broke-up on the right-hander beyond the pits.

After the Monza fracture of a rim the whole batch were found to be wrongly machined, which allowed a fatigue crack to develop between cooling holes drilled in the cone. New wheels had been ordered, but could not be made-up in time for the Canadian race, so at St Jovite each rim had been crack-tested and the soundest wheels raced. Colin had arranged for new wheels to be fitted at Watkins Glen, but the weary mechanics overlooked them and one of the dicey Canadian wheels had found its way on to Jackie's car. 'The Old Man' was livid when he found what had happened, and five very chastened mechanics set about preparing the surviving Hill and Andretti cars for the race.

Mario lapped smoothly and shatteringly fast in his Lotus 49B to take pole position in his first-ever Formula 1 race, his time of 1min 4.2sec being 0.07 second quicker than Stewart, while Graham was next up with 1min 4.28sec. Siffert started on the outside of the sixth row with a time of 1min 6.17sec.

Andretti took an immediate lead at the start with Stewart and Hill on his tail, but at the Loop Stewart dived through to snatch the lead, while Graham ran wide and slowed out of the corner. Under braking his steering column had slid forward, trapping his fingers between the wheel rim and the dash panel and knocking all the switches off! He recovered as Amon nipped through, but was troubled by his 'adjustable' steering column for the rest of the race.

After five laps Andretti appeared with his nose cowl breaking-up, and on lap 13 he was ordered into the pits, where it was taped-up before he rejoined in 13th place. Mario tore through the field into ninth place, but then he developed bad clutch slip and dropped out after 32 laps. Hill chased Stewart all the way, but the Matra was 24.68 seconds ahead of the Lotus at the end of the 108 laps.

Hulme had crashed heavily and Ickx was still nursing his broken leg, so this result gave Graham 39 points to lead the World Championship from Stewart with 36 and Denny with 33, Ickx now being out of contention with his 27 points.

The Mexican Grand Prix in November was the

exciting climax to the Championship battle with Stewart, Hulme or Hill all with a chance of clinching the title for Matra, McLaren or Lotus. The McLaren team performed a brilliant rebuild on Denny's wrecked car in time for the race, and Colin gave Graham a choice of 49B/6 or 49B/2, while Jackie had his usual 49B/5 and Siffert the Walker car. Graham's number-one car had a new full-width wing, hinged and sprung by rubber bungee-belts to fall into the operating position through corners and feather along the straights, an extra pedal to the left of the clutch feathering the wing through a Bowden cable. No wings were fitted to 49B/5—to keep the opposition guessing and waste time trying their cars in a similar trim—and 2-inch wide wheel spacers were brought along so that 17-inch wheel rims could be

Jo Siffert was in searing form for practice, and he hurtled round to take pole position at 1min 45.22sec, 0.4 second quicker than Amon. Graham was on row two, with 1min 46.01sec, and Moises Solana qualified the spare car, 49B/2, on the inside of the sixth row, 0.77 second quicker than Jackie Oliver on the row behind. Overnight both Graham's and Jo's cars were found to have cracked their rear suspension frames and rapid repairs were necessary before they formed-up on the grid for this all-important race.

Both front-row cars were slow away, and Graham led to the first corner before Surtees took a brief lead and was then repassed. Stewart quickly established himself on the Lotus' tail and on the third lap Graham pressed the feathering pedal on the straight and found that it had gone limp. He fiddled with his mirrors to examine the wing struts, and saw the bungee-bands on one side were fluttering free. With only one band still attached the wing didn't feather fully, but it snapped into position as he braked and worked well enough.

High kerbs marked the inside of the corners after corner cutting had been much in evidence in previous years, and Graham kept rigidly within them early on until he realised Stewart and the pack were happily bouncing and planing over the kerbs and taking fractions off him every time. So he, too, took to the kerbs, changing gear as he hit them to ease the load on his fragile transmission.

On lap five Stewart grabbed the lead with Graham and the flying Siffert on his tail, then Hulme crashed when his car broke under him. Graham rushed back into the lead on lap 10 and seven laps later Siffert stole second place. Five more laps saw the Walker car in the lead after outbraking Hill into the hairpin, but the Swiss held out for only three laps before his throttle linkage came apart and he had to stop. He lost two laps, rejoined in 12th place and began to fly round even faster than before.

Graham maintained a narrow 2 seconds margin over Stewart until lap 38, when the Matra dropped back with a failing fuel pump, and while the Scot was reduced to cruising pace, eventually to finish seventh, Graham built a commanding lead and flashed over the line 1min 9sec ahead of Bruce McLaren to clinch his second World Championship title, and bring Lotus bouncing back after the hardest series of blows they had ever suffered. The Lotus pit exploded with delight, Colin Chapman running along the pit lane to greet his new Champion as his wife, Hazel, just burst into tears. . .

Meanwhile, poor Solana had gone out after 15 laps, his car unmanageable since its wing had collapsed on the second time round, but Jackie Oliver had driven a very consistent race to take a rousing third overall. Siffert was sixth after his troubles and set a new lap record of 1min 44.23sec, 107.26 mph, which compared with Clark's previous record of 1min 48.13sec—an indication of the progress achieved by wing and tyre developments.

A tragic year for Lotus had ended with splendid success, the Ford-powered Lotus 49 having achieved all that its designers had intended for it the previous year. In addition to Indy, Lotus had contested all 12 World Championship rounds, the three non-title Formula 1 races and eight Tasman rounds during the season, winning four Grandes Epreuves, a fifth going to Jo Siffert's Walker car at Brands Hatch. Down-under, four major races had fallen to the Gold Leaf Lotus-Fords, so of the 23 major events the Lotus 49s had won nine. In South Africa John Love, who had bought 49/3, had a most successful season in national Formula 1 events, and won five races, was second in a sixth, and retired in two more to clinch the South African Championship. The year was a most memorable one for Lotus, with final triumph following early tragedy. . .

1968 RACING RECORD
Other formulae and classes

The Formula 2 season was saddened by the tragic loss of Jim Clark at Hockenheim, a body blow from which Gold Leaf Team Lotus never recovered fully. Graham Hill had eight races during the season with the Lotus 48s and finished only two of them scoring a fourth place at Reims and a distant seventh at Vallelunga.

It was left to Jackie Oliver to uphold some of the marque's flagging Formula 2 prestige, and he began the season armed with the original Lotus 48-FVA, the car which Graham Hill had driven in Australia the previous year. It was still finished in the famous old green-and-yellow colours, and backing for the unofficial 'works' team came from Roger Frogley's Herts & Essex Aero Club. Derek Wilde looked after the old car, and his impeccable preparation gave it 11 finishes from 11 starts in the European season, allowing Oliver to take fifth place overall in the non-graded Drivers' Championship. Jackie's best placing was second at Hockenheim, and he added three fourth places and four fifths to this record. At the end of the year the car was sold to Irishman Gerry Kinnane, but before it was delivered 'Oli' took it out to the Argentine for the Temporada races in December. This series was dominated totally by the works Ferrari Dinos, but

Jackie managed a strong third place in one of the Buenos Aires rounds to finish a good season in an obsolete car.

Beyond the luckless 48s there was little Lotus interest in the formula, apart from a pair of spaceframe 41Bs shared by Bruno Frey, Walter Habegger and Manfred Behnke. None of these drivers was exactly a hot property, and the cars appeared just as make-weights in most of the Championship rounds . . .

This was a sad state of affairs, and although the Lotus works teams were fighting hard to regain their Formula 1 World Championships and were running the futuristic turbine cars at Indianapolis, there was little of note available to private customers. The company had shifted their emphasis much more towards the new road car ranges, and Lotus Components were having a poor time on the international competition front. The saving grace was the huge success of Formula Ford, which helped to keep the production lines full of Lotus 51s, and in fact production of this model eventually totalled no less than 218—way in advance of the almost legendary success of the Lotus 18 and Lotus 23!

The most significant development of the year was the adoption of a wedge-shaped body in Formula 3, John Miles' works development car appearing in this new guise at the Silverstone International Trophy meeting. The car was based on the previous season's Lotus 41C, but front suspension modifications included the use of Lotus 47 uprights and wheels, and the body-line in profile was very reminiscent of the Indianapolis Lotus 56s, although the panelling was much more rounded in section. From a wide and shallow air intake the nose cone rose in a constant slope to the rear of the cockpit, from which point a tilt-tailed engine cowl completed the wedge effect. This prototype car was given the Lotus 41X classification, but the proposed production version, the Lotus 55, never materialised and the idea was shelved.

On its debut Miles blasted round Silverstone in the 41X 0.9 second under the class lap record to take pole position, and the new body shape proved highly effective in the slipstreaming battle of the race which followed. The front suspension changes had made the frame very much more stable under heavy braking than hitherto, and John was a happy winner by just 0.3 second from Roy Pike's Titan. He scored three more big wins as the season progressed, but as in Formula 2 Lotus involvement in the 1 litre class was limited. While John won at Silverstone, Brands Hatch, Croft and Zandvoort, the indefatigable Mo Nunn forced his Lotus 41C to a splendid victory at Jarama. In Scandinavia Freddy Kottulinsky threw away his Lotus 41 and stepped-down to his old Lotus 35 with which he won handsomely at Jyllandsring and Keimola. Roland Binder and Ernst Maring were also prominent on the Continent with their Lotus 35s, although they achieved relatively little success, and in Spain Palomo, Baturone and Giro also ran Lotus 41s. In all, Lotus won seven of the 65 major European Formula 3 races of the year, as the Italian Tecno company became undisputed masters of the formula with 32 victories to their credit. Their most successful customer was a young Swede named Reine Wisell, who notched 10 major wins during the year, and of whom much more was to be heard in the future . . .

Group 5 racing attracted no works team for the first time since 1963, but Brian Robinson ran his ex-works Cosworth FVA-powered Lotus-Cortina to such effect that he finished second in the 2 litre class behind Frank Gardner's Alan Mann Escort no less than seven times in the British Saloon Car Championship rounds. Barry Pearson usually drove Robinson's second car, while Tony Dean and Willy Kay both campaigned BRM Phase 4 Lotus-Cortinas in the series.

The new Escort Twin-Cam completely outclassed the Cortina on a pure power-to-weight basis, but early in the season Gardner won the Aspern round of the European Touring Car Challenge in one of the Alan Mann Cortinas' last important appearances.

At home in club and National races Mo Nunn drove some superb races in his self-prepared Lotus 41, fitted towards the end of the season with a 119 bhp Broadspeed engine. This basically two-year-old car beat a lot of 1968 machinery and earned for Nunn a Gold Leaf Team Lotus Formula 3 drive late in the year; he took over the Lotus 41X while Miles was fulfilling GT commitments elsewhere, and secured a regular seat in the new Formula 3 team for 1969. Ken Crook forsook his Lotus 23s and an old 31 for the later Lotus 41C and put up some smooth performances, while in Formula Ford the Lotus Championship was won by Bob Ellice's type 51. Another Lotus single-seater champion was Eddie Heasell, whose near-prehistoric 1 litre Lotus 20 clinched the Monoposto Register's title.

Overseas, the American Formula B attracted several Lotus 41Bs fitted with 1,600 cc twin-cam engines. One of their leading pilots was Canadian Lotus dealer Bill Brack, who also drove a Lotus 49 in the Canadian Grand Prix. He laid plans to enter 5 litre Formula A racing the following year, using one of the Lotus 42 monocoques originally intended for Indianapolis and modified by Racing Frames to carry a tubular engine bay and V8 power unit. At the end of the 1968 season the Sports Car Club of America decided to adopt Formula Ford, although modified to allow the use of racing tyres while in Britain Formula A was imported as Formula 5000.

Meanwhile, the 1968 club season saw Gold Leaf Team Lotus picking up many awards with a brace of Lotus 47s driven by John Miles and Jackie Oliver. John Hine and Trevor Taylor also drove 47s but posted regular retirements, while Alan Fowler's Mercury-bodied Lotus 23GT was generally capable of giving any Lotus 47 a hard time . . . in more ways than one. George Silverwood picked up many Northern class wins in his 1,150 cc 23GT, and in Scotland John Nicholson's Lotus 23-based Jaynick GT was extremely competitive, but unfortunately this promising driver lost his life in a road accident late in the year.

Barry Flegg, Robin Hall, Trevor Elliott and Bob

Robertson were all very successful in various-engined Lotus Sevens, and at club level at least the Lotus ball kept rolling. In hill-climbing the marque's day seemed to be over, for big American-engined specials, preferably with four-wheel drive, were now the order of the day, apart from such exotic one-off vehicles as the V8-powered 4wd BRM. Geoff Rollason was the most successful Lotus driver, piloting a 1.6 litre Cosworth FVA-engined 41B, and he was placed equal fourth in the RAC Hill-Climb Championship. After Peter Watkin's success in the Autocross competition the previous season, Lotus fortunes waned, but one notable competitor was Paul Kerridge, whose supposedly totally unsuitable Lotus Europa proved surprisingly competitive.

But although the Lotus marque was well-represented in most classes of motor racing and other speed events, success at any significant level was rather limited . . . a situation which Mike Warner, head of Lotus Components, was all set to alter. Lotus' first serious new Formula 3 contender since the Lotus 41 was unveiled at the 'Boxing Day' Brands Hatch meeting on December 27. This was the Lotus 59, and although the boxy and rather ugly-looking car had hardly turned a wheel before the race John Miles brought it home in fourth place. It was a promising debut, and in fact the car was to put Lotus squarely back on the production competition car map . . .

Below: John Miles' Lotus 41X (alias Lotus 55) leads Roy Pike's Titan at Silverstone. He won. Bottom: One-point landing for Oliver's Lotus 48 at Nurburgring. Right, top to bottom: All kinds of funny things qualified as GTs in Club racing—John Markey's Lotus 23 at Brands Hatch. The GLTL Lotus 47 coupes had a good year. The De Dion-axled Lotus 57 Formula 2 car was never raced; it felt good but was just plain slow!

1969

Storm clouds over Hethel

After the huge success of the road-car side of the Lotus organisation in 1968, Lotus Components set-out to make a real success of their new spaceframe Lotus 59s during 1969. Under the energetic leadership of Mike Warner the division sold cars to many of the leading drivers in their class, and the 59's successes did much to offset a poorer year by the touring-car division.

A major upheaval at BRM in mid-season resulted in their long-standing chief engineer, Tony Rudd, leaving the concern, and subsequently joining Lotus to take charge of powertrain engineering. Steve Sanville had left to establish his own twin-cam engine-preparation company, and Rudd assumed responsibility for the development of the new Lotus LV-series engines in his place.

For the first time in Lotus history production was hindered due to a strike, involving 115 men in the paint area in September. In addition the whole Group was subject to a financial 'squeeze'—in common with the rest of the British industry—and these two aggravations combined to produce the first fall in Lotus profits for years.

In April, the first deliveries took place of the new Lotus Plus 2S model. This was a luxurious up-date of the existing Elan Plus 2, featuring cast wheels and the 115 bhp Special Equipment engine, and costing £2,244. The Plus 2 range dropped the Elan name, kit cars being dropped from the range simultaneously. In June, the Europa was introduced to the British market, priced at £1,667 and the same month saw a record number of 450 touring cars being delivered to customers. The Lotus Seven S3 began assembly in Buenos Aires, where it was fitted with Fiat 1500 engine/ gearbox units, and at Alexandra Park in July a special Lotus Show attracted a comprehensive display of Lotuses (from the Mark 3 onwards) and a tremendous number of visitors.

The trusty old Seven still refused to lie down, and with a general growth in the fun-car market Lotus Components jumped on the bandwagon and produced the new Seven S. It was originally built by Lotus Components purely as a display car for the Racing Car Show, but it attracted so much attention that Graham Nearn, who ran Caterham Car Sales, the Seven concessionaires, talked Warner into building replicas to order. It was intended to build no more than a dozen of them, and the Seven S specification was a considerable advance on the standard Seven Series 3.

Power came from a Holbay CFR (Fast Road) 1,599 cc Cortina crossflow engine, which used a flowed and ported head, special Hepolite pistons, a high-lift camshaft and double twin-choke Weber 40DCOE carburettors. Compression ratio was 10:1, and output stood at 120 bhp at 6,200 rpm. A special spray and upholstery job gave the necessary 'Special' appearance, and Dunlop alloy wheels carrying massive SP Sport Aquajet tyres completed the ensemble. The model was offered in fully assembled form only, and cost £1,600. Top speed was 108 mph, and through the gears the Seven S would hit 34 mph in first, 55 mph in second and 87 mph in third. Acceleration from 0-60 mph took 7.2 seconds (which interestingly was no better than the 1,340 cc Cosworth-engined car of 1961-62) and 90 mph came up in 16.2 seconds. Fuel consumption hovered around 21 mpg, and understandably the appeal of the car was limited to the wealthy enthusiast who could afford an impractical but impressive adrenalin pump!

Another Lotus Components project, and one which brought them some very favourable publicity, was the Lotus 47D specially built for GKN and Vandervell, who used it as a guinea pig for all kinds of product testing. The car consisted of a special backbone chassis lengthened by 3 inches to accomodate a 3.5 litre Rover V8 engine. This 185 bhp unit was mated to a ZF five-speed and reverse Formula 1-type transaxle, driving to 7½ inch wide, 13 inch diameter wheels shod with Goodyear tyres. Two ducted radiators were mounted in parallel in the nose, and interior trim was sumptuous in the extreme, with tan leather, full carpeting, a radio and airflow ventilation.

GKN wanted a car with tremendous performance in order to test a whole range of components, including a new type of camshaft and experimental dry steering bushes. The car caused a great deal of interest World-wide, and appeared at numerous exhibitions and race meetings in between carrying out its original intended duties, and there were many requests for 'replicas', all of which were resisted firmly!

In August a new twin-cam powered Seven SS model was released, and during September—despite the paint area dispute—production exceeded 100 units per week for the first time. In October the Elan won a Coachwork Gold Medal at the London Motor Show for the second year running, and November saw the largest-ever shipment to one dealer, when 108 cars left for Canada. The labour dispute was finally settled after a strained 13 weeks, and another Lotus landmark was passed as the company celebrated 21 years of production, the original Mark 1 having first run in November 1948. In December Colin was awarded the CBE for 'services to exports', and during the year 55 per cent of total deliveries were exported compared with 46 per cent in 1968. During the year two ex-RAF hangars standing on the airfield had become available, giving an extra 56,000 square feet of space, and £135,000 was spent on buying further land to build new manufacturing facilities.

The upset of the season undoubtedly was the Indianapolis set-back when the complex Lotus 64s were withdrawn after hub failures had put Andretti into the wall and left too little time for adequate replacements to be made. This episode saw the end of the Lotus-STP association, in which the first chinks had appeared the previous year. The sale of the cars and spares to Granatelli after Indianapolis had developed into something of a haggling match, as Colin liked to name his price for spare parts—many of which were available off-the-shelf from outside contractors.

Before the first failure occurred the promising Ford-powered four-wheel-drive cars looked set to stamp all over the opposition during qualifying, and Colin tried desperately to get new parts made, but the first batch of replacement components was fudged and the programme just ran out of time. Consequently the decision was taken to withdraw the cars, and 10 minutes before this was announced publicly Granatelli gave his verbal agreement to buy the cars, at a price of 95,000 dollars.

Shortly afterwards the STP and Lotus executives got together in the Speedway Motel to finalise the deal and sign over the cars. Andrew Ferguson was late for the meeting by a couple of minutes, and as he walked into the motel car park he was nearly flattened by Colin, reversing his car across the asphalt with foot hard down and tyres squealing. He caught sight of Ferguson, who saw that the 'Old Man' was visibly upset. 'We're not selling the cars', he roared. 'Hide them; take them away and don't let Granatelli have them. Don't let him find them.' He then floored the throttle and screamed away to the airport and home, leaving Ferguson to carry out his orders.

Andrew walked into the Motel, and into the suite where the meeting had been held. The STP hierarchy were still there, looking as bemused as the Lotus Racing Manager felt. Apparently Granatelli had agreed to buy

Left: New instruments, tumbler switches and hood release were interior features of the new S4 version of the Elan, which was offered in both Coupe and Convertible forms. Right: A Lotus LF/115 twin-cam engine in one of the test cells of the new engine development facility at Hethel. Below: The Vauxhall-based Lotus LV220 engine, though an experimental project, marked an important step forward for the company into the area of engine manufacture.

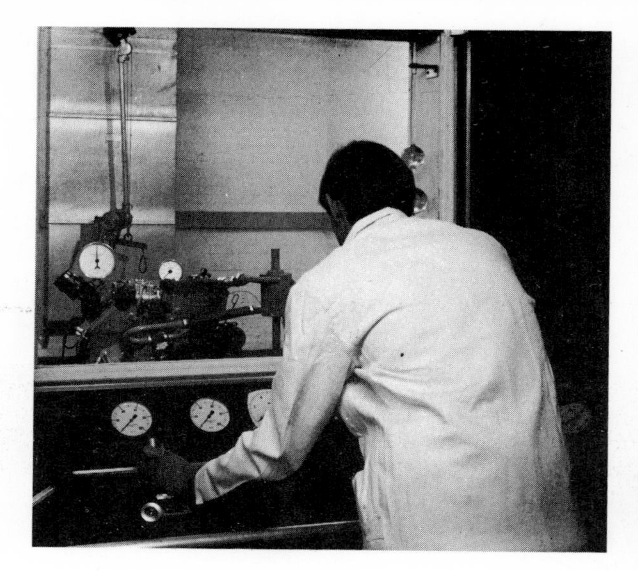

Following criticisms concerning the trim of the early Europas Lotus instituted a programme of refinement on their mid-engined coupe with the commendable result seen in the picture below. However, a more fundamental redesign to give more interior space had to wait until later.

the cars for the quoted price, but then queried the cost of spares from Lotus. Colin, smarting from the loss of face caused by withdrawing from the '500', took this as an immediate challenge, leapt to his feet and stormed out after a brief but fierce interchange. The whole incident lasted just a few minutes, and Ferguson was now left to sort-out the loose ends, and hide the cars to prevent STP slapping an injunction on them.

This wasn't easy. In Indiana you can rent a lock-up garage, but if you try to work on a car in it you are breaking the law. The Lotus 64s' Ford engines had to be craned-out and returned to Dearborn, and so Andrew had to find somewhere secluded and private where his mechanics could do the job. Eventually he contacted the secretary of Lotus' shipping agent at Indianapolis Airport, and she 'phoned her husband who cleared the family cars out of his garage at home, about 40 miles upstate.

Andrew then got hold of a single car trailer, coupled it to a hire car, and with a Lotus 64 under wraps on the back drove off to this new-found hide-out, keeping a sharp eye out for STP scouts! Mechanics Arthur Birchall, Dale Porteous and 'Hughie' Absalom made a string of high-speed return trips until the poor girl's garage was bulging with cars and spares, and meanwhile Andrew had been told a sheriff was looking for him at the Speedway. He thought this was an STP sheriff with a writ to impound the cars, so he hid himself, but in fact it was a Ford sheriff who had been sent along because they had the impression that their engines were being stolen!

Finally Andrew met the sheriff, who was reassured,and Ferguson hired a hydraulic trolley lift to help remove the engines and return them to Dearborn. One by one the engines filtered back via the most remarkable cross-country routes, while the householder whose premises Lotus were using rapidly became cheesed-off with having his garage jammed to the rafters.

Ferguson was under orders from Chapman to stay in America and beat-out some form of agreement with STP, and he was there for two and a half months while the now bare chassis were shifted from hide-out to hide-out.

Eventually the whole deal collapsed, agreement could not be reached on the supply of spares, and as a parting shot Granatelli told Andrew he knew where the cars had been all the time! Colin finally passed sentence on the Lotus 64s with one of his favourite sayings: 'Andrew, bring the cars back to Hethel, where I will personally put a hack-saw through them, I will personally dig a hole and I will personally bury them!'. Of course he didn't, but these most complex Lotus racing cars ever built were never to be raced, and two years later were still mouldering in one of Hethel's hangers.

Later in the year Andrew left Lotus after nine hectic seasons to concentrate on his constructors' associations, and Peter Warr eventually was brought back in his place. Peter had been with Lotus Components in the early 'Sixties, and had been running a commercial slot-racing centre in Hammersmith in the interim.

The year was a turbulent one for Lotus' racing programmes and for Colin, and the bad publicity resulting from Jochen Rindt's forthright outbursts and problems with the unsuccessful four-wheel-drive cars and aerofoils must have made it a year forever imprinted on his memory.

Jochen was the first foreigner to be signed-on as a front-line Lotus driver, and his Teutonic bluntness did not fit in well with Colin's tender sensibilities. Colin Chapman: 'Jochen was a very good racing driver . . . a very temperamental racing driver . . . brilliant on occasions . . . but very moody. I wouldn't say there was animosity between us—more a lack of appreciation and understanding of each other's problems. I always had a very great respect for him, and I think eventually he grew to respect me and Lotus.

'His bluntness was never a serious obstacle, but it was difficult for the team to have the same enthusiasm for working with Jochen as they had for working with Jimmy. He was very critical of the team and of everyone in it, but since he was a foreigner it was difficult for him to convey shades of opinion. He said what he thought and I respected him for that, but the way he put it in English tended to make one over-react, and then he wouldn't quite understand the precise opinion I was trying to convey and the whole thing would spiral. One tends to get upset easily by difficulty of communication, and although Jochen spoke far from pidgin English it was difficult to convey conflicting attitudes without being offensive . . .'

Colin's main difference with his explosive new driver seems to be summed up in the following: 'Jochen used to listen to a lot of detractors that were around at the time . . . it seems the more successful one becomes the more detractors one seems to attract. Really there was a certain reservation between us, but I wouldn't say it was a serious problem.'

While the works team was having its difficulties, Lotus Components staged a remarkable recovery with their new 59-series cars, Mike Warner persuaded leading drivers to run them and reinstated the Lotus marque as a credible commercial contender. During the years of the Formula 3 monocoque and the Lotus 41 the name had sunk to a nadir, particularly on the Continent where the Formula 2 and Formula 3 boys wouldn't even look at a Lotus. But now confidence was being restored, and a reputation being built as a foundation for great sales in the new year. Lotus Components sold £670,000-worth of racing and Lotus Seven road cars during the year, compared with £450,000-worth during 1968, and despite tremendous overheads this division of the company was proving really successful. The Lotus 59s won the British Formula 3 Championship, the Formula 2 (Graded) Championship and the Formula B Canadian title, while Lotus 61s scored in the British, Belgian and Irish Formula Ford Championships.

Overall, a total of 4,506 Lotuses were built during

the year, 1,458 more than in the preceding year, this increase being more than the total Lotus production in 1965! Turnover was up by £842,000 to £5,285,000, but due to the general problems encountered during the year, and unsold stock at the year's end, profits slumped by £125,000 to £606,000, a fall from the 16.5 per cent profitability of the previous year to the 11.5 per cent which had been achieved in 1967. Was the bubble bursting?

1969 RACING RECORD
Grands Prix and other major formulae

For the first time the South African Grand Prix was moved away from the start of the year, and the 1969 International season opened in January at Pukekohe with the New Zealand Grand Prix.

Gold Leaf Team Lotus shipped two 49Ts South of the equator, and this time Graham Hill was to contest the whole series, with his new joint number-one, Jochen Rindt, in the other car. As in 1968 Cosworth's Ford 2.5 litre short-stroke DFW engines were fitted to the cars, and both used old nose cones and ZF trans-axles, Graham having 49T/8 and Jochen 49T/5.

Chris Amon's Ferrari led the Grand Prix from the start, but Jochen was ahead on the second lap to lead his first race in a works Lotus. Hill retired with deranged suspension on lap 13, and five laps later the Austro-German spun on oil. Despite all his efforts to recover, Amon won handsomely, but Jochen was placed second and set a new lap record of 58.6 seconds on the way. Leo Geoghegan was out again in his evergreen Lotus-Repco 39, and finished fifth.

Levin the following weekend saw a scrambled start in the first 14-lap preliminary race which left Rindt fumbling for a gear on pole position. Derek Bell and Amon powered their Ferraris to the front, with Graham on their tails, while Jochen rushed furiously through the field to tack on to his team-mate's exhausts. It was immediately evident he was taking his joint status seriously, and he pressed Hill hard under braking into the tight Levin corners, Graham slamming the door shut on him every time! Finally the Londoner ran over Jochen's left-front nose spoiler with his right-hand rear wheel, and they finished third and fourth in that order.

There was a certain amount of flak flying around the pits after this encounter, but in the main 63-lapper Rindt stole an early lead from Amon, with Hill fifth. On lap 3 the Lotus new-boy spun and fell back behind his team-mate, only to spin again two laps later. This time the new car rode up a bank and toppled upside-down, contriving to damage itself quite severely in the process. Jochen was OK, but somewhat chastened by the experience. After 13 laps Hill's car sheared a drive-shaft universal joint so Amon made it two-in-a-row. Jochen's fastest lap of 45.3 seconds in the heat bettered his main race time by 0.4 second.

The wrecked car was beyond repair locally, so after some hasty work back at Hethel one of the Mexican Grand Prix cars was put on a plane for New Zealand. The car appeared at Christchurch for the Lady Wigram Trophy, complete with top-ducted nose and Hewland transmission in place of the earlier plain nose and ZF transmission. Hill won the 11-lap preliminary heat by 0.1second from Rindt after a race-long battle, Graham averaging 103.24 mph and Jochen setting a new record at 1 min 18.8 sec in his new 49B/10 (49/2 rebuilt).

Jochen started the main 44-lap race on pole position with Hill and Piers Courage in Frank Williams' Brabham-Ford alongside. He took an instant lead and won his first race for Gold Leaf Team Lotus by 34 seconds from Hill, equalling the new lap record of 105.08 mph. Chris Amon was third to maintain his Tasman Championship lead with 22 points to Courage's 13 and Hill's six.

Teretonga Park was again the last New Zealand round of the series, and Hill's older Lotus 49 was updated with a Hewland transmission to bring it into line with Rindt's replacement car. The Austrian led the ten-lap preliminary event from start to finish while a disgruntled Hill fell back to sixth with fuel-feed troubles.

Jochen averaged 97.05 mph in this heat and set a new lap record of 57.9 seconds, so started on pole position for the 62-lap main race. As the flag fell he stalled his car as a drive-shaft shattered, and Bell savaged his Ferrari's nose on the Lotus' rear wheel. Brabham had a long battle for third place with Frank Gardner's Mildren-Alfa Romeo, and finally got ahead after 33 laps, then took second place from Amon on lap 53 to finish just behind Courage's meteoric Brabham.

So the circus moved to Australia with Amon and Courage sharing the points lead with 22 each, from Rindt with 15 and Hill with 12. The Lotus 49Bs destined for Lakeside and the Australian Grand Prix were delayed by Customs and missed much of practice, then just as the final session closed Graham had a nasty moment when the left wing support buckled and the wing toppled backwards. This was a bigger wing than the adjustable type used in New Zealand, and so the smaller wing was refitted for the race, with a fixed incidence.

Both Lotuses had engine problems, and Graham raced with the spare Williams DFW installed, Jochen using Graham's discarded unit. He was a struggling fourth when a camshaft broke on lap 44, by which time Hill was soldiering on with an inoperative rev counter and a wildly flexing rear wing. Only four laps after Jochen's retirement the whole structure collapsed completely, and after a stop to cut-away the remains Hill went on to finish fourth behind Geoghegan's old Lotus 39 and the two Amon-entered Ferraris.

After this race there were only two serviceable Ford DFWs among the three cars using them, and Mike Costin flew out from England to rebuild Jochen's engine in time for the Warwick Farm '100' the following weekend. Hill's car had its larger adjustable

An interesting special project during 1969 was the development for GKN, the automobile component manufacturers, of a super-luxury version of the Europa powered by the Rover 3.5 litre light-alloy V8 engine. The car was intended to do double duty as a test vehicle and as management express transport.

wing refitted for this race, and Geoghegan's car appeared with a more modest structure.

Jochen took pole position, 0.7 second quicker than Amon, and he was soon in the lead despite a rather poor start. Courage spun in the damp and collected Amon, but with his only rival joining him in the fencing Chris won his Tasman title. Jochen won the Warwick Farm race from Bell's Ferrari Dino, while Geoghegan had a troubled run into fifth place. Hill had been second until rain affected his car's electrics, and after a long stop to have them dried out he finished 11th and last, although the fastest lap was his at 1min 40.3sec.

The last round of the series was at Melbourne's Sandown Park, for which Mike Costin had rebuilt a second engine for Graham Hill. But Jochen was still quicker, and he started from pole position beside Amon with Hill next-up on the second row. The new Tasman Champion hauled the red Ferrari Dino away from the Austrian and beat him fair-and-square by 7.3 seconds, while Hill stopped after one lap with throttle linkage troubles and lost three laps in the pits. He rushed back through the field to finish sixth, and a rather unhappy down-under series for Lotus ended with Amon leading Rindt by 14 points, with Hill fifth, a further 14 points behind.

Two weeks later the South African Grand Prix opened the new World Championship series at Kyalami. Graham and Jochen were joined by Mario Andretti in the Formula 1 GLTL cars, and Hill was running his old 49B/6 once again, while Jochen made his debut in a brand-new 49B/9 and the Italo-American took over another new car, 49B/11. Siffert was out in the Walker-Durlacher team's 49B/7 once more, and John Love had his supremely successful Team Gunston 49/3 to make a record field of five 3 litre Lotus-Fords.

All three works cars used strutted wings at front and rear, all acting directly on the wheel uprights and adjustable by pedal, cable controls and bungee-bands as seen on Graham's victorious car in Mexico the previous year. In compliance with new FIA regulations each car had an on-board fire-extinguisher system and higher and stronger roll-over hoops. Andretti's 49B/11 was 49/5 rebuilt.

The Walker car was similarly bi-planed and had three-gallon supplementary fuel tanks tacked-on outside the hull, with the oil tank and cooler re-sited above the gearbox. Love's car had a wing system of his own design, which was operated by a compressed air bottle containing 2,000 psi. When this was expended the wing remained in the operating position and the whole thing seemed very scientific compared with the devices on the works cars.

In the middle of practice Rindt suddenly appeared with his rear wing collapsed around the car's tail, and while the wreckage was being examined Andretti limped in with a similar failure on his car. He explained that as the wings swayed under cornering the struts fouled the tyres, were instantly twisted and so collapsed. Team Lotus had no spares, so they hastily borrowed back the struts they had loaned to Walker.

Below: A grim-looking Graham Hill prepares to practise for the Race of Champions. Bottom: An even grimmer Jochen Rindt contemplates a collapsed wing during the same training session; but worse wing trouble was to follow. Right: Hill uses his wings to maximum advantage at Brands Hatch. Bottom right: Hill at Monaco, where the wing ban was imposed after the Barcelona disasters.

The following day Jochen and Graham both ran with equal-height wings at front and rear, with the struts steeply inclined away from the wheels, while Andretti had just a rear wing fitted, and Siffert's forward wing was re-sited at the rear, both cars having nose canards fitted as in 1968.

Jochen qualified for the middle of the front row with 1min 20.2sec, 0.2 second down on Brabham's new Ford-powered car, while Andretti was 0.6 second slower on row three with Hill alongside, 0.3 second slower again. Siffert was on the middle of the fifth row and Love on the outside of row four.

At the end of the first lap Rindt and Hill were third and fourth as Love led Siffert and Andretti further down the field, the American having made a bad start.

CASTROL

Left: Full-width front wing supplementing nose tabs on Jo Siffert's Walker-Durlacher Lotus 49B was an extreme measure tried before the new regulations were enforced. Below: Siffert's earlier Lotus 49 looks positively bare during its final race (at Rouen) of the 'pre-wing' era. Bottom: Jochen Rindt and Graham Hill at Zandvoort; though team-mates they were intense rivals on the GP circuits during 1969.

Brabham lost the lead when his car's wings collapsed, and Stewart inherited it for Matra with the two GLTL cars on his tail and looking most menacing. But Graham took second place when Jochen's engine began to misfire, and Siffert and Andretti rushed through the field to take third and fourth places. At one point four Lotus 49s trailed the leading Matra, and while Jochen slowed Andretti drove furiously to close on Hill until he abandoned abruptly without gears on lap 31. Love's ignition failed at the same time, dropping him from 10th place, and Rindt finally retired after 44 laps when his mechanical fuel pump quit. Hill went on to finish second, 28.8 seconds down on Stewart's Matra, while Hulme was third and Siffert fourth, and last to complete the full 80-laps distance. Only two of the five Lotus 49s survived but both scored Championship points.

Two weeks later came the Race of Champions at Brands Hatch, where a carbon copy of the Kyalami result saw Stewart win, with Hill, Hulme and Siffert behind him. . .

Practice was marred by a clammy mist which filled the Kentish valley, and while Jochen circulated with twin wings on his Lotus 49B/9, Siffert found his front wing giving him some bad blind spots on Brands Hatch's swoops and climbs. As the cars screamed round vortices could be seen clearly streaming off the wing tips, and clear tunnels were carved through the dank mist in their slipstreams. Andretti's South African car, 49B/11, had been sold to fellow American Pete Lovely and was painted red overall for his 3 litre Formula 1 debut.

Hill quietly took pole position at 1min 28.2sec, with Stewart 0.1 second behind him on the middle and Siffert on the outside of the front rank a whole second slower still. Jochen had a wing collapse and ended-up on row two, 0.1 second behind the Walker car, and Lovely's gentle 1min 36.4sec lap put him on the fourth row. For the race Hill ran a tall rear wing and Rindt a lower one, while Siffert bravely retained the bi-plane arrangement and Lovely had a rear foil similar to Jochen's. Stewart led all the way, to beat Hill by 7 seconds, and behind the front-runners Lovely finished sixth. Jochen had been right on Hill's tail at one stage and it looked as though he was being baulked, so the pit-crew signalled Graham to let him past, but almost simultaneously Jochen was badly baulked by a back-marker and he lost his chance. He was annoyed at this and blasted round to shatter the lap record at 1min 26.8sec, 109.91 mph, but this proved too much for his engine, which lost its oil pressure and put him back in the paddock after 38 laps.

The International Trophy race followed at Silverstone, where GLTL ran their usual car/driver pairings, supported by the Walker and Lovely entries, all unchanged from Brands Hatch trim, until Friday practice when the American VW dealer crashed his car in the wet as he was examining his instruments! The car was straight in time for the race. . .

Practice on Saturday was divided into four 30-minute sections with £100 prize money for the fastest lap in each part. Thus stimulated, Jochen skated round to win £200 in the later sessions, but on one occasion his engine died as he hurtled through Woodcote, and he only just kept control. Everybody thought his engine had broken until he walked ruefully up the pit lane saying, '. . . You try running out of fuel half-way through Woodcote in the wet—phew!'.

The works cars had missed the drier Friday sessions, so Siffert was the best-placed Lotus driver on the middle of row two, with Rindt, Hill and Lovely on the third and fourth rows. Race day was very wet and Stewart started from the back of the grid in his older Matra since his new car did not have suitable rim sizes for rain tyres. Brabham led away while Jochen's engine misfired in the opening stages due to damp ignition leads. Graham made the mistake of disconnecting his front anti-roll bar in the hope of improving his car's wet-weather handling, and made it unmanageable. . .

Jochen was 11th after five laps when his engine cleared, and he began to saw his way through the field, gaining 2 seconds per lap on Brabham. He plumed round the airfield circuit in a fantastic display of knife-edge control, with the car dancing across the wet surface. He passed Stewart as though the Scot was stationary and after 29 laps he was 27 seconds behind Brabham. Ten laps later the gap was 20.5 seconds, on lap 42 it was 18.5 seconds and on lap 44 it was 17.5 seconds. With three of the 52 laps to go the gap was 15 seconds and Brabham seemed safe, but next time round there were only 11 seconds between them. Jack's car was running out of fuel, and Jochen slid and sawed his way closer and closer. With one lap left there were 9.8 seconds between them past the pits, and after the Brabham gulped itself dry under the bridge before Woodcote, Jack coasted across the line to win by only 2.2 seconds from his former team-mate.

Amid this drama Siffert had been troubled by poor handling and after a stop he finished 11th. Hill was seventh and unhappy, and poor Pete Lovely had been forced to start on dry tyres and understeered into a bank just after the start.

Meanwhile, on the other side of the World, Leo Geoghegan ran his venerable Lotus-Repco 39 in the Japanese Grand Prix at Mount Fuji, and won easily for his Total-sponsored team.

The first European round of the World Championship was the Spanish Grand Prix, held for the first time in Barcelona's Montjuich Park. This twisty circuit had some very fast sections which could place a premium on aerofoil performance, and Colin experimented with the cars throughout practice. Extra aluminium-strip tabs were fitted to the rear wing's trailing edge, and the increased downthrust demanded extra incidence on the nose fins to balance the effect and keep the front wheels on the ground. Jochen hit and killed a stray dog in practice, but stormed round to take pole position at 1min 25.7sec. Amon's Ferrari was alongside, 0.5 second slower and Hill took the outside of the row a further 0.4 second down. Siffert suffered from excessive understeer and was on row three.

Race day brought brilliant sunshine, and Jochen bulleted away to underline his claim as Stewart's only real challenger in modern Grand Prix racing. Amon trailed him while Siffert and Hill were hot on the Ferrari's tail. On lap seven Graham stole third place from the Swiss and set off after Amon, and on lap nine he was closing the gap past the pits into a 150 mph curve downhill towards the hairpin. This curve breasts a hump before falling left-handed downhill, and as Graham's car hammered over the brow the suspension snapped down on to full droop. This was too much for the wing, which wasn't stressed for negative loads such as this, and it 'topped-out', collapsed and folded back over the tail. This sudden loss of downthrust made the light tail go wild, and the car spun.

It smashed nose-first into the inside Armco barrier, then spun madly across the circuit into the other barrier, careering to a stop with Graham safely strapped in the cockpit. He thought he'd lost a wheel, until he examined the wreck, then noticed Jochen howling past with a slight crease in the underside of his wing. The mechanics had just run up from the pits, and as Graham realised his wing had collapsed he sent them back to report to Colin while he ran down to the hairpin to warn Jochen if he could. But Jochen only came by in the lead once more, and before he could be stopped his wing topped-out over the hump and collapsed.

He had just begun his 20th lap, and the car snapped into a 140 mph spin, clumped the inside rail and spun into Graham's wreck, cartwheeling over it to finish upside down in the road, bent like a banana, with the unfortunate driver hanging from his belts.

Graham helped the marshals heave the wreck upright and he stood on the distorted monocoque to bend the steering wheel and column out of the way so that Jochen could be released. He was battered and bloody, but still conscious, and escaped from this terrifying accident with facial cuts, a broken nose and cheekbone, and concussion. Both cars were write-offs.

These disasters left Amon leading from Siffert, but on lap 31 the Walker engine blew-up because its oil pump had shaken loose and allowed the lubricant to drain away, so the Lotus challenge was at an end. Amon retired, leaving the race to Stewart, but Jochen had a new lap record of 1min 28.3sec, 96.03 mph, to his credit as he went to hospital.

It was abundantly obvious that Formula 1 design was moving into dangerous realms where barely understood forces prevailed. Colin knew now that his wings must be stressed against this topping-out condition in which the loadings were reversed, but he was not to get the chance. The CSI, as the governing body of the sport, gave the aerofoil question some thought, and came to a decision, although sadly it was typically abitrary and ill-timed, being announced in the middle of practice at Monaco. . .

The month of May brought the usual hive of activity at Indianapolis, and USAC had made some far-reaching rule changes since the Lotus 56 turbines had so nearly won the '500' the previous year. At first they banned four-wheel drive, and further limited the maximum turbine annulus area to 11.999 square inches for 1969, making them quite uncompetitive. Later the four-wheel drive ban was moderated to a 10-inch rim-width limitation as compared to the 14-inch rims allowed with two-wheel drive, but notice was given that four-wheel drive would be out completely in 1970.

This effective ban on turbines encouraged Lotus/STP to invest in the latest 2.65 litre turbocharged four-cam Ford V8 engines, and these were mounted in new Lotus 64 chassis. These were based closely on the turbine Lotus 56 hull and running gear, and at the time were the most complex cars ever built by the company. The four-wheel drive system was Lotus-developed, using ZF and Hewland parts, and the plumbing and piping for the engine and transmission made the car's system a complete maze of minute parts. . .

Early in training Andretti wound his Lotus 64 up to 170.197 mph, but Graham was hard-pressed to better 160 mph and Jochen, who had been passed fit, was even slower and spun his car. Huge duck-tail spoilers were fitted to the cars, but the rear hubs began to overheat and so new finned components were made and fitted. The first qualifying weekend was rained-out and the following Wednesday Andretti survived an enormous accident when his car's right-rear hub failed and the car lost a wheel and slammed into the wall. 'Superwop' escaped with facial burns, and later qualified his old Hawk-Ford for the race. The hub failure was attributed to poor heat treatment, and there was insufficient time for new parts to be made and tested, so the surviving Lotus 64s had to be withdrawn.

Meanwhile, the old Lotus 56 chassis had been revised and their turbines replaced by piston engines. The Granatelli brothers ran two cars for Art Pollard, one with a turbo-Ford V8 and the other with a 5 litre Plymouth V8 'stock-block' unit. The Plymouth failed in qualifying so Pollard put the Ford-engined car on the fourth row of the grid at 167.123 mph. In the race his transmission failed after only seven laps, but such are the rewards at Indianapolis that in being classified 31st he won 10,816 dollars. Gary Bettenhausen attempted to qualify a third Lotus 56, with a turbocharged Offenhauser four-cylinder engine, but failed and raced a Gerhardt instead. Lotus had not returned to Indy up to the end of 1971.

In the midst of these trials and tribulations the Monaco Grand Prix was held in mid-May. Despite losing both team cars at Barcelona, two Gold Leaf 49s appeared at Monte Carlo, a real tribute to the energy of the mechanics at Hethel. The two Tasman cars, 49B/8 and 49B/10, had been dusted-down and brought up to latest Formula 1 specification, and while Jochen was still recovering from his concussion Richard Attwood was roped-in to join Hill.

Attwood's older car retained the original nose-mounted oil tank, while both cars had full-width rear wings suitably modified after the Barcelona disasters, with wide nose fins. New front wheels were fitted, cast in one piece, while Siffert reappeared in Walker's always immaculate 49B/7.

First practice was on Thursday afternoon, and Attwood's 1968 record of 1min 28.1sec with the BRM immediately palled as Stewart went round in 1min 24.9sec. Siffert was also well under the record and getting typically crossed-up due to his car's instability under braking (this was a familiar Lotus 49 shortcoming), then he caught his left nose fin in the fence as he skittered into the Gasworks Hairpin, and spun to a halt in a shower of glass-fibre. But immediately after the session the CSI called a meeting and announced a ban on aerofoils for the rest of the meeting, consequently discounting all the day's times, trials and tribulations; UPROAR!

Ken Tyrrell, whose Matra MS80 was the only car designed since the advent of wings, was in a towering rage, but with Colin Chapman absent at Indy he lacked a strong ally. All the cars were stripped overnight, and new suspension settings had to be guessed-at before the first practice session of another new era of motor racing. . .

But everybody soon proved themselves adept at good old-fashioned suspension-sorting without the issue being clouded by incidence angles and negative lift, and Stewart finally took pole position with a lap in 1min 24.6sec, 3.5 seconds under the old record and quicker than his best time with wings, while Hill's was the fastest Lotus time, 1.2 seconds slower on the outside of the second row. Siffert was 0.2 second behind him on row three and Attwood did a reasonable 1min 26.5sec for row five.

Graham's car used an upswept engine cover similar to that on the car with which he had won the previous year, and he ran third in the early stages while Amon chased Stewart for the lead. But both Tyrrell Matras, driven by Stewart and Beltoise, retired with broken universal joints, and Amon's differential failed, so Graham Hill the Monte Carlo master was left with the lead. He went on to win his fifth Monaco Grand Prix, his second consecutive win there in a GLTL Lotus 49B, and received an ovation. Siffert was third, despite a sick engine and a hastily patched nose-cone, and Attwood was a reliable and smooth fourth. He was the last finisher to cover the full distance, and there were three Lotus-Fords in the first four in the race which Team Lotus could never win in the days of Climax engines and Jim Clark; it was some consolation for the troubles at Indy.

As the Belgian Grand Prix was cancelled, there was a long breathing space before the next World Championship round at Zandvoort, and Team Lotus took the opportunity to rebuild Graham's crashed 49B/6 from Barcelona, and completed the new Lotus 63 four-wheel drive Formula 1 cars. In these the Ford engine was turned about-face, the drive being taken from the clutch/flywheel assembly immediately behind the cockpit. The drive was stepped to the left side of the car, where propeller shafts drove fore and aft to offset differentials at either end. The whole system was mounted in a complex bathtub-type monocoque similar to that used in the Lotus 56 and 64, and the engine sat between monocoque pontoons as used in the earliest Lotus 25/33 series chassis. Small 13-inch diameter wheels were fitted all round, carrying 12-inch wide Firestones at the front and 14-inch tyres at the rear. These small wheels left little room within the rim for the upright, suspension links, constant velocity joints and so on, so inboard mountings were provided for the ventilated disc type brakes, which were connected to the wheels through drive-shafts. The layout of the car forced the cockpit far forward and slightly to the right, and the driver had to wriggle his feet under the forward drive unit to reach the pedals. The transmission itself was a combined effort between Lotus and Hewland Engineering.

The design had been inspired by road-racing experience with the Lotus 56 turbine cars of 1968, in which the four-wheel drive and stable ride qualities had proved very effective. Pitch was very limited compared with the rear-wheel-drive Lotus 49, and this improved stability into corners, giving more effective braking and promising better lap times. The idea was to bring these pitch-free, smooth riding qualities, plus the additional traction of four-wheel drive, to Formula 1. But it was destined not to work. . .

Following the CSI's arbitrary ban on wings at Monaco, the teams arrived at Zandvoort with their own ideas of what constituted 'aerodynamic assistance fixed and part of the bodywork'. The interim rules demanded that such assistance should not extend beyond the inner edges of the tyres at front and rear, and the GLTL cars—49B/10 for Hill and 49B/6 for Rindt—had small wings mounted on two fins above the oil tanks, which were wrapped over the gearbox. Siffert's car used a delta-wing upturned tray formed around the oil cooler, and each arrangement was accepted by the scrutineers. After practice Matra lodged an official complaint about the Lotus wings, but it was rejected, and then Ferrari announced their disapproval of the wings and their intention to race only under protest. . .

The new Lotus 63s originally had been intended for Mario Andretti to run in this race, but after the organisers had offered £1,500 starting money for him the little American found his USAC commitments would prevent him attending. He was a great advocate of four-wheel drive, but both Team Lotus' regular drivers were dubious and Jochen in particular was opposed to the whole car on principle; he felt the driving position was dangerous, and loudly refused to run the car.

Graham did some shake-down laps in 63/1 while Jochen's 63/2 was finished-off in the paddock, but when his Lotus 49's engine went off-song the mechanics had to take the engine from the new car and fit it to the old one. Jochen was fastest in practice with 1min 20.85sec to take pole position, 0.29 second quicker than Stewart, who in turn was 0.87 second faster than

Hill; Graham's best lap in the unsorted Lotus 63 was 1min 25.75sec, and Siffert was on row four at 1min 23.94sec.

Graham made a superb start to block-off Stewart and Rindt into Tarzan, and out of the hairpin the Gold Leaf cars were side-by-side and touching! The pair elbowed and shouldered their way round, but going into Tarzan for the third time Jochen dived over the grass to nip inside his joint number-one and take the lead. Immediately he began to pull away, and Stewart nipped past the second Lotus but could not challenge the Austrian's rampaging pace. But after 16 laps a drive-shaft universal joint shattered as the leading Lotus 49B howled past the pits. Flying pieces cut McLaren team manager Teddy Mayer's leg as Rindt pulled off the circuit and retired, leaving Stewart's Matra in total command of the race. Hill became involved in a tremendous battle for third place, and eventually Siffert took it from him by skittering around the outside at Tarzan and leading away through the dunes!

Graham held fourth place until the end of lap 27 when he headed into the pits to complain of vicious oversteer, but nothing could be found wrong with the car so he rejoined to soldier round into an unhappy seventh place. Siffert inherited second place behind Stewart when Rindt retired, and drove a splendid race to score six World Championship points as Stewart took the lead in the table with 27 points to Hill's 15 and Siffert's 13. . . Jochen had yet to score.

The beautiful Charade circuit at Clermont-Ferrand was the next destination for the Formula 1 teams, for the French Grand Prix in July. GLTL produced the Zandvoort Lotus 49Bs for Rindt and Hill, and Colin entrusted 63/2, the unused Zandvoort car, to John Miles, the son of actor Bernard Miles and a fine GT and Formula 3 driver, for its race debut. A rear wing was fitted, similar to those on the Lotus 49Bs, but hung behind the tail on two tapering struts.

The acrobatic Clermont circuit proved too much for Rindt, who was still not fully recovered from his concussion, and in practice he was sick and dizzy, and substituted an open-faced helmet for the all-enveloping Bell Star type he had adopted since Barcelona. But it was to little avail. After setting third fastest practice time in 3min 2.5sec, 1.9 seconds slower than Stewart on pole position, he ran fourth in the opening stages of the race until Denny Hulme made a stop and elevated the Lotus one place, but Jochen was already feeling nauseous and dizzy, and almost immediately he lost his place to Beltoise's Tyrrell Matra, and then to Amon's Ferrari; after 23 laps he pulled into the pits and retired with double-vision to add to his troubles.

Meanwhile John Miles had qualified the Lotus 63 at 3min 12.8sec on the penultimate row after suffering excessive understeer throughout practice and had made a good start, but he was out after one lap when the mechanical fuel pump drive belt broke and the engine consequently died. Hill had put his car on the fourth row with a lap in 3min 5.9sec, 0.4 second quicker than Siffert on the next row, but he performed miserably during the race to finish sixth, completely out of touch. Jo Siffert tackled Hill in the early stages, got out of shape braking into the corner above the pits and ploughed into the bales, tearing his car's nose-cone, but he continued after a couple of stops for attention to finish ninth.

Once again there was just a fortnight between races, the next event being the British Grand Prix at Silverstone. Colin was determined to prove the potential which he felt certain the Lotus 63 had to offer, and finally he lost patience with his drivers and decided he would sell 49B/8 to Jo Bonnier and 49B/10 to John Love, so leaving the team with a solitary Lotus 49B and the two Lotus 63s. Neither of the 'equal number-ones' was happy with the prospect of running one of the experimental four-wheel drive cars, and Rindt was absolutely adamant that he would not race the Lotus 63. This discord within the team was only alleviated when Jo Bonnier was persuaded to loan his 'new' car back to the works for Hill to drive, and was lent 63/1 to run in its place. Rindt stuck to his 49B/6 and John Miles, as ever, was happy to be in Formula 1 with 63/2.

Graham practised his original Lotus 63 in both major sessions but it wasn't as quick as either of the competitive four-wheel drive machines from McLaren and Matra. Then he took out the 'Bonnier' car, and the front-wheel bearings collapsed before he completed a lap, while at the same time Rindt's Lotus 49B was sitting streaming fuel in the paddock as a sprung rivet had chafed a hole in a fuel bag. Later in practice the team began to pull together as the final two hours were divided into four 30-minute sections with £100 going to the fastest lap set in each. Stewart took the first two prizes, then crashed in the third session, which left Jochen to even the score. The Scot was fastest overall, but Jochen was just 0.2 second slower, and since the crashed Matra could not be repaired for the race Stewart had to qualify in team-mate Beltoise's car, and he left pole position to Rindt's 1min 20.8sec, taking the middle of the front row at 1min 21.2sec. Siffert was on row four with a 1min 22.7sec, Hill behind him on 1min 23.6sec after his troubled practice, and Miles and Bonnier followed with the Lotus 63s at 1min 25.1sec and 1min 28.2sec, respectively.

In the race Bonnier's engine failed after just six laps at the tail of the field, while Jochen and Jackie Stewart began a tremendous battle for the lead, with Siffert and Hill eighth and ninth, and Miles involved in the four-wheel drive race at the tail of the field.

Rindt led Stewart by inches for the opening five laps, then the Matra kept ahead for ten laps, before the Lotus howled by once more. So the race went on with these two outstanding drivers of the year rushing round and completely out-pacing the rest of the field. Stewart held back and trailed the Lotus for lap after lap until the left-hand end-plate on the Lotus 49B's wing came adrift and began to foul the tyre. On lap 62 the Matra rocketed by into the lead again as Jochen thundered

The Lotus 63—a costly and unsuccessful experiment in four-wheel drive. Above: Graham Hill tested the car briefly before the Dutch Grand Prix at Zandvoort. Below: Two 63s, with differing tail sections, were taken to Zandvoort but Rindt and Hill showed more interest in their 49Bs. Bottom: The complicated steering geometry needed to obtain adequate lock. Right: John Miles' French Grand Prix lasted one lap with the Lotus 63, now with an extended rear wing.

into the pits to have the offending piece removed. He rejoined without losing second place, but on lap 76 his engine cut and spluttered at Stowe as the pumps refused to pick up the last remaining gallons of fuel, and he staggered into the pits after another lap while the Lotus mechanics found some extra fuel. His second stop cost him dear, and when Piers Courage nipped by to take fourth place Jochen let him go, thinking he was just unlapping himself, but at the last moment he realised his mistake and powered back into fourth place, to score his first three World Championship points in a Lotus.

Meanwhile, Hill and Siffert had made their way through the field, and while the battle raged for the lead an equally entertaining struggle developed in the mid-field. Siffert got the better of the works car around half-distance, but Graham hacked his way back again and by lap 77 was running fifth ahead of Courage and the Swiss. But next time round the works Lotus was spluttering as its pumps failed to scavenge, and on lap 79 Graham stopped for fuel, followed by Siffert on lap 80. The reigning Champion rejoined to finish seventh and 'Seppi' was eighth, one lap behind. John Miles soldiered round in the Lotus 63 without a clutch for much of the distance, and when he could no longer find top gear he stopped for attention to the linkage. He finally rejoined stuck in third, and made it to the finish, his engine wailing away at 9,000 rpm almost all the way round the circuit; he finished 10th, 10 laps behind Stewart.

Following the wash-out of 1968, the Nurburgring was hot and sun-drenched for the German Grand Prix in August. After the shambles of Silverstone practice Gold Leaf Team Lotus was in better shape, with 49B/10 for Hill, Rindt in his usual car, and that great four-wheel drive protagonist Mario Andretti on hand with 63/2. Bonnier's 49B/8 had been repainted red and was being looked after by the Parnell team, and Siffert was out again in the immaculate Walker-Durlacher 49B/7. The fuel system plumbing had been revised on the Lotus 49Bs to prevent the Silverstone failures recurring; of the 42 gallons carried for the race in Britain, there had been six left when the pumps refused to scavenge. . .

Early in practice Andretti's engine broke a camshaft and left him stranded out on the 14-mile circuit on a day which was marred by the death of Gerhard Mitter, one-time Lotus guest driver, who crashed his Formula 2 BMW. Rindt could not get in tune with the circuit, but Siffert was flying round, although handicapped by low gearing along the main straight. He was powering through the corners and twists in splendid style, but his practice ended abruptly when the left-front suspension collapsed and he ground to a halt. Jacky Ickx took pole position in his Brabham, his 7min 42.1sec bettering Stewart by 0.3 second and Rindt by 5.6 second, giving some perspective to the pair who had come to look upon Grand Prix racing as their own private game.

Siffert was next up with 7min 50.3sec, but Hill was way back on the fourth row with 7min 57.0sec.

Below: Fourth year of the Lotus-STP association and Andy Granatelli seems to be very interested in the small print of the Indianapolis contract. Right: Mario Andretti in the Lotus 64 which promised so much but was withdrawn from the race following a hub failure. Bottom: Granatelli's back-up cars included this Super Wedge for Art Pollard, the design of which leant heavily on experience gained in running wedge-shaped Lotus cars at Indy.

2
STP
STP
Ford
2
LOTUS
STP
AMERICAN
AMERICAN
WAGNER

Above: A damaged rear wing, caused by the left end blade rubbing on a rear tyre when cornering, stopped Jochen Rindt's exciting battle with Jackie Stewart in the British Grand Prix, and possibly cost him his first GP victory. Below: Rindt comes in to land neatly after the violent hump at Brunnchen, Nurburgring, which has since been levelled-off.

Andretti had a new engine installed in his Lotus 63, and his standing lap was covered in 8min 58sec, and his first flyer at 8min 15sec before another camshaft broke and wrecked the engine. His times gave some promise of better four-wheel drive things to come. He started from the penultimate row with Bonnier behind him at the back of the grid. Jo was so cramped in his new acquisition's cockpit that he had to reach across to the right-hand gearchange with his left arm! One Lotus 59B started in the Formula 2 race run concurrently with the Grand Prix, a Winkelmann car driven by Rolf Stommelen, the young German Porsche driver who was making his single-seater debut.

Ickx was engulfed by the pack at the start and Stewart howled away into the woods with Siffert and Rindt on his tail. Two-thirds of the way round that opening lap Andretti's Lotus 63 grounded on full tanks and instantly bounded off the road, wiping off a wheel and other bits and pieces on some fence posts. The unfortunate Vic Elford crashed heavily after hitting some of the flying debris and wrote-off his Antique Automobiles-entered McLaren; he broke an arm and Andretti helped rescue him from the battered wreckage, while the Lotus 63 was very severely damaged.

The young Belgian Brabham driver quickly disposed of the Lotuses and challenged Stewart for the lead, eventually going ahead and winning comfortably after Stewart hit transmission trouble. Siffert was followed through by Rindt, Hulme and Graham Hill and after four laps Bonnier trundled into retirement with a leaking fuel bag. Jochen's engine went off-song and he dropped back, and Hill was passed by Bruce McLaren, but Siffert ran confidently in third place and looked all-set for another good result when his front suspension collapsed approaching the Karussel on lap 13. He saw the left front wheel fall outwards, muttered 'Merde, alors', ducked-down, and escaped uninjured as the car tore into the undergrowth and crashed into a tree.

Graham scored again by finishing fourth, while Jochen retired at the pits after ten laps with ignition trouble. Poor Andretti had unintentionally cost Team Lotus a fortune, with his two broken engines and a wreck which was to require a complete strip-down and reskinning before it could run again . . . Stommelen was most impressive in the Formula 2 section and finished fourth with the car on fire!

Two weeks after the German race the non-championship Oulton Park Gold Cup was held in England. The atmosphere within the Lotus team had moderated considerably after Colin and Jochen had had a deep heart-to-heart at the Nurburgring, and Rindt made his debut in 63/1. Graham drove his Winkelmann Racing Formula 2 Lotus 59B, suitably ballasted to run in the mixed Formula 1/Formula 5000 field, and the only Lotus 49B on hand was Bonnier's, now on Goodyear tyres and entered by Filipinetti. But the unfortunate Swede crashed heavily in practice when a bottom wishbone pulled loose on the approach to Island Bend; he was lifted from the wreck unconscious, but was spectating next day although the car effectively was written-off.

Bonnier's best time was sufficient to leave an empty space on the outside of the front row, and after breaking the fuel pump drive on the Lotus 63 Jochen started from row two, 3.2 seconds slower than Stewart's Matra on pole position, while Hill was back on row four with his 1,600 cc car. When Stewart made a pit stop in the race Ickx ran away to an unchallenged win and Jochen was a consistent second to score the Lotus 63's greatest success. Graham dropped out after 36 laps when his oil pressure gauge feeder pipe burst.

While Hill and Rindt had their usual Lotus 49Bs for the Italian Grand Prix at Monza in September, John Miles appeared in 63/1. Smaller wings were fitted to reduce drag on this super-fast slipstreaming circuit, and front suspensions were modified with stronger rocker arms and new pins retaining the bottom of the uprights after the problems at Nurburgring.

Development work on the Lotus 63 had shown that its strong basic understeer could be reduced by altering the central torque-split and feeding less power through the front wheels. This made the car easier to drive, but naturally reduced the advantages of having four-wheel drive at all! The problem was that a driver could set-up the car nicely into a corner, but as he accelerated through the nose of the car would run wider and wider until the driver had no more lock available. He would then lift-off the throttle, whereupon the front wheels would grip and the nose of the car would dive smartly into the inside of the bend. It was impossible to hold a smooth, fast line through the turns, and this zig-zag course cost time. In addition the 90lbs weight penalty of the four-wheel drive system didn't help. . .

Despite a spate of Ford camshaft breakages in practice, Jochen took pole position with a lap in 1min 25.48sec. Miles had a transmission oil seal fail, and when his engine developed an untraceable misfire the spare Walker unit was craned-in overnight. Graham had a camshaft break and drove into the pits on one bank of cylinders, much to everyone's astonishment, and Siffert's engine also had to be changed. The Walker car had been completely re-jigged since its accident in Germany, and 'Seppi' put it on row four, with Hill on row five (browned-off at being consistently slower than the Walker car) and Miles second-slowest, 5.2 seconds down on Rindt.

John's race ended on lap four when yet another camshaft snapped on the way down to the Parabolica, but Jochen led as the race developed with Stewart, the works McLarens, Courage, Siffert, Beltoise and Hill all in a huge bunch battling for the lead.

This titanic race thundered on for lap after lap, and then Graham suddenly heard his engine note change and thought it had broken, but in fact the exhaust system was falling apart and the engine kept running. One tail pipe eventually dropped off and hit Surtees' fast BRM, and after losing about 5 seconds Graham slipstreamed skilfully back into contention, taking a consistent third place while Jochen and Jackie were still working-out the finishing order between them. Stewart led consistently past the pits whereas Jochen's gold nose-cone only led across the line seven times in the whole race. Siffert fell back when his engine lost power and finally blew-up, while Hill went ahead of Rindt to see what he could do about Stewart. He was running a consistent second for 16 laps until the left-hand exhaust camshaft snapped with only six of the 68 laps left, and he toured in to a tremendous reception from an enthralled crowd.

There were now four cars left in the leading bunch, with Stewart and Rindt hotly pursued by McLaren and Beltoise. On the final lap Jochen burst ahead through Lesmo and led towards the last corner, the Parabolica. Then Beltoise weaved through to outbrake Stewart and lead into the corner, but slid wide and took Jochen with him as Stewart backed-off, pointed his Matra to the inside and fled away to the line. He held his specially-selected second gear all the way as Jochen rushed up under the pits barrier but had to change-up as his rev-limiter began to cut-out his engine. Stewart won the race by inches and clinched his first World Championship title, and in a flurry of colour and sound Jochen was second, Beltoise third and McLaren fourth, with a bare 0.19 second covering all of them!

Two weeks after this wonderful motor race the Formula 1 circus arrived at Toronto's Mosport Park circuit for the Canadian Grand Prix. The Lotus 49Bs were unchanged while John Miles appeared in the re-jigged, re-skinned and rebuilt 63/2 which Andretti had crunched in Germany. The Walker-Durlacher car was present as usual and Pete Lovely made his reappearance with 49B/11, now finished in the white-and-blue American national racing colours.

Jochen and Colin had buried the hatchet and the Austrian tried the Lotus 63 only to spin it before the pits. Siffert got going very quickly until his foot slipped off the brakes and jammed behind the pedal on the same corner, and the Walker car crashed into the banking, folding up the left-side suspensions and creasing the hull. But Tony Cleverley and Stan Collier rebuilt it next day, and on race morning Jo showed his thanks by running over Tony on the warming-up lap!

Ickx took pole position again at 1min 17.4sec, and Beltoise took the middle of the rank with Jochen outside him, equalling the Matra time, 0.5 second slower than Ickx. Graham was on the middle of row three, quicker than Siffert (at last) by 0.2 second, while Miles was on row five with a self-respecting 1min 20.0sec, and Lovely was two rows behind, 2.9 seconds slower.

Jochen led the race initially only to be displaced by Stewart and the flying Belgian, and later in the race when the Brabham nudged Stewart into a bank while trying to overtake, Ickx was left with a long lead. Meanwhile, Rindt was having a hard time staving-off Jack Brabham in the second green-and-yellow car, and eventually had to let him by and settle for third place, the only driver on the same lap as the two Brabham-Fords at the finish.

Siffert and Hill both ran in a bunch battling for fourth place until 'Seppi' broke a drive-shaft after 40 laps and Graham spluttered to a halt with another broken camshaft two laps later. Seconds earlier Miles had dropped out at the same spot with the Lotus 63's gearbox seized.

The richest Grande Epreuve of them all followed early in October, the United States Grand Prix at Watkins Glen, which was worth 200,000 dollars in prize fund. GLTL presented their usual pair of Lotus 49Bs and Mario Andretti had his second go in 63/2 on the circuit where he had made such an impression on his Formula 1 debut the previous year. Once again five Lotus-Fords were running, with Siffert and Lovely making up the total.

Friday practice was damp and cold, and it was then that the four-wheel drive blind-alley was finally recognised as such. The cars should have been at an advantage in these conditions, but neither the Matra MS84 nor the Lotus 63 were impressive. Saturday was dry and after early problems with overheating tyres caused by incorrect suspension settings Jochen flew round to snatch pole position at 1min 3.62sec, 0.03 second quicker than Hulme's McLaren. Stewart and Hill were on the second row, Siffert on row three, while the unfortunate Andretti was rapidly losing his faith in four-wheel drive back on row seven. He would have liked to have had a go in a Lotus 49B but neither of the regular drivers were too keen on the idea! Lovely was behind him at the back of the grid.

Hulme was in transmission trouble on the front row of the grid and Jochen took an immediate lead from Stewart, with Hill and Siffert battling for third place. On lap three the blue Walker car went ahead but next time round Siffert stopped and retired with a broken fuel metering unit drive belt. Andretti was shunted at the start and stopped after four unhappy laps with bent rear suspension. Hill's suspension had been re-set with reduced camber to prevent the experimental Firestone tyres overheating, but this affected the car's handling adversely and he fell back through the field while Rindt and Stewart continued their season-long struggle.

It was Silverstone all over again as Stewart went ahead on lap 12, but Jochen was in command from lap 21 as his great friend dropped back with an oil leak finally to retire on lap 35. This left Rindt with a huge lead, and he lapped his team-mate after 31 laps and rushed on with Graham a slow and unhappy sixth. At 77 laps Hill moved up a place as Ickx's engine broke, and he was still fifth past the pits at the end of lap 88 when his mechanics noticed a rear tyre deflating. Jochen had eased-up because there was oil on the circuit, and Graham spun on this oil at the loop. The engine stalled and wouldn't restart, so Graham undid his belts, push-started it and climbed aboard, being unable to refit his belts. There were only 18 laps to go, and he pointed to his bald and chunking rear tyres as he passed the pits, intending to stop next time round, but he never made it. . .

Along the straight the deflating right-rear tyre

popped off the rim and Graham suffered the kind of explosive decompression which had probably killed Jim Clark. The car veered off the circuit, hit a bank and cartwheeled end-over-end, throwing out its unbelted driver and writing itself off. Graham was picked up with serious knee injuries and was taken to the Arnott Ogden Memorial Hospital in Elmira.

Jochen rushed on to score his lucrative first Grande Epreuve victory, tempering Team Lotus' near-loss of their ex-World Champion with a fine drive. Rindt won at 126.36 mph and set a new lap record of 1min 4.34sec, 128.69 mph, on his 69th lap. Pete Lovely retired his Lotus from 12th place when a drive-shaft universal joint failed.

As usual, Mexico City was the scene of the final Championship race later in October, and GLTL fielded Jochen in his Watkins Glen-winning 49B/6 with Miles returning in 63/2, even though four-wheel drive had been virtually given-up as a bad job. Hill, of course, had started his long and painful recovery back in England, but Siffert and Lovely were in their usual cars. None of the Firestone runners could compete with the cars using Goodyear's latest mix, and Jochen and Jo wound-up on row three with the Walker car quicker at 1min 43.81sec against the rather tired Gold Leaf car's 1min 43.94sec. John was on the inside of row six with a lap in 1min 47.76sec and Lovely was on row eight with a dismal 1min 50.34sec.

The Lotus 63 misfired on the warming-up lap and retired after three laps and a pit stop, during which nothing could be done to rectify fuel pump maladies, while Jochen blinded into fourth place, but was passed by Hulme and stopped on lap 21 with a broken front rocker arm. Siffert took eighth place after four laps, then tried to outbrake Courage at the hairpin and ran wide. He tried again at the next corner, but the two cars collided and 'Seppi' was left on the verge with the Lotus 49B's front suspension folded-up and the bodywork tattered. Lovely soldiered-on and scored the last Lotus finish of the year in ninth place, three laps behind Hulme's winning McLaren.

The STP Lotus 56 wedges were raced widely during the USAC season, and Art Pollard's Offenhauser-powered car won the Milwaukee 150 and was second in the Langhorne 150 races. In the Rex Mays 300 George Follmer and Sam Posey drove the vermilion Lotuses, fitted with Plymouth stock-block engines, automatic transmission and—of course—four-wheel drive; Follmer eventually was 14th but Posey retired with magneto failure. The Dan Gurney 200 at Seattle closed the season, and Posey finished third on aggregate in the two-heat event. Jim Malloy also ran one of the Plymouth-engined cars at Trenton, and generally the wedge-shaped Lotuses were quite competitive.

So the 1969 season ended with Gold Leaf Team Lotus cars having contested 21 major Internationals during the year. Of the seven Tasman rounds the Lotus 49Bs had won two, and two of the 11 World Championship races also fell to the cars. Three non-championship races were contested without success, and Indianapolis was a complete debacle. It had not been a good year, in fact with the failure of both the Indy cars and of the four-wheel drive experimental vehicles, and the serious injury to Graham Hill, it was one of Lotus' more forgettable seasons.

Emerson Fittipaldi used a Formula 3 Lotus 59 to good effect during his rapid rise to stardom from Formula Ford to Formula 1. Here he is winning a Lombank Championship race at Brands Hatch.

1969 RACING RECORD
Other formulae and classes

Lotus' minor-leagues 'Car of the Year' was without doubt the Lotus 59, which doubled-up as Formula 2 and Formula 3 transport for some of the top drivers in both classes. With Jochen Rindt joining the company for 1969 it was obvious that he would be anxious to retain his Formula 2 crown, and he brought with him the Formula 2 expertise of the Winkelmann Racing Team's management and mechanics.

The Lotus 59, which had made its debut in Formula 3 trim at the Brands Hatch 'Boxing Day' meeting the previous year, was a simple square-tube spaceframe design created by Lotus Components' Dave Baldwin. The front suspension was by upper and lower wishbones with outboard coil-spring/damper units interposed, and at the rear a conventional system was used with reversed lower wishbones, single top links and twin radius rods on each side. Special cast-magnesium rear uprights were used, while the familiar old modified Triumph Herald components reappeared at the front. Cast magnesium spoked wheels were fitted with knock-on centre-lock fixings, and although the front disc brakes were buried within the wheels in conventional style the rears were mounted in a direct air-stream just inboard of the hubs. The entire oil system, including the tank, pump, cooler and catch-tank, was mounted on the Hewland gearbox, and in original form power was provided by a Holbay Ford R68 down-draught engine. The Lotus 59's wheelbase was 93 inches, track front and rear 56 inches, and in Formula 3 trim the car was right on the 400Kg minimum weight limit (just over 881 lbs). A very compact glass-fibre body-shell was used, with a truncated top-ducted nostril nose. Later development on production models provided mounts for spoilers on either side of the nose-cone, plus an upswept engine cowl with a sunken air intake to feed the oil cooler.

In Formula 2 trim the car used bigger fuel tanks, had a Cosworth FVA/Hewland FT200 power-and-transmission package, and until the ban on aerofoils used canard wings on either side of the nose with a tall strutted aerofoil mounted on the rear-wheel uprights.

This model was known as the Lotus 59B, and apart from the Winkelmann Racing cars for Jochen Rindt and Graham Hill (when they were available), only one other was supplied to a private entrant. This went to Len Street Engineering, the London Lotus specialists, who planned a full season for it with Max Mosley as driver, but the talented barrister unfortunately wrote-off his new acquisition in practice for the Eifelrennen, and subsequently retired from race driving to become the 'M' of March Engineering . . .

Hill and Rindt gave the new cars their debut in the Easter meeting at Thruxton, where they drove numbers 59/F2/20 and 59/F2/21, respectively. The cars had turned a wheel for the first time at Snetterton only the previous Thursday, but they needed very little development and appeared at the Hampshire circuit for official practice the next day. Jochen was delighted with the car, and his best practice lap of 1min 13.2sec (compared with his standing lap record of 1min 16sec) was a clear 2.2 seconds faster than his nearest rival.

Jochen had a puncture in his heat, and the consequent stop put him way back on the eighth row of the grid for the final, but undeterred he rushed through the pack in a terrific race, caught and passed Stewart's Matra, and scored a first-time victory for the latest Lotus.

Graham had a chequered time with his car, for the cockpit was rather cramped for his tall frame and the steering wheel fouled his thighs. He spun in the Esses when his hand caught his leg, and after the meeting the car's entire dash panel was cut away from the spaceframe, lifted one-and-a-half inches and welded back on to spacer pieces to give him more room.

The season developed with Jochen winning four times, adding Pau, Zolder and Langenlebarn to his Thruxton trophy. He had eight outings in the Lotus 59B, and was third at Albi, retired with suspension dramas at the Nurburgring (as did Hill in the sister car), and had two minor shunts; one at Reims (as did Hill in the sister car!) and the other at Vallelunga.

Graham also had eight races, and his record was enhanced by a win at Albi, where he was over-geared and inherited the lead when Stewart retired . . . his first Formula 2 win since the 1 litre Brabham-BRM days. He was sixth at Enna and third at Langenlebarn in his only other finishes of the year.

When neither of the works Formula 1 drivers was available, team manager Alan Rees called on John Miles, Roy Pike, Alan Rollinson, Andrea de Adamich, Rolf Stommelen and Hans Herrmann to stand-in. The bespectacled Miles had a rather wretched time, although in his four outings he managed to snatch a fifth at Hockenheim and a third at Vallelunga. Roy Pike drove in both Hockenheim events, retiring from the first and finishing an unhappy seventh in the second after so many years in Formula 3. Stommelen was fourth in the German Grand Prix Formula 2 class, as already mentioned, and de Adamich placed seventh in the team's third car at Vallelunga.

Gerry Kinnane's Team Ireland Lotus 48s appeared in their traditional green-and-yellow colours during the year, and John Watson drove an incredible race in the ex-Oliver car at Thruxton. He was 18th at the end of the first lap of the final and he rocketed through the field into fifth place, humbling many works drivers in the process. But sadly this brilliant effort came to an abrupt end against the bank at Cobb, with two wheels torn off and the monocoque badly creased, ending the old car's career although happily Watson escaped unhurt. Subsequently another Lotus 48 was built up, and at Vallelunga John Pollock finished sixth in one car while John l'Amie was eighth in the other. This race must have been remarkable for the number of bespectacled Lotus drivers, Miles, de Adamich and l'Amie all 'goggling' their way to the finish!

Other Lotus Formula 2 participation during the season was mainly of academic interest, but Kurt Stumpf drove a BMW-engined Lotus 35 briefly at Neubiberg —a German airfield race organised hurriedly at the end of the year—and one Helmut Vetter finished seventh there in a Holbay-Ford powered Lotus 61 'wedge' . . . it was that kind of race.

Of the 15 Formula 2 races held during the season Lotus won five, as did Matra, Brabham four and Tecno one. For Lotus it was a very much better year than 1968, and equalled the marque's 1967 total of victories, although the percentage success was much improved. Things were looking up . . .

In Formula 3, Gold Leaf Team Lotus ran Holbay-powered 59s for Roy Pike and Morris Nunn, and Lotus Components arranged deals with a bevy of leading drivers to run similar cars. This arrangement resulted in a very profitable feed-back of information, and the cars were developed to become extremely competitive later in the year. Unlike the Formula 2 variants, early problems were found with spring-rates and the compact oil system, and like their bigger-engined sisters the Formula 3 59s proved rather slow on circuits which placed a premium on maximum speed. Their boxy body-shells, with a nose-line that looked like crash damage, were largely to blame, but after some development the cars proved capable of putting their power on to the road better than anything else then available. For the first time here was a Lotus customer car which was really manoeuvrable and easy to handle, and Baldwin's forgiving spaceframe chassis allowed its drivers to take some tremendous liberties in relative security.

Unfortunately for Roy Pike the season was

Gold Leaf versatility. Top: Brian Muir co-drove the Lotus 62 with John Miles to a class win in the BOAC 1000 at Brands Hatch. Above: Mo Nunn leads team-mate Bev Bond in a Formula 3 race at the same circuit; they finished second and third on this occasion behind Reine Wisell's Chevron.

characterised by a series of torrid slipstreaming battles which the quiet Californian stylist did not relish, and it was left to Freddy Kottulinsky, the Swedish Lotus dealer, to score the Lotus 59's first big International success when he won at Brno in Czechoslovakia in June. Pike and Nunn scored a Gold Leaf one-two victory at Mallory Park in July and in this same race Emerson Fittipaldi made his first appearance in a Lotus 59, and finished fifth.

Emerson was a Formula Ford discovery, and he won three of his nine races in England between April and July, after emigrating from his native Brazil. He was introduced to Jim Russell, proprietor of the Snetterton-based racing drivers' school, by fellow countryman Carlos Avallone, and Russell offered him a deal whereby he sold his Formula Ford Merlyn and bought a Lotus 59 rolling chassis. Mike Warner of Lotus Components helped to arrange an engine, and in his second race at Brands Hatch Fittipaldi finished second behind ex-kartist Bev Bond's Brabham. The following weekend he beat Bond at Mallory Park to score his first Formula 3 win, and his first in a Lotus, and he followed-up with eight more wins to clinch the Lombank Formula 3 Championship after only half a season. Later he crashed his car at Clearways in practice for the big Motor Show meeting at Brands Hatch, having spun out of the lead at the Bank Holiday International meeting at the same circuit when he raised his arm to warn his immediate competitors of oil on the track—he was leading Tim Schenken and Reine Wisell at the time . . .

Bev Bond ended the season third in the Lombank Championship, and late in the season abandoned his Brabham when he won a drive in the third GLTL 59.

Dave Walker, who had driven Formula Fords for Jim Russell in 1968 and for much of the 1969 season, followed Emerson into Formula 3 with a Lotus Components-entered 59, and he was second to the Brazilian in a late Mallory Park meeting, then followed Bond and Fittipaldi home at Brands Hatch and repeated the result at Thruxton where he beat Roy Pike into fourth place.

Mike Warner loaned the Lotus Components car to the redoubtable Ronnie Peterson for the big August meeting at Brands Hatch, and Andy Sutcliffe was another of its drivers, although he met with limited success.

Tetsu Ikuzawa, the forceful Japanese driver, found the forgiving Lotus 59 ideally suited to his driving style, and he notched a major International success at Mallory Park although his season was liberally punctuated with spins and crashes. Mike Beckwith drove a similar car for the late Mike Spence's Maidenhead-based dealership, but he was not happy with it and left the team—and the formula—after a mid-season disagreement.

In older cars Mike Watkins and Ken Crook went well in Lotus 41Cs, the former's being Mo Nunn's old car, but naturally they could not compete with the later spaceframe design. The new car was a great improvement over its predecessors, but it still had to reach full maturity, and of the 61 major Internationals held during the year only four fell to the Lotus 59. Tecno still ruled the Formula 3 roost with 29 wins, compared with the Brabham total of 16. In home events Lotus Components' aid programme succeeded, and the 59's percentage success was much greater; they scored eight significant wins, compared with Brabham's ten and Chevron's two, so at long last that gap was closing . . .

Once again Gold Leaf Team Lotus took an interest in GT racing, and the new season's Group 6 Prototype cars were the nearest yet to an all-Lotus product. Externally the Lotus 62s were similar to the Lotus 47 coupes, but the rear body section was much more bulbous, with flared wheel arches to accomodate the Formula 1-size wheels and tyres. A large spoiler appeared on the tail, and others were mounted on the nose, which was top-ducted to feed hot air away from the radiator.

The Lotus 47's fabricated backbone chassis was completely replaced by a multi-tubular spaceframe structure, which carried the new Lotus-Vauxhall LV/220 slant-four engine behind the cockpit, and Formula 1-style rear suspension. This included reversed lower wishbones, single top links and twin radius rods on either side, with coil-spring/damper units interposed. At the front another conventional double-wishbone system was used, and the 12-inch ventilated brake discs were mounted outboard on the hubs all round. The wheel rims were 12 inches wide at the front and 15 inches at the rear, and in the interests of access the whole front and rear body sections hinged open, leaving just the cockpit section permanently fixed.

The new engine used a Lotus-developed twin-cam 16-valve head on a suitably modified Vauxhall Victor 2000 cylinder block. The camshaft drive was by an internally-toothed rubber belt, as on the single-cam original, and with Tecalemit-Jackson fuel injection the

Rolf Stommelen drove a Winklemann Racing Lotus 59 impressively in the Formula 2 section of the German Grand Prix; he finished the race with his car on fire!

unit produced around 220 bhp at 8,000 rpm, with torque of 160 lb ft at 5,700 rpm. Bore and stroke were 3.75 inches by 2.75 inches, giving a total capacity of 1,995 cc. The engine weighed 325 lbs, and was mated to a ZF 5DS12 five-speed-and-reverse transaxle.

The car was designed by Lotus Components' Martin Wade, and was intended as a test-and-development vehicle for the new LV/220 and LV/240 engine programme. The wheelbase was 91 inches, track 52 inches, overall length 154 inches and height 38½ inches, the all-up weight being around 1,350 lbs. These were the rortiest-looking Lotus coupes yet, and one car made its debut in the BOAC '500' at Brands Hatch, where John Miles and Brian Muir won their class.

A second car was added later, and the pair of them ran regularly in club and minor International events. Roy Pike joined Brian Muir when Miles was fulfilling his four-wheel-drive Formula 1 commitments, and several victories were scored, although usually against limited opposition. The best performance was Miles' third place in the TT, while in the Trophy of the Dunes at Zandvoort he finished fourth with Muir sixth.

The new engine made a glorious rasping noise, but as the operation proceeded and development on the head was completed basic weaknesses in the touring block were revealed. By the end of the season sufficient data had been collected to begin serious design work on the new Lotus block, and the cars were withdrawn having served their purpose.

During the year the Lotus 62s had been run under the Lotus Europa name, which seemed to be stretching things rather far, but Lotus Components also made available normal twin-cam Ford-engined Lotus 47A competition coupes. These differed from the original 47 in having a detachable backbone chassis in place of the original to which the body-shell had been bonded. This gave a huge bonus in accessibility and ease of maintenance but although production proceeded at a leisurely pace the Lotus 47s continued to find only limited success.

Lotus Components' production lines were full of Formula Ford cars, however, and the international acceptance of the class caused a business boom. Following the success of the old Lotus 22-based 51 in the class' first half-season, a much more sophisticated vehicle was developed for the new year, borrowing the successful wedge-shaped profile from Indianapolis. This body-style rose from a 3-inch deep section at the nose to 30 inches at the tail, and incorporated a humped cockpit section with a tiny tinted windscreen as on the Lotus 56 turbine cars. The body was hung on a brand-new round-tube spaceframe chassis carrying completely conventional racing suspension, but much extra rigidity was found by the use of a stressed-steel undertray. A Hewland Mark 6 gearbox was offered as standard while customers could fit any eligible engine of their choice. A 105 bhp Lotus-Holbay-developed LH/105 'guaranteed output' unit was available from the works, and extras included adjustable dampers and springs. In a Lotus press conference on the eve of the

Racing Car Show, Colin Chapman announced that the Lotus 51 would continue in production for the time being, and that seven of the earliest Lotus 61s were to go to Jim Russell, who would operate a couple of Formula Ford teams.

Many of the cars were exported to the United States and to Europe, but in Britain the Lotus 61s only seemed to win when driven by Dave Walker or Mo Harness of the Jim Russell team. The Australian scored nine wins to find his way into Formula 3 before the end of the year, and the Russell cars were always immaculately prepared. Some early cooling problems were encountered, which led to extra slots being cut in the nose section to feed the canted radiator, but the cars were rather overshadowed by the predominantly Merlyn and Alexis opposition. Walker won the Les Leston FF Championship, but the most successful driver of the class, Dick Barker, scored most of his 17 wins in an Alexis after selling his 'wedge' early in the year.

Another British club competition to fall to the marque was the 'Motoring News' GT Championship which Martin Warren won in his little 1,100 cc Holbay-powered Lotus 23. Les Aylott won the 1,600 cc class in the same Championship with his ancient twin-cam-powered Lotus 11, and Tim Goss won his class in the Clubmans Championship with the old Lotus 37, which he had resurrected after a season's lay-off. He revised the rear suspension to accept extremely wide wheels and scored a dozen wins during the year. At the Boxing Day Mallory Park meeting which rounded off the season he won first time out in the experimental Lotus 7X, and he was to drive this car throughout the following season. Other notable Lotus Clubman's contenders included Barry Flegg, Clive Santo, David Wragg, Sid Turner and John Moulds.

Formula 5000 had run its first season in Europe as the imported version of America's Formula A. Plans were laid early in the year to build a car for John Miles' use, running a Ford V8 engine, probably developed by Holbay, but these never came to fruition, and the season saw just a handful of Lotus 'specials' contesting the class. These included the old ex-Formula 1 Lotus 43s, modified with spaceframe engine bays and 4.7 litre Ford V8 engines for Robs Lamplough and Scotsman Jock Russell. Neither had much success, and the latter had a miraculous escape at Brands Hatch when his clutch exploded and in the ensuing shunt his car was torn in half. Chris Summers brought out his venerable old Chevvy-powered Lotus 24 but was similarly unsuccessful, and a Dutchman named Jan van Straaten also produced a Lotus 24, this with a Ford V8 installed, but never finished a race. An astonishing would-be competitor was one Mike Panico, who turned up at Mallory Park with a creaky old Lotus 18 but didn't make it to the starting grid. During the previous season Bob Waters had run one of the old Lotus 40s in British club events, and during the Winter this was modified by ex-Chequered Flag chief mechanic Chas Beattie to form the Conchord F5000, but it was completely uncompetitive and quickly left the class . . .

While the original Formula 5000 plans had been rather vague, to say the least, in June Colin finally decided to build a car and set a target date in September for the big American Formula A round at Riverside. So, with just ten weeks to design and build the car Martin Wade and Lotus Components set to work, and they produced the first car—the Lotus 70—in the required time, but then it was decided that a hurried American debut might do more harm than good and instead a development programme was carried out in England.

Wade's design was simple and clean, using a wedge-shaped monocoque hull formed by twin side boxes in 16- and 18-gauge aluminium sheet, mated by an 18-gauge aluminium undertray. Stiffness was derived from folds on the inner skins of the side bays and small mild-steel braces which provided mounts for various components. There were no bulkheads as such, and the monocoque terminated in a sheet panel backing the driver's seat at the rear, and a mild-steel box arrangement at the front. The Shelby-modified Ford Boss 302 V8 engine formed the rear part of the car, bolted rigidly to the monocoque with the rear suspension loads fed-in through the bell-housing and the Hewland LG600 gearbox. Tubular stay rods served to steady the engine, and although the Ford was fitted as standard, it was intended to allow Chevrolet engines in the production cars. These were slightly longer than the Ford so longer radius rods were supplied to adapt the rear suspension. Single radius rods were used on each side, with single top links and double lower links locating the uprights, while at the front heavy double wishbones were formed by half-pressings welded together. Outboard coil-spring/damper units were fitted all round, and 12 inch diameter Lockheed ventilated disc brakes were buried within the four-spoke cast wheels. The wheelbase was 98 inches, front track 61 inches, rear track 58 inches and the overall length 152 inches.

The original idea had been to form a perfect wedge shape, carrying the radiator above the gearbox as on the experimental De Dion-axle 'wedge' which had been run during 1968, but tests quickly showed that this would not work in high ambient temperatures, so the perfect wedge nose-line had to be broken and adapted to accept a steeply canted radiator in a top-ducted nose cone.

The prototype car was given the Lotus 68 type number and was acquired by Koshland Competition, who ran it in the Formula A final at Sebring in December, where Mario Andretti gave it its debut. He just ran away and hid from his top-class competition in Heat One, but after 12 laps, when nearly 18 seconds in the lead, the engine blew apart. Mario was intended to run the car in the new year's West Coast races, but his other commitments prevented him doing so. The Lotus 70 was to prove another of the company's mistakes, and only seven were built, few of which proved really competitive with the McLaren, Lola and Surtees Formula 5000 cars . . .

1970

Victory without joy

This was to be Lotus' year of truth, a year of change which saw the Group's fantastic growth arrested and temporarily reversed. It also saw Team Lotus win the World Championships once again, though tragically this success was to be marred by the loss of Jochen Rindt. It was also witness to preparations which were made for a resurgence in 1971.

Three reasons were given for the set-back to the Group's fortunes. Selling and advertising expenses were excessive in relation to the sales actually accomplished, while the profit shown by racing car sales in 1969 was converted into a substantial loss in 1970 by ever-increasing overhead costs. The final blow came from heavy interest costs arising from abnormal stock levels. Lotus Cars' unsold vehicles were filling the hangars and overflowing on to the airfield, and corrective measures were badly needed by the end of the year.

The year also marked the introduction of three new models, together with a new version of the supremely successful twin-cam engine. An informal ceremony took place at the Racing Car Show in London at which Walter Hayes of Ford was presented with the 25,000th Lotus-Ford twin-cam engine, suitably mounted. Powertrain engineering, under its new director, Tony Rudd, who had joined from BRM, introduced the 'Big-Valve' 128 bhp unit during the year, and this was to appear in the new Elan Sprint which was also released at the January show.

Modifications to this engine included larger inlet valves, an opening-out of the ports, a 10.3:1 compression ratio and new jets in the Weber 40DCOE carburettors. This gave a rise in permitted rpm to 6,800, but up in these dizzy regions the unit sounded far from happy. Speeds in the gears were 40 mph in first, 58 mph in second and 82 mph in third, while maximum speed was up to 118 mph. Transmission surge had been largely eliminated by the use of less flexible Rotoflex couplings, and a stronger differential and drive-shafts were also adopted. Unfortunately, some aspects of the Sprint did not reflect a car with nine years' development behind it, and the crude bonnet catches and crowded engine bay were still legitimate criticisms, while for £1,700 one might have expected better detailing. On the other hand, where else could one find such a combination of performance and comfort in a two-seat soft-top? Coupe models were available, and driving a well-prepared Elan on winding roads was probably still the second greatest pleasure known to man . . .

Rudd's Big-Valve engine also appeared in the Plus 2 S130, which became the most expensive car in the range at £2,627, and this model had a similar maximum speed to the Sprint, but slightly reduced acceleration (in deference to its greater weight) of 0-50 mph in 6.1 seconds compared with 5.5 seconds.

The Europa S2 was still selling well on the British market as well as abroad, although it was not cheap at £1,828, and it was decided to offer the model in component form for £1,449. The Elan Sprint was also available as a kit for £1,663, and the third new model of the year—the Seven Series 4—was priced at £945 in component form.

This was probably the most interesting of the trio, for it formed a civilised fun car without losing the basic spartan tenets of the original concept. Had Britain's club-racing Formula F100 regulations been slightly different, this car might well have been mid-engined. When the class was first announced a plan was proposed for a car based on the Lotus 61 Formula Ford, using the same suspension but with a wider chassis frame. This was to double as both a road and a racing car but Formula F100 specified an all-enveloping body and this would have made the car expensive and would have masked the Seven identification.

Designer Peter Lucas adopted a similar multi-tubular chassis to the preceding Series 3, but now this employed a fabricated-steel forward part and stressed-steel side panels in place of the old alloy skins. The Escort rear axle was retained, now from the Twin-Cam, and a new suspension arrangement included a quadruple-link system. Two of them picked-up on top of the axle and at the rear of the chassis frame, while the other two trailed in conventional fashion. An angled transverse link formed a wide-based wishbone with the offside trailing arm, and the complete linkage

A busy 'road' year for Lotus. Left: The Seven S4; first major redesign of an ever-popular enthusiast's car. Below: The luxury Lotus, the Plus 2S 130. Bottom right: The Elan Sprint, available in open and closed forms. Bottom left: Tony Rudd's big-valve Lotus twin-cam engine with Weber carburettors.

was suspended on co-axial coil-spring/damper units.

The front suspension was of double-wishbone proprietary type, similar to that of the Europa, with Burman rack-and-pinion steering. Front brakes were 8½ inch discs with 9 inch drums at the rear, and 5J-13 inch steel wheels were standard with Dunlop 165 SP Sport tyres. Attractive Brand Lotus cast alloy wheels were optional, with 195 Goodyear Rally Special tyres.

The most noticeable difference about the S4 was its moulded glass-fibre body-shell, maintaining the old sweeping front wing line and boxy snout, but adding a fully enveloping tail section over a foot longer than its immediate predecessor. The new shell was unstressed but a hefty windscreen frame was bolted through it to the chassis and added considerable rigidity.

Although the new model had moved away slightly from the Seven's original road-racing origins it was very much in keeping with the modern beach-buggy fun-car idiom, and was offered with two basic engine options—a choice of 84 bhp Ford 1600GT Crossflow or LF/115 Lotus-Ford twin-cam power units. Prices in kit form were set at £895 and £995 respectively, and Holbay versions of both engines were available as special options.

This new model took the Lotus 60 type number, while the Lotus 65 also appeared during the year, being a special-bodied version of the Europa which complied with the plethora of American Federal Safety Regulations. At the time of writing the Lotus 66 had still not been disclosed, while the Lotus 67 was a proposal for a Tasman Formula car which did not come to fruition.

Lotus Seven production during the preceding years had been allowed to dwindle at one point around 1964, but demand continued and actually built-up as the new fun-car age began to dawn. Lotus Components, in fact, built 1,350 Series 2 cars, and 330 Series 3s before the new S4 came along. A total of 430 of these were to be built before Lotus Components as such ceased to exist late in 1970.

The Lotus Components name did not go down too well, particularly in America and Canada, where they thought it was some kind of spare-parts organisation. Consequently, the name was changed to Lotus Racing at the start of 1971 when, despite their financial problems, the division was ready to capitalise on the past two seasons' ground-work.

During this period there had been many rumours of Colin developing a Lotus aircraft, and indeed it would have seemed a logical move, with the works situated on an airfield and Colin's personal interest in aviation being so great. But understandably in view of the economic climate nothing came of the rumours. Colin, of course, is an extremely accomplished pilot, and has this to say of his 'hobby': 'It's the only thing which enables me to run two businesses, one of building and running racing cars, and the other of building road cars, either of which normally would keep one man fully occupied. I've been mad enough to try to do both all these years, and maybe it's beginning to tell! Flying is my only relaxation now that I don't drive (racing cars) any more, and it offers the same sort of satisfaction and sense of achievement'.

He had learned to fly in the University Air Squadron, and bought his first plane way back at the close of the 'Fifties. This was a little Miles Messenger of doubtful vintage, and from that there stemmed a whole line of Chapman transports, including a Cessna 180, three Comanche 250s, a couple of Twin Comanches and then a brace of Navahos.

As a fully qualified 'Zoomer' in the Brabham and Graham Hill mould, Colin has had his share of incidents, including one closely involved with running Team Lotus during practice for a Race of Champions at Brands Hatch. The 'airfield' at Brands was an unpretentious grass strip. After a dry spell the clay ground had baked hard, and then it rained, which produced a surface '. . . with a coefficient of friction akin to melting ice. I came in a little bit over-weight, with too many people, too much stuff and too much fuel on board, and despite making a very short approach I realised we weren't going to stop before we

It seemed a good idea at the time, but the Lotus 70 Formula A/5000 car was not destined for success. This was the prototype car, designated the Lotus 68, which was equipped with rear-mounted radiators, which enabled a pure wedge nose to be adopted. The radiators were moved to the front on later production cars of which only seven were built.

ran into the hedge on the other end of the field. In this situation there's only one thing to do, and that's to apply reverse thrust. Now the only way you can do that with a light 'plane is to spin it and point it in the opposite direction, to use the thrust from the propellers. I got it about half-way round when very unfortunately a wheel dropped into a hole and one undercarriage leg folded up, digging a wing-tip in and doing the 'plane no good at all. Nobody was hurt or anything, but it was all experience . . .'

Early in the season something of a furore was caused by press reports of Team Lotus mechanics walking out, and although this was not really the case, Formula 1 Chief Mechanic Leo Wybrott moved to McLaren, Indy Chief Mechanic Arthur Birchall moved elsewhere within the company (since there was no longer an Indy programme) and Bill Cowe and Bob Dance of the Grand Prix team also moved on.

At Monaco Colin had a chance encounter with his Pratt & Whitney contact from Indianapolis days, and in conversation it became apparent that P&W's 3 litre-equivalent turbine engine was nearly ready. As the Lotus 56B chassis was still lying unused in Team Lotus' workshop the old Formula 1 turbine project was restarted, and the car was extensively tested during the latter part of the year. It was hoped to spring a surprise on the opposition and run the car at Monza in the Italian Grand Prix, but braking and throttle-lag still proved thorny problems for road-racing and the car was held in reserve until 1971.

The set-backs suffered during the year were not reflected in the general activity at Hethel, and further investment was made in new research and development facilities in addition to new manufacturing processes. A new body-laminating unit, the most modern in Europe, was commissioned at a cost of £300,000, and extra warehousing, workshop and office accomodation also came into use. All the old engineering functions, together with quality, inspection and warranty activities, were lumped together into one company, but in order to reduce stocks of finished vehicles Group production was curtailed to a total of 3,373 cars compared with the 1969 total of 4,506. Redundancies and some dismissals occurred in the Group's efforts to redress the balance, and one of the well-known Lotus personalities to leave at this troubled time was Graham Arnold, the Sales Director. Over 900 employees were on the books at the start of the year, and this figure was pruned to around 650 by the end of the period. With production curtailed Group turnover fell by £353,000 to £4,933,000, and gross profit was cut by £284,000 to £322,000. Profitability, which had fallen from 16.5 per cent in 1968 to 11.5 per cent in 1969, now plummeted to 6.5 per cent. One redeeming feature of the situation was that some £201,000 of the profit had been made in the last six months of the year, so the remedial measures were certainly working. Despite its recent problems Group Lotus was continuing to consolidate and develop and in the new year it was to reach its full maturity as a major motor manufacturer.

1970 RACING RECORD
Grands Prix and other major formulae

The Tasman Formula was changed for the beginning of 1970, allowing Formula 5000 cars to be run in mixed fields with 2.5 litre Formula 1-based machinery, and the result was a series which was a mere shadow of its former self. Ken Smith kept the Lotus flag waving feebly with his Lotus 41, seeing off much of the heavier metal in the New Zealand rounds with a 1,600 cc twin-cam engine, and at Teretonga Digby Taylor's even older Lotus 27 twin-cam also went well.

The Australian rounds began at Surfers' Paradise, where Leo Geoghegan gave the old Repco V8-engined Lotus 39 another outing and finished seventh. He was seventh again at Warwick Farm, but at Sandown the place fell to Tony Roxburgh's 1965 ex-Clark Lotus-Climax 32B. Lotus were represented only by historic racing cars in the 1970 Tasman series. . .

One week after the final Tasman race the new World Championship season began at Kyalami, where a new unknown quantity in Grand Prix racing, March Engineering, were represented in force by works, Tyrrell and STP-entered cars. Meanwhile, Gold Leaf Team Lotus had been reorganised during the Winter months.

While Graham Hill lay in hospital for many weeks recovering from his severe leg injuries and writing his memoirs, Colin adopted Jochen Rindt as sole number-one with John Miles as his regular number-two. Graham was an unknown quantity as his full recovery at times seemed doubtful, but Porsche had bought Jo Siffert a promising drive with the works March team and Rob Walker was pledged to his Lotus support, so he took on Graham as his regular driver.

The Walker-Durlacher team brought along their veteran 49B/7 for Hill to race, but Rob had Brian Redman on hand to qualify the car and be prepared to race it should Graham's legs prove too weak. GLTL provided Jochen with his regular 1969 car and John Miles took over 49B/10 which had been completely rebuilt following Hill's crash in it at Watkins Glen. Both works cars and the Walker Lotus 49 were updated to 'C'-specification, which entailed fitting modified front suspension, with new hubs accepting 13-inch front wheels. This change gave lower unsprung weight, better penetration and lighter steering, and finally made the Lotus 49 a stable car under braking after three full seasons' racing. Previously the drivers had not dared to run too close to the edge of the road entering a corner, as the cars were prone to weave and need a lot of room with the brakes hard-on. John Love was out again at Kyalami with his ancient 49/3, and Dave Charlton, the Lotus 22 charger of old, had the rebuilt ex-Bonnier car which also had 49C modifications.

Jochen was on row two at the start, 0.6 second slower than Stewart's March on pole position, while Charlton was on row five, Miles on row six and the grimly determined Graham Hill on the penultimate row, his time of 1min 21.6sec comparing with Stewart's 1min 19.3sec. Graham could only apply limited pressure to his brake pedal, and even with a small master cylinder fitted to reduce pedal pressure he was losing time in having to brake earlier than his fitter opponents. As a precaution Rob Walker had Brian Redman standing by in the pits, ready to take over the car if the need should arise.

The field surged away in blistering sunshine, and at the first corner Amon's March jostled Rindt's Lotus, which bounded over Brabham's left-front wheel. Jochen careered round with two wheels in the air before coming to rest, then tore off after the field in ninth place. He was followed by Charlton and Miles, while John Love's old car was disappointingly at the tail of the field. After 55 laps Jochen and John inherited seventh and eighth places, then Ickx's ailing Ferrari fell past them on lap 59, and when Surtees' private McLaren retired the two Gold Leaf cars became fifth and sixth. But after 72 laps Rindt's engine suddenly failed, elevating Miles to fifth despite acute discomfort caused by petrol leaking into the cockpit. Meanwhile, the dark blue Lubysil-sponsored Walker car had gone round reliably and increasingly quickly, while Hill made ground from retirements and finished sixth behind Miles to score probably the best deserved World Championship point of his career. Jochen was disappointed but philosophical at his failure, for he knew that the forthcoming new car was going to make the opposition look obsolete overnight. . .

Immediately after the South African Grand Prix many of the cars were air-freighted to England for the Race of Champions at Brands Hatch, but there was no room on the 'plane for Miles' Lotus 49C so he was left without a ride while Rindt and Hill ran their Kyalami cars and Pete Lovely shipped his 49B/11 over from the United States. Practice ended with Jochen qualifying on row two, 0.4 second slower than Stewart on pole position, with Hill on row three and Lovely slow but happy at the back.

The quicker Lotus-Fords both made good starts, with Rindt third and Hill fifth on the first lap. But Graham soon lost second gear, which cost him dearly round Druids Hairpin, and he fell back through the field. Jochen ran fourth until Oliver and Brabham had trouble ahead of him, and he finished a poor second, 36.2 seconds behind Stewart's victorious March. Hill also profited from retirements to finish fifth to a tremendous reception. Pete Lovely inexplicably hit the barrier at Paddock Hill Bend after 11 laps, honestly ascribing the accident to 'brain fade. . . '.

Two weeks after Brands Hatch the new Lotus 72 was demonstrated to the press at Hethel by Rindt, Miles and Hill. This was the car Jochen had been waiting for, and once again Lotus had set the pace in Grand Prix design.

Colin Chapman and Maurice Phillippe evolved the car from their experience with four-wheel drive, wedge body shapes and the rear-wheel drive Lotus 49s. The latter suffered from pitch and attitude changes under acceleration, and compared to the smooth-riding Lotus 56 turbines and the 63/64 series they were really rather crude. Four-wheel drive and piston-engined power had proved unsuccessful together, so the Lotus 72 design set out to combine smooth-riding characteristics with wedge-body aerodynamics and penetration, and the all conquering Ford V8 engine with two-wheel drive.

A single nose-mounted water radiator could not be incorporated into a true wedge shape, so hip radiators replaced the traditional type, hung on either side of a shallow full-monocoque nacelle which carried perfectly wedge-shaped nose panels.

The Lotus 72 also incorporated a completely new suspension system. Coil-springs had disappeared completely in favour of compound torsion bars at front and rear consisting of an outer tubular component, internally jointed at one end to a solid bar, which passed back through the middle of the tube. The tubular section was rigidly mounted on the chassis at one end, with the free end of the inner bar protruding and picking up on a linkage attached to the wheel. The geometry of this linkage was such that the more the wheel deflected the torsion bar was twisted at a rising rate, thereby providing a progressive system which allowed very soft springs to be used without the penalty of bottoming under full tanks. In practice the suspension automatically adjusted itself to maintain constant handling characteristics as the fuel was consumed and the car became lighter.

Compound torsion bars were adopted because there was insufficient space to accommodate a simple bar of similar 'rate'. They were machined with extreme accuracy on equipment normally used for making gun barrels, and crowded roller races were used at the business end of the bar to maintain clearance between the two parts.

Suspension location was by conventional upper and lower wishbones, exquisitely fabricated from nickel-chrome-molybdenum sheet. At the front these wishbones were mounted on the front chassis subframe at a steep angle, the front mountings lower than the rearward ones, to give a strong 'anti-dive' characteristic which prevented the car dropping its nose under braking. At the rear the forward mountings were higher than the rearward ones, to give a similar characteristic in reverse—'anti-squat' to prevent the tail dipping under hard acceleration. This arrangement, it was hoped, would provide the required smooth-riding, low-pitch characteristics.

Both the front and the rear brakes were mounted inboard and operated on the wheels through drive-shafts. Solid discs were used, cooled through flush NACA ducts at the front, with 'chimnies' formed in the body above them to expel cooling air.

The monocoque structure was fabricated from multi-curvature panels formed over steel bulkheads, and to achieve the necessary shapes soft 18-gauge NS4 alloy sheet was used for the outer skins, with thinner but stiffer inner panels of 20 gauge L72 Alclad. The whole monocoque tapered gently forward in a semi-

Above: First time out in the Lotus 72. Jochen Rindt found that there was still some chassis development to be done when he drove the new wedge-shaped Lotus in the Spanish Grand Prix at Jarama. Below: Last time out in the old Lotus 49C. Rindt's great drive in the Monaco Grand Prix was rewarded with a surprise victory after Jack Brabham crashed at the last corner.

wedge shape and the outer surfaces were flush-riveted and waisted towards the radiator ducts to provide optimum air-flow. The inner panels sloped sharply inwards at the base of the cockpit to accomodate the necessary fuel tankage, and a collector tank resided behind the sloping seat back as in the Lotus 42/43/49 series cars. The front end of the monocoque was formed around a 5/8-inch square-section steel tube structure which carried the suspension and provided mounts for a spidery forward frame carrying the battery and body pick-ups. At the rear the V8 engine was bolted rigidly to the monocoque nacelle, and suspension loads were fed in via sandwich plates on the Hewland FG transaxle. Since the suspension was relieved of braking torques with the discs mounted inboard, only upper radius rods were fitted at the rear, one on either side.

A new three-tier wing was mounted above a three-gallon oil tank wrapped over the gearbox, with its aerofoil slats set initially at 10, 20 and 30-degrees incidence from bottom to top, although the upper slats were adjustable. This system allowed the effective wing to be set at a much greater incidence angle than had been possible with a conventional one-piece wing. The necessary trim was provided by the flat sloping front body and wide fins on either side of the wedge nose-cone.

The Lotus 72's debut came at Jarama in April, when the Spanish Grand Prix returned to its alternate venue North of Madrid. Two of the new cars were unloaded from the giant Gold Leaf transporter, together with 49C/6 and 49C/10, the two older cars from Kyalami.

Team manager Peter Warr was running a rent-a-car scheme once again, and local man Alex Soler-Roig was to drive one of the Lotus 49s, the car being entered in the name of 'Garvey Team Lotus', enabling other than Gold Leaf advertising to be carried.

Jochen was soon out in his new Lotus 72, bedding it in and attempting to set it up for the tight and twisty circuit, but on one lap, as he barrelled down the long straight past the pits and stood on the brakes for the tight right-hander at the end, a thump came from the front end and the car spun like a top. Luckily it came to rest without hitting anything, and when the smole had cleared it was found that the bolts holding one front brake disc on the shaft had sheared, leaving braking on only three wheels. Maurice and Colin decided that the insulating spacer between the shaft and the disc had overheated and broken-up, allowing the bolts to fidget until they stretched and broke. Ventilated discs, which would cool more quickly than the original solid components, were hurriedly substitued on Rindt's car, but with no such parts available for Miles' 72 it looked as though he would race a Lotus 49C.

Meanwhile, the Walker-Durlacher team continued happily with their 49C/7, though keeping an interested eye on Lotus 72 developments, and Pete Lovely entered his car, but scratched when he discovered that he would have to qualify it for a start.

Further problems attended the Lotus 72s' debut

Left: Four views of the Lotus 72 showing the fan coolers for the inboard brakes, the extinguisher mounting, the triple wing and the oil tank of the prototype car. Bottom: The epic battle between Rindt and Brabham which resulted in Jochen's luckiest victory.

when the radiator ducting proved too restricted to cool efficiently under the hot Spanish sun, so the glass-fibre pods were hastily enlarged by fitting 'spacer' sections against the hull sides. New 17-inch wide rear rims were tried by Jochen but they caused excessive understeer and he hastily reverted to the standard 15-inch wide wheels.

The tight circuit proved to be hard on Hill's weak legs and he spun the Walker car, damaging the suspension, wing and oil coolers as he took out yards of chain-link fencing. Practice became a complete shambles as the organisers attempted to amend the number of qualifiers from 16 to 20, and finally allowed 20 cars to form up on the grid before ordering four of them to be removed. These were the Lotus 49Cs of Miles and Soler-Roig, Siffert's March and de Adamich's McLaren-Alfa Romeo, and chaos ensued as the police chased them off. They even tried to manhandle some drivers out of their cockpits, including Graham Hill, which must have been agonising for his injured legs; eventually he was allowed to settle back into the car, moustache bristling within his Bell Star helmet. . .

Jochen qualified the Lotus 72 on the inside of row three with a time of 1min 24.8sec, 0.6 second slower than Stewart's March on pole position, and Hill was on the inside of row six, 0.74 second slower still.

The Lotus 72's engine failed to fire at the last moment, but finally stirred into life just as the dummy grid rolled forward. On the first lap there was a horrendous accident as Oliver's BRM and Ickx's Ferrari collided and both cars were completely burned out. The race ran most of its length with the wrecks still blazing, and every other car was quickly coated in foam and grime from the incident.

The accident broke the field into two groups, with Jochen trailing McLaren in the second group and running eighth overall, but after 10 laps he pulled on to the verge after his electronic ignition cut-out had shorted.

This left Graham Hill alone to uphold the marque's honour, and he pressed on, liberally covered in foam, to finish fourth for Rob Walker among only six survivors, and score three more title points.

It was apparent that much development work was required on the Lotus 72, for at Jarama it had looked very softly suspended and had rolled badly through the corners. But only a week after this rather abortive outing GLTL were back in England for the International Trophy race at Silverstone, which was to be run in two 26-lap heats for both Formula 1 and Formula 5000 cars. The Lotus 72s were hastily modified with thicker anti-roll bars, bigger fins on

Above: About to score his first GP win with the Lotus 72, Jochen Rindt beats Jackie Stewart away from the line at Zandvoort. Below: Rindt's new team-mate, John Miles leads Regazzoni, Beltoise and Piers Courage, whose tragic death later in the race made Jochen's win such a sad occasion.

either side of the nose and modified front disc mountings. John's 72/1 retained the original solid discs, while Jochen's 72/2 ran ventilated components as fitted at Jarama. The Walker Lotus for Graham Hill carried huge Brooke Bond-Oxo food combine stickers, proclaiming its new-found sponsorship, and Pete Lovely was out again in his 49B/11. Alan Rollinson's Lotus 70 was the marque's only Formula 5000 representative.

The Lotus 72s looked promising in practice, and although Stewart's March took two of the half-hourly, £100 prizes for fastest lap during the final session, Jochen skated round through frequent rain showers to take the other two. He lapped in 1min 42.1sec, and at one point Miles was third fastest behind Stewart. The wet weather made it impossible for newcomers to sort-out their cars, and Rollinson withdrew the Lotus 70 for this reason.

Race day was dull and cold, but dry, and the organisers based grid positions for both heats on the practice session times which, since the works Lotuses had missed the only dry session, put them at a distinct disadvantage. Hill was the quickest Lotus qualifier on row two, his 1min 24.2sec time being 2.8 seconds down on Chris Amon's March in pole position. Jochen was three rows behind and Miles was on the back, slower than Lovely who managed some laps in the dry.

Having had no chance to set the wedge-shaped cars' revised suspension to dry conditions Gold Leaf Team Lotus had a miserable first heat in which Miles' rear anti-roll bar snapped and left him struggling round in 11th place, while Rindt ran a lonely fifth, Hulme failing to catch him on the line by 0.3 second. Meanwhile, Lovely stopped for clean goggles after following an oil-spewing Formula 5000, and Hill's steering column came loose; they finished 17th and 14th, respectively.

Jochen retired after only seven laps of the second heat when the Lotus 72's ignition went awry once more, and five laps later, when John's throttle pedal broke, both the futuristic Lotuses were out of the race. Hill elected to run dry tyres as the threat of rain held off, and he pleased his new sponsors no end with a rousing fourth place. Lovely was 13th in this heat, and on aggregate the two Lotus 49s were classified ninth and 13th overall.

Monaco followed two weeks later and Hethel became a frenzied hive of activity as the design of the unmanageable Lotus 72 was revised. Consequently, while Jochen's 72/2 was torn down in the racing shop, the team fell back on the trusty old Lotus 49Cs and the other Lotus 72 as spare car for this important race.

Jochen was in his 49C/6 while John Miles gave his ex-Hill 49C/10 another outing in practice, feeling his way round on his first visit to Monte Carlo. Both cars had been fitted with the three-tier Lotus 72-type rear wing, as had Hill's 49C/7. It rained on Friday, and while Jochen settled-in a new engine Graham charged round in the Walker car until he slid too wide out of the Gasworks Hairpin, bumped the kerb and broke two wheels and bent the rear suspension cross-member.

The dark blue Lotus was repaired overnight, but on a damp and windy Saturday Graham crashed into a guard-rail near the Casino, wrecking the front suspension and putting another crease in the old monocoque. He was unhurt, and when Miles failed to qualify his Gold Leaf car it was loaned to the Walker team for Graham's use in the race. So the two Lotus 49Cs started, with Jochen on the outside of row four with a 1min 25.9sec best lap, 1.9 seconds slower than Stewart on pole position. Hill had to start right at the back in his borrowed and hastily resprayed car.

Jochen ran seventh in the early stages, but fell back behind Henri Pescarolo's Matra as the race progressed. He felt he had little chance with his obsolete car and had no great interest in the race at this stage, but when Beltoise retired after 22 laps Jochen followed Pescarolo into sixth place, and when Stewart stopped six laps later he was fifth, still trailing the Matra. The pair of them gradually closed on Hulme, who was in third place behind Amon and Brabham, the leader.

On lap 36 Jochen finally made up his mind to go motor racing, and as the Frenchman tired he tore ahead under braking for the Gasworks and rushed past the pits towards the right-hander at Ste Devote well ahead of the pale blue Matra. He was after Hulme with a vengeance now, and set a new lap record in 1min 24.3sec as he hurtled after the orange car. He pinned himself on to the McLaren's tail for five laps before blasting by on lap 41, and then Amon was in his sights, although he made little impression on the second placed car.

The gap between the leaders held consistently at 2½ to 3 seconds until Amon was suddenly baulked by Rodriguez's BRM, which allowed Brabham to get away while Jochen closed to within 9 seconds of the delayed March. Chris finally got by the BRM, but with only 20 laps to go a bolt dropped out of his suspension and put him out, so Jochen inherited second place behind Jack Brabham.

He was 13½ seconds behind with 20 laps to go, and five laps later he seemed to have no chance of victory, for Jack was still maintaining a clear 13 seconds lead over the old Gold Leaf car. The Team Lotus pit crew were well satisfied with what looked like a safe second place, but Jochen thought otherwise and began to hurl his car round in a way too seldom seen in Grand Prix racing.

With 10 laps to go the gap was 10 seconds, and Brabham was nursing his car whose brakes were losing their edge. Jochen began to take off two seconds a lap, hurling the Lotus up the hill, flinging it through the Casino Square, and slithering downhill past the Mirabeau and the old station. With less than four laps to go suddenly he could see the turquoise and yellow Brabham ahead, the gap now being less than four seconds! Brabham had hustled round the left-hander to the Casino only to find Siffert's March weaving all over the road as the Swiss tried to persuade his fuel pumps to pick-up the last remaining gallons in his tanks, and Jack had been forced almost to a stop in avoiding him. The

Lotus was now within challenging distance as the two cars fled into their closing laps. But it was one thing to catch Brabham, and quite another to get past, and on the last lap Jochen was trying desperately to close the gap as they hurtled along the quayside, a second apart, towards the Gasworks Hairpin—the last corner. Jack swept past Courage's De Tomaso and Peterson's March before braking into the corner, hoping to leave the back-markers to cover his tail, but in passing them he misjudged his braking point, locked-up the front wheels and slid straight into the outside barrier. Jochen rushed by on the inside open-mouthed at his good fortune, for the veteran Australian triple-World Champion so seldom made a mistake. But the race was Rindt's and he howled over the line to an ecstatic reception from the crowd, including Jackie Stewart, the Lotus crew and Colin Chapman. His sensational last lap was a new record at 1min 23.2sec, 84.56 mph, while Brabham recovered to stagger across the line second with his car's nose cone split and torn. Jochen's victory took him to third place in the World Championship table, with nine points behind Stewart's 13 and Brabham's 15.

Graham Hill soldiered round and round in his borrowed car, getting used to it as the race progressed and finally finished fifth, only one lap down on the winner. If the race had been its original 100-lap length the finish would almost certainly have been even more dramatic, for 20 minutes after the flag the heavens opened and a savage thunder storm enveloped the little Principality, and flooded those historic streets of Monte Carlo. . .

There followed a long gap before the Belgian Grand Prix at Spa-Francorchamps in June, and Team Lotus arrived there with their two 72s redesigned and rebuilt after some frantically busy weeks at Hethel. In an effort to prevent the rear wheels lifting when cornering the anti-squat characteristic had been removed from the rear suspension of 72/2, which also had the anti-dive removed from the front. This feature had tended to make the already light steering feelingless as it stiffened the suspension under braking. The anti-dive was retained on 72/1 although it, too, featured the new 'parallel' rear suspension system. Although these changes sound relatively simple in fact they were anything but because once the suspension pick-ups and subframes had been altered at either end the monocoque skins would not fit. In effect, therefore, the more-modified of the two cars was virtually new, having a new and stiffer monocoque rebuilt around the original rear cockpit bulkhead and the four engine mounts.

Jochen managed only a few practice laps in his much-revised car before a wheel bearing seized out on the circuit. He borrowed the Monaco-winning 49C/6 which had originally been allocated to John Miles to set sixth fastest time, while John took out 72/1 and professed himself happy with both car and circuit. Hill circulated in the rebuilt Walker 49C/7 without wings, as was his practice on the faster circuits, but his tyres failed to work properly without the added downthrust and the handling went to pieces.

Jochen stuck to the 49C and finally lapped in 3min 30.1sec, which was good enough for the middle of the front row but 2.1 seconds slower than Stewart. Miles put 72/1 on the outside of the fifth row with a creditable 1min 33.8sec, and Hill was right at the back in the Walker car with a best time of 3min 37.0sec. Alex Soler-Roig took over 72/2 late in practice but predictably failed to qualify.

The works Lotus 49C and Amon's March alongside it made the best starts but as the field sped away into the hills Stewart forced ahead of Rindt to chase the New Zealander. However, Stewart's engine soon went off song and he fell back as Rodriguez forced his BRM ahead of Jochen followed by Ickx in his Ferrari. John Miles had a frightening spin at Les Combes on lap four, by which time Jochen's engine was beginning to lose its edge; he lost fourth place after 11 laps when a piston finally broke at Malmedy. Miles had been running last, and two laps after Rindt's retirement he came into the pits; the gear selectors were failing and fuel siphoning through the breathers was being sucked into the intake trumpets and making the engine run very rich. In this sorry state the car was duly retired, leaving Hill's Lotus last on the circuit where he and Jim Clark had fought such epic battles for the lead in the past. He stopped when a rear tyre chunked, but on lap 19 his engine failed and Lotus interest in what was likely to be the last Belgian Grand Prix at the fabulous Spa circuit died with it. . .

There followed the customary two-week pause before the Dutch Grand Prix at Zandvoort, and after the rent-a-car entry for Soler-Roig had been scratched Team Lotus set about providing two truly competitive cars for their regular drivers. During private practice cracks had developed in the Lotus 72s' rear frames and consequently these had been replaced. Jochen was in 72/2, with the fully revised and stiffened monocoque and all-parallel suspension, and John took over 72/1, which had the earlier hull and anti-dive front suspension. The Walker car was unchanged, and Pete Lovely arrived with his car but had no chance of qualifying for the select 20 places on the grid.

Jochen shone throughout practice, and proved that this latest Lotus could do as well as its illustrious antecedents. Minor damage resulted from a spin at Tarzan, but Rindt took pole position with a time of 1min 18.50sec, 0.23 second faster than Stewart and 0.43 second faster than Ickx. Miles also went well to start on the outside of row three, and Gold Leaf Team Lotus really seemed to be coming in from the cold. Hill put the aged Lotus 49C on the back row with a best of 1min 21.75sec.

Ickx booted the Ferrari into an immediate lead at the start, with Jochen second and Miles fifth as they sped away between the dunes. The Lotus 72's wedge nose inched ahead under braking into Tarzan on lap three, and Jochen had already set a new lap record of 1min 19.19sec despite his full tanks. The Lotus 72 had soon established a two-seconds lead, and looked as smooth and fast as had Clark's Lotus 25 in 1962 and the 49 in 1967. As John Miles was rushing round in a consistent sixth place, Jochen built his lead to a clear five seconds over the Ferrari team-leader in the first ten laps. After 20 laps the lead was a full seven seconds, but three laps later Piers Courage was killed as his De Tomaso ploughed off course. Piers was one of Jochen's closest friends and the sight of the burning wreckage made the greater part of the race an agonising chore. But he never let his concentration fail, and he went on to lap all but Stewart's March in second place and win his second Grande Epreuve of the season by a clear 30 seconds. He averaged 112.95 mph for the 80 laps, but his was a cheerless victory with success so cruelly overshadowed.

Miles finally finished seventh after a great battle with Surtees' McLaren during which they both spun in separate incidents, while Hill's car handled badly and he was an unhappy 12th. It was a sombre and cheerless day at Zandvoort, and the prize-giving ceremony was cancelled after a sad dusk had settled over the circuit.

Nevertheless, his win had put Jochen in a much stronger position in the Championship table, for he had 18 points to Stewart's 19, while Jack Brabham was third with 15 followed by Rodriguez with 10.

The next round was at Clermont-Ferrand in July, when the French Grand Prix returned to the tight and mountainous circuit above Royat. Further development work on the Lotus 72s had improved chassis stiffness, with robust cross-bracing within the monocoque behind the drivers' shoulders. Stronger suspension pick-up points were also provided, and the shock absorbers were repositioned away from the radiators where they had been thoroughly cooked by a direct hot-air stream. In addition to the two Lotus 72s Soler-Roig returned to the fray with 49C/6, entered under the Lotus subsidiary Wideworld Racing, again to enable different advertising material to be carried, while Hill and Lovely ran their usual cars.

Jochen became rather despondent in practice, for after his unpleasant experience the previous year he now found that the Lotus 72 was understeering excessively. Once again he exchanged his all-enveloping helmet for an open-faced type, still not trusting his rather nervous stomach, but he had only been out for a short time when he returned with a cut cheek and lip. Beltoise's Matra had thrown up a stone which had caught him full in the face, but the damage wasn't serious and Soler-Roig, the son of an eminent Spanish surgeon, stitched the wound.

The Austrian finally lined-up on the outside of row three with a best lap in 2min 59.74sec, while Miles (similarly plagued by excessive understeer) could not better 3min 4.16sec and only Graham Hill was slower at 3min 7.84sec. Lovely again failed to qualify.

For the first time in years the 12-cylinder cars from Matra and Ferrari pushed the Ford V8s off the front row of the grid, and the race developed with Ickx and Beltoise pushing and shoving their way round the circuit while Stewart sat on their tails and awaited developments. Amon's March and Jochen's Lotus ran nose-to-tail some distance behind, and when Stewart's ignition faltered on lap five they took over third and fourth places, Jochen nipping ahead on the uphill straight beyond the pits.

Ickx dropped out after 14 laps, which left Beltoise with a handsome lead over Rindt and Amon, but on lap 25 the familiar wedge shape appeared in the lead by the Rosier Memorial, and as Jochen howled by the pits the Matra crept in with a flat tyre.

Jochen paced himself carefully but gradually hauled away from the March, completing the 38 laps to score a rather lucky second consecutive victory by 7.6 seconds. For the first time he led the World Championship table, with 27 points to the 19 shared by Stewart and Brabham. Miles climbed steadily through the field from his lowly grid position, and stayed ahead of Stewart's delayed March in the closing stages to finish eighth in a car which was still far from right. Hill had circulated rather sadly in Miles' wake, his engine starving as it began to run low on fuei and finally blowing-up on the line as he finished in 10th place.

The British Grand Prix followed at Brands Hatch in July and GLTL appeared with a new driver line-up. The young Brazilian Formula 3 prodigy Emerson Fittipaldi had attracted much interest from many Formula 1 teams, and Colin was quick to sign him on as the Lotus team's third driver. He was to run 49C/10, while Rindt and Miles retained their usual cars, further modified since their French outing.

Jochen's 72/2 now had a neat airbox fitted over the injection trumpets, collecting its air through two ducts either side of the driver's head. The roll-over bar brace had been re-sited on the moncoque rather than on the engine to accomodate the airbox, and the oil cooler had been resited at the tail. It had been starved of air by the wing and was moved from a position above the oil tank to low down on the side. Miles' car was unchanged apart from the oil-cooler modification, and it was obvious from the impeccable preparation of the Lotus 49C that Fittipaldi's Formula 1 debut was meant to be a serious one.

The lengthy development of the Lotus 72 had seriously delayed the delivery of Rob Walker's car for Graham Hill, and so he reappeared in the faithful old 49C/7, while Pete Lovely had his 49B/11 on hand, and finally made the race. . .

Jochen was shatteringly fast in practice, clipping a full second off Stewart's Race of Champions lap record in the first session. He went on to take pole position at 1min 24.8sec, but Jack Brabham later equalled this time for the middle of the rank with Ickx on the outside, 0.3 second slower. John Miles was handicapped by excessive understeer and wrong gear ratios but in a characteristically calculated performance qualified on the middle of row three. The three Lotus 49s formed the last row of the grid, with Fittipaldi quickest at 1min 28.1sec followed by Hill at 1min 28.4sec and Lovely at 1min 30.3sec. The Walker team had blown two engines at Clermont, and when another failed in practice at Brands their Lotus 49 made it to the line only with the help of the Brabham Racing Organisation, who loaned them their spare engine.

Ickx and Brabham led away from the line with Jochen third until the Ferrari broke its differential after only seven laps and coasted to a halt. As the Italian car broke Brabham was on its tail with Jochen forcing his nose through on the inside at Paddock Hill Bend, and as Jack was baulked the Lotus rushed past into the lead. The race developed with Jochen holding a narrow one-second lead from Brabham, but his advantage looked most precarious for when Jack was delayed in traffic he seemed to close the gap again with consummate ease, his car being faster into the corners although Jochen won the acceleration battle away from them. With 20 laps to go Brabham was still doggedly trailing the Lotus, daring its driver to make a mistake, then with just 11 laps left he suddenly asserted himself, surged ahead out of South Bank Bend and just pulled away as he liked, setting a new lap record on the way. The Goodyear-shod Brabham now proved far superior on the slick and oily circuit, and going into the last lap Jack had a 14-seconds lead. But on that final lap the Australian's wretched luck returned and he ran out of fuel at Stirling's Bend. Jochen rushed past at the last corner for the second time that season, and rocketed across the line to score his third successive win in the Lotus 72. Brabham coasted across the line second as once again the Lotus pit erupted in delight.

Meanwhile, John Miles had been running eighth until his engine went badly off-song and he stopped to have the spark box changed. But it made no difference, and after two more stops he retired with a damaged camshaft. Graham Hill put on a splendid performance before his home crowd, and took seventh place on lap 29. Surtees displaced him in his brand-new TS7 before retiring, and when Stewart dropped out of sixth place Graham took it over. He closed on Chris Amon and they began a splendid battle for fifth place which the Walker driver seemed to have won until his clutch pedal came loose, he missed a gear, and the red March shot through to hold the place to the finish. Fittipaldi was a smooth and impressive seventh despite a rough-sounding engine (the exhaust system had fallen apart).

Once again Gold Leaf Team Lotus had scored a lucky win at Brabham's expense, but 90 minutes after the finish Jochen was disqualified. Scrutineer Cecil Mitchell found that the struts supporting the Lotus 72's rear wing were bent, and he formed the opinion that with straight struts the upper edge of the wing would be 1½ centimetres above the maximum height limit. It was not clear if the car had started the race with bent struts, or whether the struts had been bent either deliberately after the race, or by air-pressure during the race. Since the standard struts were angled anyway it wouldn't have made much difference to the height of the wing, and the farcical measuring and remeasuring in the unevenly surfaced scrutineering bay went on for some time. The wing was dismantled and rebuilt, and measurements from ground level to the top of the wing were averaged and found to be correct. Then Mitchell decided the wing had been assembled differently, and so it was torn down and rebuilt once more. After 3½ hours of haggling Jochen Rindt was finally reinstated as winner of the British Grand Prix. . .

The German Grand Prix followed in August, but the Grand Prix Drivers' Association had contrived to have it removed from Nurburgring—which they considered unsafe—to Hockenheim. The circuit was modified with chicanes included on the near-straight sections through the pine forest so as to break up slipstreaming groups, and the stadium held a huge crowd throughout the practice and the race days.

Team Lotus arrived with Jochen's successful 72/2 and a similar, all-parallel suspension, brand-new car numbered 72/3 for John Miles. Fittipaldi was to race 49C/10 once again, while Rob Walker brought out his veteran 49C/7 for Graham Hill to race for the last time.

Miles' engine blew in a race morning test session and was replaced only just in time for the race, for which Jochen's best time of 1min 59.7sec had given him the middle of the front row, 0.2 second slower than Ickx's Ferrari on pole position. Miles' 2min 1.6sec placed him on row five and Fittipaldi was 0.9 second slower on row seven. Hill's ancient Lotus 49C was 0.5 second slower still on the penultimate row.

Jochen's rear wheels spun madly at the start, and Ickx just arrowed away as the Lotus 72 hung fire, its tail wreathed in tyre smoke. But the two drivers slipstreamed each other round until lap seven, when Jochen demonstrated the wedge's edge on maximum speed and stormed ahead into the first chicane, holding his advantage for three laps while Regazzoni in the second Ferrari followed him through. But Jacky was quickly back in second place and on lap 10 he retook the lead with Rindt being dogged by Regazzoni's Ferrari on his tail.

Not until lap 18 could Jochen stream ahead again to retake the lead, and after four more laps Regazzoni blazed past to lead only his third-ever Formula 1 race! The two Ferraris were working hard to shut Jochen out, but he had their measure, and Regazzoni dropped out of contention when his gearbox tightened and he slid and spun after 31 laps. With 19 to go the German Grand Prix developed into a straight fight between Rindt and Ickx, and Jochen let the Belgian go ahead while he sorted out his tactics for the finish. On lap 44 he led into the stadium and across the timing line, and stung Ickx into surging ahead again on the fast section out into the pines. The Ferrari led for two more laps, and with four to go Jochen forged ahead again. Two laps to go and the Lotus skittered wildly on to the grass at the right-hander ending the straight, which gave Ickx his chance, but he thought the Lotus was about to spin back in front of him and he momentarily lifted-off. This allowed Jochen to stay in contact as he snapped back on to the asphalt, and going into the last lap he was ahead again and there was nothing the Ferrari team-leader could do about it. The pair catapulted

Above: Jochen Rindt used his old open-fronted helmet for his winning drive in the French Grand Prix to reduce the nausea he felt from the undulating Clermont-Ferrand circuit. Below: In contrast, the Hockenheim track is almost billiard-table smooth, and this time Rindt's main trouble came from the Ferrari of Jacky Ickx, who chased him all the way to the line. This was Jochen's final GP success.

Below: Jochen Rindt, a great driver and motor racing's first posthumous World Champion. Right: Emerson Fittipaldi's great drive in a Lotus 49C at Hockenheim led to him being selected as team-leader following Rindt's death, and fittingly his victory at Watkins Glen (centre right) confirmed Jochen's title. Bottom: After recovering from his 1969 Watkins Glen injuries, Graham Hill drove Rob Walker's Lotus during 1970.

across the line with just 0.7 second between them, and for the first time since Zandvoort Jochen had won a Grand Prix purely on merit. He averaged 123.90 mph, but the fastest lap in this splendid race went to his adversary.

Meanwhile, Miles climbed through the field into seventh place,but dropped out after 25 laps when the engine sheared another camshaft. Fittipaldi was as fast and smooth as he had been in Formula 3, and he profited from mechanical mayhem to finish in a points-scoring fourth place, the last runner to complete the full distance. Hill trundled the Brooke Bond-Oxo car round near the tail of the field, until his engine broke its crankshaft in a massive blow-up after 38 laps, ending 49B/7's career after three full seasons' racing.

Jochen now took an enormous World Championship lead with 45 points to Brabham's 25 and Hulme's 20, and he was looking to the next round in his home country to clinch his first World Championship title.

The Austrian Grand Prix had been revived for the first time since 1964 on a brand-new circuit laid-out in the hills overlooking the old airfield venue at Zeltweg. This was the Osterreichring, where the Lotus 72s ran into more scrutineering problems. The cooling pods surrounding the hip radiators exceeded the legal maximum width of 110 centimetres since they were still at the larger size adopted in practice at Jarama. Consequently the ducts were pruned to size, and GLTL began practice with the same line-up as in Germany. Rob Walker's Lotus 72 had yet to materialise, and since the 49C was now too old for serious work Graham Hill's entry was scratched.

With slimmer centre-sections benefiting from the cut-down radiator ducts, the Lotus 72s pulled an extra 200 rpm along the main straight, and Jochen stole pole position before his home crowd with a best lap in 1min 39.23sec, 0.77 second quicker than Regazzoni's Ferrari. Miles was on the outside of row five with 1min 41.46sec and Fittipaldi started from the outside of row eight with a time of 1min 41.86sec.

The Ferraris of Regazzoni and Ickx blasted away from the line and swamped Jochen completely as they set-out to dominate the race. He was third until lap three, when he had a wild spin on spilled oil and dropped to sixth, but he recovered and forced his way back into fourth place, until on his 22nd lap the engine tightened behind the pits and he coasted to a halt. John Miles had retired after only five laps when one of his front brake drive-shafts had sheared and he skilfully controlled a nasty moment to retire unhurt, so only Fittipaldi remained, and he dropped through the field, made a stop to refuel, and finished 15th and last.

The following Saturday saw the non-championship Oulton Park Gold Cup race in England, which was run in two 20-lap heats for a combined Formula 1/Formula 5000 field. Miles' Austrian brake-shaft failure had caused some worry. Examination suggested that the failure had originated from a flaw on the central drilling, which ran right through the shaft to give it some spring and reduce its weight. Consequently, some stop-gap solid shafts were made-up, far in excess of original design strengths, and these were fitted to the Lotus 72s. Jochen ran 72/2 at Oulton, while Rob Walker's 72/4 appeared at last, immaculate in his dark blue and white colours. Heavy rain in practice following an early dry session made a mockery of grid positions, and Jochen started in row four with Graham behind him.

The Walker Lotus 72 only went as far as the first corner of Heat One before Graham threw up his hand as the throttle slides stiffened, but he continued for two laps, when the untested car's oil pressure failed so he retired. Jochen's car was under-geared, and Surtees' new TS7 won from Oliver's BRM with the Gold Leaf car third.

Grid positions for Heat Two were decided on the finishing order in Heat One, and Oliver led Surtees and Rindt away from the line. On lap three Jochen dived ahead of Surtees, and two laps later outbraked Oliver at Old Hall Corner to take the lead he was to hold to the finish, although Surtees managed to stay close enough to win on aggregate. Immediately after crossing the line Jochen pulled up on the Avenue, collected his travelling bag from a marshals' post, hopped over a bank and climbed into his 'plane to be whisked away to Vienna and a Formula 2 race the next day. . .

Gold Leaf Team Lotus went to Monza for the Italian Grand Prix in September knowing that Jochen could clinch his World Championship there. The transporter disgorged three Lotus 72s, the usual cars for Rindt and Miles, and a new 72/5 for Fittipaldi which was identical to the others apart from modified front brakes and bearing carriers in an attempt to cure the heat build-up problems experienced when the cars stood stationary after some fast running. These three cars were joined by Walker's now properly prepared 72/4 and the Lotus line-up looked formidable indeed.

Fittipaldi crashed in practice when he missed his braking point for the Parabolica, ploughed over the bank and bounced between stout trees to become a non-starter. Then, on Saturday afternoon, Jochen went out in his 72/2 and lapped in 1min 26.75sec on new tyres (compared with Ickx's eventual pole position time of 1min 24.14sec) then failed to reappear out of the Parabolica. He had been running in company with Hulme's McLaren, but Denny had taken the second part of Lesmo incorrectly and had pulled over to let Jochen go ahead so that he could slipstream him and turn the lap into a quick one for both of them. The cars breasted the rise after the speedbowl bridge, then swept left-handed through Vialone and on to the 190 mph straight down towards the Parabolica, where they would brake just inside the 200-metres boards.

Denny saw Jochen's car dip as he braked, hitting his own brakes simultaneously as he was only about 30 feet behind. Suddenly the Lotus twitched right, then left, then right again, just as it would normally under heavy braking, but then it took charge and turned hard left, arcing across the grass and into the Armco barrier on the outside of the circuit. . .

Colin Chapman and Maurice Phillippe later pieced together the sequence of events from stills and movie film of the disaster. The car's wedge nose dived beneath the high-mounted barrier, and the left-front wheel popped after it, running down behind the barrier at very high speed. A joint in the barrier parted and allowed the car to plough into the end of the next section almost head-on. It hit a solid upright and the front of the car collapsed under the enormous impact. The tail spun round, and with one wheel trapped behind the barrier the whole suspension and front end were torn out of the monocoque. The instruments and steering column were torn out of the dash panel with such force that the top skin of the monocoque was peeled away, and the remaining centre-section of the car, connected to the engine and rear wheels, centrifuged to rest on the grass. Jochen was not in the habit of wearing the two crutch straps provided in his seat harness, and although the shoulder straps held he 'submarined' under the initial impact. He was fatally injured and died almost immediately.

A stunning, dreadful quietness descended on the Autodrome, and as the news was confirmed Team Lotus withdrew their entries and Rob Walker's crew also loaded their Lotus 72 on to their transporter. The Italian Grand Prix was run without Lotus participation and was won by Regazzoni for Ferrari.

The Monza police impounded the remains of Jochen's car, and the right-hand brake-shaft was found to be broken, but it was extremely doubtful whether this was the cause or an effect of the impact. The shaft was new and had only covered 15 laps while the shear itself was nothing like the fatigue failure on Miles' car in Austria. Damage was so severe that little could be proved, and at the time of writing the cause of Jochen Rindt's tragic loss has still to be established.

Inevitably the Lotus team were shattered by Jochen's death on the eve of achieving his greatest ambition. During his first season with Lotus there had been differences and a certain animosity, but in 1970 he and the team had grown together and became an entity, working together towards the goal for which they both existed.

The next Grand Prix was at St Jovite in Canada, and predictably GLTL cancelled their entries. Rob Walker arrived with his Lotus 72 for Graham Hill, unchanged apart from the use of solid front brake-shafts. It suffered a minor fuel fire in practice when a union leaked, and later the clutch exploded. Graham qualified last on the grid with a time of 1min 35.8sec compared with Stewart's pole-position time in the new Tyrrell of 1min 31.5sec. He ran well down the field, and stopped on lap 28 with a loose rear wishbone and without fourth gear. He lost 11 laps before pressing-on to carry out some race development on the car, finally finishing 12th, but too far behind to be officially classified.

At Watkins Glen a revamped Gold Leaf Team Lotus appeared for the United States Grand Prix at the beginning of October. John Miles had been shattered by the loss of his team-leader, and while he took time to consider whether he wanted to continue in the team he was replaced by Reine Wisell, the Swedish Formula 3 star who had made a name for himself handling big McLaren Formula 5000 machines. He joined Fittipaldi, and for the first time Lotus were without a British driver.

Wisell took over Miles' 72/3 while Fittipaldi was in 72/5, rebuilt since his Monza excusion, the two cars and Walker's 72/4 had 60-thou-oversize solid brake-shafts. Pete Lovely completed the Lotus entry with his old 49B.

Emerson excelled himself in practice and set third-fastest time to start on the inside of row two with a best lap at 1min 3.67sec, only 0.6 second slower than Ickx's Championship-contending Ferrari on pole position. Few people liked the idea of a posthumous World Champion, but Jochen had earned his points total, and it would be too ironic now for the young Belgian to steal his final glory. Wisell started on row five with a lap in 1min 4.79sec, 0.02 second quicker than Hill, while Lovely had gearbox problems in practice and didn't make it to the grid. . .

Race day was cold and dull, but the circuit remained dry. Emerson felt his way along in eighth place in the opening stages, then took seventh place from Surtees and inherited sixth when Oliver's BRM retired after 15 laps. When Regazzoni stopped, the leading Lotus 72 moved up into fifth, and when Stommelen took his Brabham into the pits after 48 laps it moved into fourth place. Ickx's Ferrari broke a fuel tank breather pipe and began splashing fuel on the circuit, so he also took to the pits on lap 57 and the young Brazilian inherited third place. This was the highest he had yet run in a Formula 1 race, but shortly afterwards he took second place as Stewart's leading Tyrrell began to smoke and soon retired, elevating Rodriguez's BRM and the Lotus 72.

The tough little Mexican knew his lead was precarious for the BRM engine's consumption was so great he would have to stop for fuel. Sure enough, the BRM fluffed and starved after 100 laps and Pedro rushed into the pits, leaving a delighted and astonished Fittipaldi in the lead. Emerson fled round the last seven laps in his smooth and heady style to score his first Grande Epreuve victory in his fourth Formula 1 outing. Reine Wisell had kept up his end of the bargain and had followed Emerson through the field into third place, and this staggering success so close on the heels of the ugliest adversity clinched Jochen's World Championship. In Dick Scammell's words, '. . . it was too good to be true. Winning at the Glen was just like a fairy tale . . . we couldn't believe it'. Just as in 1968, when Graham Hill had won the Spanish Grand Prix immediately after the loss of Clark and Spence, Lotus had won their first race after suffering another savage blow. Jochen's points total was untouchable—he and his Lotus-Ford were Champions of the World. . .

Only the Mexican Grand Prix remained to be run, and on October 25th Jacky Ickx won this closing round of a tragic series. All three Lotus 72s had cooling problems in practice, and were affected by the thin air of high-altitude Mexico City. Emerson and Graham Hill both had oil pressure problems, and Reine's engine broke its timing gears, so all three had engine changes overnight.

The start of the race was badly delayed by a totally unmanageable crowd, but the race went ahead with most of the drivers pussy-footing round in an attempt to stay on the road and not plunge into the mass of humanity lining the verges. Graham Hill doubted his fastest time of 1min 44.13sec, but was credited with a fourth-row position, more than 2 seconds slower than Regazzoni on pole position. Wisell was two rows behind with a best time of 1min 44.59sec and Fittipaldi was right at the back with 1min 48.13sec.

Emerson's unhappy meeting ended on the first lap when his engine tightened-up again and he coasted to a halt out on the circuit, and Hill lasted only three more laps before his Lotus 72 expired with overheating. Wisell drove well within himself, forging slowly through the field and benefiting from retirements to finish 10th and last, covering only 56 of the 65-laps distance.

In retrospect the season had gone full-circle, from initial adversity through great success to tragedy, before late recovery confirmed eventual success. Gold Leaf Team Lotus' programme had been very much reduced with only Formula 1 being contested. They ran cars at 12 of the 13 World Championship-qualifying races, non-starting in one and winning six of them. Gold Leaf cars also ran in all three non-championship events, and were beaten each time. But Jochen Rindt became the first posthumous World Champion racing driver, and his performances in the Lotus 72 and his great drive at Monaco in the Lotus 49 had made him a thoroughly worthy owner of that title. . .

1970 RACING RECORD
Other formulae and classes

After the promising successes of the Lotus 59s and 59Bs during 1969, Lotus looked all-set for a good minor-formulae season in 1970. New regulations came into force which demanded the use of bag-type fuel tanks in Formula 2, and most of the interested constructors modified their cars accordingly. Dave Baldwin took the opportunity to design what effectively was a completely new car, and with the withdrawal of Roy Winkelmann from racing Jochen Rindt took over the Lotus Formula 2 operation. Bernie Ecclestone, his manager, looked after team administration, and the new Lotus 69s made their debut in the hands of Jochen Rindt Racing Ltd and several prominent privateers in the first European Championship meeting at Thruxton at Easter.

Baldwin had taken his existing Lotus 59 spaceframe and cut it in half, throwing away the forepart and mating the surviving engine bay to a bulbous forward monocoque nacelle. Minor front suspension modifications were made, including new destruction-tested bottom wishbones, and the old snub-nosed bodywork which had handicapped the cars so much on fast circuits was scrapped. In its place a wedge-nosed low-line shell appeared, with an underslung shark's mouth intake feeding air over the radiator. A single top duct exhausted radiator air, replacing the twin ducts featured on the Lotus 59s.

Although only Jochen's car, 69-F2-4, appeared in the team's dark green colours at Thruxton (John Miles' not being ready), other customers' Lotus 69s appeared for Emerson Fittipaldi (69-F2-1) in Jim Russell's colours and Tetsu Ikusawa (69-F2-2) in the white and red of Japan. Jochen proved conclusively that he still ruled the formula, and after taking pole position he won the 108-mile race easily. He went on to score three more wins at Pau, Nurburgring and Zolder, but these were the limit of Lotus Formula 2 success, and they ended the season third in the constructors' rankings, for both Tecno and BMW notched six wins apiece out of the 20 major events held.

Jochen drove in ten of them, but apart from his victories he only finished one other race, when he was ninth at Rouen. He had a collision with Carlos Reutemann's Argentinian-entered Brabham at Hockenheim, and retired with mechanical troubles in his other outings. His last win in any race was in the first heat at the Salzburgring; one week later he was at Monza for the Italian Grand Prix . . .

Graham Hill drove the second team car five times, and scored three fifth places, at Crystal Palace, Ricard-Castellet and the Salzburgring, while Eugenio Baturone, Alex-Soler-Roig and John Miles made other appearances with no real success.

Of the other Lotus 69 drivers Emerson Fittipaldi was by far the most successful. He split with Russell early in the season and ran his Lotus Components car in yellow and green Team Bardahl colours from the Crystal Palace meeting onwards. He contested 12 races, and finished third in the European Trophy, his best performance of the year being second place to Regazzoni's Tecno at Imola. He added a trio of thirds and fourths and two fifths to a splendidly consistent record, which earned him his place in the Gold Leaf Formula 1 team in July.

Although Ikuzawa was regarded with something approaching mistrust by certain of his fellow competitors, he proved much more gentlemanly than his Formula 3 reputation would have people believe, and he went particularly well in the slip-streaming races such as at Hockenheim, where he was second to Regazzoni, the perennial Lotus-baiter . . .

Other Formula 2 69s were run by John Blades (one of the ex-Winkelmann 59Bs updated), Peter Gaydon and Adam Potocki, but with very little success. At Thruxton D&A Shells produced one of the ex-Team Ireland Lotus 48s for Barrie Smith, but it ran its bearings in practice and did not start. Another fleeting appearance was put in by David Cole in Mike Stow's Lotus 59, which failed to qualify at Crystal Palace.

Formula 3 ran its final 1 litre season in 1970, and the spaceframe Lotus 59s continued unchanged until mid-season when the wedge-nose of the 69 was adopted to form the new Lotus 59A. The season was tremendously close and hard-fought, but with the promotion of so many of the previous season's stars to greater things standards fell slightly at the top. There were some petrifyingly close races for the lead, and a fair amount of pushing-and-shoving led to some serious accidents in mid-season. Many of the leading drivers chose Lotuses for their season, and the Gold Leaf works cars were piloted by Bev Bond and Dave Walker. The latter was much the more successful, and although forced to concentrate on home events he notched eight good wins during the season, and was willing and ready to mix it with anybody. Bond scored a couple of club wins, but did not have a very happy year.

A tremendously good impression was created by the Team Bardahl Lotus 59s of Wilson Fittipaldi (Emerson's elder brother) and Carlos Pace, who was rated as better than Fittipaldi Jr in his native Brazil. They won three major British events each, and Wilson also won at Montlhery (as had his brother the previous year) while Carlos won the Croft International in Yorkshire. Fritz Jordan was another Brazilian to appear in England with a Lotus 59A (the aerodynamic wedge-nosed variant introduced in May) and quite a South American 'colony' developed around the Hethel works! David Cole, James Hunt, Tom Walkinshaw, and Tony Trimmer all drove Lotus 59s at some time during the season, and on the Continent Freddy Kottulinsky and Sten Axelsson formed a Lotus 59 team with sponsorship from Liptons Tea and proved very successful. Andy Sutcliffe drove the Lotus Components and later Kent Messanger newspaper-sponsored car in a full season, and of the year's five major Formula 3 Championships one of them, the Forward Trust (British) fell to Carlos Pace, who scored all his points in a Lotus 59, and another, the Motor Sport/Shell (International) to Tony Trimmer. Trimmer scored most of his points in a Brabham, but won the early Snetterton International in a borrowed Lotus Components car, and was second in the same machine at Pau.

Of the 60 major Internationals held during the year Brabham were on top with 25 wins, while Tecno cornered 14 and Lotus 13, but in major National and club-level British events Lotus excelled with 14 wins to Brabham's seven and Chevron's three . . .

It had been a good year for the Lotus 59s in the last season of 1 litre racing, and some of the older Lotuses also ran successfully. Notable among their drivers was Mike Watkins in his old ex-Nunn 41, who continued to show the way home to drivers of much more modern machinery.

For Formula Ford, by this time as important as an international nursery class as Formula 3 had been in its early days, Lotus Components produced a revised version of their partially successful 'wedge' known as the Lotus 61M, for 'Modified'. This featured a 4-inch lower body line which reduced the car's cross-sectional area by over 72 square inches, and other changes included strengthened gearbox side plates, redesigned engine mountings, long range fuel tanks as standard equipment and a lengthened steering rack. The dash panel was re-shaped to suit the lower body-line, and a Lotus 59-like oil system was adopted with a repositioned oil cooler, a four-pint catch tank and a revised breather system. Five of the new cars had made their debut in the late-December 1969, Formula A meeting at Sebring, and many of the final Lotus 61 total of 248 cars were sold throughout the United States. During the European season there was no quasi-works team as there had been in the shape of Jim Russell's flotilla the previous year, but Mike Warner provided a fair amount of assistance for several leading privateers.

Another interesting Formula Ford project was the 'degrading' of the Lotus 59. The first FF 59 had been built-up by Russell mechanics for Brooks Firestone, scion of the tyre family, in America, and during 1970 Lotus Components made a revised-suspension, narrow-wheeled 59F available to Belgian Claude Bourgoignie. Other cars appeared for Peter Wardle and Brian Smith, and they made their debut in the Euro-Trophy round at Zandvoort in March. Bourgoignie, whose car ran under the familiar Russell colours, finished second there to Tony Trimmer's Lola, but beat a flock of Lotus 61Ms in the process. Later in the year these 59s adopted the new wedge nose cones, forming the Lotus 59AF model.

The Lotus 61Ms' great success story during the year was in the BUA-sponsored Brazilian Formula Ford Torneio, where Emerson Fittipaldi won three of the five races and Ian Ashley in another 61M one of the others. Emerson won the title with a clear 42 points from Ashley's 27 in second place, while Wilson Fittipaldi was fourth and M. Fernandez sixth in similar cars.

Without drivers of Emerson's calibre the 61Ms' European season was less rosy, and the Euro-Trophy went to Bourgoignie very narrowly from Colin Vandervell's Merlyn which was the most successful car in the class overall. Other leading Lotus FF pilots were Reg James and Jeremy Gambs, while the Dutch Radio Veronica Team's cars were driven dramatically by Ton Strous until he up-ended one rather efficiently at Zolder.

In Formula A and Formula 5000, the handful of Lotus 70s built met with some success in the United States, but none at all in Europe. Cars were sold to the American Echlin Ignition team for comedian Dick Smothers and George Wintersteen, and Bill Brack bought another, all three being fitted with Chevrolet engines. George Follmer had a fourth car, fitted with a Falconer & Dunn-prepared Boss Mustang 302 engine, and he was most successful Lotus 70 driver of the year, winning at St Jovite and Mid-Ohio, being placed second at Lime Rock and third at Elkhart Lake to finish well-up in the L&M Formula A Championship. Wintersteen was second at Laguna Seca and third at Edmonton, while Smothers trailed him home on the Monterey Peninsula, but otherwise had an unlucky season's racing. Two older Lotuses appeared in the US series, both converted ex-Indy cars; one was a Lotus 38 driven by Frank Eggers, and the other one of the Foyt Lotus-Coyotes, fitted with a Chevvy engine and campaigned by Crocky Peterson.

On the home front Alan Rollinson began the year in Lotus Components' Vegantune Chevvy-engined 70, but it bottomed over the bumps at Brands Hatch in the Easter meeting, crashed heavily and was torn in half. Another car was built up subsequently, using the Boss Ford engine, and Dave Walker gave it its debut at Oulton Park in the penultimate meeting of the year, but he went off the road at the first corner, did the car an injury, and retired on the second lap. Rollinson took over the new car for the final Brands Hatch meeting, but the rear suspension collapsed on the warming-up lap! Subsequently this car was taken to Sebring for the Formula A final, then Vince Granatelli took it down to the Tasman series for Chris Amon and David Oxton. Jock Russell had the only Lotus 70 in private captivity in Europe, but it was pretty uncompetitive, and his best result from very few outings was a distant seventh at Silverstone.

The face of sports car racing had changed since Lotus 19s and 30s had promised to rule the waves, and with specialised 5 litre and 3 litre machinery contesting the classic long-distance races a special 2 litre Championship was introduced for the smaller cars, although Lotus took no part in this competition, leaving it to Chevron, Lola and Abarth.

But the American and Canadian Formula B was a different matter, and several Lotus 59s and 69s appeared with twin-cam engines. Mike Eyerley's Chevron won the title, but the Jim Russell Racing Drivers' School transatlantic division ran Lotus 69Bs for Jacques Couture and Dave McConnell, the former taking third place after scoring good wins at Elkhart and St Jovite. Bob Hebert and Craig Hill (a one-time Lotus 30 driver) ran Lotus 59Bs in the Championship with varying success, and another Lotus title across the Atlantic fell to Dan Carmichael's old 23B sports-racer. He won his class in the SCCA National Championships.

In Britain, the Lotus club racing story of the year was the Clubman's Formula 7X, which had made its debut at Mallory Park in December, 1969. Lotus Components put the finishing touches to the car on Christmas Day, and Tim Goss drove it to a victorious debut three days later; he had prompted the project after his two so-successful seasons in the old 'Three-Seven'.

The new car was based on a conventional square-tube chassis with stressed aluminium panelling, carrying all-independent suspension. At the rear an Elan differential and drive-shafts were combined with Lotus 41-type suspension, while conventional double wishbones and Triumph Herald uprights were used at the front. Disc brakes were used fore and aft, and wrap-round mudguards were fitted both front and rear. A 140 bhp Holbay-Ford engine was used, driving through a Ford gearbox as used in the Elan, and Goss scored a dozen wins during the season to take the Gregor Grant Championship. But even this victory-run was surpassed by the more conventional Lotus Seven driven by Barry Flegg, who notched 14 wins during his 1970 season.

The modified sports car classes were enlivened by the entry of Lotus Elans during the year, and Jon Fletcher's car notched no less than 16 first places. Norman Cuthbert won 14 times in his similar car, and John Sabourin was also successful in an Elan prepared by Ian Walker's company. Elans were also raced widely in the United States, with considerable success. Nevertheless, Worldwide Lotus racing seemed to have contracted during the year, although the concentration on major formulae certainly paid off. In South Africa Dave Charlton won the National Formula 1 Championship in his Lotus 49C, while in Australia Leo Geoghegan had finally forsaken his faithful Lotus 39 in favour of a Waggott twin-cam-engined 59B and a series of victories in his new car gave him the coveted National Gold Star award.

Below: Tim Goss' very sophisticated Lotus 7X was a spectacular newcomer to the British Club scene which earned him many awards. Bottom: The wedge-shaped Lotus 61M sold prolifically to Formula Ford drivers; Reg James holds off two determined challengers.

1971

The end of an era

During 1971 Group Lotus recovered completely from the set-backs of 1969 and 1970, but did so in the role of a touring car manufacturer rather than as the most successful racing marque in the history of motor sport. This was a year of Lotus eclipse on the circuits of the World, and for the first time since 1959 Lotus failed to win a single Formula 1 event during the season. The production of customer competition cars also failed during the year, and after the promise and the apparent boom of the previous two years the closure of Lotus Racing, formerly Lotus Components, came as a shock to the racing world. At the close of the year new sponsorship plans for Team Lotus' Formula 1 programme were announced, as a result of which the cars became 'John Player Specials' and the Lotus name was submerged beneath cigarette packet livery. It was the end of an era, and heralded the beginning of a new phase of Group Lotus development.

The Lotus Racing year had begun promisingly, with all the established customers returning apart from James Hunt, who finalised a Formula 3 deal with March Engineering after Mike Warner had refused to back a Formula 2 programme with him. Cars were offered for Formula 2, Formula 3, Formula B, Formula Ford and Formula Atlantic, as well as Formula 5000. Warner had lined-up Gus Hutchison as Texas agent and Lotus 70 Formula 5000 driver, while USAC variants of the Lotus 70 were planned for Bill Brack, George Follmer and Sam Posey. Allan Lader, who had shone in 1970 Formula B races with a Brabham, was enticed into the Lotus fold by the promising performances of the marque, and was slated to run a Lotus West Coast entry, while Fred Stevenson, a Lotus driver of old, was backed by Lotus East. Back in England Ian Ashley was down to run a works-backed Formula 3 Lotus 69, and Lotus Racing looked well set for a very successful year.

Towards the end of 1970 Warner had been faced with cutting his staff and reducing Lotus Components' staggering overheads, and to this end he devised a plan to renovate the original glass-fibre shops into which the first Lotus contingent had moved from Cheshunt. He set himself a target date of December 30 to renovate, reform and revise, and he set-up shop in the old buildings on the appointed date. Lotus Racing made its public debut at the Racing Car Show in January with the complete range of cars, and just like the original move to Hethel, which had coincided with the completion and release of the Elan Plus 2 and Europa, this was 'one hell of a programme'. But the ground work of the previous years had succeeded, and the market was looking towards Lotus once again for their competition cars. Between January and March 68 racing cars were delivered, including some 35 Formula Fords, 15 Formula 3s and eight Formula 2s. The division seemed to be heading for an excellent year, but there were intramural rumours that the management were leaning away from commercial racing car production after the 1970 traumas and were looking towards other projects, such as power boats in place of the old aircraft ideas.

Colin and Fred Bushell flew to California for talks with Kjell Qvale, one of America's leading motor distributors, and Mike Warner began to believe, wrongly, that they were there to sell-off his division. When he received a telephone call asking him for a full stock check by the following weekend, he naturally (but mistakenly) assumed that this was the precursor to a take-over offer. He felt the deal had been done over his head, and when he saw Chapman and Bushell he tendered his resignation. This was rejected, and in fact the terms of his contract were quoted to him with emphasis on the time he had to work out.

On Monday, April 5, Mike issued a Lotus Racing press release on his own, rather than on the division's, behalf stating that after a disagreement with the directors he had no alternative but to resign, and this prompted instant action in the form of a massive shout-up with Colin. Not surprisingly Warner was out of the company that Monday evening, and although he has never discovered the true reason for that stock-take his suspicions may not have been entirely ill-founded for Lotus Racing ceased production after 13 more orders were fulfilled, and Team Lotus took over their renovated buildings while the staff were redistributed throughout the Group. John Standen was appointed Director of Lotus Racing, but seems to have had little

After extensive mechanical and body revisions the Europa reappeared in Lotus 74 form as a car offering much wider appeal. The Renault 16 engine was replaced by the Ford-based Lotus twin-cam power unit to substantially improve power, and the more luxuriously equipped cockpit was both wider andlonger as a result of changes to the floor pan.

to direct, and the Lotus 73 Formula 2 car, based on the wedge configuration of the Lotus 72, failed to appear during the 1971 season. So it happened that an operation which had been an integral part of the Lotus image since the very beginning came to an end.

Where Warner had been so very wrong was in assuming that the talks with Qvale were mainly concerning his division's future, for in fact Qvale had just gained control of the Jensen company and was negotiating for an engine for the new Jensen-Healey project. The deal was duly finalised under the terms of which a new Lotus LV/240-based slant-four engine would be fitted to these cars as standard, to mark another major milestone in Lotus history as a manufacturer and supplier of complete engines to another car manufacturer!

Designed the Lotus type 907, the new engine, though derived from the earlier LV-series racing engines, had been developed specifically for road use and to meet the stringent emission laws already enforced or proposed. Based on a light-alloy block, with four linered cylinders, the 907 had a four-valve cylinder head with twin overhead camshafts, and a bore and stroke of 3.7 inches by 2.7 inches to give a displacement of 1,973 cc. Despite a fairly modest compression ratio of 8.7 to 1, power output was quoted as 140 bhp, and maximum torque as 150 lb ft, while the engine, which weighed only 278 pounds, was capable of being revved to 7,000 rpm. A new production facility had been added at Hethel for the machining, assembly and testing of the new engine, giving a production capacity of 15,000 power units per year. At the time of the introduction it was confirmed that the engine would appear in an all-new Lotus road car to be announced in 1972, while it was no secret that Colin Chapman and his staff were planning a V8 derivative as a longer-term project.

Some of the rumours which had led Mike to his rather precipitate decision were true, however, and during the year Moonraker Boats became part of the Lotus Group, these strikingly aggressive power craft taking over where customers' competition cars had left off. At the final count 57 customer Lotus 69s had been completed before Lotus Racing's cessation of car production.

Another long-standing Lotus employee to leave Hethel was Dick Scammell, Team Lotus' Racing Manager, who left in March to join Tom Wheatcroft, the Leicester builder and Grand Prix car collector, as manager of the Wheatcroft Grand Prix Collection.

While the Plus 2 S130, Seven S4 and Elan Sprint continued into 1971, the Europa was revised and appeared in new Lotus 74 form as a twin-cam-powered car. This was a very extensive revision, and to the company's credit much attention had been paid to long-standing road test and customer criticism. The bodyshell incorporated cut-away rear fins to increase three-quarter vision, and modified seats and a lower floor pan contributed to a better driving position. Wider foot-wells and revised pedal location also helped

Below: The cut-down tail of the new Europa was universally welcomed, but conflicting emission-control regulations in different countries in 1971 called for variations in engine specification. The US Federal version (centre) had Stromberg and the UK version (bottom) Dellorto carburettors. Right: The interior of the Plus 2 S130; tasteful luxury. Below right: Federal requirements not asked for on 'home market' Plus 2 models included side repeater lights and 'safety' hub nuts.

the driver, and a revised gearchange linkage and suspension were other very worthwhile modifications.

The engine was the well-tried LF/105 twin-cam unit fed by a pair of Dellorto DHLA 40 carburettors in place of the well-tried old Weber 40DCOEs. They gave quite incredible economy, and one independent road test report quoted consumption at a steady 30 mph of a staggering 74.4 mpg! At a steady 70 mph consumption was still outstandingly low at over 35 mpg, and in normal motoring a constant 30 mpg-plus could be maintained easily. Output from the 1,558 cc engine was still 105 bhp at 6,000 rpm and with the new carburettors this was allied to hefty torque of 103 lb ft at 4,500 rpm. This made for a very smooth and responsive top-gear car, and added a new dimension to the well-established Europa appeal. Acceleration from 0-60 mph occupied 8.2 seconds, and 100 mph came up in 25.5 seconds, while the top speed was around 120 mph.

In the interests of economy the LF105 engine was mated to the existing Renault Europa transmission, and this dictated the choice of engine as more powerful versions would have necessitated a new and very much more costly gearbox.

Suspension modifications involved repositioning the steering rack to compensate for suspected geometry errors on the original models, and new lower rear-link pick-ups on the Lotus-built gearbox bell-housing. New engine mountings stiffened the rear of the car and eliminated much of the bump-steer tendency of the

Lotus milestones. Below: Built on kit-car manufacture, the company was still serving the do-it-yourself enthusiast. Bottom: The first all-Lotus engine; 2 litres, 4 cylinders, 16 valves and 140 bhp. Right: For the first time Team Lotus began a new season without a British driver, and ended it without a Formula 1 win, though Emerson Fittipaldi drove with distinction.

original models, and 4½J-13 steel wheels were standard equipment with 5½-inch Brand Lotus alloy wheels also being available. Disc/drum servo brakes were fitted, and the car's interior trim and equipment was also improved. Sound-deadening was particularly effective, and the Europa's fine aerodynamic shape produced very little wind-noise, while road and engine noises were very effectively damped-out. The Twin-Cam Europa was generally a very pleasant car, although it still suffered the rearward-vision deficiencies of most mid-engined coupes and was very strictly a two-seater. Its price was set at £1,595 in component form.

Lotus staged a tremendous recovery during the year, and with the emphasis now squarely upon the production car ranges and the new breed of slant engines in the pipeline the future looked bright. Colin foresaw the slant-four engines being evolved into V8s for a large-capacity prestige model in the years ahead.

The first half-year's results for 1971 showed that the remedial measures put in hand during 1970 were genuinely effective. For this six-month period turnover totalled £2,275,000 (more than that for the whole of 1966), and £1,090,000-worth of exports were achieved. Gross profit on these figures was £324,000, exactly the same figure as for the whole of 1967, and already £2,000 in excess of that achieved in the whole of 1970.

Group Lotus was clearly set on an upward path, and although the enthusiast may regret the passing of the company as a major commercial racing car manufacturer, their products will still be seen in Formula 1, where they belong, and from time to time in other selected classes as well. Lotus already has an illustrious history, as the most successful racing marque of all time. Its future lies mainly in the field of road car manufacture, and when the time comes to write the sequel to this book the story may well be that of Britain's leading manufacturer of high-performance prestige cars . . .

1971 RACING RECORD
Grands Prix and other major formulae

The new season's Tasman Championship, held in January and February, catered again for combined 2.5 litre and Formula 5000 fields, and was dominated by 5 litre McLarens. STP ran a Lotus 70 and a March 701 for Chris Amon and David Oxton, under Vince Granatelli's management, and when the Formula 1 car proved uncompetitive Amon took over the Lotus for the later rounds. His best placing was second at Warwick Farm (where Dave Walker made a brief appearance in a similar works-backed car) but he could not better fifth place overall in the Championship.

In the middle of this series, Amon took time off to race his new Matra in the Argentine, where the Formula 1 season was opening for the first time since 1960. The Argentine Grand Prix was held in the Buenos Aires Autodrome, and consisted of two 50-lap, 106-mile heats. Gold Leaf Team Lotus had been contesting the Brazilian Formula 3 series for some weeks with Dave Walker, and Peter Warr flew down to Buenos Aires to join Dick Scammell with the team's usual Lotus 72s—72/5 for Emerson Fittipaldi and 72/3 for Reine Wisell. Emerson's elder brother Wilson had shone in the Formula 3 series, and after deciding against taking the Lotus 56B turbine car to the Argentine, Team Lotus entrusted him with 49C/6.

The Autodrome's 2.12-miles Circuit No 9 was used, where in practice Emerson found his car oversteering savagely in the wet, while Reine's misfired and Wilson's had spongy brakes and similar oversteering problems to those of his brother. After overnight gales had demolished the scaffolding-type pits, Wisell tore round in 1min 16.03sec late in practice to take the inside of row two, just 0.25 second faster than Emerson alongside. Stommelen's Surtees TS7 and Amon's Matra were on the front row, both under 1 min 16.0 sec.

In the first heat Emerson lost one of his car's nose fins (one had fallen off in practice and landed at Colin's feet) and with his handling upset he dropped back through the field. He stopped when in ninth place, and rejoined after losing three laps for a replacement fin to be fitted, tailing Stommelen's leading car easily for the rest of the heat. Wisell and Amon had a long duel for fourth place, which the Swede lost when his rev limiter slipped and his engine began to misfire at the top end, although he still managed to record fastest lap of the heat, at 1min 15.1sec, 101.62 mph. Wilson was eighth, with the old Lotus 49C still skating round in lurid oversteers, and Emerson was placed tenth.

The Brazilian team-leader suffered further misfortune when his oil pressure disappeared on the warming-up lap for the second heat and he was pulled off the grid. Wisell's engine was still misfiring and the Lotus 72's handling was not to his liking, so only the elder Fittipaldi seemed at all happy. Sure enough, he shot off in seventh place ahead of the Swede, and inherited fifth place when Stommelen and Amon collided (allowing Amon to win on aggregate after the German retired) and Siffert spun his privately owned March 701. Then, after 21 laps, Wilson's engine clattered its death knell and the historic Lotus 49 was retired. Wisell made several stops to complain of bad handling, and with only three laps to go he missed fourth gear entering the right-hander just after the pits and spun into the Armco barrier, doing little damage but ending GLTL participation in the first Argentine Grand Prix for 11 years. He was classified seventh overall, and Wilson was ninth.

A long break in the Formula 1 calendar followed before the South African Grand Prix opened the World Championship series at Kyalami in March. As a mark of respect to Jochen Rindt no 'number one' was allocated, but the Gold Leaf 72s of Fittipaldi and Wisell were numbered two and three in deference to the marque's Constructors' Championship title. Dave Charlton and

John Love deserted the Lotus fold for a works Brabham and a private March drive, respectively, so there were just the two Lotuses running for the first time for several years.

Emerson's Lotus 72 looked as twitchy in practice as it had at Buenos Aires, but his best time of 1min 19.1sec was sufficient for the outside of row two, behind Stewart's Tyrrell on pole position with 1min 17.8sec. Wisell was down on the sixth row, despite being only 0.8 second slower than his team-mate.

Fittipaldi was second into the first corner behind Regazzoni's Ferrari, but he dropped back through the field as his engine gradually went off-song and finally expired after 58 laps when running sixth. Wisell progressed in the other direction, and from 14th on the opening lap he was 10th after 10 laps, fifth after 60 laps and he finally inherited fourth place with only two laps remaining to score the team's first three points of the season.

Back in England two weeks later, the non-title Race of Champions at Brands Hatch was decided on the choice of tyres, for the threat of rain decided many runners to use wet-weather rubber, but the rain held off, so those who gambled on dry tyres had a tremendous advantage.

Colin decided to give the Lotus 56B turbine its debut in this race, and after many hundreds of test miles with Dave Walker, John Miles and Emerson Fittipaldi at the wheel it was judged to be raceworthy, despite some doubts about its braking ability due to the lack of 'over-run' help from the engine. The car remained very similar in overall design to the Lotus 56 turbine cars in their original Indianapolis form, with the turbine mounted amidships in a complex monocoque hull.

To achieve Formula 1 3-litre equivalency Pratt & Whitney engineers had taken one of their STN6/76 turboshaft engines (which were widely used as stationary power plants and in boats, helicopters and railway locomotives) and removed one axial compressor stage and reduced the area of the high-pressure nozzle. This fed into a single axial compressor stage and one centrifugal stage feeding an annular combustion chamber, while the output stage drove through an epicyclic reduction gear to the output drive-shaft.

The drive was stepped to the left side of the car, via a two-inch wide Morse Hy-Vo chain, and overall gear-ratio changes were made by removing the chain's magnesium cover and replacing the sprockets. An epicyclic differential controlled the torque-split between the front and rear wheels, and with no gearbox the driver was left with just two pedals—an accelerator and what must have been the biggest brake pedal ever fitted in a racing car!

Once again the team encountered problems in preparation for this race. Brands Hatch director John Webb had arranged for his protege Tony Trimmer to run the spare Lotus 49C/6, but its engine ran badly on the Cosworth brake after a rebuild and so Webb persuaded Gold Leaf Team Lotus to rush Emerson's 72/5 down from Hethel for Trimmer. The car had been prepared for the following weekend's Questor Grand Prix at Ontario, in California, but it was hurriedly transported down to the Kentish circuit to enable the Formula 3 star to make his Formula 1 debut.

Reine Wisell was out again in his usual 72/3, which had been modified with new uprights to accept Firestone's latest low-profile tyres, and before Trimmer practised his Lotus 72 it was modified similarly.

The Friday sessions were marred by driving rain, but in these conditions the Lotus 56B proved very controllable and it plumed round to set second-fastest time behind Stewart's Tyrrell. Braking was still a problem, for a good lap time necessitated holding the brakes on hard while keeping up engine revs with the other foot, and this 'push-me-pull-you' technique increased pad wear enormously. The huge front discs heated-up, and this began to affect the front dampers, so cooling slots were cut in the wedge nose. Emerson was the quickest Lotus qualifier, starting on the centre of the third row with a time of 1min 28.7sec, 4.1 seconds slower than Stewart in pole position. Wisell was alongside the 56B with a time of 1min 29.0sec, and Trimmer's few exploratory laps put him at the back with a best lap in 1min 37.9sec.

Unfortunately, Tony's Formula 1 debut was marred on the first lap when he stopped with fuel-pressure problems, and he lost seven laps before rejoining; the electrical pump was failing, and after two more slow laps the latest Lotus 72 was out.

Meanwhile, the turbine was bottoming all round the circuit, showering sparks as it graunched and ground over the bumps. Emerson came in after 11 laps with the rear anti-roll bar stays broken away, and this cost him two laps. He continued with the car still bottoming, the thumps and bangs being clearly audible above the swishing exhaust note, and after 33 laps the right-rear suspension collapsed and the car lurched to a halt on the grass beyond the pits.

Reine's race wasn't much happier, for his engine had over 800 miles on it when he began practice, and he lost fifth place in the race on lap 43 when it 'broke'. He walked home quite cheerfully, surprised that it had lasted that long, but in the paddock the engine fired-up on the starter button and the problem was proved to have been electrical!

There was little respite for the Lotus team's hard-working mechanics, and two days later the cars were air-freighted to California for the Questor Grand Prix at Ontario Motor Speedway. The turbine was beld back at Hethel as Fittipaldi and Wisell were to race their usual Lotus 72s. Pete Lovely was hoping to give his ancient Lotus 49B/11 a final International airing, and George Follmer was the only other Lotus runner with a Chevrolet-engined Lotus 70 Formula A car. The race was billed as a face-off between Formula 1 and Formula A, and it took little imagination to predict the result . . .

Reine had an alarming practice moment when a bolt dropped out of the suspension and allowed the left-rear wheel to skew inwards, while Emerson's best lap at 1min 43.358sec (OMS were very proud of their electronic timing gear!) put him on the fifth row of the two-by-two grid. Follmer's TransAm saloon car-engined Lotus 70 went very well to range alongside Emerson with a best lap in 1min 43.474sec, and Wisell was right behind with 1min 43.535sec. Lovely's best of 1min 47.269sec was disregarded as he was a reserve entry and failed to find a place on the grid.

Once again a two-heat system was used with the overall result being based on aggregate times, and each 32-lap heat fell to Mario Andretti's raucous flat-12 Ferrari. The two GLTL cars were running seventh and eighth at half-distance in the first heat, with Reine trailing and lacking fourth gear. His race ended abruptly when his brand-new 11-series (1971) engine seized and he stammered to a halt at the end of the pit lane, while Emerson's metering unit adjusted itself to full-rich and caused his car to run out of fuel with seven laps to go.

Only Fittipaldi started the second heat and he dropped out with the transmission stuck in fourth to be classified a dismal 21st overall and win 8,350 dollars for an unhappy day's racing. Wisell was classified 27th, and poor Follmer was 30th and last after retiring on lap four of the first heat with a broken rocker--at the time he had been running in company with the Formula 1 72s . . .

Oulton Park on Good Friday saw the next Formula 1 non-championship race in a busy year, and the Rothmans International field included three generations of Lotus Formula 1 cars. Reine Wisell was to have his first race in the rebuilt 56B turbine car, while 72/5 reappeared for Emerson Fittipaldi, and Tony Trimmer finally obtained his ride in 49C/6.

The Lotus 56B had been modified with proper cooling ducts for the over-worked brakes, and bump stops to prevent any recurrence of the Brands Hatch bottoming problems. These were very necessary since low-profile Firestone tyres were fitted, 2.3 inches smaller in diameter than those used at Brands Hatch. The solitary Lotus 72 had a new single-plane wing, plus a different oil tank, to help clean-up its slipstream.

During first practice Trimmer lost control of the Lotus 49C over the hump topping Clay Hill, and one side of the car was damaged against a bank. Fortunately, old R10 was on display in Normand's Garage at Bradford, and parts were cannibalised from it to repair the damage in time for the race.

Emerson could not better 1min 29.4sec in practice, 3.5 seconds slower than Stewart's Tyrrell on pole position, and only good enough for the centre of the third row. The next row consisted of Wisell at 1min 33.6sec and Trimmer with a best time of 1min 34.6sec which he set before his crash.

In the race Emerson disappeared after four laps, but rejoined after a mechanic had sprinted out with a replacement spark box. A stone had broken the Lotus 72's windscreen in the opening stages, and he completed a windy race in seventh and last place. Trimmer drove a smooth race before stopping to have his over-rich fuel mixture adjusted and finally placed sixth, four laps behind Rodriguez's winning BRM. Wisell had been running fifth in the turbine, but after 17 laps he came whooshing into the pits and retired after a tyre had burst and damaged the suspension.

One week later came the first European World Championship round at Barcelona, and after some rather dismal displays the Lotus team arrived in Spain with only two of their ten engines in running order, and no spare; a sorry state of affairs for a works team.

The usual two Lotus 72s were fielded for their Brazilian and Swedish drivers, but neither handled well on the tight and tricky Montjuich Park circuit. Emerson's best of 1min 27.9sec compared unfavourably with Ickx's 1min 25.9sec pole-position time, and he started on the sixth row with Reine 0.7 second slower on the row behind.

In the race a fierce battle developed around eighth place between Gethin's McLaren, Cevert's Tyrrell and Emerson's Lotus, and when the orange car jumped out of gear the latter pair swept past. Meanwhile, Reine was in serious trouble with his car jumping out of gear, and on lap 30 he headed for the pits with only third and fifth safe to use on the Armco-lined circuit. Emerson followed him in almost immediately, for his car had started to weave badly under braking and had lost most of its brake fluid. The Swede lost 14 laps and finally finished 12th and last, while Fittipaldi struggled on until lap 55 when the rear cross-member locating the lower wishbones broke, and he lurched into the pits to retire from 12th place . . . the two Lotuses had been running last and second-to-last for some time.

Morale in the Hethel racing shop was probably at its lowest ebb for years as the cars were prepared for the International Trophy race at Silverstone in May. This was another combined Formula 1/Formula 5000 event, run in two 26-lap heats. The Silverstone circuit was well-suited to the characteristics of the Lotus 56B turbine, and consequently Emerson raced it for the second time, leaving Reine to appear again in his repaired 72/3. Larger brakes had been fitted to the 56B since its Oulton appearance, and it was a favourite with the crowd during practice, when it qualified on the front row of the grid, one second slower than Amon's Matra on pole position at 1min 20.0sec, and 0.8 second slower than Stewart's Tyrrell; Wisell was still not happy with his car and took the inside of the seventh row, down among the 5000s with a best time of 1min 27.9sec.

On a dry and sunny Sunday the first heat began with Emerson in fifth place as the field streamed past the pits on the opening lap. But on lap two a top wishbone bearing seized solid, wrenching the mounting point on the monocoque, and a bitterly disappointed Fittipaldi toured in to retire. Reine progressed slowly through the field from his lowly starting position and finished seventh.

During the interval the Lotus 56B's damage was repaired, and Emerson started from the back of the grid for the second heat, while Reine had been promoted to the second row as a result of his finishing position in the first heat.

Free of the rumbling 5000s, Reine soon scratched into fifth place as his team-mate whooshed through the field behind him into eighth position. When Rodriguez's BRM hurtled into the pits with a puncture the Lotus 72 was elevated into fourth place, but on lap 23 the engine cut dead at Copse Corner. Meanwhile, Fittipaldi disposed of Pescarolo's March and Gethin's McLaren, and then inherited third place when Surtees retired his car, and held it to the finish, but after their respective retirements only Wisell was classified on aggregate, in 13th place, Emerson being unplaced because he had lost too much time in the first heat. In the Formula 5000 section Scotsman Jock Russell ran a Lotus 70, but after placing 22nd in the first heat he retired without oil pressure from the second race and was unclassified.

The serious business of the Monaco Grand Prix followed later in May, and Emerson's 72/5 arrived there with much revised rear suspension in an attempt to cure the continual poor handling which the new low-profile tyres had prompted during the season. This '72D' had the original single upper radius rods on either side augmented by lower radius rods, and parallel lower links replaced the original wishbones to limit bump-steer. New upper links were also adopted, and the rectangular structure which originally carried the main suspension pick-ups was replaced by an upper cross-member and a small tubular sub-frame bolted beneath the gearbox casing, as on the Lotus 49. Wisell's 72/3 retained the earlier '72C' suspension layout, so he was prepared to suffer the rapid transition from understeer to oversteer which had plagued the cars throughout the early part of the season.

There had been no time to test the new layout before leaving Hethel, and rain in practice gave Emerson little chance to get it all sorted-out. Wisell likes Monaco and powered his way round in lurid style, but even so his best time of 1min 26.7sec could not compare with Stewart's pole position time of 1min 23.2sec and he started from the sixth row, while Emerson was right at the back with a best time of 1min 27.7sec.

Happily, race day was dry, and the Grand Prix developed with Wisell running a rather lonely seventh and Emerson in a huge bunch scrapping for eighth place. But on lap 21 Regazzoni had closed on Wisell and their Ferrari and Lotus collided just before the Tir aux Pigeons tunnel. The Italian car ground along the barriers and rejoined the race after changing two wheels, but the Lotus 72 was out with the right-hand rear hub bearing collapsed.

At half-distance, 40 laps, Emerson was holding a consistent seventh place, and was generally happier with both car and circuit although his clutch had long since disappeared. When Beltoise's Matra transmission began to fail, the surviving Lotus moved into sixth place, and on lap 59 Jo Siffert's BRM engine expired and gave Emerson a reliable fifth place which he held to the finish, scoring his first Championship points of the year.

Once again there was no Belgian Grand Prix, and the weary Lotus mechanics had a break until the non-championship Jochen Rindt Memorial Race at Hockenheim in June.

Sadly, Emerson had injured himself in a road accident and was still recovering in a Lausanne hospital, but three Gold Leaf cars arrived at the Baden circuit. Reine Wisell's usual 72/3 had been updated to Lotus 72D specification with the new rear suspension arrangement, and Tony Trimmer returned to the team to drive Emerson's usual 72/5. Hockenheim, with its super-fast straights, should have been an ideal turbine circuit, and Dave Walker was on hand to drive the 56B in his Formula 1 debut.

The tough Australian Formula 3 king really had the turbine whistling round in practice, blowing off Trimmer's 72 along the straights, but he suddenly felt it falter and hastily switched off when he saw flames belching from the 'chimney'. The supposedly 100 per cent reliable gas turbine engine had been returned to the factory in Canada after high inter-turbine temperatures had been seen at Silverstone, and it had been returned with 'improved characteristics'. Evidently something had gone astray in reassembly, for the whole unit was in an ugly shambles, and the car was withdrawn and the engine flown back to Canada.

Dave took over Trimmer's 72D, leaving Tony without a drive, and when one of the oil coolers fell off the engine seized and had to be changed before the race. Reine's best time of 1min 59.6sec put him on the second row alongside Regazzoni's Ferrari (1.9 seconds quicker) and behind Ickx, who was fastest overall at 1min 56.8sec. Walker started on row six with a best lap in 2min 2.8sec.

In the race as Ickx drove his Ferrari to victory Wisell had a tremendous dice with Peterson's March for second place, but finally had to give best to his fellow countryman when his brakes disappeared. He stopped for fluid to be added, and rejoined two laps down.

Meanwhile, Dave Walker's first Formula 1 race was marred first by low fuel pressure and then by the loss of fourth gear. He was having to drive on the starting pump, but he spun at the Sachs Curve and dropped back, and then began a duel with Alex Soler-Roig's March. But the Spaniard capitalised on the Lotus' shortage of gears and Dave finally tailed him across the line in ninth place, immediately ahead of Wisell.

One week later came the Dutch Grand Prix at Zandvoort, where both Lotus 72Ds and the 56B were on hand, the latter pending the arrival of a replacement turbine. Emerson was still in hospital, so Colin enlisted South African charger Dave Charlton to join Wisell and Walker in the team.

The Australian took out Fittipaldi's Lotus 72/5 in practice on Friday since the turbine car was still not a runner, but he crashed it heavily on his second lap, writing off the rear suspension. This left Charlton without a drive as Wisell hung on to his 72/3 and Walker

The conversion of the Lotus turbine from an Indianapolis Lotus 56 to a Formula 1 Lotus 56B involved much more than a different-size Pratt and Whitney power installation, and the different chassis requirements of road racing called for a prolonged development programme. Above: Reine Wisell raises a heat haze at Silverstone. Below: Dave Walker during practice before the Dutch Grand Prix; the body-bulge amidships was necessary to carry more fuel.

took over the turbine. Reine qualified sixth fastest, on the inside of the third row, with a time of 1min 18.70sec, 1.28 seconds slower than Ickx's Ferrari on pole position. Walker's best of 1min 21.83sec in the re-engined 56B was good enough for the middle of the last full row.

It was cold, wet and misty on race day, and Wisell was seventh on the opening lap while Walker prepared to make the most of his four-wheel drive and smooth turbine power in the treacherous conditions. On lap five he was tenth as he whooshed past the pits, but on his own admission he left his braking too late into Tarzan and crashed through the fencing, escaping unhurt but leaving the turbine with its front-end wiped out. Two laps later Reine felt something amiss with his car and he pulled up beyond the pits and reversed smartly into the pit lane. This manoeuvre horrified the officials, and although Wisell continued after loose rear wheel nuts were tightened he was soon black-flagged and disqualified.

The new Ricard-Castellet circuit in the South of France was the scene of the fourth FFSA French Grand Prix and Emerson returned to the fold with his ribs firmly bandaged but feeling fit to drive. He took over his repaired 72/5, while Wisell ran his usual 72/3 and the turbine was left at home in Hethel with its nose in plaster. Sadly, practice showed the latest Lotus 72Ds to be a shadow of their 1970 selves, and Wisell was quickest on row six of the three-two-three grid with a best time of 1min 53.75sec compared with Stewart's pole-position time of 1min 50.71sec. Fittipaldi was on the row behind, 0.47 second slower still.

But in the race the Brazilian began a wonderful mid-field dice with Tim Schenken's Brabham, and as the race progressed these two disposed of their rivals in no uncertain terms and made ground through the field, profiting from accidents and retirements but still lapping very quickly. They moved forward to such effect that Emerson took over fourth place and finally caught Siffert's BRM to finish a good third behind the victorious Tyrrells of Stewart and Francois Cevert.

Reine Wisell had been running consistently two places down on his team-mate, and was involved for much of the race in a battle with Beltoise's Matra, Surtees' TS9 and Pescarolo's March 711, only to spin on oil at the chicane. This dropped him behind his immediate opponents, but the Swede began driving with a fire seldom seen since his Tecno Formula 3 days and he regained sixth place at the finish. With both Lotus drivers earning World Championship points the atmosphere at Hethel lightened considerably.

The British Grand Prix returned to Silverstone in July, and as Dave Charlton was back in England negotiating to buy one of the Lotus 72s he was given a Grand Prix ride in 72/3 while Wisell took over the 56B turbine. Emerson was in his usual 72/5, still suffering tender ribs and so foregoing a drive in the heavier turbine car. Both Lotus 72s had tall ram boxes fitted above the injection intakes as was now current practice, the Lotuses having been among the first to

All change! Reine Wisell (below) was brought in to Gold Leaf Team Lotus to replace John Miles (bottom), who in turn had joined the team in place of the injured Graham Hill. But Wisell's position as Lotus number-two driver was to pass to Dave Walker (right), whose reputation was only temporarily tarnished when he put a Lotus 72 into the bank during practice at Zandvoort and had to make that embarrassing walk back to the pits.

experiment with this idea the previous season.

In practice Emerson was a revelation, always within fractions of the fastest times set by Stewart and Regazzoni and acting as the spur which forced them on. Team Lotus had recaptured their old form for this meeting and Emerson took fourth place on the grid, on the inside of the second row with a best time of 1min 18.3sec, 0.2 second slower than Regazzoni and Stewart on the front rank. Charlton went well to set a time of 1min 20.05sec for the outside of row five while Wisell's turbine times compared with Emerson's International Trophy figures at 1min 20.66sec, which put him on row eight. The young Brazilian didn't get a chance to challenge the final front-row times as an engine mounting cracked, and while an oil leak was repaired on Charlton's car, both Lotus 72s had their engine mounts strengthened.

Race day was brilliantly hot and sunny, but things didn't shine for Dave Charlton, whose car was surrounded by smoke on the grid after a piston had failed on the warming-up lap. The start was very confused and Graham Hill's Brabham was dragged into the pit road with deranged suspension, so as the South African trundled in to retire after an expensive first lap he very nearly collided with the wreck, sending marker cones bouncing as he swerved past!

Emerson made a dreadful getaway after the starter dithered with the flag, and he was 11th at the end of the first lap, though really flying. After six laps he was eighth, and he stole past Hulme's McLaren for seventh place on lap 10. It took him three more laps to dispose of Schenken, and Ronnie Peterson was deposed for fifth place on lap 22.

But the March team leader proved a tough nut to crack, and he stayed in close contact before repassing on lap 34. The Lotus' torsion bar suspension had been stiffened before the race to prevent bottoming on full tanks, and as Emerson's fuel load lightened the car's handling progressively deteriorated as the springs proved too stiff. In common with all users of the latest ultra-wide, low-profile tyres, Fittipaldi also had a vibration problem through Silverstone's fast bends, and Schenken repassed him only to break his transmission near the finish. Emerson finally crossed the line in third place, and although he never managed to contest the lead he drove a fine race.

Poor Wisell never managed to persuade his turbine car to show anything near parity with the 3 litre piston-engined cars, and as the race progressed it lost power. He made two stops, in the first of which a lengthy examination found nothing amiss although some adjustments were made. During the second the throttle linkage was found to be awry and this was rectified, although the car never ran as well again and finished only 57 of the races's 68 laps to be unclassified. However, Fittipaldi's good performance had proved that although GLTL perhaps were down, they most certainly were not out.

After Silverstone there were two weeks in hand before the German Grand Prix returned to its rightful home at the Nurburgring. Reine's old 72/3 was shipped off to South Africa for Dave Charlton to run under its new Lucky Strike tobacco company sponsorship, and the Swede took over Emerson's faithful 72/5 while the Brazilian had a brand-new car—72/6. This was very similar to the finalised 72D series design, but ventilated disc brakes were fitted front and rear on both cars to contend with the Nurburgring's continual twists and turns without overheating.

Emerson went well in practice in his new car, even taking the opportunity to lap with full tanks, but he could not compete with the Tyrrell and Ferrari opposition. His best lap of 7min 27.5sec on the extensively smoothed-out and re-graded circuit was fully 8.5 seconds slower than Stewart on pole position, and it put him on the inside of the fourth row. Wisell had a radiator break away from his ex-Fittipaldi car and managed very little practice, finally taking a ninth-row position on the two-by-two grid with a best time of 7min 39.96sec.

Reine was left at the start with no fuel pressure, and finally screamed off after the pack 30 seconds late. Almost simultaneously his team-mate's new car broke an anti-roll bar and began handling viciously, but Fittipaldi quickly adapted himself, and second time round passed his old sparring partner Tim Schenken in the Brabham to take eighth place. When Denny Hulme retired he became seventh, but first Pescarolo and then Schenken nipped by as the new Lotus began to suffer gear-selection troubles. Emerson came into the pits after seven laps when the broken anti-roll bar was spotted, but after rejoining the race his engine blew out all its oil and he retired on lap nine when he had no pressure left. Wisell soldiered round after his early delay, but could make little impression upon the front runners and finally finished eighth, completing the full distance but over six minutes behind Stewart's winning Tyrrell.

The second Austrian Grand Prix on the superb new Osterreichring circuit followed in mid-August. Gold Leaf Team Lotus entered the Nurburgring cars, using modified drive-shafts in an attempt to cure the wide-tyre vibration problems which had been afflicting most of the Formula 1 teams. Emerson's new car also had a weaving problem under braking, but when differential expansion of one brake caliper was discovered, due to its being made of magnesium on one side and aluminium on the other, the problem was effectively solved. Reine had more brake problems, and never settled down, and consequently Emerson's practice performances far overshadowed those of his Swedish team-mate. The Brazilian qualified on the third row of the grid with a best time of 1min 37.90sec, only 0.46 second slower than Siffert's BRM on pole position, while Wisell was back on row five, with 1min 38.95sec to his credit.

Both Lotus-Fords made fine starts, and as Siffert, Stewart and Regazzoni led away, Ickx headed the main pack with Emerson and Reine on his tail. Tim Schenken then displaced both cars and as the race developed the two Gold Leaf cars were fighting hard in fifth and sixth places. Fittipaldi and Schenken joined battle, leaving Wisell in their wake, but ahead of the mid-field runners in a rather lonely position until Graham Hill in the second Brabham caught and passed him; there were now two furious Brabham/Lotus duels for fourth and sixth positions.

Siffert was holding a commanding lead with the Tyrrells of Francois Cevert and Jackie Stewart in pursuit. Jackie was set to clinch his second World Championship title in this race, but with a mysterious vibration coming from his car he was content just to stay in contact with the leader. Colin signalled to Emerson that he was less than 10 seconds behind the Champion elect, with Schenken between them, and as the Lotus 72's fuel load lightened he really went to town, and on lap 31 dashed by the Brabham into fourth place. Wisell had already disposed of Hill, whose Brabham had developed a slow puncture, and as Emerson closed on the third-placed Tyrrell it broke a drive-shaft, threw a wheel and sent Stewart sliding off the track. But as his only contender for the World title, Jacky Ickx, had also retired he had already clinched the Championship.

But more excitement was being caused by Emerson's spectacular progress. He was hard after the second-placed Tyrrell of Francois Cevert, and as the young Frenchman's transmission began to wilt the red-white-and-gold Lotus closed inexorably. With only 12 laps to go the Tyrrell's engine blew-up in front of the pits and Fittipaldi screamed by into a strong second place behind Siffert, and although the BRM driver held on to win, Emerson scored Team Lotus' best finish of the season, four seconds behind after the winning car had suffered a slow puncture in the final laps. Schenken was third, and Reine Wisell a fighting fourth after another best drive of the season.

Team Lotus had been the only Formula 1 organisation to contest every race of the season thus far, giving the company and their sponsors maximum publicity—though without major success—throughout the World. But only one week after the Austrian Grand Prix the non-title Gold Cup race was taking place at Oulton Park, and this time GLTL decided to give the race a miss. Another non-title Formula 1 race had been organised at the Salzburgring in Austria, but this event died on its feet as the organisers proved unable to bring their dangerous slipstreaming circuit up to the required standard before the race.

The Italian Grand Prix followed at Monza early in September, but the aftermath of the 1970 disaster prevented Gold Leaf Team Lotus from attending under their own name. Colin had received certain writs in connection with Rindt's death, and since it seemed likely that he could be detained, other Lotus personnel put at risk and the cars impounded if they raced in Italy, GLTL refrained from making entries. However, Monza seemed to be an ideal turbine circuit, and the old Lotus 56B was dusted off at Hethel and repainted in a gold-and-black colour scheme. This was regarded with great interest, as John Player & Sons had just released a new brand of cigarettes known as 'John Player Specials', which sold in smart black-and-gold packs. There was much speculation about the team cars being repainted in these colours for 1972 and sure enough, after the racing season had ended, came the announcement that this was to be so, and that the cars would run as John Player Specials.

Peter Warr's original plan for the team had been to run the Lotus 72s at Salzburgring, while the turbine was entered at Monza under World Wide Racing's licence, and taken down to Italy on the BRM transporter. World Wide Racing was a Lotus subsidiary company, registered in the Bahamas, which originally had been used as a vehicle for Indianapolis entries, and later entered the Soler-Roig cars during 1970 in order to qualify for non-Gold Leaf advertising on the cars. But with the cancellation of the Austrian race Lotus arranged their own transport for the turbine car, and the only untoward incident of the whole trip concerned the BRM transporter, whose crew had to explain why they had no Lotus on board at the frontier!

Emerson Fittipaldi was to drive the car, but unfortunately the Monza track was hot and arid over race weekend and the high ambient temperature robbed the turbine of some of its power. He qualified the car on the ninth row of the grid, his best time of 1min 25.18sec hardly comparing with Chris Amon's pole position time in the Matra at 1min 22.40sec.

The car was barely competitive in the race and ran 12th for many laps until retirements occurred further up the field, and Emerson finally finished eighth, one lap behind Peter Gethin's winning BRM. The car suffered two cracked brake discs during the race, owing to their long periods of cool running on the straights being abruptly interrupted by savage braking into the slower corners at Lesmo and the Parabolica. A wishbone had also collapsed in practice, but it was an instructive outing, and provisional plans were laid for a lighter and more powerful two-wheel-drive turbine car for the future.

One week after Monza Emerson drove the Lotus 56B in a Formula 1 class provided in the Preis der Nationen Formula 5000 race at Hockenheim. He started on the front row of the grid and finished second behind Frank Gardner's Lola-Chevrolet. The fastest race lap fell to the turbine at 1 min 59.5 sec., which was 0.1 second quicker than the Lola.

The Lotus 72s returned to the fray at Mosport Park for the Canadian Grand Prix later in September, the cars being unchanged since their last race in Austria. Once again Emerson was fast and smooth, qualifying fourth-fastest overall with a time of 1min 16.1sec, which put him on row two behind Stewart's pole-position Tyrrell at 1min 15.3sec. Reine completed the fantastic total of 158 practice laps on a circuit he had not seen before (race distance was a mere 80 laps!), but they helped him to a place on the centre of row three, only 0.2 second slower than Fittipaldi's time.

Veteran Lotus private entrant Pete Lovely arrived with a new Formula 1 car. He had long since been sure that his old 49B/11 was completely obsolete, and had purchased the ex-Rindt/Graham Hill Formula 2 Lotus 69/5. The actual monocoque was little changed, but the engine and suspension from the old Lotus 49 were grafted on at the rear and the nose was altered to accept a larger radiator. The wheelbase was about 5 inches longer than on a standard Lotus 69, and with insufficient fuel capacity for a full Grand Prix distance the American intended running it mainly in National Formula A events. He was to qualify on the back of the grid and complete the race, though he was unclassified.

Race day was wet and misty, and the race started late in horrible conditions after a fatal accident in a supporting race had delayed the proceedings. The two Lotuses ran fifth and sixth in team order for many laps, until they both dropped back and Reine moved ahead of the Brazilian. Emerson's car was understeering badly in the treacherous conditions, and Wisell drew right away as they both benefited from similar problems afflicting Ickx's Ferrari. As dusk drew near the race was flagged off 16 laps early, Stewart winning his sixth Grand Prix of the season with Reine fifth and Emerson seventh, wet and unhappy . . .

With the cancellation of the Mexican Grand Prix following the breakdown of crowd control in 1970, there was only one more World Championship round to run—the richest of them all—the United States Grand Prix at Watkins Glen.

The old 2.3-mile circuit's lap record had been perilously approaching the sub-one minute lap, and this year an extra 1.1-mile loop had been added making the whole circuit much more interesting, though considerably slower. For this race Emerson reappeared in his old 72/5 while Wisell took over the later 72/6. New 13-inch diameter rear wheels were fitted carrying taller-profile tyres in the hope of gaining greater feel and limiting still further that elusive tyre vibration. Pete Lovely broughthis Lotus 69/49 special down from Canada, so once again there were three Lotuses on the grid.

Emerson was all-out to score another 50,000 dollars victory, yet Team Lotus were perilously close to scoring a duck in a season's Formula 1 racing for the first time since 1959! Fittipaldi flickered round to qualify on the middle of the front row, with a superb 1min 42.659sec lap, a whiskery 0.017sec slower than Stewart on pole position. This was the first Lotus front-row placing of the year, and Wisell did not disgrace himself with the inside of row four, at 1min 44.024sec. However, both works drivers still suffered severely from tyre vibrations on the new high-speed curves of the Glen. Lovely was right on the back with a time of 1min 52.140sec.

Emerson scrambled his start and was eighth ending the first lap, with Reine right on his tail amid the jostling bunch of screaming Grand Prix cars. The Lotus team-leader slowly forged through the field, but after five laps Reine lost his brakes as a practice master cylinder leak recurred, and he creamed along a barrier to retire with the car creased. Emerson fell back from sixth place when he hurtled into the pits on lap 11 to have sticking throttles freed-off; he rejoined way down in 21st place, and stopped again four laps later to have a flat rear tyre changed. This failure had damaged a ball joint on the left-rear suspension as it grounded and after another three slow laps the Lotus 72 was back in again for attention. The previous year's winner was totally out of contention before the race had really got under way, and he had another stop on the 34th lap when the fuel pressure gauge feeder line burst and treated him to a petrol shower. He finally completed the race, but with only 49 laps to his credit, and was placed 19th. The only runner he beat was Pete Lovely, whose special ran out of petrol and also completed 49 laps.

So the World Championship series ended, but three weeks later came a hastily organised non-Championship Formula 1/Formula 5000 race at Brands Hatch, taking the date of the cancelled Mexican Grand Prix and acting as a celebration of Jackie Stewart's World Drivers' Championship and Ken Tyrrell's Constructors' title. Lotus had to win this race to maintain their record of Formula 1 wins in every season for the previous 11 years.

Gold Leaf Team Lotus entered just 72/5 for Emerson to drive, while Reine Wisell—despite some good performances in the latter part of the year—had had his last Lotus Formula 1 drive and was at the wheel of a Formula 5000 McLaren.

Practice saw Emerson hurling the Lotus round Brands Hatch's bumpy curves with wonderful abandon, but when a front wishbone pick-up broke his final session was limited to just five laps. Nevertheless his best time of 1min 23.6sec was good enough for the outside of the front row, beside the BRMs of Peter Gethin and Jo Siffert, who was 0 .8 second quicker on pole position.

As Siffert made a poor start Gethin flashed into the lead with Fittipaldi right on his tail and the rest of the 27-strong field howling and bellowing their way round the valleys. As Gethin rushed round holding a narrow lead from the charging Brazilian's Lotus, the pair of them drew away from Stewart in the Champion Tyrrell in third place. Emerson felt he was being baulked by the BRM, but the two cars seemed very evenly matched as they feinted, parried and thrust their way round under a low Autumn sun.

Jo Siffert had recovered after his poor start and was tearing through the field in tremendous style, taking fourth place behind Stewart and catching the Scot all round the circuit, although unable to do much about the BRM and the Lotus contesting the lead. On the 15th lap the great Swiss driver's car unaccountably left the road before Hawthorn's Bend, plunged into the bank and exploded into flames. Jo died in the inferno, and with blazing petrol blocking the circuit the race was stopped immediately. So Peter Gethin won for BRM, with Emerson classified second, 0.2 second behind the last time they crossed the timing line, and for the first time since Buenos Aires fastest lap went to a Lotus, Emerson forcing his 72 round at 1min 24.0sec, 113.57 mph . . .

On this shatteringly tragic note the season came to an end and Lotus' record run of victories was broken. Team Lotus cars (although once in disguise) had contested all of the 11 World Championship events, and all but one of the eight non-Championship races, without a win; Gold Leaf Team Lotus had carried out a more comprehensive Formula 1 operation than any other team during the season, but despite some fine late-season performances success had still eluded them. Lotus-Ford were fifth in the Constructors' Championship, with 21 points compared with Tyrrell-Ford's winning total of 73, while Emerson Fittipaldi took fifth place in the drivers' table and Reine Wisell was ninth equal, on a par with the late Pedro Rodriguez, Denny Hulme, Chris Amon and Peter Gethin. It had not been a good Grand Prix year for Lotus, but they had only experienced the kind of fortune which had been so well known to most of their opposition for so many years, and there was hope at Hethel that a change of colours would bring with it a change of luck as the 'John Player Specials' were prepared to continue the magnificent Lotus Grand Prix story . . . . . .

1971 RACING RECORD
Other formulae and classes

For 1971 Lotus' Formula 2 programme was entrusted to a newly formed team, known as London International Racing Associates, which consisted of youthful ex-journalists Justin Haler and Chris Witty, and was backed by Aberdonian driver Richard Scott. Reine Wisell was contracted to drive for them, and a strong team of mechanics was assembled to look after the two LIRA-Team Lotus 69 FVAs. But sadly the organisation was grossly under-financed, and it collapsed after Wisell had an injunction placed on his car in a Swedish court-room. Their only success was a lucky win for Reine in the Pau race, where he inherited the lead two laps from the end after Beltoise's March had expired. Francois Migault, a promising French newcomer, also drove for the team on two occasions, but he and Scott both had an indifferent Formula 2 season.

The early demise of Lotus Racing left all the Lotus 69 runners somewhat out on a limb, and the lack of works development was very apparent after such promising results in 1969 and 1970. Some teams were reduced to fabricating their own parts towards the end of the season as the spares situation became desperate, and few drivers had a kind word for the cars. They were twitchy and unpredictable, but one driver stood head-and-shoulders above the rest in his Lotus. This was Emerson Fittipaldi, and although bound to the car by contract he got on with the job in hand in his

Below: Emerson Fittipaldi came within four seconds of winning the Austrian Grand Prix for Lotus. Centre: Emerson's brother Wilson in a Formula 2 Lotus 69 at the Nurburgring. Right: The man in the pits; Lotus' team manager Peter Warr. Centre right: Rear-end modifications to the Lotus 72 in 1971 included changes to suspension, air intake and lubrication systems. Bottom: Dave Walker winning the Monaco Formula 3 race in a Lotus 59/69 powered by a Novamotor Ford engine.

characteristically quiet and intelligent manner and sorted it out into a race-winner. His yellow Team Bardahl car scored wins in the European Championship rounds at Madrid, Crystal Palace and Albi, and right at the close of the season, during the last races of the 1,600 cc Formula 2, he scored two more wins in the Brazilian Torneio at Interlagos. By this time his car was very highly developed, with a massive fenced rear aerofoil cantilevered over the tail and a full-width March-like nose apron. Emerson was joined in Team Bardahl by his elder brother Wilson, and he, too, ran a Lotus 69 in the early part of the season, but soon gave up the unequal struggle and invested in a March.

Gerry Birrell, one of the most intelligent and capable of all the 'coming men', drove another Lotus 69 for John Stanton, but this car was never developed as effectively as Fittipaldi's and the Scot had to fight it every inch of the way. Tetsu Ikuzawa retained his 69 and put up some more fast and fearless performances with it, and Johnny Blades also-ran his 59/69. Polish Count Adam Potocki invested in another new Lotus 69 but soon decided that Formula 2 was perhaps beyond his powers and he took to entering the car for Jose Dolhem, although little success attended this venture.

Where Lotus triumphed in the face of all this adversity was in Formula 3 and Formula Ford. A new Formula 3 came into operation this year, catering for 1,600 cc engines which originally had to breathe through a 20mm restrictor plate. The idea was to limit power output to around the 120 bhp of the previous year's high-revving 1 litre engines, but the restrictor placed a strict rev limit on the new units and even with fuel injection power output was nearer 105 bhp. This made for dull and nearly silent motor racing, and in August the CSI relented and allowed 21.5mm restrictors to be adopted. This gave another 12 horsepower on average and by the end of the year huge Formula 3 grids were being assembled and some very close racing was seen.

The works Gold Leaf Team Lotus 69 of Dave Walker was completely dominant wherever it appeared, and in 32 starts he scored 25 wins. These gave the 32-year-old Australian both the Forward Trust and the Shell Super Oil Championships, and although his international forays were few he won convincingly at Monaco, Zandvoort, Ricard and Silverstone in major events supporting the Formula 1 Grands Prix. During the year Walker emerged as a driver of great stature, and his earlier win-or-bust reputation was modified to that of a master tactician.

The Formula 3 69 differed from the Formula 2 cars in being a spaceframe design from nose to tail, but in order to accomodate rubber fuel bags as required by the regulations, stressed alloy sheet side boxes gave a very 'monocoque' external appearance. The works car used a Novamotor-modified twin-cam Ford engine, and was fitted with inboard rear brakes. It was only beaten fair-and-square on one occasion, by Roger Williamson's March 713 at the Oulton Park Gold Cup meeting. This car was backed by Tom Wheatcroft and tended by former Lotus man Dick Scammell . . .

The way ahead. The 1971 season marked the end of direct Lotus involvement in motor racing with cars bearing their own name. For 1972 the Grand Prix challenge was to be carried by 'John Player Specials'.

Other Lotus 69 Formula 3 exponents were Claude Bougoignie, Freddy Kottulinsky and Harald Ertl, the latters' cars being interesting in using BMW and Alfa Romeo engines, respectively, although neither had much success. Ian Ashley's Lotus Racing-backed drive collapsed when the division shut-up shop.

In Formula Ford, Jim Russell's protege Mo Harness clinched the Johnson Wax Euro-Trophy Championship in a Lotus 69F (the chisel-nosed, narrow-wheeled variant of the spaceframe design), but the new manufacturers such as Merlyn, Elden, Palliser and Hawke began to share many individual race victories between them.

Band-leader Chris Barber bought one of the old GLTL LV240-powered Lotus 62 coupes and Dave Brodie campaigned it during the year, while the same driver also excelled in a big-engined Elan. The Elans were now eligible for modified sports car racing in Britain and were given a new lease of life, while ancient sports-racers such as Alan Edgar's 1,150 cc Lotus 23B and John Markey's Pink Stamps-sponsored Lotus 30/40 were still winning races. Edgar was second in the Motoring News GT Championship, and he bought the ex-Walker Lotus 69 at the close of the season.

In America and Canada what had looked to be such a promising year for Lotus Racing took a tremendous dive. Bill Brack, George Follmer and Bruce Eglinton appeared in Lotus 70s in Formula 5000 (the British title having been adopted in place of Formula A) but had little to show for their efforts, and in Europe only Jock Russell raced a Lotus 70 in Formula 5000, and his works-loaned Boss Ford engine did not have enough muscle to compete with the Chevrolet opposition.

For Lotus the Formula 3 and Formula Ford successes were the major contributions in a mainly dismal year of minor league activities, while Emerson Fittipaldi made the most of his initially uncompetitive car to score his splendid Formula 2 successes. But achievements in the minor leagues of motor racing in all parts of the World are not to be measured in just one season, and over more than two decades they have helped to make Lotus the most successful marque in the history of the sport, and have provided the Lotus Group of Companies with a firm foundation on which to base their further programmes of consolidation, development and expansion.

A.C.B. (COLIN) CHAPMAN

Appendix 1

LOTUS SPECIFICATIONS

1961-1971

1961: LOTUS 19—Sports-racer developed from Lotus 18. Engine 2,495 cc Climax or 1,998 cc Climax. Spaceframe chassis. Wheelbase 7ft 6in; max. track 4ft 1in; length 11ft 9in; weight 1,120 lbs. 13 off.

LOTUS 19B—One-off sports-racer with Ford V8 engine and revised suspension for Dan Gurney (1962/63).

LOTUS 20—Formula Junior production car. Engine 997 or 1,097 cc Ford, 90-100 bhp. Wheelbase 7ft 6in; max. track 4ft 1in; length 11ft 7in; weight 805 lbs (997 cc) or 882 lbs (1,097 cc). 118 off.

LOTUS 20B—Disc-braked version of Lotus 20 using 1,498 cc Ford engine for Formule Libre or US Formula B. Included in Lotus 20 production total.

LOTUS 21—Formula 1 developed from Lotus 18. Engine 1,498 cc Climax, 151 bhp. Wheelbase 7ft 6in; weight 995 lbs. 11 off.

1962: LOTUS 22—Formula Junior developed from Lotus 20. Altered suspension, canted engine. 77 off.

LOTUS 23—Sports-racer developed from Lotus 20/22. Wide choice of engines, 997 cc, 1,097 cc and 1,599 cc Fords most popular. Wheelbase 7ft 6in; max. track 4ft 3½in; length 11ft 8in. 131 off.

LOTUS 23B—Sports-racer using modified and strengthened chassis and Lotus-Ford twin-cam engines. All late-model 23s produced to this chassis specification. Included in Lotus 23 production total.

LOTUS 24—Formula 1 V8 developed from Lotus 21. First Lotus V8 F1 car and last F1 spaceframe. Engine 1,498 cc Climax V8, 174-182 bhp. Wheelbase 7ft 6in; weight 1,000 lbs. 12 off, plus three built-up by outside agents.

LOTUS 25—Formula 1 monocoque; World's first monocoque racing car. Engine 1.5 litre Climax V8, up to 200 bhp. Wheelbase 7ft 7in; max. track 4ft 5¼in; length 11ft 10in; weight 995 lbs. 7 off.

LOTUS 25B—Formula 1 monocoque developed from Lotus 25, using revised suspension as on the Lotus 33 to accept 1964-size wheels and tyres. Climax or BRM V8 engines.

LOTUS 26—Elan production sports tourer. First Lotus convertible. Engine 1,558 cc Lotus-Ford twin-cam, 105 bhp. Wheelbase 7ft 0in; max. track 3ft 11in; length 12ft 1¼in; weight 1,290 lbs.

1963: LOTUS 27—Formula Junior development of Lotus 25 monocoque. Engine 1,097 cc Ford, 110 bhp. Wheelbase 7ft 6in; max. track 4ft 3½in; length 11ft 7in; weight 882 lbs.

LOTUS 26R Series 1 competition Elan—52 off.

LOTUS 26R Series 2 competition Elan—43 off.

LOTUS 28—Lotus-Cortina saloon based on Ford Cortina production model. Engine 1,558 cc Lotus-Ford twin-cam, 105 bhp. Wheelbase 8ft 2½in; max. track 4ft 3½in; length 14ft 0in; weight 1,857 lbs. Racing Lotus-Cortina produced by Lotus Components—49 off.

LOTUS 29—Indianapolis car. Engine 4,200 cc Ford V8 pushrod, 370 bhp. Wheelbase 8ft 0in; max. track 4ft 5¼in; length 13ft 0in. 3 off.

1964: LOTUS 30—Sports-racer using Ford V8 power. Engine 4,727 cc Ford V8, 350 bhp. Wheelbase 7ft 10½in; max. track 4ft 5in; length 13ft 9in. Series 1 23 off. Series 2 10 off.

LOTUS 31—Formula 3 car, developed from Lotus 22. Engine 997 cc Ford, 85 bhp. Wheelbase 7ft 6in; max. track 4ft 1½in; length 11ft 8in; weight 882 lbs. 12 off.

LOTUS 32—Formula 2/Formula B monocoque developed from Lotus 27. Engine (Formula 2) 997 cc Cosworth SCA, 115 bhp. Wheelbase 7ft 6in; max. track 4ft 3½in; length 11ft 7in; weight 995 lbs. 12 off.

LOTUS 32B—Tasman Formula version of Lotus 32 using 2,495 cc Climax FPF four-cylinder engine. One-off.

LOTUS 33—Formula 1 monocoque developed from Lotus 25. Revised suspension and steering to accept wider wheels and tyres. Engine 1.5 litre Climax V8, up to 205 bhp. Wheelbase 7ft 8in; max. track 4ft 8in; length 11ft 10in; weight 995 lbs. 5 off plus one built-up by outside agent.

LOTUS 34—Indianapolis car developed from Lotus 29. Engine double-overhead-camshaft 4,200 cc racing Ford V8, 410 bhp. Wheelbase 8ft 0in; max. track 4ft 5¼in; length 13ft 0in. 3 off.

1965: LOTUS 35—Formula 2/Formula 3/Formula B monocoque developed from Lotus 32/27. Engine (Formula 2) 997 cc Cosworth SCA, 130 bhp. Wheelbase 7ft 9½in; max. track 4ft 4in; length 12ft 3in; weight 926 lbs. 22 off.

LOTUS 36—Elan Fixed-head Coupe with detail bodywork and trim revisions.

LOTUS 37—'Three-Seven' Clubman's Formula sports car. Engine 1,499 cc Ford, 125 bhp. Wheelbase 7ft 4in; max. track 4ft 1½in; length 10ft 3in. One off.

LOTUS 38—Indianapolis 'full-monocoque' (unlike 'bath-tub' Lotus 29/34) with longer nose to prevent lift. Engine 4,200 cc Ford V8, 500 bhp. Wheelbase 8ft 0in; max. track 5ft 0in; length 13ft 0in; weight 1,350 lbs. 5 off.

LOTUS 39—Formula 1/Tasman car with truncated monocoque intended for flat-16 Climax engine, modified with tubular engine bay housing 2.5 litre Climax FPF four-cylinder engine for 1966 Tasman series. Wheelbase 7ft 7½in; max. track 4ft 8¼in; length 11ft 8in; weight 995 lbs. One off.

LOTUS 40—Beefed-up sports-racer using 5.8 litre Ford V8 engine, heavier suspension. About 410 bhp. Three off.

1966: LOTUS 41—Formula 3 spaceframe. Engine 997 cc Ford, 115 bhp. Wheelbase 7ft 6in; max. track 4ft 8½in; length 12ft 0in; weight 926 lbs. 61 off.

LOTUS 41B—Formula 2 spaceframe car run by Lotus Components for Jack Oliver in 1967. Type number also allocated to Formula B cars for US sale.

LOTUS 41C—Formula 3 spaceframe developed from standard Lotus 41 for 1967-68 racing, using modified front suspension on Europa lines.

LOTUS 42—Indianapolis car with truncated monocoque to carry 4.2 litre BRM H16 engine, subsequently fitted 4,200 cc Ford V8 for 1967 '500'. Wheelbase 7ft 6in; max. track 4ft 8½in; length 12ft 0in. Two off.

LOTUS 42F—Indianapolis 1967 car. Basic Lotus 42 monocoque modified to carry Ford V8 engine in tubular engine bay.

LOTUS 43—Formula 1 truncated monocoque to carry 3 litre BRM H16 engine, 2,996 cc, 405 bhp. Wheelbase 8ft 0in; max. track 5ft 0in; length 13ft 6in; weight 1,250 lbs. Two off.

LOTUS 44—Formula 2 monocoque based on 35 with Lotus 41-type rear suspension. Engine 997 cc Cosworth SCA, 140 bhp. Wheelbase 7ft 9½in; max. track 4ft 6in; length 12ft 3in; weight 926 lbs. Three off.

LOTUS 45—Elan Drop-head Coupe replacing Lotus 26 and known as the Series 3 or Elan S3.

LOTUS 46—Europe mid-engined coupe for export. First mid-engined Lotus production car. Engine 1,470 cc Renault, 78 bhp. Wheelbase 7ft 7in; max. track 4ft 5in; length 13ft 0½in; weight 1,350 lbs. In full production 1967.

LOTUS 47—Group 4 sports-racing coupe sometimes known as Europa but powered by Cosworth-Ford twin-cam, 165 bhp, and racing suspension. Wheelbase 7ft 7in; max. track 4ft 5in; length 13ft 0½in; weight 1,230 lbs. In full production 1967. 55 off.

1967: LOTUS 48—Formula 2 monocoque car with tubular engine bay for new 1,600 cc class. Engine 1,599 cc Cosworth FVA, 220 bhp. Wheelbase 7ft 7¾in; max. track 4ft 10in; length 12ft 5½in; weight 926 lbs. Four off.

LOTUS 49—Formula 1 truncated monocoque carrying 3 litre Cosworth-Ford DFV V8 engine as stressed member as on BRM-engined Lotus 42/43, 410-425 bhp. Wheelbase 7ft 11in; max. track 5ft 1¼in; length 13ft 2¾in; weight 1,102 lbs. '12' off (see text) including 1968/9 49Bs and 1970 49Cs.

LOTUS 49B—Formula 1 monocoque developed from standard Lotus 49 for 1968-69. Revised details and suspension, 8ft 1in wheelbase. Included in Lotus 49 production total.

LOTUS 49C—Formula 1 monocoque developed from Lotus 49B for 1970. Revised front suspension with 13-inch diameter wheels. Included in Lotus 49 production total.

LOTUS 49T—Tasman Formula monocoque developed from Lotus 49 series cars, using 2.5 litre Cosworth-Ford DFW V8 engines. Included in Lotus 49 production total.

LOTUS 50—Elan Plus-2 Coupe. Engine 1,558 cc Lotus-Ford twin-cam, 118 bhp. Wheelbase 8ft 0in; max. track 4ft 7in; length 14ft 1in; weight 2,086 lbs.

LOTUS 51—Formula Ford spaceframe based on Lotus 31/22. Engine 1,599 cc Ford pushrod, 100 bhp. Wheelbase 7ft 6in; max. track 4ft 1½in; length 11ft 8in; weight 882 lbs. 218 off.

LOTUS 51A—Formula Ford spaceframe for 1968. Included in Lotus 51 production total.

LOTUS 52—Lotus 1,558 cc twin-cam-engined Europa road car project for home market which was shelved. Europa TC released 1971.

1968: LOTUS 53—Sports-racing car project based on Lotus 23 which was shelved.

LOTUS 54—Europa Series 2 or S2 with detachable chassis and improved trim and equipment.

LOTUS 55—Formula 3 Lotus 41X for Gold Leaf Team Lotus use only. One-off.

LOTUS 56—Indianapolis turbine car. Engine Pratt & Whitney 14.999 sq in annulus area ST6 turbine, 500-plus bhp. Wheelbase 8ft 6in; max. track 5ft 2½in; length 14ft 2in; weight 1,350 lbs. Four off.

LOTUS 57—Formula 1 De Dion-axled car which completed design stage but was never built.

LOTUS 58—Formula 2 experimental De Dion-axled car which was completed and tested but quickly shelved. Said also to have been run with 3 litre Cosworth-Ford Formula 1 engine installed (see above). One-off.

1969: LOTUS 59—Formula 3 square-tube spaceframe developed from Lotus 55. Engine 997 cc Ford, 117 bhp. Wheelbase 7ft 8¾in; max. track 4ft 8in; weight 882 lbs.

LOTUS 59B—Formula 2/Formula B spaceframe similar to above with larger tanks and 1,600 cc Cosworth FVA or Lotus-Ford twin-cam engines.

(1970): LOTUS 60—Seven Series 4 or S4, latest development on long-established theme. Engine 1,599 cc Ford pushrod, 86 bhp. Wheelbase 7ft 6in; max. track 4ft 4in; length 12ft 1¾in; weight 1,300 lbs. 430 off by Lotus Components/Lotus Racing before production transferred to Lotus Cars in mid-1971.

1969: LOTUS 61—Formula Ford 'wedge'. Engine 1,599 cc Ford pushrod, 102 bhp. Wheelbase 7ft 6in; max. track 4ft 3½in; length 12ft 6in; weight 820 lbs. 248 off.

LOTUS 61M—As above, 'Modified' for 1970/1971, with lower frontal area.

LOTUS 62—Tubular-framed Europa using 1,992 cc, 220 bhp LV 220/240 Lotus-Vauxhall engines in experimental racing programme. Wheelbase 7ft 7in; max. track 4ft 4in; length 12ft 10in; weight 1,350 lbs. 2 off.

LOTUS 63—Experimental Formula 1 four-wheel-drive cars. Engine 2,993 cc Cosworth-Ford DFV V8, 430 bhp. Wheelbase 8ft 2in; max. track 4ft 11in; length 12ft 8in; weight 1,170 lbs. 2 off.

LOTUS 64—Indianapolis piston-engined four-wheel-drive 'wedge' car. Engine turbocharged 2,605 cc Ford V8, 530 bhp-plus. Wheelbase 8ft 4in; max. track 4ft 2in; length 13ft 4in. 4 off.

(1970): LOTUS 65—Federal-bodied Europa for the United States market.

1969: LOTUS 66—Allocation undisclosed at time of going to press.

LOTUS 67—Proposed 1970 Tasman Championship car, not built.

LOTUS 68—Prototype 'wedge' Formula A/5000 car, built in late 1969 and subsequently renumbered as Lotus 70. Engine 4,945 cc Ford Boss V8, 480 bhp. Wheelbase 8ft 2in; max. track 5ft 1in; length 12ft 8in; weight 1,300 lbs. 1 off, subsequently modified to Lotus 70 specification with tail radiators re-sited in nose.

1970: LOTUS 69—Formula 2 monocoque variant of preceding Lotus 59B model, continued in slightly modified form in 1971. Spaceframe variants carried same classification for Formula Ford and Formula 3. 57 off.

LOTUS 70—Production Formula A/5000 car developed from Lotus 68. Engine 5 litre Ford or Chevrolet V8s, 480 bhp. Dimensions, as Lotus 68. 7 off.

LOTUS 71—Allocation undisclosed at time of going to press.

LOTUS 72—Formula 1 torsion bar-suspended, side-radiator 'wedge' car. Engine 2,993 cc Cosworth-Ford DFV V8, 440 bhp. Wheelbase 8ft 4in; max. track 4ft 9in; length 13ft 9in; weight 1,170 lbs. 6 off, continued into 1971.

1971: LOTUS 73—Formula 2 wedge shelved during 1971 and held over to 1972 season.

LOTUS 74—Twin-cam Europa introduced as high-performance version of Lotus 46 with many detail changes. Engine 1,558 cc Lotus-Ford twin-cam, 105 bhp. Wheelbase 7ft 8in; max. track 4ft 5½in; length 13ft 1½in; weight 1,513 lbs.

Appendix 2

LOTUS FORMULA 1

REGISTER 1960-1971

LOTUS 18

369 Coventry-Climax '4' Team Lotus 1960—Works prototype, sold to Mike Taylor, written-off in Belgian Grand Prix practice crash 1960.

370 Coventry-Climax '4' Team Lotus 1960—Written-off Belgian Grand Prix 1960 in Alan Stacey's fatal accident.

371 Coventry-Climax '4' Team Lotus 1960—Retained and converted to 18/21 1961—Sold to Jim Hall and won 1962 Hoosier Grand Prix—Subsequent history unknown.

372 Coventry-Climax '4' Team Lotus 1960—Retained and converted to 18/21 1961—Sold to J. Wheeler Autosport for Peter Ryan late 1961—Subsequent history unknown.

373 Coventry-Climax '4' Team Lotus 1960—To Wolfgang Seidel in 1961—To Kurt Kuhnke 1962, fitted with Borgward engine to form BKL-Borgward, written-off Karlskoga 1963.

374 Coventry-Climax '4' Team Lotus 1960—To Jim Diggory 1961—Subsequent history unknown.

375 Number allocated to 18 chassis but car never built.

Subsequent production Lotus 18s built by Lotus Components:

901 Vanwall '4' G.A. Vandervell 1960—Test vehicle for rear-engined Vanwall F1/InterContinental project, retained until 1964—Sold to Chris Ashmore less engine, had 1.5 litre Climax installed—To Paul Ridgeway 1965—Subsequent history unknown.

902 Maserati '4' David Buxton 1960—To Scuderia Centro-Sud 1960—To Prince Gaetano Starrabba 1961—Subsequent history unknown.

903 Coventry-Climax '4' Mrs Louise Bryden-Brown 1960—Retained 1961—To Ron Flockhart for Tasman Series 1961/62—Dan Gurney won 1962 Pipeline '200' and 1963 Hoosier Grand Prix—Subsequent history unknown.

904 Coventry-Climax '4' Reg Parnell 1960—Tim Parnell 1961—Philip Robinson 1962—Fred Sloman 1965—Subsequent history unknown.

905 Coventry Climax '4' Ian Burgess 1960—Camoradi International 1961—Jay Chamberlain 1962—Subsequent history unknown.

906 Coventry-Climax '4' R.R.C. Walker 1960—Driven by Stirling Moss, retained 1961 and converted to 18/24 with Coventry-Climax V8 engine—loaned to UDT-Laystall team 1962, written-off in Moss' Goodwood crash Easter 1962.

907 Coventry-Climax '4' Jim Hall and Carroll Shelby 1960—Jim Hall 1961—Subsequent history unknown.

908 Less engine Camoradi International 1961—Car unraced and sold later by John Ewer to P. Bailey.

909 Coventry-Climax '4' Tony Marsh 1960—Retained 1961—To Gerry Ashmore 1962, driven by Graham Eden—To Tom Norton 1963—Adrian Andrew 1964—Subsequently to Lionel Hickman.

910 Coventry-Climax '4' Chris Summers 1960—To Tom Norton for hill-climbing—Subsequent history unknown.

911 Less engine to Helmut Menzler 1961, later fitted with Borgward '4'—To Vern McWilliams 1962—Subsequent history unknown.

912 Coventry-Climax '4' R.R.C. Walker 1960—Converted to 18/21 1961, Moss' famous Monaco and German Grand Prix winner—To Scuderia SSS Republica di Venezia 1962—Returned to Walker—To Tim Parnell 1963—Frank Lythgoe 1964 for Dave Rees—Robin Darlington 1964—Tom Wheatcroft 1965 and fully restored for Wheatcroft Grand Prix Collection 1972.

913 Coventry-Climax '4' Ernesto Prinoth 1961—To Scuderia Sud-Ouest 1965 for Colin Davis—Jo Siffert/Jo Bonnier 1965 (exhibited in Berne showroom)—Subsequent history unknown.

914 Coventry-Climax '4' Wolfgang Seidel/Scuderia Colonia 1961—To Kurt Kuhnke 1962/3 fitted with Borgward '4' as BKL-Borgward —Subsequent history unknown.

915 Coventry-Climax '4'—UDT-Laystall Racing Team 1961—To Tim Parnell 1963—Subsequent history unknown.

916 Coventry-Climax '4' UDT-Laystall Racing Team

1961—Converted to 18/21 and retained—To Tim Parnell for Andre Pilette 1963—Alf Lovejoy 1963—Vic Wilson 1964—Tony van Moyland 1966, written-off at Bo'ness hill-climb.

917 Coventry-Climax '4' UDT-Laystall Racing Team 1961—Converted to 18/21 and retained—To Tim Parnell for himself and Andre Pilette—B.J. Hough (unraced) 1964—Albert Rodgie fitted 1.5 litre Ford Cortina engine 1965—Subsequent history unknown.

918 Coventry Climax '4' UDT-Laystall Racing Team 1961—Converted to 18/21—Loaned to R.R.C. Walker 1962—To Tim Parnell 1963—To Jock Russell who later fitted Ford V8 and renamed car Russell-Ford, burned-out in garage fire 1967.

919 Coventry-Climax '4' Gerry Ashmore 1961—Converted to 18/21, also driven by David Piper—To Mark Rigg 1963—Kurt Kuhnke 1964, who fitted Borgward '4' as BKL-Borgward—Subsequent history unknown.

Two 18/21s were produced by agents outside the works and carried no official works number. These were as follows:

'P1' Coventry-Climax '4' Tony Shelly 1962—John Riley 1965—Converted to sports car (Lotus 19B) and fitted with 3.5 litre Oldsmobile V8; subsequently rebuilt with replica McLaren bodywork.

'P2' Coventry-Climax '4' Tim Parnell 1962—Driven by Tim Parnell, John Dalton, Gary Hocking—To Clive Puzey 1963; later broken-up and rebuilt as special.

LOTUS 21

930 Coventry-Climax '4' Team Lotus 1961—Scrapped 1961

931 Coventry-Climax '4' Team Lotus 1961—Written-off in Monaco Grand Prix practice 1961 by Innes Ireland.

932 Coventry-Climax '4' Team Lotus 1961—Written-off in German Grand Prix practice 1961 by Jim Clark.

933 Coventry-Climax '4' Team Lotus 1961—Retained for Tasman series 1962—To Ray Fielding 1963—Gray Mickel later fitted 3.5 litre Buick V8—To Ernie Blakeman.

934 Coventry-Climax '4' Team Lotus 1961—Crashed Italian Grand Prix 1961 in collision with Von Trips' Ferrari, wreckage impounded by Italian authorities and bought by Tom Wheatcroft and fully restored for the Wheatcroft Grand Prix Collection 1972.

935 Coventry-Climax '4' R.R.C. Walker Racing Team 1961—Debut in Tasman series 1962 driven by Moss—To John Mecom Jr 1962—Subsequent history unknown.

936 Coventry-Climax '4' Brabham Racing Organisation 1962—Ordered by Jack Brabham as stop-gap until own Formula 1 design complete but never raced, destroyed in garage fire—Subsequently rebuilt with new chassis and sold to Jim Hall 1962—Subsequent history unknown.

937 Coventry-Climax '4' Team Lotus 1961—To Ernie Pieterse (Lawson Organisation) 1962—Lawson Motors fited Maserati '4'—Dave Clapham 1967.

938 Coventry-Climax '4'—Team Lotus 1961—To Scuderia Filipinetti for Jo Siffert 1962—Clement Barrau 1963—Subsequent history unknown.

939 Coventry-Climax '4' Syd van der Vyver—To Aldo Scribante for Neville Lederle 1962—Written-off at East London 1964.

952 Coventry-Climax '4' Scuderia Scribante 1964—Driven by Neville Lederle and Jackie Pretorius—Subsequent history unknown.

LOTUS 24

940 Coventry-Climax V8 R.R.C. Walker Racing Team 1962—Written-off Natal Grand Prix practice 1962 in Gary Hocking's fatal accident.

941 Coventry-Climax V8 R.R.C. Walker Racing Team 1962—Written-off in Mexican Grand Prix practice 1962 in Ricardo Rodriguez's fatal accident—One car was built up for 1963 from this wreck and the remains of 940, and sold to Reg Parnell (Racing) 1963 fitted BRM V8 engine—To J. Frank Harrison 1963—Subsequent history unknown.

942 Coventry-Climax V8 UDT-Laystall Racing Team 1962—To Reg Parnell (Racing) 1963—Chris Summers 1964, fitted with Chevrolet V8 engine—Subsequent history unknown.

943 Coventry-Climax V8 UDT-Laystall Racing Team 1962—British Racing Partnership 1963, unraced—To Brian Gubby 1964—To Warner Bros for 'Day of the Champion' 1966—Subsequent history unknown.

944 BRM V8 UDT-Laystall Racing Team 1962—British Racing Partnership 1963—To Peter Hawtin 1965, fitted Ford V8 engine—Surrey Racing Cars 1970.

945 BRM V8 UDT-Laystall Racing Team 1962—British Racing Partnership 1963—To Bob King 1964, fitted Coventry-Climax '4' and driven by Tony Lanfranchi—To John Lewis (intended for Martin V8 engine) 1966—Warner Bros for 'Day of the Champion' 1966—John Dillamore 1967—Fred Opert 1967—Subsequent history unknown.

946 BRM V8 Wolfgang Seidel/Autosport Team 1962—To Gunther Seifert 1963, Loaned to Paddy Driver for South African Grand Prix, written-off in practice.

947 Coventry-Climax V8 Brabham Racing Organisation 1962—To Bowmaker Racing Team 1962—Syd van der Vyver 1962, burned-out in garage fire—Remains to Vern McWilliams 1963—Subsequent history unknown.

948 Coventry-Climax V8 Team Lotus 1962—Written-off Belgian Grand Prix 1962 in Trevor Taylor's collision with Mairesse's Ferrari.

*949 Coventry-Climax V8 Team Lotus 1962—To Bernard Collomb 1963, burned-out 1965.

*950 BRM V8 Team Lotus 1962—To Scuderia Filipinetti 1962 for Jo Siffert—Siffert 1963, fitted with Coventry-Climax '4' 1965—Subsequent history unknown.

*These chassis numbers were reversed when the two cars were owned by Team Lotus.

951 — BRM V8 Scuderia Filipinetti 1963—To Andre Wicky 1964—Subsequent history unknown.

At least three 24s were produced from parts by agents outside the works and carried no official works number. These were as follows:

'P1' — BRM V8 Tim Parnell 1963, used by Reg Parnell (Racing) 1963—Revson Racing (America) 1964 fitted with Lola Mark 4 bodywork—Peter Hawtin 1965, fitted Ford V8 engine—Bob Walton 1966—Jeff Roberts 1967—Sold by J.A. Pearce to Jan van Straaten 1969.

'P2' — Less engine Tim Parnell 1963—To Mark Rigg 1964, fitted Maserati '4' engine—David Prophet 1966—David Snowden 1967—Tony Broster 1968, fitted Chevrolet V8 engine, sold in USA—Subsequent history unknown.

'P3' — Less engine Tim Parnell 1963—To Phil de Banks 1965, unraced—Dulon Cars, converted to Formula Ford Dulon LD3 1968—Charles Allen 1969.

LOTUS 25

25-R1 — Coventry-Climax V8 Team Lotus 1962—Written-off French Grand Prix 1962 in Trevor Taylor's collision with Trintignant's Walker Lotus 24.

25-R2 — Coventry-Climax V8 Team Lotus 1962—Written-off Mediterranean Grand Prix 1963 in Trevor Taylor's accident.

25-R3 — Coventry-Climax V8 Team Lotus 1962—Reg Parnell (Racing) 1964, fitted BRM V8 engine, later 2.7 litre Climax '4' installed, then 2 litre BRM V8 refitted, crashed Mexican Grand Prix practice 1966—Subsequent history unknown.

25-R4 — Coventry-Climax V8 Team Lotus 1962—Reg Parnell (Racing) 1964, fitted BRM V8 engine—Written-off Belgian Grand Prix 1965 in Richard Attwood's accident.

25-R5 — Coventry-Climax V8 Team Lotus 1962—Written-off Belgian Grand Prix practice 1963 in Trevor Taylor's accident.

25-R6 — Coventry-Climax V8 Team Lotus 1963—Jo Bonnier 1966—To MGM for 'Grand Prix' 1966—Subsequent history unknown.

25-R7 — Coventry-Climax V8 Team Lotus 1963—Reg Parnell (Racing) 1964, fitted BRM V8 engine, later 2.7 litre Climax '4' 1965—John Campbell-Jones 1966 for Emery-Godiva Climax V8—Returned to Parnell—Loaned to MGM for 'Grand Prix' 1966—Rebuilt with 1.6 Cosworth FVA engine as Parnell F2 1967--Reconverted to Lotus F1 and modified to accept 3.0 BRM V12 but unraced in this form—Tom Wheatcroft 1969 and subsequently restored to works Lotus trim for Wheatcroft Grand Prix Collection 1972.

LOTUS 33 (Numbering continued from Lotus 25 series)

33-R8 — Coventry-Climax V8 Team Lotus 1964—Severely damaged in Jim Clark's accident Aintree 200 1964—To Dickie Stoop for Paul Hawkins 1965—To MGM for 'Grand Prix' 1966—Subsequent history unknown.

33-R9 — Coventry-Climax V8 Team Lotus 1964—Jo Bonnier 1966—To MGM for 'Grand Prix' 1966—Subsequent history unknown.

33-R10 — Coventry-Climax V8 Team Lotus 1964—Written-off Brands Hatch Race of Champions 1965 in Jim Clark's accident.

33-R11 — BRM V8 Team Lotus 1965—To Earl Chiles 1967, driven by Mike Fisher and Pete Lovely—Paul Scott 1969, fitted Oldsmobile V8 engine.

*39-R12 — Coventry-Climax flat-16 Team Lotus 1965—Only Lotus 39 built for still-born Climax engine and unraced in Formula 1—Fitted 2.5 Climax '4' 1966 for Clark in Tasman series—To Leo Geoghegan 1966, fitted Repco 2.5 V8 1967, retained.

33-R13 — BRM V8 Reg Parnell (Racing) 1965—Rebuilt R4 renumbered by Parnell—Peter Yock 1967/8—Peter Hughes, fitted 2.5 Daimler SP250 V8 1969.

33-R14 — Coventry-Climax V8 Team Lotus 1966—Presented to Leonard Lee of Coventry-Climax in thanks for their services since 1955 and in Formula 1 since 1958.

*Solitary Lotus 39 was produced within the Lotus 33 production cycle so took the next chassis number in sequence.

LOTUS 43

43/1 — BRM H16 Team Lotus 1966—To Robs Lamplough, then Jock Russell 1968, fitted 4.7 Ford V8 engine—Severely damaged Brands Hatch 1969—Wreckage retained.

43/2 — BRM H16 Team Lotus 1966—To Robs Lamplough, fitted 4.7 Ford V8 1968—Mike Woolley—Subsequent history unknown.

LOTUS 49

49-R1 — Cosworth-Ford DFV V8 Team Lotus 1967—Written-off Monaco Grand Prix 1968 in Jackie Oliver's accident. Rebuilt as 49B-R9.

49-R2 — Cosworth-Ford DFV V8 Team Lotus 1967—Loaned to R.R.C. Walker for Jo Siffert 1968—Subsequently rebuilt as 49B-R10.

49-R3 — Cosworth-Ford DFV V8 Team Lotus 1967—To Team Gunston for John Love 1968—Peter Parnell 1970.

49-R4 — Cosworth-Ford DFV V8 Team Lotus 1967—To R.R.C. Walker Racing Team 1968, severely damaged in Brands Hatch Race of Champions practice and destroyed in garage fire next day.

49-R5 — Cosworth-Ford DFV V8 Team Lotus 1968—Rebuilt as 49B—Rebuilt once more as 49B-R11.

49B-R6 — Cosworth-Ford DFV V8 Team Lotus 1968—Written-off French Grand Prix practice 1968 in Jackie Oliver's accident—Subsequently rebuilt and written-off Spanish Grand Prix 1969 in Graham Hill's accident—Rebuilt again and retained.

49B-R7 — Cosworth-Ford DFV V8 R.R.C. Walker Racing Team 1968—Retained to 1971—Loaned to Wheatcroft Grand Prix Collection 1972.

49-R8	Cosworth-Ford DFV V8 Team Lotus 1968—Rebuilt as 49B—To Jo Bonnier 1969,severely damaged in Oulton Park Gold Cup practice—Dave Charlton 1969/70 rebuilt as 49C.
49-R9	Cosworth-Ford DFV V8 Team Lotus 1969—Rebuilt as 49B—Written-off Spanish Grand Prix 1969 in Jochen Rindt's accident.
49B-R10	Cosworth-Ford DFV V8 Team Lotus 1969—Written-off in Graham Hill's accident in US Grand Prix 1969, subsequently rebuilt—Retained as exhibition car.
49B-R11	Cosworth-Ford DFV V8 Team Lotus 1969—To Pete Lovely 1969.
49-R12	Cosworth-Ford DFV V8 Ford Motor Company 1969—Exhibition car, unraced.

LOTUS 63

63/1	Cosworth-Ford DFV V8 Team Lotus 1969—To Tom Wheatcroft 1970—Wheatcroft Grand Prix Collection 1971.
63/2	Cosworth-Ford DFV V8 Team Lotus 1969—Retained.

LOTUS 56B

56B/1	Pratt & Whitney turbine Team Lotus 1968/71—Retained.

LOTUS 72

72/1	Cosworth-Ford DFV V8 Team Lotus 1970—Basis of 72/4.
72/2	Cosworth-Ford DFV V8 Team Lotus 1970—Written-off Italian Grand Prix practice 1970 in Jochen Rindt's fatal accident.
72/3	Cosworth-Ford DFV V8 Team Lotus 1970—Retained 1971—To Team Lucky Strike for Dave Charlton 1971.
72/4	Cosworth-Ford DFV V8 R.R.C Walker Racing Team 1970—To Jo Siffert 1971.
72/5	Cosworth-Ford DFV V8 Team Lotus 1970—Retained 1971.
72/6	Cosworth-Ford DFV V8 Team Lotus 1971.

Appendix 3

LOTUS WORLD CHAMPIONSHIP RACING RECORD 1961-1971

1961

MAY 14—MONACO GRAND PRIX, MONTE CARLO:

1st	Stirling Moss	Lotus-Climax '4' 18	912
8th	Cliff Allison	Lotus-Climax '4' 18	916
10th	Jim Clark	Lotus-Climax '4' 21	930
Rtd	Michel May	Lotus-Climax '4' 18	914
DNS	Innes Ireland	Lotus-Climax '4' 21	931
DNQ	Henry Taylor	Lotus-Climax '4' 18	915

MAY 22—DUTCH GRAND PRIX, ZANDVOORT:

3rd	Jim Clark	Lotus-Climax '4' 21	930
4th	Stirling Moss	Lotus-Climax '4' 18	912
13th	Trevor Taylor	Lotus-Climax '4' 18	371
DNS	Ian Burgess	Lotus-Climax '4' 18	905

JUNE 18—BELGIAN GRAND PRIX, SPA-FRANCORCHAMPS:

8th	Stirling Moss	Lotus-Climax '4' 18/21	912
12th	Jim Clark	Lotus-Climax '4' 21	932
Rtd	Innes Ireland	Lotus-Climax '4' 21	933
Rtd	Lucien Bianchi	Lotus-Climax '4' 18	373
Rtd	Willy Mairesse	Lotus-Climax '4' 18	909
DNQ	Tony Marsh	Lotus-Climax '4' 18	909
DNQ	Wolfgang Seidel	Lotus-Climax '4' 18	373
DNQ	Ian Burgess	Lotus-Climax '4' 18	905
DNQ	Cliff Allison	Lotus-Climax '4' 18	918

JULY 2—FRENCH GRAND PRIX, REIMS-GUEUX:

3rd	Jim Clark	Lotus-Climax '4' 21	932
4th	Innes Ireland	Lotus-Climax '4' 21	933
10th	Henry Taylor	Lotus-Climax '4' 18/21	916
11th	Michel May	Lotus-Climax '4' 18	914
14th	Ian Burgess	Lotus-Climax '4' 18	905
Rtd	Stirling Moss	Lotus-Climax '4' 18/21	912
Rtd	Willy Mairesse	Lotus-Climax '4' 21	930
T-car	Juan-Manuel Bordeu	Lotus-Climax '4' 18/21	915
Rtd	Lucien Bianchi	Lotus-Climax '4' 18/21	917
T-car	Wolfgang Seidel	Lotus-Climax '4' 18	373

JULY 15—BRITISH GRAND PRIX, AINTREE:

10th	Innes Ireland	Lotus-Climax '4' 21	933
13th	Tony Maggs	Lotus-Climax '4' 18	903
14th	Ian Burgess	Lotus-Climax '4' 18	905
17th	Wolfgang Seidel	Lotus-Climax '4' 18	373
Rtd	Jim Clark	Lotus-Climax '4' 21	932
Rtd	Lucien Bianchi	Lotus-Climax '4' 18/21	917
Rtd	Stirling Moss	Lotus-Climax '4' 18/21	912
Rtd	Tony Marsh	Lotus-Climax '4' 18	909
Rtd	Tim Parnell	Lotus-Climax '4' 18	904
Rtd	Gerry Ashmore	Lotus-Climax '4' 18	919
Rtd	Henry Taylor	Lotus-Climax '4' 18/21	916

AUGUST 6—GERMAN GRAND PRIX, NURBURGRING:

1st	Stirling Moss	Lotus-Climax '4' 18/21	912
4th	Jim Clark	Lotus-Climax '4' 21	930
11th	Tony Maggs	Lotus-Climax '4' 18	903
15th	Tony Marsh	Lotus-Climax '4' 18	909
16th	Gerry Ashmore	Lotus-Climax '4' 18	919
Rtd	Wolfgang Seidel	Lotus-Climax '4' 18	373
Rtd	Innes Ireland	Lotus-Climax '4' 21	933
DNS	Michel May	Lotus-Climax '4' 18	914

SEPTEMBER 10—ITALIAN GRAND PRIX, MONZA:

11th	Tim Parnell	Lotus-Climax '4' 18	904
12th	Henry Taylor	Lotus-Climax '4' 18/21	918
Rtd	Stirling Moss	Lotus-Climax '4' 21	933
Rtd	Prince Gaetano Starrabba	Lotus-Maserati '4'	902
Rtd	Masten Gregory	Lotus-Climax '4' 18/21	917
Rtd	Innes Ireland	Lotus-Climax '4' 18/21	912
Rtd	Wolfgang Seidel	Lotus-Climax '4' 18	373
Rtd	Jim Clark	Lotus-Climax '4' 21	934
Rtd	Gerry Ashmore	Lotus-Climax '4' 18	919

OCTOBER 8—UNITED STATES GRAND PRIX, WATKINS GLEN:

1st	Innes Ireland	Lotus-Climax '4' 21	933
7th	Jim Clark	Lotus-Climax '4' 21	930
9th	Peter Ryan	Lotus-Climax '4' 18	372
11th	Olivier Gendebien/ Masten Gregory	Lotus-Climax '4' 18/21	918
Rtd	Jim Hall	Lotus-Climax '4' 18	371
Rtd	Lloyd Ruby	Lotus-Climax '4' 18	907
Rtd	Stirling Moss	Lotus-Climax '4' 18/21	912
Rtd	Masten Gregory	Lotus-Climax '4' 18/21	917

1962

MAY 20—DUTCH GRAND PRIX, ZANDVOORT:

2nd	Trevor Taylor	Lotus-Climax V8 24	948
9th	Jim Clark	Lotus-Climax V8 25	25-R1
Rtd	Innes Ireland	Lotus-Climax V8 24	942
Rtd	Masten Gregory	Lotus-Climax '4' 18/21	917
Rtd	Jack Brabham	Lotus-Climax V8 24	947

JUNE 3—MONACO GRAND PRIX, MONTE CARLO:

Rtd	Jack Brabham	Lotus-Climax V8 24	947
Rtd	Innes Ireland	Lotus-Climax V8 24	943
Rtd	Jim Clark	Lotus-Climax V8 25	25-R1
Rtd	Trevor Taylor	Lotus-Climax V8 24	948
Rtd	Maurice Trintignant	Lotus-Climax V8 24	940
DNQ	Jo Siffert	Lotus-Climax '4' 21	938
DNQ	Masten Gregory	Lotus-BRM V8 24	944
DNQ	Nino Vaccarella	Lotus-Climax '4' 18/21	912

JUNE 17—BELGIAN GRAND PRIX, SPA-FRANCORCHAMPS:

1st	Jim Clark	Lotus-Climax V8 25	25-R1
6th	Jack Brabham	Lotus-Climax V8 24	947
8th	Maurice Trintignant	Lotus-Climax V8 24	940
9th	Lucien Bianchi	Lotus-Climax '4' 18/21	918
10th	Jo Siffert	Lotus-Climax '4' 21	938
11th	John Campbell-Jones	Lotus-Climax '4' 18	373
Rtd	Trevor Taylor	Lotus-Climax V8 24	948
Rtd	Masten Gregory	Lotus-BRM V8 24	944
Rtd	Innes Ireland	Lotus-Climax V8	943
DNS	Dan Gurney	Lotus-BRM V8	950

JULY 8—FRENCH GRAND PRIX, ROUEN-LES-ESSARTS:

7th	Maurice Trintignant	Lotus-Climax V8 24	940
8th	Trevor Taylor	Lotus-Climax V8 25	25-R1
Rtd	Jim Clark	Lotus-Climax V8 25	25-R2
Rtd	Masten Gregory	Lotus-BRM V8 24	944
Rtd	Jack Brabham	Lotus-Climax V8 24	947
Rtd	Jo Siffert	Lotus-Climax V8 24	950
Rtd	Innes Ireland	Lotus-Climax V8 24	942

JULY 21—BRITISH GRAND PRIX, AINTREE:

1st	Jim Clark	Lotus-Climax V8 25	25-R2
5th	Jack Brabham	Lotus-Climax V8 24	947
7th	Masten Gregory	Lotus-Climax V8 24	942
8th	Trevor Taylor	Lotus-Climax V8 24	949
15th	Jay Chamberlain	Lotus-Climax '4' 18	905
16th	Innes Ireland	Lotus-Climax V8 24	943
Rtd	Wolfgang Seidel	Lotus-BRM V8 24	946
Rtd	Tony Shelly	Lotus-Climax '4' 18/21	'P1'

AUGUST 5—GERMAN GRAND PRIX, NURBURGRING:

4th	Jim Clark	Lotus-Climax V8 25	25-R2
12th	Jo Siffert	Lotus-Climax '4' 21	938
Rtd	Maurice Trintignant	Lotus-Climax V8 24	940
Rtd	Heinz Schiller	Lotus-BRM V8 24	950
Rtd	Trevor Taylor	Lotus-Climax V8 24	949
DNQ	Wolfgang Seidel	Lotus-BRM V8 24	946
DNQ	Tony Shelly	Lotus-Climax '4' 18/21	'P1'
DNQ	Jay Chamberlain	Lotus-Climax '4' 18	905
DNQ	Gunther Seifert	Lotus-Climax '4' 18	373

SEPTEMBER 16—ITALIAN GRAND PRIX, MONZA:

9th	Nino Vaccarella	Lotus-Climax V8 24	941
12th	Masten Gregory	Lotus-BRM V8 24	944
Rtd	Innes Ireland	Lotus-Climax V8 24	942
Rtd	Trevor Taylor	Lotus-Climax V8 25	25-R2
Rtd	Maurice Trintignant	Lotus-Climax V8 24	940
Rtd	Jim Clark	Lotus-Climax V8 25	25-R3
DNQ	Gerry Ashmore	Lotus-Climax '4' 18	919
DNQ	Jo Siffert	Lotus-BRM V8 24	950
DNQ	Ernesto Prinoth	Lotus-Climax '4' 18	913
DNQ	Jay Chamberlain	Lotus-Climax '4' 18	905
DNQ	Tony Shelly	Lotus-BRM V8 24	946

OCTOBER 7—UNITED STATES GRAND PRIX, WATKINS GLEN:

1st	Jim Clark	Lotus-Climax V8 25	25-R3
6th	Masten Gregory	Lotus-BRM V8 24	944
8th	Innes Ireland	Lotus-Climax V8 24	942
9th	Roger Penske	Lotus-Climax V8 24	943
10th	Rob Schroeder	Lotus-Climax V8 24	940
12th	Trevor Taylor	Lotus-Climax V8 25	25-R2
Rtd	Maurice Trintignant	Lotus-Climax V8 24	941
DNS	Jim Hall	Lotus-Climax '4' 21	936

DECEMBER 29—S. AFRICAN GRAND PRIX, EAST LONDON:

5th	Innes Ireland	Lotus-Climax V8 24	942
6th	Neville Lederle	Lotus-Climax '4' 21	939
10th	Ernie Pieterse	Lotus-Climax '4' 21	937
Rtd	Jim Clark	Lotus-Climax V8 25	25-R5
Rtd	Trevor Taylor	Lotus-Climax V8 25	25-R2

1963

MAY 26—MONACO GRAND PRIX, MONTE CARLO:

6th	Trevor Taylor	Lotus-Climax V8 25	25-R5
8th(Rtd)	Jim Clark	Lotus-Climax V8 25	25-R4
Rtd	Jack Brabham	Lotus-Climax V8 25	25-R3
Rtd	Innes Ireland	Lotus-BRM V8 24	944
Rtd	Jim Hall	Lotus-BRM V8 24	945
Rtd	Jo Siffert	Lotus-BRM V8 24	950
DNQ	Bernard Collomb	Lotus-Climax V8 24	949

JUNE 9—BELGIAN GRAND PRIX, SPA-FRANCORCHAMPS:

1st	Jim Clark	Lotus-Climax V8 25	25-R4
Rtd	Jim Hall	Lotus-BRM V8 24	945
Rtd	Jo Siffert	Lotus-BRM V8 24	950
Rtd	Trevor Taylor	Lotus-Climax V8 25	25-R3
T-car	Innes Ireland	Lotus-BRM V8 24	944

JUNE 23—DUTCH GRAND PRIX, ZANDVOORT:

1st	Jim Clark	Lotus-Climax V8 25	25-R4
7th	Jo Siffert	Lotus-BRM V8 24	950
8th	Jim Hall	Lotus-BRM V8 24	944
10th	Trevor Taylor	Lotus-Climax V8 25	25-R2
T-car	Chris Amon	Lotus-Climax V8 24	942
T-car	Innes Ireland	Lotus-BRM V8 24	944

JUNE 30—FRENCH GRAND PRIX, REIMS-GUEUX:

1st	Jim Clark	Lotus-Climax V8 25	25-R4
6th	Jo Siffert	Lotus-BRM V8 24	950
8th	Maurice Trintignant	Lotus-Climax V8 24	942
11th	Jim Hall	Lotus-BRM V8 24	945
13th(Rtd)	Trevor Taylor	Lotus-Climax V8 25	25-R2
Rtd	Phil Hill	Lotus-BRM V8 24	951
Rtd	Masten Gregory	Lotus-BRM V8 24	'P1'
DNS	Peter Arundell	Lotus-Climax V8 25	25-R3

JULY 20—BRITISH GRAND PRIX, SILVERSTONE:

1st	Jim Clark	Lotus-Climax V8 25	25-R4
6th	Jim Hall	Lotus-BRM V8 24	945
8th	Mike Hailwood	Lotus-Climax V8 24	942
11th	Masten Gregory	Lotus-BRM V8 24	'P1'
Rtd	Jo Siffert	Lotus-BRM V8 24	950
Rtd	Trevor Taylor	Lotus-Climax V8 25	25-R2
T-car	Innes Ireland	Lotus-BRM V8 24	944

AUGUST 4—GERMAN GRAND PRIX, NURBURGRING:

2nd	Jim Clark	Lotus-Climax V8 25	25-R4
5th	Jim Hall	Lotus-BRM V8 24	945
8th	Trevor Taylor	Lotus-Climax V8 25	25-R2
9th(Rtd)	Jo Siffert	Lotus-BRM V8 24	950
10th	Bernard Collomb	Lotus-Climax V8 24	949
Rtd	Innes Ireland	Lotus-BRM V8 24	944
DNQ	Tim Parnell	Lotus-Climax '4' 18	915
DNQ	Andre Pilette	Lotus-Climax '4' 18/21	917
DNQ	Kurt Kuhnke	'BKL-Borgward'	914

SEPTEMBER 8—ITALIAN GRAND PRIX, MONZA:

1st	Jim Clark	Lotus-Climax V8 25	25-R4
8th	Jim Hall	Lotus-BRM V8 24	945
13th(Rtd)	Mike Spence	Lotus-Climax V8 25	25-R3
Rtd	Jo Siffert	Lotus-BRM V8 24	950
Rtd	Masten Gregory	Lotus-BRM V8 24	'P1'
DNQ	Andre Pilette	Lotus-Climax '4' 18/21	917

OCTOBER 6—UNITED STATES GRAND PRIX, WATKINS GLEN:

3rd	Jim Clark	Lotus-Climax V8 25	25-R4
10th(Rtd)	Jim Hall	Lotus-BRM V8 24	944
Rtd	Jo Siffert	Lotus-BRM V8 24	950
Rtd	Rodger Ward	Lotus-BRM V8 24	'P1'
Rtd	Pedro Rodriguez	Lotus-Climax V8 25	25-R3

Rtd	Trevor Taylor	Lotus-Climax V8 25	25-R6
Rtd	Hap Sharp	Lotus-BRM V8 24	940

OCTOBER 20—MEXICAN GRAND PRIX, MEXICO CITY:

1st	Jim Clark	Lotus-Climax V8 25	25-R4
7th	Hap Sharp	Lotus-BRM V8 24	940
8th	Jim Hall	Lotus-BRM V8 24	944
9th	Jo Siffert	Lotus-BRM V8 24	950
Rtd	Pedro Rodriguez	Lotus-Climax V8 25	25-R3
Rtd	Trevor Taylor	Lotus-Climax V8 25	25-R6
Rtd	Chris Amon	Lotus-BRM V8 24	'P1'

DECEMBER 28—S. AFRICAN GRAND PRIX, EAST LONDON:

1st	Jim Clark	Lotus-Climax V8 25	25-R4
8th	Trevor Taylor	Lotus-Climax V8 25	25-R7
14th	Brausch Niemann	Lotus-Ford '4' 22	22-J-17
Rtd	Ernie Pieterse	Lotus-Climax '4' 21	937
Rtd	Paddy Driver	Lotus-BRM V8 24	946

1964

MAY 10—MONACO GRAND PRIX, MONTE CARLO:

3rd	Peter Arundell	Lotus-Climax V8 25	25-R4
4th(Rtd)	Jim Clark	Lotus-Climax V8 25	25-R6
6th	Mike Hailwood	Lotus-BRM V8 25	25-R7
8th	Jo Siffert	Lotus-BRM V8 24	950
DNQ	Chris Amon	Lotus-BRM V8 25	25-R3
DNQ	Peter Revson	Lotus-BRM V8 24	'P1'
DNQ	Bernard Collomb	Lotus-Climax V8 24	949
DNS	Innes Ireland	Lotus-BRM V8	944

MAY 24—DUTCH GRAND PRIX, ZANDVOORT:

1st	Jim Clark	Lotus-Climax V8 25	25-R6
3rd	Peter Arundell	Lotus-Climax V8 25	25-R4
5th	Chris Amon	Lotus-BRM V8 25	25-R3
12th(Rtd)	Mike Hailwood	Lotus-BRM V8 25	25-R7

JUNE 14—BELGIAN GRAND PRIX, SPA-FRANCORCHAMPS:

1st	Jim Clark	Lotus-Climax V8 25	25-R6
9th	Peter Arundell	Lotus-Climax V8 25	25-R4
Dis	Peter Revson	Lotus-BRM V8 25	25-R7
Rtd	Chris Amon	Lotus-BRM V8 25	25-R3

JUNE 28—FRENCH GRAND PRIX, ROUEN-LES-ESSARTS:

4th	Peter Arundell	Lotus-Climax V8 25	25-R4
8th	Mike Hailwood	Lotus-BRM V8 25	25-R7
10th	Chris Amon	Lotus-BRM V8 25	25-R3
Rtd	Jim Clark	Lotus-Climax V8 25	25-R6

JULY 11—BRITISH GRAND PRIX, BRANDS HATCH:

1st	Jim Clark	Lotus-Climax V8 25	25-R6
9th	Mike Spence	Lotus-Climax V8 25	25-R4
Rtd	Peter Revson	Lotus-BRM V8 24	'P1'
Rtd	Trevor Taylor	Lotus-BRM V8 24	945
Rtd	Mike Hailwood	Lotus-BRM V8 25	25-R7
Rtd	Chris Amon	Lotus-BRM V8 25	25-R3

AUGUST 2—GERMAN GRAND PRIX, NURBURGRING:

8th	Mike Spence	Lotus-Climax V8 25	25-R6
9th	Gerhard Mitter	Lotus-Climax V8 25	25-R4
11th(Rtd)	Chris Amon	Lotus-BRM V8 25	25-R3
14th(Rtd)	Peter Revson	Lotus-BRM V8 24	'P1'
Rtd	Jim Clark	Lotus-Climax V8 33	33-R9
Rtd	Mike Hailwood	Lotus-BRM V8 25	25-R7

AUGUST 23—AUSTRIAN GRAND PRIX, ZELTWEG:

8th	Mike Hailwood	Lotus-BRM V8 25	25-R3
Rtd	Mike Spence	Lotus-Climax V8 33	33-R8
Rtd	Jim Clark	Lotus-Climax V8 33	33-R9
Rtd	Chris Amon	Lotus-Climax V8 25	25-R4

SEPTEMBER 6—ITALIAN GRAND PRIX, MONZA:

6th	Mike Spence	Lotus-Climax V8 33	33-R8
13th	Peter Revson	Lotus-BRM V8 24	'P1'
Rtd	Jim Clark	Lotus-Climax V8 25	25-R6
Rtd	Mike Hailwood	Lotus-BRM V8 25	25-R4

OCTOBER 4—UNITED STATES GRAND PRIX, WATKINS GLEN

5th	Walt Hansgen	Lotus-Climax V8 33	33-R8
7th(Rtd)	Mike Spence/ Jim Clark	Lotus-Climax V8 25	25-R6
8th(Rtd)	Mike Hailwood	Lotus-BRM V8 25	25-R7
Rtd	Jim Clark/ Mike Spence	Lotus-Climax V8 33	33-R9
Rtd	Chris Amon	Lotus-BRM V8 25	25-R4

OCTOBER 20—MEXICAN GRAND PRIX, MEXICO CITY:

4th	Mike Spence	Lotus-Climax V8 25	25-R6
5th(Rtd)	Jim Clark	Lotus-Climax V8 33	33-R9
10th	Moises Solana	Lotus-Climax V8 33	33-R8
Rtd	Chris Amon	Lotus-BRM V8 25	25-R4
Rtd	Mike Hailwood	Lotus-BRM V8 25	25-R7

1965

JANUARY 1—SOUTH AFRICAN GRAND PRIX, EAST LONDON:

1st	Jim Clark	Lotus-Climax V8 33	33-R10
4th	Mike Spence	Lotus-Climax V8 33	33-R9
11th	Tony Maggs	Lotus-BRM V8 25	25-R4
DNQ	Neville Lederle	Lotus-Climax '4' 21	952
DNQ	Brausch Niemann	Lotus-Ford '4' 22	22-J-17
DNQ	Ernie Pieterse	Lotus-Climax '4' 21	937
DNQ	Dave Charlton	Lotus-Ford '4' 20	20-J-867
DNQ	Clive Puzey	Lotus-Climax '4' 18/21	'P2'

MAY 30—MONACO GRAND PRIX, MONTE CARLO:

10th(Rtd)	Paul Hawkins	Lotus-Climax V8 33	33-R8
Rtd	Richard Attwood	Lotus-BRM V8 25	25-R3
Rtd	Mike Hailwood	Lotus-BRM V8 25	25-R7

JUNE 13—BELGIAN GRAND PRIX, SPA-FRANCORCHAMPS:

1st	Jim Clark	Lotus-Climax V8 33	33-R11
7th	Mike Spence	Lotus-Climax V8 33	33-R9
13th	Innes Ireland	Lotus-BRM V8 25	25-R7
14th(Rtd)	Richard Attwood	Lotus-BRM V8 25	25-R4

JUNE 27—FRENCH GRAND PRIX, CLERMONT-FERRAND:

1st	Jim Clark	Lotus-Climax V8 25	25-R6
7th	Mike Spence	Lotus-Climax V8 33	33-R9
Rtd	Chris Amon	Lotus-BRM V8 25	25-R3
Rtd	Innes Ireland	Lotus-BRM V8 25	25-R7

JULY 10—BRITISH GRAND PRIX, SILVERSTONE:

1st	Jim Clark	Lotus-Climax V8 33	33-R11
4th	Mike Spence	Lotus-Climax V8 33	33-R9
13th	Richard Attwood	Lotus-BRM V8 25	25-R3
Rtd	Innes Ireland	Lotus-BRM V8 25	25-R7
DNS	Brian Gubby	Lotus-Climax V8 24	943

JULY 18—DUTCH GRAND PRIX, ZANDVOORT:

1st	Jim Clark	Lotus-Climax V8 33	33-R9
8th	Mike Spence	Lotus-Climax V8 25	25-R6
10th	Innes Ireland	Lotus-BRM V8 25	25-R7
12th	Richard Attwood	Lotus-BRM V8 25	25-R3

AUGUST 1—GERMAN GRAND PRIX, NURBURGRING:

1st	Jim Clark	Lotus-Climax V8 33	33-R11
Rtd	Gerhard Mitter	Lotus-Climax V8 25	25-R6
Rtd	Mike Spence	Lotus-Climax V8 33	33-R9
Rtd	Richard Attwood	Lotus-BRM V8 25	25-R3
Rtd	Chris Amon	Lotus-BRM V8 25	25-R7
Rtd	Paul Hawkins	Lotus-Climax V8 33	33-R8

SEPTEMBER 12—ITALIAN GRAND PRIX, MONZA:

6th	Richard Attwood	Lotus-BRM V8 25	25-R3
9th	Innes Ireland	Lotus-BRM V8 25	25-R13
10th(Rtd)	Jim Clark	Lotus-Climax V8 33	33-R11
11th(Rtd)	Mike Spence	Lotus-Climax V8 33	33-R9
Rtd	Giacomo 'Geki' Russo	Lotus-Climax V8 25	25-R6

OCTOBER 3—UNITED STATES GRAND PRIX, WATKINS GLEN:

10th	Richard Attwood	Lotus-BRM V8 25	25-R3
12th	Moises Solana	Lotus-Climax V8 25	25-R6
Rtd	Jim Clark	Lotus-Climax V8 33	33-R11
Rtd	Innes Ireland	Lotus-BRM V8 25	25-R13
Rtd	Mike Spence	Lotus-Climax V8 33	33-R9

OCTOBER 24—MEXICAN GRAND PRIX, MEXICO CITY:

3rd	Mike Spence	Lotus-Climax V8 33	33-R9
6th	Richard Attwood	Lotus-BRM V8 25	25-R3
Rtd	Moises Solana	Lotus-Climax V8 25	25-R6
Rtd	Bob Bondurant	Lotus-BRM V8 25	25-R13
Rtd	Jim Clark	Lotus-Climax V8 33	33-R11

1966

MAY 22—MONACO GRAND PRIX, MONTE CARLO:

Rtd	Jim Clark	Lotus-Climax V8 33	33-R11
Rtd	Mike Spence	Lotus-BRM V8 25	25-R13
T-car	Phil Hill	Lotus-Climax V8 25	25-R6
T-car	Jo Bonnier	Lotus-Climax '4' 25	25-R3

JUNE 12—BELGIAN GRAND PRIX, SPA-FRANCORCHAMPS:

Rtd	Mike Spence	Lotus-BRM V8 25	25-R13
Rtd	Jim Clark	Lotus-Climax V8 33	33-R11
DNS	Peter Arundell	Lotus-BRM H16 43	43/1

JULY 3—FRENCH GRAND PRIX, REIMS-GUEUX:

Rtd	Pedro Rodriguez	Lotus-Climax V8 33	33-R11
Rtd	Mike Spence	Lotus-BRM V8 25	25-R13
Rtd	Peter Arundell	Lotus-BRM H16 43	43/1
DNS	Jim Clark	Lotus-Climax V8 33	33-R11

JULY 16—BRITISH GRAND PRIX, BRANDS HATCH:

4th	Jim Clark	Lotus-Climax V8 33	33-R14
Rtd	Peter Arundell	Lotus-BRM V8 33	33-R11
Rtd	Mike Spence	Lotus-BRM V8 25	25-R13

JULY 24—DUTCH GRAND PRIX, ZANDVOORT:

3rd	Jim Clark	Lotus-Climax V8 33	33-R14
5th	Mike Spence	Lotus-BRM V8 25	25-R13
Rtd	Peter Arundell	Lotus-BRM V8 33	33-R11

AUGUST 7—GERMAN GRAND PRIX, NURBURGRING:

12th	Peter Arundell	Lotus-BRM V8 33	33-R11
Rtd	Mike Spence	Lotus-BRM V8 25	25-R13
Rtd	Jim Clark	Lotus-Climax 33	33-R14
Rtd	Pedro Rodriguez	Lotus-Cosworth '4'	44-F-3*
Rtd	Piers Courage	Lotus-Cosworth '4'	44-F-2*
DNS	Gerhard Mitter	Lotus-Cosworth '4'	44-F-1*

*Formula 2 cars in race run concurrently with Formula 1 Grand Prix

SEPTEMBER 4—ITALIAN GRAND PRIX, MONZA:

5th	Mike Spence	Lotus-BRM V8 25	25-R13
8th	Peter Arundell	Lotus-BRM V8 33	33-R11
9th	Giacomo 'Geki' Russo	Lotus-Climax V8 33	33-R14
Rtd	Jim Clark	Lotus-BRM H16 43	43/1
T-car	Giancarlo Baghetti	Lotus-BRM V8 25	25-R3

OCTOBER 2—UNITED STATES GRAND PRIX, WATKINS GLEN:

1st	Jim Clark	Lotus-BRM H16 43	43/1
6th	Peter Arundell	Lotus-Climax V8 33	33-R14
Rtd	Mike Spence	Lotus-BRM V8 25	25-R3
Rtd	Pedro Rodriguez	Lotus-BRM V8 33	33-R11

OCTOBER 23—MEXICAN GRAND PRIX, MEXICO CITY:

7th	Peter Arundell	Lotus-BRM V8 33	33-R11
Rtd	Pedro Rodriguez	Lotus-Climax V8 33	33-R14
Rtd	Jim Clark	Lotus-BRM H16 43	43/1
DNS	Mike Spence	Lotus-BRM V8 25	25-R3

1967

JANUARY 2—SOUTH AFRICAN GRAND PRIX, KYALAMI:

Rtd	Piers Courage	Lotus-BRM V8 25	25-R13
Rtd	Jim Clark	Lotus-BRM H16 43	43/2
Rtd	Graham Hill	Lotus-BRM H16 43	43/1

MAY 7—MONACO GRAND PRIX, MONTE CARLO:

2nd	Graham Hill	Lotus-BRM V8 33	33-R11
Rtd	Jim Clark	Lotus-Climax V8 33	33-R14

JUNE 4—DUTCH GRAND PRIX, ZANDVOORT:

1st	Jim Clark	Lotus-Ford V8 49	49-R2
7th	Chris Irwin	Lotus-BRM V8 25	25-R13
Rtd	Graham Hill	Lotus-Ford V8 49	49-R1

JUNE 18—BELGIAN GRAND PRIX, SPA-FRANCORCHAMPS:

6th	Jim Clark	Lotus-Ford V8 49	49-R2
Rtd	Graham Hill	Lotus-Ford V8 49	49-R1

JULY 2—FRENCH GRAND PRIX, BUGATTI CIRCUIT LE MAN

Rtd	Jim Clark	Lotus-Ford V8 49	49-R2
Rtd	Graham Hill	Lotus-Ford V8 49	49-R1

JULY 15—BRITISH GRAND PRIX, SILVERSTONE:

1st	Jim Clark	Lotus-Ford V8 49	49-R2
Rtd	Graham Hill	Lotus-Ford V8 49	49-R3
T-car	Graham Hill	Lotus-Ford V8 49	49-R1

AUGUST 6—GERMAN GRAND PRIX, NURBURGRING:

5th	Jackie Oliver	Lotus-Cosworth '4' 48	48/3
Rtd	Graham Hill	Lotus-Ford V8 49	49-R1
Rtd	Jim Clark	Lotus-Ford V8 49	49-R2
T-car	Graham Hill	Lotus-Ford V8 49	49-R3

AUGUST 27—CANADIAN GRAND PRIX, MOSPORT PARK:

4th	Graham Hill	Lotus-Ford V8 49	49-R3
11th	Mike Fisher	Lotus-BRM V8 33	33-R11
Rtd	Eppie Weitzes	Lotus-Ford V8 49	49-R1
Rtd	Jim Clark	Lotus-Ford V8 49	49-R2

SEPTEMBER 10—ITALIAN GRAND PRIX, MONZA:

3rd	Jim Clark	Lotus-Ford V8 49	49-R2
Rtd	Graham Hill	Lotus-Ford V8 49	49-R3
Rtd	Giancarlo Baghetti	Lotus-Ford V8 49	49-R1

OCTOBER 1—UNITED STATES GRAND PRIX, WATKINS GLE

1st	Jim Clark	Lotus-Ford V8 49	49-R2
2nd	Graham Hill	Lotus-Ford V8 49	49-R3
Rtd	Moises Solana	Lotus-Ford V8 49	49-R1

OCTOBER 22—MEXICAN GRAND PRIX, MEXICO CITY:

1st	Jim Clark	Lotus-Ford V8 49	49-R1
Rtd	Moises Solana	Lotus-Ford V8 49	49-R2
Rtd	Graham Hill	Lotus-Ford V8 49	49-R3
DNS	Mike Fisher	Lotus-BRM V8 33	33-R11

1968

JANUARY 1—SOUTH AFRICAN GRAND PRIX, KYALAMI:

1st	Jim Clark	Lotus-Ford V8 49	49-R4
2nd	Graham Hill	Lotus-Ford V8 49	49-R3

MAY 12—SPANISH GRAND PRIX, JARAMA:

1st	Graham Hill	Lotus-Ford V8 49	49-R1
Rtd	Jo Siffert	Lotus-Ford V8 49	49-R2

MAY 26—MONACO GRAND PRIX, MONTE CARLO:

1st	Graham Hill	Lotus-Ford V8 49B	49B-R5
Rtd	Jo Siffert	Lotus-Ford V8 49	49-R2
Rtd	Jackie Oliver	Lotus-Ford V8 49	49-R1

JUNE 9—BELGIAN GRAND PRIX, SPA-FRANCORCHAMPS:

5th	Jackie Oliver	Lotus-Ford V8 49B	49B-R6
7th	Jo Siffert	Lotus-Ford V8 49	49-R2
Rtd	Graham Hill	Lotus-Ford V8 49B	49B-R5

JUNE 23—DUTCH GRAND PRIX, ZANDVOORT:

9th(Rtd)	Graham Hill	Lotus-Ford V8 49B	49B-R5
Unc	Jackie Oliver	Lotus-Ford V8 49B	49B-R6
Rtd	Jo Siffert	Lotus-Ford V8 49	49-R2

JULY 7—FRENCH GRAND PRIX, ROUEN-LES-ESSARTS:

11th	Jo Siffert	Lotus-Ford V8 49	49-R2
Rtd	Graham Hill	Lotus-Ford V8 49B	49B-R5
DNS	Jackie Oliver	Lotus-Ford V8 49B	49B-R6

JULY 20—BRITISH GRAND PRIX, BRANDS HATCH:

1st	Jo Siffert	Lotus-Ford V8 49B	49B-R7
Rtd	Jackie Oliver	Lotus-Ford V8 49B	49B-R2
Rtd	Graham Hill	Lotud-Ford V8 49B	49B-R5

AUGUST 4—GERMAN GRAND PRIX, NURBURGRING:

2nd	Graham Hill	Lotus-Ford V8 49B	49B-R5
11th	Jackie Oliver	Lotus-Ford V8 49B	49B-R2
Rtd	Jo Siffert	Lotus-Ford V8 49B	49B-R7

SEPTEMBER 8—ITALIAN GRAND PRIX, MONZA:

Rtd	Jo Siffert	Lotus-Ford V8 49B	49B-R7
Rtd	Jackie Oliver	Lotus-Ford V8 49B	49B-R5
Rtd	Graham Hill	Lotus-Ford V8 49B	49B-R6*
DNS	Mario Andretti	Lotus-Ford V8 49B	49B-R5

*Car rebuilt with new monocoque chassis

SEPTEMBER 22—CANADIAN GRAND PRIX, ST JOVITE:

4th	Graham Hill	Lotus-Ford V8 49B	49B-R6
Rtd	Jackie Oliver	Lotus-Ford V8 49B	49B-R2
Rtd	Jo Siffert	Lotus-Ford V8 49B	49B-R7
Rtd	Bill Brack	Lotus-Ford V8 49B	49B-R5

OCTOBER 6—UNITED STATES GRAND PRIX, WATKINS GLEN:

2nd	Graham Hill	Lotus-Ford V8 49B	49B-R6
5th	Jo Siffert	Lotus-Ford V8 49B	49B-R7
Rtd	Mario Andretti	Lotus-Ford V8 49B	49B-R5
DNS	Jackie Oliver	Lotus-Ford V8 49B	49B-R2

NOVEMBER 3—MEXICAN GRAND PRIX, MEXICO CITY:

1st	Graham Hill	Lotus-Ford V8 49B	49B-R6
3rd	Jackie Oliver	Lotus-Ford V8 49B	49B-R5
6th	Jo Siffert	Lotus-Ford V8 49B	49B-R7
Rtd	Moises Solana	Lotus-Ford V8 49B	49B-R2

1969

MARCH 1—SOUTH AFRICAN GRAND PRIX, KYALAMI:

2nd	Graham Hill	Lotus-Ford V8 49B	49B-R6
4th	Jo Siffert	Lotus-Ford V8 49B	49B-R7
Rtd	Jochen Rindt	Lotus-Ford V8 49B	49B-R9
Rtd	John Love	Lotus-Ford V8 49	49-R3
Rtd	Mario Andretti	Lotus-Ford V8 49B	49B-R11

MAY 4—SPANISH GRAND PRIX, BARCELONA:

Rtd	Jo Siffert	Lotus-Ford V8 49B	49B-R7
Rtd	Jochen Rindt	Lotus-Ford V8 49B	49B-R9
Rtd	Graham Hill	Lotus-Ford V8 49B	49B-R6

JUNE 8—MONACO GRAND PRIX, MONTE CARLO:

1st	Graham Hill	Lotus-Ford V8 49B	49B-R10
3rd	Jo Siffert	Lotus-Ford V8 49B	49B-R7
4th	Richard Attwood	Lotus-Ford V8 49	49-R8

JUNE 21—DUTCH GRAND PRIX, ZANDVOORT:

2nd	Jo Siffert	Lotus-Ford V8 49B	49B-R7
7th	Graham Hill	Lotus-Ford V8 49B	49B-R10
Rtd	Jochen Rindt	Lotus-Ford V8 49B	49B-R6*

*Car rebuilt with new monocoque chassis

JULY 6—FRENCH GRAND PRIX, CLERMONT-FERRAND:

6th	Graham Hill	Lotus-Ford V8 49B	49B-R10
9th	Jo Siffert	Lotus-Ford V8 49B	49B-R7
Rtd	Jochen Rindt	Lotus-Ford V8 49B	49B-R6
Rtd	John Miles	Lotus-Ford V8 63	63/2

JULY 19—BRITISH GRAND PRIX, SILVERSTONE:

4th	Jochen Rindt	Lotus-Ford V8 49B	49B-R6
7th	Graham Hill	Lotus-Ford V8 49B	49B-R8
8th	Jo Siffert	Lotus-Ford V8 49B	49B-R7
10th	John Miles	Lotus-Ford V8 63	63/2
Rtd	Jo Bonnier	Lotus-Ford V8 63	63/1

AUGUST 3—GERMAN GRAND PRIX, NURBURGRING:

4th	Graham Hill	Lotus-Ford V8 49B	49B-R10
8th	Rolf Stommelen	Lotus-Cosworth '4'	59-F2-19*
11th(Rtd)	Jo Siffert	Lotus-Ford V8 49B	49B-R7
Rtd	Jochen Rindt	Lotus-Ford V8 49B	49B-R6
Rtd	Jo Bonnier	Lotus-Ford V8 49B	49B-R8
Rtd	Mario Andretti	Lotus-Ford V8 63	63/2
DNS	Hans Herrmann	Lotus-Cosworth '4'	59-F2-20*

*Formula 2 cars in race run concurrently with Formula 1 Grand Prix.

SEPTEMBER 8—ITALIAN GRAND PRIX, MONZA:

2nd	Jochen Rindt	Lotus-Ford V8 49B	49B-R6
8th(Rtd)	Jo Siffert	Lotus-Ford V8 49B	49B-R7
9th(Rtd)	Graham Hill	Lotus-Ford V8 49B	49B-R10
Rtd	John Miles	Lotus-Ford V8 63	63/1

SEPTEMBER 20—CANADIAN GRAND PRIX, MOSPORT PARK:

3rd	Jochen Rindt	Lotus-Ford V8 49B	49B-R6
7th	Pete Lovely	Lotus-Ford V8 49B	49B-R11
Rtd	Graham Hill	Lotus-Ford V8 49B	49B-R10
Rtd	Jo Siffert	Lotus-Ford V8 49B	49B-R7
Rtd	John Miles	Lotus-Ford V8 63	63/2

OCTOBER 5—UNITED STATES GRAND PRIX, WATKINS GLEN:

1st	Jochen Rindt	Lotus-Ford V8 49B	49B-R6
Rtd	Graham Hill	Lotus-Ford V8 49B	49B-R10
Rtd	Pete Lovely	Lotus-Ford V8 49B	49B-R11
Rtd	Mario Andretti	Lotus-Ford V8 63	63/2
Rtd	Jo Siffert	Lotus-Ford V8 49B	49B-R7

OCTOBER 19—MEXICAN GRAND PRIX, MEXICO CITY:

9th	Pete Lovely	Lotus-Ford V8 49B	49B-R11
Rtd	Jochen Rindt	Lotus-Ford V8 49B	49B-R6
Rtd	Jo Siffert	Lotus-Ford V8 49B	49B-R7
Rtd	John Miles	Lotus-Ford V8 63	63/2

1970

MARCH 7—SOUTH AFRICAN GRAND PRIX, KYALAMI:

5th	John Miles	Lotus-Ford V8 49C	49B-R10
6th	Graham Hill	Lotus-Ford V8 49C	49B-R7
8th	John Love	Lotus-Ford V8 49	49-R3
12th(Rtd)	Dave Charlton	Lotus-Ford V8 49C	49B-R8
13th(Rtd)	Jochen Rindt	Lotus-Ford V8 49C	49B-R6
T-car	Brian Redman	Lotus-Ford V8 49C	49B-R7

APRIL 19—SPANISH GRAND PRIX, JARAMA:

4th	Graham Hill	Lotus-Ford V8 49C	49B-R7
Rtd	Jochen Rindt	Lotus-Ford V8 72	72-2
DNQ	John Miles	Lotus-Ford V8 72	72-1
DNQ	Alex Soler-Roig	Lotus-Ford V8 49C	49B-R10

MAY 10—MONACO GRAND PRIX, MONTE CARLO:

1st	Jochen Rindt	Lotus-Ford V8 49C	49B-R6
5th	Graham Hill	Lotus-Ford V8 49C	49B-R10
DNQ	John Miles	Lotus-Ford V8 49C	49B-R10
DNS	Graham Hill	Lotus-Ford V8 49C	49B-R7

JUNE 7—BELGIAN GRAND PRIX, SPA-FRANCORCHAMPS:

Rtd	Graham Hill	Lotus-Ford V8 49C	49B-R7
Rtd	John Miles	Lotus-Ford V8 72	72-1
Rtd	Jochen Rindt	Lotus-Ford V8 49C	49B-R6
DNQ	Alex Soler-Roig	Lotus-Ford V8 72	72-2

JUNE 21—DUTCH GRAND PRIX, ZANDVOORT:

1st	Jochen Rindt	Lotus-Ford V8 72	72-1
7th	John Miles	Lotus-Ford V8 72	72-2
Unc	Graham Hill	Lotus-Ford V8 49C	49B-R7
DNQ	Pete Lovely	Lotus-Ford V8 49B	49B-R11

JULY 5—FRENCH GRAND PRIX, CLERMONT-FERRAND:

1st	Jochen Rindt	Lotus-Ford V8 72	72-2
8th	John Miles	Lotus-Ford V8 72	72-1
10th	Graham Hill	Lotus-Ford V8 49C	49B-R7
DNQ	Alex Soler-Roig	Lotus-Ford V8 49C	49B-R6
DNQ	Pete Lovely	Lotus-Ford V8 49B	49B-R11

JULY 18—BRITISH GRAND PRIX, BRANDS HATCH:

1st	Jochen Rindt	Lotus-Ford V8 72	72-2
6th	Graham Hill	Lotus-Ford V8 49C	49B-R7
8th	Emerson Fittipaldi	Lotus-Ford V8 49C	49B-R10
Unc	Pete Lovely	Lotus-Ford V8 49B	49B-R11
Rtd	John Miles	Lotus-Ford V8 72	72-1

AUGUST 2—GERMAN GRAND PRIX, HOCKENHEIMRING:

1st	Jochen Rindt	Lotus-Ford V8 72	72-2
4th	Emerson Fittipaldi	Lotus-Ford V8 49C	49B-R10
Rtd	Graham Hill	Lotus-Ford V8 49C	49B-R7
Rtd	John Miles	Lotus-Ford V8 72	72-3

AUGUST 16—AUSTRIAN GRAND PRIX, OSTERREICHRING:

15th	Emerson Fittipaldi	Lotus-Ford V8 49C	49B-R10
Rtd	Jochen Rindt	Lotus-Ford V8 72	72-2
Rtd	John Miles	Lotus-Ford V8 72	72-3

SEPTEMBER 6—ITALIAN GRAND PRIX, MONZA:

†	Jochen Rindt	Lotus-Ford V8 72	72-2
DNS	Graham Hill	Lotus-Ford V8 72	72-4
DNS	John Miles	Lotus-Ford V8 72	72-3
DNS	Emerson Fittipaldi	Lotus-Ford V8 72	72-5

SEPTEMBER 20—CANADIAN GRAND PRIX, ST JOVITE:

Unc	Graham Hill	Lotus-Ford V8 72	72-4

OCTOBER 4—UNITED STATES GRAND PRIX, WATKINS GLEN:

1st	Emerson Fittipaldi	Lotus-Ford V8 72	72-5
3rd	Reine Wisell	Lotus-Ford V8 72	72-3
Rtd	Graham Hill	Lotus-Ford V8 72	72-4
DNQ	Pete Lovely	Lotus-Ford V8 49B	49B-R11

OCTOBER 18—MEXICAN GRAND PRIX, MEXICO CITY:

Unc	Reine Wisell	Lotus-Ford V8 72	72-3
Rtd	Graham Hill	Lotus-Ford V8 72	72-4
Rtd	Emerson Fittipaldi	Lotus-Ford V8 72	72-5

1971

MARCH 6—SOUTH AFRICAN GRAND PRIX, KYALAMI:

4th	Reine Wisell	Lotus-Ford V8 72	72-3
Rtd	Emerson Fittipaldi	Lotus-Ford V8 72	72-5

APRIL 18—SPANISH GRAND PRIX, BARCELONA:

12th	Reine Wisell	Lotus-Ford V8 72	72-3
13th	Emerson Fittipaldi	Lotus-Ford V8 72	72-5

MAY 23—MONACO GRAND PRIX, MONTE CARLO:

5th	Emerson Fittipaldi	Lotus-Ford V8 72	72-5
Rtd	Reine Wisell	Lotus-Ford V8 72	72-3

JUNE 20—DUTCH GRAND PRIX, ZANDVOORT:

Dis	Reine Wisell	Lotus-Ford V8 72	72-3
Rtd	Dave Walker	Lotus-P&W 56B turbine	56B-1

JULY 4—FRENCH GRAND PRIX, PAUL RICARD CIRCUIT, LE CASTELLET:

3rd	Emerson Fittipaldi	Lotus-Ford V8 72	72-5
6th	Reine Wisell	Lotus-Ford V8 72	72-3

JULY 17—BRITISH GRAND PRIX, SILVERSTONE:

3rd	Emerson Fittipaldi	Lotus-Ford V8 72	72-5
Unc	Reine Wisell	Lotus-P&W 56B turbine	56B-1
Rtd	Dave Charlton	Lotus-Ford V8 72	72-3

AUGUST 1—GERMAN GRAND PRIX, NURBURGRING:

8th	Reine Wisell	Lotus-Ford V8 72	72-6
Rtd	Emerson Fittipaldi	Lotus-Ford V8 72	72-5

AUGUST 15—AUSTRIAN GRAND PRIX, OSTERREICHRING:

2nd	Emerson Fittipaldi	Lotus-Ford V8 72	72-5
4th	Reine Wisell	Lotus-Ford V8 72	72-6

SEPTEMBER 5—ITALIAN GRAND PRIX, MONZA:

8th	Emerson Fittipaldi	Lotus-P&W 56B turbine	56B-1

SEPTEMBER 19—CANADIAN GRAND PRIX, MOSPORT PARK

5th	Reine Wisell	Lotus-Ford V8 72	72-6
7th	Emerson Fittipaldi	Lotus-Ford V8 72	72-5
Unc	Pete Lovely	Lotus-Ford V8 69	69-F2-5*

*Special built by Lovely using front-end of ex-Rindt Lotus 69 Formula 2 car and rear-end of Lovely's 49B-R11

OCTOBER 3—UNITED STATES GRAND PRIX, WATKINS GL

19th	Emerson Fittipaldi	Lotus-Ford V8 72	72-5
20th	Pete Lovely	Lotus-Ford V8 69	69-F2-5
Rtd	Reine Wisell	Lotus-Ford V8 72	72-6

Appendix 4 LOTUS FORMULA JUNIOR STATEMENT

"During the past few weeks allegations have been made in German magazines and newspapers concerning the size of engines used in some Formula Junior cars; British cars, including Team Lotus, have been named in particular. A German driver and an Austrian driver are stated to have admitted to irregularities. The trouble started with an article in issue No 22 of 'Das Auto Motor und Sport' in which Richard von Frankenberg claimed to have positive proof that Team Lotus drivers have been using 1,450 cc engines in Formula Junior races.

"Normally we would not even bother to repudiate such ridiculous and completely unfounded charges, but as the matter has been raised again in issue No 23 of 'Das Auto Motor und Sport' we have had translations made of this and the original article and feel it necessary to answer the more obvious allegations point for point. It is claimed, for instance, that 'Lotus threatened a law suit'. This is not true.

"It is alleged that Alan Rees was not seriously injured and not heavily drugged at the time of the conversation on which most of Von Frankenberg's evidence is based, yet Rees was still in hospital in England for three weeks afterwards as a result of his accident.

"Von Frankenberg claims to have proof for all his allegations, but upon inspection his evidence is farcical. Alan Rees was asked if he would sell the engine of the car in which he crashed during practice for the Eifel races in September; Rees said he could not sell the engine as it belonged to the works; this is cited as PROOF that the engine was oversize.

"As further evidence, Alan Rees is said to have admitted that Team Lotus use special crankshafts. This is true. The crankshafts are made of steel instead of cast iron as is the standard shaft, but they still have the standard stroke as permitted by the regulations. It is also alleged that Lotus has offered oversize engines to customers; Von Frankenberg assumes that we would not do this unless we were using oversize engines ourselves. Lotus make no secret of the fact that larger versions of the Ford engine are available. The Lotus 20B is a version of the Type 20 specifically developed for and sold with a 1,500 cc Ford engine. It was widely advertised, and several of these cars have been sold for use in Formula 1 and Formula Libre races, particularly in South Africa and New Zealand in which they have been extremely successful. 1,500 cc engines have been and still are being sold for use in sports cars, but this does not mean that they were used in Team Lotus Junior cars.

"Von Frankenberg states that engine sizes have never been checked, yet the bore and stroke of the first three cars were measured at Goodwood on both 23rd April and 18th August this year; in neither case were there any irregularities. The scrutineers are empowered to check the size of any engine at any race. It seems unfortunate that the German scrutineers neglected to do this; had they done so at the Nurburgring on 29th-30th September there could never have been any excuse for Von Frankenberg's article.

"Team Lotus categorically deny ever having used oversize engines in any form of racing and would never consider doing so, if only for the harm it would do to the firm were it discovered—which it undoubtedly would be. Any intelligent observer can detect the difference in the exhaust notes even of 1,100 cc and 1,340 cc engines.

"We have accepted Von Frankenberg's challenge to take a car to any circuit of his choice, to repeat our race-winning speeds, and to allow the size of the engine to be checked, against a wager to cover all our expenses and provided he undertakes to retract all his allegations. Yet even if all this is done it can never completely overcome the harm caused—quite unjustifiably—by the publication of such defamatory remarks as 'It will take a long time to overcome the lack of confidence in the English'—all because a German driver and an Austrian driver have admitted using oversize engines. Von Frankenberg headed his original article 'The Biggest Disgrace in International Motor Sport'. In fact the biggest disgrace in International motor sport is that this libellous attack should ever have been published."

Von Frankenberg chose the Monza circuit and Peter Arundell had to reproduce his Monza Lottery Grand Prix figures; an average of 113.47 mph over 30 laps, and fastest lap of 1min 50.8secs, 115.99 mph. He covered the 30 laps in 55min 48.7secs, an average of 115.16 mph, and his fastest lap was timed at 1min 50.4secs, 0.4 second under his previous best. Peter did three extra laps after completing the distance, and recorded a best time of 1min 49.8secs, 117.14 mph, a clear second under his race time. Scrutineers immediately dismantled the engine which was found to have dimensions of 85mm x 48.15mm, giving a precise capacity of 1,092.348 cc (the stroke was less than the standard Ford stroke of 48.41mm). The car weighed 403Kg, three over the minimum limit, and Colin Chapman accepted a cheque for £1,000 and a lengthy published retraction from Richard von Frankenberg . . .

Index